Certificate in Higher Education: Skills for the Workplace Student Yearbook

Certificate in Higher Education: Skills for the Workplace Student Yearbook

Andrew Maund
Michaela Schriek
Paul K. Tinkler

PRIFYSGOL CYMRU
Y Drindod Dewi Sant
UNIVERSITY OF WALES
Trinity Saint David

Los Angeles | London | New Delhi
Singapore | Washington DC | Melbourne

Los Angeles | London | New Delhi
Singapore | Washington DC | Melbourne

SAGE Publications Ltd
1 Oliver's Yard
55 City Road
London EC1Y 1SP

SAGE Publications Inc.
2455 Teller Road
Thousand Oaks, California 91320

SAGE Publications India Pvt Ltd
B 1/I 1 Mohan Cooperative Industrial Area
Mathura Road
New Delhi 110 044

SAGE Publications Asia-Pacific Pte Ltd
3 Church Street
#10-04 Samsung Hub
Singapore 049483

Typeset by: C&M Digitals (P) Ltd, Chennai, India
Printed in the UK
Printed on paper from sustainable resources

First published 2017

British Library Cataloguing in Publication data

A catalogue record for this book is available from the British Library

ISBN 978-1-5264-3971-0 (pbk)

At SAGE we take sustainability seriously. We print most of our products in the UK. These are produced using FSC papers and boards. We undertake an annual audit on materials used to ensure that we monitor our sustainability in what we are doing. When we print overseas, we ensure that sustainable papers are used, as measured by the PREPS grading system.

Contents

PART 1

EFFECTIVE TEAM WORKING
AND COMMUNICATION

Introduction to Teams

Griffiths, B.A. and Dunham, E.B.

Working in teams to solve problems and achieve collective goals is a common experience for many. While teams can achieve extraordinary results, they can also deteriorate into an ineffective and immobilized group of frustrated individuals. This chapter introduces the concept of teams and describes common team problems as well as the conditions that are associated with team success. As individuals join together and build trust, groups develop a shared identity and a common purpose as they progress through predictable stages of development. Team leaders that understand those stages are able to facilitate growth. The chapter concludes with a look at the current trends in team research.

CASE 1.1: ALTERNATIVE SPRING BREAK

Alternative Spring Break (ASB) began at Vanderbilt University in 1986, when four students decided to form a team and spend their spring vacation together serving others. Although they had the best of intentions, being with a group of friends under stressful conditions for a week can be quite a challenge. Under duress, the very best of human nature comes out and the very worst of human nature comes out. The sheer logistics of organizing and planning a week-long service trip can be daunting. Once teams are on site, interpersonal problems often emerge as people start working together. As soon as a leader or a coalition of members decides to do one thing, other people will question those decisions and advocate a different direction. Even though ASB participants are well meaning and eager to contribute to the common good, problems almost inevitably emerge.

Whitney was a typical student and would be quick to attest to the life-changing power of her ASB experience. She spent every spring break during her college career volunteering at different ASB sites. She remembers her first spring break as setting the stage for involvement in a student group that would forever change her life. During that year, her team conducted conflict resolution workshops in some of the most troubled public schools in Detroit, Michigan. While the work was overwhelming at times, it was also extremely meaningful. Team members called the Detroit experience that year the "all-star site" because of the incredible friendships they forged and the important work they accomplished together.

The "all-star site" was not without its problems, though. One of the memorable experiences for Whitney was an argument that took place between two of the male members of the team. It was a heated debate about whether or not sports should be presented to urban kids as a viable career option. One member viewed sports as an opportunity for disadvantaged youth, while the other saw it as an unrealistic dream and barrier to educational success. Interestingly, Whitney found herself pleased that group members had become comfortable enough with one another that they were able to disagree so openly after only spending a short amount of time together. Because of the amount of time ASB participants spend with one another and because of the issues they face, they tend to go through the stages of group development quickly. While some teams get bogged down in communication misunderstandings and interpersonal squabbles, most become cohesive units that not only make a difference in the communities in which they serve but also in the lives of the members themselves.

Case Study Discussion Questions

1. If you were screening applications of students who wanted to go on an ASB trip, what are the qualities for which you would seek?

2. What are some of the tasks that need to be done ahead of time to prepare for a spring break trip?

3. Describe the general climate of ASB. What are the collective values and beliefs of students who are involved with this organization?

4. What would you do if you were on a team in which two of the members were hostile toward each other? How do you respond to interpersonal conflict?

5. From an administrative level, what do ASB leaders need to do to ensure a safe and successful experience for students?

In their article "The Discipline of Teams," Katzenbach and Smith (2005) suggest that "The essence of a team is shared commitment. Without it, groups perform as individuals; with it, they become a powerful unit of collective performance. This kind of commitment requires a purpose in which team members can believe" (p. 3). ASB students who are willing to forgo a fun and relaxing spring break in order to provide meaningful service to others are certainly committed to the mission of their teams. But their level of commitment does not ensure a smooth and successful experience. There are a multitude of things that can go wrong because of site leaders who are inexperienced or activities that are poorly planned or team members who do not get along with one another. Any one of these, which come from a much longer list of potential team obstacles, can serve to create disappointment and frustration. As the title of this text suggests, a collection of high-potential individuals does not always develop into a high-performance team. In fact, it is quite the exception (Wheelan, 2005). But with a little bit of knowledge and planning, teams can be rewarding and extremely successful enterprises (Hertel, 2011).

WHAT IS A TEAM?

Perhaps we should begin by defining what a team is. Kozlowski and Bell (2003) define teams as groups of people "who exist to perform organizationally relevant tasks, share one

WRITE YOUR NOTES HERE

or more common goals, interact socially, exhibit task interdependencies, maintain and manage boundaries, and are embedded in an organizational context that sets boundaries, constrains the team, and influences exchanges with other units in the broader entity" (p. 334). First and foremost, according to this definition, teams exist to accomplish specific tasks that are related to common goals. In order to do this, people must interact with one another in some form or fashion to accomplish those tasks.

Summarizing the existing definitions, Wageman, Gardner, and Mortensen (2012) define a team as a "bounded and stable set of individuals interdependent for a common purpose" (p. 305). Team boundaries are created so that members know who is on the team and who is not. And finally, we must acknowledge that teams exist within a larger organizational context that influences them to varying degrees. While some organizations give tremendous autonomy to their teams, others require strict adherence to a set of rules, roles, structures, and operating procedures.

Businesses and corporations are well aware of the potential of teams and frequently use them to carry out the missions of their organizations. Take Ford Motor Company, for example. When Henry Ford, the founder and chief engineer of Ford, envisioned his company, he wanted to find a way to efficiently create cars that were both affordable and reliable for the consumer. He developed several teams—each consisting of two to three members—that worked together on a specific part of the assembly process instead of separately building a car from start to finish. This innovative approach pioneered the assembly line method. With several teams working toward a common goal, Ford Motor Company went on to make millions of reliable automobiles and is now the world's fifth-largest automaker in the world. The 21st century business world is marked by the need for quick responses to rapidly changing market conditions. Keeping up with the complexities of a global economy requires businesses to draw upon multiple perspectives and multiple sources of input in order to be able to compete. For this reason, task-oriented teams can be found almost anywhere, from factory assembly lines to corporate executive suites (Polzer, 2003).

WHY DO WE NEED TO LEARN ABOUT TEAMS?

Individuals who affiliate with groups and learn to cooperate with others increase their chances of solving shared problems and meeting personal needs (Qin, Johnson, & Johnson, 1995). Families, neighborhoods, communities, work teams, organizations, and cultures are all attempts to increase collective stability in ways that meet individual needs for survival, personal development, and social interaction. Given the shift in our economy to a more team-based, collaborative, and interdependent approach to work, it is not surprising that an Association of American Colleges and Universities (AACU) survey showed that 71 % of employers want colleges to place a greater emphasis on teamwork (AACU, 2010). It is more important than ever for college graduates to be prepared to work in a team-based environment.

While it is not uncommon to encounter group projects and team-based assignments throughout the college experience, the robust working knowledge and subtle interpersonal skills required for team success may not be effectively developed within the undergraduate curriculum. Another AACU report, "College Learning for the New Global Economy: A Report from the National Leadership Council for Liberal Education and America's Promise" (AACU, 2007) identifies teamwork as 1 of 15 "Essential Learning Outcomes" in college. Success in most work environments after graduation requires individuals to work well with others in collaborative team efforts. Whether in business, government, not-for-profit organizations, or a vast array of other professional pursuits, being able to work within and to lead teams is of central importance to individual success and organizational sustainability.

The primary focus of this text is to prepare students for task-oriented groups in which individuals have joined together to accomplish specific goals. The evidence-based concepts and skills that are presented can help both leaders and members alike as they work together to achieve collective success. After reading the text, students will be able to create meaningful social contexts that foster the development of individual members, changing "high-potential" teams into "high-performance" teams.

TEAMS VERSUS WORKGROUPS

Groups of people who join together to accomplish a specific task do not always exemplify the characteristics of a true "team." Hackman (2009) has identified five basic conditions that must be met if a group is to be considered a team versus a workgroup:

1. "Teams must be real." While many organizations assign people to teams, some of those structures are teams in name only. Real teams are groups of identifiable people who actually work together to achieve a common set of objectives.

2. "Teams need a compelling direction." In order for everyone to be pulling in the same direction, they need to understand and embrace a shared purpose.

3. "Teams need enabling structures." This means involving the right number of the right kind of people on the right tasks in the right ways, and governing them by the right norms and shared values.

4. "Teams need a supportive organization." Everything must facilitate success, from the behaviors and output that are most prized or rewarded, to the structure of the teams' people, systems, and processes.

5. "Teams need expert coaching." An expert third party must lend insight and guidance at key points in any groups' evolution. Too much coaching focuses on the individual, when it should be focused on teamwork and team process.

Clearly, teams and teamwork are nuanced, dynamic, and highly variable. In addition, they are increasingly valued across industries as instrumental in organizational success.

COMMON PROBLEMS

While teams have tremendous potential to accomplish tasks well beyond the reach of any single individual, they are not without problems. As a matter of fact, working in teams can be quite frustrating. Research about teams, personal observations, and personal experience point to five common problems that people experience when working in teams:

- Lack of commitment

- Productivity losses

- Poor communication

- Interpersonal conflict

- Poor leadership

One of the perennial problems in working with others is a lack of commitment among members. It is not uncommon for a majority of the work to be done by only a few members. While this may be extremely frustrating for those who are doing the work, those same team members are often reluctant to give up control in order to allow others to rise to the challenge. As a result, those who are doing little or nothing are content to ride the coattails of higher performing members. This free riding, or social loafing, is a regular irritant for countless team leaders.

Losses in productivity that come from poor structure and a lack of planning and organization are called "process losses." They occur because of the additional layers of complexity that come from working in teams. For example, it may take longer to come to a decision, time may be wasted in trying to schedule meetings, and individual contributions must be integrated into the larger project. Furthermore, conflicts about goals, task assignments, and operating procedures all threaten to slow down the work of a team. Unless a team has specifically defined roles and responsibilities, and has established a sound system of coordinating its efforts, there will likely be losses in productivity.

Poor communication is often at the heart of poorly performing groups. Team members can emerge from the same meeting with completely different perspectives of what was said or what was or was not accomplished. In general, as the number of people working on a task increases, so does the chance for communication problems. Most of what team members perceive comes from highly subjective interpretations of nonverbal behavior including tone, facial expression, and body posture. In addition, members often do a poor job supporting or providing evidence for their positions. Thus, there is a great propensity to miscommunicate or misunderstand what is being said.

Communication problems easily give way to interpersonal conflict. On any given team, there are likely to be people with whom we get along better than others—and there may even be some whom we strongly dislike. Strong dislike for a person is frequently quite evident to them even despite our best efforts to hide it. Furthermore, some members are prone to taking questions or challenges far too personally, and do not realize that banter and spirited debate actually sharpen the ability of the group to make good decisions. When members are emotionally fragile, they are likely to feel threatened by those who play the important role of the deviant or devil's advocate.

Finally, poor leadership can compromise the ability of teams to perform effectively (Sivasubramaniam, Murry, Avolio, & Jung, 2002). Leadership is a delicate dance that both guides and empowers. There is no shortage of cases in which team members were so discontent with their leaders that they disengaged, resisted, or even sabotaged their own teams. Team leaders who do not balance members' need for structure with their need for autonomy will hinder performance.

CONDITIONS FOR TEAM SUCCESS

Druskat and Wolff (2001) have identified three essential conditions for team success: trust among members, a sense of group identity, and a sense of group efficacy. Team leaders and organizers can impact their teams by nurturing the development of each of these components. As teams begin their journey together, trust, identity, and efficacy must be established for optimal performance.

Trust

According to Doney, Cannon, and Mullen (1998), trust can be defined simply as the willingness to rely upon others. Organizational researchers have become increasingly interested in its causes, nature, and effects (Costa, Roe, & Taillieu, 2001; Kramer, 1999; Mayer, Davis, & Schoorman, 1995). Lencioni (2002) suggests that trust is necessary for effective team functioning. Without it, a host of dysfunctions may emerge, including a fear of conflict, lack of commitment, avoidance of accountability, and inattention to results.

Levels of trust are related to the personal characteristics of both those who trust and those who are trusted. Some people, by nature, are more trusting than others. This quality stems from positive past experiences and relationships that have proven others to be generally trustworthy. Thus, core beliefs in the goodness of people are established, which enables attraction and attachment to others. On the other hand, for those who have had negative experiences with people in the past, relying upon others will not be an easy thing to do. Group members with painful past experiences and negative beliefs will likely be less trusting of others and seek to be independent.

Trust in groups is also related to the trustworthiness of the group members. Members are trusted when they are perceived to have characteristics that engender trust. These include competence, benevolence, and integrity (Mayer, Davis, & Schoorman, 1995). First, members will rely upon those who are competent and have ability in an area of concern to the group. In other words, members must be relatively sure that the person has the capacity to perform the task at hand. Second, members will trust colleagues who exhibit benevolence. Benevolent members are kind and generous, and are opposed to intentionally harming or manipulating other people. The third quality that begets trust is integrity. Members who have integrity are true to their word and do what they say they will do before the deadline. If enough members consistently demonstrate these qualities of competence, benevolence, and integrity, the group will establish a foundation of trust that will lead to success and satisfaction.

While trust takes time to establish, it can be compromised after just a single negative interaction. Distrust can become a group norm if members have a lack of confidence in one another or suspect that others are harmful or malicious (Kramer, 1999). Imagine a scenario in a local coffee shop in which a cashier takes an order from a customer and communicates that order to the barista. The line is long, the customers are in a hurry, and the barista inadvertently makes a mistake. When the customer comes back to complain, the cashier makes a condescending remark to the barista. The barista is upset and quickly tries to correct the mistake, only to find that she is still out of the vanilla syrup that the backroom person promised to bring 20 minutes earlier. At this point, the barista thinks the cashier is being overly critical (questioning his benevolence) and that the backroom person is not reliable (questioning her integrity). Meanwhile, the cashier is annoyed at the barista's error (questioning her competence) and no longer wants to work the same shifts because she makes him look bad. One can see how quickly trust can be violated. In a matter of a few short minutes, trust was lost—and it can be difficult to regain.

Team Identity

Team identity is Druskat and Wolff's (2001) second element necessary for team success. Teams that spend enough time together eventually develop a unique identity. When individuals derive their own identity in part from their team affiliation, they become invested in, loyal, and committed to it. Teams develop norms, values, and characteristics that separate them from other teams, and these characteristics can be the difference between an average team performance and a stellar performance.

Alternative Spring Break (ASB) teams are a good example of how team identity can produce superior results. Service organizations such as ASB, Teach for America, or Boys & Girls Clubs are known for their commitment to the common good and enlist members who are aligned with those goals. Their training programs seek to build a sense of camaraderie and unity among their team members that can stand up to the adverse circumstances they will likely encounter together. In the opening case study, the ASB team that went to Detroit dubbed itself the "all-star site." This demonstrated the members' belief that they were both special and unique. This clear sense of identity was one of the reasons the team was so successful.

Collective Efficacy

Collective efficacy concludes the shortlist of the most vital elements leading to team success. We know that optimism and self-confidence can go a long way in enhancing personal achievement. Teams are no different. In order for teams to be most successful, they need to believe they can accomplish their goals (Porter, Gogus, & Yu, 2011). Visit the locker room of any high school football team and you will be inundated with messages of "We Can,"

"Believe," "No Limits," and the like. When members are confident that they can accomplish ambitious goals, their chances of success are much greater (Katz-Navon & Erez, 2005). There exists no shortage of examples of small groups of people accomplishing amazing feats simply because they believed they could.

IDEAL TEAM CLIMATE

Teams are often created and assembled to solve important problems within communities and organizations. For example, a marketing team might be asked to improve annual sales by 10%, a school improvement task force might be asked to identify strategies to reduce student absenteeism by 5%, or a product design group might be tasked with the responsibility of creating a new potato chip bag that will keep chips fresher longer. In each of these cases, team members must "think outside the box" to solve the problem presented to them. Anderson and West (1998) have found four team characteristics that lead to innovation and effective performance. The ideal team climate includes a shared vision, participative safety, task orientation, and support for innovation.

Shared vision describes the importance of developing clear, objective goals that are visionary in nature but also attainable. A shared vision can be dictated by the de facto leader of the group, or it can emerge organically through a collaborative process. Whatever the case, the group ultimately needs to agree upon the purpose of members' collective efforts. Members need to know the answers to questions such as "Where are we headed?," "What are we doing?," and "What are our goals?" Often, the leader can jump-start this process by asking those very questions. Some of the most successful groups begin their work with the question "What do we want to accomplish with this team?" The ensuing conversation invariably covers topics such as goals, benchmarks, balance of responsibility, commitment level, and other similar logistical concerns. A clear vision within the team is essential in order to produce and sustain long-term results.

Participative safety exists when levels of trust and support are such that members feel safe participating freely in group discussions and decisions (Kessel, Dratzer, & Schultz, 2012). This can be established with as little effort as setting ground rules and holding members accountable to those rules. As with shared vision, participative safety is something that the group can facilitate by establishing explicit rules of engagement and expectations for participation during meetings. For example, is everyone expected to "participate fully"? If so, what does that mean? If it's something that everyone understands, this will allow all group members to refer to that "ground rule" to encourage contributions *and* to discourage negative dynamics like condescending or judgmental behavior that hinder the willingness of other team members to offer ideas, voice dissent, or contribute to the shared process.

A task orientation is achieved when teams uphold their commitment to high performance standards by monitoring performance, holding one another accountable, giving one another honest feedback, and engaging in constructive conflict in order to reach their goals. As with other dimensions of successful teams, it is helpful to have an open discussion about this and lay out expectations. Structure is the product of intentional and earnest conversation about the things that matter most to members with regard to the *task* at hand. Leaders should be willing to discuss it in concrete and specific terms. They can begin by saying something like, "I think it will be important for us to have some shared expectations about our group and the work we do. I know we all have our own ways of doing work, so can we take a few minutes to talk about how we work best in teams, giving special attention to how we can stay on task and accomplish our goals." It may be particularly helpful to have an agenda for each meeting and to have someone take minutes in order to record major decisions, action items, and assigned responsibilities.

Groups that have strong support for innovation are open to examining existing ways of doing things and are willing to take risks and experiment with new ideas. Innovation often means change, and change can create anxiety. Teams that support innovation are willing to endure the discomfort of thinking "outside the box" in order to explore new ways of understanding problems and creating solutions. These types of teams also give great latitude to creative members who at first might seem totally off base, but who often see things in very different ways.

Research and development (R&D) teams are often called upon to create new and innovative products and services. The amount of time it takes to design a new product or concept can be the difference between success and failure in a fast-paced, market-driven economy. In a study of 33 R&D teams over a nine-month period, Pirola-Merlo (2010) found that three of the four team climate scales (participative safety, support for innovation, and task orientation) were significantly related to project performance as rated by managers and customers. In addition, two of the scales (support for innovation and vision) were associated with higher levels of project innovation. Those teams with a stronger climate were also able to complete their projects more quickly.

Not only does team climate affect innovation and efficiency, it also influences levels of member satisfaction and general team performance. In a study of 654 general practitioners and staff and 7,505 chronically ill patients from 93 primary health care practices in Australia, researchers found that a strong team climate is related to higher levels of job satisfaction as well as higher levels of patient satisfaction (Proudfoot, Jayasinghe, Holton, Grimm, Bubner, Amoroso, Beilby, & Harris, 2007). An optimal team climate creates both the structure and interpersonal dynamics that can lead to success. But it often takes time and intentional effort to develop that type of atmosphere. It doesn't happen by accident, and it doesn't happen overnight. But an understanding of the typical stages of group development can help team leaders shape the direction and destiny of their teams.

STAGES OF GROUP DEVELOPMENT

Groups are dynamic social systems that change over time; the first few meetings of a newly formed group are substantially different from the twentieth meeting (Arrow, Poole, Henry, Wheelan, & Moreland, 2004). Group development models attempt to explain these differences and identify typical stages through which groups evolve. Knowledge of these stages can help leaders and members alike to understand the changes and manage expectations. Bruce Tuckman (1965) was the first to suggest the stages of development known as forming, storming, norming, performing, and adjourning. Sometime later, Susan Wheelan (1999) constructed a similar linear model that includes many of the same concepts.

During the first few meetings, while the group is in the forming stage of its development, members are sizing one another up while self-consciously assessing their own competence. At this stage, members are typically concerned with acceptance and belonging. They have an over-reliance on the leader and are generally cautious and tentative due to both a lack of role clarity and an understanding of the rules of operation (norms). Coincidentally, when existing groups add new members or change the composition of the group, they will often return to the forming stage as the existing members and the new members size one another up. New members can provide a fresh perspective that encourages an examination of the existing team structure that propels the group into the next stage of development.

Storming is the stage of group life characterized by members becoming increasingly impatient with the existing structure and directly or indirectly challenging the leaders of the group. Because there is rarely one right way to solve problems or achieve goals, it is nearly impossible for everyone in the group to be completely happy with decisions and plans.

Disagreement over procedures, role assignments, and any number of details related to group life are inevitable, and as the newness of the group wears off, members become bolder in questioning and challenging one another. "Individual" roles emerge at this time as members take a passive, passive-aggressive, or aggressive stance against the group (avoider, resister, and dominator roles, respectively). Groups will often become polarized as members form coalitions and alliances with one another as they jockey for status and power (Carton & Cummings, 2012). Although uncomfortable for some, this stage is necessary for optimal cohesion and group functioning.

The norming stage is an attempt by the group to restore stability and cohesion after the storm and to develop a more effective structure toward achieving goals. Having gone through conflict, the group has tested its boundaries and (hopefully) developed trust. At this stage, groups not only become more unified, but also better organized. Relationships deepen at the same time that task efficiency increases. During this stage, the storming period has officially given way to a renewed commitment to the goals and purpose of the group, resulting in an examination and redefinition of norms, roles, and relationships.

In the performing stage the group's focus is on getting work done. Relationships and cohesion have been built, optimal strategies have been constructed, and the underlying group structure has solidified. The group is now positioned for maximum productivity. During this stage, effective groups spend 80% to 85% of their time on task completion (Wheelan, 1999; Wheelan, Davidson, & Tilin, 2003). In terms of time frame, Wheelan (2004) suggests it takes approximately six months for a group to get to this level of functioning. Unfortunately, not all groups make it to this productive stage. Many groups remain stuck in one of the earlier stages.

In the adjourning stage of group development, groups are preparing to disband. The group is coming to an end and members need to prepare for its demise. For some this is a joyful event, but for others there may be disappointment or even sadness. Some group experiences are so positive and so powerful that members do not want them to come to an end. In either case, it is important for members to discuss what they have learned from the experience and to say their goodbyes to one another.

OTHER MODELS OF GROUP DEVELOPMENT

Not all experts agree with the stage model of group development. In Connie Gersick's (1988, 1989) research on team development, she found that by the end of the first meeting, groups had formed an initial structure that remained fairly stable until the middle of the project or life of the group. At that midpoint, Gersick observed a burst of energy and transition whereby members critically examined their progress and reorganized themselves for more effective functioning. Interestingly, whether the groups she studied met four times or twenty-five times over seven days or six months, they all had a major transition at the chronological midpoint of the project. As a result of her studies, Gersick postulated that groups do not progress through stages of development, but phases.

According to her phase theory, the first phase is defined by the stable structure that is established by the end of the first meeting. Thus, the first meeting is extremely important in setting the climate, culture, and direction of the group. Then, at the midpoint, the group goes through a period of instability and transition before entering phase two, with the newly defined structure that will guide the project through to the end. Gersick also noted a flurry of activity and effort toward the end of the project as the deadline approached.

Research partially supports both the Tuckman and Wheelan models and the Gersick model (Chang, Bordia, & Duck, 2003). One way to reconcile them is to use the Tuckman and Wheelan models to describe the relationship dimension of group work while the Gersick model is more aligned with the task dimension. These dimensions of group dynamics (task and relationship) are the two primary components of group dynamics that require the attention of group members and leaders alike. The forming and storming stages often set the relational tone for the later, more task-oriented stages of norming and performing. Both dimensions are important for long-term group success.

Table 1.1   Comparing Models of Group Development

Tuckman (1965)	Wheelan (1999)	Gersick (1988)
Forming	Dependency and inclusion	Phase 1 (stability)
Storming	Counterdependency and fight	Transition (instability)
Norming	Trust and structure	
Performing	Work and productivity	Phase 2 (stability)

THREATS TO EFFECTIVE COLLABORATION

Collaboration is the ability of team members to work together effectively, efficiently, and meaningfully. Thompson (2004) asserts, "When groups perform highly uncertain tasks, they need to integrate large amounts of information, form multiple perspectives, and collaborate closely. In such situations, collaboration is necessary" (p. 238). Yet only about a quarter of all teams progress through the normal stages of group development and reach their full potential (Wheelan, 1999). There are numerous threats to effective collaboration, including the size of the team, the degree of virtual participation, the amount of diversity, and the education level of the members (Gratton & Erickson, 2007). Each of these threats will be discussed in detail.

Size of the Team

In the last few decades, teams in organizations have become significantly larger in size (Gratton & Erickson, 2007). Technology has made it easier to include geographically remote members with presumably greater levels of expertise. Yet as teams grow in size, it becomes harder and harder for members to coordinate their efforts (Walsh & Maloney, 2007). Due to process losses and logistical challenges, large teams can be inefficient and, therefore, less effective. Furthermore, interaction among members is often more superficial, and thus less meaningful. Working closely with others to achieve mutual goals is often one of the most rewarding dimensions of team participation, but one that teams that are large and dispersed often lose.

Degree of Virtual Participation

As teams become more "virtual," the quality of collaboration decreases (Gratton & Erickson, 2007). Because the communication process relies heavily on nonverbal cues to interpret verbal statements, electronic messages can be ambiguous at best and grossly misunderstood at worst. Virtual teams have been studied at length, and while there are many benefits, there are drawbacks as well. In order to minimize potential misunderstanding and miscommunication, team leaders have to implement specific strategies that support collaboration in a technology-rich environment.

Amount of Diversity

Similar to technology, diversity can be both a benefit and a threat to collaboration. Differences of opinion and perspective can create innovative and fresh ways to understand and solve problems, but they can also generate distrust and frustration. For example, a university task force that is charged with addressing the role of the Greek system on campus would probably include members from the administration, faculty, and student body. However, such a task force would likely begin with some tension as each group sought to understand the motives and positions of the other stakeholders. Though diverse perspectives are important to the overall discussion, groups might regard one another with suspicion. Theoretically, a diverse team composition creates a more comprehensive approach to problem-solving, yet, in practice, diversity can put a strain on interpersonal dynamics and the ability to collaborate. Diversity can be found in any number of member differences, including personality, gender, age, race/ethnicity, functionality, education level, or length of tenure within the organization or industry.

Education Level

Interestingly, level of education is negatively correlated with group collaboration. According to Gratton and Erickson (2007), "the greater the proportion of highly educated specialists on a team, the more likely the team is to disintegrate into unproductive conflicts" (p. 5). Members who are very knowledgeable and highly trained tend to be resistant to perspectives and ways of doing things other than their own. Simply put, they have a hard time compromising. It is no wonder that academic departments that aspire to the highest ideals of virtue and learning can become mired in endless squabbles over relatively insignificant decisions. True collaboration requires an openness and willingness to understand and agree with other perspectives. The following section will describe specific strategies to increase team collaboration.

IMPROVING COLLABORATION

Team researchers have identified a number of things that can be done to overcome the inherent challenges in teamwork and increase the chances for effective collaboration. Specifically, team composition, meeting space, and leadership practices can all contribute to the conditions conducive for success (Gratton & Erickson, 2007).

Team Composition

New teams that are comprised of members who have successfully worked together in the past are at a distinct advantage as they have a history of trust and interpersonal strengths from which to draw, whereas team members without any history must go through the typical posturing and interpersonal jockeying that take place at the start of a new team. Thus, when possible, designing teams in which 20% or more of the members have successfully worked together in the past can help establish a strong foundation of collaboration (Gratton, 2007). The opposite is also true. People who have had negative experiences working together in the past may not be a good fit for a new team. While a small amount of interpersonal tension can be helpful, too much can engender negative emotional contagion that can sabotage trust and good will.

Meeting Space

The physical or virtual setting where meetings take place can also have a significant impact on collaboration. The setting should reflect the values of the organization and the goals of the team, and it should be conducive to effective and balanced communication. Rooms that are inviting and conducive to allow members to see and hear one another are obviously the most effective. Thus, consideration should be given to seating arrangements and the layout of the room. A study group that meets in a classroom would feel very different from a group meeting in a dorm room. Each setting has its relative strengths and weaknesses. Furthermore, eating a meal together, or simply sharing snacks or soft drinks, may increase the sense of community and cohesion.

Leadership Practices

Team leaders impact team collaboration through the behaviors and attitudes they model, by publicly acknowledging collaborative behavior, by coaching individual members, and by focusing on both task and relationship dimensions of the team. Modeling is a powerful communicator of team norms and values. Thus, what a team leader does is often more important than what he or she says. Leaders that model collaborative behavior are setting the standard for the rest of the group (Ibarra & Hansen, 2011). For example, a leader who is transparent about personal goals and willing to admit mistakes opens the door for others to do the same. In a similar way, when a leader responds nondefensively to a direct challenge or personal attack, he or she increases the team's capacity for collaboration.

In addition to modeling collaborative behavior, team leaders can reward it publicly and coach members on it personally. Acknowledging a member who went above and beyond the call of duty for the sake of the team reinforces collaborative behavior. When leaders "encourage the heart," both the recipient of the comment as well as the rest of the team are reminded of the importance of ideal team behavior. Members who are not aware of their own behavior may need personal feedback and coaching. Effective leaders regularly pull individual members aside to facilitate conversations on how they view their own level of collaboration and team behavior.

TRENDS IN TEAM RESEARCH

Technological advances and trends in globalization are radically changing the ways individuals participate in teams (Wageman, Gardner, & Mortensen, 2012). Technology and globalization have increased both the scope and practice of our work with others. While it is unfathomable to think of a world without e-mail, social networking, and the Internet, these technologies have only been used by a majority of the workforce since the mid-1990s. For example, the popular social networking platform Facebook was only launched in early 2004. In just a few short years, it has revolutionized the ways in which individuals connect with one another. So are Facebook groups that are created to address social problems or discuss political issues actual teams? When some computer programmers voluntarily work together to develop the next release of an open source operating system, are they part of a team? When people join a virtual support group to help one another find medical solutions to diseases from which they all suffer, are they operating as a team? While these groups may not fit the standard definition of a team, they certainly have many characteristics of a team, including shared commitment to a common goal.

Teams in the 21st century are not as stable or bounded as they have been in the past. In contemporary social settings, people float in and out of teams, move quickly among teams, and are part of multiple teams (O'Leary, Mortensen, & Woolley, 2011). Technology has made it easy to be involved in multiple projects at the same time. Since formal team membership is a more loosely understood construct in today's world, researchers are just beginning to explore how to capture the complexities of multiple team membership and its effect on interpersonal dynamics and team performance.

```
┌─────────────────────────────────────┐
│                                     │
│        WRITE YOUR NOTES HERE        │
│                                     │
│                                     │
│                                     │
│                                     │
│                                     │
│                                     │
│                                     │
│                                     │
│                                     │
│                                     │
└─────────────────────────────────────┘
```

Another trend in team research has been to reexamine the way we understand the concept of interdependence. Once again, technology has allowed us to contribute to collective tasks in novel and creative ways. The person who takes our order at the drive-thru menu of a fast food restaurant may actually be located many miles from the pickup window and may be taking orders from multiple stores at once (Friedman, 2006). This certainly challenges the way we have traditionally understood collaborative work teams. Contemporary team structures are more elusive, dynamic, and difficult to measure. Teams themselves have greater levels of autonomy than in the past to define their own goals and operating procedures. Thus, researchers are concluding that not only is team membership dynamic, so is the way people work together to define and accomplish shared tasks (Wageman, Gardner, & Mortensen, 2012).

LEADERSHIP IN ACTION

Effective team leaders pay attention to both the task and relational dimensions of teams. Clear roles, responsibilities, deadlines, and accountability can go a long way in accomplishing tasks and achieving goals. But on the relational dimension, members must learn to trust one another and create a sense of community in order to work together effectively. The best leaders are able to address both dimensions directly.

First of all, teams must have a clear vision of what they are trying to accomplish. A team mission, charter, or project statement can give a clear vision of the purpose of the group. Then, leaders must coordinate the work of the team to accomplish those goals. For example, a team leader might begin a meeting by asking members to give a status update on their individual tasks. At the end of the meeting, he or she might ask whether or not everyone knows exactly what they need to accomplish before the next meeting. Action plans, deadlines, and meeting agendas help keep teams focused and on task.

On the relational dimension, team members want to feel like they are appreciated and valued. They want to feel connected to the team on some level. This is where team-building activities come into play. It can be hard to trust others when you do not know them. So at the beginning of a new group, it makes sense to do an icebreaker or two to allow members to get to know one another. In addition, leaders can create a positive atmosphere by being enthusiastic about the team and by supporting team members both publicly and privately. When this happens, the group is well on its way to becoming a high-performing team.

KEY TERMS

DISCUSSION QUESTIONS

1. Hackman identifies five basic conditions that distinguish a team from a workgroup. Name and describe each condition.

2. Although teams have great potential to accomplish tasks effectively, there is an array of common problems that can hinder performance. Describe three of those common problems.

3. Druskat and Wolff (2001) state that there are three conditions that are essential to a team's success. Name and explain the importance of each condition.

4. Levels of trust are strongly related to team success. Identify individual qualities that are related to trustworthiness.

5. Explain why each the following characteristics of team climate can impact team success: shared vision, task orientation, open communication, support for innovation, and interaction frequency.

6. Describe Tuckman's five stages of group development. Provide an example of each.

7. Name and describe the four threats to collaboration. What can be done in order to increase collaboration? Give at least two examples.

GROUP ACTIVITIES

EXERCISE 1.1 PAST TEAM EXPERIENCES

Get into groups of four to five and describe the positive experiences you have had in groups and/or teams in the past:

- What made the team exceptional?

- What was the shared goal of the group or team?

- Were members committed to the team? How do you know?

- Describe your past experiences with unsuccessful teams. What made them frustrating? Why did they fail? What was lacking in the leadership of the team?

Create a list of the top three reasons teams succeed and a list of the top three reasons teams fail. Be prepared to share your list with the rest of the class.

EXERCISE 1.2 BUILDING TRUST

Trust is an important component of relationships. Form groups of three or four and discuss the following questions:

1. What is trust?
2. Can you describe a trusting relationship in your life?
3. What does it take to form trust/a trusting relationship?
4. How do trusting relationships differ from relationships that may lack trust?
5. What ground rules and team guidelines will help build trust?

Be prepared to present your ground rules to the rest of the class. After all the groups have shared, you will have a final opportunity to add additional items to your list of ground rules.

CASE 1.2 WORKING WITH THE LONE WOLF

You have just finished a summer-long stint with your family's business, an office products supplier. The company generates about $3 million of revenue per year and employs 27 people. Employees are organized in three primary teams: sales and marketing, warehouse operations and distribution, and the executive team. Your mother, the CEO, has brought you on for the summer so you can rotate through each team to get a first-hand look at how the company operates.

You spent the first month with the warehouse team, sweating in the June heat with warehouse workers and delivery people. In spite of the backbreaking work, this crew proved to be a tight, strong community that ate lunch together, spent breaks playing basketball on the temporary hoop behind in the back parking lot, and often grabbed a beer together after work. Though they didn't immediately trust you as "the owner's kid," you worked hard to prove your worth through hard work and a minimal amount of complaining.

The second month, you went out with the sales team. Rick, your mentor for the month, referred to himself as "the lone wolf." He has been the top salesperson for the last two years and is vocal about his financial success and the value he brings to the company. Rick confides in you that he thinks other salespeople are jealous of his success and are actively trying to steal his customers. At the weekly sales team meetings, you notice a lot of competitive jabbing among sales representatives. There are also a lot of complaints about the commission structure and criticism of the "lazy warehouse workers" who drag their feet and take too long to process orders.

By August, you moved inside the main office with the executive team. The executive team is made up of middle-aged, highly educated professionals who are the highest-paid people in the company. You often hear them complain about the "lack of effort" they see from the salespeople and the hourly employees. Lately, company executives have appeared frazzled and stressed out due to what they describe as "shrinking profits." At executive meetings nobody seems to know what to do to turn the company around. There appears to be a growing sense of pessimism about whether or not the company is going to make it.

By the end of the summer, you have experienced three different teams with three distinct cultures operating within the organization.

Describe and assess each of the teams according to the following:

- The problems each team is experiencing

- The conditions for team success they may or may not be experiencing

- Whether or not they have the characteristics associated with the ideal team climate.

Team Design

Griffiths, B.A. and Dunham, E.B.

Team design affects how a group of individuals interact as a unit and serves as a key determinant of success. This chapter will describe the major components that make up team design, including member roles and responsibilities and team culture. In order to build a successful team, leaders need to be well versed in the specific goals and tasks that need to be completed, as well as the levels of interdependence needed among members. Once team members have been selected, work can begin. The first few meetings in the life of a team strongly influence its ongoing structure, so planning *how* to launch a project and *how* to conduct those first few meetings is an important consideration in developing an effective and efficient team structure. Thoughtful planning and active participation increase the chances for outstanding team performance.

CASE 2.1: JOINING THE STARBUCKS TEAM

Jennifer is like many college students. She enjoys her classes and the whole college experience—but she's broke. It's only November, and the money she saved from her summer job as a retail clerk is almost depleted. As she withdraws the last of her final paycheck, she can't help but recount how the hours in the clothing store seemed to drag on and on while the workers continuously engaged in petty bickering and complaining. Jennifer stayed to herself that summer in an attempt to avoid the store drama. She hated going to work and often felt irritated by her demeaning customers or demanding bosses. Now that the hard-earned money she made during those months was gone, she knew she would have to find another part-time job, but she couldn't bear the thought of having another experience like the one she had over the summer.

One of Jennifer's favorite places to study had always been the local Starbucks. She loved to drink her coffee and enjoy the atmosphere of the shop—particularly the friendly and helpful staff who worked there. The obvious enjoyment the employees seemed to get from their jobs soon convinced Jennifer to apply for a position. After an interview that went pretty well, she got the job. When Jennifer arrived for her first of several days of training, she was encouraged by the store manager's kind words of introduction to the rest of the team. He named several of the achievements that he remembered from her résumé and assured them that she would be a great asset to the team.

Her training program allowed Jennifer to acquire new knowledge and to learn new skills. She was taught a host of information about the coffee industry and the Starbucks philosophy, while simultaneously gaining

experience in every area from drink mixing to cashiering and inventory logging. Her coworkers were patient, help-
ful, and kind to her during her training process, and she soon began to build meaningful relationships with them.
She even went out to dinner a few times with them and genuinely enjoyed their company.

Jennifer was both surprised and pleased with the positive environment at Starbucks and soon became loyal to
the company's mission. Instead of simply putting in her time and counting down the hours, Jennifer saw herself
as part of a group of people working toward a common goal. This job proved to be nothing like the experience she
had over the summer. Working at Starbucks began as a simple solution to her financial woes, but it quickly became
something much more.

Case Study Discussion Questions

1. What was Jennifer's primary reason for working at Starbucks? What kind of environment was she looking for?

2. What are some of the typical problems in working with others in a team environment?

3. List some characteristics of successful team experiences.

4. What is the primary mission of each Starbucks location? How does each store maintain high levels of commitment to that mission?

5. Field experiment: Next time you find yourself inside a Starbucks, observe the employees. What do you see? Ask them if they enjoy working there, and why. Ask them how their performance is measured as individual employees and as a team.

Jennifer's experiences as a team member at the clothing store and then at Starbucks were very different. When people join new teams, they eagerly observe the way team members communicate with one another and the way they work in order to figure out how they are supposed to act and what they are supposed to do. These observed "operating procedures" can be understood as the group's structure. As expectations, roles, and relationships become clear, team members find their place on the team and attempt to fit in. A well-conceived team design provides (a) predictability, by reducing ambiguity and, thereby, lowering anxiety; (b) efficiency, by maximizing resources and reducing coordination losses; and (c) member satisfaction, through improved relationships and task achievement. Unfortunately, work environments like the one Jennifer experienced at the clothing store are not uncommon. Much of the frustration and inefficiencies can be linked back to a faulty or ill-defined structure.

Team design can be imposed from an external source, or it can emerge organically from within the team itself. In a democratically oriented group, structure is mutually decided upon by members and emerges from the bottom up. Team members might volunteer for specific jobs and have the freedom to vote on when and where they will meet. For example, a group of community volunteers who have come together to address rising property taxes in their town will likely decide for themselves what they want to accomplish and how they will do it. This kind of empowerment and shared decision making can be an adjustment for many (Thoms, Pinto, Parente, & Druskat, 2002). Members who are conscientious, open to new ideas, and emotionally stable will be most successful and satisfied with self-structured groups (Molleman, Nuata, & Jehn, 2004).

Conversely, teams that operate in strict, hierarchical social systems, organizations, or cultures will have their structure defined from the top down. Some institutions have stringent regulations about the behavior and expectations of their members in terms of dress code, rules about communication, and policies regarding attendance, to name just a few. Employee handbooks and office protocol can take a lot of the guesswork out of knowing what is expected of members. Though individuals tend to experience higher levels of satisfaction when teams function more democratically in nature (Foels, Driskell, Mullen, & Salas, 2000), teams that are defined by the larger organizations within which they operate may be more efficient. In some cases, it may be more effective to be told exactly what to do and how to do it instead of spending a lot of time creating the right set of rules, roles, and interpersonal dynamics that satisfy the particular tastes of any given team. Furthermore, teams that need to respond quickly in crisis situations require strong autocratic leadership in order to maximize efficiency and minimize coordination losses. For example, the military requires a highly structured, top-down hierarchy of authority in order to accomplish tasks in potentially confusing and life-threatening situations. Surgical teams and cockpit crews are other groups in high-intensity situations where rules and roles are dictated by strict institutional policies and predetermined task assignments.

Figure 2.1 The Search for Stability

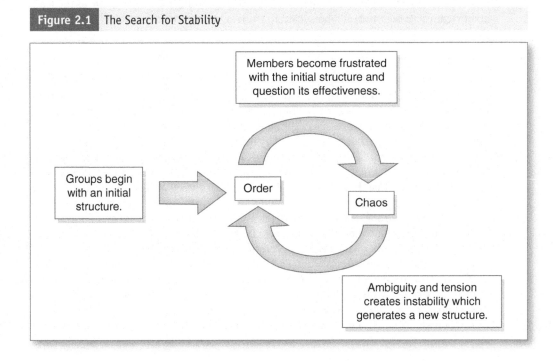

While initial structure provides security and stability for teams, it is important to note that social systems don't remain stable for very long. They frequently oscillate from stability (order) to instability (chaos) and back again (order). This fluid dynamic makes groups unpredictable, yet it also provides the potential for learning and development. Because of the diversity of opinion and experience within teams, members bring multiple perspectives regarding how they should operate; as a result, they often challenge the existing structure. The "storming" and "norming" stages of group development are necessary to move the team into "performing." In this way, ongoing reorganization and restructuring can be seen as a creative force that has the potential to maximize group effectiveness.

For example, imagine a fraternity that has just elected a new set of officers. Not surprisingly, the brothers were elected on the basis of popularity and not necessarily on their administrative experience or skills. After the "chaos" of elections, the new executive board is in the forming stage and the members settle into their roles and responsibilities according to their positions. Unfortunately, the new treasurer is not a detail person, and bills from outside venders start to fall through the cracks. Things get so bad that the president gets a letter from the local electric company threatening to turn off the house's electricity if it is not paid immediately. The president confronts the treasurer, but he gets defensive and blames the secretary for not delivering the bills to his mailbox. The rest of the officers are briefed on the situation and there is full-blown "storming" between those loyal to the treasurer and those critical of him. How can this team pull out of the downward spiral? The executive committee needs to have a "norming" session to get all the issues on the table and redefine procedures or reassign responsibilities to ensure the board is able to "perform" its function properly. These types of meetings can be messy, but they are necessary. After this, things will settle down as the leadership team stabilizes and members learn to work together more effectively.

ROLES AND RESPONSIBILITIES

As teams work on common goals, members fill various roles and responsibilities to contribute to the group effort. Roles are a "set of prescriptions that define the behaviors required of an individual member who occupies a certain position" (Bray & Brawley, 2002, p. 234). These roles can be assigned by the leader, decided by the team, or volunteered for by specific members. For example, the leader of a team working to raise money for a worthy cause might ask a certain member to contact various agencies with whom they might partner. Presumably, the leader perceives that the member to whom he or she gives the assignment either has the skills, commitment, or appropriate attitude to carry out the task. Other, less formal roles evolve through the group's process. After a few meetings, the service team mentioned above might realize that it would be advantageous to partner with other organizations and suggest that a particular member who has strong community ties explore that possibility.

Finally, members will often volunteer for those tasks that they feel most comfortable, confident, and competent doing (Bray & Brawley, 2002). For example, a member who has a lot of experience working for nonprofit organizations might be quick to volunteer to make initial contact with other groups.

As individuals consistently take on similar tasks and functions, other members will come to expect to see them in those roles. This is one way groups become predictable and

WRITE YOUR NOTES HERE

stable. When roles are ambiguous and unclear, members experience frustration and group performance suffers. But when everyone understands their role within the group, misunderstandings and process losses can be minimized. Consistent patterns of behavior from individual members can be associated with one or more of the three major categories of group roles: task roles, relationship roles, and individual roles (Forsyth, 2006).

Task roles are roles that contribute to the ultimate goal of the group. Members who primarily fill these roles provide critical thinking and strong organizational skills. They are able to analyze problems and overcome obstacles to success. These roles include the ability to make plans and create accountability structures. Sometimes perceived as driven, those immersed in task roles are goal-oriented and keep the group focused and on track. Productivity, efficiency, and achievement are important values to those who are in task roles, causing them to become frustrated if the group wastes time or becomes inefficient.

Relationship roles, on the other hand, are roles that build cohesion in the group. They fulfill the important functions of creating trust and increasing member satisfaction (Ilgen, Hollenbeck, Johnson, & Jundt, 2005). Members who fulfill relationship roles are aware of the interpersonal dynamics of the group and strive to encourage and validate others. While some may perceive these roles as overly concerned with non-task-related issues, both task and relationship roles are needed to balance the group experience and increase the chance for success.

The third type of role describes behavior patterns that are not often beneficial to the group. Individual roles work against the group's goals and distract the group from its mission. People who are playing individual roles are often frustrating to other members, as they passively or actively resist the work of the group. While they may serve a function by challenging and thereby establishing boundaries, individual roles are generally seen as more of a hindrance than a help to performance. The following list of team roles is adapted from a larger list of functional group roles originally developed by Benne and Sheats (1948).

At times, roles can become overly rigid to the point where members either get stuck in less than optimal roles or they become stagnant. This not only hurts their own development but can also prevent others from having the opportunity to experience that role. Family systems theory suggests that the healthiest families allow members to try different roles at different times. For example, the "rebel" of the family does not always have to be the rebel. Likewise, the family "hero" does not always have to be perfect. Applied to groups, the person who has played the role of "recorder" does not always have to be the one who takes notes. He or she may like a break, and someone else may want to take on that task for a while. Members who previously served as negative forces in the group should also be

Table 2.1

Task Roles	Function
Information seeker	Asks for facts, opinions, and ideas from the group, and for clarification and elaboration about existing concepts
Information giver	Contributes facts, opinions, and novel ideas to the group
Discussion facilitator	Facilitates the discussion by engaging the group
Task manager	Keeps the group on task and focuses on practical details
Skeptic	Challenges ideas and evaluates potential solutions
Recorder	Takes notes and records the decisions of the group

Table 2.2

Relationship Roles	Function
Encourager	Validates, affirms, and supports others
Harmonizer	Mediates conflict among group members
Process observer	Observes and periodically comments on the groups progress
Advocate	Helps quieter members to speak up and be heard in the group

Table 2.3

Individual Roles	Function
Resister	Opposes the group by being negative and passive-aggressive
Dominator	Dominates discussions and intimidates others
Avoider	Tries to do as little work as possible
Attention seeker	Calls attention to self to meet personal needs

given the opportunity to participate in more productive roles. However, groups often make it challenging, even for members playing negative roles, to change roles. Once initial impressions have been formed, it can be difficult to change them.

Interestingly, a given role can change the typical behavior of the role carrier. Commonly held beliefs about how a particular role should be carried out can determine an individual's behavior regardless of whether or not that behavior had previously been characteristic of that individual. The classic Stanford Prison Experiment is an example of the strength and influence of role expectations. In 1971 social psychologists at Stanford University enlisted 24 male students to participate in an experiment conducted in the psychology building on campus. Each was assigned, by the flip of a coin, to act as either a prisoner or a guard in a convincing mock prison that was constructed in the basement.

On the first day of the experiment, prisoners were "arrested" by local law enforcement officers, taken to the Palo Alto police station, and charged with armed robbery. They were booked, fingerprinted, had their mug shots taken, and then placed in a holding cell. When they were transported to the mock prison, their individual identity was largely taken from them; they were given ill-fitting muslin smocks to wear and were no longer referred to by name, but by number. The guards were dressed in military-style uniforms and wore mirrored sunglasses to prevent eye contact. They wore whistles around their necks and carried billy clubs borrowed from the local police department. Although the guards were forbidden to use physical force, they were otherwise encouraged to use any means possible to control the prisoners and maintain order in the prison.

By the second day of the experiment, the prisoners had already become weary of the humiliating environment and attempted to stage a rebellion. They ripped off their numbers, barricaded themselves in their cells, and began taunting the guards. The guards responded with anger and hostility, using a fire extinguisher to force prisoners back as they entered their cells. The guards then stripped the prisoners naked, put the leaders into solitary confinement, and began to harass and intimidate them. As they strongly identified with their arbitrarily assigned roles, the guards became abusive and the prisoners became passive and depressed. The entire experiment had to be stopped prematurely after only six days into the projected two-week timetable. The power of roles in conjunction with the power of peer influence ensured that everyone knew their place and were expected to behave accordingly. After a short time, the roles were no longer roles—they became identities.

In the case of the Stanford Prison Experiment, roles were exaggerated and, ultimately, dysfunctional. But well-defined roles can also be used in a very positive way. Members with clear roles know what they are expected to do and can execute their responsibilities with efficiency. Little time is wasted in confusion about which responsibilities belong to whom. In contrast, without clearly defined roles and agreed-upon division of responsibilities, teams sacrifice productivity and potentially even induce chaos. This would certainly be the case during the morning rush at Starbucks if the employees didn't have clearly defined roles for cashiers, baristas, backroom staff, and supervisors. Over time, standard operating procedures and interpersonal patterns are established and become part of the culture. These patterns of interaction create stability, predictability, and efficiency.

TEAM CULTURE

Culture is the learned set of shared beliefs, values, customs, and history that unifies a group of people, helps them make sense of their world, and influences their behavior. Southwest Airlines has been proactive and deliberate about creating a corporate culture that fosters mutual respect and a commitment to customer service. It devotes significant time and resources transmitting these particular values to new and existing employees. The culture of a group or organization can be communicated in many ways and through many symbolic mediums (Bolman & Deal, 2003). Organizational developers and team leaders often pay close attention to how these messages are communicated.

Myths, folklore, and stories represent and perpetuate the values and shared beliefs that tie a group of people together. For example, the hallways of Southwest Airlines' corporate headquarters are lined with pictures of the early days; these images of heroes, heroines, and milestones reinforce the company's shared set of beliefs and values. They are reminders of what is important to the organization. Group and organizational histories are rich with clues about the development of their cultures.

Company logos, team names, performance measures, and job titles all communicate distinct messages. The way people dress, the physical layout of offices and meeting rooms, and the way people talk to one another impact the overall environment. These symbolic messages are always present to influence what people are to believe and how they are to behave. Some team leaders are very deliberate about the kind of culture they want to create, while others let the group culture emerge organically. In either case, a team culture takes shape.

Rituals and ceremonies celebrate important moments in the life of the team (Martin, 2002). For example, initiation rituals indoctrinate new members, enhancement rituals recognize exemplary conduct, and degradation rituals publicly reprimand or remove poorly performing members from the group. Ending rituals signal the time when a member transitions out of a group. Whether they operate within a prison gang or on a corporate executive board, rituals reinforce the identity and structure of groups. This is because rituals are explicit ways that groups communicate and reinforce group culture. Walmart's founder, Sam Walton, conducted the following ritual with over 100,000 employees over TV satellite in the mid-1980s: "Now, I want you to raise your right hand—and remember what we say at Walmart, that a promise we make is a promise we keep—and I want you to repeat after me: From this day forward, I solemnly promise and declare that every time a customer comes within ten feet of me, I will smile, look him in the eye, and greet him. So help me, Sam" (Walton and Huey, 1992, p. 223.) This ritual helped create a culture that is reinforced every time a customer walks past a Walmart greeter. When customers walk into a Walmart store, they are welcomed with a warm, friendly greeting that is distinctly personal and engaging.

As individuals work together and form relationships, they develop a shared identity that distinguishes their group from others. According to social identity theory, this happens when individuals "identify themselves in the same way and have the same definition of

WRITE YOUR NOTES HERE

who they are, what attributes they have, and how they relate to and differ from specific out-groups or from people who are simply not in-group members" (Hogg, 2005, p. 136). As people experience various groups, either as members or outsiders, they create categories with which to associate individuals of that group. Thus, if a person has created an internal definition, or schema, that describes "chess players," then all new people who describe themselves as chess players are ascribed those attributes (Hogg & Reid, 2006).

Characteristics and attitudes that define a group's identity can have a strong influence on its members (Hogg & Reid, 2006). Social identity theory suggests that members adopt a common set of beliefs and behaviors when they associate with a certain group. Those that are strongly associated with a particular group will readily adopt the beliefs and goals that define that group (Christensen, Rothgerber, Wood, & Matz, 2004). Social norms that are integrated into personal identity then become standards against which to evaluate one's own beliefs and behavior. For example, in the highly polarized world of national politics, those who identify as either Democrats, Republicans, or independents are prone to having an overly optimistic assessment of their own party's views while discounting any ideas or proposals coming from a different group. When this happens, meaningful dialogue is compromised, as groups engage primarily in offensive and defensive posturing to gain or maintain power.

WRITE YOUR NOTES HERE

In the same way that individuals construct internal working models that include beliefs, goals, and strategies for daily functioning, groups create a shared working model or mental model to define the life and structure of the group (Ilgen, Hollenbeck, Johnson, & Jundt, 2005). Internal working models are cognitive roadmaps that provide a framework for understanding experiences (what is) and for defining ideals (what should be). They are established from previous group experiences and influenced by the larger sociocultural context within which they exist. Because groups establish unique and distinct mental models, two groups might perceive the same event in very different ways. For example, a group of homebuilders might be very enthusiastic about a large, highly desirable piece of land that was rezoned for residential building and put up for sale. But a neighboring homeowners' association might be upset due to potential problems with overcrowded schools or additional traffic. The local school administration could interpret this event in an altogether different way, seeing it as a way to increase funding and visibility in the district. But then, a group of conservation enthusiasts might be concerned about the potential impact on the environment. Each group has a unique set of shared beliefs, goals, and strategies that influence the way it interprets and evaluates new information.

Shared mental models include a common set of beliefs, attitudes, and values that guide group thinking and decisions. They define beliefs about the team in terms of group description, collective self-esteem, and group efficacy. As a result, an assessment of one's team can create a sense of pride and confidence. Individual members experience increased personal self-esteem when they are affiliated with a highly desirable and successful group (Aberson, Healy, & Romero, 2000). Because of these benefits, groups have a tendency to view their own group in overly inflated ways while viewing other groups, especially competing groups, in an overly negative way. This tendency is called the ingroup/outgroup bias, whereby individuals consider their group as better than other groups.

Members are not only influenced by the culture, but they also impact the culture in a reciprocal fashion. The personality of individual members contributes to the personality and identity of the larger group. The personalities of leaders, especially, can have a ripple effect upon a social context. Because of their stature and influence, they have the ability to establish and enforce policies that reflect their own values. For better or worse, charismatic leaders such as Herb Kelleher, CEO of Southwest Airlines, have tremendous influence over their organizational cultures. But it is not only top leaders that have influence; leaders and influential members (i.e., culture carriers) at all levels contribute to the collective atmosphere and often set the tone for group meetings. For example, skilled facilitators can create warm, inviting environments, where discussion is vibrant and engaging in contrast to ineffective facilitators, who can shut down conversations and discourage members from speaking up.

Have you ever wondered while you're placing an order for a vanilla latte or caramel macchiato at Starbucks, why the baristas are so friendly and helpful? They seem to enjoy their jobs and seem to be enjoying the camaraderie of their fellow teammates. In his autobiography, Howard Schultz, chair and CEO of Starbucks (Schultz & Yang, 1997), describes the passion and devotion of his employees as their "number one competitive advantage. Lose it, and we've lost the game" (p. 138).

By harnessing the power of teams, Starbucks grew from a single Seattle location in 1971 to 20,000 stores in 59 countries by 2012—and its success is not just numerical. Starbucks has won a multitude of awards including the "Ten Most Admired Companies in America" by *Fortune* magazine in 2003, 2004, and 2005, a trend that continues to date. In fact, Starbucks is one of the most admired companies in the world. It is frequently listed by the press and business literature in categories such as "most admired," "most influential," "top performers," and "best companies to work for." This last distinction deserves further discussion. What makes Starbucks so effective, and why is it such a great place to work?

One reason may be the shared culture that the company works to inspire among its employees. New Starbucks baristas receive a full 24 hours of in-store training that informs them not only about how to mix drinks and operate a cash register, but also about the coffee industry and the Starbucks franchise itself. And note that the term is always *barista* or *partner,* and not merely *worker* or *counter help,* thus further individuating Starbucks employees from other standard coffee shop workers. And finally, the company accepts and responds to an average of 200 mission review queries per month from employees with concerns or suggestions regarding the company mission. The care that Starbucks takes to institute both a unique training and team environment, coupled with the empowering feedback-oriented relationship established around the company's mission, help to make employees feel as though they are a valued part of a greater shared vision. It comes as little surprise to learn that the first of Starbucks' six-point mission statement is to "provide a great work environment and treat each other with respect and dignity."

With the shift away from hierarchal authority structures in recent decades, organizations have relied upon self-managed groups to establish their own unique ground rules and operating procedures that produce results (Pfeffer, 1992). This popular management strategy of empowerment utilizes the dynamics of group conformity to hold members accountable to high standards. High-performance standards and "cult-like cultures" often exist in the most successful organizations (Collins & Porras, 2002). A concrete ideology reinforced by strong methods of indoctrination can create cohesive group environments that socialize members into proven strategies for success.

However, it is important to note that a strong team culture can have negative consequences as well. Groupthink is a condition that occurs when teams are overly cohesive or when one or more members have too much power and influence over the group as a whole. For example, the Senate Intelligence Committee (2004), which assessed the U.S. intelligence systems' conclusion in falsely identifying Iraq's possession of weapons of mass destruction, identified groupthink as one of the contributing factors to the error. Apparently, the general presumption that Iraq had such weapons was so strongly felt by top members of the administration that individuals were reluctant to question what they perceived as the majority position. When a single dominant member or small group of members have enough influence to make judgments that others in the group are reluctant to question, the checks and balances of group decision making are compromised. The process and potential pitfalls of team decision making is discussed in length in Chapter 7.

BUILDING A TEAM

Team design begins with a clear understanding of the task that the team is being asked to accomplish. After that has been established, it is time to begin identifying and enlisting the members that will give the team the best opportunity to fulfill its purpose. Some important and highly interrelated aspects to consider are the complexity of the task; the amount and type of interaction that will be required of members; and, finally, the number and type of members to enlist. Not all teams have a discreet beginning. In fact, most group memberships evolve over time. In those cases, existing teams can regularly evaluate their performance to determine if they have the right mix of people along with an enabling structure and positive culture that lead to results. If not, the following concepts can help improve performance.

Task Complexity

Groups that engage in complex tasks require greater levels of coordination, participation, and decentralized communication (Brown & Miller, 2000; Lafond, Jobidon, Aubé, & Tremblay, 2011). There are simply more details and interdependencies to monitor and manage. Task complexity increases with the following:

- Task unfamiliarity (lack of previous experience)

- Task ambiguity (absence of clear mission or goals)

- The volume of information required to understand the task

- The number of alternatives available in reaching the desired outcome

- The number of subordinate tasks to be defined and coordinated

For example, restructuring a student organization would be a more complex task than collaboratively writing a research paper. Imagine yourself as an executive council member of a fraternity that has had repeated alcohol violations and must either restructure the house or face possible expulsion from campus. The leadership team is likely to have had little or no previous experience with the task before it. In addition, the students will be challenged by the relative ambiguity of the goal of "restructuring." In contrast, writing a group research paper for a history class does not have this same level of complexity. The desired outcome is fairly straightforward, as students will have had plenty of experience writing papers by the time they have reached college.

Group members performing highly complex tasks need to work together closely to determine their best options for success. These higher levels of interdependence and cooperation mean that, depending on the type of interdependence required (see next section), extra attention may need to be paid to selecting team members with superior communication skills. When task complexity stems from a lack of familiarity or background information, teams will benefit from the advice of experts in the field. If a team doesn't have the expertise within its ranks, it must find it outside the team. Finally, regardless of the source of complexity, teams performing complex tasks must clearly define their vision, create detailed action plans, and have regular status updates to ensure that members are informed of the team's progress.

Types of Interdependence

As stated in the previous section, the amount of cooperation needed for success is strongly related to the type and complexity of the tasks being undertaken. When high levels of interdependence are required, clearly defined roles must be in place in order for teams to be successful (Allen, Sargent, & Bradley, 2003). The nature of these roles will largely be determined by the type of interdependence needed to accomplish the task. Thompson (2004) identifies three distinct types of interdependence within groups: pooled, sequential, and reciprocal interdependence.

Pooled interdependence refers to group work that may simply be divided among members in order to be compiled into a finished product at a later time. For example, a group of workers cleaning up after a big football game might each take a section of the stadium from which to pick up trash and sweep. Though they work independently of one another, the workers collectively clean the entire stadium. These types of tasks require the least amount of cooperation and communication.

Pooled interdependence is more effective when teams have the following structural procedures in place: (a) a reporting structure in which a supervisor or leader can hold members accountable for their part of the project, (b) regular team meetings where members can discuss potential problems and improve policies and procedures, and

Figure 2.2   Pooled Interdependence

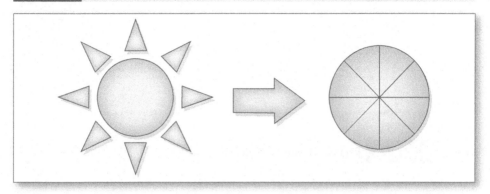

(c) a way to keep members committed to the overall task by reinforcing and updating each member's understanding of how their part will be integrated into the finished product.

Other tasks require more coordination among members. Sequential interdependence occurs when group members are dependent on the completed work of other members prior to being able to complete their own part. As one person finishes a portion of the task, he or she hands it off to the next person. The "hand off" can be a bottleneck in the process, so it requires thoughtful attention. In the case of a relay team, track and field athletes will rehearse the simple act of handing the baton to the next runner countless times before competing in an actual race. Efficiency in the handing of the baton could be the difference between victory and defeat, especially in a sport that is decided by milliseconds.

In another example, before a Starbucks barista can make a coffee drink, he or she is dependent upon someone else to order and then to stock the ingredients that are needed to brew the coffee. Thus, each member's work is dependent on other members fulfilling their portion of the task. Therefore, sequentially interdependent groups must pay close attention to the transition points between each member's portion of the task. Groups may want to establish a routine for notifying the next member in sequence when a task has been completed. It may also be beneficial to create a procedure for informing the next member of delays or changes that will affect their segment of the work. High-performance teams identify mistakes or problems early on and learn from them as opposed to hiding them or covering them up.

Reciprocal interdependence requires the greatest level of interaction among members as they work together simultaneously. Members influence one another as tasks are accomplished simultaneously with input from others. For example, sailing teams in the America's Cup races have a highly defined structure that dictates who does what and when. Every member is needed to successfully complete the task, and there is little room for role negotiation.

Figure 2.3 Sequential Interdependence

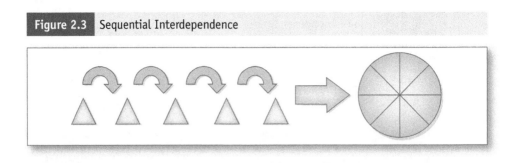

Figure 2.4 Reciprocal Interdependence

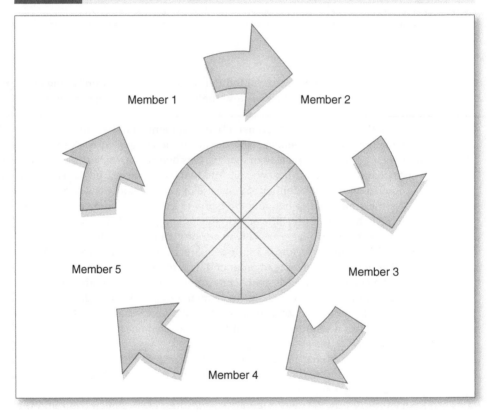

Examples of this type of interdependence include zone defenses in football, marching bands, and Broadway plays. Each member is required to do his or her part according to well-defined protocols in order for the whole group to be successful.

Team Composition

The success or failure of a team is strongly related to the quality of its membership. Collins's (2001) popular book, *Good to Great: Why Some Companies Make the Leap . . . and Others Don't,* stresses the importance of finding the best people possible. Metaphorically speaking, he suggests that "getting the right people on the bus" is even more important than deciding where the bus is going, because high-caliber individuals will be able to figure out where the bus needs to go and determine the best route for getting there. Research on sports teams suggests that "the best individuals make the best team" (Gill, 1984, p. 325). This correlation between individual talent and team performance is strongest in sports such as baseball (.94) and football (.91). However, it is entirely possible for a group of highly skilled players to be a poorly performing team. For example, though a soccer team of eleven all-star goalies may boast an extraordinary amount of individual talent, their performance as a team may suffer because their one-dimensional level of expertise does not encompass all of the skills required to play a well-rounded game of soccer. Thus, not only do teams need to have talented members, those members need to have skills that complement one another.

Ideally, each member will possess task-related knowledge and skills along with interpersonal skills that enable them to work with others. The relative amount of each type of skill that a given member should possess will depend on the complexity of the task and the level of interdependence required to achieve the desired outcome. More specifically, task-related knowledge and skills are especially important on tasks that are complex and that require highly specialized knowledge and skills to achieve results. On the other hand, members of reciprocally interdependent teams will need stronger interpersonal skills than do members of groups that use sequential or pooled methods. Regardless, group work will always call upon some mixture of both sets of skills; thus, it is important to be aware of each when building a team.

While task-related competence is important to consider in choosing potential members, ideal members also possess strong interpersonal skills. Members who are considered "team players" are enthusiastic, optimistic, collegial, cooperative, and flexible (Rousseau, Aubé, & Savoie, 2006). Furthermore, they are self-motivated and conscientious, and have strong communication skills. Communication skills such as active listening and assertiveness are used both to support and to challenge other team members. Yet individuals who have strong interpersonal skills are self-aware enough to know that they are not being overly assertive, derogatory, or offensive. In addition, they are able to accept negative feedback from others and respond in a nondefensive manner. Of course, those with strong interpersonal skills also know how to give critical feedback in a way that is motivated by a desire to help others, not tear them down. Spirited banter through which members challenge one another's assumptions is often the hallmark of high-performing teams; it is described in detail in Chapter 6, on communication.

Stevens and Campion (1999) have developed the Teamwork-KSA Test to measure team knowledge, skills, and abilities (KSAs). After reviewing the research, they determined five specific areas associated with effective participation in groups:

Interpersonal Knowledge, Skills, and Abilities

Conflict resolution: Recognizing types and sources of conflict; encouraging desirable conflict but discouraging undesirable conflict; and employing integrative (win-win) negotiation strategies rather than distributive (win-lose) strategies.

Collaborative problem-solving: Identifying situations requiring participative group problem-solving and using the proper degree of participation; recognizing obstacles to collaborative group problem-solving and implementing appropriate corrective actions.

Communication: Understanding effective communication networks using decentralized networks where possible; recognizing open and supportive communication methods; maximizing the consistency between nonverbal and verbal messages; recognizing and interpreting the nonverbal messages of others; and engaging in and understanding the importance of small talk and ritual greetings.

Self-Management Knowledge, Skills, and Abilities

Goal-setting and performance management: Establishing specific, challenging, and accepted team goals, and monitoring, evaluating, and providing feedback on both overall team performance and individual team member performance.

Planning and task coordination: Coordinating and synchronizing activities, information, and tasks among team members, as well as aiding the team in establishing individual task and role assignments that ensure the proper balance of workload among members.

Sources: Miller (2001, p. 748); Stevens and Campion (1994, p. 505).

The Teamwork-KSA Test is just one of many assessment tools available commercially for assessing current and potential members, and its results are often used for member selection or staff development.

Team Size

After team designers clarify the team's task, predict the level of interdependence that will be required for success, and identify potential members, they must decide how many members to enlist. In smaller groups of three or four, members may have to take on multiple roles and responsibilities. But in groups of more than eight or ten members, coordination can become cumbersome. The complexity and breadth of the task to be completed will help to inform the minimum number of members required to complete the task. In other words, the number of specializations or fields that the task will call upon, added to the human capital that will be required in order to carry out the job, will yield an estimate as to the number of individuals that should be called to the team. Noted team expert J. Richard Hackman (2002) emphasizes the importance of team size and specifically warns against the common error of placing too many members on a team.

What are the risks associated with oversized teams? Coordination losses increase as the number of people involved on any given task increases and relational bonds weaken (Mueller, 2012). As group size grows, individual members may also become passive due to a diffusion of responsibility, a lack of accountability, and ultimately a reduction in commitment

| **Figure 2.5** | Effects of Group Size on Cohesion and Coordination Problems |

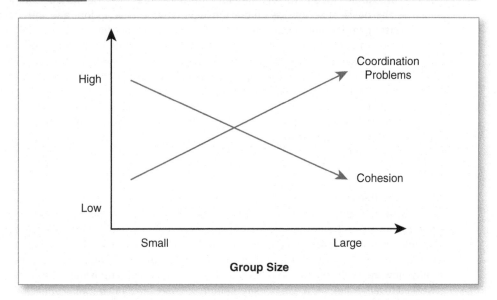

(Wagner, 1995). In a study of group performance on a decision-making task, three-person groups consistently outperformed seven-person groups (Seijts & Latham, 2000). This means that not only did having an extra four people fail to contribute positively to the outcome of the group, the additional members actually hindered performance. One reason for this is that smaller groups tend to have higher levels of commitment among their membership. Similarly, they have fewer members who engage in social loafing, which is the desire to do as little work as possible. Smaller groups simply cannot afford to have members slacking off. It's also harder for members to fly under the radar in smaller groups. Laughlin, Hatch, Silver, and Boh (2006) found that three-, four-, or five-member groups outperformed individuals and dyads on a problem-solving task but did not differ from one another.

As groups increase in size, it is also more difficult to maintain a sense of connection with fellow group members. Individuals have a limited capacity for the number of people with whom they may feel reasonably close. As groups get larger, it is increasingly difficult to establish and maintain high levels of cohesion (Gammage, Carron, & Estabrooks, 2001). Hackman (2002) suggests that the optimal size for a group is the fewest number of members who can feasibly accomplish the tasks assigned to them. The ideal size for most groups is typically between four and eight members, once again depending upon the complexity and breadth of the task.

LAUNCHING A TEAM

Once team membership is determined, team builders must give thought to how they will introduce team members to their task, and to one another. The first face-to-face meeting is a critical event in the life of a team. Patterns of relating and general operating procedures can become established in the opening minutes of the first meeting. Various components such as the physical setting, seating arrangements, task description, and introductions forge a lasting impression on the members of the team. In addition, interpersonal dynamics such as communication patterns and status hierarchies will influence the emerging structure of the group. Thus, it is important to conduct a well-structured and thoughtfully planned launch meeting, since it is generally much easier to establish effective team processes at the beginning of a team's development than to correct faulty ones later (Polzer, 2003). This first meeting sets the foundation upon which the group and its work will be built, so consistency, foresight, transparency, and candor must be used throughout the following four preliminary steps.

Introductions

One of the first tasks of running a successful launch is taking the time to make thorough and thoughtful introductions. Introductions help begin the process of forging bonds and developing trust. Tasks that are highly interdependent require significant amounts of mutual trust, and it is difficult for members to trust those they do not know. Members often come into new teams with some measure of anxiety and uncertainty because they don't know how they will compare to other members. For teams with individuals who have never worked together before, it can be very helpful to share brief biographies of each member to familiarize the team with one another. This allows members to become aware of the unique value and expertise each member will bring to the team, including their own potential contribution. Take, for example, the introduction that Jennifer's manager at Starbucks made on her first day of work. Not only did his kind words infuse a feeling of initial respect from her new coworkers, they helped contribute to her own self-confidence in that new and unfamiliar work setting.

Since introductions can be stressful, leaders might want to consider ways to minimize the need for members to try to prove themselves or promote their own superiority. Thus, leaders can use a prepared description of each member so that the members themselves do not feel put on the spot. In this way, the team designer or leader can highlight the strengths that each team member brings to the team in order to establish the norm that all members have been carefully selected and are important for the team's success. Another strategy is for members to pair up, interview one another, and then introduce their partner to the rest of the team. In general, this is a time for members to learn about one another. They should have more confidence in their teammates after going through this exercise.

Ground Rules

The launch meeting is also a prime opportunity to establish initial rules and expectations for members. Setting concrete ground rules is an effective way to reduce uncertainty and establish what will be expected of each member. Ground rules differ from implicit norms. Implicit norms, which we will cover in more depth in a later chapter, are the unstated yet generally accepted rules that are established based on the team members' experiences together. Ground rules, on the other hand, are the specifically stated regulations and standards to which every member is expected to adhere. The launch meeting provides the team leader with an important opportunity to establish these rules because everyone is likely to be present, attentive, and eager to comply with what is asked of them. Here are some typical ground rules established at the first meeting: (a) meetings will start and end on time, (b) members should let others know if they cannot attend or will be late, (c) texting and cell phones are not appropriate during team meetings, (d) everyone is expected to contribute to discussions, and so on. Publicly stating these guidelines, even those that seem obvious, will eliminate ambiguity and serve as a foundation for other rules and norms that will be added throughout the team members' time together.

Some rules will be established by the leader while others will be left up to team members themselves. In fact, it can be helpful to ask members to describe how they best work in teams or about the types of team dynamics that have worked best for them in the past. This will help them to establish ownership in the functioning of the group and create a collaborative team environment.

Shared Vision

High-performance teams go much further beyond mere compliance or perfunctory obedience to group expectations. The most effective teams are committed to a shared vision. An engaging vision defines the purpose for which the group exists. From that purpose, specific goals emerge that have the potential to motivate members and guide collective efforts (Van Mierlo & Kleingeld, 2010). A compelling direction that captures the hearts and minds of team members separates true teams from mere workgroups (Hackman, 2002). Launching the team in a way that lays out the task in a compelling way can help motivate and jump-start the process.

In the movie *Braveheart*, William Wallace (played by actor Mel Gibson) rode to the battlefield at Stirling, Scotland, to confront a group of Scottish peasants fleeing before a superior British army. In the film, Wallace was faced with the daunting task of inspiring a shared vision of such proportions that the peasants would be willing to give up their own lives to fight the British in order to become a free nation. Much to Wallace's credit, the peasants, who had been nothing more than pawns with which the Scottish nobles bargained for their own personal gain, began to embrace Wallace's vision as they considered the possibilities for their children and grandchildren. Because of their shared vision, the peasants were willing to make great personal sacrifice and commit themselves to battle. According to the Hollywood version of this thirteenth-century historical event, Wallace challenged the enemy to a battle, and with the help of the peasants, nobles, and some clever strategy, managed to defeat the British in a surprising victory.

Motivational speeches alone rarely generate the long-term commitment required for group success. Eventually, motivation must come from within the group itself, not imposed from an outside source (Liu, Zhang, Wang, & Lee, 2011). A shared vision often begins with one or two members and then spreads to the rest of the group. In the case of William Wallace, fighting for a free Scotland was his passion, and he was willing to pay the ultimate price for it. In his petition to the Scottish peasants he offered few extrinsic rewards, yet the vision he inspired regarding the possibility of a better life for future generations was enough to motivate the ragtag army.

A shared vision stimulates the interest, enthusiasm, and creativity of group members (Cohen & Bailey, 1997). More important, it generates commitment. Personal goals are put aside as members work for the common good of the group and the ultimate mission of the organization. For instance, if a Starbucks employee is only serving coffee and cleaning tables, he or she may feel disengaged or lack motivation. However, if the employee sees his or her job as providing a meaningful service to others and contributing to the success of the team, then pouring coffee and emptying trash cans take on a whole new meaning. This transformation of thinking can be a wonderful benefit of working in teams or groups. Collaborating with a group of friendly, outgoing people on a meaningful task can make an otherwise wearisome 5:00 a.m. shift significantly more enjoyable.

Levels of Commitment

WRITE YOUR NOTES HERE

Thompson (2004) suggests that the most common leadership challenge identified by more than half (56%) of the leaders in her study is developing and sustaining high levels of team motivation. Consequently, team leaders should use the launch meeting to set the stage for true commitment from the membership. People are drawn to groups for collective benefits. However, they will also want to preserve personal interests. The result is a tension between conforming to the will of the group and preserving individuality and autonomy. Not all members will be committed to the group's goals; some will resist. This resistance can come in many forms, including a passive response (do nothing to help the group), an aggressive response (actively resist the leader or other members of the group), or a passive-aggressive response (resist indirectly while appearing to be supportive of the group's goals). Leaders can overcome member resistance by creating a shared vision around which members can rally.

Group members can experience various degrees of commitment at different times. The following levels describe the possible ways members might relate to the goals of the team (Senge, 1990):

- *Commitment:* These members are committed to the goal and motivated to achieve it. They are also committed to the group and have interest in and concern for the other group members.

- *Compliance:* Members who are compliant will do what they are asked in spite of not having embraced the importance of the group's mission. While they rarely volunteer or go above and beyond what is expected, they consistently fulfill their responsibilities.

- *Resistance:* Group members who are resistant are working against the group. They are actively trying to sabotage particular members or even the group as a whole for their own personal reasons. If the leadership of the group is fairly authoritarian, these resistant members tend to be passive-aggressive, as they secretly try to enlist other members to join in working against the group.

- *Disengagement:* These members are physically present but are apathetic toward the work of the group. Their clear disinterest and lack of engagement likely render them undependable in the eyes of their colleagues.

One undergraduate student offered the following example of how member commitment affects the team:

My junior year of high school, I played bass and guitar for a band with some friends from church. After performing three songs for a local battle of the bands, we got a call from a guy at the Dallas House of Blues to play in a battle of the bands downtown. The winning band got a recording contract and $3,000. We had one month to get ready. Immediately, I started writing original songs for the battle of the bands. In the meantime, we asked the other band members to begin learning some cover songs that we would perform as well. When it came time to practice five days later, I asked everyone if they were ready to practice the covers. The female vocalist said she "never got around to it." The drummer and other guitarist nodded in agreement. "What do you mean 'you never got around to it?'" the band's male vocalist asked. "Learning those cover songs was the only thing we told you guys to do. How can we have a productive practice if no one knows their parts?" "Okay, I'm sorry," the female vocalist said. "Let's just go to dinner, and practice next weekend." Reluctantly, TJ and I agreed. "But for next time we need everyone to know those cover songs, because we will really need to practice our original songs as well." A week passed and I practiced and spent some more time writing with TJ and our other guitarist, Matt. When next week came, once again, no one knew the cover songs. TJ and I cancelled practice and sent everyone home to learn the covers for a practice in the next few days. However, when TJ asked everyone when they could practice, no one could practice until the next weekend. Two weeks from the House of Blues battle of the bands, the band had no songs prepared. By the weekend before the battle of the bands, my band only knew one cover and had half of a song written and rehearsed. After briefly discussing practicing during the weekdays, everyone decided it would be best if we just did not perform at the battle of the bands, and focused on other things. After that the band never played together again.

Each member's commitment level contributes to the collective strength of the group. Compliant members are loosely connected to the group, while resistant or disengaged members are negative forces that serve to weaken the group. Effective leaders pay attention to group interactions from day one to assess the commitment level of each member and appropriately address those members whose commitment is lacking.

LEADERSHIP IN ACTION

Throughout this chapter, we have provided theories, suggestions, and examples outlining the foundational steps of building a healthy team. However, think back to the last time you were a part of forming a team. Was it a structured, logical, and effective process? More likely, you found yourself and your team down a road you hadn't planned to take, fumbling along toward a general outcome or product without a formalized system of values, expectations, or shared agreement about how often you would meet, the quality of the ultimate deliverable, and the distribution of responsibilities. At that point, the enthusiasm and optimism of a new team most likely deteriorated into frustration and even dread.

In order to start a new team in the right direction, there are a few key agreements to strike early. Much of this can be achieved by calling the foundational components by name and requiring the group to engage the issues directly and explicitly. For example, in the first meeting of a group of students working together on a class project, members should introduce themselves to one another. Introductions should include each member's name, where they are from, what they are studying, what they like to do in their free time, and what they think their academic strengths are. Leaders should take notes during this round-robin introduction session so they can identify common interests, complementary strengths, and levels of motivation. A discussion about ground rules can easily emerge with the following prompt: "Okay, now that we see how much potential we have, I think we should take a few minutes to set up a few ground rules for how we want to work together."

Ground rules include "rules of engagement" that regulate participation, interaction, conduct, and productivity. One of the ground rules that most teams should adopt is "everyone must offer their full and earnest participation." This bars individuals from holding back, biting their tongue, or "checking out." From those rules and from the shared personal details that emerged from the introductions, trust begins to form. Trust builds upon the safety and consistency provided by the ground rules (and their necessary enforcement). Next, the leader can describe the task and, thus, begin building a vision for success. And from the vision, common ground, shared rules, and trust, the group can achieve an identity. This may seem or feel like a forced or overly intentional approach to building a team, but the best results don't occur by accident. They are the result of an earnest, consistent, and dedicated architecture. Real-world examples include the 1980 U.S, men's Olympic hockey team portrayed in the movie *Miracle*; the 2008 U.S. men's Olympic basketball team; and Earnest Shackleton's Antarctic expeditionary crew that survived against all odds in the face of isolation, starvation, and hopelessness from 1914 to 1917. They are all the products of an effectively and intentionally built team.

The complex challenge of assembling, coordinating, and motivating high-performance teams requires dedication and know-how. By applying the key concepts described in this chapter and building a solid structural foundation, teams are positioned for success.

KEY TERMS

Predictability   20
Efficiency   20
Member satisfaction   20
Task roles   23
Relationship roles   23

Individual roles   23
Ingroup/outgroup bias   28
Groupthinkm29
Pooled interdependence   30
Sequential interdependence   31

DISCUSSION QUESTIONS

1. Explain the difference between task roles, relationship roles, and individual roles.

2. Discuss the importance of rituals in respect to corporations such as Walmart, Southwest Airlines, and Starbucks.

3. Describe the three types of interdependence in groups: pooled interdependence, sequential interdependence, and reciprocal interdependence. Give examples of each.

4. Describe Stevens and Campion's five types of skills associated with ideal team members.

5. Describe the strengths and weaknesses of a large versus a small team. How do you know how many members to place on a new team?

6. Explain the importance of introductions and facilitating a successful launch. How do these contribute to a shared vision?

7. Group members can have any of the following attitudes toward the group's main goal: commitment, compliance, resistance, and disengagement. Describe each of these attitudes and provide examples.

GROUP ACTIVITIES

EXERCISE 2.1 GROUP ANALYSIS

Get into groups of four and complete this task: Compare and contrast two different student groups on campus. Before you begin, assign roles for the discussion. Each person should either be a task leader, recorder, time keeper, or skeptic.

What is the primary objective or goal of the groups? How are members selected to be a part of the groups? Describe the culture of each of the groups. What are the strengths and weaknesses of each of the groups?

You are to submit a written analysis at the end of the prescribed time and present your analysis to the rest of the class.

EXERCISE 2.2 PRESENTATIONS ABOUT GROUP STRUCTURE

Form groups of five to seven people and prepare a three-minute presentation on the three most important concepts in this chapter. Describe the concepts, illustrate the concepts with examples, and apply the concepts to an actual group or team that could benefit from this information. Assign one of your team members to observe how you accomplish this task. That person will watch and take notes but will not participate in the actual task. After each group presents, the observer will describe how his or her group approached this task.

CASE 2.2 PLANNING A COMMUNITY OUTREACH

It's the first week of your summer internship at Futura Industries, and you've been asked by Jasmine, the company's internship coordinator, to meet with her in the conference room. She lets you know that she is putting together a group of interns to form a team charged with the responsibility of planning a community outreach event for the company to raise money for a local animal shelter. Because you have had a class on teams, she is asking you to be the team leader and to identify potential members. She has given you a deadline and some goals in terms of how many summer associates at the company she would like to have participate and how much money Futura Industries wants to raise.

- What kind of team members would you pick from the other interns? Describe their characteristics.

- How many people would you ideally like to have on your team, and why?

- Create a detailed agenda for your first meeting with the internship coordinator.

Communication

Griffiths, B.A. and Dunham, E.B.

Verbal and nonverbal communication among group members defines much team life. Individual goals, team goals, structure, and norms are evident in the communication patterns that develop among members. Tasks are accomplished and relationships managed through interpersonal interaction. Yet not all communication is positive, and as a result, team performance can be compromised. This chapter describes communication skills and patterns that lead to team success. It also identifies specific strategies members can adopt to improve their ability to communicate effectively. The chapter ends with a discussion about virtual communication and the benefits and challenges of virtual teams.

CASE 5.1: *THE APPRENTICE*

The TV reality show The Apprentice *first aired on NBC during the winter of 2004 and quickly became the hit that it is today. At the beginning of each season, 16 contestants are divided into two teams that compete against each other for the ultimate prize of becoming the president of one of Donald Trump's companies. Every week the two teams face off in various challenges, ranging from selling lemonade on the streets of New York City to organizing charity events. The project leader of the losing team must face Trump in the boardroom and explain why the team did not succeed. Trump then identifies a member of the team who, in his opinion, was most responsible for the loss and issues his now famous decree, "You're fired."*

In week two of the first season, the two teams, Versacorp (all men) and Protégé (all women), were given the task of designing an advertising campaign for a private jet service. Each team chose a project leader and began to structure the task. The men made a strategic error when they decided not to conduct customer interviews. Not knowing the distinguishing characteristics or the desires of the customer proved to be fatal and led to Versacorp's downfall. In addition, one of the more eccentric members of the team, Sam, talked excessively during planning sessions, frequently getting off topic. In one of the meetings, when he spent valuable project time lying on the floor of a conference room taking a nap, his credibility was compromised. As a result, when he later tried to interject his ideas and influence other members, he was interrupted by the project leader, Jason, and marginalized.

In contrast to the men, Protégé met with the customer and eventually decided upon an advertising campaign that used sexual overtones in its print ads. However, not all the members were comfortable using that approach, as it risked offending the customer. In the process of discussing options and making decisions, a number of members had different opinions, and tempers flared. Even though the women won the competition, it became obvious that there were serious interpersonal problems on their team. Two of the members, Omarosa and Ereka, had engaged in a number of arguments, and other members of the team were concerned that their dislike for each other would hurt the team's performance in the future.

For this challenge, Trump asked Donny Deutsch, the principal of a successful advertising agency in New York City, to decide the winning proposal. Deutsch and his two associates were torn between the men and the women. The sex appeal in the women's presentation may not have been appropriate for an actual print campaign, but it showed that they were more creative and willing to take risks. Ultimately, those qualities persuaded Deutsch to declare the women victorious. In addition, he commented that their presentation was sharper and more persuasive than that of the men. Their ability to communicate their ideas with passion and enthusiasm connected well with Deutsch.

After losing the task, Jason, the project manager for the men's team, identified Sam as the team's biggest problem. Jason explained to Trump how Sam failed the group by literally falling asleep during the project and not caring about the team's performance. Sam told Trump that Jason was just an average leader who made many mistakes, including not meeting with the customer. He added that because the team did not take the time to thoroughly understand the customer's needs, the project plan was flawed from the start. Thus, Sam didn't respect Jason's leadership and became passively detached. In the end, Trump held the team leader, Jason, responsible and fired him; Sam was spared. However, the group members became so frustrated with him that they decided to make him team leader for the next project in an effort to get him to "put up or shut up." While this may have been a strategic move to deal with Sam, the team suffered, losing the next competition. Although the women's team was winning competitions, interpersonal conflicts began taking their toll. Hostility and mistrust among members began to compromise the team's ability to perform.

Case Study Discussion Questions

- What should the men do about Sam? How do you view members who don't exactly fit in with the group? Is Sam a resource or a liability to the team? Explain.

- Two of the women strongly dislike each other. How would you handle that situation?

- What do you typically do in group situations when people are angry and start attacking one another? What do you do when others challenge you?

- What communication skills are needed in the men's group? In the women's group?

In an article in *Business Communication Quarterly,* Kinnick and Parton (2005) describe the results of a content analysis they performed on all 15 episodes from the first season of *The Apprentice.* They examined the following communication skills in each of the episodes: oral and written communications, interpersonal communication, teamwork skills, intercultural communication, negotiating skills, and ethical communication. In addition, they examined Trump's view of how those skills influenced individual and team performance. Trump and his associates identified poor communication skills as a factor in 5 of the 15 team losses. Poor communication was also cited as a factor in more than half of the individual firings. The last five players in the competition at the end of the season were considerably more likely to be praised for their communication skills than were the first five who were eliminated.

Communication skills are foundational for individual, team, and organizational success (Kinnick & Parton, 2005). For example, oral communication and interpersonal skills are often cited as the most important criteria in evaluating job candidates. Interpersonal skills were mentioned more frequently than any other competency listed in classified ads for entry-level jobs in 10 major metropolitan newspapers. Not surprisingly, the U.S. Department of Labor has identified communication and interpersonal skills as core requirements for future workers. Colleges work hard to prepare individuals for professional success by helping them develop these skills through team-based learning activities and class projects (Kalliath & Laiken, 2006). And once employees are hired, organizations invest significant resources to enhance their communication skills. According to one study, 88% of U.S. companies provide communication skills training for their employees (*Industry Report,* 1999). The importance of communication cannot be overstated. Thus, it is important to thoroughly understand this powerful interpersonal process.

ENCODING AND DECODING MESSAGES

Communication is the exchange of thoughts, information, or ideas that results in mutual understanding between two or more people. The process requires at least one sender, one receiver, and a message that is transmitted within a communication medium. It begins with an idea or concept in the mind of the sender. He or she encodes the idea into meaningful symbols in the form of words, pictures, or gestures (i.e., language). The sender then selects a medium to transmit those symbols so the receiver can access them through one or more senses. The medium can be a face-to-face conversation, a piece of artwork hanging in an

Figure 5.1 Sending and Receiving Messages

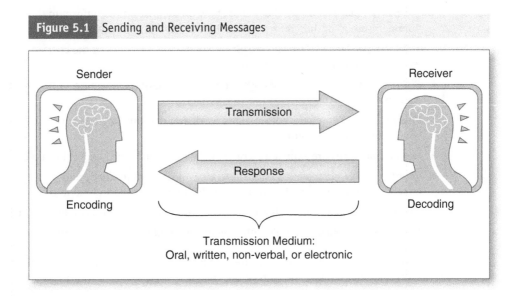

art gallery, a text message, or any growing number of electronic transmission media. When the receiver receives the message, he or she must decode the symbols in order to interpret the message and understand the intent of the sender, as depicted below.

Meaningful communication takes place when the receiver accurately understands the message transmitted by the sender. However, this does not always happen perfectly. A multitude of potential problems can hinder the process and block understanding. The rest of the chapter examines the many ways in which a message can become distorted or mis-understood; it also suggests ways to minimize the potential for communication missteps.

VERBAL COMMUNICATION

The use of verbal statements is one of the most common ways individuals communicate with one another. As team members work together to understand problems and manage projects, hundreds, if not thousands, of verbal comments are exchanged. A team member might be communicating a message at face value, or he or she may be implying hidden meanings or even multiple layers of meaning in a single statement. Because members do not always know the exact intent of one another's comments, there can be multiple interpretations and frequent misunderstandings. In the early stages of group development, team members have to learn the most effective way to interact with and understand that particular group.

Wheelan and her associates have developed a classification system called the Group Development Observation System (GDOS) as a way of categorizing and analyzing the verbal interactions that take place among group members (Wheelan, Davidson, & Tilin, 2003). The GDOS classifies statements into one of eight categories, and while statements can some-times fit more than one category, trained observers are in agreement 85% to 95% of the time. The eight GDOS categories are as follows:

- *Dependency statements* are those that show an inclination to conform to the dominant mood of the group and to solicit direction from others.
- *Counterdependency statements* assert independence by resisting the current leadership and direction of the group.
- *Fight statements* directly challenge others using argumentativeness, criticism, or aggression.
- *Flight statements* are attempts to avoid work and demonstrate a lack of commitment to the group.
- *Pairing statements* are expressions of warmth, friendship, and support toward others.
- *Counterpairing statements* demonstrate an avoidance of intimacy and interpersonal connection by keeping the discussion distant and intellectual.
- *Work statements* are those that represent goal-directed and task-oriented efforts.
- *Unscorable statements* include unintelligible, inaudible, or fragmentary statements.

After observing 26 task groups in various stages of development, researchers identified 31,782 verbal statements made during one meeting for each of the groups. Wheelan,

Davidson, and Tilin (2003) found that established groups utilized twice as many task-related statements as compared with newly formed groups. In the early stages of group development, for example, there are more fight, flight, and dependency statements communicated among members than in later stages (Wheelan, 2005). Interestingly, they found that the number of pairing statements remain relatively stable. Approximately 17% of the statements made at any stage of development are supportive of others and meant to engender positive relationships (Wheelan, 2005).

The verbal statements of members of any group can be evaluated to determine whether or not members are committed, compliant, resistant, or disengaged from the team at any given time. Observing a member's consistent pattern of verbal statements over time is one possible way to determine that person's commitment to the task and people of the group. Dependency statements suggest compliance, whereas counterdependency and fight statements suggest resistance. Flight and counterpairing statements often indicate disengagement. Finally, pairing statements suggest commitment to other group members, while work statements suggest commitment to team goals.

NONVERBAL COMMUNICATION

As verbal messages are being communicated, an equally important process of communication is taking place on a nonverbal level. Nonverbal cues from a speaker such as smiling, eye contact, or fidgetiness help listeners interpret the meaning behind the words a person is using to communicate a message. Listeners perceive these messages subconsciously and often have a difficult time articulating why they arrived at a certain understanding of a person's message. As the title of Malcolm Gladwell's (2005) book *Blink: The Power of Thinking Without Thinking* suggests, this process of rapid cognition takes place in the blink of an eye and often outside of awareness. For instance, although the words are the same, the message below may be interpreted as having entirely different meanings based upon the nonverbal cues associated with it:

Table 5.1 Using Nonverbal Cues to Interpret Messages

Verbal Message	Nonverbal Cues	Possible Meanings
We need to be more prepared for the next project.	The speaker scans the group and gestures widely. Her facial expression demonstrates sincere pleading as she emphasizes the word *need*.	The speaker is desperate. For her, there is a lot riding on the success of the group.
We need to be more prepared for the next project.	The speaker emphasizes the word *prepared* as she looks intently at and leans toward a particular member. Her brow is furrowed and she appears frustrated.	The speaker is blaming one of the other members for the group's recent failure and hopes to shame that person into doing better in the future.
We need to be more prepared for the next project.	The speaker says this in a monotone voice with no energy, facial expression, or hand gestures. Her body is facing slightly away from the group.	The speaker is disengaged, does not actually care whether the group sees improvement, and does not plan to put in any extra effort.

Mehrabian's (1981) seminal research on the importance of nonverbal communication suggests that messages, especially those that express feelings, are overwhelmingly understood through nonverbal cues. The following percentages represent the relative contributions of the verbal and nonverbal components that a listener uses to interpret a message:

- 7% from verbal cues (words)

- 38% from vocal cues (volume, pitch, rhythm, etc.)

- 55% from facial expressions (smiling, frowning, etc.) and other body movements (arms crossed, eye contact, etc.)

Nonverbal cues such as physical appearance, facial expressions, level of eye contact, body movements, vocal qualities, and the physical space between members all contribute to the way a message is interpreted. An accurate perception of nonverbal communication helps the listener understand the intent of the speaker and is strongly related to social intelligence and interpersonal sensitivity (Goleman, 2006). So while an individual's "words" can be difficult to understand, nonverbal cues are even more subject to personal interpretation as listeners use their own subjective frame of reference to interpret the nonverbal expressions of others.

Nonverbal cues not only help members interpret verbal messages, they also help regulate the flow of conversation (Goleman, 2006). For example, when members want to interject a comment into a discussion, they may use any number of nonverbal prompts such as leaning forward, clearing their throats, making direct eye contact with the current speaker, or posing a facial expression that indicates a desire to speak. Additionally, if speakers receive positive nonverbal feedback from others while they are speaking (i.e., head nodding, eye contact, or smiling), they will continue with confidence that they are being heard. Speakers signal the end of their comments by relaxing their body posture, reducing verbal volume, or leaning back in their seat. These cues prompt others to respond or add their own thoughts. A more direct invitation might be to nod or gesture toward a particular member with an open hand, palm facing upward. Effective group facilitators frequently use these types of nonverbal cues to move members in and out of the conversation and to otherwise regulate the discussion.

POSTURING

Individuals use both verbal and nonverbal means to establish credibility and communicate ideas in a persuasive manner. Because people desire to be understood and respected, the use of posturing is common. Posturing and the use of identity markers are used to influence the perception, opinion, and approval of others and to bolster one's status within the team (Polzer, 2003). According to Polzer, "We do not communicate identity-relevant information solely for the benefit of others. . . . When we bring others to see us in a favorable light, we tend to boost our own self-image as we bask in their approval" (p. 3). Identity markers might include the following:

- *Physical appearance:* This includes how people are dressed, whether they have a well-groomed appearance, or their fitness level.

- *Personal office or room decorations:* The presence or absence of plaques, framed diplomas, photographs, or other indicators of success.

- *Body posture:* How much space a person takes up, whether their arms or legs are crossed, whether they stand up straight or slouch, the direction they are facing, strength of eye contact.

- *Demeanor:* Loud voice or soft, smiles or frowns, engaged or withdrawn, warm or cold, attentive or aloof.

- *Explicit statements:* Success stories that are shared verbally, statements of one's strengths, subtle references to past accomplishments.

The communication and utilization of these markers is driven by the need for self-enhancement. The self-enhancement motive relates to the desire to present oneself in a positive light to garner respect and admiration from others. This is commonly demonstrated on college campuses, for example, by identity markers such as fraternity or sorority T-shirts, sweatshirts, and accessories to identify as a member of an elite social group or by clothing, automobiles, and vacation trips to communicate wealth and social status. Leaders need to be attuned to both the subtle and blatant attempts of members to promote themselves. Self-promoting behavior can intimidate others and restrict the free expression of ideas, and it can be off-putting and hinder the development of trust and cohesion. It might also signal a strong need for recognition and admiration on the part of those who employ such tactics.

Unfortunately, members posture and perform for others in order to gain their respect and admiration at the expense of authenticity. Teams can become like families in which the members (siblings) compete for the approval of the team leaders (parents). This type of "sibling rivalry" in which the members compete for the favored child status can be a distraction for the team. One way a leader can help minimize this dynamic is by establishing the norms of authenticity, honesty, and transparency early on in the life of the team by sharing his or her own mistakes or weaknesses. This sends a strong message that members do not need to compete with one another for performance-based status but, instead, will be valued for their genuineness and humanity.

COMPONENTS OF EFFECTIVE COMMUNICATION

Communication skills, such as active listening and assertiveness, help make information processing more transparent. Actively trying to understand and interpret the verbal messages of others takes work. Simply asking another person to provide the evidence that led to certain conclusions can be very enlightening. Similarly, it is helpful to others when we describe the specific data and interpretation of that data that led to our conclusions. Advocating our ideas in a confident and comprehensive way is demonstrated in the practice of assertiveness. In a typical workgroup setting, assertiveness can take many forms such as promoting a new idea, lobbying for a policy change, or publicly supporting one method of resolving a problem over any number of alternatives. The following section describes the communication skills of active listening and assertiveness in detail.

Active Listening

Active listening is the key to accurately understanding what another person is saying. It requires effort and discipline. Yet group members are often preoccupied or distracted, and thus do not give 100% of their attention to one another (McKay, Davis, & Fanning, 1995).

WRITE YOUR NOTES HERE

Instead, listeners may be busy comparing themselves with the speaker, mentally rehearsing what they will say next, daydreaming about a past experience, or wishing they were somewhere else. They might also be speculating about what is going on in the mind of the speaker (mind reading), filtering out parts of his or her message, or jumping to conclusions and offering premature advice. It is also all too common for some listeners to be more focused on debating and critiquing than actually hearing what is being said. In contrast to the benefits reaped when a person feels heard, contentiousness can elicit either a defensive reaction or passive detachment, compromising meaningful dialogue.

An accurate understanding of others is needed before a meaningful response can be made. Effective listeners suspend judgment in order to first understand the perspective of the speaker. This advanced developmental skill requires listeners to attempt to "get into the shoes" of the speaker and see the issue through his or her eyes before responding (Kegan, 1994). The comments of others will make more sense if understood from within that person's perspective. Paying attention to posture, paraphrasing what is heard, and probing for deeper meaning are skills that facilitate this type of perspective taking and lead to a more accurate understanding of the messages that are communicated.

First, active listeners pay attention to their *posture*. Specifically, they use their physical posture to help them focus on what is being said. It also creates an interpersonal dynamic that signals to speakers that the listener is paying attention. The acronym SOLER describes five specific behaviors that encourage a listening posture:

S—Square: Face the person squarely.

O—Open: Keep an open posture without crossed arms or legs.

L—Lean slightly forward to communicate interest and engagement. Head nods and verbal encouragers like "uh-huh" and "yes!" are also effective.

E—Eye contact: Maintain direct eye contact according to appropriate social norms.

R—Relax: Stay relaxed. Listeners should be comfortable with silence where appropriate and allow the conversation to unfold without force.

By following these guidelines, listeners will be perceived as engaged and interested in what is being said. This approach helps the speaker to feel more comfortable in sharing information.

Paraphrasing is a powerful listening skill that validates others, builds trust, and invites deeper levels of disclosure. A paraphrase restates the message that was communicated in order to clarify and confirm an accurate understanding of that message. For example, in the following dialogue, Mary responds to her roommate's comments regarding the cleanliness of their room without appearing defensive or minimizing the problem. In this way, the paraphrase is an attempt to understand the roommate's concern before responding to it.

Sue: I hate that our room is constantly a mess. We can't live like this! I try to keep my side of the room clean, but yours is always a mess. I want to hang out with friends here, but I can't because I don't want them to see this place!

Mary: Okay, I understand that you're feeling frustrated with our room and the way it looks, and you're even embarrassed to have friends here because you don't want them to think you're sloppy. Am I hearing you right?

This paraphrase invites Sue to elaborate on her frustration because Mary has neither become defensive nor has she discounted Sue's concern. At this point, Mary is simply listening and gaining a better understanding of the issue. Thus, the paraphrase ensures an accurate understanding of the situation, maintains a peaceful interaction, and affirms Sue that she has been heard before moving to the problem-solving phase of the conversation.

Probing is the third skill that facilitates active listening. In order to understand the ideas, opinions, and perspectives of others, a listener may need information beyond that which the speaker has already provided. A good question is often the catalyst to an information-rich response. Open-ended questions lead to a deeper understanding of the issues at hand because they stimulate reflective thinking and can be used to identify underlying assumptions. Once an accurate paraphrase has been communicated, probing questions can be used to solicit more specific, useful, or otherwise relevant information. Returning to the example of the messy roommate situation, Mary's response might include some of the following probing questions:

- What do you consider the messiest parts of our room?

- When were you thinking of having friends over?

- What are some realistic expectations for both of us?

- How can I be more sensitive to you in the future?

- What do you need from me right now?

These questions can be used to address issues and create meaningful dialogue. Instead of avoiding difficult issues, probing questions address them directly. Additionally, they validate the speaker by showing genuine interest or concern on behalf of the listener.

Probing with *open-ended questions* is an excellent way to gather information about someone's priorities, beliefs, and concerns because you give the respondent complete control over the content of his or her response. The material on which the respondent chooses to focus is likely the material most pressing or important to that person. Open-ended questions often begin with the words *how, what,* or *why.* Examples may include "What motivates you?" or "How could this process have been improved?" Open-ended questions can also come in the form of an invitation for the speaker to provide more detail. For instance, one might begin with "Describe for me . . ." or "Tell me in your own words . . .".

Hypothetical questions give insight into the state of mind of the speaker as well. These types of questions allow you to discover the nuanced thought process of your respondent and/or his or her comfort level with a given skill. Respectively, examples may include "Suppose you were the project manager on this task. How would you proceed?" or "If I were to give you the lesson plans, would you feel confident teaching the class tomorrow morning?"

Unlike the types of questions that we have discussed thus far, *closed-ended questions* aim to gather specific information, facts, or details. The range of responses available to your question's recipient is quite small, and his or her answer is likely to be short and to the point. Examples of closed-ended questions include "Did Kevin complete the spreadsheet for the meeting?" or "What is the fastest route to 6th Avenue?"

Finally, *forced-choice* questions call upon the respondent to make a choice. The answer to one of these questions will demonstrate the respondent's priorities and may guide a decision about how to move forward in a given scenario. Consider the following example: "The printing company is wondering whether or not it should go ahead and ship the signs with the typo. Would you rather the signs arrive on time, or that they are printed accurately?" Forced-choice questions are also frequently used in a negotiation if one is trying to limit the other person's options.

While the previous types of questions can all be productive within certain discussions, the following, however, are not. Leading questions, loaded questions, and multiple questions asked in rapid fire make it challenging for a recipient to respond productively. Instead, recipients are likely to feel challenged, intimidated, and confused. Leading and loaded questions often use harsh language and make unflattering assumptions in order to embed an accusation within a question. An example may be "Do you always pawn off your work onto other people?" or "How long have you been wasting the company's time dealing with personal issues at work?" Obviously, questions like these will be perceived negatively by the recipient and have the potential to compromise trust and goodwill in the relationship. It is rarely beneficial to make enemies, so questions should not be used as weapons.

Multiple questions refers to a string of questions asked in rapid progression that, while they may be related to the subject at hand, confuse and disorient the recipient. The following is an example of multiple questions: "How could the team have missed the deadline, and how do you know, and what are the consequences that we now face, and did you notify everyone, and who was supposed to have been keeping track of this?" By the end of this five-question series, it would be difficult for the responder to decide where to begin or to which question the asker truly wants an answer. Stressful situations can instigate the use of multiple questions. Therefore, when intensity mounts, it is helpful for members to slow down their speech and make discrete, productive, and answerable questions.

Assertiveness

Assertiveness is the ability to express oneself directly and honestly without disrespecting or dishonoring another person. Assertive people are able to stand up for themselves and communicate their ideas firmly without bullying, patronizing, or manipulating others. Because group discussions can move quickly, teams frequently arrive at conclusions that are not well thought out or supported. Thus, it is important that members speak up either to promote other perspectives or to challenge ideas that are ill-conceived. Assertive members, therefore, are actively engaged in group discussions and avoid the extremes of being either too passive or too aggressive.

Baney (2004) suggests that assertiveness can best be expressed by including the following three components: I think, I feel, I want. The first step in this assertiveness formula is to describe one's thoughts about a particular situation. For example, a member of the team is often late for meetings, so the project leader might say something like: "I've noticed that you've been late to most of our recent meetings." Next, the leader describes his or her feelings about the situation: "It's frustrating to be interrupted when you arrive, and I never know if I should stop and bring you up to speed." Finally, the assertive person would make a respectful request: "Do you think you could make it a priority to arrive on time from here on out?" This interchange shows respect for the other person but also values one's own needs. According to the social style framework, drivers and expressives do much better at advocating their positions than do analytics or amiables.

When making a point in a group setting, especially when responding to a particularly complex or important set of questions, assertive communicators pay attention to the introduction and conclusion of their comments. To start, a brief overview of their position will let others know what to expect. For example, an explanation of one's position may begin with "I'd like to discuss a few key areas where I think that the team could have been more organized." At the end of the comments, a concise summary can be given to reinforce the main ideas. Returning to the example at hand, a person might end his or her comments with "and I believe that these were the problem areas that led to the poor performance of our team." Opening and closing with clarity are useful practices that reinforce effective communication.

It is often beneficial to provide specific examples or anecdotes to give texture and nuanced understanding. Some people are more likely to remember interesting statistics or quotes, for example, than general concepts. Memorable stories or illustrations not only reinforce the main concepts, they also help listeners remember the main concepts. In addition, supporting comments with data and examples not only makes the argument more interesting and informative, but also credible. However, there is a difference between this tactic and attempting to establish credibility by overusing confusing jargon that others do not understand. This can alienate others and decrease their desire to engage in meaningful dialogue.

At times, strong, assertive statements will provoke negative responses or questions from others. As discussed, an initial overview at the beginning of a response can be a useful tool in rephrasing and perhaps softening the nature of the question. For this reason, this strategy is an excellent one to employ when asked a leading or loaded question. If faced with multiple questions, the speaker can slow down the pace of the conversation by calling attention to the multitude of questions and acknowledging the desire to answer the questions one at a time. For example, an appropriate response to a hostile barrage of questions might be, "You clearly have a lot on your mind and are looking for some clarity. Let me see if I can explain my position, beginning with your first question." Finally, it is perfectly acceptable to acknowledge feeling ill-prepared or uncomfortable answering a question and, instead, choose not to respond at that particular time. For example, if one team member pushes another team member into making a commitment about a certain problem, he or she might need to say something like "There are several aspects of this situation about which I know very little, and I do not want to speculate. Can you give me a few days to think about it and get back to you?" In that way, he or she can buy time and formulate a more thoughtful response.

CENTRALIZED VERSUS DECENTRALIZED COMMUNICATION

Group researchers have observed that one of the most important features of group communication is the level of centralization (Brown & Miller, 2000). When one or two members do most of the talking and comments are routinely directed toward these members specifically, the group is said to have a centralized communication structure (Huang & Cummings, 2011). Conversely, when groups exhibit more balance in terms of who speaks and with what frequency, the group has a decentralized communication structure. In a decentralized structure, members engage in both advocacy (proposing their own views) and inquiry (exploring the views of others). Of course, due to logistical and time constraints on any given meeting, not everyone can be expected to comment on every topic. In larger groups, it can be very easy to situate oneself on the periphery and become marginally involved. In smaller groups, it is more difficult to be anonymous, and members may choose to confront those who are consistently not speaking up. Nonetheless, who speaks, how often they speak, and to whom they speak are each important characteristics of communication structure. The degree of communication centrality within a given group is influenced by the level of complexity of the group's task as well as the characteristics of individual group members.

```
┌─────────────────────────────────────┐
│                                     │
│        WRITE YOUR NOTES HERE        │
│                                     │
│                                     │
│                                     │
│                                     │
│                                     │
│                                     │
│                                     │
│                                     │
│                                     │
│                                     │
│                                     │
└─────────────────────────────────────┘
```

Groups tend to adopt a more centralized communication structure if the task is relatively simple and become more decentralized as the tasks become more complex (Brown & Miller, 2000). This trend is due to the fact that task uncertainty and ambiguity lead to wider participation and a more open exchange of information. Put another way, complex tasks require cognitive flexibility and open discussions in order to thoroughly understand the issues and to make well-reasoned decisions (Roy, 2001). Relatively straightforward tasks, on the other hand, are conducive to one or two people directing the discussion and coordinating the efforts of the group. Simpler tasks benefit from the efficiency of centralized communication, allowing group discussions to be more organized, efficient, and concrete.

In addition to task complexity, individual member characteristics influence the communication structure of the group. Some members speak often and with confidence, while others tend to be more hesitant. Individual member traits such as interpersonal dominance, perceived competence, and commitment to the group's task all serve to influence the degree of centrality in group communication. People with high interpersonal dominance have a strong need to be in control. Even if they are not the designated leader, they may attempt to take charge and direct the group. When members acquiesce and allow plans and meetings to be controlled by their dominant teammates, the communication becomes centralized. But sometimes members resist. When faced with dominant members, some group members form alliances or subgroups in order to create a balance of power and, thus, ensure a decentralized communication pattern where everyone's voice is heard.

During the "forming" stage of group development, members assess one another's knowledge, skills, and competencies. This is done partly to see how they might compare with their new teammates, but it is also done with the intent of taking inventory of the group's resources. Those who are perceived as competent and who possess important abilities are allotted greater amounts of influence over the decisions, direction, and dynamics of the group. However, the criteria used in this assessment are not always related to the task at hand. Sometimes members are given status based upon characteristics such as gender, physical attractiveness, education level, or professional success. For example, when medical doctors are given too much status while nurses or other health care professionals are marginalized, patient safety is compromised (Lingard et al., 2004). As a result, the health care industry has gone to great lengths to improve the quality of communication on health care teams (Brock, Abu-Rish, Chiu, Hammer, Wilson, Vorvick, Blondon, Schaad, Liner, & Zierler, 2013).

Once a member is perceived to have high levels of competence, regardless of the reasoning behind this perception, and is granted status in the group, members will naturally direct their questions and comments to him or her. Members who perceive *themselves* as having competence are also more likely to speak up in discussions. Interestingly, there is a slight tendency for men to overestimate their knowledge and abilities (Lemme, 2006), possibly explaining why men tend to be more frequent contributors in mixed-gender groups (Dindia & Canary, 2006; Krolokke & Sorensen, 2006).

Commitment to the group's tasks and goals will also affect the level of member engagement. Highly motivated members will tend to be more active and contribute more frequently to discussions. They are more invested in the group's success, and will subsequently seek to be involved in major decisions. At the same time, there may certainly be members who are very committed to the task but withhold their comments and ideas from conversations. In these cases, other personal or circumstantial variables have intervened to reduce their perceived involvement. In order to establish balanced communication within the team, leaders have to figure out the reasons for poor participation and help low talkers become more active.

As group members interact, each establishes his or her place in the group relative to other members. A systems view of groups suggests that individual communication styles will depend upon the particular group composition within which members find themselves. For example, a dominant member might take over if there are no other dominant members in the group. As that member exerts control, submissive or passive members become more passive, in turn encouraging the dominant member to become even more dominant. Each member reacts to others in a reciprocal fashion. If there are a number of dominant members in a group, control and management of the group may be shared. Similarly, if no particular person has a great deal of competence in a given area, a member with moderate competence will likely be forced to become an active participant. The assessment of one's own competence is related to the perceived competence of other members. The same holds true for commitment to the group's task. If nobody is passionate about the goal or interested in taking charge, a member who normally does not take a leadership role might find him or herself doing just that. Each group has a unique configuration that influences how people act, interact, and communicate with others in that particular group. For this reason, the tasks and interpersonal roles that people fill will vary with each new group they experience.

The process of communication is complex and highly idiosyncratic. Different people can hear the same message but have completely different interpretations. The practice of reflection can help group members slow down the interpretation and evaluation of messages to improve the accuracy of understanding and thoughtfulness of responses. In addition, certain listening skills (posture, paraphrasing, and probing) can increase the likelihood that accurate understanding is taking place.

Group members can also learn to express themselves more intentionally. They can become more aware of how they are communicating observations, thoughts, feelings, or needs. Members can provide the data and reasoning that led to certain conclusions. In addition, members can enhance their ability to communicate by avoiding mixed messages and becoming more assertive. Assertiveness is a form of communication that respects the opinions of others while directly stating one's own thoughts and perspectives.

Effective communication requires members to suspend their assumptions and judgments of others in order to stay open to new ideas. Members can learn to minimize their reactivity even when dialogue becomes spirited or difficult. In the most effective groups, members feel comfortable to freely express their views and engage in a balanced level of participation. When this happens, communication contributes to the effectiveness and efficiency of group processing and team success.

VIRTUAL COMMUNICATION

Virtual teams bring geographically dispersed members together though electronic information and communication technologies to accomplish organizational tasks (Powell, Piccoli, & Ives, 2004). The use of technology can significantly improve team efficiency and increase productivity, but they need to be actively managed (Hertel, Geister, & Konradt, 2005). Technology has become such an integral part of organizational life that some teams never meet face to face; they only exist in a virtual environment. Virtual teams and the technology that drives them offer the following benefits: (a) team compositions that increase quality and outcomes, (b) efficiency of communication, and (c) the development of intellectual capital.

Putting the right mix of people together without regard to geographic location allows managers to maximize knowledge, skills, and abilities (Blackburn, Furst, & Rosen, 2003). These types of diverse and specialized teams are especially necessary to solve complex organizational problems and tasks. For instance, a team of school principals and district administrators working on educational reform might be able to benefit from the experience and knowledge of parallel committees in other states. The team might also benefit from the perspective of a curriculum specialist at a university who consults with school districts.

Virtual teaming allows diverse members to collaborate in ways that were heretofore difficult if not impossible. Virtual teams allow team members in various locations to interact without the need for face-to-face (F2F) meetings. Scheduling and attending meetings may be easier when workers can stay at their own desk (wherever

WRITE YOUR NOTES HERE

that may be) and participate in virtual meetings instead of flying in from various places around the world to meet in a central location. Since physical spaces and other arrangements such as travel and accommodations are not necessary, organizations can save both time and money. While virtual meetings may not be as efficient as F2F meetings (Levenson & Cohen, 2003), the financial and logistical benefits are attractive. Without the benefit of nonverbal clues, group communication can be ambiguous and cohesion can be difficult to build. These obstacles, however, can be overcome by effective leadership.

Improved Knowledge-Sharing

When geographical obstacles are removed, teams have access to subject matter experts from all over the globe. But those experts might live in different time zones and have technological limitations that prevent them from engaging in virtual meetings. Knowledge management systems assist members in capturing, storing, and cataloguing what they know so that others can access that knowledge and experience. Knowledge-sharing links team members together through a virtual repository of expertise. For example, Proctor and Gamble (P&G) has an electronic network that links 900 factories and 17 product development centers in 73 countries. In the past, it was difficult to know what new products were being developed in different locations, centers, and departments around the world. To address this issue, P&G purchased collaborative knowledge-sharing software that permits product developers to search a database of 200,000 existing product designs to see if a similar design or process already exists in another part of the company. As a result, the time it takes to develop new products has been reduced by 50 % (Ante, 2001).

Buckman Labs, a chemical manufacturing company, has effectively pooled the expertise of 1,400 employees in over 90 nations through an electronic knowledge base (Buckman, 2004). For example, when one of its customers has an outbreak of a bacterial contamination that threatens production in a paper mill in Brazil, the local Buckman engineer in that part of the world can access the company knowledge base for possible solutions based upon the knowledge and experiences of engineers at other locations. In this way, problems can be solved more quickly and effectively than when field offices operate independently from one another. This type of quality customer service earned Buckman Labs the 2005 MAKE Award (Most Admired Knowledge Enterprise) from a panel of leading knowledge management experts.

Inherent Problems

Virtual teams are not without their problems; they tend to be abstract and ambiguous, and, by their nature, are challenging to manage. Davis (2004) found that problems within virtual teams take longer to identify and solutions longer to implement. The distance inherent in virtual teams may serve to (a) amplify dysfunction, (b) dilute leadership, and (c) weaken human relations and team processes. Virtual teams can be especially difficult to manage in terms of goal definition, task distribution, coordination, and member motivation.

Teamwork requires interdependence. Members need to have a level of trust that their teammates are equally committed to the goals of the group and will do their part to achieve those goals (Aubert & Kelsey, 2003). In organizational contexts, trust is built by assessing the ability, benevolence, and integrity of other group members (Mayer, Davis, & Schoorman, 1995). In virtual groups the lack of face-to-face interaction makes it difficult to carry out this assessment. Therefore, virtual teams struggle to gain a level of trust that maximizes group potential. When group members interact in person, they are able to observe one another and draw conclusions about a number of variables including intellectual ability, past experiences, interpersonal style, and personality type. Virtual members have less information from which to make assessments. Thus, virtual environments can be more tenuous and less trusting (Gibson & Manuel, 2003).

In addition to developing trust, virtual groups may also have a difficult time creating a shared vision. Shared vision includes not only an understanding of the group's goal but also a shared commitment to achieving it. In a virtual environment, it can be difficult to assess commitment levels. Because virtual members typically interact less frequently and with less perceptual richness, they do not have the opportunity to observe interpersonal characteristics such as vocal tone, body language, and facial expressions. Thus, it is difficult to determine who is invested in the success of the group.

Communication Challenges

Communication is more of a challenge in virtual teams than in F2F teams (Martins, Gilson, & Maynard, 2004). Since trust is difficult to achieve, members are more reluctant to express their opinions in virtual discussions (Baltes, Dickson, Sherman, Bauer, & LaGanke, 2002). Contributions in a virtual environment lack the nonverbal and social context to understand others accurately and to be understood. Teams take longer to make decisions and arrive at a shared understanding. In an F2F meeting, an idea can be acknowledged and agreed upon through nods, smiles, or verbal responses. Puzzled looks, shrugs, and raised eyebrows signal a lack of understanding and a request for more information. Even the most sophisticated computer-mediated communication channels are not able to capture the richness of F2F exchanges (Driskell, Radtke, & Salas, 2003).

WRITE YOUR NOTES HERE

Obviously, it is more difficult to communicate complex information by phone or e-mail than it is in person. Even video conferencing has its limitations. For example, consider the experience of going to a college football game or hearing an orchestra perform a symphony. Live action includes the sights, smells, sounds, and various intangibles that cannot easily be put into words. Even watching a game or musical performance on TV does not capture all the details of the experience. Listening on the radio or reading a *New York Times* review does even begin to convey the nuances of a live performance. Likewise, virtual environments are limited in capturing all the detail and "feel" of F2F meetings.

Virtual teams, by nature, tend to be more diverse than F2F teams since they often span multiple geographic locations. Greater geographical distances can translate into differences in regional, national, and organizational cultures. Diversity introduces the potential for increased creativity and problem-solving, but it also creates a context for miscommunication and misunderstanding. Therefore, in addition to the challenges noted above, virtual teams also have to contend with the lack of a common set of assumptions and social norms that facilitate effective communication (Hinds & Weisband, 2003). Members may not even be communicating in their native language. Yet even with a common language, different words and phrases have different meanings from culture to culture. It is easy to see that the potential for miscommunication and misunderstanding is great.

LEADERSHIP IN ACTION

In many team discussions, there is too much talking and not enough listening. To test this hypothesis, try monitoring your next interaction with friends, family, or colleagues. People are often more interested in delivering a message than receiving one. This is certainly true in meetings where emotions are running high. What happened the last time you had a disagreement with someone or were in a tense or stressful situation? Why did your voice rise in volume and pitch? Why did your words hasten? It was probably because you wanted to make sure you got your point across before it was too late. This chapter emphasizes the fact that communication is critical when it comes to leading people, working in teams, and facilitating interpersonal dynamics.

Team leaders can model active listening and manage the dialogue so that understanding takes place and everyone feels heard. It is amazing how much can be accomplished when members are invited to participate and feel validated when they do so. Because leaders want to encourage a high standard on clear, concise, and well-supported dialogue, they might need to push members to explain their position and to develop their ideas more completely. While leaders will have their own position on various subjects, they should not discount the value of open dialogue or minimize the contributions of others. Effective communication involves members verbalizing their ideas clearly *and* listening carefully to the ideas of others in order to create a fertile environment for understanding, exploration, and innovation.

So, the next time members are locking horns with one another, try using an engaged posture, probing questions, and paraphrases to help them explain their perspectives and arrive at a mutual understanding. Once all the information is on the table and understood by the team, members will be closer than they originally thought. This nuanced and challenging skill set can be difficult to master, but with conscientious practice and risk-taking, it can be learned. And there is no better time or place to hone one's communication skills than when working on a team.

KEY TERMS

Self-enhancement 97

SOLER 98

Advocacy 102

Inquiry 102

DISCUSSION QUESTIONS

1. Name and describe the eight GDOS categories of verbal communication. Give an example of each.

2. Compare and contrast verbal versus nonverbal communication.

3. What impact does nonverbal communication have on a conversation? What are some examples of nonverbal cues?

4. Name and describe the SOLER acronym. What is this communication strategy designed to do?

5. Recall a time when you either misunderstood a message or were misunderstood in a group atmosphere. What were the repercussions?

6. What are the three skills of active listening? How can you apply these in group situations?

7. Describe the difference between advocacy and inquiry. Create three examples of each.

8. What are the benefits and challenges of virtual teams? As a leader, how would you address some of the inherent challenges?

GROUP ACTIVITIES

EXERCISE 5.1 THE OLD RUMOR MILL

We have all played "Telephone." This exercise is designed to illustrate distortions that can occur as information is relayed from one person to another.

The instructor enlists the help of six volunteers. The rest of the students remain to act as process observers. Five of the six volunteers are asked to leave the classroom so they can't hear the class discussion. One remains in the room with the instructor and the observers.

The instructor reads an "accident report" (or a detailed account of an event) to the first volunteer. One of the volunteers who is waiting outside the room comes back in the room and the first volunteer reports the details of the story to him or her. The process observers record what information was added to the original story, what information was left out of the original story, and what information was distorted.

A third volunteer returns to the classroom and the second repeats the story that was reported from the first volunteer. Again, the process observers write down what was added, deleted, or distorted. The process is repeated until all the volunteers are back in the room. The last volunteer will write the details of the event on the board. Compare that version with the original version.

Class observers should report their observations and identify where the message went awry.

EXERCISE 5.2 HIGH TALKER/LOW TALKER EXERCISE

Place yourselves into one of two similar-sized groups: high talkers (people who are more expressive) and low talkers (people who are quieter). Make sure that everyone agrees with who is in which group (some high talkers do not see themselves as high talkers, and vice versa). Adjust groups accordingly and form a circle with the low talkers in the middle and the high talkers in the outside circle. *Note: high talkers and low talkers are just labels—one group is not better than the other.*

The goal of this exercise is for low talkers and high talkers to gain a better understanding of one another's experience. When one group is talking (the group in the fishbowl or inner circle) the other group (the group on the outside of the circle) is to remain quiet.

Ask the low talkers the following questions:

- What is it like to be a low-talking member of this class?
- What would you like the high talkers to know about what it is like to be a low talker in this class?
- Have the high talkers paraphrase what they heard. Then have the low talkers either confirm or clarify.

Have students switch places (the high talkers are now in the fish bowl and the low talkers are on the outside of the circle). Remind the low talkers that they cannot speak while they are on the outside.

Ask the high talkers the following questions:

- What was it like for you not to be able to speak?
- What did you hear the low talkers say about their experiences as low talkers?
- What would you like the low talkers to know about what it is like to be a high talker in this class?
- Have the low talkers paraphrase what they heard. Then have the high talkers either confirm or clarify.

After everyone has returned to his or her original seat, discuss what you learned from this experience.

CASE 5.2: ENEMY LINES AND FRIENDLY FIRE

It's the third week of the semester and you have met with your class project team several times. You've already noticed that two of your teammates, Sam and Alex, seem to be very friendly with each other. On e-mails, texts, and in person, this duo strikes you as fun, light-hearted, and occasionally flirtatious. After the next team meeting, Sam and Alex are the last two people left in the meeting room. As they are walking out the door, Sam turns to Alex and says, "Hey, Alex, I really enjoyed getting to know you these last couple of weeks. With Homecoming next weekend, I'd love to hang out and grab a bite to eat before we hit some of the parties together." After an awkward silence, Alex turns to Sam and says, "Gosh, Sam. That's so sweet. I'm not sure if my roommate has anything planned for us, but let me check and see. I'll shoot you an e-mail."

The e-mail from Alex never comes. Sam doesn't know what to think, but feels angry and hurt that Alex didn't follow through. At the next meeting, Sam pulls up a chair next to Alex and says, "Hey, what's up? I never heard from you." Alex curtly snips, "Yeah, I can't make it. It's not going to work out," just as the meeting was beginning.

During the meeting, Alex withdraws and takes an aloof posture. Sam is visibly agitated and very critical of everyone else's contributions. The two have spread a negative dynamic over the team. You, as team leader, pull Sam aside during the break and say, "Hey, Sam, I've noticed that you're not yourself today. What's going on?"

- *Using active listening skills from this chapter, what would you do to find out the source of the tension between Sam and Alex that has affected the team? Please write out a hypothetical conversation that might follow.*

- *If you were Alex, how could you have been more assertive in setting boundaries between work relationships and potentially romantic ones?*

Verbal and Non-Verbal Communication

Quintanilla, K.M. and Wahl, S.T.

O ver the past 10 years, verbal and nonverbal communication have increasingly taken place in a digital environment. Traditional media such as newspapers and magazines have struggled to maintain their readership in this online environment. However, in May 2015, Facebook launched Instant Articles, a feature that allows publishers to host their news stories and content directly on Facebook, giving traditional media a new foothold in the digital world (Rezab, 2015). Along with print news articles, publishers are also able to post pictures and other nonverbal communication to one of the largest websites in the world. The increasing popularity of the Internet caused the media landscape to shift completely from the physical to the digital; Facebook News Feed and Twitter Timeline are now two of the biggest discovery channels for consumers to find and consume verbal and nonverbal communication.

This new platform gives traditional publishers access to rich, standardized features. Facebook also offers an audience of roughly 1.3 billion active users for publishers to choose from. As students, business professionals, and scholars continue to adapt both verbal and nonverbal communication to the digital environment, features such as Instant Articles can enhance and replace many of the communication methods that have lost popularity in the Internet age. As you read this chapter, remember to reflect on how the Internet and social media have altered the way you communicate both verbally and nonverbally in the social and professional environments.

VERBAL COMMUNICATION

What is verbal communication? Verbal communication encompasses both our words and our verbal fillers (e.g., *um*, *like*). Verbal messages are created through language. Effective communication involves accurate interpretations of others' verbal messages as meaning is cocreated. Otherwise, the meanings of the words you communicate will not be understood. As a professional, you must make effective use of your language skills and improve your abilities to interpret other people's messages. Robinson and Robinson (1982) concluded that if speakers are to be consistently efficient at conveying verbally their intended meanings to listeners, they must understand that intended meanings may not be fully conveyed by a message and that many factors can lead to a listener's failure to understand what a speaker means.

WRITE YOUR NOTES HERE

The symbols communicators use are abstract, vague, and sometimes arbitrary. Because symbols can make things a bit off or fuzzy, we have to interpret the meaning. So we construct meanings as we interact with other people and by processing the information in our own heads (Duck, 1994; Keyton & Beck, 2010). This process of meaning construction is also symbolic, because we use words to think about what things mean (Keyton & Beck, 2010; Wood, 2009).

When you really think about it, it is an absolute miracle that we can communicate with one another at all. Really, think about it for a moment. We have selected a bunch of arbitrary symbols we call words and gestures to represent "things." These can be things we have never seen or never can see, such as feelings. Nevertheless, we use those symbols to express our thoughts, desires, and emotions, and somehow communication does occur. Because of the need for interpretation of meaning, being an audience-centered communicator is a must for professional excellence. It is obvious that communication affects how we are perceived by our audience(s). Still today, some people believe that communication works like a pipeline (i.e., if you send a message, the target will no doubt be reached); if you said something and another person heard it, then effective communication occurred. We should know from experience that this simply is not the way it works. With little effort, you could give a dozen examples of times when you said something and the listener completely misunderstood the message.

Let's look at an example from the retail industry to illustrate the point. A customer comes into a grocery store and asks for green beans. Trying to provide good customer service, a manager explains, "The green beans are on Aisle 8." Twenty minutes later, the customer is still wandering around the store frustrated. Why? Because canned green beans are on Aisle 8, fresh green beans are on Aisle 1, frozen green beans are on Aisle 14, and the prepared green beans she wanted are in the deli across from Aisle 10. "Green beans" is an arbitrary symbol with various interpretations of meaning.

Verbal communication concerns communication rules—shared understanding of what communication means and what constitutes appropriate communication given the context. Two kinds of rules guide communication (Pearce, Cronen, & Conklin, 1979). Regulative rules describe when, how, where, and with whom to talk about certain things. These same rules also dictate appropriateness. For instance, it might be appropriate for your boss to call you at home after hours, but would it be appropriate for you to do the same if you had a concern about your travel schedule? What's appropriate for the person with power or control may not be appropriate for those serving in a subordinate role. To demonstrate professional and workplace excellence, you must be able to monitor your own appropriateness when communicating. In addition, constitutive rules define what communication means by prompting us to count certain kinds of communication. In other words, we learn what counts as paying attention (e.g., eye contact) and showing affection (e.g., kissing, hugging), as well as what counts as being inappropriate (e.g., interrupting conversations, rolling one's eyes; Duck, 2007; Wood, 2009).

Step Back and Reflect:
CONFIDENT CONNIE

As you read this passage and answer the questions, step back and reflect on what went wrong in this professional situation.

Connie works in the accounting department of a manufacturing company. She often complains to her family and friends that her coworkers do not like her and treat her differently than they do the other staff. She is not invited to lunch outings, and she notices that people walk away when she approaches. She considers herself a friendly, outgoing person and cannot figure out what she is doing wrong. Connie believes her coworkers may resent her because she is able to work well with all her clients and is skilled in accounts reconciliations, resulting in company savings of thousands of dollars each month. She is confident in her abilities and speaks proudly in meetings, providing guidance to her teammates about work issues. She enjoys sharing her success stories and has no apprehension about asking questions in meetings. She has been with the company longer than everyone, including her boss, and she often reminds him of the history of why things are done a certain way. Connie is confident that even if her coworkers are jealous of her abilities, her boss recognizes her value as an employee. However, when she receives her performance review, she is shocked by her supervisor's comments:

"Feedback has been shared with Connie several times on her engagement in team meetings. Connie constantly repeats points discussed and closed in meetings, which is a distraction for several analysts. It is evident that Connie is having a hard time following along in meetings, as points and topics are constantly being repeated for her to understand. Feedback has been shared with Connie on staying on point and not drifting off to other tangents. At times, Connie's body language, comments, and tone of voice during meetings seem aggressive and indicate that she disagrees with her manager. This has been shared with Connie and she has been asked to improve."

STEP BACK AND REFLECT

1. What went wrong?
2. How could Connie use the KEYS approach to improve her communication interaction?
3. How can the KEYS process be a reflexive exercise for both Connie and her manager?

Being aware of yourself can make the difference between losing your job and nurturing a promising career. We see examples of this in the news headlines and front-page stories of our favorite magazines and newspapers. In early 2012, radio talk show host and political commentator Rush Limbaugh caused controversy after he made inflammatory remarks about Georgetown University law student Sandra Fluke. Despite the fact that his career is based on sharing his opinions, the words he chose on that fateful day resulted in public and sponsor backlash. What factors led to such an outcry? If he had spoken out in disagreement without name-calling, would the reaction have been the same? What are the ethical considerations in this situation? What might you take from this story when considering your verbal communication in the workplace? Undoubtedly, the words we say are extremely important. Yet, of equal importance is what we communicate without words.

NONVERBAL COMMUNICATION

What is nonverbal communication? Put simply, nonverbal communication (also referred to as body language) includes all those ways we communicate without words. A more technical definition for nonverbal communication is "communication other than written or spoken language that creates meaning for someone" (Ivy & Wahl, 2014, p. 5).

The literature provides considerable support for the effectiveness of nonverbal communication as a tool for conveying thoughts, attitudes, perceptions, and meaning. Research indicates that about 55% of interpersonal messages are conveyed nonverbally (Lavan, 2002). This seems logical, because most human beings are visually dominant and live in a society dominated by visual images and are thus more inclined to believe the evidence

ETHICAL CONNECTION
TAKING THE SPOTLIGHT

As you read this passage and answer the questions, consider how the way you communicate has an ethical dimension.

Sheila and David work for an advertising firm and are partners assigned to work on a major advertising campaign. Sheila is a seasoned account manager, while David is a recent college graduate hired as a junior account executive. He is very enthusiastic and has several ideas that he shares excitedly with Sheila via e-mail. Sheila never responds to the e-mail. In a meeting with management to propose their ideas, however, Sheila takes the lead on presenting; as a result of her nonverbal and verbal communication, management concludes that she was responsible for the work. In fact, when commended on the ideas, she accepts the praise and makes no reference to David. David, by contrast, is afraid to say anything, and his bosses have no clue that the majority of the ideas were his.

QUESTIONS TO CONSIDER

1. What are the ethical considerations and dilemmas in this scenario?
2. What did Sheila communicate or not communicate during her presentation and how?
3. How could David use his verbal and nonverbal skills in the future to keep this situation from happening?
4. What do you believe should be the appropriate, professional response in this situation?
5. Does communicator intent affect the ethics in situations such as this?
6. Do you believe the outcome of this situation would have changed if David had talked directly to Sheila instead of using e-mail?

of the eyes than that of the other senses (Sampson, 1995). In fact, a widely held viewpoint among scholars is that communication is optimized when verbal and nonverbal elements operate in an integrated fashion, producing a coordinated and synchronized effect (Jones & LeBaron, 2002; Laplante & Ambady, 2003). Harrison and Crouch (1975) suggested that verbal communication is only the tip of the communication iceberg and that "nonverbal communication precedes and perhaps structures all subsequent communication" (p. 77).

Nonverbal symbols are everywhere, even though we tend to use verbal forms for our most formal communications. In fact, the nonverbal system accounts for 65% to 93% of the total meaning of communication (Birdwhistell, 1970; Mehrabian, 1981). Nolan (1975) concluded that the many theories of language evolution had one impor-

> WRITE YOUR NOTES
> HERE

tant argument in common: "Nonverbal behavior precedes verbal behavior in the evolution of communication" (p. 101).

What kinds of behavior are included in the term *nonverbal communication*? Your "walk, stance, posture, and footsteps are a form of nonverbal communication. What you wear and how you look, move, and gesture, as well as the facial and eye expressions you make all count as nonverbal communication" (Ivy & Wahl, 2014, p. 6). What are the purposes of nonverbal communication? Why is nonverbal communication important?

Argyle (1988) suggested that nonverbal behavior serves four purposes. The first function is to express emotion. Consider a moment when you may have had a conflict with a friend or family member. When that person asked you what was wrong, you probably responded, "Nothing," but you could not control your facial expressions, which indicated otherwise. Displaying appropriate emotion is vital to professional excellence. One should show passion and drive but also demonstrate resilience and be able to triumph over day-to-day disappointments in the workplace. Could you imagine a classroom environment where students displayed extreme emotion each time they received a grade that was lower than expected? How do you think your productivity would be affected?

The second function of nonverbal communication is to convey interpersonal attitudes. Being skilled in observing and interpreting the nonverbal behavior of others will give you an edge over other professionals. For example, a young woman competing for a promotion with another employee noticed that her coworker would always approach their boss with issues first thing in the morning. The coworker would then complain that he had to repeat himself and that their supervisor seemed to forget what he had been told. The young woman observed that her supervisor always seemed rushed and distracted until he had his coffee and had checked and responded to pressing e-mails. She made sure always to approach him when he seemed more relaxed and focused. When he offered her the promotion, her supervisor said he appreciated her timing and how she always kept him in the loop.

The third function is to present one's personality, such as character, disposition, or temperament. Think about the different work environments you frequent during your week—the bank, the school library, restaurants, etc. What are the character traits of employees at each of these establishments? Do you expect that the librarian will be as outgoing as a server in a crowded bar? Make a list of the top five jobs you have considered, and write down some of the personality traits that might be expected. How might your verbal and nonverbal communication vary between the positions?

Finally, the fourth purpose of nonverbal communication is to accompany verbal communication. Ekman (1965) specified the important ways that verbal and nonverbal behaviors interrelate during human communication. Nonverbal communication can simply *repeat*

A DAY WITH THE CHIEF

As you evaluate the passage below, consider whether this behavior is appropriate for this professional context.

Mark is a top-performing salesperson at a pharmaceutical supply company. As a reward for his performance, he is treated to a trip to the corporate office in California to meet the chief executive officer, Ms. Mills. Ms. Mills is known around the office as the "Wicked Witch of the West" because of her short and sometimes abrasive demeanor. Mark's coworkers share "horror stories" of their encounters with her, stating that she rarely makes eye contact, never smiles, and dislikes being approached unless she initiates the conversation. Although he is excited to travel, he is also nervous about what he and Ms. Mills might talk about. He prepares by thinking about how he can share his sales strategies and techniques. On the day of the meeting, he waits patiently for Ms. Mills's assistant to call him into her office. When he is escorted in to meet her, he is shocked to see a petite woman behind the large desk smiling back at him with kind eyes. He approaches, shakes her hand, and waits for her permission to sit. Ms. Mills is nothing like the horrible person they made her out to be. Ms. Mills asks Mark several thoughtful questions about why he is

successful, ways the staff can be supported, and how the company fits in with his professional goals. Mark feels more and more comfortable as she leans forward to listen intently to what he is saying. Mark loosens his tie, crosses his legs, and begins sharing stories of how he feels his immediate supervisor has dropped the ball on more than one occasion and that the team would be better if more money were allocated to incentives and bonuses. Mark immediately sees Ms. Mills's eyes begin to squint and her brow furrow. She stands up abruptly and says in a gruff voice that their time is up and that her assistant will show him out.

QUESTIONS TO CONSIDER

1. Given the professional context, what would you have done the same and/or differently if you were in Mark's position?

2. Do you think Mark accurately evaluated the context? Why or why not?

3. What communication factors led to the change in the chief executive officer's disposition?

4. How could the KEYS process help Mark improve his communication skills?

WRITE YOUR NOTES HERE

what is said verbally. It can also *conflict* with what is being said. Verbal and nonverbal communication can be incongruous, or in disagreement. Think of a time at home, work, or school when you experienced someone saying he or she was being truthful yet could not look you in the eye. Did you assume that person was being deceptive? Or think of a time when a loved one said, with a raised voice and tear-filled eyes, that nothing was bothering him or her. When verbal communication carries one message and body language a conflicting message, the result is likely to be communication failure (Jones & LeBaron, 2002; Laplante & Ambady, 2003).

Ekman (1965) also found that nonverbal communication can *complement* or accent a specific part of the verbal message. This can include placing emphasis on certain words by slowing down your speech or changing your tone. Nonverbal behavior can also be a *substitute* for a word or phrase within a verbal message. How many of you have ever nodded instead of saying yes when your professor asked you if you understood the curriculum? Or perhaps you have looked away to avoid eye contact instead of saying that you do not want to be called on to answer the question being asked.

Nonverbal communication may also *accent* (amplify) or *moderate* (tone down) parts of the verbal message. As well, nonverbal communication is distinct in its ability to *regulate* verbal behaviors by coordinating our verbal and nonverbal behavior in the production of our messages or those of our communication partner (Ekman, 1965). Imagine the last time you had a conversation with a roommate or friend. How did you determine whose turn it was to speak? Did you use eye contact to end the conversation or to let the other person know you were listening? What hand gestures or sounds might you have made to show your partner that you wanted to speak?

Recall the definition of human communication as presented earlier in the text: the process of understanding our experiences and the experiences of others through the use of verbal and nonverbal messages. In fact, in an effort to categorize the meaning associated with nonverbal behavior, Mehrabian (1981) identified three dimensions that indicate how we use nonverbal communication to make sense of things in both personal and professional contexts:

- *Immediacy:* We react to things by evaluating them as positive or negative, good or bad.

- *Status:* We perceive behaviors that indicate various aspects of status to us, for example, rich or poor, strong or weak, superior or subordinate.

- *Responsiveness:* We perceive activity as being active or passive. This signals the intensity of our feelings about a person or subject.

Knapp and Hall (2009) proposed that these three dimensions are basic responses to our environment and are reflected in the way we assign meaning to both verbal and nonverbal behavior.

Now that we have explored the value and importance of nonverbal communication and how we assign meaning, it is crucial that we examine the *components* of nonverbal communication to understand it on a deeper level. Although we focus on these nonverbal communication codes in Western culture, remember that perceptions or reactions to nonverbal communication can vary in other cultures.

CODES OF NONVERBAL COMMUNICATION

The primary categories or codes of nonverbal communication include vocal expression; space, environment, and territory; physical appearance; body movement, gestures, and posture; facial and eye expressions; and touch (see Table 2.1; Ivy & Wahl, 2014).

VOCAL EXPRESSION

Vocalics, sometimes referred to as paralanguage, refers to how people use their voices to communicate and express themselves (Foley & Gentile, 2010; Ivy & Wahl, 2014). Vocalic cues include tone (quality) of voice, volume, articulation, pitch (highness or lowness), rate of speech, and use of silence. The voice reveals our emotions, our thoughts, and the relationships we have with others. A growing body of evidence from multidisciplinary research in acoustics, engineering, linguistics, phonetics, and psychology suggests that an authoritative, expressive voice can make a big difference in one's professional career. Scientific studies show that someone with authority characteristically speaks low, slow, and with vocal intonation (Louet, 2012). Vocalics provide information about our self-confidence and knowledge and influence how we are perceived by others (Hinkle, 2001). Think about the direct impact that tone of voice can have in a professional setting. What does your voice say about you to others?

SPACE

The impact of space on communication is called proxemics, or how people create and use space and distance, as well as how they behave to protect and defend that space (Foley & Gentile, 2010; Hall, 1959, 1966; Ivy & Wahl, 2014). Violations of territory and our personal space can be detrimental in business and professional settings.

Have you ever been on a crowded elevator and been uncomfortable because it seemed as though people were invading your personal space? When you go to the library, how many of you place your backpacks on the table or chair next to you to claim your space? What would happen if someone sat down in that chair anyway? Violations can be alarming,

TABLE 2.1

NONVERBAL COMMUNICATION CODES: CONSIDER THE PROFESSIONAL CONTEXT

NONVERBAL CODE	CONSIDER THE PROFESSIONAL CONTEXT
Kinesics (body movement, gestures, and posture)	How do you think gestures and body movement impact professional contexts?
Facial/eye behavior	Can you think of some examples of professional face and eye behavior? How can face and eye behavior lead to negative perceptions?
Vocalics (paralanguage)	What vocal qualities do you perceive as professional? Unprofessional?
Space/territory	How can space and territorial violations impact business and professional contexts?
Touch	Can you think of positive ways to use touch in professional contexts? In contrast, can you think of some negative uses of touch?
Environment	What are the qualities of a professional environment?
Physical appearance	In what ways does physical appearance impact business and professional communication?

WRITE YOUR NOTES HERE

possibly even threatening. Our relationships with others, power and status, and our cultural backgrounds determine how physically close we get to others and how close we let others get to us (Burgoon & Jones, 1976).

What preferences do you have related to space and distance? Edward T. Hall (1963) identified four zones of space in middle-class U.S. culture. The first is the *intimate zone* (0 to 18 inches). This is usually reserved for our significant others, family members, and closest friends. It is rare that a stranger can enter this space without making us feel violated. These interactions mostly occur in private and signify a high level of connection, trust, and affection. The *personal zone* (18 inches to about 4 feet) is reserved for personal relationships with casual acquaintances and friends. The *social zone* (4 to 12 feet) is the distance at which we usually talk to strangers or conduct business. If you went to your professor's office to discuss a grade, for example, you would most likely remain at a distance of 4 to 12 feet. The *public zone* (more than 12 feet) refers to the distance typical of large, formal, public events. In large lecture classrooms, campaign rallies, or public speeches, the distance between speaker and audience is usually more than 12 feet. Understanding these spatial zones is important to your everyday nonverbal communication competency.

ENVIRONMENT

The constructed or natural surroundings that influence your communicative decisions, attitude, and mood are termed the environment (Foley & Gentile, 2010; Ivy & Wahl, 2014). People are influenced by environmental factors such as architecture, design, doors, windows, color, lighting, smell, seating arrangements, temperature, and cleanliness (Harris & Sachau, 2005; Jackson, 2005). Take a moment to think about what preferences would be related to your work environment. How does the environment (e.g., temperature, lighting, color, furniture) impact your communication?

WRITE YOUR NOTES HERE

Consider other things in the environment that can serve as nonverbal cues about who you are. These environmental factors you create and control are what serve as nonverbal messages to others who enter the space. As one scholar put it, "People cannot be understood outside of their environmental context" (Peterson, 1992, p. 154). The environments we create for ourselves often speak volumes about those relationships we consider most important (Lohmann, Arriaga, & Goodfriend, 2003).

The way we perceive our environment and the environments of others is an important factor in how we respond. Overall, we perceive the environment in six distinct ways (Knapp & Hall, 2006). The first is *formality*, which is an understanding people have of environment that relates to how comfortably they can behave, in light of their expectations. Sometimes it is more about the atmosphere of a certain place than the place itself. The second way we can perceive the environment is *warmth*. This means that the environment gives off a certain sense of warmth, comfort, or a welcoming context based on our past or current experience. Think of a favorite smell from your childhood, for example. Smells in an environment contribute to our perception of warmth.

Know Yourself:
NONVERBAL COMMUNICATION

As you read the index below and answer the questions, think about how this knowledge can help you be a better communicator.

NONVERBAL IMMEDIACY SCALE0—OBSERVER REPORT

This measure will allow you to assess your own nonverbal immediacy behaviors.

Directions: The following statements describe the ways some people behave while talking with or to others. Please indicate in the space at the left of each item the degree to which you believe the statement applies to [fill in the target person's name or description]. Please use the following 5-point scale:

1 = *never*; 2 = *rarely*; 3 = *occasionally*; 4 = *often*; 5 = *very often*.

___ 1. I use my hands and arms to gesture while talking to people.

___ 2. I touch others on the shoulder or arm while talking to them.

___ 3. I use a monotone or dull voice while talking to people.

___ 4. I look over or away from others while talking to them.

___ 5. I move away from others when they touch me while we are talking.

___ 6. I have a relaxed body position when I talk to people.

___ 7. I frown while talking to people.

___ 8. I avoid eye contact while talking to people.

___ 9. I have a tense body position while talking to people.

___ 10. I sit close or stand close to people while talking with them.

___ 11. My voice is monotonous or dull when I talk to people.

___ 12. I use a variety of vocal expressions when I talk to people.

___ 13. I gesture when I talk to people.

___ 14. I am animated when I talk to people.

___ 15. I have a bland facial expression when I talk to people.

___ 16. I move closer to people when I talk to them.

___ 17. I look directly at people while talking to them.

___ 18. I am stiff when I talk to people.

___ 19. I have a lot of vocal variety when I talk to people.

___ 20. I avoid gesturing while I am talking to people.

___ 21. I lean toward people when I talk to them.

___ 22. I maintain eye contact with people when I talk to them.

___ 23. I try not to sit or stand close to people when I talk with them.

___ 24. I lean away from people when I talk to them.

___ 25. I smile when I talk to people.

___ 26. I avoid touching people when I talk to them.

Scoring for Nonverbal Immediacy Scale—Observer Report:

Step 1. Start with a score of 78. Add the scores from the following items:
1, 2, 6, 10, 12, 13, 14, 16, 17, 19, 21, 22, and 25.

Step 2. Add the scores from the following items:
3, 4, 5, 7, 8, 9, 11, 15, 18, 20, 23, 24, and 26.

Total score = *Step 1* minus *Step 2.*

SOURCE: Richmond, V. P., McCroskey, J. C., & Johnson, A. E. (2003). Development of the Nonverbal Immediacy Scale (NIS): Measures of self- and other-perceived nonverbal immediacy. Communication Quarterly, 51, 502–515.

How did you score? What surprised you about your score? You can also try the measure on others. Simply fill out the measure with another person's behaviors in mind. For instance, you might find it interesting to fill out the survey for your least and most favorite professors to determine whether their nonverbal immediacy might play some role in the degree to which you like them. Do you notice differences in their use of nonverbal immediacy behaviors? Did you learn more in one class? What class did you enjoy more?

Privacy is another way the environment can be perceived. Do you prefer a crowded and noisy restaurant or a peaceful and quiet one? Do you choose a seat in the back of a movie theater or in the middle next to many other moviegoers? Another perception we have is *familiarity*, which means that we tend to react cautiously when we meet new people or are confronted with an unfamiliar environment. Not knowing where we are and what to expect makes us feel less comfortable. We like knowing what to expect and how to behave in the environment.

Another perception of environment is that of *constraint*. Think about your living situation. Do you like sharing a room or home with another person? Whenever we feel that our personal space is being invaded, we feel constrained. Most of our perceptions of constraint are shaped by the amount of privacy and space available to us. The final perception of environment is *distance*. Our perceptions of distance in an environment pertain to physical arrangements. We like to know how far away the closest door is or

TOOLS FOR PROFESSIONAL EXCELLENCE 2.1
SETTING UP AN EFFECTIVE WORKSPACE

To set up an effective workspace, take note of these useful tips:

KEY POINTS	PRACTICAL TIPS
Think beyond the desk.	• Incorporate movement into the office: a workspace that breaks the "bond between user and desk" can bring physical and psychological benefits to its employees. • Create work areas where employees can both sit and stand. • Bring in different sizes of tables, chairs, and even sofas for meetings or lunch breaks.
Your office is an extension of your culture and brand.	• Consider what you want your workspace to say about the culture of your company, which can help foster a sense of belonging in employees. • Think carefully about what furnishings and décor items are used in the workspace. • Don't be afraid of color: a workspace that is all white or gray can have negative health effects on employees, while a workspace that incorporates colors like blue or red can help keep employees productive and motivated.
Include an area for meaningful play.	• Incorporate a play area to help employees break free from the monotony of e-mail and phone calls. • While something as simple as a couch or two will do, don't be afraid to get creative and incorporate games, such as ping-pong, into the play area. • "Play means connection": Play areas can help employees build bonds with one another and fosters communication and success.
Allow employees to design their own workspace.	• Let employees have a say in the design process, especially when it comes to expressing who they are; doing so can boost employee morale, which further improves the company's productivity. • Give employees some control in how the workspace should look by letting them pick the color, allowing them to personally decorate their section of the workspace, or inviting them to bring in their pets.

SOURCE: Vozza, S. (2013, March 11). Rethink your office design: Designing a more effective workspace. *Entrepreneur*. Retrieved and adapted from www.entrepreneur.com/article/226034

how many people can fit into an elevator. We create distance by avoiding eye contact or taking a longer route to avoid saying hello to a person we find annoying.

PHYSICAL APPEARANCE

Physical appearance—"the way our bodies and overall appearance nonverbally communicate to others and impact our view of ourselves in everyday life" (Ivy & Wahl, 2014, p. 153)—also plays an important role in communication. Making the connection between physical appearance and nonverbal communication is important for two reasons: (1) The way we represent ourselves and our physical appearance reveals a lot about who we are, and (2) the physical appearance of other people influences our perception of them, how we talk to them, how approachable they are, how attractive or unattractive we think they are, and so on.

Clothing is also a part of our physical appearance that is often critical to professional situations. Clothing helps you convey a sense of professionalism. Clothing and other appearance aspects, termed artifacts (e.g., jewelry, tattoos, piercings, makeup, cologne, eyeglasses), send nonverbal messages and help others form perceptions of us, both good and bad (Okoro & Washington, 2011; Roach, 1997). The nonverbal message sent by your clothing is a powerful part of professional excellence. Appearance is extremely important in our society. In fact, according to Armour (2005), employers also agree that physical appearance matters. An Intranet software firm in the Northeast requires formal business attire on the job. Men must

```
┌─────────────────────────────────┐
│      WRITE YOUR NOTES HERE       │
│                                 │
│                                 │
│                                 │
│                                 │
│                                 │
│                                 │
│                                 │
│                                 │
│                                 │
│                                 │
│                                 │
│                                 │
└─────────────────────────────────┘
```

wear ties, cannot have beards, and cannot wear their hair past shoulder length. "Clients like to see a workforce that looks conservative," says the chief operating officer. Although the criteria for what is acceptable in each environment might vary, physical appearance undoubtedly can affect one's perceived professional excellence.

BODY MOVEMENT

Kinesics is a general term for the study of human movement, gestures, and posture (Birdwhistell, 1970; Foley & Gentile, 2010; Ivy & Wahl, 2014). Kinesics provides valuable information about a person to others. Have you ever heard someone make reference to how a certain person carries himself or herself? Have you ever talked about a person who has a certain presence in the room? Perhaps you have said, "He/she walks like a leader." Some people carry themselves in ways that convey pride and confidence, while others have poor posture and seem to lack confidence. Ekman and Friesen (1969b) classified movement and gestures according to how they function in human interaction. The five categories of kinesics are emblems, illustrators, affect displays, regulators, and adapters.

Emblems are specific, widely understood meanings in a given culture that can actually substitute for a word or phrase. An example of this would be placing your pointer finger in front of your lips to indicate to someone to be quiet. Illustrators are gestures that complement, enhance, or substitute for the verbal message. If you were describing the length of the biggest fish you ever caught, you might use your hands to illustrate the size. Or when you are giving directions, you might point to show which way to go. Affect displays are facial expressions and gestures that display emotion. A smile can be an affect display for happiness, while a scowl can display frustration. Regulators are gestures used to control the turn-taking in conversations. For example, you might make a hand motion to encourage someone or raise your own hand to get a turn at speaking. When we are eager to speak, we typically make eye contact, raise our eyebrows, open our mouths, take in a breath, and lean forward slightly. We do the opposite if we do not want to answer. Head nods, vocal expressions (such as *um*), facial expressions, body postures, and eye contact can be seen as connectors that keep the conversation together and make it coherent. When these sorts of nonverbal cues are absent from a conversation, it might trigger a negative reaction, and we could come to believe that our conversational partner is not listening at all. Adapters are gestures we use to release tension. Playing with your hands, poking, picking, fidgeting, scratching, and interacting nonverbally with your environment are all adapters that reveal your attempts to regulate situations and to make yourself feel more at ease and able to function effectively. Adapters can alert us that another person is uncomfortable in some way (Ekman & Friesen, 1969b).

FACIAL BEHAVIOR

Facial expressions (including the study of eye behavior, called oculesics) are also critical codes that have been studied by nonverbal communication scholars (Ivy & Wahl, 2014). The face can be considered a gallery for our emotional displays (Gosselin, Gilles, & Dore, 1995). What does another person's face tell you about him or her? What emotion is she expressing? How is he feeling? Are your coworkers surprised to see you? Did your colleagues find your presentation to be entertaining, or were they disappointed? Your face and eye behavior play a huge role in the messages you send in business and professional contexts.

It is important not only to have a basic understanding of the emotions communicated by the face but also to be aware of how we manage our faces in daily interactions. Social norms and communication expectations in our culture set the rules for what kinds of emotional expressions are appropriate in certain situations. Facial management techniques are categories of behavior studied by Ekman and Friesen (1969a, 1969b) that determine the appropriate facial response for a given situation. The four most common techniques are neutralization, masking, intensification, and deintensification.

The process of using facial expressions to erase how we really feel is called neutralization. People who neutralize their facial expressions are often referred to as having a poker face. Masking means hiding an expression connected to a felt emotion and replacing it with an expression more appropriate to the situation. If we use an expression that exaggerates how we feel about something, it is called intensification. By contrast, if we reduce the intensity of our facial expression connected to a certain emotion, it is called deintensification.

A significant part of facial expressions involves use of the eyes. About 80% of the information in our everyday surroundings is taken in visually (Morris, 1985). Kleinke (1986) purports that eye contact and gaze functions provide information, regulate interaction, express intimacy, exercise social norms, and facilitate personal, situational, and relational goals. Evasive glances and limited-duration eye contact

Your Communication Interaction
TO TWEET OR NOT TO TWEET

As you read the passage below, consider what would be a more effective communication strategy in this situation.

Ryan is the new digital media intern at a public relations firm. During one of his first meetings, members of the digital media team outline new hashtags they would like to test on the company's social media accounts, and get consumer feedback. Eager to show off his social media savvy, Ryan immediately logs on to his personal Twitter account and shoots off a series of tweets using the new hashtags. Later that day, Ryan receives an e-mail from the head of the digital media team, reprimanding him for using a personal social media account while on the job.

QUESTIONS TO CONSIDER

1. Was Ryan justified when he tweeted during the meeting? Why or why not?
2. To promote the company, what other communication channel(s) could Ryan have used instead of his personal Twitter account?
3. When, if ever, is it acceptable to use a personal social media account while on the job?
4. If you were the head of the digital media team, how would you handle Ryan's situation?

on the part of a communicator tend to reduce compliance with requests (Gueguen & Jacob, 2002). What can people tell about you by looking into your eyes?

TOUCH

Touch, also called haptics in nonverbal research, "is the most powerful form of nonverbal communication; it's also the most misunderstood and has the potential for severely negative consequences if not enacted appropriately" (Ivy & Wahl, 2014, p. 49). Several different systems for categorizing touch have been developed to help us better understand this complex code of nonverbal communication. One of the best means of classifying touch behavior was developed by Heslin (1974). The first, functional/professional touch, serves a specific function. These touches typically take place within the context of a professional relationship and are low in intimacy. An example would be the essence of greeting rituals in business situations, the *professional handshake* (Hlemstra, 1999). The handshake is critical to making a good first impression as a professional. Think about what you look for in a handshake. What does a professional handshake feel like?

Social/polite touch is connected to cultural norms, such as hugs or pats on the back. Once again, these touches convey relatively low intimacy within a relationship, whereas friendship/warmth touch is the type people use to show their platonic affection toward each other. Hugs and kisses on the cheek might be exchanged between two close friends, for example. Love/intimacy touch, by contrast, is highly personal and intimate. People communicate strong feelings of affection toward each other with these kinds of touches; in this case, hugs may last longer and kisses may be on the lips. The last category involves sexual arousal. These touches are extremely intimate.

FORMING RELATIONSHIPS WITH VERBAL AND NONVERBAL COMMUNICATION

Developing interpersonal, verbal, and nonverbal communication skills requires you to differentiate between the content and relational layers of messages. As you communicate with other people, your messages have two layers (Dillard, Solomon, & Palmer, 1999; Watzlawick, Beavin, & Jackson, 1967). The first is the content layer. The content layer consists of the "information being explicitly discussed" (Adler & Proctor, 2007, p. 16). The content layer may include descriptive information such as the time of a meeting, a project due date, or the names of the coworkers assigned to a team. You exchange content with others to function and retrieve basic information.

The second layer is relational. The relational layer reveals "how you feel about the other person; whether you like or dislike the other person, feel in control or subordinate, feel comfortable or anxious, and so on" (Adler & Proctor, 2007, p. 16). The relational layer may be communicated by your choice of words. For example, an executive may call her employees by their first names, while the employees are required to refer to the executive as Mrs. Villarreal. The difference in formality of names signifies a difference in control. The relational level can also be communicated nonverbally through tone of voice, use of space, and eye contact.

For example, Jason is really nervous about making a deadline, but he can't finish until Rachel completes the financial section of the project. Jason could ask Rachel, "What time will you be done with financials?" to retrieve a specific time reference, such as "Sometime this evening." These words reflect the content layer. If Jason wants to send the message that he's annoyed with Rachel, he could add a negative tone: "What *time* will you be done with financials?" If Jason is indeed annoyed, then he has effectively communicated both the content and relational layers of his message. However, if Jason did not intend to express annoyance, then his message is ineffective on the relational level.

ACTION ITEMS
SKILLS FOR OBSERVING NONVERBAL COMMUNICATION

SKILL	STRATEGY	APPLICATION
Listen	Listen for different verbal inflections and tone of voice.	Watch a political speech and observe the ways that vocalics influence message reception.
Observe	Inspect nonverbal cues to determine how a person responds to verbal communication.	Pay attention to the body language of people as you give them either positive or negative reinforcement.
Understand	Gain data from multiple interactions with different people in an attempt to generalize your findings.	After several communication interactions, step back and reflect on whether there were any nonverbal cues that are reliable across contexts.

There are communicators out there who do not pay attention to the relational layer of their messages. As a result, they don't realize how they're coming across to others. To achieve professional excellence, you must think beyond the content layer of your messages and also assess the relational layer. This can be supported by using the KEYS process.

VERBAL AND NONVERBAL COMMUNICATION AND THEIR IMPACT ON PROFESSIONS

In this chapter, we have explored verbal and nonverbal communication—why they are important, their definitions, their principles, and their components. As you consider your professional goals, think about how you will use verbal and nonverbal communication to succeed in your career. We have included the following examples of the importance of verbal and nonverbal communication in a variety of industries. Even if your desired profession is not listed in the sections below, know that developing your professional excellence and communication competence is invaluable no matter what path you may take in life.

WRITE YOUR NOTES HERE

CUSTOMER SERVICE AND SALES

Recall the importance of proxemics, or the impact of space on communication. Manning and Reece (1989) found that success in productivity and sales was linked to the distance between sales representatives and prospects, salesperson posture, handshake techniques, facial expressions, arm movements, hand movements, and placement of the legs and feet. Those sales representatives who rely primarily on the spoken word to communicate with prospects may be neglecting an important tool for conveying their ideas. In addition, Leigh and Summers (2002) conducted an investigation that examined the effectiveness of nonverbal communication in a sales context. Using videotaped presentations, they found that nonverbal cues (eye gaze, speech hesitations, gestures, clothing, and posture) influenced the experimental buyers' perceptions of the sales representative and their evaluation of the sales presentation.

JOURNALISM AND TELEVISION BROADCASTING

Those in the public eye must demonstrate effective nonverbal and verbal communication. How many times have you seen a clip of an on-camera flub being played over and over again on YouTube or the local news? In the opinion of some scholars, as well as television commentators, arrogant body language on the part of many journalists in the United States has led to low public respect and esteem for them (Lehrer, 1998).

PUBLIC SERVICE

Individuals who work in environments such as libraries or government offices (e.g., Department of Motor Vehicles, utility companies) are sometimes criticized for their communication and viewed as distant and unhelpful. Evidence indicates that individuals who are trained in nonverbal communication can replace negative perceptions of themselves with positive ones (Sampson, 1995).

HOSPITALITY MANAGEMENT

Customer service is especially important in the hotel and restaurant industries. A number of hotel and restaurant managers have improved their organizations' image among guests by providing client services employees (e.g., hosts, servers, desk clerks, bellhops) with training in verbal and nonverbal communication (Jafari & Way, 1994). In restaurants, eye contact, facial expression, body position, and posture of the staff, including servers and cashiers, affect how customers rate the value of the service (Martin, 1986).

MEDICAL PROFESSIONS

Many people can probably share a story about an unpleasant experience at the doctor's office. As physicians compete to attract and retain a strong client base, their services can be interpreted positively by potential patients through correct body language on the part of the physicians and their employees. Patients often choose a physician based on their perceived image of the doctor, as revealed by verbal and nonverbal communications (Hill & Garner, 1991).

TEACHING PROFESSIONS

There is evidence that the nonverbal communication of teachers influences the evaluation direction (positive or negative) and level of performance they receive from their students (Babad, Avni-Babad, & Rosenthal, 2003). Consider the different teaching and communication styles of your current professors. What do you find are the common communication traits of the professors you enjoy most?

WRITE YOUR NOTES HERE

WRITE YOUR NOTES HERE

LEGAL PROFESSIONS

A study has indicated that lawyers can project a favorable impression of themselves and their firms for prospective clients through sustained eye contact and other forms of body language, such as an erect but relaxed sitting position and close proximity to the clients (Clarke, 1989).

ACCOUNTING AND FINANCE

In the same vein as lawyers, accountants can benefit through the technique of maintained and appropriate eye contact, good posture, and close proximity to clients (Pickholz & Zimmerman, 2002).

MANAGEMENT
(PRIVATE AND PUBLIC)

Managers in both business and not-for-profit organizations can more effectively convey ideas to their employees through correct use of nonverbal communication (Hancock, 1999; McCaskey, 1979). Further, job evaluations of employees by their supervisors have been found to correlate with smiling, gaze, hand movement, and body orientation (DeGroot & Motowidlo, 1999). In a similar vein, managers can effectively convey impressions of empathy and power through body language (Gabbott & Hogg, 2000).

KEYS TO EXCELLENCE IN VERBAL AND NONVERBAL COMMUNICATION

In the opening of this chapter, we discussed the ways verbal and nonverbal communication can be conveyed in different communication contexts. Do you believe that this also affects your business communication? Think about how using the KEYS strategies can positively affect your nonverbal communication with others. The first step, *know yourself*, asks you to inventory the types of nonverbal cues you display to others. This can be difficult, but try to be aware even of the small, unconscious nonverbal cues you create. Sometimes the worst nonverbal cues we display are the ones we are not even aware of making.

The next step, *evaluate the professional context*, requires that you assess what nonverbal signals are considered acceptable in your workplace. Are your meetings informal, or is there a set decorum on how people interact? Notice how both your coworkers and superiors convey nonverbal cues during workplace interactions, and gauge how your nonverbal cues line up with those of others in your company.

The third step, *your communication interaction*, involves taking an immediate reflexive inventory of both your nonverbal communication and your partner's. How do you react to your partner's nonverbal signals? How does he or she react to yours? Think about what sets you at ease when communicating with others, and try to accomplish the same goal when talking with customers, employees, or superiors. The more open people feel when talking with you, the more likely they are to disclose information more honestly and comfortably.

The final task, *step back and reflect*, requires you to analyze your communication after the interaction has ended. Did you walk away feeling satisfied with your nonverbal communication? Did your communication partner seem at ease when talking with you?

Assess what seemed to be the most effective nonverbal cues and which ones appeared to create a negative perception.

Much like the relationships between traditional and new media, new venues for business communication can help or hinder your professional career. Remember that nonverbal communication does take place in digital contexts, and learn how to use nonverbal cues appropriately. This can lead to better (and more honest) communication and allow you to practice professional excellence in the workplace.

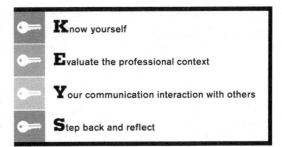

Know yourself

Evaluate the professional context

Your communication interaction with others

Step back and reflect

EXECUTIVE SUMMARY

Now that you have finished reading this chapter, you should be able to:

Define verbal communication:

- Verbal communication is both our words and verbal fillers (e.g., *um*, *like*). Verbal messages are created through language. Effective communication involves accurate interpretations of others' verbal messages as meaning is cocreated (p. 27).

Define nonverbal communication:

- Nonverbal communication (also referred to as body language) includes all those ways we communicate without words (p. 29).

Appraise your verbal and nonverbal communication skills:

- Developing interpersonal, verbal, and nonverbal communication skills requires you to differentiate between the content and relational layers of messages. As you communicate with other people, your messages have two layers (p. 39).
- The content layer consists of the "information being explicitly discussed" (Adler & Proctor, 2007, p. 16). The content layer may include descriptive information such as the time of a

meeting, a project due date, or the names of the coworkers assigned to a team (p. 39).
- The relational layer reveals "how you feel about the other person; whether you like or dislike the other person, feel in control or subordinate, feel comfortable or anxious, and so on" (Adler & Proctor, 2007, p. 16). The relational layer may be communicated by your choice of words (p. 39).

Discuss examples of how verbal and nonverbal communication are related:

- Some communicators do not pay attention to the relational layer of their messages. As a result, they don't realize how they're coming across to others. To achieve professional excellence, you must think beyond the content layer of your messages and also assess the relational layer (p. 40).

Apply the KEYS approach to conduct yourself with professional excellence through verbal and nonverbal communication in the workplace:

- The first step, know yourself, asks you to inventory the types of nonverbal cues you display to others. This can be difficult, but try to be aware even of the small, unconscious nonverbal cues you create. Sometimes the worst nonverbal cues we display are the ones we are not even aware of making (p. 42).

- The second step, evaluate the professional context, requires that you assess what nonverbal signals are considered acceptable in your workplace. Are your meetings informal, or is there a set decorum for how people interact? Notice how both your coworkers and superiors convey nonverbal cues during workplace interactions, and gauge how your nonverbal cues line up with those of others in your company (p. 42).
- The third step, your communication interaction, involves taking an immediate reflexive inventory of both your nonverbal communication and your partner's. Think about what sets you at ease when communicating with others, and try to accomplish the same goal when talking with customers, employees, or superiors. The more open people feel when talking with you, the more likely they are to disclose information more honestly and comfortably (p. 42).
- The final task, step back and reflect, requires you to analyze your communication after the interaction has ended. Did you walk away feeling satisfied with your nonverbal communication? Did your communication partner seem at ease when talking with you? Assess what nonverbal cues seemed the most effective and which ones appeared to create a negative perception (p. 42).

EXPLORE

1. Visit a website that defines Internet slang and/or emojis (e.g., Internetslang.com, Urbandictionary.com). How often do you use Internet slang in your online (and professional) communication? List several types of slang or acronyms you were previously unfamiliar with.
2. Observe a social gathering, and compare and contrast the nonverbal displays present versus what you would see in a business or professional setting. Are there significant nonverbal communication differences when people are relaxing or at work? List several examples that support or refute this claim.
3. Watch any video of your choosing that features someone giving a speech or presentation to a group of people. In what ways does the speaker blend verbal and nonverbal communication. Write a brief statement describing how nonverbal cues can both enhance and hurt verbal communication.

REVIEW

Check your answers to these questions at **http://edge.sagepub.com/quintanilla3e.**

1. Define verbal and nonverbal communication.
2. Explain the difference between regulative rules and constitutive rules.
3. _____ refers to how people use their voices to communicate and express themselves.
4. The impact of space on communication, or how people create and use space and distance, is known as _____.
5. The constructed or natural surroundings that influence your communicative decisions, attitude, and mood refers to _____.
6. List and briefly describe the six different perceptions of environment.
7. The general term for the study of human movement, gestures, and posture is known as _____.
8. Identify the four facial management techniques that determine the appropriate facial response for a given situation.

DISCUSSION QUESTIONS

1. What two rules guide communication? Why is appropriateness important when communicating? Share an example of a time when you experienced inappropriate communication. Who was the communicator? Why was it inappropriate?
2. Ethical consideration: In a workplace, when, if ever, is it appropriate to verbally communicate something that is not true? Does this apply to your personal relationships? Ask three people this same question, and note their responses.
3. What are the principles of nonverbal communication? Discuss at least two nonverbal communication codes. Which codes discussed in this chapter are the most important to you as a professional?
4. Name three reasons why nonverbal communication is important. Work through a personal example of a time when you needed to improve your verbal or nonverbal communication. What changes would you have made in the situation?
5. Step back and reflect on a time when you received criticism at work or school. How did you respond verbally? How did you respond nonverbally? How did the environment contribute to your communication?

TERMS TO REMEMBER

Review key terms with eFlashcards. **http://edge.sagepub.com/quintanilla3e.**

adapters (p. 37)
affect displays (p. 37)
artifacts (p. 37)
codes (p. 33)
communication rules (p. 28)
constitutive rules (p. 28)
content layer (p. 39)
deintensification (p. 38)
emblems (p. 37)
environment (p. 34)

friendship/warmth touch (p. 39)
functional/professional touch (p. 39)
haptics (p. 39)
illustrators (p. 37)
intensification (p. 38)
kinesics (p. 37)
love/intimacy touch (p. 39)
masking (p. 38)
neutralization (p. 38)
nonverbal communication (p. 29)

oculesics (p. 38)
physical appearance (p. 36)
proxemics (p. 33)
regulative rules (p. 28)
regulators (p. 37)
relational layer (p. 39)
sexual arousal (p. 39)
social/polite touch (p. 39)
verbal communication (p. 27)
vocalics (p. 33)

Listening

*Quintanilla, K.M. and
Wahl, S.T.*

Retailer Best Buy is listening to its customers more than ever by focusing on its customer reviews. The company has begun to share customer feedback with vendors and has taken multiple actions based on web reviews (Reid, 2014). To encourage honest feedback, Best Buy has instituted a program that rewards customers for completing reviews with special points to use toward future purchases. More than ever, companies are empowering their customers to influence business decisions. The convergence of social, mobile, and cloud technologies has drastically altered the way people buy, and looping customer feedback into the company's decision-making processes is critical (Reid, 2014). Today, companies have a multitude of tools and technologies available to get immediate and effective customer feedback. The data available to retailers such as Best Buy make it inexcusable for companies not to be customer centric. Whether companies have physical locations (Best Buy) or are entirely digital (Amazon), customer insight is critical to long-term success.

As you study this chapter, think about the variety of methods people can use to listen effectively. From a professional standpoint, critical listening skills are invaluable. However, being an effective listener can benefit your academic, social, and romantic life as well. Use the tools and information gained in this chapter to continually assess the communication around you.

How important is listening in the communication process? What role does listening play in developing professional excellence? According to Crockett (2011), the average person remembers between 25% and 50% of what he or she hears. That means that when you talk to your boss, your colleagues or customers, your friends and family, they are likely to retain less than half of the conversation. Our poor memories are not to blame; rather, most of us simply do not listen well. To compound matters, the diversity and environment of today's workforce makes listening more difficult. In many workplaces, it is not uncommon for work teams to consist of people from several countries or ethnic backgrounds as well as varying levels of technological communication knowledge and practice. Even if everyone speaks English, some might use different dialects and speech patterns. Maximizing performance in such a multicultural and highly technological work environment means learning to listen. We will explore the concept of diversity and communication further in Chapter 5 ("Getting to Know Your Diverse Workplace"). Understanding why listening is important is crucial to help us improve our listening skills overall. The ability to be an effective listener plays a role in one's business and professional communication and is a prerequisite to demonstrating professional excellence. Listening is also vital to the needs of companies of all sizes and dynamics.

According to Stengel, Dixon, and Allen (2003), the most basic principle in the consumer products industry is "listen to the customer." Without an intimate knowledge of ever-changing trends and tastes, you are likely to lose out to competitors who are more tuned in. The notion that success also depends on listening to employees might seem just as basic. Yet this is not as easy as it sounds, and, due to poor listening, a company's leaders—regardless of industry—are often oblivious to what employees are concerned about and why. A good example is the Jayson Blair episode at the *New York Times*. Jayson fabricated and plagiarized multiple articles. By the time senior leaders got around to listening to their employees' concerns about the reporter's misdeeds, damage had been done to the organization's reputation. The problem of managers not hearing what staffers are saying is common in corporate life (Stengel et al., 2003). But the problem is not necessarily whether managers are hearing their staff. The problem lies in the ability to listen. Listening is a fundamental and complex part of the communication process. Let's explore it in more detail.

HEARING AND LISTENING

In casual conversation, most of us use the words *hearing* and *listening* as if they mean the same thing. However, as a professional striving for communication excellence, it's important for you to have a clear understanding of the difference between these terms. Hearing is your physical ability to detect sounds. It is the physiological process or function of receiving sounds. Your hearing is what they test at the doctor's office. Listening, however, is not one's physical ability. Recall the importance of nonverbal communication skills, which help you differentiate between the content and layers of messages. Listening requires you to concentrate on the verbal and nonverbal messages being sent and to determine the meaning of those messages. Effective listening is central to fostering interpersonal relationships with coworkers, leaders, and clients. Effective listening can affect one's relationship satisfaction and can be a determining factor in whether someone is an effective communicator.

The effects of one's listening abilities are far-reaching. Sypher, Bostrom, and Seibert (1989) reported that an individual's listening ability has implications for the effectiveness of productivity, teamwork, the overall organization, and perhaps the individual's own success. Listening, in addition to other communication abilities, is a likely predictor of who gets promoted or receives other relevant rewards, such as status and power. Sypher et al. (1989) found that better listeners hold higher-level positions and are promoted more often than those with less-developed listening abilities.

Wouldn't life be fantastic if everyone were an excellent listener? Can you imagine an entire career without any misunderstandings? The trouble is, many people make the mistake of thinking excellent hearing equals excellent listening. You have no doubt already experienced communication misunderstandings in the workplace—you know firsthand that excellent hearing does not necessarily equal excellent listening.

Developing excellence as a listener can be difficult, but to achieve professional excellence, you must hone your ability to listen effectively. In fact, Haas and Arnold (1995) state that a growing body of research suggests that listening ability, or the perception of effective listening, is inextricably linked to effective individual performance in organizations. Nichols and Stevens (1957) found that good listeners regularly engage in mental activities while listening. A good listener periodically reviews and mentally summarizes the talking points completed thus far. Throughout the talk, the listener "listens between the lines," in search of meaning that is not necessarily put into spoken words. He or she pays attention to nonverbal communication (facial

> WRITE YOUR NOTES HERE

expressions, gestures, tone of voice) to see if it adds meaning to the spoken words. The listener may also weigh the evidence used by the talker to support the points he or she makes. It takes a lot of practice to become a good listener, and listening has become a lot more difficult.

So how can you develop your skills as a listener? The first step is to admit that listening is difficult. Don't fall into the trap of assuming that because you have good hearing, you have good listening skills, too. Take Carey, for example. Carey was born deaf, and

Step Back and Reflect:
TROUBLE AT HOME, TROUBLE WITH TRAINING

As you read this passage and answer the questions, step back and reflect on what went wrong in this professional situation.

Jennifer is a recent college graduate who started a new job as a recruiter for a local nonprofit. Her job consists of placing individuals with employment barriers into jobs. She must build relationships with employers, secure job leads, screen candidates, and report her monthly hires/placements. Her position is commission based, which means she must make placements to earn money. While in training, she found herself preoccupied by several things going on at home. She was fighting with her boyfriend and in a conflict with her roommate. Her boyfriend sent her numerous text messages while her new manager explained the job responsibilities to the class of new hires. Between worrying about her relationship and the pressures of learning a new job, she heard the new manager say that she should do anything in her power to get placements, as this was the most important thing to remember of all the training content.

A few weeks into her position, Jennifer found that she felt really lost about how to do her job well. She was not making any placements. Whenever she approached her

coworkers, they did not seem to listen to her. They rarely looked up from their computers or phones, and she had to repeat her questions several times before they answered. When they did respond, they answered only parts of her questions. Jennifer was left confused and frustrated. They all said the same thing, however: Getting placements was the most important thing to focus on, no matter how she met her goal. She followed their lead and began claiming credit whenever any of her clients found a job, whether she had assisted them or not. Jennifer was cutting corners to reach her placement outcomes. She had "heard" the message loud and clear. A few months later, Jennifer, her coworkers, and their immediate supervisor were terminated and the nonprofit was under investigation for fraudulent reporting.

STEP BACK AND REFLECT

1. What went wrong?
2. What role did listening play?
3. What are the ethical considerations?
4. What critical listening strategies can Jennifer employ to help her in the workplace?
5. How could Jennifer use the KEYS approach to improve her communication interaction?

while she could not physically hear others speak, she was an excellent listener. She used an interpreter, lip reading, and a highly developed ability to read nonverbal cues to make sense of the messages she received. In fact, her inability to hear may have caused her to develop her exceptional listening abilities. Carey outperformed many of her colleagues who did possess perfect hearing. Although they sat beside Carey in meetings, hearing every word, they fell victim to the barriers to listening excellence. These barriers include failing to limit distractions, failing to focus on the message, and failing to be active listeners. In any business and professional situation, you'll encounter some or all of these barriers. An important part of professional excellence is being able to develop your listening skills and overcome the barriers.

BARRIERS TO LISTENING

FAILING TO LIMIT DISTRACTIONS

As we covered in Chapter 1, noise is part of every communication interaction. External noise includes distractions such as audible talking during a meeting, ruffling of papers, or a cell phone going off in the next cubicle. Whenever possible, you should take steps to control the external noise that might interfere with your ability to listen to others, as well as their ability to listen to you. For example, when you are talking to someone on the phone, turn away from your computer if you're distracted by messages in your inbox. If you're running a meeting, begin by asking everyone to turn off their cell phones. If the work environment is such that it's difficult for people to break away from distractions, hold a retreat away from your worksite to maximize the team's ability to listen effectively. For example, Jennifer (in "Step Back and Reflect" on page 49) failed to limit her distractions when she did not turn off her cell phone prior to the new-hire training. Instead, she focused on reading the messages from her boyfriend, increasing her inability to listen to the trainer. We must be conscious of the extent to which environmental, physical, psychological, and experiential factors affect the quality of listening (Highet, 1989, p. 65).

Internal noise encompasses any internal condition or state that interferes with the communicator's ability to focus on the message. Even when we are listening in real time—on a cell phone, for example—listening has become more multilayered. During a cell phone conversation, we expect the speaker to be doing something else. Whether we think about it consciously or not, during the conversation we assess what the speaker is saying as well as what she or he is *not* saying because of where she/he is or whom she/he is with. Technology has changed not only the tools we use to listen but also when and where we use them, and even what we think about as we listen (Jalongo, 2008).

Controlling internal noise in others can be difficult, as it may be hard to predict. Still, you can minimize some internal noise in others. For example, holding long meetings without food or bathroom breaks will guarantee internal noise in your team. Minimize the noise by providing food and giving breaks. Say you are a health care provider who has to deliver bad news. News such as "You have cancer" or "You will need surgery" will create tremendous internal noise. In situations such as these, allow the listener time to deal with the news before giving additional information or instructions he or she will need to listen to, comprehend, and remember.

WRITE YOUR NOTES HERE

Your Communication Interaction
THE PROMOTION

As you read the passage below, consider what would be a more effective communication strategy in this situation.

Cara has worked at her employer for a few years and considers herself an asset to the company. Her annual review is coming up, and she is debating whether or not to ask her boss for the promotion she feels she deserves. Cara decides to get on her boss's good side in the days before her review, and does so by making coffee runs, taking on extra duties around the office, and even taking him lunch. Feeling confident that she has won him over, Cara casually mentions the promotion, to which her boss responds with a big smile and several head nods. A week later, one of Cara's coworkers excitedly announces that she received the promotion. Feeling hurt and confused, Cara immediately texts her boss and asks him why she did not receive the promotion.

QUESTIONS TO CONSIDER

1. What could Cara have done differently in the face-to-face interactions with her boss to avoid miscommunication?
2. Was texting the best communication channel for Cara to have used when confronting her boss? Why or why not?
3. If you were Cara, how would you handle the news that you were passed over for the promotion?
4. If you were Cara's boss, how would you respond to her text?

As for the internal noise within *you*, you must reflect on what is causing your internal noise and address those factors. If you have an urgent matter to deal with, don't try to hold a conversation with someone. You simply won't be able to listen. Tell the other party you will need to reschedule your conversation for a time when you can give your undivided attention. If matters in your personal life are affecting your ability to listen on the job, you must become aware of those issues and address them. For example, Jason has been experiencing a personal conflict with his wife. They both feel he's been spending too much time at work and not enough time at home. Jason's conflict at home serves as internal noise when his coworker, Rachel, tells him she will not have her part of the project to him on time. As she explains how her workload has doubled over the past few weeks due to some vacant positions in her department and she really wants an extension, all Jason can think about is the fact that his part of the project will now have to be completed over the weekend. For Jason, developing professional excellence includes learning to manage his internal noise so that he can listen. If Jason had listened to Rachel, he could have supported her desire for an extension and they could have jointly requested a solution that would benefit them both. Like Jason, Jennifer (from "Step Back and Reflect" on page 49) was experiencing internal noise as a result of her relationship conflicts at home. Her failure to limit external distractions and to address the factors leading to internal noise prevented her from developing professional excellence.

FAILING TO FOCUS ON THE MESSAGE

In the ever-changing world of social media and emerging technology, we are locked into a mode of continuous partial attention, where we are always scanning our smartphones for the next bit of news or the latest update. Multitasking is the norm, despite some evidence that it prevents us from doing anything to the best of our abilities (Fryer, 2009). In addition to distractions and noise, or maybe because of noise, you may fail to focus on the message being sent. As a result, you are not listening effectively. Beyond noise, some additional factors that may distract your focus on the message include jargon, message overload, receiver apprehension, and bias. Or you may fail to focus on the message because it is difficult to comprehend.

WRITE YOUR NOTES
HERE

If a speaker uses jargon (technical words used by specialized groups) with which you are not familiar, you may think, "What in the world is she talking about? Why should I even pay attention to this stuff?" and then simply tune out. Jargon is a language of familiarity. It can be a useful tool when everyone has a common understanding of the terms at hand. If there is no common understanding, language can separate, insulate, and intimidate. Good communication is the result of the use of common terms that are clearly understood by both parties (Morasch, 2004).

Message overload can have the same impact as jargon. Message overload occurs when a speaker includes too many details in a message, making it difficult for the listener to comprehend. As the listener tries to make sense out of the specific details, he or she loses focus on the primary message. Presenters sometimes make the mistake of including too many graphs and charts during their talks, which leads the audience to message overload. As a listener with professional excellence, you must stay engaged even if the message is difficult to comprehend. Listen for the main points, and request a copy of the notes or PowerPoint slides after the presentation. If the jargon or message overload comes as part of a conversation, not a presentation, engage in active listening.

Have you ever been nervous about listening to a presentation on a unfamiliar subject or about being involved in a conversation with a person you want to impress? You might be listening to someone give you specific directions about a complicated task or sitting in a lecture trying to take notes on classroom material. In any of these cases, you might be apprehensive about listening to the speaker. This feeling is called receiver apprehension. Receiver apprehension refers to "the fear of misinterpreting, inadequately processing, and/or not being able to adjust psychologically to messages sent by others" (Wheeless, 1975, p. 262). This could mean having a fear of coming across new information or of being judged on your ability to remember the information correctly (Wheeless, Preiss, & Gayle, 1997). Research has demonstrated that a person with high receiver apprehension tends to have more problems with information processing and general listening effectiveness (Chesebro & McCroskey, 2001).

We also need to limit our bias in order to be better listeners. Bias is any assumption we make or attitude we have about a person, an issue, or a topic before we have heard all the facts. If you equate a speaker with subject matter or experiences

ETHICAL CONNECTION
LISTENING TO EMPLOYEES

As you read this passage and answer the questions, consider how the way you communicate has an ethical dimension.

Jennifer and Daniel are both personnel managers at a large company. Although both jobs are identical in size and duties, the feedback that Jennifer and Daniel each receive could not be more different. Jennifer's employees feel safe approaching her with new ideas and concerns and are overall satisfied with the feedback they receive. Employees who work for Daniel, on the other hand, often complain that talking to him is like talking to a brick wall. They say that their concerns go unaddressed and that when they forward a new idea for the company, their suggestions are shrugged off without any discussion. At a recent supervisor meeting, the company executives discussed

the disparity between Jennifer's and Daniel's employee satisfaction surveys and retention rates. Daniel seemed at a loss as to why his department was underperforming in comparison with Jennifer's.

QUESTIONS TO CONSIDER

1. What is the ethical dilemma involved in being a poor listener?
2. Why would employees be happier working in an environment with a manager who effectively listens to their ideas and concerns?
3. Why is it so important that Jennifer provides feedback relating to her employees' communication?
4. How can Daniel use the KEYS process to become a more effective listener?

that have made you feel frustrated or angry in the past, chances are good that you will be biased about that person before he or she gives the speech. That bias may prevent you from listening to what that person has to say, and you may miss some important information. Bias is not limited to individuals; it can also apply to groups. For example, if you feel strongly about a particular topic because of your values, you may refuse to listen to any other perspective, no matter whom it comes from. Effective listening requires you to put your biases aside and regard the other as having a valid point of view worthy of your time and careful attention. To reduce bias, you need to acknowledge that bias might exist and try to remove it from your evaluation of the message.

WRITE YOUR NOTES HERE

FAILING TO BE AN ACTIVE LISTENER

Just as there is a difference between hearing and listening, there are also differences between various types of listening. In your professional career, you will engage in three types of listening: informational, critical, and empathetic. Informational

---

Evaluate the Professional Context

MIGUEL AND THE MULTITASKING MISHAP

As you evaluate the passage below, consider whether this behavior is appropriate for this professional context.

Miguel had a successful career as an event planner. He started off as an assistant at an agency, but through hard work and consistent results, he had developed his own client list and saved enough money to start a company out of his home. He specialized in weddings and took pride in helping couples plan their dream events. As his client base continued to grow due to word-of-mouth referrals, he struggled to keep up with all the client requests but did not have the funds to hire additional employees. Miguel found himself multitasking on most days, and he was often double booked. The summer months were especially hectic.

One of his repeat clients, Tamara, hired him to plan a 50th anniversary party for her parents, as she had been so pleased with how her wedding turned out. It was an especially important event because Tamara's father had been diagnosed with cancer a few months before. A few weeks before the party, Miguel was meeting with a new client when the phone rang. Tamara was on the phone, extremely upset because they needed to move up the event

due to a medical procedure scheduled around the original event date. Miguel took the call while working with the new client. While showing the new client fabric samples and place settings, he listened to Tamara, assured her he would take care of it, and they agreed on an available date.

On the day of the event, Tamara, Miguel, her parents, and their guests arrived at the venue to find that another event had already begun. Miguel was mortified when he realized that he had forgotten to reschedule the event with the venue. Although he attempted to apologize and offered alternatives, the damage was done. The family was extremely upset. Tamara began to cry, called Miguel an insulting name, and told him she would be sure to tell all her friends and acquaintances about the experience.

QUESTIONS TO CONSIDER

1. What could Miguel have done differently to avoid this situation?
2. Should Tamara have handled the situation differently?
3. How could the KEYS process help Miguel manage his clients' needs and expectations despite his hectic schedule?

WRITE YOUR NOTES HERE

An active listener makes sense out of the message and then verifies that the sense making is accurate.

listening occurs when you focus on the content of the message to acquire knowledge. Part of learning a new position involves listening to information during new-employee orientation and one-on-one training. Critical listening asks you to evaluate the information being sent. For example, Trey has been asked to seek three separate bids from business-development consulting firms. Trey must critically listen and then evaluate the advantages and disadvantages of each proposal. Empathetic listening is listening to understand the speaker's point of view without judgment. If a customer comes to you with a complaint and you listen to him to try to understand the problem from his perspective, without countering, criticizing, or judging, you have engaged in empathetic listening. Research tells us that listening with empathy is the basis for a host of important workplace skills and strategies: assessing situations, making rational decisions, generating connections between theory and practice, arriving at deeper understandings of beliefs, adapting to new perspectives, informing instructional decisions, challenging traditions, improving teaching and learning, and validating ideals (Jalongo, 2008).

Where does active listening fit in? Isn't it a type of listening? No, it is not a type of listening; rather, it is a *way* to listen. Every time you engage as a listener, you must consciously decide if you are going to be an active listener or a passive listener. As a passive listener, you will simply receive a message and make sense out of that message without feedback or verification. For example, watching the news on television is passive listening, because there is no need to provide feedback since a response is not expected. Poorly run meetings often have everyone but the leader acting as passive listeners. In contrast, as an active listener, you are required to make sense out of the message and then verify that your sense making is accurate. In other words, you must verify that you understand the message as the speaker intended. To achieve professional excellence in interpersonal relationships, you must always be an active listener.

An active listener focuses on asking questions and will often listen to the message and then paraphrase it for the sender. Let's say an employee complains to you by saying, "I'm sick of the attitude around here. Some people stroll into work whenever they feel like it, and the customers suffer. The poor customers have to be put on hold forever, and they get really upset." As an active listener, you can summarize that message to check your understanding: "You feel irritated when people are late for work because it means the phones are not covered and we are not providing the best service we are capable of." In some situations, paraphrasing is critically important. At the same time, many professionals view continual paraphrasing as unnatural or mechanical in style. Still, when there's a high likelihood of misunderstanding, a little paraphrasing can make a big difference in the communication interaction.

WRITE YOUR NOTES HERE

Kerry Washington stars in the television hit *Scandal* as Olivia Pope, a beautiful and shrewd image expert who can "fix" even the most desperate and disastrous public relations blunders. Her particular expertise calls for a constellation of communication skills that enable her not only to understand the circumstances surrounding a client's problem, but to discover his or her interests and needs. What communication skills do you think Olivia Pope consistently needs to be successful in her role?

Another technique is reflection. Jalongo (2008) categorizes reflective listening as different from ordinary listening in four important ways. Reflective listening means the listener (1) listens thoughtfully to the meaning of the speaker's words; (2) considers the content of the message, both stated and implied; (3) thinks about the feelings associated with the message, attending to the speaker's verbal and nonverbal cues; and (4) makes every effort to reflect that message accurately. Questions are another tool used by the active listener. By asking questions, you can develop a better understanding of the speaker's message and provide support to the speaker.

Graham, Santos, and Vanderplank (2008) highlight the importance of developing a sense of being "in charge" of the listening process. Being in charge of listening includes both knowing how and knowing when to use which strategies. We have defined listening, discussed why it is important, and revealed the various barriers that may prevent one from listening effectively. Now we will explore in more detail some of the different styles and categories of listening.

TOOLS FOR PROFESSIONAL EXCELLENCE 3.1
EFFECTIVE NOTE-TAKING

To take effective notes in the workplace, follow these practical tips:

KEY POINTS	PRACTICAL TIPS
Don't just take notes; read them.	• Simply taking notes in the moment is not enough to recall the information: Rereading what you've written later on is vital. • Notes are meant to be used as storage for information that can be accessed at any time, not just once and then forgotten.
Digital or handwritten?	• There are varying opinions on which method is the best when it comes to note-taking: Some people argue that digital note-taking can be a distraction, while others argue that digital note-taking is more efficient and improves information recall. • Use whichever method works best for you and provides the most useful set of notes.
Supercharge your notes.	• Notes with hierarchical ordering or numbered sections prove to be the most accurate. • Notes that contain some sort of organizational pattern are more useful for information recall than are freestyle notes.
Doodling isn't just for fun.	• Using visual note-taking methods, such as mind-mapping, can enhance the material and improve your ability to recall and present the information. • If a piece of information seems important, underline it to make it stand out and help you remember it later.
Take breaks.	• Continuous listening and note-taking can result in fatigue and decrease the effectiveness of the notes. • Whenever possible, take short breaks from note-taking: This ensures the quality of future notes, and helps you process those you've already taken.

SOURCE: Codrea-Rado, A. (2013, March 20). The complete guide to taking notes effectively at work. *Quartz*. Retrieved and adapted from qz.com/64539/complete-guide-to-taking-notes-effectively-at-work/

LISTENING STYLES AND CATEGORIES

Barker and Watson (2000) classified four listening preferences or styles. People-oriented listeners are interested in demonstrating concern for others' emotions and interests, finding common ground, and responding. These listeners demonstrate a genuine concern for others' feelings and identify with emotional states of human behavior. This type of listener can become "over-involved with the feelings of others" (Watson & Barker, 1995, p. 3). Action-oriented listeners are interested in direct, concise, error-free communication that is used to negotiate and accomplish a goal; these listeners are easily frustrated by disorganized presentations. Content-oriented listeners are interested in intellectual challenge and complex information; they want to evaluate information carefully before forming judgments and opinions. At times, it appears as though "they are looking under a microscope and dissecting information" (p. 5). Time-oriented listeners prefer brief communication; such listeners seek interaction that is concise and to the point, and they want to know the length of time available before the communication begins. What type of listener are you? Do you recognize the styles of your boss, family, or friends?

Listening can also be divided into a variety of categories. Listening in interpersonal situations is usually categorized as either conversational or presentational. When the speaking role shifts from one person to another with some degree of frequency, we call it conversational listening. In a conversational situation, the person who was actively listening one minute can assume the major speaking role the next, while the previous speaker becomes a listener. Conversational listening is an integral part of meaningful one-on-one social relationships and professional interpersonal exchanges. Conversational listening most often emerges in face-to-face situations but may also take place over the telephone. Presentational listening is a type of listening that takes place in situations where a clear role of speaking and listening functions is prescribed. In presentational listening, roles are usually formal and defined as active speaker and responsive listener. The listening environment is based on the following conditions: mode (conversational or presentational), environment (formal or informal), and relationship (social or business; Nelson & Heeney, 1984).

IMPROVING YOUR LISTENING

Now that you have an understanding of the types, styles, and categories of listening, we can share additional ways to improve your listening skills. Becoming a better listener takes time and effort. The HURIER model provides a framework for skill-based listening by defining listening as six interrelated components: Hearing, Understanding, Remembering, Interpreting, Evaluating, and Responding (Brownell, 1994, 1996).

Hearing refers to concentrating on and attending to the message. The first step toward better listening is making sure you can properly hear the other person. Be sure that you limit any distractions that would prevent you from doing so. Understanding is the process of attaching meaning to the verbal communication, or comprehending the literal meaning of the message. We often do this unconsciously. Understanding a message requires that we first hear the message, but it also includes being able to understand the speaker's use of language and the basic context of the information. Remembering includes recalling the message so that it can be acted on. Listening not only requires us to be present, in the moment, and mindful but also necessitates anticipating future interactions. One way to help yourself remember the message is to create an outline of the main points.

Interpreting is the step where we make sense of the verbal and nonverbal codes to assign meaning to the information received or the sensitivity to nonverbal and contextual aspects of the message (Brownell, 1994). Interpreting is an important part of the collaborative process of communication. Ethically interpreting a message means you are not intentionally letting your own bias or beliefs interfere with your interpretation. Evaluating is the logical assessment of the value of the message (Brownell, 1994). Learning to evaluate a message without bias, distractions, apprehension, or gender/cultural differences takes time and patience.

After interpreting and evaluating the message, you must decide how to reply or respond. Responding is the last step and involves giving some form of *response* to the message, either verbally or nonverbally. Communication would not be collaboration if not for this vital step. Paraphrasing, summarizing, reflecting, and asking questions all demonstrate responsiveness. Using nonverbal cues such as head nods, emotional expressions, or verbal utterances is also a good way to show you are listening. The six-step process, when used in combination with active listening skills and barrier avoidance, will result in development of your professional excellence.

Research in listening has just begun to explore the many aspects of this complex and central communication process. According to Nixon and West (1989), listening is the most basic communication skill and supersedes all learning processes. Historically, listening has been the most neglected instructional and research area. However, now professional organizations such as the International Listening Association, academic institutions, and other organizations are providing increased training materials devoted to listening research. Through proficient use of listening instruction, people learn listening guidelines and can develop listening skills in ways similar to learning mathematics, physical fitness, reading, and writing (Nixon & West, 1989).

Gibbs, Hewing, Hulbert, Ramsey, and Smith (1985) assert that listening awareness and instruction can accomplish four major objectives: (1) increasing understanding of

---

Know Yourself:
LISTENING ANXIETY

As you read the index below and answer the questions, think about how this knowledge can help you be a better communicator.

The following statements apply to how various people feel about listening to others. Indicate to what degree these statements apply to how you feel. Please use the following 5-point scale:

5 = *strongly agree,* 4 = *agree,* 3 = *are undecided,*
2 = *disagree, or* 1 = *strongly disagree.*

1. ___ While listening, I get nervous when a lot of information is given at once.
2. ___ I get impatient and anxious when listening to someone discuss theoretical, intellectual issues.
3. ___ I have avoided listening to abstract ideas because I was afraid I could not make sense of what was said.
4. ___ Many classes are annoying and uncomfortable because the teacher floods you with detailed information in the lectures.
5. ___ I feel agitated or uneasy when someone tells me there is not necessarily a clear, concrete way to deal with an important problem.
6. ___ While listening, I feel tense when I have to analyze details carefully.

7. ___ It is frustrating to listen to people discuss practical problems in philosophical and abstract ways.
8. ___ When I hear abstract material, I am afraid I will be unable to remember it very well.
9. ___ I experience anxiety when listening to complex ideas others tell me.
10. ___ When I listen to complicated information, I often fear that I will misinterpret it.
11. ___ I do not feel relaxed and confident while listening, even when a lot of information is given at once.
12. ___ Listening to complex ideas is not a pleasant, enjoyable experience for me.
13. ___ When listening, I do not feel relaxed and confident that I can remember abstract ideas that are being explained.

Add all scores together: _____
The higher the score, the higher your listening anxiety.

SOURCE: Adapted from Wheeless, L. R., Preiss, R. W., & Gayle, B. M. (1997). Receiver apprehension, informational receptivity, and cognitive processing. In J. A. Daly, J. C. McCroskey, J. Ayres, T. Hopf, & D. M. Ayers (Eds.), Avoiding communication: Shyness, reticence, and communication apprehension (pp. 151–187). Cresskill, NJ: Hampton Press.

NOTE: This is a modified version of the Listening Anxiety Test.

WRITE YOUR NOTES HERE

Technology has affected our ability to listen. Limit distractions by turning off your cell phone before a presentation or professional meeting.

the nature of listening and its importance in the total communication process, (2) diagnosing listening abilities and practices, (3) developing skills and techniques to improve listening effectiveness, and (4) creating awareness of the importance of effective listening to personal and professional success. In schools that have instituted listening instruction, students' listening comprehension has as much as doubled in just a few months. Continuous evaluation of one's own listening abilities and participating in listening instruction or learning measures increases retention, promotes critical thinking, and facilitates learning.

Being mindful of your listening effectiveness is valuable in the professional environment. According to Haas and Arnold (1995), listening plays a pivotal role in conceptions of communication competence in coworkers. In other words, your ability or inability to listen will directly affect whether your coworkers perceive you as possessing communication competence. In turn, you will also judge your coworkers' abilities to communicate effectively by how well they demonstrate listening skills. Failure to recognize that listening is just as important as verbal communication is inevitably detrimental. In fact, many Fortune 500 companies, as well as several management training programs used across the United States, identify listening as one of the most important communication skills in the workplace (Haas & Arnold, 1995).

Nelson and Heeney (1984) explain that a truly competent listener goes beyond simply hearing; listening includes comprehending meaning, analyzing relationships, interpreting impressions, and evaluating content. The ancient adage still rings true today—the beginning of wisdom is silence. The second stage is listening (Gibbs et al., 1985). Will you value the knowledge gained in this chapter and improve your listening skills to develop professional excellence? How have your listening skills affected your work, school, or home life?

ACTION ITEMS
SKILLS FOR BEING AN ACTIVE LISTENER

SKILL	STRATEGY	APPLICATION
Observe	Watch the verbal and nonverbal cues your communication partner is expressing.	Use a debate-style forum that encourages you to focus entirely on the other person before you are allowed to respond.
Focus	Don't do anything else while listening.	Block out all other distractions and give your undivided attention to the other person.
Acknowledge	Acknowledge the message, even if you don't agree with it.	Your acknowledgment can be verbal (*uh huh*, *yes*) or nonverbal (a head nod).
Respect	Let the speaker finish.	As tempting as it can be to voice your opinion, remember to respect the other person's time first.

KEYS TO LISTENING EXCELLENCE

The opening of the chapter discussed the listening strategies used by Best Buy to increase customer satisfaction and revenue. Try to apply Best Buy's practices to the KEYS strategy. The first step, *know yourself*, allowed Best Buy to realize there was a better way to deliver the products that the company's customers want (by listening).

The second step, *evaluate the professional context*, involved Best Buy executives assessing the professional makeup of the company. Best Buy is a major retailer of electronic media that saw online competition (such as Newegg) having great success using customer feedback and ratings for their products. Taking inspiration from this model, Best Buy began to model their consumer marketing strategy to focus on listening to what their customers liked or disliked about their products.

The third step, *your communication interaction*, involved Best Buy offering rewards to customers who offered them feedback. The result was an increase in customer involvement and overall satisfaction with Best Buy. The company developed a better understanding of what products their customers prefer and what platform they choose to buy from (in person or online).

Know yourself

Evaluate the professional context

Your communication interaction with others

Step back and reflect

The final strategy, *step back and reflect*, allowed Best Buy to quantitatively measure the success of their new business approach. Best Buy saw an increase in market share and an overall more favorable public perception after taking customer feedback. By taking an active role in listening to consumer demand, Best Buy allowed itself to grow as a major retail company.

What listening skills do you use when interacting with others? Can Best Buy's example be used by other companies to generate both profit and goodwill?

Want a better grade?

Get the tools you need to sharpen your study skills.
Access practice quizzes, eFlashcards, video, and multimedia at
http://edge.sagepub.com/quintanilla3e.

$SAGE edge™

EXECUTIVE SUMMARY

Now that you have finished reading this chapter, you should be able to:

Explain the difference between hearing and listening:

- Hearing is your physical ability to detect sounds. It is the physiological process or function of receiving sounds (p. 48).

- Listening requires you to concentrate on the verbal and nonverbal messages being sent and to determine the meaning of those messages. Effective listening is central to fostering interpersonal relationships with coworkers, leaders, and clients (p. 48).

Discuss the barriers to listening and how to avoid them:

- External noise includes distractions such as audible talking during a meeting, ruffling of papers, or a cell phone going off in the next cubicle. Whenever possible, you should take steps to control the external noise that might interfere with your ability to listen to others, as well as their ability to listen to you (p. 50).
- Internal noise encompasses any internal condition or state that interferes with the communicator's ability to focus on the message. Controlling internal noise in others can be difficult, as it may be hard to predict. Still, you can minimize some internal noise in others. For example, holding long meetings without food or bathroom breaks will guarantee internal noise in your team. Minimize the noise by providing food and breaks (p. 50).
- Message overload occurs when a speaker includes too many details in a message, making it difficult for the listener to comprehend. As the listener tries to make sense of the specific details, he or she loses focus on the primary message. If the jargon or message overload comes as part of a conversation, not a presentation, engage in active listening (p. 52).

Describe strategies for developing and sustaining professional excellence using active listening skills:

- An active listener focuses on asking questions and will often listen to the message and then paraphrase it for the sender (p. 54).
- Another technique is that of reflection. Jalongo (2008) categorizes reflective listening as different from ordinary listening in four important ways. Reflective listening means the listener (1) listens thoughtfully to the meaning of the speaker's words; (2) considers the content of the message, both stated and implied; (3) thinks about the feelings associated with the message, attending to the speaker's verbal and nonverbal cues; and (4) makes every effort to reflect that message accurately (p. 55).
- Questions are another tool used by the active listener. By asking questions, you can develop a better understanding of the speaker's message and provide support to the speaker (p. 55).

Define the six-step process of listening:

- The HURIER model refers to a six-step listening process: **H**earing, **U**nderstanding, **R**emembering, **I**nterpreting, **E**valuating, and **R**esponding (Brownell, 1994, 1996). Hearing refers to concentrating on and attending to the message. The first step toward better listening is making sure you can properly hear the other person (p. 56).

- Understanding is the process of attaching meaning to the verbal communication, or comprehending the literal meaning of the message (p. 56).
- Remembering includes recalling the message so that it can be acted on. Listening not only requires us to be present, in the moment, and mindful but also necessitates anticipating future interactions (p. 56).
- Interpreting is the step where we make sense of the verbal and nonverbal codes to assign meaning to the information received or the sensitivity to nonverbal and contextual aspects of the message (Brownell, 1994). Interpreting is an important part of the collaborative process of communication (p. 56).
- Evaluating is the logical assessment of the value of the message (Brownell, 1994). Learning to evaluate a message without bias, distractions, apprehension, or gender/cultural differences takes time and patience (p. 57).
- Responding is the last step and involves giving some form of response to the message, either verbally or nonverbally. Communication would not be collaboration if not for this vital step. Paraphrasing, summarizing, reflecting, and asking questions demonstrate responsiveness (p. 57).

Apply the KEYS approach to conduct yourself with professional excellence while developing your listening skills in the workplace:

- Know yourself. Understand the components of being an active listener and critically apply them to your professional interactions. Realize your strengths and weaknesses as a listener and adapt accordingly (p. 59).
- Evaluate the professional context. Learn whether your professional environment uses formal or informal communication. Also, pay attention to jargon used at your work. Use active listening to create understanding of words or phrases you are not familiar with (p. 59).
- Your communication interaction. Take what you have learned from the first two steps and try communicating with fellow business professionals. Are you using the workplace jargon correctly and effectively? Be critical about the responses you receive from your peers (p. 59).
- Step back and reflect. Ask yourself if you and your communication partner(s) came away from the interaction with mutual understanding. Think about what was effective and what was not. Repeat the process to gain greater and more effective strategies for being a good listener and a good communicator (p. 59).

EXPLORE

1. Visit Best Buy's website and look at their customer reviews and feedback. Do you believe the company does an effective job of listening to its customer base? Are there any improvements you would recommend to make the company a more effective listener?
2. Think about the ways you use the Internet and social media to gain knowledge about businesses and products. How important is peer and customer feedback to you in your own

purchasing decisions? Write about a time you used either word-of-mouth or online reviews to reach a purchasing decision.
3. Identify a movie or television show in which a character engages in poor listening techniques. What nonverbal cues does he or she give off that show a lack of interest? What critical listening skills could be used to improve the communication in the given situation?

REVIEW

Check your answers to these questions at **http://edge.sagepub.com/quintanilla3e.**

1. Define hearing versus listening.
2. Explain the difference between external noise and internal noise.
3. Technical words used by specialized groups are known as _____.
4. _____ is any assumption we make or attitude we have about a person, an issue, or a topic before we have heard all the facts.
5. _____ are interested in demonstrating concern for others' emotions and interests, finding common ground, and responding.
6. Identify the different components of the HURIER model.
7. _____ occurs when a speaker includes too many details in a message, making it difficult for the listener to comprehend.
8. _____ listening asks you to evaluate the information being sent.

DISCUSSION QUESTIONS

1. What is the difference between hearing and listening, and why does it matter?
2. List three barriers to listening. Which barriers most frequently affect your ability to listen? List the steps you will take to improve your ability to avoid these barriers.
3. What is listening bias, and how has it affected your communication interactions in the past? What can you do to avoid it in future interactions?
4. List and define the four listening styles. Which style do you most relate to? Will this change now that you know how listening affects your professional excellence?
5. What is the difference between active and passive listening? Conversational and presentational listening?

TERMS TO REMEMBER

Review key terms with eFlashcards. **http://edge.sagepub.com/quintanilla3e.**

action-oriented listeners (p. 56)
active listener (p. 54)
bias (p. 52)
content-oriented listeners (p. 56)
conversational listening (p. 56)
critical listening (p. 54)
empathetic listening (p. 54)
evaluating (p. 57)
external noise (p. 50)
hearing (p. 48)

HURIER model (p. 56)
informational listening (p. 53)
internal noise (p. 50)
interpreting (p. 56)
jargon (p. 52)
listening (p. 48)
message overload (p. 52)
paraphrase (p. 54)
passive listener (p. 54)
people-oriented listeners (p. 56)

presentational listening (p. 56)
questions (p. 55)
receiver apprehension (p. 52)
reflection (p. 55)
remembering (p. 56)
responding (p. 57)
time-oriented listeners (p. 56)
understanding (p. 56)

PART 2

BUSINESS SKILLS AND RESEARCH METHODS

Chapter Outline

Technology and Media

Duck, S. and McMahan, D.T.

ow much time each day do you think the average person spends watching television, listening to music, reading, playing video games, and using the Internet? If you base your answer on how much time you personally spend engaging in these activities, then doubling that number will provide a more accurate answer, with a recent study showing that 51.9% of students are addicted to the Internet (Pontes, Szabo, & Griffiths, 2015).

The so-called Middletown Media Studies discovered that people actually spend twice the amount of time using media than they believe they do. These studies also established that people do not use media in isolation but often use two or more media systems simultaneously, an activity referred to as concurrent media use. For example, you may be reading this book while listening to the radio or watching television. Including concurrent media use, the most media-active person observed in these studies spent more than 17 hours using media each day, and the least media-active person observed spent a bit more than 5 hours using media each day. The average amount of time spent using media daily was nearly 11 hours (Papper, Holmes, & Popovich, 2004). However, more recent research suggests that these data have been overtaken in light of the growth of use of smartphones and their value as mobile devices in all contexts, even in the classroom, where BYOD (bring your own device) is a developing educational tool (Cochrane, Antonczak, & Wagner, 2013).

Now consider how often people send text messages in a given day. Focusing only on teenagers, the median (half send more, and half send fewer) number of texts sent each day is 60, with 18% of teenagers sending more than 200 text messages daily (Lenhart, 2012). Adults send fewer texts on average than teenagers do (Smith, 2011). However, the frequency of adult texting is rising as teenagers become adults and continue their texting habits. Not surprisingly, texts are exchanged most often with people we know and with whom we have relationships. For the same reason, technology and media use at home occurs in the presence of family members, close friends, and romantic partners, whereas technology and media use outside the home often occurs with those with whom you share more social relationships, such as classmates, coworkers, and acquaintances. This just means that because we spend more time with technology and more time with close folks, the time spent on technology is more likely to be spent in the company of close folks!

This observation encourages us to take a relational perspective on technology and media, exploring the relational context for the use of technology and

FOCUS QUESTIONS

1 How do people generally perceive technology and media?

2 What are the relational uses of technology and media?

3 How are smartphones used in the construction of identities?

4 How do smartphones influence relationships?

5 How are identities constructed online?

6 How does online communication influence relationships?

concurrent media use: use of two or more media systems simultaneously

By the way . . .

Early Technological Fear

Perhaps the earliest recorded instance of technological fear is attributed to Socrates. He was concerned that writing would ruin people's memories. Ironically, his concerns are remembered because Plato wrote them down.

QUESTIONS TO CONSIDER

1. Why do you suppose people tend to view emerging technologies with such fear?

2. In contrast, why do you suppose some people view emerging technologies as lifesavers?

media, given that the predominant reason for using them in the first place is relational. Finally, we specifically examine the ways in which people construct identities and relate through two prominent technologies: smartphones and the Internet.

Perceptions of Technology and Media

A person's perspective will influence how something is understood and how it is studied. Accordingly, your view of technology and media will influence how you comprehend and evaluate the information provided in this chapter. We first discuss how people traditionally view emerging technologies in general along with the roles that relationships play in the uses and understandings of technologies. We will also address whether technology and media influence people, whether it is the other way around—or a bit of both.

Cave Drawings and Other Key Concerns

When a new technology is introduced in a society, it is generally framed both as something that will save the world and as something that is intrusive and threatening. The new technology also tends to be evaluated according to standards and criteria associated with previously existing technology rather than being studied and evaluated according to its own unique standards and norms. More often than not, technological fears are more common than technological praises.

The emergence of any new communication technology has historically elicited choruses of concern and anxiety, surprisingly similar in nature. People tend to worry about the effects of emerging technologies on family, community, and, of course, children. Although no evidence exists, we imagine focus groups were developed by well-meaning cave people to examine the potentially negative impact of cave drawings on innocent and susceptible cave children.

Documented criticism of more recent technologies shows that people expressed similar fears about the printing press and the telephone. Indeed, when radio began appearing in homes in the 1920s, these fears were nearly identical to those expressed about television when it began appearing in homes during the 1950s. Comic books were going to turn children into criminals, and video games were going to rot their brains. The Internet was going to destroy society by isolating people, and Twitter was going to make people illiterate. Many of these criticisms are still being expressed, even though most have been proven wrong. In some cases, rather than isolating people, the Internet has brought them together, and Twitter has been credited with a key role in the Arab Spring revolutions of 2011 (Elbelghiti, 2016).

Every Technology Is Relational

Technologies do influence the world in which you live. Regardless of whether its influences are positive or negative, each technology changes how people communicate and interact. The one constant among all technologies, from cave drawings to Twitter or Snapchat to whatever technologies are next, is that they are inherently relational in their understanding and use: *communication* fosters *community*.

At the center of all criticism and even praise of technologies rest their influence and effect on social interaction and connections among people. This influence is probably why criticism and praise surrounding each emerging technology have sounded so similar—relationships among people have been the one constant throughout all human technological development. Adapted to accomplish and meet relational needs, all technologies have influenced how you interact and relate with others.

Impact of Technology

Technologies do influence your world, and this influence is especially evident when it comes to relationships. However, a question arises as to whether technologies are affecting humans or humans are affecting technologies. If you ask us—and we are certainly glad that you did—the answer is both. Three primary views are associated with the impact of technology.

Technological Determinism

Technological determinism is the belief that technologies determine social structure, cultural values, and even how we think. People are essentially viewed as powerless against the force of technology. As you might gather, people viewing technologies as deterministic are the same people most likely to evaluate emerging technologies with fear and suspicion. Karl Marx laid the basis for this kind of observation when he noted the relationship between material experience and social consciousness—that is a fancy way of saying that the "stuff" that you have will influence the way in which you experience the world. For example, we have no idea of what it felt like to have no easy access to telephone communications or fast cars, but presumably the change in society that made these available to people considerably affected the way they understood the nature of distance and connection.

This point about the role of technology in framing our experience is different from the claim that company decisions about the nature and "shape" of technology may affect our lives. Jo-Elle Public might experience relationships differently when in possession of a smartphone instead of a piece of paper and a quill pen, but it is also true that the companies that research and market technology tend to make decisions about the future styles of technology whether we like it or not, as when the company might encourage us to use Cortana. The "Push" and "Tracking" services used by large companies tend to influence our decisions and our lives. Although we need to be aware of these factors in our social lives, we are more concerned here with the uses of technology and their impact on relational experience.

Somewhat related to technological determinism is the belief that people are powerless against media content. Taken to the extreme, whatever is shown on television, for instance, will have the intended impact of producers and affect everyone in the audience in the exact same manner. Of course, people are not passive consumers of media. Rather, they actively interpret and evaluate media in a variety of ways for a variety of reasons. Rachid Elbelghiti (2016) noted, for example, that the

> WRITE YOUR NOTES HERE

technological determinism: belief that technologies determine social structure, cultural values, and even how people think (compare with *social shaping of technology* and *social construction of technology*)

"Arab Spring" of 2011 failed to take much hold in Morocco because high illiteracy and poverty rates meant that few citizens had access to social media, so the message of optimistic revolution was less easily spread there.

Social Construction of Technology

Social construction of technology (SCOT) is the belief that people determine the development of technology and ultimately determine social structure and cultural value. The social constructionist view of technology reminds us that many factors are involved in the development and emergence of technologies beyond the technology itself (Bijker, Hughes, & Pinch, 1987). These factors include human innovation and creativity, economics, government regulation, and characteristics of users of technology.

We can use radio as an extended example when looking at the ways in which these human factors influence the emergence of technologies in society. Radio was created through the innovation and creativity of Guglielmo Marconi, based on the earlier electromagnetic work of Nikola Tesla. However, radio really took hold after November 1920 when promoted by Westinghouse—a radio set manufacturer interested in selling more sets! The government got involved via the Radio Act of 1927 to establish more control over licensing and then the Federal Communications Commission (FCC) was created in 1934 to "ensure decency" on the airwaves. Ultimately, however, actual users exert tremendous influence on the development of any technology, their preferences determining its use, development, and place within society. In the case of radio, users influenced such factors as where it would be used and thus be made available (home, automobile, and outdoors), along with establishing the relative popularity of different types of content that should be offered by broadcasters in pursuit of larger audiences.

Social Shaping of Technology

Social shaping of technology (SST) is the belief that both people and technologies exert influence on social structure and cultural values. Many factors determine the development, popularity, or adoption of technologies, including characteristics of the technology itself (MacKenzie & Wajcman, 1985). We can use the development of smartphones as an example. People may ultimately determine what to do with a smartphone but once they saw the possibility of using apps to replace calendars, mirrors, GPS, shopping list, address books, cameras, or computer terminals, people exerted strong consumer influence on the development of smartphones toward those abilities (http://www.businessinsider.com/11-things-the-iphone-has-made-obsolete-2015-11; http://www.buzzfeed.com/jeffrubin/30-things-you-no-longer-need-because-of-smartphones#.xw8j5MWGv).

So, social shaping of technology views both humans and technology as responsible for what happens in the world. This perspective influenced research conducted by David (McMahan & Chesebro, 2003) concerning political structure and primary technologies of all the world's nation-states. It was discovered that a nation-state's primary technology influences its political system and any political transformation that may take place. For instance, orality is more likely to support certain political systems, with literacy, electronic, and digital systems more likely to support other types.

At the same time, humans (especially governments) exert influence on technologies and society through such factors as innovation and creativity, economics, regulation, and

social construction of technology (SCOT): belief that people determine the development of technology and ultimately determine social structure and cultural value (compare with *social shaping of technology* and *technological determinism*)

social shaping of technology (SST): belief that both people and technologies exert influence on social structure and cultural values (compare with *social construction of technology* and *technological determinism*)

the actual use of technology, encouraging some uses and not others. Although governments may like to include speed record in all funds to determine whether you exceed the limit when driving, for example, people are likely to resist this use of smartphones.

Ultimately, both technology and humans influence the developments of societal systems, ways of thinking, and ways of relating.

The Relational Uses of Technology and Media

Individuals do not use technology and media as solitary beings. Rather, *people* use technology and media as *relators*. It might sound like we are getting too technical or abstract. However, we make that distinction for a very specific reason. Your use of technology is most often done with relationships in mind. Accordingly, a relational context is the most valuable way to understand technology and media in everyday life. In this section, we talk about their various relational uses.

The Use of Technology and Media Is a Shared Relational Activity

People often use technology and media for specific relational reasons. Most technologies—especially digital and electronic technologies—enable interaction to take place and quite frequently are the actual basis for interaction, whether by text, Skype, or Yik Yak.

Especially when people are not at the same location, a sense of connection is created through shared experience with technology and media. In the case of television, sometimes millions of people are watching the same material as you, frequently at the exact same time. This sense of connection is being enhanced through the growing number of people texting and chatting with others online while watching the same television program (Proulx & Shepatin, 2012).

The use of technology and media as a shared relational activity enables people to accomplish certain relational needs (Table 13.1).

Technology and Media Inform People About Relationships

People base their understanding of relationships and their actions within relationships partly on media representations. Books, magazines, newspapers, the Internet, movies, songs, and television programs feature both fictional and real social and personal relationships. Of course, a variety of sources inform your understanding of relationships, and you can compare the information you gain from one source with the information you gain from other sources as you develop your own understanding of relationships. However, that is not just information about content that is important, and Georg Simmel (1950) observed that by access to such information people establish reference points for their own relationships and establish some kind of understanding about whether they are obtaining from their relationships as much as they "should."

> WRITE YOUR NOTES HERE

> Do you think using the Internet as a family will become a shared media experience like watching television as a family?

Table 13.1　Relational Needs and the Shared Use of Technology and Media

Promoting Interaction

Technology and media enable interactions to take place. Even in technology- and media-rich households with multiple television sets, computers, and other technology and media systems, families often use technology and consume media together, which provides an opportunity for interactions to occur. Walter Gantz (2013), for example, found that sports are often viewed on TV with others, and watching sports is an activity that can maintain and enhance existing relationships.

Withdrawing From Interactions

Technology and media also allow people to withdraw from social interaction. Texting and accessing materials using smartphones and tablets allow people to disengage from others when desired. People sometimes even pretend to use their smartphones to avoid interactions (Baron & Campbell, 2012).

Differentiating Relationships

The shared use of technology and media has even been shown to distinguish particular relationships from others. Nearly 40 years ago, it was discovered that watching television was the most frequent activity shared by spouses—it even outranked sex (Argyle & Furnham, 1982)! More recently, Laura Padilla-Walker, Sarah Coyne, and Ashley Fraser (2012) found that smartphones and watching television and movies to be among the most common media shared by families.

Enacting and Evaluating Roles

The shared use of technology and media also enables people to establish and enact specific relational roles, expectations, and boundaries. For instance, relational boundaries must be evaluated when parents and children "friend" one another on Facebook (Kanter, Afifi, & Robbins, 2012).

Make your case

Positive and Negative Influences

Although there is often resistance to new technology on the grounds that it will destroy society and these ideas are too often overstated, there are nevertheless several negative impacts (DeLoatch, 2015): (1) Technology changes the way children think and reduces their ability to remember; (2) technology changes the way children feel and reduces their sense of well-being; (3) technology put safety and privacy at risk; (4) technology reduces physical activity and overuse leads to obesity.

QUESTIONS TO CONSIDER

Consider these points and make a list of arguments for and against the value of technology:

1. After making your arguments, which position do you support the most, and why?
2. Which position do you support the least, and why?

Media Representations Inform About How Relationships Should Look

Media representations of relationships provide information about relational roles. Essentially, people can learn about what relationships look like and what to expect from them based on media depictions; in particular (Simmel, 1950) they learn what other people do in relationships or what they have as relationship goals and achievements. All those Cosmo quizzes really tell you what you "should" expect from relationships—even if you hadn't thought of doing it for yourself!

Relationships depicted on television and through other technologies are not always realistic, however. People have the ability to compare media depictions of relationships with relationships observed or enacted in their physical lives, but media representations of relationships may nevertheless create unrealistic expectations and beliefs about how relationships should look (e.g., Osborn, 2012).

Further, relationships depicted in media do not always look like those that audiences personally experience. Multiple races, religions, sexual orientations, socioeconomic categories, and relationship configurations are underrepresented in television and in all media (http://phys.org/news/2015-02-women-minorities-underrepresented-actors-directors.html). Even though media portrayals of relationships are often less than realistic, people may tend to believe that those relationships are normal and that their relationships should be compared with those in media. Thus, the media depictions of relationships can inadvertently set your own goals and expectations for relational outcomes and give you criteria for assessing your own "success" in them.

Media Representations Inform About How to Behave in Relationships

Media representations also inform people about behaviors and interactions within relationships. These depictions provide models of behavior that inform people about how to engage in relationships. This use of media encompasses the socialization impact of media.

Like relational roles, however, media portrayals of relationship interactions and behaviors may not always mirror those in people's lives. Family life on television, for instance, has historically and consistently been portrayed as quite positive (e.g., Bryant, Aust, Bryant, & Venugopalan, 2001). Actual family life is not always positive and may be quite violent, yet unrealistic media depictions may create unrealistic expectations about relationship behavior (Duck, 2011).

Technology and Media Function as Alternatives to Personal Relationships

Technology and media provide many of the same uses and benefits as personal relationships. Needs and desires satisfied by personal relationships, such as companionship, information, support, control, intimacy, and entertainment, can be gained through media.

Notice that the header for this section of the chapter labels technology and media as *alternatives* to rather than *substitutions* or *compensations* for personal relationships. People do not necessarily turn to technology and media to compensate for a lack of companionship. Rather, technology and media use have been found to enrich already satisfied social and personal lives (Perse & Butler, 2005). Furthermore, such words as *substitution* imply an inferior entity is filling in or taking the place of a superior reality, but that is not how everyone experiences it.

Companionship and Relational Satisfaction From the Actual Use of Technology and Media

The relational and social satisfaction derived through technology and media comes partly from their use and position within the home. Some people may prefer the companionship provided by technology to that provided by those in their social network. Certainly, on some occasions people would rather browse the web, listen to music, or watch a movie than be with other people.

ETHICAL ISSUE

Do you believe that producers of such media products as television programs have an ethical obligation to combat the underrepresentation of certain groups in media content?

ANALYZING EVERYDAY COMMUNICATION

Media Depictions of College

Before coming to college, most of what you knew about the experience probably came from media depictions. You probably found some depictions of college life more accurate than others.

QUESTIONS TO CONSIDER

1. What are the differences between what you now know about college and what you thought you knew based on media portrayals?

2. Have you had any difficulty managing expectations about college versus the realities?

3. What advice would you give to an incoming freshman?

socialization impact of media: depictions of relationships in media provide models of behavior that inform people about how to engage in relationships

The use of technology and media can actually provide the same amount of relational satisfaction, if not more, than engaging in a personal relationship. Jonathan Cohen and Miriam Metzger (1998) previously observed that many motives for using technology and media correspond with motives for engaging in personal relationships. These authors specifically compared social and relational needs surrounding feelings of security, such as intimacy, accessibility, control, and relaxation. In all instances but intimacy, media seem to have the advantage.

Byron Reeves and Clifford Nass (2002) discovered that people interact with technology using the same basic patterns of interaction used with other humans. The media equation maintains that interactions with technology are the same as interactions with other people, and people use the same social rules and expectations when interacting with both. You interact with your computer and other technologies as if they are actual persons. Okay: Reality time! Have you ever cursed at your computer or urged it to "hurry up"?

When they first hear about the media equation, many people deny that they treat technology similarly to people. Yet, why, just as some people seem more trustworthy than others, are some GPS voices perceived to be more trustworthy than others (Verberne, Ham, & Midden, 2012)? Perhaps the digital "voice" of some automobiles sounds more confident than that of others. It may not be so inconceivable that your interactions with technology mirror your interactions with other people, especially given the interactive nature of more recent technological innovations.

A number of studies have been conducted in support of the media equation. Table 13.2 provides three of Reeves and Nass's (2002) initial findings.

media equation: people use the same social rules and expectations when interacting with technology as they do with other people

parasocial relationships: "relationships" established with media characters and personalities

Companionship and Relational Satisfaction From Parasocial Relationships

Although technologies themselves can assist satisfaction of relational needs, when these needs are met through relationships established with media characters and personalities, they are known as parasocial relationships (Horton & Wohl, 1956). As illustrated by the findings presented in Table 13.3, relationships that people form with

Table 13.2   Media Equation Research Findings

Personality

When it comes to being dominant or submissive, people generally prefer to be around and interact with people who are similar to them rather than people who are different. It turns out people can not only perceive computers as having dominant or submissive personalities, through prompts and other means, but also prefer computers whose "personalities" are similar to their own.

Flattery

People like other people who compliment them, and the same evaluative response holds true for computers. People, it was discovered, like computers that offer them praise more than computers that offer no evaluation.

Politeness

When someone asks for your feedback on a completed project or performance on a task, you generally provide a positive response. If someone else asked you about that person's performance, your response may be more negative than if that person asked you directly. Not necessarily deceitful, you are just not being as negative as you could be because you do not want to hurt a person's feelings. The same patterns of interaction were found to take place with computers. When asked to evaluate a computer while using the same computer to type their responses, people responded much more positively than when typing their responses on a different computer.

SOURCE: Reeves, B., & Nass, C. (2002). *The media equation: How people treat computers, television, and new media like real people and places.* Stanford, CA: Center for the Study of Language and Information.

Table 13.3   Parasocial Relationships Research Findings

- Similar to other relationships, people are often attracted to media characters and personalities with whom they perceive a certain degree of similarity (Turner, 1993).
- People use similar cognitive processes when developing parasocial relationships and other relationships (Perse & Rubin, 1989).
- People follow the same attachment styles used in physical relationships in their other relationships (Cole & Leets, 1999).
- Tweeting increasingly enables public figures to establish both parasocial and social relationships with followers (Frederick, Lim, Clavio, Pedersen, & Burch, 2012).
- Parasocial and other relationships provide similar levels of satisfaction (Kanazawa, 2002).
- As with face-to-face contact, parasocial contact has been shown to lower levels of prejudice (Schiappa, Gregg, & Hewes, 2005).
- Parasocial relationships are measured using similar criteria to those used to evaluate other relationships (Koenig & Lessan, 1985).
- Parasocial relationships influence the body images of both men and women (Young, Gabriel, & Hollar, 2013; Young, Gabriel, & Sechrist, 2012).
- Parasocial relationships and relationships with people in physical social networks have been found to follow similar patterns of development, maintenance, and dissolution. When parasocial relationships end (e.g., when a television character "dies"), people experience this loss in much the same manner as they do losing a close friend (Cohen, 2003).

media characters and personalities have proved just as real and meaningful as those within their physical social networks. People consider and treat media characters and personalities just like they do family and friends, paralleling relationships in physical social networks.

As with the media equation, when first learning about parasocial relationships, students often consider the concept a bit outrageous and claim they do not form such relationships. Students think of these relationships like stalkers or those who are obsessed with particular characters or media personalities. However, parasocial relationships are actually more common than you would expect and much less negative. We bet that you have formed parasocial relationships with media characters and, at a minimum, thought of and talked about fictional characters as if they were actual people.

Technology and Media Are Used in Everyday Talk

Technology and media frequently provide the basis for conversation in social and personal relationships. Reports have indicated that anywhere from 10.5% to half of all conversations involve media content to some extent (Alberts, Yoshimura, Rabby, & Loschiavo, 2005). Even using a conservative estimate, these numbers position technology and media as among the most frequent topics—if not the most frequent topic—of conversation among people.

 **By the way . . .**

Love and Sex With Robots

People's relationships with technology may become especially close in the relatively near future. David Levy (2007) convincingly argues in the book *Love and Sex With Robots* that by the year 2050 "robots will be hugely attractive to humans as companions because of their many talents, senses, and capabilities. They will have the capacity to fall in love with humans and to make themselves romantically attractive and sexually desirable to humans" (p. 22).

QUESTIONS TO CONSIDER

1. Do you believe that this will be the case in the year 2050?

2. What might be some social drawbacks to your having a robot as a romantic partner?

Technology and Media Provide a General Topic of Conversation

Technology and media have long been recognized as providing people with a general topic of conversation (Lazarsfeld, 1940). Much like discussing the weather, the topic of media enables people to establish a shared topic of discussion that in many cases will not lead to a heated disagreement and plays a social and relational role. Yet, even when media simply appear to provide a topic of conversation, important social and relational *work* takes place, and other functions of technology and media talk discussed here are ultimately accomplished.

Talk About Technology and Media Affects Their Value and Understanding

Talking about technology and media significantly affects the meanings derived from them as well as emotional responses and attitudes. You may have previously discussed with others the value of certain types of technology and media. For instance, you and a friend may have discussed the release of a new smartphone or a great website that one of you discovered. Although not always immediately recognized as doing so, such discussions have likely influenced your use and understanding of technology and media, for example, by influencing your decisions about whether to purchase a particular item (Duck, 2011).

Talk about such media content as a song, a movie, or an online video often results in new understandings of those products. An example is discussing a particular newsfeed with friends at work or school. Such discussions of media products can clarify the meanings attached, alter convictions about their significance, and adjust levels of appreciation. Increasingly, such discussions are taking place through texting or online discussions (Proulx & Shepatin, 2012).

Talk About Technology and Media Affects Their Dissemination and Influence

Discussions of technology and media aid in the dissemination (spread) of their use and messages. The use of technology spreads through word of mouth (WOM) among friends more than through any other means. When you learned of the most recent digital tablet, smartphone, gaming system, or other technological product, chances are that information from someone you know was more influential than was an advertisement by the manufacturer (see Kawakami, Kishiya, & Parry, 2013).

Media content also spreads through interactions with others. Even when someone has not watched a TV or Netflix show, discussing it with others can still spread the information contained within the program or site, for example alerting you to the latest *Game of Thrones* trailer. You may not have caught a recent video online, but when friends who have watched the video tell you about it, the content of that video has nevertheless been spread to you. Especially with online content and podcasts, these conversations may lead to personal viewing or co-viewing (Haridakis & Hanson, 2009). Media information is being spread, and relational connections are being enhanced at the same time.

The influence of media content may also be enhanced through discussion with others (Kam & Lee, 2012). Because of the issues of trust and concern inherent in close relationships, information gained from media but conveyed through a friend, a family member, or another close relationship is more reliable than is information received directly from an advertiser. A newsfeed about the dangers of texting while driving, for instance, may not convince you to stop this dangerous and completely stupid behavior. However, a friend may pass along the information to you and because this information comes from someone with whom you share a close personal relationship, you may view it as more meaningful than if it came to you from another source.

Talk About Technology and Media Promotes the Development of Media Literacy

media literacy: the learned ability to access, interpret, and evaluate media products

Media literacy is the ability to access, interpret, and evaluate media products. Discussion of media content affects people's understanding and evaluation of this material, as well as their comprehension of its production and influence. Talking about media with those with whom you share close relationships significantly influences your development of media literacy.

Communication regarding the use and interpretation of media often occurs among family members (see Davies & Gentile, 2012). Parents, for instance, influence children's television literacy both indirectly and directly (Evans, Shaw, & Bell, 2000). *Indirect influences* include children's modeling of viewing behaviors exhibited by their parents. *Direct influences* include rule making and actively controlling children's interpretations of television content through communication about observations on television.

Of course, the promotion of media literacy through discussions of media is not limited to those occurring among family members (Geiger, Bruning, & Harwood, 2001). Much media literacy and the ability to critically evaluate media products have developed from interactions with friends, classmates, coworkers, romantic partners, and others with whom you share a relationship.

Talk About Technology and Media
Influences Identification and Relationship Development

Talking about technology and media enables people to recognize and promote shared interests, understanding, and beliefs, while highlighting differences among people. Perceptions derived from conversations about technology and media are fundamental in the evaluation of others and play a strong role in the development of relationships.

For example, a discussion with someone about movies may promote feelings of similarity. These discussions are influential because they allow people to recognize shared media experiences as well as shared understanding of those experiences. At the same time, feelings of division or separation with someone can develop if there exists little or no overlap of such experiences or understanding of these experiences.

Of course, discussions of media content can uncover areas of similarity and difference beyond actual media use and evaluation. For example, discussing a blog entry can lead to the realization that you share certain political views with someone else. Talking with a romantic partner about a romance portrayed in a movie can provide a sense of how that person views relationships and whether you share such views. The topics included in media are essentially limitless, and so too are the areas of similarity and difference that can be explored through their discussion.

Talk About Technology
and Media Enables Identity Construction

Technology and media that you use and enjoy are a significant part of who you are as an individual and play a major role in informing people of your identity. Discussions of technology and media allow people to enact identities related to technology use and media preferences, which are just as meaningful as other identities (McMahan, 2004). For instance, someone may be a fan of a particular television program or Internet site. These discussions can provide a sense of voice and empowerment (Jewkes, 2002), while serving a vital role in the modeling of multiple types of identities, such as age and gender (Aasebo, 2005). Such discussions have also been found to enact professional and workplace identities (Stein, Galliers, & Markus, 2013).

Your **technology and media profile**, a compilation of your technology and media preferences and general use of technology and media, informs others about your personal identity. David, for instance, loves watching television. He has numerous favorite shows, with *The Andy Griffith Show* at the top of the list. He enjoys most music and especially likes blues, classic soul, alternative music from the 1980s and 1990s, and anything by Eric Clapton and Prince. Thanks to Steve's introduction, David also enjoys listening to the music of Ralph Vaughan Williams but does not care much for Symphony No. 7. His favorite movie of all time, *The Blues Brothers*, is probably responsible for his initial interest in and enjoyment of blues and soul music. He rarely plays video games but tends to do well when he does play them. He never reads fiction (except for the Jack Reacher series by Lee Child, introduced to him by his friend, Julia) but is a voracious reader of history, newspapers, and academic literature. His Internet use is primarily dedicated to news sites along with watching television programs and listening to music. He prides himself on having had a Facebook account and a Twitter account before most people had even heard of the sites. Paradoxically, he rarely uses them.

What does David's technology media profile inform you about him? What does it tell you about who he is as a person, where and when he grew up, his past experiences, and his additional interests and preferences, along with the beliefs, attitudes, and values he might hold? You might also pause to ponder what the emphasis on these categories tells us about the marketing wishes of the owners of the relevant websites. How do they profit by asking us to define ourselves in terms of musical and technological preferences?

technology and media profile: a compilation of your technology and media preferences and general use of technology and media; informs others about who you are as a person or at least the persona you are trying to project

Smartphones: Constructing Identities and Relationships

Having discussed technology and media in general to this point, we want to focus on two technologies that are extremely prevalent in society. We first examine smartphones and then turn our attention to the Internet, especially social networking sites. Specifically, we will explore the use of smartphones and the Internet

Table 13.4 Creating Your Technology and Media Profile

1. Do you like watching television? If so, what are some of your favorite programs?
2. Do you like listening to music? If so, what are some of your favorite artists and songs?
3. Do you like watching movies? If so, what are some of your favorite movies?
4. Do you like to read? If so, what are some of your favorite books, newspapers, and magazines?
5. Do you like playing video games? If so, what are some of your favorite games?
6. Do you like using the Internet? If so, what are some of the sites you visit most often?
7. What television programs, music, movies, print material, video games, and Internet sites do you dislike?
8. Do you access television programs, music, movies, and books/newspapers/magazines through the Internet or your smartphone?
9. How often do you use e-mail? To whom are you most likely to send an e-mail message?
10. How often do you use your smartphone to call or text someone? To whom are you most likely to contact through voice or text?
11. Do you use a social networking site? If so, what are your primary reasons for using it, and how often do you use it?

in the construction of identities and their use in the development and maintenance of relationships.

Constructing Identities Using Smartphones

Smartphones do not merely connect you with other people or provide you with information, music, and video. Personal and relational identities are created and maintained through your *use* of

COMMUNICATION + YOU

Your Own Profile

Create your own technology and media profile, using the questions listed in Table 13.4 as a guide.

QUESTIONS TO CONSIDER

1. What do you think your technology and media profile would tell people about you?
2. Do you discuss aspects of your technology and media use and preferences with some people and not others? If so, why do you think this is the case?

them. We view smartphones, along with iPods, tablets, and other such devices, as relational technologies to emphasize the relational functions and implications of their use in society and within specific groups.

The Meaning of Relational Technology

Identities constructed through relational technologies are based partly on what it means for specific groups to use them. For instance, some groups view the smartphone less as a device to contact others and more as a means of displaying social status and membership (Suki, 2013). Perceiving and using technology in a manner consistent with these groups assists in establishing membership into these groups and developing particular identities.

Relational Technology and Generations

A major influence on people's perceptions and use of technology is the generation in which they were born. Looking specifically at such technologies as print and television, communication scholars Gary Gumpert and Robert Cathcart (1985) were the first to suggest that the traditional notion of separating generations according to time can be replaced by separating generations according to technology and media experience.

What separates generations is not just the chronological era in which they were born but also the technology that encompasses their world. Technology and media generations are differentiated by unique technology grammar and consciousness based on the technological and media environment in which they were born. Accordingly, members of different technology and media generations view the use of certain technology and media differently. For example, if you were born into a generation that does not know a time when smartphones were not used, you perceive their use differently than does someone born before the introduction of smartphones, and vice versa.

Relational Technology and Social Networks

Your social network is an equally powerful force in guiding perceptions and use of technology. Although generational influence is largely determined by the *availability* of technology, the influence of social networks on your use and perceptions

relational technologies: such technologies as smartphones, iPods, and Twitter, whose use has relational functions and implications in society and within specific groups

technology and media generations: those differentiated by unique technology grammar and consciousness based on the technological and media environment in which they are born

of technology is determined by the actual *use and incorporation* of technology and the social meanings that subsequently develop.

Friends, family, classmates, coworkers, and others with whom you share a particular relationship direct and shape your assumptions about the value of technology and what its use represents both relationally and personally. Smartphone adoption is often shared among members of a social network. Likewise, your use of relational technologies and your attitude toward them are likely to mirror those of your friends and other members of your social network (see Archambault, 2013).

Skills You Can Use: **Medium and Appropriateness**

The medium through which you contact someone can make a difference in his or her perception of your message. The purpose of your message and the technological preferences of the person you are contacting will determine the appropriateness of face-to-face, telephone, or online communication. Think what impression you would form if someone sent you a letter on fine paper written with a quill pen.

Technological Products and Service Providers

In addition to adoption and incorporation of relational technologies, identities are created through the use of specific products and services. Specific meanings are associated with the use of particular products and service providers within a social system.

Smartphones and other relational technologies are symbolically connected to certain lifestyles, activities, or media personalities. The use of these devices allows people to associate themselves with accompanying perspectives and attitudes. One study (Lobet-Maris, 2003) found that, when purchasing a smartphone, young people are influenced less by quality or available features and more by the images or personas associated with that particular phone. Through both consumer adoption and manufacturer advertising, phones and other relational technologies may be associated with hipsters, youth, elderly, or other groups.

The service provider may even be associated with particular groups or issues. Individuals in the study just mentioned linked smartphone networks with humanitarianism, professionalism, and family. Thus, the use of specific networks may enable people to feel associated with groups sharing preferred values.

Ringtones

Ringtones and other notifications do not simply inform someone of an incoming call or message; they can be viewed as a method of identity construction (see Pfleging, Alt, & Schmidt, 2012). People frequently select favorite music or dialogue from television programs or movies. Using these media products as ringtones announces your media preferences to others and underscores their importance in your life. Other ringtones are humorous or simply unique in some way. The selection of ringtones is meaningful and is based largely on how a person wants to be perceived by others.

Of course, some people tend to keep their smartphone set on silent or vibrate rather than an audible ringtone. This decision could be an indication that the person does not desire to draw attention to his or her use of the technology. It could also indicate that the person does not want to be socially compelled to answer, which provides greater choice in social contexts. Indeed the whole concept of phone etiquette has become quite sophisticated in the last 10 years (Daum, 2013) and is not just personal but also relational, influenced by how a person wishes to be perceived by others.

Performance of Relational Technology

Finally, the use of relational technologies can be considered a performance through which identities are constructed. The proper use or performance of technology has been established socially and will likely change over time. However, behaviors are judged according to present norms and prevailing expectations. Violating social standards associated with the use of technology often leads to negative responses and evaluations by others (Miller-Ott, Kelly, & Duran, 2012).

The appropriate use of technology is often determined by location and occasion. You know that there are numerous locations and occasions where the use of technology may be deemed socially unacceptable. For instance, the use of relational technology is usually discouraged in the classroom. Your instructors may ban the use of smartphones in the classroom, but they are not the only ones who disapprove. Other students consider smartphones ringing or vibrating during class to be just as distracting and annoying as faculty do (Saskia et al., 2013).

Relating Through Smartphones

Relationships and changes in technology can be seen as both relatively simple and more complex. In a very basic way, changes in technology simply allow people to achieve relatively stable relational goals in new ways. For instance, people exchange birthday greetings through sending e-cards rather than sending a traditional card through the postal service. From a more advanced view, technological transformations also change what can be accomplished, creating new relational goals and norms.

Smartphones are changing how people communicate and form relationships with others, as well as altering established relational goals and norms. In what follows, we examine the impact of smartphones on interactions among people.

Constant Connection and Availability

Smartphones position people as being constantly connected and constantly available to others. If you have your smartphone with you, you have your social network with you as well. The ability to make instant contact with another person regardless of geographic location creates a symbolic connection unlike that created by any previous communication technology, and it means that you have telemarketers with you wherever you go! How comforting is that thought!

This constant connection has led people to make contact with others more often than ever before. Sometimes the content of these messages is less important than the contact itself. Such instances are similar to how seemingly mundane everyday talk keeps relationships going without necessarily adding much of substance. Connecting with another person reestablishes the existence and importance of the relationship, confirming for both parties its existence and value in their lives.

New relational expectations have also developed because of this constant availability. For instance, when you text someone or call a smartphone, you have an expectation of an immediate response. No response, or that a response does not occur in a timely manner, can constitute a violation in the relationship (Ling, 2004). Constant availability has also influenced how relationships develop, are maintained, and dissolve, especially among teenagers and younger adults (Bergdall et al., 2012).

Boundaries and Closeness

Smartphones have come to represent constant connection to those who possess your smartphone number, and how freely people give out that number varies. Giving or denying someone access to your smartphone number establishes both the *boundaries* and the *degree of closeness* desired and expected within the relationship. Limiting the availability of contact with a person establishes specific relational boundaries. How that person views and evaluates such limits depends on your relationship. Refusing to provide a number to a friend may be viewed negatively; physicians not providing clients with their personal numbers may be viewed as legitimate (Wong, Tan, & Drossman, 2010).

Providing another person with your number suggests a desire for connection with that individual and perhaps an indication of the type of relationship you want to establish. For instance, making your number available to an acquaintance could imply a desire to develop a closer type of relationship. As mentioned earlier, the evaluation and the meaning of this action generally depend on your relationship with the other person.

Shared Experience

We can discuss shared experience derived from the use of smartphones in two ways. First, the use of smartphones constitutes shared technological experience, as was discussed earlier. More than simply transmitting information, the act of sending and receiving text messages both announces and establishes shared membership and acceptance into a group.

Smartphones also enable people to engage in shared experience even when physically separated. The immediate transmission of voice, picture, sound, and video provides people with the sense of experiencing an event or occasion together.

Social Coordination

One of the greatest relational consequences of the smartphone encompasses its use in coordinating physical encounters with others. Face-to-face interactions are frequently created and synchronized using smartphones. Coordination of physical encounters can be accomplished through phone calls and text messages as well as through location-sharing applications (Patil, Norcie, Kapadia, & Lee, 2012).

Smartphones enable people to synchronize their activities to the point of **microcoordination**. Making plans to meet someone previously involved establishing a fixed time and physical location for the interaction to occur, but the massive adoption of smartphones has resulted in time and physical location for contact becoming increasingly fluid. *Microcoordination* refers to the unique management of social interaction made possible through smartphones. Rich Ling (2004) has observed three varieties of microcoordination: (1) midcourse adjustment, (2) iterative coordination, and (3) softening of schedules (see Table 13.5).

> **ETHICAL ISSUE**
>
> Do you believe physicians have an ethical obligation to provide their smartphone numbers to their patients?

microcoordination: the unique management of social interaction made possible through smartphones

Table 13.5   Ling's Three Varieties of Microcoordination

Midcourse Adjustment	Involves changing plans once a person has already set out for the encounter—for example, contacting the other person to change locations or to request that he or she pick up someone else on the way.
Iterative Coordination	Involves the progressive refining of an encounter. Smartphones have made actually establishing location and time unnecessary. Instead, people increasingly plan to meet without specifying an exact time or location. For instance, friends may agree to meet sometime tomorrow. As a result of progressive calls or messages, they eventually "zoom in on each other" (p. 72).
Softening of Schedules	Involves adjusting a previously scheduled time. If you planned to meet a friend for coffee at 3:30 p.m. but a meeting with your advisor took longer than expected and you are running late, smartphones make it much easier to reach your friend and inform him or her of the delay.

SOURCE: Ling (2004).

Constructing Identities and Maintaining Relationships Online

Having discussed the influence of smartphones on the construction of identities and on relationships, we now turn our attention to online communication. Internet use is transforming knowledge, realities, commerce, politics, education, and essentially all aspects of everyday life (see Chesebro, McMahan, & Russett, 2014).

Even though there are a number of areas to investigate, we specifically examine the online construction of identities and maintenance of relationships. These are intriguing topics and are fundamental to many of the other changes taking place.

WRITE YOUR NOTES HERE

In what ways could the use of a smartphone create shared experiences?

Social Networking Sites and the Construction of Identities

Social networking sites such as Facebook and Twitter are generally promoted for their social or relational benefits. However, they also happen to be locations where many of the transformations listed earlier are taking place.

We examine the use of social networking sites relative to relationships later in the chapter. Now, we want to explore an aspect of social networking sites that people may tend to overlook: They have become important tools in the construction of identities.

Friends

The list of connections on a person's social networking site profile is an important tool in the construction of identities. For instance, others can use the number of friends listed on a social networking site when they make social judgments about the user. People with a large number of friends are often perceived to be outgoing

---

WRITE YOUR NOTES HERE

What activities are related to identity construction on social networking sites such as Facebook?

and socially connected (Tong, Van Der Heide, Langwell, & Walther, 2008). However, there is a point at which an excessive number of friends actually diminishes a person's appearance as socially connected (Zwier, Araujo, Boukes, & Willemsen, 2011). When someone lists 10,000 friends, others begin to wonder just how legitimate that list and those friendships actually are!

Appearance is another way in which friends influence the identity construction of users. It has been discovered that the physical attractiveness of friends influences perceptions of the user's physical and social attractiveness (Jaschinski & Kommers, 2012). Essentially, people with good-looking friends are more likely to be perceived as good looking. People with not very attractive friends are more likely to be perceived as less attractive. Quick! Check your friends list! Make sure you come back when you are done, though. As always, we will be here waiting on you.

This next item does not require you to give immediate attention to your social networking site profile. However, you may want to examine the posts left by your friends, regardless of their level of physical attractiveness. The same study mentioned earlier (Walther, Van Der Heide, Kim, Westerman, & Tong, 2008), discovered that socially complimentary or positive posts left by friends can improve perceptions of a user's social attractiveness and credibility. Likewise, it is smart these days to make every effort to clean up your "digital dirt" and remove those posts that looked so funny at the time (when you are young and irresponsible and possibly even drunk) but which now could be found by potential employer who wouldn't see you as a reliable and responsible employee).

Gender differences appear when it comes to posts left by others, however. Female users were judged positively when friends left socially positive comments and were judged negatively when friends left socially negative comments. Male users, on the other hand, were actually judged positively when friends left comments about drinking, promiscuous behavior, and similar morally questionable behavior.

Photographs

The display of photographs on the pages of social networking site users is another tool in the construction of identities. One study

---

By the way . . .

The Future of Social Networking Sites

The number of adults in the United States using social networking sites reached 50% in 2011. When data were first gathered 6 years earlier, only 5% of adults in the United States reported using social networking sites. By the time adults finally reached 50%, teenagers in the United States were already at 76%. When the Internet-using population is specifically examined, the percentages of social networking site users increase to 65% of adults and 80% of teenagers (Lenhart et al., 2011), a proportion that continues to increase (Baym, 2015).

QUESTIONS TO CONSIDER

1. What percentages of the population do you believe will be using social networking sites in 10 years?
2. What percentages of the population do you believe will be using social networking sites in 20 years?

(Pempek, Yermolayeva, & Calvert, 2009) discovered that the majority of users indicate that these photographs help them express who they are to other users. Furthermore, users tend to be very selective about the photographs that are posted online.

The selection of photographs is frequently based on which ones are the most physically flattering. Likewise, dissatisfaction with their personal appearance is the primary reason users give for "untagging" themselves in photographs of other users.

Another reason for untagging themselves in photographs is when they are shown engaging in morally questionable activities. Ironically, given the earlier discussion about friends' posts, male users are more likely than female users to cite being engaged in such activities as a reason for untagging themselves.

Media Preferences

As mentioned earlier in the chapter, technology and media preferences are frequently a basis for identity construction. In addition to the development of identities through talk, technology, and media, identities can be constructed through social networking sites.

Many social networking sites encourage users to list favorite media. Technology and media are also topics included in posts, and users have the opportunity to "like" certain technology or media products on Facebook. Of course, the corporations owning social media usually also sell other kinds of media that they encourage people to use in defining themselves on their profiles—such as music, movies, and books.

Media preferences, in particular, have been found to be an even more important aspect of identity for social networking site users than such "classic identity markers" as gender, political view, hometown, relationship status, and other categories frequently listed on a user's profile (Appel, Gerlach, & Crusius, 2016).

Strategic

Identity construction on social networking sites tends to be quite strategic. Research indicates that users put thought into their comments and profiles (Bareket-Bojmel, Moran, & Shahar, 2016). This is possible because, compared with face-to-face communication, online communication in general provides more time for people to develop their thoughts and actions.

As discussed earlier, people tend to carefully consider the photographs posted on their sites and consider whether to remain tagged in the photographs of others. Beyond photographs, all comments and activities on social networking sites can be used in the construction of identities and may be given a great deal of attention. It is not surprising to find that people believe they are better able to convey their identities online than off-line (Appel et al., 2016).

Public Disclosure

The *good news* about social networking sites is that they provide an opportunity for a great deal of self-disclosure. The *bad news* about social networking sites is that they provide an opportunity for a great deal of self-disclosure. We do not care how much you restrict access to your profile or how many privacy measures you enact on these sites. Consider everything that you post online to be within the public domain. Your relatives, elementary school teachers, and future employers, along with such scandal and tabloid programs and sites as TMZ, will be able to see it all.

ETHICAL ISSUE

- Students have been suspended from some schools for content on social networking sites. Should schools be allowed to suspend students for this content? Would your assessment change depending on whether the content did or did not pertain to school-related issues, activities, or people?
- Employers have based hiring decisions on social networking site content. Do you believe these actions are justified? In what ways do employers using social networking sites for the evaluation of job candidates compare and contrast with school officials using these sites for student discipline?

By the way . . .

Early and Developing Social Networking Sites

It can be argued that social networking sites began in the form of online communities. If so, Well.com, launched in 1985, would be among the first. In their current form—in which people create a profile, compile a list of connections, and visit the profiles of other members—Classmates.com, launched in 1995, and SixDegrees.org, launched in 1997, were among the first social networking sites. There are now more than 200 sites based throughout the world and dedicated to a variety of groups and interests.

QUESTIONS TO CONSIDER

1. If you were to create a social networking site, on what group or interest would you focus?
2. What is the strangest social networking site you have ever come across or heard about?

With that said, we are here to provide an education along with such helpful advice. So, we want to look at what this massive public disclosure actually means when it comes to identity construction.

For the study of communication, this public disclosure of information challenges traditional beliefs about self-disclosure and relationship development (Altman & Taylor, 1973). These views maintained that self-disclosure takes place gradually, with information shared becoming more personal as relationships gain intimacy or closeness. When it comes to disclosure on social networking sites, the disclosure of personal information takes place immediately. Further, this information is provided to everyone, regardless of relational closeness.

For users of social networking sites, this public disclosure of information provides opportunities for public confirmation and comparison. Activities and thoughts publicly shared through updates are confirmed by others and given social legitimacy (Manago, Graham, Greenfield, & Salimkhan, 2008). This confirmation occurs off-line as well, but not publicly and not by as many people.

Furthermore, the public disclosure of others enables comparison among users when evaluating themselves. Once again, of course, this behavior takes place off-line. There are a couple of important distinctions, though. First, many people are offering public disclosure, which provides more opportunities for comparison. Second, the information being shared tends to be strategic (as discussed earlier) and therefore more likely to be favorable and positive. Comparisons are being made with idealized images of others, which may lead to more negative evaluations of the self and to increasing pressure to enhance the image being portrayed on one's own profile.

Online Communication and Relationships

Having discussed the construction of identities online, we now turn our attention to online communication and relationships. Online communication enables people to maintain and enhance existing relationships, reinvigorate previous relationships, and create new relationships. Increased use of the Internet actually leads to increased interaction with friends and family, not only online but also face-to-face and over the telephone (Jacobsen & Forste, 2011).

Fears that the Internet will decrease social interaction and diminish the quality of relationships appear unfounded. Some people still champion face-to-face communication as the superior form of interaction (e.g., Turkle, 2012). However, these arguments tend to be based on opinion rather than on unbiased evidence or studies.

DISCIPLINARY **DEBATE**

The Value of Social Networking Sites

The relational benefits of social networking sites seem overwhelming. However, a few scholars in the discipline view social networking sites negatively. For these scholars, relationships maintained online are not as valuable or genuine as those maintained through face-to-face communication.

QUESTIONS TO CONSIDER

1. What do you consider the strengths of this position?
2. What do you consider the weaknesses of this position?

Maintaining Relationships and Social Networks

Although online communication can lead to the creation of new relationships, it tends to be used more for the maintenance or continuation of existing relationships. This is especially true when it comes to social networking sites (Baym, 2015). The average Facebook user, for instance, has met 93% of his or her *friends* at least once. High school friends represent the largest category of Facebook friends, followed by extended family, coworkers, college friends, immediate family, people from volunteer groups, and neighbors (Hampton, Goulet, Rainie, & Purcell, 2011). As mentioned earlier, relational maintenance does not just occur online. Rather, online communication is associated with increased interactions using other forms of communication.

Online communication is also positively influencing social networks. Studying the impact of the Internet on social networks, Jeffrey Boase, John Horrigan, Barry Wellman, and Lee Rainie (2006, p. 5) distinguished two types of connections in social networks: **core ties** and **significant ties**.

Internet users tend to have a greater number of significant ties than nonusers do. Internet activity does not appear to increase the number of core ties. However, Internet use has been shown to increase the diversity of core ties. For instance, Internet users are more likely to have nonrelatives as members of their core networks (Hampton, Sessions, Her, & Rainie, 2009).

Another consequence of online communication is the geographic diversity of social networks. Physical proximity still plays a large role in the development of social networks. However, online communication has resulted in more geographically dispersed networks (Boase et al., 2006). At the same time, Internet users are still just as likely as nonusers to visit with their neighbors (Hampton et al., 2009).

Overall, social networking site users, in particular, also indicate feeling less isolated. They are also more likely to receive social support (Hampton, Goulet, Marlow, & Rainie, 2012).

The increased likelihood of receiving support may not be based solely on Internet users being more helpful than nonusers. The greater number of significant ties and the overall diversity of an Internet user's social networks also increase the network resources. In other words, they increase the likelihood of finding someone who is willing to help. Perhaps more importantly, they increase the likelihood of finding someone who possesses the ability to help.

Explaining the Benefits

Internet use seems to greatly assist the maintenance of relationships and enhance social networks. However, we have not discussed why this may be true. Accordingly, we will examine the nature of both online communication and social networking sites as possible reasons why this is so.

WRITE YOUR NOTES HERE

In what ways does a webcam affect the nature of online communication?

core ties: people with whom you have a very close relationship and are in frequent contact; a person often discusses important matters in life with these people and often seeks their assistance in times of need (compare with *significant ties*)

significant ties: people who are more than mere acquaintances but with whom a strong connection does not exist; a person is not overly likely to talk with these people or seek help from these people, but they are still there when needed (compare with *core ties*)

Characteristics of Online Communication. A characteristic of online communication is that it can be both synchronous and asynchronous. In synchronous communication—for example, an interaction through Skype—people interact essentially in real time and can send and receive messages at once. In asynchronous communication—for example, an interaction through e-mail—there is a delay between messages, and interactants must alternate between sending and receiving. Each type of communication has advantages and disadvantages.

When it comes to maintaining relationships, the asynchronous nature of online communication makes it easier for people to interact. People do not have to coordinate their schedules to interact. Rather, interaction can take place whenever it is most convenient for those involved. The ease with which contact can be made online may very well increase the likelihood that contact will take place at all.

Asynchronous communication also provides time for people to be more thoughtful and strategic. This additional time can make the interactions more meaningful and more likely to convey what a person wants to share and get across. Alternatively, asynchronous communication takes a lot more time overall.

Characteristics of Social Networking Sites. The characteristics of social networking sites also explain why users are better able to maintain larger and more diverse social networks, why they feel less isolated, and why they are more likely to receive assistance when needed (see Chesebro et al., 2014).

One responsible characteristic is the *list of connections* users compile on these sites. These lists help people keep track of their social networks and can make these connections more real and available. Relative to maintenance, we talked about Stuart Sigman's (1991) relational continuity constructional units in Chapter 8. These lists can serve as introspective units, reinforcing the existence of a relationship when people are physically apart.

Participation is easy on social networking sites. For one thing, you may have a power user in your list of connections. Power users are a group of users who tend to be active when it comes to posting, making comments on other users' walls, making friendship requests, and engaging in other activities (Hampton et al., 2012). It does not take a great deal of effort to participate, regardless.

Another characteristic of these sites, which helps explain the findings, is that they *normalize the sharing of the mundane*. We have maintained that it is not the discussion of deep subjects or the sharing of private information that is most responsible for the development of relationships. Rather, it is the more common discussions of everyday, seemingly mundane information that drive the development and maintenance of personal relationships.

Social networking sites often encourage users to post what they are doing at a given moment. Most people are not saving the world; they are throwing out moldy bread or scraping something off of their shoes. Stephanie Tom Tong and Joseph

synchronous communication: communication in which people interact in real time and can at once both send and receive messages (contrast with *asynchronous communication*)

asynchronous communication: communication in which there is a slight or prolonged delay between the message and the response; the interactants must alternate between sending and receiving messages (contrast with *synchronous communication*)

emojis: text-based symbols used to express emotions online, often to alleviate problems associated with a lack of nonverbal cues

Walther (2011) have observed that these sites normalized the discussion of these undistinguished events.

Despite the existence of and potential for negative experiences, participation in social networking sites tends to be quite *positive*. The vast majority of both teen and adult users believe that people are mostly kind on these sites. Twice as many teen users, specifically, report positive outcomes when using these sites as report negative outcomes (Lenhart et al., 2011). These positive experiences are liable to increase the likelihood that people will continue using these sites and gain relational satisfaction and comfort from doing so.

A final characteristic of social networking sites explaining their benefits is that *relating is the point*. These sites are constructed in ways that enable connection to take place. Intimacy, security, entertainment, knowledge, self-worth, and other needs generated from relationships are also provided through their use.

Further, people are able to learn more about relationships in general and their own relationships specifically through these sites. Relationships are played out through these sites, with some entirely documented through updates, photos, and other features. Relational knowledge, developed using these sites, may assist in the development and maintenance of relationships online as well as off-line.

⟫⟫ FOCUS QUESTIONS REVISITED

 How do people generally perceive technology and media?

Society frequently views technology and media with suspicion, especially initially. Ultimately, all technology and media have influenced relationships in some manner, which has made responses to technology and media historically quite similar. Some view technology and media as controlling societal development but by others as being merely tools without great influence.

 What are the relational uses of technology and media?

The use of technology and media is a shared relational activity that enables people to come together, withdraw from relationships, and enact specific relational roles. Media content informs people about how relationships "should" look and how people "should" behave in relationships. Technology and media function as alternatives to personal relationships. Technology and media are also used in everyday talk. Beyond providing a general topic of conversation, talk about technology and

media influences their interpretation and understanding. Such talk also affects their distribution and influence, promotes the development of media literacy, influences identification and relationship development, and enables identity construction.

 How are smartphones used in the construction of identities?

Identities constructed through relational technologies are based partly on what it means for groups to use them, such as generations and social networks. Identities are also created through the use of specific products and services, as well as through ringtones and the actual performance of smartphones.

 How do smartphones influence relationships?

Smartphones have come to represent constant connection to those who possess your number. Giving someone your smartphone number or denying someone access to your number establishes both the boundaries and the degree of closeness desired and expected within your relationship with that person. A new relational expectation of constant availability has subsequently developed. Also, shared experience develops from the actual use of smartphones and from the immediate transmission of voice, picture, sound, and video. Finally, the use of smartphones makes possible the microcoordination of physical social interaction.

 How are identities constructed online?

Examining social networking sites specifically, identities are constructed through lists of connections, photographs, media preferences, strategic work, and massive public disclosure.

 How does online communication influence relationships?

Although online communication can lead to the creation of new relationships, it tends to be used more for the maintenance or continuation of existing relationships. By examining social networking sites specifically, we can explain benefits to relationships by the nature of online communication and the general characteristics of such sites.

》》》 KEY CONCEPTS

asynchronous communication   270
concurrent media use   249
core ties   269
emojis   270
media equation   256
media literacy   258
microcoordination   264
parasocial relationships   256
relational technologies   261

significant ties   269
social construction of technology (SCOT)   252
social shaping of technology (SST)   252
socialization impact of media   255
synchronous communication   270
technological determinism   251
technology and media generations   261
technology and media profile   260

》》》 QUESTIONS TO ASK YOUR FRIENDS

1.   Ask your friends to estimate the amount of time they spend using media every day. How do their responses compare with the average daily media use revealed by the Middletown Media Studies? If there is a significant difference between your friends' estimations and the numbers discovered in the Middletown Media Studies, why do you think this discrepancy exists?

2.   Ask a few of your friends separately to describe their technology and media profile, and then compare their responses. Do you notice any similarity among their responses? If so, why do you think this similarity exists? What impact would this similarity of technology and media uses and preferences have on the relationships among your friends?

3.   If you have your own page on a social networking site, ask your friends to compare how you present yourself on this page with how you present yourself off-line. In what ways are they different and similar?

》》》 MEDIA CONNECTIONS

1.   Examine how characters on television programs are portrayed using technology and whether it specifically involves relational uses. To what extent does their use of technology parallel your use of it with your friends, family, coworkers, or classmates?

2.   Describe how relationships are featured in the television, print, and Internet advertisements of smartphone companies. For example, pay attention to the number of times in which they illustrate users having relationships with one another or doing something connected with business applications.

3.   Compare recent media depictions of relationships with media depictions of relationships from previous decades. What changes do you recognize?

Sharpen your skills with SAGE edge at http://edge.sagepub .com/duckciel3e

SAGE edge for students provides a personalized approach to help you accomplish your coursework goals in an easy-to-use learning environment.

Conducting a Literature Review

Wilson, J.

—**Learning Objectives**—

After reading this chapter, you should be able to:

- understand the nature of a literature review;
- be able to explain the importance of conducting a literature review;
- know the stages in the literature review process;
- plan a literature search and know various sources of literature;
- explain the typical structure of a literature review;
- know how to present a literature review; and
- understand the difference between a good and a poor literature review.

Introduction

This chapter is about how to conduct a literature review. When undertaking your research project it is essential that you are aware of and acknowledge existing research in your chosen area. Most student researchers therefore spend a considerable amount of time reviewing the literature: first, in order to identify possible gaps or ideas that can help refine their own research and, second, to examine relevant sources so as to become fully conversant with the literature.

This chapter starts by introducing the nature of a literature review and briefly stresses why it is an essential part to your research project. The next section aims to answer a common question among student researchers, namely, 'Why conduct a literature review?' This is then followed by a discussion on the literature review process, in particular the stages that you are likely to go through when searching the literature and conducting your review. Next, planning your literature search emphasizes the necessity of planning your review, while the section on sources of literature provides a relatively brief overview of the main places to look in order to determine what has been written on your chosen topic. These sources include books, journals,

Internet sites and abstracts. A key part of conducting a review is recognizing where to search. Therefore, this section sets out not only the process of searching the literature, but also the range of sources that can be accessed.

The ability to carry out a critical review of the literature remains a challenge for many students. The intention of the following section is to alleviate these concerns by discussing how to adopt a critical approach. Another common cause of concern for students is structuring and presenting the literature review. Therefore, an illustration of how to divide up the review section is provided, along with an example of an introduction. Next, our attention turns to what constitutes a good or a poor literature review. Although by no means exhaustive, I have included examples of good practice, along with the most frequent problems students encounter. Finally, the last part of the chapter serves as a reminder of the importance attached to a critical review of the literature. In short, how to write a good literature review is something that many students find particularly challenging. This chapter should help you to deal with this challenge as it explains the common issues that students typically face when undertaking this part of their research.

Nature of a Literature Review

In the context of your research, 'literature' means all sources of published material. A *literature review* can be described as 'identifying, evaluating and critically assessing' what has been published on your chosen topic. Reviewing the literature critically will allow you to develop an understanding of previous research that is relevant to your own study. In addition, it should allow you to understand how the literature has developed. An important part of conducting your literature review is to establish the current state of findings in your chosen area. For example, an environmental scientist studying climate change is unlikely to conduct research without first referring to previous studies into climate change. Similarly, as a student researcher you also need to be aware of existing research. Once you have chosen your topic, e.g. mergers and acquisitions involving UK companies, you then need to find out what has been written about it across a wide variety of media. This is likely to include books, textbooks, academic journals, government reports, trade magazines, Internet websites, newspaper articles and quite possibly unpublished dissertations.

Conducting a methodical review is not an easy task. To be sure, it is not something that you can do over the course of a weekend! In truth, your review is likely to take several months. The length of time that you spend on your review is usually dependent on three factors: (1) the amount of literature available; (2) the accuracy of data; and (3) access to data.

Jeffrey W. Knopf (2006: 127) suggested that a literature review has two key elements. First,

it should concisely summarize the findings or claims that have emerged from prior research efforts on a subject. Second, a literature review should reach a conclusion about how accurate and complete that knowledge is; it should present your considered judgements about what's right, what's wrong, what's inconclusive, and what's missing in the existing literature.

Why do I have to conduct a literature review?

Students have asked me on many occasions, 'Why do I have to conduct a literature review?' Understandably, for some students the process of conducting a literature review is totally alien to them. Often, these are international students who originate from countries with markedly different educational systems from that of the UK. However, in some instances UK students may also experience difficulty conducting the review. In short, conducting a thorough, critical literature review is no easy task for the novice researcher. Yet it forms an integral part of your research. Through compiling a literature review you are demonstrating an important set of skills.

> Undergraduates researching for their dissertation or thesis are expected to show familiarity with their topic. Usually, this takes the form of a summary of the literature, which not only demonstrates the skills to search and compile accurate and consistent bibliographies, but also summarizes your key ideas, showing a critical awareness. They are required to demonstrate, on the one hand, library and information skills, and on the other, the intellectual capability to justify decisions on the choice of relevant ideas and the ability to assess the value of those ideas in context. (Hart, 1998: 9)

Several reasons support the carrying out of a literature review. First, you should review the literature on your chosen topic because it can provide much-needed inspiration for research topic ideas. Second, although you may already have a significant level of knowledge on a particular topic, a review of the literature is likely to further this knowledge. Third, it can help to identify new and emerging research areas. Fourth, it can ensure that you are actually contributing to an area of research by avoiding what has been done already. Fifth, previous researchers often make explicit recommendations for further research. Sixth, by reviewing previous literature you are able to identify methods and approaches used by others in similar research areas, as well as identify gaps in knowledge. Finally, the review is a way of organizing your own thoughts. It is also a record of the evidence/material you have gathered.

Conducting a literature review can have several benefits:

- It can give you a general overview of a body of research with which you are not familiar.
- It can reveal what has already been done well, so that you do not waste time 'reinventing the wheel'.
- It can give you new ideas that you can use in your own research.
- It can help you to determine where there are problems or flaws in existing research.
- It can enable you to place your research in a larger context, so that you can show what new conclusions might result from your research.

(Knopf, 2006: 127)

Literature Review Process

The best way to think of the literature review is as a *process*. Each subsequent step builds on the previous one, building a solid understanding of the literature.

I am aware that you may decide not to follow each step to the letter. For example, it is likely that you may already have what you perceive as relevant literature. Therefore, you do not need to go out and actively search for your sources. Still, wherever possible, try to follow the process as closely as you can in order to ensure that you adopt a thorough, efficient approach to your literature review. The literature review process involves the following:

Research questions and objectives

By now you should be familiar with how to formulate research questions and objectives, as this is something that was covered in Chapter 2. Once you are confident that you have a suitable range of objectives and research questions, you are then ready to proceed to the next step of defining your parameters. At this stage, it is worth noting that your research questions and objectives will ultimately determine the literature that you will read and refer to in your literature review. For example, if one of your objectives is 'To determine the marketing metrics used by UK national newspapers', then one would expect to see reference to articles on different types of marketing metrics, as well as the UK newspaper industry. In simple terms, the marker of your project will be looking to see if there is a clear 'link' between your research questions and literature review.

Define parameters

Essentially, the term 'parameters' means you are setting *boundaries* to your study that help you to narrow down what it is that you intend to search. One way of doing this is establishing *key words* (see below). The ability to be clear about what it is that you are trying to study can help set your parameters. In some cases, parameters linked to a given topic are reasonably clear, particularly in relation to certain theories. On the other hand, you may find it difficult to set parameters. This is where reviewing existing articles can help, especially to determine parameters to similar studies and how these relate to your own work.

Key words

Both Internet search engines and search engines specific to applicable databases rely on *key words* to find relevant information. It is therefore essential that you are able to identify your topic, sub-topics, main variables, theories, key concepts, etc., in the form of key words. You will then be able to search for works by both single and combined key word searches (O'Leary, 2004: 70). An example of how to do a key word search is illustrated later in the chapter. For now, it is worth considering possible key words for your study. Ideally, you do not want to be in a position where you are unclear or have too many or too few key words, as this is likely to make your literature search all the more difficult.

Conduct search

A key part to conducting your search is identifying possible sources of literature. The majority of your search will involve reading through articles in academic journals. After all, your project is of an academic nature. The main thing to do at the beginning of your search is to identify the leading journals in your discipline. It is usually in leading and/or specific journals relating to your chosen topic that you will find the greatest wealth of information.

Jill Hussey and Roger Hussey (1997: 87) provide the following useful guide to conducting a literature search:

- It is very important to start exploring the literature as soon as possible. If, initially, your research project is still fairly unfocused, your search will be in general terms only.
- Decide the scope of your research and set your parameters accordingly (e.g. by period of time, geography or industry).
- Determine the key words, including alternative spellings, synonyms and differences in usage.
- Only collect articles, books, papers, etc. which are relevant to your research (e.g. in terms of subject matter, methodology, research instrument, theoretical discussion). Good research articles should review the literature, describe the research methodology used in the study, discuss the results and draw conclusions.
- Use the references given in the literature you have collected to guide you to other articles you should collect.
- When you start to recognize the references cited in other works, you are nearing the end of your first search.
- In order to keep up to date with the literature, it is important that you continue your literature search throughout your study.

Today, student researchers are in the fortunate position of having access to a wide range of electronic sources, in particular electronic databases that contain articles from academic journals. As a student, your library card is likely to offer you free access to a large number of articles relevant to your research project. Perhaps one of the more well-known electronic databases in the field of business and management is 'Emerald'. It is something that is certainly popular with my own students, largely because it is easy to access and holds full articles on many different business-related topics.

Basically, Emerald is an online database covering 24,000+ articles and 104+ journal titles. It covers mainly management and business subjects, e.g. marketing, human resources, finance, general management and strategy. Although there is no substitute for actually using Emerald, Table 3.1 gives you an insight into how to perform a *key word search*. The first column shows the words entered into the 'quick

search' facility, while the right-hand column shows the actual number of 'hits' or, in other words, articles that contain the terms entered.

In Table 3.1, you can see that through experimenting with key words, the student has managed to refine their search to a manageable number of sources. Obviously, simply searching for just 'trust' or 'commitment' is far too general, and likely to encompass a wide range of articles. Table 3.2 shows the same search terms; however, this time an 'Advanced search' has been selected, followed by 'Content item title' in the 'All fields' box.

Clearly, searching the literature takes time. However, undertaking searches using the key words or themes set out in your research questions will ultimately help you to identify the most relevant and leading studies in your selected area of research.

TABLE 3.1 How important is trust and commitment in business-to-business relationships?

Search item	Hits
'Commitment'	43,607
'Trust'	35,169
'Business-to-business'	671
'Trust and commitment'	657
'Business-to-business relationships'	5
'Trust and business relationships'	3

TABLE 3.2   How important is trust and commitment in business-to-business relationships? (2)

Search item (Advanced search)	Hits
'Commitment'	593
'Trust'	796
'Business-to-business'	1
'Trust and commitment'	12
'Business-to-business relationships'	0
'Trust and business relationships'	0

What if I can't find any relevant sources?

'I can't find any literature on my research topic' tends to be an issue for those students who have not gone about their literature review in an appropriate, systematic way. Often, literature is always available. In general, if you experience problems finding literature on your chosen topic, it is probably due to the following causes:

- you are looking for the wrong type of source;
- you are looking in the wrong place;
- you have problems with the parameters or key words for your research; or
- you really have found an uncharted research area.

How do I plan my literature search?

When it comes to the best way to plan the literature search, there is no one definitive answer. Fundamentally, two key factors need to be considered – *organization* and *time*. In terms of the former, I have already stressed the importance of keeping an accurate record of your findings. It is also a good idea to plan when and where you intend to conduct your literature search. In terms of the latter, make sure that you allocate sufficient time to searching the literature. Personally, I find that it is the kind of task that very rarely can be undertaken in short time periods. Preferably, you should allocate a minimum of half a day to conduct an efficient review of key sources.

Obtain literature

Obviously, in order to do a literature review you need to obtain literature. Try to use a wide range of sources. Some students have a tendency to mainly use web-based sources when conducting their literature review. By only referring to a very narrow range of online literature, key studies in your chosen area are likely to be ignored. You will find that the majority of literature is accessible in your college or university library. By now, you should be familiar with the sources made available by your institution's library. These will almost certainly include textbooks, journals, reports, magazines, encyclopaedias and directories, to name but a few. Of course, in some cases these sources may only be available in hard copy or electronic format. Still, this should not detract from your ability to obtain the literature.

For part-time or mature students, a useful source of literature is often their employer. I have known several cases where students are actively encouraged by their employer to make use of all available literature within their place of work. Yet this support is usually because the employer has sponsored the student to base their research on the company.

Evaluate

Two key reasons exist why researchers use a wide range of sources when reviewing the literature. First, different sources are open to varying degrees of bias. For example, if you cite an article written in the UK's *Guardian* newspaper on government education policy, you will most probably get a largely critical viewpoint. In other words, being a left-wing newspaper, the journalist is more likely to write something that takes on a left-wing political bias. Obviously, as a researcher, you need to be aware of bias, as this will affect your own evaluation and interpretation of the findings. Second, different sources are aimed at different audiences. As a result, they go through a variety of processes prior to publication.

Recording the literature

At the beginning of your project, as soon as you are able to, get into the habit of *organizing* your literature. Ultimately, by the end of your project you will have gathered a wide range of sources. Each one that you refer to needs to be included in the bibliography section at the end of your project. Believe me, a situation where you are frantically searching for your sources at the last minute is best avoided! Therefore, it is a good idea to make a note of each source from the outset. Ideally, enter the full reference (Harvard system) and comments in Word. This is for the simple reason that you can do a 'cut and paste' when it comes to finalizing your references. In addition, organizing articles electronically is far less cumbersome than storing hard copies. Hussey and Hussey (1997: 102) recommended the following reasons for maintaining a database:

- You need to be able to identify the full and accurate reference in order to find or order the material.
- You can develop links among authors, topics, results and periods of time by re-sorting your database.
- It prevents duplication of effort.
- You will need to refer to your sources of information in your proposal and final research report.
- Others reading your finished work will be able to trace the original sources of information easily.

By the time you start your research project, you should have some experience of *referencing*. Basically, referencing your work involves two things. First, if you are citing a piece of work in the main text of your research, then you need to acknowledge within the text the source from which you have gathered the information. If you are using the *Harvard referencing system*, this involves citing within the main text (as opposed to footnotes). Some institutions may insist on an alternative referencing system that requires students to cite work within footnotes. Always check with the project guidelines published by your college or university to find out which referencing system you are required to follow.

Another aspect of referencing that tends to vary between institutions is use of the term 'references' and 'bibliography'. In general, *references* is a comprehensive list of sources that have been cited in the main text of a research project, whereas *bibliography* refers to those items that a student has read but not necessarily cited in the text. There appears to be no consensus between institutions as to the preferred method. For example, you may find that all references, both those consulted and cited, are required to be listed underneath the one heading of 'bibliography'. On the other hand, your project guidelines may require you to distinguish between bibliography and references. In short, it is best to consult your project guide or ask your project supervisor to determine what is required.

Using research management software to organize your literature search

There a number of *research management programs* available. These are designed to make it easier to organize and store literature in a searchable library. One that I have personally used and is ideal for students doing a research project is ReadCube which is a free academic software and reference manager for researchers. This can be downloaded at www.readcube.com. Alternatively, you could simply organize your journal articles on a thematic basis by creating a folder for each theme. For instance, if we use the earlier marketing metrics and UK national newspaper example, in the broadest terms, you could have one folder for 'Marketing metrics' and another folder for 'UK newspaper industry'. It is important to take an organized approach from the outset, otherwise you will find it difficult when it comes to locating literature and writing your review.

Start drafting review

If you are fully conversant with the literature and you have organized it into something that is manageable and easily accessible, then you are ready to begin drafting your literature review. Notice that I use the word 'draft'. This is because in all likelihood you will end up writing your literature review several times. Not only because you discover new literature that you wish to incorporate, but also because your supervisor may require you to rewrite it. On the other hand, you may simply wish to rewrite it several times until you hit upon a final version that you are comfortable with. Still, the main reason that you will write several drafts is because you should continue conducting your literature search up to a few weeks prior to submission.

Sources of Literature

Incorporating an eclectic mix of sources into your research project is likely to be deemed good practice by your supervisor and/or your marker. It illustrates that you have gone to great lengths when conducting your literature review.

Different sources of literature have different advantages and disadvantages. The important thing is that you are fully aware of these strengths and weaknesses, and that you refer to each one when conducting your review. This section examines the main sources that you are likely to draw on when reviewing the literature.

General reports

These may include *government reports, country data reports* such as those produced by the Economist Intelligence Unit (EIU), and market research reports such as those produced by Mintel. In some cases, these reports are difficult to access and can only be accessed by paying a subscription fee, although the majority of university and college libraries subscribe to the leading reports. Their usefulness should not be ignored, particularly if you are conducting research into a topic that may make use of macroeconomic data. You may find that market research reports produced, and commissioned, by different companies may contain conflicting data. This can make an interesting inclusion to your research.

Theses

These include major projects such as those associated with MPhil and PhD degrees. You may be able to access these in your own institution. Alternatively, the British Library keeps a large number of *theses*. The advantage of referring to research of this nature is that it may provide you with ideas for your own study. Generally, the structure is likely to be very similar to your own research project. For example, you will certainly see reference to some kind of introduction, methodology, data analysis, etc. But be wary of the fact that a thesis submitted for the award of an MPhil or PhD is usually in the region of 60,000–80,000 words. It will certainly be more in-depth and probably more theoretical than your own submission. Also, a PhD thesis needs to 'make a contribution to knowledge'. This is not the case for undergraduate studies.

Conference reports

The majority of *conferences* have a theme that is quite specific. For example, the Industrial Marketing and Purchasing (IMP) conference examines topics relating to interactions, relationships and networks in business-to-business markets, while the annual Association of Chartered Certified Accountants (ACCA) conference explores all areas of accounting and finance. An *academic conference* usually invites academics to write and present a paper based on a particular theme associated with the conference. In essence, it is largely an opportunity for academics to get together to discuss each other's research interests. How does this apply to student researchers? Well, in many cases, the entire body of papers presented at the conference are put on to the conference organizer's website. Some of these are available for public access free of charge. The IMP is such an example. More than 1,600 articles can be viewed free of charge at www.impgroup.org.

Newspapers

When considering *newspapers* as a possible source, make sure to review what is commonly referred to as the *business press*. For instance, the *Financial Times* is a great source for leading articles on company performance, mergers and acquisitions, the financial markets, and information on sectors ranging from construction to IT. Yet, although newspapers can be a useful source, remember that they are only likely to provide a practical insight into companies and markets. As you are conducting a research project that also requires reference to theory and possible theoretical application, you must not confine your sources just to newspapers. The majority of your theoretical content will come from academic journals.

Academic journals

An *academic journal* can be defined as 'a peer-reviewed periodical containing scholarly articles in a particular field of study'. Unlike newspaper articles, articles in academic journals are different both in terms of content and the process of publication. Table 3.3 summarizes the key differences between a newspaper article and an article featured in an academic journal. Academic journals are rated on their quality and standing within the academic community. In general, the leading research tends to be published in top journals that are rated four or five stars. Still, this should not dissuade you from reviewing the other journals. Even those rated as one star are of a sufficient standard for you to refer to them in your research project.

Of course, there are a large number of academic journals in the discipline of business and management. Table 3.4 provides examples of some of the academic journals you may consider referring to when undertaking your research. This has been divided on the basis of Marketing, Human Resources (HR), Strategy and Finance. I have purposely chosen these journals to illustrate the plethora of different areas of research within each discipline. For example, some journals focus on a

TABLE 3.3 A comparison of academic and newspaper articles

Academic article	Newspaper article
Authors: Usually academics who are experts in their field. Most are affiliated to an academic institution.	Authors: Journalists. Usually one journalist will write an article. Their credentials are often not supplied.
Bibliography: A detailed list of references using the Harvard referencing system at the end of the article.	Bibliography: Often not featured within the article.
Content/structure: Specialist content, research based. Typical structure includes an abstract, introduction, literature review, methodology, analysis and results, conclusion and bibliography.	Content/structure: Based on current affairs and topics of general interest. Often in line with the view of the target readership, and generally in narrative format.
Length: Longer articles (typically 5,000–8,000 words) based on an analytical approach.	Length: Short articles.
Peer review: Often peer-reviewed by experts in the field. Reviewers may accept an article outright, or accept it subject to modifications, or decline it outright.	Peer review: Reviewed by the editor or editorial board of the newspaper.

TABLE 3.4 Academic journals

Subject	Journals
Marketing	• *Journal of Marketing* • *Asia-Pacific Journal of Marketing and Logistics* • *European Journal of Marketing* • *Journal of Marketing Management*
Human Resources	• *Journal of Human Resources* • *Human Resources for Health* • *Asia-Pacific Journal of Human Resources* • *Advances in Developing Human Resources*
Strategy	• *Business Strategy and the Environment* • *Journal of Business Strategy* • *Journal of Economics & Management Strategy* • *Strategy & Leadership*
Finance	• *Journal of Property Finance* • *Managerial Finance* • *Pacific Accounting Review* • *Accounting Review*

particular geographical region, such as the *Asia-Pacific Journal of Marketing and Logistics*, while others may focus on one specific area of research within a broader discipline, such as the *Journal of Property Finance*.

Table 3.4 is by no means exhaustive and does not include journal rankings. My intention here is not to list the most prestigious journals in each subject area, but to provide you with an insight into some of the key journals that are likely to be relevant to your own research.

Textbooks

Textbooks need no introduction, as I know that you are likely to have read many different titles during the course of your study! As a potential source for your research project, they can prove invaluable. Yet you should still be careful when searching through the various titles covering your chosen topic. In short, make sure that you choose a good book. Jennifer Rowley and Frances Slack (2004: 33) propose that a good book should fulfil the following criteria:

- It should be relevant to the research topic.
- It should be written by an authoritative author; the bibliographical details given in the book will summarize the author's experiences in the field.
- It should be up to date, as signalled by the publication date.
- It should be published by a reputable publisher in the discipline.
- It should include extensive reference to other associated literature.
- It should be clearly structured, well presented and easy to read.

Certainly, textbooks can be a great source of information. By the time you begin working on your research project you should be very familiar with the layout, content and style of writing associated with textbooks. Of course, some textbooks tend to be more comprehensive than others. Typically, the larger texts that tend to focus on a broad discipline, such as Finance, Marketing or Human Resource Management, can be as long as nearly 1,000 pages. Although these may seem too general for your chosen topic, an interesting feature included in many of the leading textbooks is a glossary and company index. The former is helpful when generating key words associated with your study, while the latter can aid your research if you have decided to adopt a *case study approach*, i.e. you have chosen to research a particular company or companies.

Despite the obvious strengths associated with textbooks, the main downside is that they are unlikely to feature the latest innovative research. Moreover, textbooks do not always explore issues within a particular discipline in any great depth. In short, they are intended to cater for students engaged in a module over the course of one or two semesters, not as an aid to student researchers. Finally, remember that in some disciplines, especially those referring to the technology sector, material can soon become dated. Be wary of reviewing literature that may be deemed to be out of date, as this may impact on the credibility of your literature review.

Internet websites

In recent years, I have noticed an increasing number of students making reference to *Internet websites* within their research project. Given the growth in the Internet this is to be expected. Although Internet websites can provide ease of access to a wide range of sources, you still need to take a cautious approach when searching through various websites. In considering whether or not to use a particular web-based source, you should determine the *reliability* of the source and its perceived standing among the academic community. First, reliability can be relatively easy to determine. For instance, most students are familiar with *Wikipedia*. Although Wikipedia claims to be the biggest multilingual free-content encyclopaedia on the Internet, there are questions over its reliability. It is unable to guarantee the accuracy of the information appearing on its website. For this reason, several colleges and universities prefer students to refrain from quoting from Wikipedia. Similarly, some external examiners prefer not to see Wikipedia featured among references. If in doubt whether or not you are able to use Wikipedia, check with your college or university.

In brief, the web is likely to be your main tool for locating relevant literature. The majority of researchers use a technique known as 'snowballing' to help build a database of relevant literature that can be used as part of their literature review. Snowballing means reading through relevant article references in order to locate other sources, then reading through those sources' references, and so on. Eventually, you know you are making progress when authors' names become familiar to you or the same references appear on a regular basis. Although the Internet holds a wealth of information, how you access, record and recognize data is vitally important. Martin Brett Davies (2007: 40) makes the following valid points when searching via the web:

1. When you are carrying out a net search – which will lead you in all manner of directions – be sure to make notes of the interesting and useful items and sites that you come across. You can use a Word file to do so, but while you're actively net searching, you may find it more efficient to make hand-written notes and references.
2. When you come across quotable items that you might want to include in your report, copy and paste them to a file straight away.
3. Save any good websites that you come across to your Favourites.
4. Remember that there is a lot of rubbish on the net. When you are using a search engine, make sure that what comes up is useful, true and reliable. Be discriminating and selective in your choices.
5. If you are stuck, your academic library will have information specialists who are there to guide you in your net searches. Make sure you can tell them just what it is that you are seeking, and be prepared to listen to their advice.

Google Scholar is another useful search tool for students. Released in November 2004, it is a freely available service that includes the content of scholarly documentation from a wide variety of sources. Google Scholar covers journals, books, conference proceedings, dissertations, technical reports, preprints and postprints, and other scholarly documents (Neuhaus and Hans-Dieter, 2008: 200).

Abstracts

An *abstract* is a summary of an article. The abstract is designed to give the reader a 'snapshot' of the article content. The majority of articles in academic journals include an abstract. Essentially, it is a short overview (usually no more than 350 words) of the entire research. It is used as a helpful guide to researchers so that they can determine to what extent the article 'fits' with their own research. In short, it can be defined as a time-saving device: because it summarizes the study, the reader does not have to read the entire article. A search using key words within an abstract is a useful way of narrowing your search. If an abstract contains your key word, it is highly likely that the article is relevant to your research.

Catalogues

A *catalogue* contains a comprehensive list of sources held by a library. Increasingly, library catalogues tend to be electronic database systems. I have found that a useful source is copac.ac.uk (Copac, 2008). Copac is a freely available library catalogue, giving access to the merged online catalogues of many major UK and Irish academic and national libraries, as well as an increasing number of specialist libraries.

Dictionaries

A *dictionary* is a 'reference book containing words and other information'. Obviously, a dictionary, together with a thesaurus, is a very useful tool for any writer. A definition from a dictionary can be used if you intend defining a word or term for the benefit of your readers. As a general rule, the *Oxford English Dictionary* is the definitive dictionary. For example, if your intention was to critically review the body of literature on cultural theory, you may start by including a definition of culture from the *Oxford English Dictionary*. A range of definitions from established researchers in the field may then follow. There is no harm in consulting a range of dictionaries in order to get an eclectic mix of definitions.

Bibliographies

A *bibliography* is a comprehensive list of books, articles, Internet websites, magazines and other sources used in a particular study. A bibliography is often found towards the end of a book or journal. Its purpose is twofold: first, to acknowledge those authors whose work has been used when conducting the study, and second, to help other researchers engaged in a similar area of research. By including a bibliography, other researchers can save a great deal of time when conducting research.

Encyclopaedias

Quite simply, an *encyclopaedia* can be a book or more commonly a set of books that contains information on a wide range of topics. In this digital age, electronic versions tend to be more popular. As already mentioned, perhaps the most famous electronic encyclopaedia is Wikipedia. It remains a popular source of information for students, but, once again, reliability remains a concern. Although an encyclopaedia may provide relatively detailed information on your chosen topic, it is unlikely that this will go into any great depth. Moreover, material published on your chosen topic is likely to be the work of one particular author. Therefore, it may be subject to bias and is probably based on a limited range of sources. Quite simply, the purpose of an encyclopaedia is to provide material of a practical nature, so you will find few references to specialist studies.

Citation indices

These provide an indication of the quality and expert nature of a piece of research, by showing how many times the work has been cited. In brief, it can help you to identify the leading authors in your subject area by indicating how many times their work has been referred to. Scopus (2008) (available online only, www.info.scopus.com) is the largest abstract and citation database of research literature and quality web sources for the social sciences. Once again, your library should allow you to access this particular facility.

In sum, this section has examined a range of possible sources you can consult when doing your literature review. The next step is to consider what to actually do with the literature. In essence, this involves conducting a critical review.

Critical Review

A key skill in doing a literature review is to be able to read and review literature *critically*. By improving your knowledge of your topic through reading a wide range of sources you are more likely to familiarize yourself with the major issues surrounding your research. Some key questions that you may ask to help you to critically review an article include:

1. What is the main topic under review?
2. What are the results?
3. What methodology has the author(s) used? Is it appropriate?
4. What are the main issues raised by the author?
5. To what extent do the findings echo existing studies?
6. What questions are raised?
7. Is the article fair/biased?
8. How does the article relate to your own views?
9. Does the article display a contemporary view or are the findings/sources dated?
10. What are your own conclusions about the literature?

Certainly, the above questions should provide you with a useful guide when attempting to critically review an article. They can also be put to good use when you are actually writing your own literature review, and are comparing, contrasting and critically reviewing a range of literature within the review section of your research project. Personally, I have found that the critical nature of the literature review is something that some students find particularly difficult to grasp. Unfortunately, some fall into the trap of being overly descriptive. As a result, rather than ending up with a critical review, the final version of the review section ends up being an almost verbatim account of extracts from several different articles. This ultimately leads to a lower mark being awarded, as it falls some way short of actually critically reviewing the literature.

Structure of a Literature Review

Although adopting a critical approach is important, it is also essential that you structure your literature review in an appropriate way. Rowley and Slack (2004: 38) provide the following useful example of how to structure a literature review:

1. Include basic definitions, e.g. What is business process re-engineering (BPR)? What is e-government?
2. Discuss why the subject is of interest, e.g. What impact can BPR have on business success? Why are e-government applications important and what is their scope?
3. Discuss what research has already been undertaken on the topic, and whether there is any research on aspects of the topic that need to be investigated, e.g. the application of BPR to support the delivery of e-government applications.
4. Provide a clear summary of the research opportunities and objectives that emerge from the literature review.

A poorly structured literature review can be both irritating and confusing for the reader. In short, the structure of your literature review should include an introduction, the main body and a conclusion.

It can be argued that no one part of the review is more important than any other. However, I personally believe that it is important to start your literature review well by defining your topic, providing a clear rationale for selecting the topic, making clear your intentions, providing adequate background, and making reference to key authors.

Example of an introduction to a literature review

What follows is an example of an introduction to a literature review. Do not be too concerned about the nature of the topic. I have intentionally included an example that gives you an insight into content, thematic structure and referencing.

This chapter discusses the development of research into relationships, interaction and networks. There is a huge body of literature on this subject, and many theories have been used to describe relationships. Understanding relationships and their importance is of great significance in Chinese culture, and has resulted in a growing Western literature on the subject (Vanhonacker, 1997; Strange, 1998; Child, 2000; Stuttard, 2000). First, a brief overview of the IMP Group's key empirical findings illustrates the work of IMP and how it links to this study. Second, relationships will be discussed. There are many definitions of relationship. It must be emphasized that this study focuses on interorganizational rather than interpersonal relationships. Third, interaction and networks will be examined, in particular work conducted by the IMP Group. Finally, FDI relationships and the key constructs of commitment, trust and cooperation will be considered.

Main body of the review

This is where you discuss the range of sources that you consider particularly relevant to your study. It is important that you adopt a critical approach to your review and organize it so that it follows a logical structure for the reader. In general, there are three options governing the structure of your review. First, you may decide to follow a thematic approach. In other words, your review takes particular themes in the literature and discusses each one in turn. Next, a methodological approach to your structure may analyze qualitative studies first, followed by quantitative studies. If some studies have adopted a mixed methods approach, this may be your final section. Or you may choose to structure your review chronologically. This involves reviewing changes in the literature over time. For instance, a timeline could be incorporated to show how a series of economic events have changed people's perception of government. Whichever option you choose, remember that your literature review needs to have a 'natural flow'.

Conclusion to the review

Your conclusion should summarize the leading articles in your chosen topic, evaluate the existing position within the area of your research, and identify gaps in and possible future areas of research. Above all, you should make the link between existing research studies and your own. For example, are you incorporating any aspects of existing research, e.g. in terms of methodology, and if so, why?

How to present your literature review

The above section should provide a useful guide in terms of structure, yet students are also frequently unsure of how to *present* their literature review. The simple answer is that there are no hard-and-fast rules on presentation. Personally, I like to see a bit of variation when it comes to presenting the review. Tables are a great way of summarizing existing key studies in your chosen area. They provide not only an interesting 'snapshot' for the reader, but also make it easier for other researchers wishing to review research of a similar nature. Table 3.5 is an excellent example of

TABLE 3.5 Comparing definitions of trust in inter-firm relationships

Author(s)	Definition	Type of relationship
Anderson and Weitz (1989)	'One party's belief that its needs will be fulfilled in the future by actions undertaken by the other party'	Sales agencies and manufacturers in the electronic components sector
Aulakh et al. (1996)	'Degree of confidence the individual partners have on the reliability and integrity of each other'	Interorganizational relationships
Chow and Holden (1997)	'The level of expectation or degree of certainty in the reliability and truth/honesty of a person or thing'	Buyer–seller in the circuit board industry
Doney and Cannon (1997)	'Perceived credibility and benevolence of a target of trust'	Buyer–seller in manufacturing
Ganeson (1994)	'Trust is the willingness to rely on an exchange partner in whom one has confidence'	Retail buyers and vendors from department store chains
Morgan and Hunt (1994)	'Trust exists when one party has confidence in an exchange partner's reliability and integrity'	Relationships between automobile tyre retailers and their suppliers
Sako and Helper (1998)	'An expectation held by an agent that its trading partner will behave in a mutually acceptable manner'	Supplier–manufacturer relationships in the auto industry

Source: Adapted from Raimondo (2000)

the type of table that can be incorporated into a literature review. As you can see, it includes all of the relevant information the reader would be interested in seeing, in this case: author(s), definitions and type of relationship.

Referencing under the Harvard system

I have already briefly mentioned the Harvard referencing system. In terms of referencing method, it remains the favoured choice for the majority of academic institutions. Following your own institution's guidelines on referencing is important as in some cases they may expect an alternative referencing system to be applied, or indeed, a slight variation on the Harvard system. Therefore, there is no excuse for not getting it right! Yet, perhaps surprisingly, poor referencing still appears to be a relatively common feature in student research projects. The next section should help you to overcome this problem by illustrating how to reference different sources within your references or bibliography.

Citing work using the Harvard system

How you cite your work in your references or bibliography is dependent on the source that you are referring to. However, no matter what the source, e.g. journal article, book, magazine or newspaper, all your references need to be laid out alphabetically, with the first named author's surname determining where each reference goes.

Examples of how to reference using the Harvard system:

- *For authored books*: Author's surname, initials (year of publication in brackets), *title of the book in italics*, place of publication, publisher.

For example: Jones, K. (2007). *Business Research*. London: Sage.

- *For journal articles*: Author's surname, initials (year of publication in brackets), 'title of the article in inverted commas', *title of the journal in italics*, **volume number in bold**, (issue number in brackets), page numbers.

For example: Henderson, T. (1995). 'International marketing: Cross-cultural issues'. *Journal of Marketing*, **24** (4): 212–224.

- *For papers published in edited books*: Author's surname, initials (year of publication in brackets), 'title of the paper in inverted commas', editor's surname, followed by the editor's initials, *title of the book in italics*, place of publication, publisher, page numbers where the paper can be found.

For example: Cole, A. (1996). 'Benchmarking in the UK retail sector', in Smith, L. (ed.) *International Business*. London: McGraw-Hill, pp. 12–19.

- *For newspaper articles*: Author, initials, (year). Title of article. *Full Title of Newspaper*, day and month of publication, page numbers and column line.

For example: Slapper, G., 2005. Corporate manslaughter: new issues for lawyers. *The Times*, 3 Sep. p. 4b.

- *Online newspaper articles*: Author and initials or corporate author, (year). Title of document or page. *Name of newspaper*, [type of medium] additional date information. Available at: include website address/URL (uniform resource locator) and additional details of access, such as the routing from the home page of the source [Accessed date].

For example: Chittenden, M., Rogers, L. and Smith, D., (2003). Focus: Targets Fail NHS. *Times Online*, [internet] 1 June. Available at: http://www.timesonline. co.uk/printFriendly/0..11-1506-669.html [Accessed 17 March 2005].

NB: the URL should be underlined.

It is good practice to keep a copy of the front page of any website you use.

- *Author's name cited in the text*: When making reference to an author's work in your text, their name is followed by the year of publication of their work, in brackets (parentheses), and forms part of the sentence:

For example: Cormack (1994, pp. 32–33) states that 'when writing for a professional readership, writers invariably make reference to already published works'.

- *More than two authors for a work*: Where there are several authors (more than two), only the first author should be used, followed by 'et al.' meaning 'and others':

For example: Green et al. (1995) found that the majority …
 Or indirectly: Recent research has found that the majority of … (Green et al., 1995).

- *More than one author cited in the text*: Where reference is made to more than one author in a sentence, and they are referred to directly, they are both cited:

For example: Jones (1946) and Smith (1948) have both shown …

What makes a good literature review?

By now, you should be familiar with the nature, approach and structure of a literature review. But what actually constitutes a good literature review? Zina O'Leary (2004: 81–82) cites a number of valid points that are worth considering when writing a good literature review. These are as follows:

- *Read a few good, relevant reviews*. There is no substitute for reading reviews produced in leading academic journals. By simply typing 'literature review' in the title search box of your search engine, you will probably find hundreds of articles that review literature within a particular topic.
- *Write critical annotations as you go*. If you begin sorting and organizing your annotations by themes, issues of concern, common shortcomings, etc., you may find that patterns begin to emerge. This can go a long way in helping you develop your own arguments.
- *Develop a structure*. We explored structure in the earlier section. Remember that your structure may alter as you discover new literature and your thinking evolves.
- *Write purposefully*. The literature review is driven by the researcher and needs to have and make a point. You can review literature without an agenda, but you cannot write a formal 'literature review' without one. Your audience should be able to readily identify the 'point' of each section of your review. If your audience does not know why you are telling them what you are telling them, you need to reconsider your approach.
- *Use the literature to back up your arguments*. It is important that when you make a statement or claim, you use supporting literature. For example, if you were to quote 'China is set to be the world's largest economy by the year 2020', then you must provide the source of the quote, e.g. 'China is set to be the world's largest economy by 2020' (Smith, 2005: 23).
- *Make doing the literature review an ongoing process*. As we have explored earlier, the literature review is a cyclical process. In reality, you should be conducting your review right up to a few weeks prior to your submission date.
- *Get plenty of feedback*. Writing a literature review is not an easy task, and your supervisor's expectations can vary widely. Don't wait until the last minute to begin the writing process or to get feedback. Be sure to pass a draft to your supervisor (although in some institutions this is not permitted), or anyone else willing to read it early on.
- *Be prepared to redraft*. It would be nice if first drafts and last drafts were the same draft. However, this is unlikely to be the case.

What makes a poor literature review?

You might think that what makes a poor literature review is essentially the opposite of what is listed above. That is certainly true to a point. Still, the following list of points are what I personally consider to be the more common mistakes made by students. Hopefully you will find these useful – not to copy, but to avoid at all costs!

- *No evidence of a literature review.* Thankfully this is somewhat of a rarity. Clearly, if you fail to include a literature review within your research project, it is likely to signal to your reader that you have failed to acknowledge work carried out by specialists in your chosen subject area. In addition, given that the literature review is a major part of your project, failure to include it will almost certainly mean a significant deduction in marks.
- *Poor length.* Your work is also likely to suffer if your review is of insufficient length. A question that I am often asked is 'How long should I make my literature review?' In general, this largely depends on your research approach – whether it is inductive or deductive. However, a useful guide is that your review is likely to be in the region of 25–30% of your overall word count.
- *Denser referencing required.* Although a review may be of sufficient length, sometimes a drawback is that a student has failed to include adequate reference to previous work in the main text. This suggests that the student has failed to examine the wide range of sources available to them. It also indicates that the student perhaps has not given enough time to carrying out their literature review.
- *The literature review is largely a verbatim reproduction of the original texts.* Unfortunately, sometimes students 'fall into the trap' of purely citing extracts from previous work in their subject area. As a result, the review becomes a very list-like style of writing. Of course, what they should be doing is adopting a critical approach to their review.
- *Poor structure.* A muddled, poorly structured review makes it difficult for the reader to fully grasp the nature of the research.
- *Literature does not correspond to research objectives.* Identifying and reviewing literature that is not relevant to a set of objectives shows poor understanding of the topic. In principle, if you fully understand your objectives, parameters and key words, then it should be easy to avoid citing work that is not relevant to your own study.

RESEARCH IN ACTION

Conducting a systematic literature review

The article below is taken from the *Journal of Knowledge Management*: 'Knowledge Management in SMEs: A literature review', Durst, S. and Edvardsson, I.R. (2012)

In this article, the authors undertake a systematic literature review of 36 refereed empirical articles on knowledge management and small and medium sized enterprises. The aim of the paper is to examine the current status of research in knowledge management (KM) in SMEs. The research questions are as follows:

- Which knowledge management topics are well researched and which are not?
- Which were the main findings of the studies?

- Which methods were used?
- How does the research handle the particular challenges small firms are facing regarding knowledge management?

The methodology of the literature review is explicitly set out within the paper. The methodology begins by explaining what is meant by a systematic review and the principles adopted when carrying out the review. In this case, the authors explain the process as beginning with mapping the field through a scoping review, followed by a comprehensive literature search, quality assessment, data extraction, synthesis and writing up.

First, the authors set out a research plan comprising the research questions, keywords, and details of inclusion and exclusion criteria. The inclusion criteria were: publications in the period of 2001–2011, empirical research papers, peer-reviewed, English language, SME focus on knowledge management and knowledge management processes, and ProQuest database. Conversely, any publications outside this timeframe, papers and reports that did not meet these criteria, and other databases were excluded from the review. The authors used an Excel data sheet to record the 'key elements' of each article. This consisted of the name of the author(s), year of publication, research aim/objectives, theoretical perspective/framework, method, main findings and name of the journal.

Second, the comprehensive literature search began with both authors accessing the ProQuest database to look for suitable articles. This process involved undertaking a key word search using 'knowledge management' and 'SMEs'. However, the researchers found that the search produced only a small number of publications. Refining the search to using 'KM' in combination with 'SMEs' resulted in 398 hits. This illustrates the importance of experimenting with a number of different key word searches when doing your own research. Durst and Edvardsson (2012) also included the highest ranked journals in their chosen area of research to make sure that the work by key authors was included in the review. In addition, three international journals in the field of small business were reviewed, thus resulting in an additional 697 hits.

Third, quality assessment entailed both authors reading through the abstracts and, if relevant, any other sections of the articles to make sure that they covered the pre-defined scope. This process yielded a final selection of 36 articles which fulfilled the criteria set and allowed for the analysis stage to be carried out.

Fourth, data extraction of the 36 papers was undertaken by dividing the papers among the two authors. Thus, each author read 18 papers. Both researchers then entered the relevant data regarding the research aim in the spreadsheet and jointly went through each data entry and discussed the content. If any of the authors had any reservations about one particular paper, then both authors went through the paper in question. The rationale behind this is to ensure consistency in terms of analysis and conclusions drawn.

Fifth, at the synthesis stage, the final Excel sheet was jointly discussed. This discussion enabled the authors to categorize the findings under KM themes, which, in turn, helped to clarify what is known about knowledge management in SMEs and to which KM areas the body of knowledge is limited.

Sixth, the final stage of the review process was devoted to writing up the findings.

The above article demonstrates one approach to conducting a literature review, and clearly shows the different steps that the authors went through when reviewing the literature. You will find many examples of literature-review-based articles on electronic databases such as Emerald and Business Source Premier. Irrespective of the topic, reading these types of articles will give you a good insight into how to conduct your own literature review, particularly in terms of structure and writing style.

A final reminder!

Remember that searching and critically reviewing the literature is likely to be a major part of your research project. After all, it is essential to acknowledge what has already been written. A thorough review will ensure that you have understood and identified the key authors who have published in your area.

Fundamentally, searching and reviewing the literature is a process that you should continue to undertake right up to a few weeks prior to submission. Moreover, make sure that you include a range of contemporary references. On occasion, I have read projects where the reference list contains little in the way of references post-2000. This illustrates a failure on the part of the student to actively seek the latest publications on their chosen topic.

Summary and Conclusion

In this chapter we have looked at various issues relating to conducting a literature review. The literature review is likely to be a major part of your research project. In essence, a literature review not only allows you to better understand your topic, but also allows you to identify 'gaps' and provides evidence of research. Here are the key points from this chapter:

- In the context of your research, 'literature' means all sources of published material.
- A literature review can be described as identifying, evaluating and critically assessing what has been published on your chosen topic.
- You are required to demonstrate library and information skills, the intellectual capability to justify decisions on the choice of relevant ideas, and the ability to assess the value of those ideas in context (Hart, 1998: 9).
- Think of the literature review as a process. Before you begin conducting your review of the literature you need to be clear about your objectives and research questions.
- When conducting your literature review, it is likely that you will use a wide source of literature.
- Reading journal articles is a great way to understand how to conduct a literature review.
- A key skill to doing a literature review is to be able to read and review literature critically.
- Searching the literature should be carried out until a few weeks prior to your submission date.

CASE STUDY — Writing a Successful Literature Review

Dirk has recently completed a workshop on how to write a literature review. Following the workshop, he felt a lot more confident in terms of how to approach the literature review for his own research project. He now realizes that key success factors include: reading relevant sources, developing a coherent structure, reviewing the literature as an ongoing process, and being prepared to redraft. However, he is unable to recall other important factors that the lecturer highlighted during the workshop, in particular, how to approach presentation, structure and writing style.

Case study question

- What other factors does Dirk need to consider if he is going to write a successful literature review?

YOU'RE THE SUPERVISOR

Sarah has emailed you a draft of her literature review. The final paragraph of her review reads as follows:

Henderson (2011) provides the most interesting study into leadership across cultures as it includes respondents from a range of different cultural backgrounds. His findings argue that cultural factors play a significant part in influencing leadership. I may make reference to this seminal piece of work later on in my own research.

Supervisor question

- What are the problems associated with finishing a literature review in this way and how would you advise Sarah to conclude her review?

COMMON QUESTIONS AND ANSWERS

1. How long should my literature review be?

Answer: This varies, and the word limit and views of your supervisor must be considered. For example, if you are working on the basis of a 10,000 word limit, then clearly one would expect to see a shorter literature review than if you were working towards completing a 15,000 word project. Your supervisor is likely to have his or her own opinions as to the appropriate length of your review. Also, noting the weighting of marks towards the literature review is a useful indicator. For instance, again, if you are working towards a 10,000 word project and 25% of the marks are allocated for literature review, then you can aim at writing in the region of 2,000–3,000 words. Finally, the amount of relevant literature and availability of sources are also factors. If you find that there is very little written on your subject, then perhaps your topic is too narrow. Conversely, if your topic is too broad, this will have a detrimental effect on your review because you will be unable to cover all relevant themes.

2. How do I write a literature review?

Answer: One of the most commonly asked questions by my project students is 'How do I write a literature review?' As noted earlier, the literature review is a process and should contain key features, such as: definitions of key terms; discuss why the subject is of interest; discuss research already undertaken; and provide a clear summary of the research opportunities and objectives that emerge from the literature review. Although you may know the structure and key features of a literature review, you may still feel apprehensive about actually writing your review. Although the likelihood is that you have been taught how to write a review as part of a workshop or research methods module, there is no substitute for reading literature reviews featured in leading academic journals. Literature review based articles give you an excellent insight into: structuring your literature review, adopting a critical approach, referencing your work, and summarizing and making a link to your own work. As a helpful guide, in the further reading section at the end of the chapter I have included details of three literature review articles. These have been purposely chosen as they are all on business-related topics and provide a basis in which you can learn how to form and develop your own review. Do not be too concerned if the topic does not fall into your chosen area of research. The important thing is to get a 'feel' for the writing style and how to produce a good literature review.

3. How many chapters shall I devote to my literature review?

Answer: This is often a matter of personal choice. However, I suggest that you seek advice on this from your project supervisor. In most cases, the majority of my students tend to devote one chapter to the literature review. This is generally for two reasons. First, the 10,000 word limit means that devoting more than one chapter to the review may mean that other sections of the project do not receive adequate attention. Second, the thematic nature of the chosen topic can easily be covered within one chapter. Sometimes a literature review may be based on two chapters. This might be because one chapter focuses on a more practical element, e.g. a case study, while the second chapter reviews relevant theoretical content. Again, if in doubt, discuss with your project supervisor.

4. What type and how many sources do I need to include in my literature review?

Answer: As you are conducting an academic piece of work there must be a certain number of academic sources within your research project, and this includes material from academic journals. Using other sources such as newspapers, magazines and websites is fine, as long as you also include academic sources such as academic journals and textbooks. In terms of websites, try to avoid obscure websites as the information they provide is likely to be unreliable. Moreover, try to avoid over-reliance on web-based sources. In short, it is best to use a range of sources when writing your literature review, although one would expect the majority of these sources to be 'academic based'. In terms of number of sources, this is difficult to answer as it depends on several factors; for example, amount of literature, chosen topic, university regulations, etc. Your referencing should be relatively dense and not rely too heavily on a small number of sources.

References

Anderson, E. and Weitz, B. (1989) 'Determinants of continuity in conventional industrial channel dyads', *Marketing Science*, 8 (Fall): 310–323.

Aulakh, P., Kotabe, M. and Sahay, A. (1996) 'Trust and performance in cross-border marketing partnerships: A behavioural approach', *Journal of International Business Studies*, 27 (5): 1005–1032.

Child, J. (2000) 'Management and organisations in China: Key trends and issues', in J.T. Li, A. Tsui and E. Weldon (eds), *Management and Organisations in the Chinese Context*. Basingstoke: Macmillan, 33–62.

Chow, S. and Holden, R. (1997) 'Toward an understanding of loyalty: The moderating role of trust', *Journal of Managerial Issues*, 9 (3): 275–298.

Copac (2008) 'Copac academic and library catalogue', online source: copac.ac.uk/, accessed 10 September 2008.

Davies, M.B. (2007) *Doing a Successful Research Project: Using Qualitative or Quantitative Methods*. Basingstoke: Palgrave Macmillan.

Doney, P.M. and Cannon, J.P. (1997) 'An examination of the nature of trust in buyer–seller relationships', *Journal of Marketing*, 61 (April): 35–51.

Durst, S. and Edvardsson, I.R. (2012) 'Knowledge Management in SMEs: A literature review', *Journal of Knowledge Management*, 16 (6): 879–903.

Ganeson, S. (1994) 'Determinants of long-term orientation in buyer–seller relationships', *Journal of Marketing*, 58 (2): 1–19.

Hart, C. (1998) *Doing a Literature Review: Releasing the Social Science Research Imagination*. Thousand Oaks, CA: Sage.

Hussey, J. and Hussey, R. (1997) *Business Research: A Practical Guide for Undergraduate and Postgraduate Students*. Basingstoke: Macmillan.

Knopf, J.W. (2006) 'Doing a literature review', *Political Science & Politics*, 39 (1): 127–132.

Morgan, R.M. and Hunt, S.D. (1994) 'The commitment–trust theory of relationship marketing', *Journal of Marketing*, 58 (3), July: 24–38.

Neuhaus, C. and Hans-Dieter, D. (2008) 'Data sources for performing citation analysis: An overview', *Journal of Documentation*, 64 (2): 193–210.

O'Leary, Z. (2004) *The Essential Guide to Doing Research*. London: Sage.

Raimondo, M. (2000) 'The measurement of trust in marketing studies: A review of models and methodologies', *Proceedings of the 16th Annual IMP International Conference*, Bath, September.

Rowley, J. and Slack, F. (2004) 'Conducting a literature review', *Management Research News*, 27 (6): 31–39.

Sako, M. and Helper, S. (1998) 'Determinants of trust in supplier relations: Evidence from the automotive industry in Japan and the United States', *Journal of Economic Behaviour and Organization*, 34: 387–417.

Scopus (2008) online source: www.info.scopus.com, accessed 15 September 2008.

Strange, R. (1998) *Management in China: The Experience of Foreign Businesses*. London: Frank Cass.

Stuttard, J.B. (2000) *The New Silk Road*. London: John Wiley & Sons.

Vanhonacker, W. (1997) 'Entering China: An unconventional approach', *Harvard Business Review*, March–April: 130–140.

Further Reading

Bruce, C. (1994) 'Research students' early experiences of the dissertation literature review', *Studies in Higher Education*, 19 (2): 217–229.

Cooper, H.M. (1998) *Synthesizing Research: A Guide for Literature Reviews*. Thousand Oaks, CA: Sage.

Fink, A. (2009) *Conducting Research Literature Reviews: From the Internet to Paper* (3rd edn). Thousand Oaks, CA: Sage.

Ismail, A.R., Melewar, T.C., Lim, L. and Woodside, A. (2011) 'Customer experiences with brands: Literature review and research directions', *The Marketing Review*, 11 (3): 205–225.

Nabi, G., Holden, R. and Walmsley, A. (2006) 'Graduate career-making and business start-up: A literature review', *Education + Training*, 48 (5): 373–385.

Oliver, P. (2012) *Succeeding with your Literature Review*. Maidenhead: Open University Press.

Ridley, D. (2008) *The Literature Review: A Step-by-Step Guide for Students*. Thousand Oaks, CA: Sage.

Soltani, E., Gennard, J. and van der Meer, R.B. (2004) 'HR performance evaluation in the context of TQM: A review of the literature', *International Journal of Quality & Reliability Management*, 21 (4): 377–396.

Using Secondary Data

Wilson, J.

Learning Objectives

After reading this chapter, you should be able to:

- know what secondary data are, and how they can be incorporated into your research;
- understand the different types of secondary data;
- be aware of the main electronic secondary sources;
- know the advantages and disadvantages of secondary data;
- know how to access secondary data;
- be aware of the possible usage of foreign language sources;
- appreciate how to evaluate secondary data;
- know how to link primary and secondary data; and
- understand how to present secondary data.

Introduction

In the preceding chapter we looked at primary data and associated collection methods. In this chapter we continue the theme of data collection, by examining secondary data.

In contrast to primary data, secondary data are data that have been collected by other researchers. Secondary data encompass a range of different sources. We explored some of these sources in Chapter 3 – general reports, theses, newspapers, academic journals, textbooks, Internet websites, abstracts, catalogues, dictionaries, bibliographies, encyclopaedias and citation indices.

Most Business and Management students rely heavily on secondary data when conducting their research. To be sure, in some cases it can be used exclusively within a research project. Conversely, other students may prefer their project to be dominated by primary data collection, with secondary data receiving limited attention. How does one make a decision on the application of secondary data? Well, a key aim of this chapter is to help you to evaluate the extent to which secondary data may feature in your research.

This chapter begins by defining the nature of secondary data. I then examine reasons that may lead you to base your project entirely on secondary data. At one level, this is often determined by the assessment regulations laid down by your university or college. However, other factors may also influence your decision. We examine these later on in the chapter. Next, the advantages and disadvantages of secondary data are presented. Unsurprisingly, time is cited as a major advantage. The plethora of electronic sources available has made searching for secondary data all the easier. Nevertheless, there are notable disadvantages, and these receive similar attention.

Non-native English speakers and those who are able to read languages other than English will be able to use foreign language sources. This of course applies to many international students. Thus, I have included a section in the chapter that highlights some of the issues surrounding the usage of foreign language sources.

The availability of secondary data is a real concern to student researchers. Undoubtedly, your institution's library will contain a wealth of sources. The degree to which these correspond with your research depends on the nature of your topic. In some cases, you may need to access more specialized data. I will therefore make recommendations as to how this can be achieved.

The concluding part of the chapter examines the evaluation and presentation of secondary data. The ability to evaluate secondary data is essential, not least to determine the degree of reliability. Also, if you have amassed a huge amount of data, how do you know what to include and what to omit? One way is to consider the following data evaluation factors – purpose, scope, authority, audience and format. Addressing questions associated with each of these five factors should make the evaluation process easier. Next, I provide a relatively brief overview of how to present secondary data. Often, it can be presented in its original form, or you may wish to present the data in your own way. As there is very little distinction between presenting secondary and primary data, I pay greater attention to presenting data in Chapters 9 and 10. Finally, we examine how to link primary data with secondary data.

What Are Secondary Data?

As noted earlier, secondary data are data that have been collected by other researchers. Of course, the researchers could be an individual, a group or a body working on behalf of an organization. Secondary data include everything from annual reports, promotional material, parent company documentation, published case descriptions, magazines, journal articles and newspaper reports to government printed sources.

Most research begins with secondary data analysis. The outcome of this analysis usually dictates whether or not the researcher will engage in primary research. For example, if you determine that there is a limited amount of secondary data on your chosen topic, you may be more inclined to conduct primary research. Conversely, if a plethora of data exists, then you may not feel the need to engage in primary data collection. The amount of existing data available is just one reason that may influence your decision to focus solely on secondary data. I discuss other reasons in the next section.

Reasons for Basing Your Research Project Entirely on Secondary Data

There are two main reasons that may lead you to base your entire research project on secondary data – the nature of your topic and your institution's assessment regulations.

Certain research topics are more likely to warrant a greater emphasis on secondary data. For example, let us say that you intend conducting a comparative study into gross domestic product (GDP) growth rates among European Union states. Given the large amount of secondary data on this particular topic, the likelihood is that you may not feel the necessity to collect primary data. You may argue that you are perfectly capable of producing a comprehensive piece of research without the need for primary research. This may be true. Nevertheless, your intentions may not be workable due to your institution's assessment regulations.

Some universities and colleges insist that primary data must feature within a research project, although this tends to be more applicable to postgraduate rather than undergraduate programmes. Therefore, if your institution permits projects solely based on secondary data, this may influence you to go down this route. If in doubt, check with your academic institution.

There are other reasons that may influence your decision. Arguably, these are less significant, but they still need to be considered. These can be summarized as:

- your choice of research design;
- whether you are undertaking international or cross-cultural research; and
- whether you are unable to conduct primary research.

First, your choice of research design may influence your decision whether or not to conduct a project based exclusively on secondary data. If, for example, you plan on undertaking a longitudinal study over several years, this will not be feasible using primary research. However, you may find that there are existing longitudinal studies relevant to your chosen topic. This would allow analysis, perhaps even comparative analysis, of existing studies.

Another example is using a case study research design based entirely on secondary data. Let us say that you are concerned with a comparative analysis of the internationalization strategies of two of the UK's leading supermarkets – Tesco and Sainsbury's. You may argue that existing comparative studies have already been undertaken by other researchers, in which case the nature of your research is to compare and contrast existing data.

Realistically, financial and time constraints make undertaking international or cross-cultural research difficult for student researchers. Nevertheless, this does not mean that it has to be ruled out altogether. An abundance of existing secondary sources (perhaps across different countries) may mean that you are in a position to conduct your research. However, you need to be cautious of potential differences in how studies are conducted and analyzed across cultures.

You may feel that an inability to collect primary data means that you have no option but to focus entirely on secondary data. For example, a primary study into pay awards among multinational company directors is likely to be beyond even the most dedicated student! Yet, if several organizations publish these data, you might ask yourself – 'Why do I need to conduct primary research?'

Finally, I am of the view that a perfectly good undergraduate research project can be written based solely on secondary data. True, certain topics are best suited to primary data. But if a suitable amount of secondary data exists, there is no reason why a project based exclusively on secondary data cannot be undertaken. This does not mean that using completely secondary sources is a 'soft option'. The real challenge for students is collecting, analyzing and interpreting someone else's data so that it corresponds to their own research problem.

Business and Secondary Data

Organizations also need to decide how to incorporate secondary data into their research. For example, if a company is about to launch a new product, it will run a market survey to collect primary data and gauge customer reactions; if it wants to evaluate general economic activity in an area, it will use secondary data prepared by the government (Waters, 1997: 73).

In business, there are two broad classifications of secondary data – *internal* and *external* data. Examples of internal sources include customer records, sales invoices, previous market research reports and minutes from board meetings. External sources tend to be more varied. These include everything from competitors' promotional brochures to government reports.

Classifying secondary data on the basis of internal and external sources makes sense when considering an organizational perspective. Yet, how does this relate to the student researcher? Arguably, a one-size-fits-all definition is neither practical nor possible. The majority of students do not have the privilege of access to internal company data. Moreover, not all students engage in organizationally based research. Therefore, I propose a 'student-based' classification of secondary data later in this chapter.

Small organizations have a propensity to use mainly secondary data when conducting market research. For example, this may include information from trade magazines, articles in the local press and internal data. One of the reasons for this is that many do not have the resources to engage in primary research. Where primary research is undertaken, this tends to be conducted on an informal basis.

Unlike small firms, large organizations often buy in secondary data, or mailing lists, from specialized agencies. To illustrate, let us say that a tyre manufacturer wishes to promote their tyres to French car dealers. If no published data are available, then one option is to buy the data from a specialized agency. This is costly, of course, and does not guarantee a high response rate. Other potential problems are associated with buying in data. First, secondary data soon become out of date. This is also a concern with internal data such as customer records. Relying on such data can help maintain close customer relationships, but it needs to be updated regularly.

Second, although buying in data can be potentially rewarding, the data have to be correct. There are likely to be literally thousands of data lists available. Companies that fail to buy from a reputable source may find that the data do not meet their expectations, particularly in terms of reliability and validity.

Third, secondary data bought for the purpose of direct marketing activities are unlikely to be exclusive to one organization. This is especially true in business-to-business markets, where several companies compete for a small number of customers.

In sum, for many organizations intent on promoting their products and services, secondary data can be a useful way to target potential customers. However, such data have several limitations: they soon become dated; it is sometimes difficult to verify the credibility of a source; and competitors have access to the same data.

Reliance on the Internet as a Secondary Data Source

In the last section we looked at how businesses might use secondary data. Of course, often an important source of secondary data for both businesses and students is the Internet. First, businesses may use it as a vehicle for gathering information from competitors' websites, accessing industry data or assessing potential environmental threats to the business. Most businesses are also aware of the importance of not overly relying on the Internet. Other, more traditional, secondary sources are equally important. These may include printed business directories, government reports and, of course, internal data.

Similarly, I am certain that the Internet is already an important source of information in your research. An increasingly common theme I have witnessed in research projects is overemphasis on Internet-based sources. This over-reliance is likely to have a negative impact on the reliability of your research, especially if your chosen sources are unknown and cannot be tested for their credibility. As we have established, the Internet has brought many benefits to researchers, but the increasing emphasis on Internet sources by some students is a concern. Not only does it mean that attention is being paid to potentially unreliable websites, but also that more traditional sources, such as books, are sometimes being excluded from their research.

The Distinction Between Literature Review and Secondary Data Analysis

By now, you should be aware of the role that secondary sources play in conducting your literature review. However, secondary data can also form a major, if not exclusive, part of your analysis. For those of you focusing your research entirely on secondary data, you need to make a clear distinction in your research between your literature review and analysis. Students sometimes find this difficult. In essence, your literature review is likely to be one or two chapters and will come before your secondary analysis. Unlike your literature review, secondary data analysis may involve using previously published survey data as the focal point for your analysis. Alternatively, the main focus might be on a particular case or multiple cases which could also feature published survey data. In short, either of these approaches is helpful in maintaining a distinction between the literature review and analysis chapters.

Whereas your literature review may *describe* your chosen survey, and compare and contrast similar studies, your secondary analysis is likely to involve a detailed analysis of your chosen survey. Typically, this might form the basis of one chapter – namely your analysis and results.

Remember to justify your choice of survey. Reasons might include: the reputation of the source, the contemporary nature of the study, the sample size, or simply that it is the only recognizable study conducted in your area of research.

Classifying Secondary Data

Secondary data can be classified in a number of different ways. A distinction can be made on the basis of format and intended audience. First, secondary data can be classified into electronic and written formats. Although this distinction has become blurred in recent years, it still applies to the majority of students engaged in research. Second, these groups can be further divided into subgroups according to their intended target audience. Usually, this means an exclusively academic or commercial audience. Figure 7.1 illustrates the classification of secondary data. Although

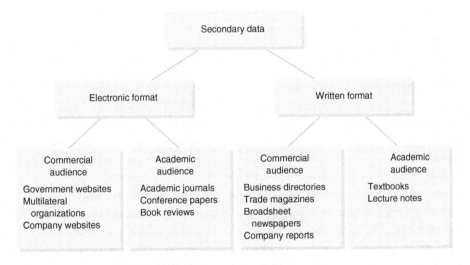

FIGURE 7.1   Classification of secondary data

it is by no means exhaustive, it classifies the main sources of secondary data used by students. Now, let us begin to look at each of these classifications in turn, starting with electronic data.

Electronic format

'Electronic data' refers to data presented in electronic format, such as Internet websites. As noted in this chapter, Internet websites are an increasingly popular source of literature for students, but the Internet is by no means the only source of electronic data. Other potential sources for you to consider are DVDs, videos and audio media. These can include an organization's in-house training video, promotional materials for a multinational company, an audio recording of a radio interview with a company director or even an audio book. Although the latter may seem an unlikely source for your research, occasionally you may find invaluable data that are only available in one particular format.

The main advantages of electronic data are that they save time because they are easily accessible, and can be easily stored. Indeed, gone are the days when student researchers were forced to keep several lever arch files of relevant articles. I remember them well!

Table 7.1 provides a list of useful government websites, multilateral organizations and general business-related sites that prove popular with business students. In addition, the American Marketing Association (2013) provides a comprehensive list of electronic data sources.

Electronic format – commercial audience

Electronic sources geared towards a commercial audience include multilateral organization and government websites. The former are particularly useful for students

TABLE 7.1 Useful electronic data sources

Source	Web address	Summary of information
World Trade Organization	www.wto.org	Data on WTO member states
OECD	www.oecd.org	Statistics on member states
International Monetary Fund	www.imf.org	Publishes a range of commercial and financial data
European Union	www.europa.eu	Statistical information on member states
Financial Times	www.ft.com	Information on financial markets
The Economist	www.economist.com	Economic data and articles
Business Week	www.businessweek.com	Provider of global business news
British Broadcasting Corporation	www.bbc.co.uk/news	Daily news on the UK and worldwide
Dun & Bradstreet	www.dnb.com	Provides global information on businesses
World Bank	www.worldbank.org	Country data and analysis on the global economy
The Guardian	www.guardian.co.uk	A leading UK newspaper

engaged in research on economics, the business environment and international trade. For instance, the WTO site contains a wealth of information on these and many other subjects.

Electronic format – academic audience

Electronic data targeted at a mainly academic audience include academic journal articles and conference papers. These are an invaluable source of data for students for the simple reason that they are aimed at a predominantly academic audience and are likely to contain many of the sections that will feature in your research project, e.g. literature review, methodology, conclusion, and so on.

Written format

Written data refer to data that are printed in hard-copy format. The main examples of secondary data are the more 'traditional' published sources, such as textbooks and academic journals. Ostensibly, we will continue to see a shift away from traditional publishing to electronic formats. This has certainly been the case in terms of publishing and accessing academic journals in recent years. Although your university or college library is likely to hold both electronic and hard copies of academic journals, once again accessing them electronically saves time and is easier to organize.

Written format – commercial audience

Written data produced for a commercial audience are generally published for convenient and functional purposes. For example, a building firm is likely to produce sales invoices, customer records and sales figures. Although the company is legally required to keep such data for accounting purposes, it is also a convenient way to develop customer relationships through direct marketing and advertising. Furthermore, such internal data can aid the organization with strategic development over the short, medium and long term.

Business data are also produced by publishers such as Dun & Bradstreet. Although such data tend to be produced in both hard-copy and electronic format, many companies still prefer hard copy. Organizations and governments can use the data produced to target potential customers and/or business partners.

Written format – academic audience

Academic data in written format still tend to include textbooks and lecture notes. The former are an essential source of data for students, as modules are often structured on a particular key text. Both textbooks and lecture notes can make worthy contributions to your research. For example, many textbooks feature contemporary case studies. You may decide that information from these cases can be used as part of your secondary analysis.

The Advantages of Secondary Data

There are several advantages of using secondary data. First, you will find that the majority of data are available through your institution's library at no or very little cost. Second, in contrast to primary data, secondary data can be relatively straight-forward to collect. Detailed advantages include:

Less resource-intensive

In general, secondary data are a convenient and cost-effective source of information for the student researcher. Given that much of your secondary data are likely to be readily available, accessing information this way will save time when it comes to analyzing and interpreting your findings. Obviously, conducting primary research involves a great deal of time to prepare, implement, collect and interpret results. By focusing on secondary data, you may be able to collect and analyze much larger data sets, like those published by an organization such as Mintel.

Can allow for comparative analysis

Another advantage of secondary data is that they can be compared to your primary findings. By comparing your primary data with your secondary sources, you can determine the extent to which you agree or disagree with existing studies. For example, if you consider a study into car ownership, you may find that a national study suggests a possible downturn in the market. However, a questionnaire survey of car owners in your area may generate contradictory data.

Secondary data also enable cross-cultural or international comparative research, as they help to overcome the obvious limitations associated with primary data col-lection. The Economist Intelligence Unit (EIU) provides country data that can be used exclusively or on a comparative basis.

Ideal for longitudinal studies

I have already noted that secondary sources provide students with an opportunity to engage in longitudinal research. This is a clear advantage. Much of the data col-lected by governments are compiled over several decades. For instance, census data and data published on the Retail Price Index (RPI) can be analyzed over many years. This lends itself well to a longitudinal study. On the other hand, you still need to be wary of how such data relate to your research problem. For example, census data are ideal if the nature of your research is to examine demographic change and/or population growth, but are unsuitable if you want to explore customers' purchasing decisions, for instance.

Easily accessible for other researchers

Finally, secondary data facilitate access for other researchers interested in your area of research. Many researchers rely on secondary data. Therefore, by making reference to secondary sources you are likely to aid other researchers engaged in developing their own research.

The Disadvantages of Secondary Data

There are numerous disadvantages associated with secondary data. The main thing to consider is that secondary data should not be used exclusively simply as a means of saving time and money! Also: data may be outdated, there may be a dearth of data relating to your study, and the data may be unreliable.

Access is difficult and costly

Often, you will find that high-quality and reliable secondary data are difficult to access. Examples include certain types of government data and internally produced organizational data. The main reason that access to this type of data is generally restricted is largely due to its sensitive nature. Normally, the only way to get hold of such valuable data is if you work for the organization that produces them. Even then, accessing such data can still prove difficult!

The cost of accessing data is also a disadvantage to student researchers. On many occasions students have told me that they have found an excellent report online, but obtaining a copy usually involves a subscription fee or a sizeable one-off payment.

May not match your research problem

You may find it problematic to find secondary data that correspond to your study. For instance, I remember supervising a student who wished to analyze the development of ecotourism in Zanzibar. Needless to say, the amount of secondary data on the subject can best be described as 'narrow'. In circumstances like these, where the nature of the topic is highly specialized, it is often essential to conduct primary research.

Another problem is that although data may appear to correspond to your research, sometimes you may find quite distinct differences in how key variables have been defined. Similarly, a different set of measures may have been employed.

You may believe you have a sufficient amount of data, but remember that secondary data are data that have been collected by other individuals or organizations for their own purposes. Such data may not therefore answer your research questions.

Difficult to verify reliability

In general, the ability to determine whether or not secondary data are reliable is largely down to the source. Certainly, academic journals offer high levels of reliability, as do established business publications such as the *Harvard Business Review* and *The Economist*. The main problem tends to be with the more obscure publications and websites.

Sometimes, it can be argued, the limitation associated with reliability can be overcome by using a varied range of secondary sources. By way of illustration, in their article into annual working hours in Britain, Gall and Allsop (2007: 801) justify the use of secondary data by making reference to the absence of standardized and longitudinal data. In addition, the authors also include a wide range of secondary sources:

> The material for this research is derived from a number of secondary sources, such as the publications of the Advisory, Conciliation and Arbitration Service (ACAS), Incomes Data Services (IDS), Industrial Relations Services (IRS), Labour Research Department (LRD) and the Institute of Personnel Management (IPM)/Chartered Institute of Personnel Management (CIPD) as well as coverage of salient developments in the quality press like the *Financial Times* and *The Guardian* and among regional daily broadsheets. Whilst there are a number of weaknesses in the robustness of the data generated using such a method, this data can help supplement other data – which itself is not without weaknesses – so that a fuller, multi-component picture of annual hours can be built up.

The secondary data cited in Gall and Allsop's article may not be familiar to you. These include publications from public sector bodies, professional bodies, and regional and national newspapers.

Not in a manageable form

Data that have experienced little, if any, processing are referred to as *raw data*, whereas data that have received some form of processing or summarizing are known as compiled or *cooked data*. For example, a successful dot.com company selling books and music CDs online might collect huge volumes of sales-related raw data each day, but such data are not very useful until they have been analyzed, interpreted and presented in a manageable form. Once processed, this type of data might be used for analyzing sales trends, launching a targeted sales promotion campaign or simply analyzing the most profitable lines. Tables 7.2 and 7.3 show raw data and cooked data respectively.

TABLE 7.2   An example of raw data

Transaction no.	Amount (£)
101293	42.96
101294	20.99
101295	11.50
101296	13.75

TABLE 7.3   An example of processed (cooked) data

Date	Daily sales achieved (£)	Daily sales target (£)	Difference (+/−)
Mon 23 March	35,000	34,750	+250
Tues 24 March	18,345	22,950	−4,605
Weds 25 March	17,234	14,750	+2,484
Thurs 26 March	29,108	28,250	+858
Fri 27 March	22,400	21,750	+650
Sat 28 March	39,100	38,250	+850
Sun 29 March	12,240	11,500	+740
TOTAL for week	173,427	172,200	+1,227

A disadvantage of raw data is that researchers need to allocate time to processing and summarizing the data. On the other hand, a major advantage is that the data can be processed in a way that suits the researcher. Table 7.2 is an extract from a daily list of sales transactions for an independent food retailer. Obviously, in its current, unprocessed, form it provides very little information for the retailer. Clearly, the only information that the list does provide is the value of each transaction, and its respective transaction number. Table 7.3 shows how the food retailer might process weekly sales transactions. As you can see, the data have been presented in a much more manageable form. Moreover, it features some interesting information that can be used to aid inventory levels, marketing and budgeting. The most notable feature is the extent to which sales have fluctuated over the course of the week, and of course the fact that the retailer has exceeded its weekly target.

Comparability

One final disadvantage with secondary data is comparability. I have already mentioned that an advantage of using secondary data is that data can be compared with your primary findings. However, if you are engaged in exclusively secondary data, then this option is not open to you. Of course, your secondary data may include both qualitative and quantitative data, e.g. a country report published by the World Trade Organization that includes quantitative statistical data such as GDP figures *and* qualitative analysis in the form of quotations from leading economics experts.

In one sense, applying a wide range of secondary sources is a good thing, but you must ensure that you can compare your findings on an equal footing. Comparability is often a problem when integrating and examining data from different sources. Differences may occur in the following aspects:

- *The reliability of the information.* In developing countries, where a substantial proportion of the population may be illiterate or difficult to access, population or economic data may be based on estimates or rudimentary data collection procedures.
- *The frequency of studies.* The frequency with which surveys are undertaken may also vary from country to country. While in the UK a population census is undertaken every 10 years, in some countries it may be more than 30 years since a complete census was undertaken.
- *Measurement units.* These are not necessarily equivalent from country to country.
- *Differences in circumstance.* Even where data may seem comparable, there may be differences in the circumstances that lie behind the data. If a researcher was to undertake a comparison of GNP (gross national product) per capita data from Sweden and the UK, the information may prove misleading. The high per capita income figures for Sweden, which suggest a high standard of living, do not take account of the much higher levels of Swedish taxation linked to the state's provision of social services.

(Wilson, 2006: 58)

The Usage of Foreign Language Sources

If you have the capability of reading foreign language sources, then this is clearly an advantage as it allows you to consult a wider range of secondary sources. In addition, if you are an international student, then you are likely to be familiar with secondary sources in your home country that might prove useful for your research. For example, given that one of my areas of research is the internationalization of Chinese brands, I tend to supervise several Chinese students. I always stress to them the importance of consulting both English and Chinese sources. This is partly because some secondary sources from different countries make for an interesting comparison, but also using secondary data from different countries can help to improve the validity of your results.

How do I reference foreign language sources? To some extent, conventions here vary depending on the referencing system. Often, non-English sources are treated the same, with direct quotes translated into English. If you are translating the text yourself, one way to illustrate this is by inserting 'translation by the author' in brackets after the quote. For example: 'Wong, 2012: 14, translation by the author.' Again, you will probably find that there are subtle variations of this approach, so if in doubt check with your project supervisor. In terms of how to reference the source in your reference list, typically, the reference will include the title of the book or article in the original language, followed by the English translation in brackets.

Evaluating Secondary Data

You may be in the position of having gathered an abundance of secondary data. Yet, on what basis do you decide what to include and what to omit from your research? Blumberg et al. (2008: 319) list five factors that should be taken into account when evaluating secondary data – purpose, scope, authority, audience and format. Table 7.4 summarizes the critical questions that a researcher might ask when evaluating secondary information sources. The questions are associated with each of these factors.

Purpose

The main point to consider here is the extent to which the purpose relates to your own research. It does not necessarily have to be a 'perfect fit'. If, for example, you are conducting research into cultural differences between Japanese and US consumers, you may find that a similar study focusing on US and South Korean consumers may be of relevance. One might argue that as South Korea and Japan are both South-East

TABLE 7.4 Evaluating information sources (adapted from Blumberg et al., 2008: 315)

Evaluating factor	Questions
Purpose	• Why does the information exist? • What is its purpose? • Does it achieve its purpose? • How does its purpose affect the type and bias of the information presented? • How does it relate to the purpose of my own research?
Scope	• How old is the information? • How often is it updated? • How much information is available? • What are the criteria for inclusion? • If applicable, what geographic area, time period or language does it cover? • How does the information presented compare with similar information sources?
Authority	• What are the credentials of the author, institution or organization sponsoring the information?
Audience	• To whom is the information targeted? • What level of knowledge or experience is assumed? • How does the intended audience affect the type and bias of the information?
Format	• How quickly can you find the required information? • How easy to use is the information source? • Is there an index? • Is the information downloadable into a spreadsheet or word-processing program if desired?

Asian states, there may be cultural similarities. Hence, you may not wish to discard the research in the first instance.

Scope

Scope covers such qualities as the age and the amount of data available, whether the information is up to date, how frequently data are updated, what period of time they cover, how information is presented, etc.

Authority

A more well-known and credible authority on a topic is likely to be more reliable than an unknown source. Assessing the credibility of the authority will allow you to determine whether or not the data warrant inclusion in your research.

Audience

The intended audience is a good indicator of the nature and quality of the data. Classifying your data on the basis of commercial and academic content can help you to form a judgement as to its appropriateness for your research.

Format

The format of the data (e.g. whether on hard copy or in an electronic version) dictates the ease with which you can access and interpret the data. Does the layout make it easy for you to find what you need, for example? Can you consult an index? Of course, if the data are vital to your research, you will want to use them irrespective of format.

In sum, it is sometimes difficult to evaluate secondary data. The source may be relatively unknown – even your supervisor may not be aware of its existence! My advice is to try to use secondary data from established sources, which can be verified in some way. In general, if a source is unknown and cannot be verified, then it is probably best avoided.

Presenting Secondary Data

Essentially, two factors are likely to determine how you present your secondary data within your research project. First, whether your data are qualitative or quantitative. Second, whether your data are raw data, or cooked data. If the latter, then you may be in a position to present the data in their original format. For example, if the

TABLE 7.5   FDI by type of investment

	1999		2002	
Type of investment	No. of projects	Value (£m)	No. of projects	Value (£m)
Joint venture	60,253	65,128.5	72,821	88,456.3
WFOE*	5,430	18,676.2	9,073	27,710.5
Total	65,683	83,804.7	81,894	116,166.8

*Wholly foreign-owned enterprise

Financial Times published a pie chart showing a breakdown of the UK's exports by industry, you could probably reproduce this in its original format, providing it is properly sourced, of course. However, if the article only quotes export figures, then you would need to consider presenting the data in your own way.

Table 7.5 illustrates the use of secondary data in its original format. You do not need to concern yourself with the actual topic. The point I am trying to make here is that tables, charts and graphs are ideally suited to many research projects. Indeed, they can form an important part of your secondary analysis.

Presenting secondary data also includes qualitative data. Let us say that you intend analyzing secondary data in the form of leading economists' views on the global economy. As you are analyzing qualitative secondary data, you may illustrate their views by quoting them directly.

There are numerous ways of analyzing qualitative and quantitative secondary data. In reality, many of these techniques are equally applicable to primary data analysis. I will therefore devote greater attention to this topic in Chapters 9 and 10.

Your Project Supervisor and Secondary Data

When a student wishes to see me to discuss concerns over secondary data, it is usually for one of two reasons. First, the student has been unable to locate sufficient secondary sources. Second, they have gathered copious amounts of data but are unsure what to give prominence to in their research. In this chapter, I have covered both these points at some length.

By now, you should be aware of just how important your supervisor is to your research project. This includes their advice on overcoming potential difficulties with secondary data. Your supervisor can provide invaluable advice on how to evaluate your data, and may also be able to recommend secondary sources that you have not yet considered. Moreover, if they feel that your topic provides access to a sparse amount of secondary data, they may be able to offer suggestions about primary data collection. Once again, when you feel yourself 'hitting a brick wall' with your research, do not forget to consult your project supervisor.

How to Link Primary and Secondary Data

If you intend including primary and secondary data in your research project, then it can sometimes be difficult to know how to link these two main sources of data. As previously noted, one way is to compare your primary data with secondary data from books, journal articles, published statistics and other sources. Part of this comparison should involve the analysis and interpretation of data. For example, let us say a UK Government report states that the main reason why joint ventures in China fail is due to cultural differences. Yet, analysis of your primary findings indicates that the leading cause is due to a failure to agree strategic objectives. The key question here is why the difference between the primary and secondary data? To be a good researcher you must compare, analyze and interpret both primary and secondary data and not fall into the trap of simply describing the data.

Secondary data can also be used to increase the credibility of your primary research findings. For instance, if your primary findings support the view of leading authors in the field, one argument that you could make is that your results are likely to be both valid and credible.

Research in Action

Examining sources of secondary data

In the academic article detailed below, an overview is provided on the sources of secondary data used in business ethics research. Irrespective of the topic, much of the content is very useful as it examines sources of secondary data which could equally apply to other areas of business research.

Cowton, C.J. (1998) 'The use of secondary data in business ethics research', *Journal of Business Ethics*, 17 (4): 423–434

The aim of Cowton's (1998) paper is to promote the interest of business ethics researchers in using secondary data, either in place of or as a complement to primary data. The article examines both sources and usage of secondary data, although the details below centre on sources of secondary data. In short, the author is making a call to business ethicists to pay greater consideration to secondary data.

In the article, Cowton highlights a number of sources of secondary data, namely: *governmental and regulatory bodies, the press, companies, other academic researchers* and *private sources*. First, the author suggests that a source of material of considerable interest to business ethicists is the legal system. Examples given here include published legal judgments, while regulatory bodies such as the Advertising Standards Authority (ASA) in the UK publish reports which are often easily accessible to the researcher.

In terms of companies, the researcher stresses that much material is publicly available, particularly in the annual report and accounts. This includes the Chairman's statement that can be analyzed using tools such as content analysis (this is something we cover in Chapter 10). Reference is made to quantitative, particularly company financial, data as an easily accessible source, as this information is now published on a number of databases.

(Continued)

(Continued)

The researcher suggests that both the press and media in general are useful sources of data. Newspaper articles can be used as sources. Also, in some articles you will find opinion polls; the advantage of these is that they distance the researcher from the evaluations. However, it is worth noting that newspaper articles should be treated with care as they have not gone through a peer review process.

Other academic researchers include data by other scholars. Unlike newspaper articles, academic articles are peer reviewed. In addition, there is scope to undertake meta-analysis. This is 'quantitative analysis of a group of studies that investigates the same research questions'. One of the benefits of meta-analysis is that it generates a large sample. One issue for the researcher, though, is the need to perhaps negotiate with the original researcher in order to gain access to the dataset.

Finally, private sources are another potential source of secondary data. Here, the author suggests that these include companies' internal reports and memoranda; this is in addition to organizational archives. However, for the student researcher there are clearly obvious difficulties in accessing such sources. Cowton makes a similar point by acknowledging the potential difficulty of negotiating access.

Cowton's (1998) article is helpful to researchers as it considers a number of different sources of secondary data. A useful exercise would be to look at the entire article, as it also discusses using secondary data. Once again, although the paper focuses on business ethics, many of the author's points are equally applicable to other areas of business.

Summary and Conclusion

This chapter has examined how secondary data can be incorporated into your study. It defined what is meant by secondary data and considered the advantages and disadvantages of using secondary data in your research. It also examined how to evaluate and present secondary data. Here are the key points from this chapter:

- Secondary data are data that have been collected by other researchers.
- Secondary data can be classified into electronic and written formats, and subdivided into commercial and academic purposes.
- The main advantage of secondary data is that such data save time and money for the researcher. The main disadvantages include the potential difficulty in verifying the reliability of the data and whether the data are applicable to your research problem.
- If you have the capability of reading foreign language sources, then this is clearly an advantage as it allows you to consult a wider range of secondary sources.
- Secondary data can be evaluated by considering its purpose, scope, authority, audience and format.
- Your university or college library is likely to contain the majority of secondary data you will need. However, consult your supervisor if you need more specialized data.
- Cooked data can often be presented in its original format, whereas raw data needs to be processed by the researcher.

Helen's chosen topic for her research project is mergers and acquisitions in the European bank-ing sector. As a BSc (Hons) Finance student, Helen has learned that the market has experienced consolidation in recent years, and she is keen to examine the impact of mergers and acquisition (M&A) on the banking sector workforce. She has chosen a case study research design, and intends to analyze two high-profile mergers and one acquisition. All of these took place within the last 12 months.

Helen is fortunate in that her research supervisor's main area of research is similar to her own proposed research topic. She has therefore sought advice from her supervisor on numerous occasions. One of the suggestions her supervisor has made is for her to include a question that examines whether or not the bout of recent mergers and acquisitions looks set to continue.

Fortunately, Helen's topic has received detailed coverage across both the business press and wider media. In addition, in recent months several empirical studies have been published in leading academic journals. Helen also has a list of all the mergers and acquisitions that have taken place in Europe since 2000, including those in the banking sector. The main problem she faces is that this is simply a list from a specialist trade magazine; it provides no detailed analysis or discussion on the companies involved.

Case study questions

1. Suggest an approach that Helen could adopt to evaluate the suitability of the secondary data she has collected.
2. Discuss the potential problems Helen might encounter by only using secondary sources.

YOU'RE THE SUPERVISOR

Pauline has decided to base her research topic on 'key changes in British family life over the last 30 years'. Although this may not seem like a business-related topic, she is interested to see how key changes, particularly household demands, might influence the marketing of cer-tain goods and services. In the first instance, Pauline was very keen to adopt a longitudinal research design, but she now realizes that this is not a realistic option given that her project needs to be fully completed inside 12 months.

Consequently, Pauline has decided to base her entire project on secondary data. She is especially pleased to have discovered the General Household Survey (GHS), and intends using this as her exclusive secondary source of analysis. The GHS includes figures on car ownership, pensions, sport participation and the use of health services. Pauline believes the GHS is ideal for her research as it fully addresses her research problem. The GHS is described thus:

> The General Household Survey (GHS) has been providing key data on life in modern Britain for over 30 years. The annual *Living in Britain* report, the printed and online document that brings its main findings to a wide audience of researchers, students, decision-makers, media and more, adds an extra dimension of explanation, insight and analysis. (National Statistics, 2002)

(Continued)

(Continued)

Much as Pauline would like to carry out primary research, she feels that this is not a viable option due to time constraints. She believes it would be impossible to generate a sample the size of the GHS. Pauline has also ruled out using other secondary data analysis because she believes the GHS fully addresses her research problem. Still, as her research supervisor, Pauline has met you to seek clarification that you share her views in relation to the GHS.

Supervisor question

* Do you agree with Pauline that the GHS should be used exclusively? Give reasons for your answer.

COMMON QUESTIONS AND ANSWERS

1. You have decided to base your research project on the current economic crisis. Your leading research question is 'How has the current economic crisis impacted on trade between the UK and USA?' Suggest possible sources of secondary data that you might use to answer this question.

Answer: Figure 7.1 provides an eclectic range of secondary sources. The majority of these are likely to be ideal for the above topic. Moreover, you may also find that each country's respective Chamber of Commerce and Embassy websites offer useful information. The important thing here is to try to consult a wide range of secondary data. At the time of writing, the global financial crisis continues to dominate daily news. Consequently, you should have no trouble in finding an abundance of information. Remember that the main advantage in consulting a wide range of secondary data is the likelihood of greater reliability.

2. Can I base my research project entirely on secondary data?

Answer: Some universities and colleges insist that primary data must also feature in a research project. However, this tends to be more applicable to postgraduate rather than undergraduate programmes. If in doubt, check with your research supervisor. If you decide to only refer to secondary data, then it is worth considering explaining to the reader why you have opted not to undertake primary research. For instance, one reason might be that there is already a plethora of data on your chosen subject so you do not feel the need to include primary data.

If you are permitted to conduct your research using purely secondary data, consider the following questions:

* Can my research problem be addressed by simply including secondary data?
* How significant might the contribution of primary data be to my research?

3. Can I use foreign language sources in my research project?

Answer: The short answer is yes. This is clearly an advantage for the student researcher as it allows access to a wider range of sources. However, one drawback is the time it takes to consult both English and foreign language sources. Hence the importance attached to considering the five factors when evaluating secondary data – purpose, scope, authority, audience and format.

4. Suggest the possible advantages of using secondary data in an electronic format.

Answer: There are two key advantages associated with using secondary data in electronic format – time and organization. The ability to access an extensive range of articles electronically will save you a great deal of time, which you can then spend on accessing a wider range of sources or analyzing your findings in greater depth. The organization of your findings can also be more easily achieved using electronic sources. For example, a vast amount of data can now be transported manually on a single USB memory stick.

References

American Marketing Association (2013) 'Secondary data sources', http://www.marketingpower.com/Community/ARC/Pages/Research/SecondaryData/default.aspx, accessed 7 August 2013.

Blumberg, B., Cooper, D.R. and Schindler, P.S. (2008) *Business Research Methods* (2nd edn). Maidenhead: McGraw-Hill.

Cowton, C.J. (1998) 'The use of secondary data in business ethics research', *Journal of Business Ethics*, 17 (4): 423–434.

Gall, G. and Allsop, D. (2007) 'Annual hours working in Britain', *Personnel Review*, 36 (5): 800–814.

National Statistics (2002) 'Living in Britain: Results from the General Household Survey', online source: http://webarchive.nationalarchives.gov.uk/20100520011438/statistics.gov.uk/lib2002/default.asp, accessed 19 September 2013.

Waters, D. (1997) *Quantitative Methods for Business* (2nd edn). Harlow: Addison Wesley Longman.

Wilson, A. (2006) *Marketing Research: An Integrated Approach* (2nd edn). Harlow: Prentice Hall.

Further Reading

Bryman, A. and Bell, E. (2011) *Business Research Methods* (3rd edn). Oxford: Oxford University Press.

Cooper, D.R. and Schindler, P. (2008) *Business Research Methods* (10th edn). Maidenhead: McGraw-Hill.

Quinlan, C. (2001) *Business Research Methods*. Andover: Cengage Learning.

Saunders, M.N.K., Lewis, P. and Thornhill, A. (2012) *Research Methods for Business Students* (6th edn). Harlow: Prentice Hall.

Stewart, D.W. and Kamins, M.A. (1993) *Secondary Research: Information Sources and Methods* (2nd edn). Newbury Park, CA: Sage.

PART 3

PROBLEM SOLVING AND DECISION MAKING

Introduction

Williams, S.

We are faced with hundreds of decisions every day. We chose when to get up this morning, what clothing we would wear, and even whether to read this book. Most of the consequences of the decisions we make throughout our day are relatively trivial or inconsequential. It probably didn't matter too much if we decided to sleep an extra 15 minutes this morning or if we selected the blue shirt rather than the green one. However, some of the decisions we make can carry substantial consequences. Choosing to get an undergraduate or graduate degree, deciding on a new job or career, or selecting one vendor out of many candidates to be our company's long-term supplier of a necessary resource are important decisions that are likely to have a significant and meaningful impact on our lives. Learning, understanding, and applying critical thinking and creative problem-solving skills can improve the quality of the decisions that mean the most to us.

Many of our decisions don't need much thought. Relatively small, routine, or mundane choices generally don't require us to spend a lot of time or energy because the outcomes associated with these types of decisions probably don't affect us very much. In other cases, however, we need to spend time to *think* about our decisions, especially those related to solving problems.

Important decisions can shape our lives, and our decision quality is improved if we critically and creatively analyze the problems facing us by considering new and different options, weighing the evidence objectively, looking at a problem from a different angle that gives us different insights, developing novel solutions that effectively solve our dilemmas, and accurately forecasting the probable impact of our decisions.

To think critically and solve problems creatively, we must first understand how decisions are made and the factors influencing our decision-making processes. Much of what is taught through formal education concerns how decisions *should* be made. Although an understanding of rational decision making helps to explain decisional processes, behavioral decision theory is concerned with how people actually *do* make decisions. If we as decision makers are aware of the factors influencing both our interpretation of problems and the methods we use to solve them, then we are better able to see subjective patterns of behavior in our own decision actions and take steps to minimize and avoid their possible negative impact on what we decide. If we are aware of how the mind processes information and how biological, physiological, and psychological factors influence thinking, we are better prepared to address their probable influence on our decisions. And if we are aware of conceptual blocks that hinder our creativity and innovation, then we are better able to overcome their constraining effects and unleash the creative potential in our minds.

Do you have trouble making decisions? If so, you're not alone. Most of us find decision making difficult, as the list in Table 1.1 demonstrates. This book distills what behavioral science has discovered related to how people, especially those in business, make decisions. Findings presented here are derived from supportive research representing what we currently know about decision making and problem solving. The information presented in the following chapters should enable decision makers to recognize and focus on the truly important decisions that require critical thinking, to analyze options more clearly and creatively, to reduce decisional time and effort, and to improve judgment quality. Awareness and application of the material contained here not only will enable us to improve our own decisions, but also will provide the means for us to understand how and why others decide as they do.

Critical thinking is a process that emphasizes a rational basis for what we believe and provides standards and procedures for analyzing, testing, and evaluating our beliefs (Rudinow & Barry, 1994). Critical thinking skills enable decision makers to define problems within the proper context, to examine evidence objectively, and to analyze the assumptions underlying the evidence and our own beliefs. Critical thinking enables us to

TABLE 1.1 Decision-Making Difficulty

Type of Decision	Percentage of People Who Have Trouble Making This Type of Decision
Making political choices	76
Buying life insurance	73
Choosing the best school for their children	72
Buying a new car	71
Selecting clothing to wear	63
Planning how to lose weight	61
Choosing a doctor	55
Deciding where to vacation	52

SOURCE: Data are drawn from *U.S. News and World Report*, February 5, 1990, p. 74.

understand and deal with the positions of others and to clarify and comprehend our own thoughts as well. When critical thinking is applied, all aspects of the decision process are involved, from defining the problem, identifying and weighing decision criteria, and generating and evaluating alternatives to estimating the consequences that will result from our decisions. However, critical thinking does *not* mean that we always make the best possible decision, never reach the wrong conclusion, and never make mistakes; it is simply a process we apply that enables us to arrive at superior decisions consistently.

Creativity results in the production of novel or new ideas (Amabile, 1988). *Creativity* means doing things differently: being unique, clever, innovative, or original. Creative solutions are those that aren't limited by self-imposed boundaries, those that consider the full spectrum of options from logical to seemingly illogical, and those that result in the creation of new and improved ways of doing things.

Critical thinking involves determining what we know and why we know it; *creativity* involves generating, considering, and using new ideas, concepts, and solutions. Applied together, the two strategies enable decision makers to analyze objectively and reason out the situation facing them and to come up with different and potentially unexpected ways of addressing and correcting problems.

This introduction provides some background information and offers an example of the *rational decision process:* the method generally believed to be used by decision makers and the method our education system teaches us to apply. However, rational decision making rarely occurs in the real world, at least for most of the complex, complicated, and unique problems facing business decision makers. To the extent we are able to meet the assumptions underlying the application of the rational process, our decisions approach optimality, but these ideal circumstances rarely (if ever) occur. Instead, we tend to shortcut the process and latch onto the first potential solution that meets our minimum expectations so we can move on to the next problem facing us in our busy lives.

Part I of this text lays the foundation for understanding the many internal factors that influence our decisions. As living beings, we have a host of biological, emotional, and psychological processes that (often without our knowledge) affect how we make decisions, and the chapters in this section analyze how these elements alter and distort our thinking ability. Part II focuses on understanding how we know what we know. The chapters in this section explore the elements of critical thinking: our attitude and belief infrastructure, which sets in motion our interpretation of what we hear, considering the source of information presented to us, weighing alternative explanations for what we are told, and testing the facts as we understand them. Part III deals with thinking creatively. In these chapters, a framework for creativity is offered, the stages of creativity are presented, and creativity-enhancing techniques are discussed.

Many of the decisions we make and the problems we face don't require much in the way of critical thinking or creativity. Applying rational decision techniques or intuition can most likely solve our everyday routine, repetitive, and minor problems. Using rules of thumb or general guidelines can speed up the decision process, and the results are generally "good enough" for the current situation—thinking critically and solving problems creatively take time and effort, and we should apply these scarce resources where they are most needed. As decisions become more important and problems become more difficult, the energy required by critical thinking skills and creative problem solving can improve the quality of our thought processes and increase the likelihood of uncovering optimal solutions.

If not all decisions require us to be critical in our thinking and creative in our problem solving, how are we to know when to apply these skills? To understand when the use of critical thinking skills and creative problem-solving techniques will be most beneficial, we need to know something about the type of decision to be made, and we need to understand how decisions *should* be made under perfect conditions. If we subjected every decision we made to what is known as the rational decision process, we would end up with the best, most optimal solution all the time. Of course, this would also mean that we would make very few decisions and that we would spend most of our time attempting to solve problems and very little time actually implementing solutions. Under ideal conditions (in other words, not in the real world), problem solving should model the following steps.

THE RATIONAL DECISION PROCESS

If decision makers had access to all the relevant information they needed, had enough time and energy to reach the best possible solution, and were unimpeded by "being human," they would always use the rational decision process. All of us strive to make the best decisions we can, but we are usually limited by certain constraints. Sometimes, we don't have enough information or enough time, or we just aren't sure what we need to do to develop an optimal answer. We would like to make the most reasonable, logical, and objective decision possible, but we are seldom able to arrive at an optimal solution. Most of the time, to the extent possible, we try to be as rational as we can by using what economists term the rational decision-making process, a problem-solving approach that involves the following sequence of events: problem identification, criteria definition, alternative generation and evaluation, and implementation (see Figure 1.1).

Problem identification. To come up with a rational solution, decision makers must first recognize that a problem exists. This sounds obvious, but research has demonstrated that problem definition is not as straightforward as it would seem. Is a 5% sales decrease a problem? What about a 2% decline? Is a 20% increase a problem if our company has limited production capacity? Rarely are the situations we confront clearly labeled as *problem* or *nonproblem*. In addition, people can distort, ignore, omit, and discount information to such an extent that they often deny they are

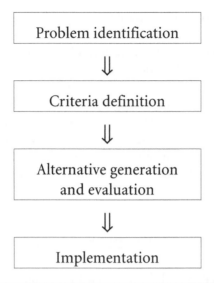

Figure 1.1. The Rational Decision Process

faced with a problem (Cowan, 1986). Managers with a morale problem in their department may convince themselves that the situation isn't quite as bad as some believe, or even that the symptoms they witness are related to something else entirely and no problem exists. Cultural factors have also been found to influence the extent to which individuals perceive a situation as a problem. For example, an American manager might define a notice from a prime supplier that necessary construction materials will be 3 months late as a problem, whereas a more situation-accepting Asian manager might not call the identical situation a problem because Asian cultures are more likely to believe that the outcome is simply fate or God's will (Adler, 1997).

Criteria definition. Most problems are multidimensional, and decision makers must determine what factors should be considered to resolve the problem they are facing. Perfectly rational decision makers would identify all the relevant criteria that might influence the decision process. The range of possible objectives for a specific problem might include price, quality, features, dependability, reputation, and so on. If certain criteria are not identified as relevant, then they have no impact on the subsequent decision process. Once the important criteria are found, the decision maker needs to recognize that not all of the factors are equally important to problem resolution. For example, people are often willing to sacrifice higher quality to gain a lower price. A difficulty many problem solvers face is that they fail to take into account an important criterion when considering their options, or they allow irrelevant criteria to influence their judgment. Although we might initially think service availability is unimportant when we make our decision to purchase office computers, we may later discover that on-site maintenance is critical after an employee experiences a computer breakdown. Or we may have identified all the important decision criteria correctly, but then we allow irrelevant factors such as persuasive sales pressure or emotional appeal to sway our judgment unduly.

Alternative generation and evaluation. At this stage, the decision maker identifies all the possible courses of action and evaluates each alternative against the established criteria. A rational decision maker would generate a list of all possible alternatives that are likely to resolve the problem and proceed to weigh the advantages and disadvantages of each. Fully rational decision makers assess the possible consequences of selecting a given alternative for each of the identified criteria, resulting in a ranking of possible solutions from most likely to resolve the problem (or the best possible solution) down to the least likely. Generating a full range of possibilities is extremely important because research has demonstrated that the quality of the final solution can be significantly improved by considering as many alternatives as possible (Maier, 1970). Rational evaluation involves considering the extent to which applying a particular solution will create additional difficulties, the extent to which those involved in the outcome will accept and be able to implement the alternative, and the extent to which the alternative considers organizational constraints and additional external factors.

Implementation. Once the optimal option has been discovered, the final step involves implementing and following up on the solution. Many decisions, especially those in organizations, require the assistance of others (those who didn't make the decision) to carry them out. Implementation concerns getting the commitment of those needed to achieve the objective and monitoring to be sure that correct implementation occurs.

Expecting a solution to be successfully implemented by participants who fail to support or even disagree with the objective is likely to be unrealistic. Again, studies demonstrate that commitment to and implementation of the solution are enhanced to the extent those responsible for implementation participate in the decision process and accept the given solution (Locke & Latham, 1988). Implementation also involves acquiring feedback to determine whether the solution adequately resolved the problem and the overall effectiveness of the solution.

AN EXAMPLE OF THE
RATIONAL DECISION PROCESS

Problem identification. To demonstrate how the rational decision process should work, consider how a manager would decide which brand of vehicles would best meet the needs of the company. The first step is to recognize that a problem exists: how to deliver our product to our customers. Notice that the problem statement dictates to a large degree what criteria and alternatives will be considered in the following phases. Asking how we can best deliver our products is a different question from asking what type of vehicle we should purchase. The range of options a manager might consider related to delivering products is much broader than those the manager would deem necessary for selecting an appropriate vehicle. For example, alternatives for delivering products might include leasing transportation, subcontracting delivery to a carrier service, and using public transportation, as well as the possibility of buying a fleet of delivery vans. Let's assume that the manager has considered all viable ways to identify the given situation and has correctly analyzed the problem as the need to purchase a number of delivery vehicles.

Criteria definition. Now, the manager needs to come up with the objectives that are important when considering the type and quantity of vehicles to buy. A thoroughly rational decision maker would develop an exhaustive list of all possible criteria and rank each factor as to its degree of importance. Table 1.2 shows how a scale of 1 to 10 might be used to weight criteria importance for this example. When considering how many and what kind of transportation vehicles the company requires, the manager might think that size, fuel economy, comfort, safety, cost,

TABLE 1.2 Possible Criteria Weighting

Criterion	Weight (from 10 to 1)
Initial price	10
Fuel economy	8
Durability	8
Performance	7
Interior comfort	4

reliability, and a host of other considerations are important. Once the criteria have been developed, the relative value of each will have to be determined. Is price more important than size? Is fuel economy more critical than comfort? How much will each vehicle carry, and how many will be required? Does reliability carry more weight than safety, and so forth.

Alternative generation and evaluation. With the relative importance of all criteria in mind, the manager will then come up with a list of possible manufacturers and the extent to which the products they offer satisfy the relevant criteria. The offerings of automobile makers such as Ford, Chevrolet, Toyota, Honda, and so on will need to be learned, and each possibility will have to be carefully assessed against the established standards. If price, availability, and fuel economy are the most important factors, how do the different styles rank? If the manager discovers all possible vehicles, weighs the possibilities against all possible criteria, and ranks the results, the optimal choice should be obvious. An example of the weighting for four possible vehicles is shown in Table 1.3, and Table 1.4 presents the final ranking of the four choices.

Implementation. Now that the manager knows which van will meet the company's needs and how many are required, the actual purchase needs to occur. The extent to which this solution resolves the identified problem needs to be determined. Does the purchase of this line of vehicles adequately solve the problem of delivering our products to our customers? Has the resolution been implemented correctly, and do any modifications or corrections need to be made?

TABLE 1.3 Examples of Decision Criteria Weighting

Alternative	Initial Price	Fuel Economy	Durability	Performance	Interior Comfort
Vehicle 1	5	6	10	7	10
Vehicle 2	7	8	5	7	6
Vehicle 3	2	7	10	4	9
Vehicle 4	10	7	3	5	3

To the extent that the manager exhaustively followed the procedures outlined above, the quality of the decision solution approaches the optimal. Unfortunately, decision makers rarely have the time, means, and cognitive abilities to apply the rational decision process. For example, problems are often identified in terms of the solution. In fact, we often bias our judgments of the strengths and weaknesses of the alternatives we consider to make them fit with the way we've identified the problem (Langer & Schank, 1994). If the company is experiencing a decrease in productivity, a manager might identify the problem as "We have to get rid of Joe because he's lazy and incompetent." Joe may indeed be the cause of a lack of performance, but the rational decision process will only derive an optimal solution to the extent that the "real" problem is identified. "How can we replace Joe?" is a fundamentally different problem than "How can we improve productivity?" As the purchasing example above demonstrated, identifying a delivery problem in terms of the need to buy trucks frames the problem in terms of the solution, which narrows the range of alternatives the decision maker will generate and consider in an attempt to resolve the identified problem. Defining the problem too narrowly or, worse yet, defining the wrong problem will result in a poorer outcome. As folk wisdom indicates, "It isn't the things you don't know that get you into trouble, but the things you know for sure that aren't so." Problems that are stated clearly and do not contain unwarranted assumptions or preconceived biases greatly influence our ability to optimize solutions. To the extent decision makers identify and frame problems correctly, the rational decision process works very well in leading to the best possible result.

TABLE 1.4 Assessment of Alternatives

Alternative	Initial Price	Fuel Economy	Durability	Performance	Interior Comfort	Totals
Vehicle 1	50	48	80	49	40	267
Vehicle 2	70	64	40	49	24	247
Vehicle 3	20	56	80	28	36	220
Vehicle 4	100	56	24	35	12	227

NOTE: In this table, the weighting values from Table 1.2 are multiplied by the data in Table 1.3 to provide final values.

If the real problem has been correctly and accurately identified, the best solution still may not be selected if the right criteria are not considered. If we have identified the problem as the need to purchase delivery vehicles, we will not be able to determine which of the many possible brands will best meet our needs if we fail to include all the criteria that could influence our judgment. We might evaluate the complete range of delivery vehicle brands available based on price, quality, fuel economy, and dependability but fail to consider the accessibility of parts for repair as an important factor. Only after we've bought our fleet of vans do we discover that repairs are difficult because replacement parts have to be shipped from the other side of the globe; if we had included the service criterion in our original list (or at least considered it more thoroughly), we would likely have made a different (and one can hope a more optimal) decision. On a more personal level, anyone who has gone through the car-buying process knows how automobile salespeople target transient or rationally irrelevant criteria in an attempt to get you to purchase the vehicle of their choice, not yours. You may have gone to the car dealer completely prepared with your list of relevant criteria indicating what was important to you in a family car: price, comfort, affordability, economy, and so forth. However, the salesperson is able to target your impulsive side by having you take the two-door speedster for a test drive, and you end up with a red convertible instead of the station wagon you meant to buy. Critical thinking skills greatly increase our ability to identify problems and develop relevant criteria.

Even if the decision maker does an excellent job of properly identifying the problem and developing and ranking all the relevant judgmental criteria, the best solution may not be achieved if the optimal possibility is not included as one of the possible solutions. In fact, many times we even fail to consider all of the alternatives we have generated because we make up our minds about the "right" decision quite early and then massage information to support our implicit favorite and convince ourselves that further consideration is unnecessary because the already-made decision was the correct one (Langer & Schank, 1994). If we have correctly identified the problem as the need to purchase delivery vehicles and accurately listed our weighted criteria, we will not be able to determine the best possible brand if we are unaware that it is a viable option or if we distort our beliefs about other candidates to justify our preferred choice. To solve our delivery vehicle problem, we generate a list of all vehicles manufactured by Ford, General Motors, and Chrysler but are unaware that Hyundai makes a commercial delivery van that suits our needs admirably. Or we consider all cargo vans but fail to include the full range of possibilities, such as other types of transportation: semitrailers and covered trucks. Or we have a preferred alternative because we prefer Ford products and fail to give subsequent options serious consideration because this predecision de-emphasizes the other options (Power & Aldag, 1985).

An even more disastrous outcome would be if we selected the best delivery van, but the solution created greater problems due to unforeseen consequences, such as a lack of enough parking space to house the fleet on arrival or an inability to find enough qualified drivers to operate the vans due to a need for specialized expertise. All possible alternatives must take into account both short- and long-term consequences; it does little good to solve the immediate problem but create a more difficult situation later on. It is primarily in the area of alternative generation that creativity can have the greatest impact on decision making.

The rational decision process has been successfully followed and the optimal solution has been found, but even the best answer may not resolve the problem if it is implemented incorrectly. After careful and thorough consideration, the optimal resolution of our delivery vehicle problem is discovered to be a fleet of Korean cargo vans. Rationally, the vehicles appear to be the "best" choice. However, certain factions within the vehicle maintenance department hold strong pro-American views and believe the company's decision to purchase foreign vehicles is "unpatriotic," and they are less than enthusiastic about seeing the new line achieve success. This lack of support manifests itself in decreased efficiency and even episodes of sabotage. To determine whether the solution has actually solved the identified problem, feedback needs to be gathered and assessed. Do the new cargo vans resolve our dilemma of how to ship our product to the customer? Does the solution generate any unforeseen complications? Has the situation been altered in some way that results in a different problem or in a less effective solution? Often, the "best" solution in the business world may be not the one that generates the most profit but instead the choice that maximizes the chances that the strategy will be accepted and completely implemented.

THE RATIONAL DECISION PROCESS

In December of 2000, Motor Trend magazine announced that it would select a winner of the Motor Trend 2001 Sport Utility Vehicle Award, a prestigious and highly sought after honor. Of the dozens of sport utility vehicles manufactured, only all-new or substantially revised SUVs available in North America by January 1, 2001, were eligible for consideration, and 12 candidates were selected for testing. The 12 vehicles were compared according to their design, engineering, performance, interior, special features, safety, off-road capability, and value.

Motor Trend's comments about the rational decision process? "Twelve vehicles. 10 editors (not to mention two photographers, plus our own road test and TV crews). Weeks of testing. Hundreds of gallons of gas. At least a gross of fast-food burgers, plus enough road snacks to feed an army. Long days and late nights." The winner? Acura's MDX at almost $40,000.

—*Motor Trend* (December 2000, pp. 35-57)

Here's a story about an employee who was faced with a tough choice. Although objective criteria favored one option, his intuition prompted him in another direction, and he couldn't make up his mind. After agonizing about the proper course of action, he finally took the problem to his boss. She listened attentively to his description of the situation and said,

Well, first of all, make sure you've identified the problem correctly. Once you've done that, develop a list of all pertinent criteria and weight them according to importance. Then generate as many alternative solutions as you can and compare each to your standards, keeping in mind that the rest of us will have to implement whatever you decide. After you've finished the process, you should have the best solution.

The employee chuckled at the manager's suggestion and replied, "No, really, this is a *serious* problem." Although the rational decision process may sound appealing, many of us feel that "serious" problem solving should somehow involve more: perhaps instinct, intuition, and gut reaction.

The rational decision process makes some fundamental assumptions about how decision makers gather and look at problem-solving information (see Figure 1.2). Under complete rationality, decision makers see problems clearly and unambiguously, and they have complete information regarding the decision situation. Possible solutions will lead to a single, well-defined goal, presenting no conflicts with other goals while allowing a maximal payoff. All criteria and alternatives can be identified, ranking preferences are clear and unchanging, and the decision maker is aware of all possible consequences associated with each. Time and resources are abundantly available to pursue various possibilities and to contemplate probable outcomes. However, most of the problems we face in the real world don't meet the required conditions to allow complete rationality (March, 1994).

Complete application of the sequence of problem identification, criteria definition, alternative generation and evaluation, and implementation as outlined above will invariably result in an optimal solution. Why don't we use the rational decision process all the time if it will lead to the best result? Decision makers, especially business people who rarely have enough time or resources to accomplish all they desire to do, don't particularly like problems. Problems amount to frustration: Things aren't going the way we would like for them to go—something is interfering with our goal attainment. Our natural tendency is to select the first reasonable solution that seems to resolve the current situation (March & Simon, 1958). Unfortunately, the first solution that meets our needs often isn't the optimal solution or even one of the better alternatives.

```
┌─────────────────────────────┐
│      Problem is clear and     │
│         unambiguous           │
└─────────────────────────────┘
               ⇓
┌─────────────────────────────┐
│    Single and well-defined    │
│     goal can be identified    │
└─────────────────────────────┘
               ⇓
┌─────────────────────────────┐
│  Alternatives (and consequences) │
│         are all known         │
└─────────────────────────────┘
               ⇓
┌─────────────────────────────┐
│  Preferences and needs are clear, │
│   recognized, and unchanging  │
└─────────────────────────────┘
               ⇓
┌─────────────────────────────┐
│     Time and resources are    │
│    abundant and accessible    │
└─────────────────────────────┘
               ⇓
┌─────────────────────────────┐
│  Decision will be implemented │
│  willingly and supported by all │
└─────────────────────────────┘
```

Figure 1.2. Assumptions of Rational Decision Making

BOUNDED RATIONALITY

Nobel prize-winning author Herbert Simon has suggested that business decision makers are constrained from making the best possible decisions due to very real limitations in their thinking abilities (March & Simon, 1958; Simon, 1957). Simon (1990) coined the term *bounded rationality* to explain that although decision makers strive to be fully rational (to make the best or most optimal decision), they are limited or bounded by a number of factors:

1. A lack of complete or fully accurate information
2. A scarcity of the time and resources required to search for more information and to formulate a full spectrum of options
3. An inability to retain more than a small amount of relevant information in the memory to attack the problem
4. Intelligence and perceptual limitations that inhibit the ability to calculate optimal outcomes

Given these constraints, decision makers "satisfice" or willingly accept a decision that is reasonable rather than continue to search for the best possible solution (March & Simon, 1958). We tend to implement solutions that are satisfactory or marginally acceptable instead of looking for the ideal or perfect response.

Even though boundedly rational problem solving leads to systematic errors in our decisions, we usually prefer satisficing instead of continuing to seek out the optimal solution. Why? Many if not most times, a solution that is good enough adequately and cheaply addresses our needs, whereas more elaborate and thorough approaches are unduly expensive and time-consuming (Conlisk, 1996). Decision makers recognize that a trade-off exists between thinking and accuracy (Pitz & Sachs, 1984). Consequently, we identify problems by lumping them with previous problems that seem similar, we limit our criteria to those we believe are most important, we rank the criteria based on our own preferences and self-interests, we come up with very few alternatives, we start with our preferred option and assess our alternatives one at a time against the criteria, we evaluate possibilities until we find one that is sufficient and satisfactory, and we allow corporate politics and power related to implementation to sway our judgments while failing to measure all the decision's possible results (see Table 1.5).

Rational decision making is a time-consuming, systematic process. The reality of business life is that we don't have the time, energy, or resources to use the rational process for most of the hundreds of decisions

TABLE 1.5 Comparing Rational Decision Making and Bounded Rationality

Decision-Making Step	Rational Decision Making	Bounded Rationality
Problem definition	Real problem is identified	Problem primarily reflects the decision maker's interests, understanding, and needs
Criteria definition	All relevant criteria are identified and weighted appropriately	Limited criteria are identified, and evaluation is influenced by self-interest
Alternative generation and evaluation	All options are considered, and all consequences are understood and taken into consideration	Limited options are identified, favored option is given priority, and consideration halts when a "good enough" solution is found
Implementation	All participants understand and support the solution	Politics, power, and self-interest influence the amount of acceptance and commitment to the solution

we face every day. For example, managers perform a different activity about every 9 minutes while at work (Mintzberg, 1975). We are simply unable to do our jobs if we attempt to be too analytical and too thorough, so we prefer to use intuitive judgment whenever possible. Businesspeople reach a speedy outcome by using simplifying strategies or rules of thumb to assist them in their decisional endeavors, and these standards work well most of the time. Painstaking application of the rational thinking process should be reserved for when decisional outcomes are of increasing importance. Even though we are constrained by many of the limitations discussed above, the closer we approximate the rational model, the more likely our decisions will approach the optimal. However, several factors affect not only our ability to make rational decisions but the intuitive rules of thumb we use as well. These internal influences on decision making will be the focus of Part I.

The rational decision process involves defining the problem, developing criteria, generating and evaluating alternatives, and implementing our decisions. It works very well under those conditions in which we have the time, resources, and willingness to practice it properly. Although it is unlikely we can ever apply the rational process completely, we can improve the effectiveness of our use of this approach if we consider the possibilities suggested in Table 1.6 (Whetton & Cameron, 1991).

SUMMARY AND REVIEW

This section introduced us to the *rational decision process,* which is a decision-making model stressing the thorough evaluation of all components of a decision. When using rational decision making, we would define the problem, identify and weight criteria that are important to the problem, generate and evaluate a comprehensive list of alternative solutions to the problem, and finally, implement our solution and follow up on it to assure that the problem has been resolved. Unfortunately, although decision makers strive to reach optimal solutions, we are generally unable to execute the rational process to its fullest extent. Decision makers are constrained by bounded rationality, a host of human limitations that lead us to satisfice or willingly settle on a solution that is good enough rather than seeking the best outcome possible.

TABLE 1.6 Effective Use of Rational Problem Solving

When Defining the Problem

- Differentiate facts from opinions
- Specify underlying causes and symptoms
- Be as explicit as possible in stating the problem
- Identify any violated standards or expectations
- Determine who actually owns the problem
- Avoid stating the problem in terms of a solution
- Encourage participation of those involved

When Identifying and Weighting Criteria

- Be as complete as possible in recognizing relevant criteria
- Maintain objectivity when weighting criteria
- Recognize that criteria that are not explicitly stated become irrelevant to the subsequent decision
- Be aware of how personal preferences influence criteria

When Generating and Evaluating Alternatives

- Postpone evaluating alternatives until completing the generation process
- Allow those who will be influenced by the decision to be involved
- Bear in mind the results desired and specify alternatives that are consistent with desired results
- Build on the ideas of others
- Be systematic and evaluate all options
- Compare to both desired results and an optimal standard
- Keep in mind potential side effects and weaknesses
- Be explicit in stating selected alternative

When Implementing and Following Up

- Be aware of implementation timing
- Provide opportunities for feedback from those involved
- Gain the acceptance of those affected by the decision as much as possible
- Establish a monitoring system to provide feedback
- Evaluate based on problem solution rather than side benefits

Strengthening Teams and Conducting Meetings

Quintanilla, K. and Wahl, S.

A s Target CEO, Gregg Steinhafel made it a critical point never to use the word *I* when talking about the company. "At Target, nothing happens without a large, collaborative effort," said Steinhafel (Dishman, 2012). What began as a single discount general store in 1962 has since become a 1,772-store-strong multibillion-dollar company. Much of Target's success is attributed to the culture of teamwork within the company, which business journalist Lydia Dishman covers below:

- **Collaborative communication–at scale.** Team members at all levels—from stores, distribution centers, and headquarters—are encouraged to use Target's vast array of social media tools to communicate (Dishman, 2012). One platform, known as Redtalk, follows the Facebook model of social communication. Target team members can post comments, respond to others' comments, and "like" posts. These social media outlets not only cement the collaborative spirit, but also make the team better equipped to sell Target products and services.

- **Mentoring and feedback not left to chance.** Customized one-on-one programs begin for every employee at the start of employment. Also, there are company-wide initiatives to gain feedback and make improvements at every level. Target also has national sales "meetings" that are more like gala events, with events that recognize individuals and teams for special achievements and performance.

- **Meeting customers where they are–online.** Plans are in place for Target to add Wi-Fi to all its stores so that customers can complete their shopping trip at the cash register or on Target.com via smartphone. "All the senior leaders like to sit down and forward think, and anticipate where the puck is going," Steinhafel said. "We benchmark against the world's best to develop ideas for future growth" (Dishman, 2012).

As you study this chapter, try to use Target's teamwork strategy as a yardstick for your own educational and professional life. Do you receive enough collaboration and feedback from your peers and professors in school? How about work? After reading this chapter, you should be able to identify what teamwork practices make for an effective organization.

Many college students make the mistake of picking a career under the assumption that it will not require them to interact with other people on a regular basis. In the communication age, however, you will almost certainly be expected to work well with others in a team environment. This chapter identifies the needs and functions of communication in a team setting and shows what benefits can be gained by working well in a group with your coworkers.

Have you had unpleasant group experiences? Are there times you'd prefer just to do the project yourself because it would be easier? Well, if you don't like working in groups, we have some bad news for you—working with others is part of every job, regardless of the field. If you want to excel in your field of interest, you need to learn how to work with others. The good news is that by using the KEYS process, you can turn your groups into innovative, functional teams. In this chapter, you'll be introduced to a variety of communication strategies that will help you lead this transformation.

Team communication is important for the following reasons: (1) Your ability to relate with other people in teams is central to achieving professional excellence, (2) team communication helps you form professional connections with coworkers and accomplish professional projects, and (3) your ability to work effectively in teams is a critical skill that will play an important role in your success as you *develop in the workplace.* Let's begin with a look at the important role of team communication at work.

HOW DO GROUPS DIFFER FROM TEAMS?

Is there a difference between groups and teams? Although executives and managers often use these terms interchangeably, their definitions do differ (Katzenbach & Smith, 1993; Kinlaw, 1991; West, 2012). For those seeking professional excellence, understanding this difference is essential. The small-group theorist Marvin Shaw (1981) states that a group is "two or more persons who are interacting with one another in such a manner that each person influences and is influenced by each other person" (p. 8). Central to this definition are the concepts of relationship, interaction, and influence.

If you go to see a blockbuster movie on opening night, you'll be part of an audience that you might refer to as a "group" of people. You may call the audience a group, but it would not fit our definition of a group since the moviegoers have no relationship, interaction, or influence on one another. For our purposes, a group is defined as three or more individuals who are working toward a common goal or share a common purpose. As a result of their common goal or purpose, they have relationships, interaction, and influence with one another.

Similar to groups, teams also have common goals and purposes. Further, like group members, team members have relationships, interaction, and influence with one another. The difference between groups and teams resides in the nature of those relationships and interactions (Levi, 2011; Myers & Anderson, 2008). A team is defined as a group in which members share leadership responsibility for creating a team identity, achieving mutually defined goals, and fostering innovative thinking (Lumsden & Lumsden, 1997; Moe, Dingsøyr, & Dybå, 2010). This definition highlights four key differences between groups and teams. First, unlike group members, team members share leadership responsibilities. There may be one team member who has a leadership title such as manager, vice president, or coach, but

all team members demonstrate leadership when it comes to defining goals, making decisions, and implementing ideas. Second, team members share an identity. They refer to their team as "us" and "we," as opposed to "the group" or "them." Third, group members work toward common goals, while team members not only work toward common goals but also help define what those goals will be. Finally, teams strive for innovation. According to Katzenbach and Smith (1993), "A working group relies primarily on the individual contributions of its members for group performance, whereas a team strives for a magnified impact that is incremental to what its members could achieve in their individual roles" (p. 88).

WRITE YOUR NOTES HERE

CONDUCTING MEETINGS

According to an old adage, groups outperform individuals, and teams outperform groups. If you wish to achieve professional excellence in the workplace, you must learn to transform your groups into teams. Effective communication is essential for this transformation.

Meetings are the central form of team communication (Boerner, Schäffner, & Gebert, 2012; Myers & Anderson, 2008). During meetings, leadership can be shared, goals and purposes can be defined, a team identity can be developed, and innovation can be fostered. The ability to effectively participate in and lead meetings is an important component of professional excellence and a key to transforming groups into teams. On the flip side, poorly run meetings are a major roadblock stopping many groups from ever becoming teams and many group members from achieving professional excellence.

WRITE YOUR NOTES HERE

For meetings to run effectively, a few basics must always be considered. These basics include the meeting environment, the meeting topics, and the meeting participants.

MEETING ENVIRONMENT

Creating the proper meeting environment is a vital but often overlooked component of effective communication. What is a meeting environment? It includes both the time a meeting is held and its location. The meeting environment is as much a part of the communication that occurs as the words that are said. Unfortunately, despite the importance of the meeting environment, most people spend little time thinking about it when they plan their meetings.

Currently, there are hundreds of shows and entire television networks dedicated to designing the perfect room or creating the perfect space. Why? The physical environment, from the color on the walls to the furniture to the lighting, has a major impact on us (Ivy & Wahl, 2014; Kupritz & Hillsman, 2011). Look around the room you are in right now. Why did you select this room for studying? How does this room make you feel? How does the room positively impact your studying? How does it negatively impact your studying? Now think about various places where you have attended meetings. How did those environments impact communication? We hope you are beginning to see the importance of meeting environment (see Tools for Professional Excellence 7.1).

Know Yourself:
UNDERSTANDING GROUP BEHAVIOR

As you read the index below and answer the questions, think about how this knowledge can help you be a better communicator.

Most students have many opportunities to develop their communication skills during class projects that require group work. The first step in developing your group into a team is to know yourself. Think about the last group project you completed for school. Take the following quiz and see how many times you displayed behaviors that did not reflect a team attitude or professional excellence while working with that group. Place a check beside every violation you have committed.

_____ 1. Came to meeting without completing your assigned task

_____ 2. Made the following statement: "No one told me what I had to do" or "I was not sure what to do, so I didn't want to do it wrong"

_____ 3. Missed a meeting without giving your group members advance warning

_____ 4. Missed a group meeting and did not proactively find out what you needed to do for the next meeting

_____ 5. Participated in a meeting without an agenda

_____ 6. Gossiped about a fellow group member

_____ 7. Pushed your ideas forward without allowing others to express their ideas

_____ 8. Did not share a concern because you did not want to start a conflict or cause the meeting to last longer

_____ 9. Discussed a problem with the professor before discussing it with your group member(s)

_____ 10. Wasted others' time by coming to a meeting late and/or discussing issues that were not relevant to the project

_____ 11. Accepted the first "okay" solution, as opposed to working toward an innovative idea

How did you do? For true professional excellence, you should not have a single check. Throughout this chapter, we will discuss why each of these areas is important for excellence in team communication. If you did earn some checks, what can you do to eliminate those behaviors in the future? Are there other behaviors that you believe should be listed here? What are those behaviors, and why do you consider them violations of excellence as a team member?

If you wish to create an effective meeting environment, what factors should be considered? First, you must consider the time. Time of day, time of week, and time of year can all influence communication. For example, holding a meeting at 8:00 on a Monday morning, 4:30 on a Friday afternoon, or right after lunch may not be the best choice if you want your team members to be fully engaged and alert. Trying to implement a large-scale change is probably a bad idea during the busy holiday season in November and December, but it may be the perfect thing to do in January to kick off the new year. When selecting meeting times, be aware of differences in team members' schedules. If team members work different shifts with different days off, meeting times should be varied. For example, if half the team works from 7:00 a.m. to 3:00 p.m. and the other half from 3:00 p.m. to 11:00 p.m., holding every meeting at 9:00 a.m. would repeatedly inconvenience the same half of the team. When team members work varied schedules, there is no ideal time to meet. Yet alternating the meetings between shifts shows that all team members are valued and respected, which positively impacts communication interactions.

Location is also an important component in creating a positive meeting environment. In fact, you should consider the convenience, aesthetics, and comfort of the location. As far as convenience, Maelia learned the impact it can have on communication in a meeting. When Maelia began her job as the district supervisor, she held all the district meetings at 8:00 on Monday mornings in her office. Her intention was to start each week fresh by clearly communicating goals and priorities. Unfortunately, this was not the message Maelia sent; both the time and the location were inconvenient for the rest of the group. Most of the managers found themselves commuting to and from Maelia's office during rush-hour traffic. Furthermore, the managers felt they were needed in their stores first thing on Monday mornings, not at a meeting across town. The location and time of the district meetings indirectly sent the message that Maelia considered herself the most important person in the group and that she didn't care about her managers' schedules or duties. This message didn't support the notion of shared goals and shared leadership necessary for transforming groups into teams. In fact, it created a negative environment that hindered communication during the meetings. Fortunately, Maelia realized her mistake. When she moved the district meetings to Mondays at 2:00 p.m., she allowed her managers to have the time they needed in their stores on Monday mornings. She also varied the location from week to week, holding meetings at different stores throughout her district. By considering the time and location, she was able to improve the meeting environment and begin transforming her group into a team.

WRITE YOUR NOTES HERE

When selecting a meeting location, you should also consider aesthetics and comfort. Many leaders get in the habit of holding all their meetings in the same room. For example, there is only one conference room in our building, so a lot of meetings are held there. The problem is that the conference room has an extremely long and narrow table. When sitting at the table, team members can't see one another, making it very difficult to hold discussions or brainstorming sessions. Further, the room is very dull and uninspired, with no windows and poor lighting. Fortunately, there is another room two floors down that has movable tables, excellent lighting, and a great view

TOOLS FOR PROFESSIONAL EXCELLENCE 7.1
THE MEETING ENVIRONMENT

To set up an effective meeting environment, consider these questions:

- Is the time convenient to those who will be attending?
- Has enough time been allotted to discuss all the topics?
- Are there too many topics?
- How long is the meeting? Will we need breaks?
- How long is the meeting? Will we need beverages and/or food?
- Are there audiovisual needs? Is the location equipped to meet those needs?
- Does the furniture support conversations? Can everyone see one another easily?
- Is the furniture comfortable? Is there enough elbow room?
- Is the location convenient to those who will be attending?
- Does the location send any unintended messages? Is the location considered anyone's turf?
- Is the location aesthetically pleasing?
- Is this the best time and location available?

Step Back and Reflect:
A DAY AT THE MUSEUM

As you read this passage and answer the questions, step back and reflect on what went wrong in this professional situation.

I (Kelly Quintanilla, one of your coauthors) have taught many successful workshops to business professionals over the years, workshops in beautiful locations with enthusiastic participants. I also taught one workshop that appeared to be doomed to fail before it even began. The topic of this 6-hour workshop was conflict management. The group was a department whose members were currently engaged in a battle with one another. Literally, half the department was not speaking to the other half. Some of the best department members had put in for transfers. Productivity and customer service were suffering.

Knowing all this in advance, I had carefully selected a large room with comfortable chairs, round tables, and good lighting. I had planned for several breaks with food and drinks in an attempt to foster informal communication. The meeting environment was ideal. Unfortunately, an emergency water outage caused the workshop to be moved to a room in one of the local museums. The meeting was scheduled to begin at 8:00 a.m., but many people arrived late due to the last-minute change in location. Those who arrived on time became increasingly agitated as they waited. Part of their agitation stemmed from the

fact that there was no coffee, no food, nothing. Despite several calls, the food order never made it to the new location. The only place to get a drink or snack was a small, extremely overpriced gift shop that did not open until 10:00 a.m. To make matters worse, the room had about 40 mounted animal heads hanging from the walls. The animal heads, most of which were in a growling pose, were very dusty, causing anyone with allergies to begin sneezing and sniffling. The final problem was the furniture. The chairs were the small, metal, folding kind. The tables were also small, and there were not enough of them, so the participants were crammed together. I could not imagine a worse meeting environment for any group, let alone a group already engaged in conflict. I needed to do something quickly.

STEP BACK AND REFLECT

1. What went wrong?
2. What would you do if you were in my position?
3. Could you overcome the meeting environment?
4. Could the situation be used to your advantage somehow?
5. Should the workshop be called off and rescheduled?
6. How could I use the KEYS approach to improve this communication interaction?

WRITE YOUR NOTES HERE

outside the window. Using this room does require proactive scheduling, a short elevator ride, and some furniture rearranging, but the aesthetics create an atmosphere that is more conducive to effective communication.

The length of the meeting should factor into your assessment of comfort. Pay close attention to the furniture. Make certain that the chairs are comfortable and that team members have enough elbow room. If you cram your team members into a small space with uncomfortable furniture for any length of time, it will be difficult for them to remain productive.

Keep in mind that comfort extends beyond furniture. For longer meetings, you should consider taking short breaks, allowing people to stretch, visit the restrooms, and refresh their perspective. If your budget allows for it, consider providing food and beverages in meetings.

In the end, you may not always have the ability to change the time or location of your meetings. Regardless, considering both time and location for every meeting is part of professional excellence.

MEETING TOPICS (AGENDA)

One essential component of any well-run meeting is an agenda. An agenda is a guide or an overview of the topics that will be covered during the meeting. An agenda can be simple or complex. Either way, an agenda is a useful channel for informing team members about meeting topics and, if used properly, can serve as a communication tool for facilitating meetings (see Figure 7.1).

Agendas should be distributed several days in advance of the meeting. This will allow team members to comment on the agenda items and give the leader time to revise the agenda if necessary. It will also give team members time to think about issues in advance of the meeting. If you'd like the participants to brainstorm ideas or share information, the agenda is a valuable preparation tool for team members.

Noting the allotted time for each topic also helps the leader determine which topics and how many can be covered in any given meeting. Leaders with professional excellence prioritize agenda items. Items should be prioritized based on importance and urgency. Items that require extensive discussion time should be handled at a separate meeting or series of meetings dedicated solely to that topic. If a leader is truly seeking the input of team members, then he or she should not try to force too many items into one meeting.

Heading: Should include date, time, and location. May include a list of participants.

I. Welcome/opening
The leader should always orient the team and focus the meeting during the opening.

II. Approve minutes from the previous meeting
Minutes are a written record of the meeting.

III. Specific points to be discussed
The majority of the agenda will be a list of the specific items that will be covered during the meeting. Beside each item, state who will lead the discussion and/or report on this item. It is also wise to include the estimated time it should take to cover each item.

IV. Old business
Allow time for the team to discuss items from previous meetings that may still be unresolved.

V. New business
Allow time for the team to discuss any new items that may have come up after the agenda was finalized or during the meeting itself.

VI. Arrangement of the next meeting
Summarize any assignments that must be completed by the next meeting. Also make certain to discuss the time and location of the next meeting.

VII. Closing
Always provide some sort of closing statement.

FIGURE 7.1
AGENDA FORMAT

ETHICAL CONNECTION
OVERTALKING VS. UNDERTALKING

As you read this passage and answer the questions, consider how the way you communicate has an ethical dimension.

Team leaders can also use an agenda as a tool for facilitating communication during meetings. Let's say one member of your team, Parker, tends to dominate conversations, occasionally leading the discussion on irrelevant tangents. Parker is an overtalker. Another member of your team, Alyssa, tends to sit silently during meetings, failing to participate or give input. Alyssa is an undertalker. The few times Alyssa has tried to communicate during meetings, she is cut off by Parker, who often moves the conversation in a different direction. During several of your one-on-one sessions with Alyssa, you have noticed that she is very insightful and has many great ideas to help out the company. Although Parker is motivated and eager to participate in meetings, you notice he has a hard time focusing

on one topic at a time. To keep your meetings moving effectively and professionally, you must find a way to curtail Parker's speeches while not cutting him off entirely. Also, you need to encourage Alyssa to interact more and to have the confidence to state her ideas to the entire staff.

QUESTIONS TO CONSIDER

1. What are the ethical issues with allowing one person to dominate or one person not to participate in a team or staff meeting?
2. How could you limit Parker's speaking without making him feel as though he is being cut off?
3. What methods or communication could you use to encourage Alyssa to be more active in team meetings?
4. Using the KEYS approach, how could both Alyssa and Parker strengthen their team communication skills?

MEETING PARTICIPANTS

When it comes to planning meetings, you should ask yourself two important questions. First, who should be at this meeting? Determining the participants in a meeting should not be based on office politics. Leaders with professional excellence avoid the trap of inviting a representative of each department in order to be politically correct. Invite people who can contribute to the purpose of the meeting. Take time to assess the meeting's purpose, and then determine who can best serve that purpose. Second, can all key members attend this meeting at this time? If key team members can't be present, the meeting should be rescheduled. For example, you should not hold a meeting about budgetary issues if the CFO (chief financial officer) can't attend. You'll waste the time of everyone who does attend, and the team will still need to meet again with the CFO.

Failing to consider meeting environment, meeting topics, and meeting participants hinders the chances for a successful meeting, but covering the basics does not, in and of itself, guarantee success. For meetings that will transform groups into teams, all members must share leadership, develop positive problem-solving strategies, strive for innovation, and participate in productive conflict. Let's take a moment to explore each of these important elements.

SHARED LEADERSHIP

As you learned earlier in this chapter, teams require members to share leadership. How do team members share leadership? What is the role of the designated leader if all members are sharing his or her duties?

There are many designated leadership titles (e.g., director, manager, supervisor, vice president, president, queen). Regardless of your title, if you're the designated leader, think of yourself as a coach. A coach has a very distinct role in meetings. Remember, a coach does not play the game. The coach must remain on the sidelines. The coach doesn't have to be an expert on everything, have all the answers, or do all the talking. However, the coach does need to call the meetings, set the agenda, and then facilitate the discussion. A coach facilitates the discussion by supporting positive team roles and norms while eliminating self-centered roles and unproductive norms.

TEAM ROLES

Within every team, members can play a host of possible roles. Some of these roles are functional roles that help the team achieve goals or maintain positive relationships among members (see Table 7.1). These roles are known as task roles and relationship roles, respectively. Unfortunately, there are also many dysfunctional roles that can interfere with the positive functioning of the team. These roles are known as self-centered roles. For a group to become a team, all team members must actively engage in the functional roles while working to limit the dysfunctional roles.

As a coach utilizing the KEYS approach, you should *know* the skills and strengths you bring to the team and *evaluate* the skills and strengths of your team members. After *your communication interaction* occurs, coaches must *step back and reflect* to determine if all the functional roles are being covered. If not, redesign the agenda or add team members who will cover the gaps. For example, if no one is giving his or her opinion, the coach might add an agenda item that calls for everyone to provide input on a topic. If the group lacks a harmonizer, the coach may add a new member to the team who is skilled at handling conflict. You should never hesitate to talk about the way the team is interacting. It's a sign of professional excellence to address weaknesses head-on. So if you're the coach, make certain your team is aware of the various tasks and relationship roles. Make it a habit to discuss the team's strengths and weaknesses. Make it a habit to step back and reflect on the communication as individuals and as a team. And when the team notes dysfunctional roles, be prepared to address those behaviors directly. (We discuss dealing with difficult people in more detail in Chapter 10.)

TEAM NORMS

When you attend class, you probably sit in the same seat every time. Why? You don't own the seat; it's not yours. Still, if someone else sat in the seat, it would bother you, right? You might even ask that person to move. There's no written rule, no seating chart stating that this is your seat—it's simply a norm.

What's a norm? A norm is an unwritten rule of behavior. Although norms are unwritten, they are as powerful as (if not more powerful than) the written rules. Think about the organizations for which you have worked. Do they have an employee handbook or a policy book? Ever taken the time to read a handbook? Many employees fail to take the time to learn the written rules. Instead, they follow the unwritten rules or norms they see other people enacting in the workplace.

Our point is this—if you want to function with professional excellence, you should read your employee handbook! You should know the written rules and expectations. (We also recommend you spend some time familiarizing yourself with your student handbooks.) Knowing both the written and unwritten rules is important for communicating

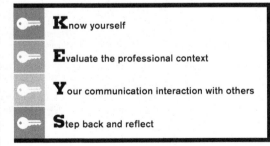

Know yourself

Evaluate the professional context

Your communication interaction with others

Step back and reflect

TABLE 7.1
TEAM ROLES

TASK ROLES: ROLES THAT HELP THE TEAM CARRY OUT TASKS AND GET THE WORK DONE	
ROLE	**CHARACTERISTICS**
Initiator	Proposes solutions; suggests ideas; introduces new approaches to problem solving
Information giver	Offers facts or generalizations; relates one's own experience to the problems to illustrate points
Information seeker	Asks for clarification of suggestions; requests additional information or facts
Opinion giver	States an opinion or belief concerning a problem and suggests solutions to that problem
Opinion seeker	Looks for an expression of feelings from group members; seeks clarification of values, suggestions, or ideas
Coordinator	Shows relationships among various ideas or suggestions; tries to pull together ideas and suggestions
Procedural developer	Takes notes; records ideas; distributes materials; guides group through the agenda
Summarizer/evaluator	Restates ideas and describes relationships; details agreements and differences
RELATIONSHIP ROLES: ROLES THAT STRENGTHEN OR MAINTAIN TEAM RELATIONSHIPS	
ROLE	**CHARACTERISTICS**
Supporter	Expresses togetherness; encourages others; gives praise; suggests solidarity
Harmonizer	Mediates and reconciles differences; suggests areas of agreement between disagreeing members; suggests positive ways to explore difference
Gatekeeper	Asks opinions of members who are not participating; prevents dominance by others; facilitates overall interaction
SELF-CENTERED ROLES: ROLES THAT INTERFERE WITH THE TEAM'S ABILITY TO COMPLETE TASKS	
ROLE	**CHARACTERISTICS**
Blocker	Gives negative responses to most ideas; is negative about any positive solutions; raises continuous objections
Dominator	Controls through interruptions, superiority of tone, and length of conversation control
Attacker	Aggressive to achieve personal status; expresses disapproval; critical of status of others
Clown	Disrupts with jokes and other diverting behavior; brings up tangents; refuses to take ideas seriously

SOURCE: Adapted from Benne and Sheats (1948).

with professional excellence. At times, these written and unwritten rules will complement each other and lend themselves to norms that are productive for your team. At other times, the written and unwritten rules can contradict each other, resulting in negative consequences for both you and the team.

Let's look at Lina for an example. In Lina's office, the written rule related to cell phones was very clear: "No use of personal cell phones during company time." Yet the norm was for employees to take personal calls all day long. Further, employees would leave meetings to answer their cell phones and/or send text messages during the middle of group discussions. This was clearly a negative norm.

All groups have both positive and negative norms. The important thing is to step back and reflect on the norms and assess how various norms are affecting your group. Your objective is to turn your group into a team by eliminating the negative norms and building on the positive norms.

But how do you eliminate negative norms? You have to address them. You can't ignore them and just expect them to fix themselves. To achieve professional excellence, you must be willing to say, "Here is something that is going wrong; let's find a way to correct the problem as a team." It's equally important to recognize the positive norms. When a norm is contributing to the success of the team, it should be acknowledged and actively supported by the team.

> WRITE YOUR NOTES HERE

PROBLEM SOLVING

In the opening section of this chapter, we introduced you to the definition of a team. If you recall, a team is defined as a group in which members share leadership responsibility for creating a team identity, achieving mutually defined goals, and fostering innovative thinking.

To achieve mutually defined goals, teams engage in problem solving. *Problem solving* and *decision making* are not interchangeable terms. Decision making is actually a step in the problem-solving process. According to Dennis Gouran (1982/1990), a leading scholar in group communication, decision making is "the act of choosing among a set of alternatives under conditions that necessitate choice" (p. 3). Problem solving involves not only making a choice but also coming up with quality alternatives from which to select and then working to implement the choice your team selects.

How can you ensure that your team generates innovative alternatives and/or successfully implements its choice? Begin by understanding all the steps in the problem-solving process. At some point in your academic career, you probably learned John Dewey's Reflective Thinking Process or some other problem-solving model based on his process. According to Dewey (1910), five steps make up problem solving:

1. Describing and analyzing the problem

2. Generating possible solutions

3. Evaluating all solutions

4. Deciding on the solution

5. Planning how to implement the solution

Your Communication Interaction

THE FUNDRAISER

As you read the passage below, consider what would be a more effective communication strategy in this situation.

Henry is the chairman of his organization's fundraising committee, and the organization's big annual fundraiser is quickly approaching. There are only a couple of meetings left before the fundraiser, and Henry and the rest of the committee are feeling the pressure to pull off another successful event. Tensions are high among the committee members, which leads to an argument between two members, Tim and Angela. During the meeting, every time Angela brings up which band to hire for the fundraiser, Tim interrupts her to talk about picking up more sponsors. After the third time, Angela snaps at Tim, demanding to know why he keeps interrupting her. Tim says that they are running out of time and that there are more important topics to discuss than what band to hire. Angela looks to Henry for support, but he stays silent.

Feeling embarrassed, Angela storms out of the meeting, leaving awkward silence behind her. Henry decides to call the meeting then and there, and stays behind to get more work done. Later that night, after having a few drinks, Henry calls Angela and leaves her a voicemail saying how much he values her as a committee member and as a person.

QUESTIONS TO CONSIDER

1. As the committee chair, what responsibility (if any) does Henry have when committee members begin to argue?
2. Do you think Henry reacted appropriately to Tim and Angela's argument? Why or why not?
3. Was Henry's response to Angela appropriate? Why or why not?
4. If you were Angela, how would you respond to Henry's voicemail?

Within each step, you have the opportunity to excel or struggle. Let's examine each of the steps to see how effective communication can help team members achieve professional excellence.

DESCRIBING AND ANALYZING THE PROBLEM

It seems only logical that the first step in problem solving is to describe and analyze the problem. After all, how can you solve a problem if you do not know what the problem is? Alas, this vital step is often shortchanged or skipped altogether. The reason for this mistake is simple. There is an assumption that "we already know what the problem is." The leader has defined the problem in his or her own mind, so he or she may feel that the group's time would be better spent discussing solutions. Group members are comfortable with skipping this step because they, too, have defined the problem in their minds. Unfortunately, the group leader and various group members, in all likelihood, do not share the same definition. Based on their individual experiences and perceptions, they probably have a different take on the nature of the problem or unsatisfactory state. By failing to understand the problem from all sides, a group limits its chances of generating a solution that will truly correct all facets of the problem.

Teams take time to discuss the problem. Team members share their own insights and experiences. In addition, they actively seek and share feedback from other employees and relevant parties who are not part of the team. When determining meeting participants, careful consideration is given to the makeup of the team in an attempt to include diverse perceptions of a problem. When analyzing a problem, group members must look at the current conditions realistically to determine the nature, extent, and probable cause(s) of the problem (Choy & Oo, 2012; Gouran & Hirokawa, 1996; Kauffeld & Lehmann-Willenbrock, 2011). Further, failure to recognize potential threats or to clearly understand the situation can result in poor decisions.

GENERATING POSSIBLE SOLUTIONS

Once a problem is clearly understood, team members can begin generating possible solutions. Avoid tossing around a few ideas; find one that is satisfactory, and then move on to the next step. Do not stop with an "okay" solution. Teams seek innovative solutions that address all facets of a problem.

For better or for worse, your formal education has trained you to look for the "right answer" (Von Oech, 1983). One consequence of taking thousands of multiple-choice exams in your lifetime is that you have become skilled at marking the right answer and then moving to the next question. This skill is useful when demonstrating your knowledge of a given subject area, but it's not very useful when trying to think critically and develop innovative solutions. There's an old proverb that states, "There are seven right answers to every question." Teams subscribe to the wisdom of this proverb.

Fortunately, there are many tools that can aid your team in generating possible solutions. Those tools include brainstorming, nominal group technique, idea writing, and role playing. See Tools for Professional Excellence 7.2 for a detailed description of each tool. (We will continue our discussion of innovative thinking later in this chapter.)

EVALUATING ALL SOLUTIONS

Once possible solutions have been generated, the team must begin the process of evaluating the merit of each solution based on criteria. Criteria are the standards used to make a decision. For example, if your company was developing a new advertising campaign, the

---

TOOLS FOR PROFESSIONAL EXCELLENCE 7.2
TOOLS FOR INNOVATION

To generate innovative ideas or solutions, consider these practical tools:

TOOL	DESCRIPTION
Brainstorming	A technique for generating many ideas quickly. The goal is quantity, not quality, so all ideas should be expressed and written down. No ideas should be criticized or praised. Members are not permitted to speak for longer than 10 seconds at a time—no long explanations. Ideas will be evaluated and elaborated on at a later point in the problem-solving process.
Nominal group technique	A type of brainstorming designed to incorporate all team members. Rather than having team members yell out their ideas, nominal group technique has members brainstorm independently, writing down their ideas on a piece of paper. After a set amount of time has passed, members stop writing and read what they have written. All the ideas are then recorded on a chalkboard or somewhere the entire group can view them.
Idea writing	This technique combines brainstorming and the nominal group technique. With this technique, team members begin brainstorming and write their first idea down on the top of a piece of paper. Each member then passes his or her paper to the right, reads the idea on the paper, and then adds another idea. This process continues until the paper is full. All the ideas are then read aloud and displayed for the group to see.
Role playing	A technique used to increase team members' understanding of various points of view. A team member will put himself or herself in the place of someone else. It may be another group member or someone not present at the meeting, such as the customer. The team member will then try to answer questions about the problem from the point of view of the person he or she is playing.

TOOLS FOR PROFESSIONAL EXCELLENCE 7.3
TOOLS FOR EVALUATION

To evaluate ideas and possible solutions, try these practical tools:

TOOL	DESCRIPTION
Keep/scratch	A technique for limiting the number of alternatives the team will discuss in detail. Display all the alternatives so that all team members can see them. Have the leader read each alternative. If a member of the team wishes an alternative to be considered further, he or she will yell "keep." If no one yells "keep," the leader will cross out or scratch the alternative. No one should ever yell "scratch."
Value rating	A technique for reducing the number of alternatives the team will discuss in detail. Team members are given a set number of points (or stickers). Each member distributes his or her points to the alternatives he or she would most like to discuss. If each team member has 10 points, he or she may give 5 points to Alternative A, 3 points to Alternative C, and 2 points to Alternative F. The alternatives that receive few or no points will be cut before the discussion begins.
T-chart	A visual representation of the pros and cons of each alternative. Team members draw a T, large enough for everyone to view easily. One side of the T is labeled "Pros," and the other side is labeled "Cons." The team then brainstorms the pros and cons of the alternative in question, recording their comments on the chart. The pros and cons are rated in accordance with the criteria.
Decision matrix	A decision matrix is similar to a T-chart. It is a visual representation of the merits of various plans. It allows team members to compare alternatives easily. The merits are rated in accordance with the criteria.

criteria might include that it must reflect the company's current image, be easy to remember, have a positive feel, reach the target audience, be in place within 6 months, and not cost more than $10,000 to implement. Your criteria should always include budgetary considerations and deadlines. Your team may come up with a highly innovative solution, but if you can't afford to implement it or if it can't be implemented by a preset deadline, then that solution is not the right choice.

How do you evaluate solutions? Teams develop a systematic process for evaluation. Just as there are tools to help generate possible solutions, there are also tools to help teams evaluate solutions. These tools include keep/scratch, value rating, T-chart, and decision matrix. See Tools for Professional Excellence 7.3 for a detailed description of each.

If the leader is actively facilitating discussion and if the team members are actively engaged, a thorough evaluation of solutions will be a natural function of the team. All teams should routinely test and question the quality of information used as the basis for both problem analysis and possible solutions. In addition, teams should routinely question their assumptions and biases.

If this type of critical evaluation is not occurring naturally, one or more team members should be assigned to the role of devil's advocate. The devil's advocate has the task of making sure dissenting points of view are discussed. The questions provided in Tools for Professional Excellence 7.4 can help guide the team through this evaluation process.

DECIDING ON THE SOLUTION

Once the merit of all the solutions has been thoroughly evaluated and discussed, it's time to make a decision. This decision will become the goal or desired state that the team will then work toward. Four approaches to decision making are available to the team. These approaches include decision by the leader, voting, compromise, and consensus.

DECISION BY THE LEADER

When the decision by the leader approach is used, members are not truly functioning as a team. The role of the members is to recommend or advise the leader. The leader then makes the ultimate decision. As a result, the goal is not mutually defined. In some instances, this approach may be the best way to make a decision. For example, if an emergency room team needs to make a quick decision about an unfamiliar medical situation, the physician in charge may ask the advice of colleagues and/or medical staff. Yet, due to the need for a quick decision, the physician will ultimately determine the course of action. Although this approach has benefits in pressure situations, it's not the preferred approach for building teams.

WRITE YOUR NOTES HERE

VOTING

The concept of voting is another way to reach a decision. With this approach, team members cast a vote for the solution they find most meritorious. The solution that receives the most votes is implemented. There are some obvious advantages to voting. First, all team members have equal input in the decision. Next, it is an easy process that often requires little more than raised hands or slips of paper for casting votes. Finally, it requires little time in comparison with the compromise or consensus approaches. However, voting as a decision-making approach also comes with some disadvantages. Because it is quick and easy, voting is often used to speed up the decision-making process and avoid any lengthy discussions or conflict. Conflict, as we discuss later in this chapter, is a valuable, needed resource in innovative problem solving and team building. Limiting this process can result

TOOLS FOR PROFESSIONAL EXCELLENCE 7.4
QUESTIONS TO GUIDE THE EVALUATION

To help guide a team through the evaluation process, consider these questions:

- Do we have enough information?
- Do we understand the information we have?
- Are we missing any information? Are any areas not covered by the information we have?
- Are our sources reliable, credible, and appropriate?
- Are the criteria appropriate given our objectives and constraints?
- Did we generate a variety of innovative alternatives?
- Did we limit our alternatives?
- Did we apply the criteria to each alternative fairly and appropriately?
- Did the team agree on the mode of decision making?

SOURCE: Gouran (1982/1990).

in quick decisions that lack innovation and cause division. Voting is a win-lose approach to decision making. Unfortunately, not everyone makes a good loser—or a good winner, for that matter—so voting can divide the group and stop it from becoming a team.

COMPROMISE

Team members approaching decision making with a "let's compromise" attitude is a positive thing, right? After all, compromise is a win-win approach, isn't it? Actually, compromise is a lose-lose approach to decision making. Although it is a commonly held belief that compromise is a good thing, compromise can limit innovation. With compromise, all parties are willing to give up something in order to gain something they want; so the goal becomes narrowing options, not developing innovative ideas. Jake and Marilyn used the compromise approach on their last date. Jake wanted to eat ribs and see an action movie. Marilyn wanted sushi and a romantic comedy. So they compromised and spent their evening eating ribs, which made Marilyn miserable, and watching a movie that Jake hated. Both parties were unhappy for half the evening; it was a lose-lose situation. If they had searched for some additional options, they would have discovered that pizza and bowling would have made them both happy for the entire evening.

CONSENSUS

The final approach to decision making is consensus. Consensus occurs when a solution or agreement that all team members can support is reached. This does not mean that the final solution is one that all team members prefer; rather, it means that the solution has the support of all team members. In an ideal world, team members might be able to come up with an idea that everyone loves and thinks is the best way to go, but most times that doesn't occur. Thus, finding a solution that everyone supports has many positive benefits. This support results in a stronger commitment to implementing the solution

---

Evaluate the Professional Context
WINTER CARNIVAL IN SNOWY MOUNTAIN

As you evaluate the passage below, consider whether this behavior is appropriate for this professional context.

The Snowy Mountain Tourist Department was tasked with developing new promotional events to attract skiers during the upcoming season. Over the years, this resort community had been steadily losing business to other ski destinations. Sasha Adams, the department manager, was willing to admit that her ideas were just not competitive, so she turned the task over to her department.

Sasha was thrilled to learn that her department generated three creative ideas. The problem was that supporters of each idea felt very strongly that their idea was the best, and they could not narrow it down to one event. Sasha honored her commitment to allow the group to make the decision, so she had department members vote. Three votes went to a winter comedy festival, three votes went to a winter sports event, and four votes went to a winter carnival.

Sasha had high hopes that the winter carnival would increase tourism, but it decreased department morale instead. The four members who had voted for the carnival were very involved, but more than four people were needed to run the event. In the end, it was not a success. The other six members felt that their events would have achieved much better results. Were they right?

QUESTIONS TO CONSIDER

1. What went wrong?
2. Was voting the best way to make this decision? Why or why not?
3. How would you have handled the decision-making process?
4. Could the KEYS approach have helped Sasha? If so, in what way?

TOOLS FOR PROFESSIONAL EXCELLENCE 7.5
IMPLEMENTING YOUR SOLUTION

To create a clear plan for implementation, take note of the following points:

- State the objective clearly and concisely.
- List the major steps that must be completed in order to accomplish the objective.
- Prioritize the steps. What are the most critical elements? Which are less critical? What can you do now? What will you need additional resources for?
- Under each major step, list all the tasks (substeps) that must be completed in order to accomplish the step in question.
- Place all the steps and tasks on a timeline. Focus on the sequence in which steps and tasks must be completed. Adjust the timeline accordingly.
- Estimate the cost of each step and begin to develop a budget. Revisit the budget often.
- Assign a lead for each step. Multiple leads may be needed for some steps—different leads for different tasks.
- Anticipate obstacles. What obstacles stand in the way of success? How will your team deal with these obstacles?

and strengthens the relationship between team members. Further, working through the consensus process lends itself to innovative decision making.

So why aren't all decisions made using consensus? Because consensus is time-consuming. Many leaders and/or groups do not see the value in spending time working through the consensus process. Although consensus is more time-consuming as a decision-making approach, decisions reached using consensus can often be implemented quickly because they have the support of all members. As a result, consensus may be less time-consuming than voting or compromise, especially when the process is looked at from beginning to end. It certainly is the most likely to result in mutually defined goals.

PLANNING HOW TO IMPLEMENT THE SOLUTION

Once the solution is reached, it must be implemented. Walking away from the table with a great solution is not a success if that solution never comes to fruition. Teams make certain their solutions are implemented by developing a thorough, detailed plan. When implementing a solution, all facets of the implementation must be accounted for in both a timeline and a budget. In addition, a lead—the person who's accountable for a given task—must be designated. Designating leads is an excellent opportunity to share leadership. The team member with the leadership title should not be the lead in all facets of the implementation plan. Rather, leads should be selected based on their areas of expertise and their passion for various parts of the plan. To ensure a thorough plan, your team should address all of the suggestions found in Tools for Professional Excellence 7.5.

CULTIVATING INNOVATIVE THINKING

Whereas groups conduct problem-solving meetings with little thought of innovative solutions, teams structure their meetings and facilitate the problem-solving process in such a way that innovation is stimulated. After all, teams, by their very definition, must foster innovative thinking.

One way to foster innovation in team problem solving is to incorporate Von Oech's (1986) explorer, artist, judge, and warrior into the process. Incorporating Von Oech's cast of characters doesn't require team members to dress up in costumes and run around acting like explorers or warriors. Rather, the skills and tools displayed by explorers, artists, judges, and warriors are meant to highlight or reinforce the skills and tools essential to creative problem solving. Let's examine each character to better understand its role in cultivating innovative thinking.

EXPLORER

When analyzing a problem and preparing to generate solutions, team members should act as explorers. Explorers seek out new information in uncharted lands. As explorers, team members follow their curiosity, create a map, leave their own turf, and look for a lot of ideas and information (Von Oech, 1986). A team in the explorer mode might ask, "What's the problem?" or "Why aren't we the leader in sales?" or "How can we do it better?" Then, team members are given the task and the time to seek new information that addresses the question(s). This task turns into a map of sorts, as it provides team members with a general guideline to follow when searching. The interesting thing is, once this map is in your mind, you will begin to see relevant information everywhere. If you have your doubts, think about the last time you purchased a car—did you suddenly start seeing similar cars (color and type) everywhere you went? Were they there before? Of course they were, but they were not on your map, so they blended into the background scenery.

As long as you have your map, leaving your turf can become a rewarding adventure. For example, the famous football coach Knute Rockne discovered his "four horsemen defense" while watching a chorus-line dance, and Picasso's art was the inspiration for World War I military camouflage (Von Oech, 1986). Looking both inside and outside your field and your type of business/industry for information and insight is what will make your team innovative. In fact, one distinct advantage of team members with diverse backgrounds is that they bring different perspectives into the team. Put simply, send the team members out to explore and make certain they come back with lots of information that can be molded into innovative solutions during the artist phase.

ARTIST

As the team begins to generate solutions, members move from the role of explorer to the role of artist. The artist puts ideas together in new ways. When you hear the word *artist*, what images come to mind? Do you see a painter, a sculptor, or someone who's handy with a hot-glue gun? That's certainly one way to look at an artist, but in reality an artist includes those images and so many more. Someone who puts ideas together in a new way is an artist. You may not be able to paint or sing, but if you can develop a chart or a schedule, you, too, are an artist. Earlier in this chapter, we discussed some tools useful to the artist (see Tools for Professional Excellence 7.2). Three additional tools your team can utilize to enhance the artist are asking "what if" questions, connecting concepts, and incubating (Von Oech, 1986).

Two small words—"what if"—are essential to finding innovative solutions. For example, a team of hospital administrators was determined to improve patient satisfaction scores. During the explorer phase, they examined successful hospitals and medical arenas for information. In addition, they left their turf and explored other places where people stay overnight, such as hotels. In the artist phase, they asked themselves "what if" questions, such as, "What if we were a five-star hotel?" By connecting hotels and hospitals, they gained a new perspective on the problem. They began to offer free valet parking at the emergency room, and they added a staff position—patient and family liaison—that functioned much like a concierge in a hotel. Not surprisingly, patient satisfaction scores increased.

Just as explorers need time to explore, artists need time to incubate. When do you have your most inspired ideas? Is it during a meeting within moments after a problem has been thrown on the table? Or does your inspiration come to you in the shower or after a good night's sleep? Maybe your creative ideas come when you're on the treadmill, sweating away your stress or singing along with your iPod. Truth be told, we have yet to meet a single person who can achieve creative inspiration on command. We certainly can't. If you want innovative solutions, your team needs time to explore resources and discover information. Then team members need time to allow that information to germinate in their minds and grow into something that is more than just okay or so-so.

JUDGE

Once a team has developed lots of innovative ideas, it moves into the judge mode as team members evaluate the possible solutions and then select one solution for implementation. Judges begin with the question, "Are we meeting our objective?" Then, they systematically examine the positives and negatives of each solution and render their decision (Von Oech, 1986).

WARRIOR

Innovative problem solving does not end with the judge mode. Warriors are needed to make certain that the plan is implemented successfully. The role of the warrior is to develop and carry out the plan. We have already discussed how to develop a thorough plan and the importance of leads who will act as warriors overseeing and/or carrying out various parts of the plan. Yet warriors must do more than that. Ask yourself, "Why did Von Oech select a warrior to represent the skills needed in this phase of innovative problem solving?" First, all plans will hit obstacles and roadblocks. As a result, team members must be strong and ready to overcome inevitable difficulties. Furthermore, innovative ideas are more likely to be criticized and attacked because they are different. When your team moves forward with a plan that is outside the box, others may want to stuff it back in the box. Therefore, team members must act like warriors, carrying out the plan with persistence (see Figure 7.2).

FIGURE 7.2
QUOTATIONS FOR WARRIORS

"Always bear in mind that your own resolution to success is more important than any other one thing."
—Abraham Lincoln

"We are all failures—at least the best of us are."
—James M. Barrie

"I didn't fail 3,000 times; I documented 3,000 ways not to make a light bulb."
—Thomas Edison

"Try not. Do or do not. There is no try."
—Yoda

"Failure is not falling down but refusing to get back up."
—Chinese proverb

"Only those who dare to fail greatly can ever achieve greatly."
—Robert F. Kennedy

ACTION ITEMS
SKILLS FOR TEAMWORK

SKILL	STRATEGY	APPLICATION
Listening	Ensure that all team members have a fair say in the decision-making process.	Offer every team member a 5-minute opportunity to list his or her ideas, expectations, and concerns at the end of every meeting.
Helping	If team members are having difficulties with their responsibilities, make sure the team is equipped to help them.	Set aside at least one team meeting during which the only goal is to help other team members in areas where they are struggling.
Participating	Be an active listener and doer in all phases of the team exercise or project.	Create benchmarks for yourself to reach before each team meeting.

SUPPORTING EACH ROLE

As you reviewed the skills and qualities of each role, you may have noticed that you are stronger in some roles than in others (this is normal). Some of us are natural artists, while others are outstanding warriors. The benefit of working in a team is that you don't have to be strong in every area to ensure innovative solutions. To ensure innovation, teams must have at least one member who is strong in each area and share leadership to maximize those strengths. In addition, meetings should be structured to support each phase of the innovative problem-solving process. For example, begin exploring the problem at your first meeting. Then send every member of the team out to explore the problem further and collect information that might aid in finding solutions. Dedicate at least one meeting, more if time allows, to the artist. Allow team members time to brainstorm, ask "what if" questions, and so on. Develop criteria and a clear process for assessing solutions during the judge phase. And finally, as a warrior, develop a clear plan and work as a team to overcome roadblocks, obstacles, and setbacks. Being innovative is not easy, but it's a central component to functioning as a team and achieving professional excellence. In the 21st century, innovation is no longer an option; it's a necessity.

CONFLICT IN TEAM MEETINGS

When was the last time you thought to yourself, "I have a meeting today. I hope it's full of conflict"? Chances are you've never had those thoughts. In fact, you may have thought the exact opposite on occasion: "I hope my meeting today has no conflict." Believe it or not, lack of conflict isn't a good thing. Lack of conflict is a strong sign that your group has some serious problems, will not develop innovative ideas, and will never reach "team" status. The whole purpose for having meetings is to get different people together to share a variety of ideas and develop innovative solutions to problems. If this is to occur, then conflict must occur, too.

The problem for most of us is that the word *conflict* has a negative connotation. So let's use a different word. If you replace the word *conflict* with something such as *discussion* or *sharing of ideas*, then the phrase sounds more appealing: "I hope my meeting today is full of discussion and sharing of ideas." To better understand the need for conflict in meetings and strategies for facilitating productive conflict, let's explore each area in more detail.

NEED FOR CONFLICT

As groups develop into teams, some naïve leaders think that a positive byproduct of this transformation will be a lack of conflict. Nothing could be further from the truth. If you're part of a group that is not experiencing conflict, chances are you're part of either a groupthink or a meetingthink situation.

GROUPTHINK

Groupthink is the tendency of highly cohesive groups to suspend critical thinking and make faulty decisions (Janis, 1982, 1989; Shirey, 2012). You may recall from history class that in 1961, President John F. Kennedy supported a group of Cuban exiles who returned to Cuba in an attempt to overthrow the communist government headed by Fidel Castro. Instead of claiming a quick and easy victory as Kennedy and his advisers had planned, the mission failed. The scholar Irving Janis studied the incident, known as the Bay of Pigs, and concluded that the defeat was a result of groupthink.

Causes of Groupthink. For groupthink to occur, several conditions must exist. First, the group must be highly cohesive. Not all highly cohesive groups suffer from groupthink; however, if highly cohesive groups are combined with other elements, the chances of groupthink increase. For example, groupthink is more likely to occur if the group functions in isolation, is very homogeneous, lacks norms for critically analyzing information, and/or is dealing with high-stress threats. In addition, these groups are often headed by a charismatic, directive leader. Because of the strong desire to maintain the cohesiveness with leader and group, group members begin to self-censor. No one in the group wants to be the voice of dissent, so members remain silent even though they have doubts or concerns. If a group member does voice disagreement, "mind guards" jump in and silence the dissent until the dissenting member begins self-censoring. (Just as bodyguards protect the group from physical harm, mind guards protect the group from conflict and dissention.) Since these groups often function in isolation, they do not receive feedback from the outside. In the end, it appears as if everyone agrees, assumptions go unchallenged, and faulty decisions are made.

Avoiding Groupthink. The way to avoid groupthink is to introduce conflict systematically. Norms should be developed for seeking additional information, testing assumptions, and incorporating the role of devil's advocate. Having the larger group divide into subgroups when brainstorming and/or having the leader withhold his or her thoughts are additional strategies used to reduce groupthink.

MEETINGTHINK

As consultants, we have seen the byproduct of groupthink occur in many different organizations—not groupthink itself but the *byproduct* of groupthink, which is the suspension of critical thinking that results in faulty decisions. The groups we have observed are not highly cohesive, don't have charismatic leaders, and don't function in isolation. Yet their members still make faulty decisions due to a lack of critical thinking. We refer to this phenomenon as meetingthink. Meetingthink has the same outcome as groupthink, but it doesn't require the same inputs. It's the suspension of critical thinking due to more common variables, such as false empowerment, overload, or poorly run meetings.

WRITE YOUR NOTES HERE

False Empowerment. False empowerment occurs when a leader acts as if he or she plans to involve the group in the decision-making process when, in reality, the leader is going to make the decision regardless of the input received from the group. At first, group members believe they are empowered to make a decision, but in the end this proves to be false. Over time, group members learn that their opinions, ideas, and thoughts are not valued, so they remain silent during meetings. As a result, critical thinking is suspended.

Overload. Overload occurs when group members have so much on their plates that they cannot truly concentrate on and engage in the meeting at hand. While the meeting is occurring, group members are thinking about the 10 other items they have to do that day at work, as well as the list of things they must take care of when they leave work. Being overloaded may also cause members to come to meetings without preparing. For example, if members fail to read a report in advance of a meeting, they may be unable to take part in the discussion. Overloaded group members also withhold valuable input because they fear it will somehow lead to more work. They are afraid the boss will say, for instance, "Great idea, Susan. I'd like you to head up a committee examining that issue and report back in 2 weeks."

Poorly Run Meetings. Poorly run meetings are a third contributor to the meetingthink problem. The next time you are at a meeting, look around the room. How many people appear to be engaged and listening? How many people's eyes are glazed over, or how many are sleeping with their eyes open, doodling, or looking out the window? If the majority of the group is not engaged, chances are the meeting is being poorly run. Poorly run meetings can be the result of some or all of the factors we discussed earlier. The meeting may be disorganized due to a lack of an agenda. It may be too long and/or include too many topics. The meeting may include the wrong participants. Overtalkers may be dominating the meeting. The leader may be doing all the talking and failing to do any facilitating. Regardless of the reason, poorly run meetings result in group members disengaging, which results in poor decision making.

Avoiding Meetingthink. What can you do about it? How can you avoid this in your own groups? First, make it a practice to follow the suggestions discussed earlier in this chapter. Consider the meeting environment. Always evaluate the meeting topics and use an agenda. When planning the meeting, ask yourself the following questions: Is this topic relevant to the participants? (If you are not positive, ask them.) Am I being respectful of my team's time? If you have a meeting scheduled but some of the key participants can't make it, cancel the meeting. Similarly, if you have a standing meeting scheduled but there are no agenda items, cancel it. Your team members will be more engaged in the meetings they do attend if you respect their time. Finally, if you have the leadership title, facilitate the discussion. Make certain all the functional roles are present. If they're not, bring it to the attention of the team.

WRITE YOUR NOTES HERE

What if you're not the leader of the meeting in question? What can you do to avoid meetingthink? On a personal level, challenge yourself to be fully prepared and engaged in every meeting you attend. Avoid becoming overloaded by actively managing the number of meetings you attend. If you are invited to participate in a meeting, ask the leader why you were selected to participate. What role does he or she want you to play? If you will play a valuable role, attend the meeting. If you were invited out of courtesy, decline to attend. Similarly, ask if you are the person who needs to attend or if a representative from your team is needed. If a representative is needed, look within your team for support. There may be equally qualified members of your team who could go in your place. What may have been a burden to you might well be an exciting opportunity for another member of your team.

Whether group members are suffering from groupthink or meetingthink, the results are the same—critical thinking is suspended, and faulty decisions occur. By design, groups and teams should have conflict. The trick is to make sure the conflict is positive and productive.

TOOLS FOR PROFESSIONAL EXCELLENCE 7.6
CONDUCTING EFFECTIVE VIRTUAL MEETINGS

To prepare for a virtual meeting, follow these practical tips:

KEY POINTS	PRACTICAL TIPS
Prepare for the meeting.	• Be upfront when preparing for the meeting: Send out the agenda ahead of time, along with any visual or supporting material, to make sure everyone is on the same page. • Decide on what technologies and software are most appropriate for the setting of the meeting, as well as for those involved. • Make sure all technologies, software, and other electronic materials for the meeting are functioning, and have backup plans in place in case of any issues or malfunctions.
Plan for technology tools and requirements.	• When it comes to technology, think small: Use only the tools that are needed, so as to avoid any potential problems or embarrassment. • Be knowledgeable of all tools that are being used, so that you know how to troubleshoot any issues that arise.
Stay focused.	• Encourage attendees to check into the meeting from a quiet, distraction-free environment. • If outside noise becomes an issue, use chat boxes or other text-based tools to conduct the meeting. • Don't try and squeeze everything into one meeting: Spread points across multiple smaller meetings to keep attendees comfortable and able to focus. • Whether directing or attending the meeting, avoid wearing clothing or accessories that can be visually distracting on camera, such as bright colors or shiny jewelry.
Use good meeting etiquette.	• Be courteous and respectful of other meeting attendees, just like you would in any face-to-face meeting. • Speak clearly and concisely, and avoid shouting. • Keep body movements to a minimum, to prevent the video quality from deteriorating. • Avoid interacting with people or objects on the side, as this may distract other attendees.
Engage participants.	• Break the ice by asking each attendee to introduce and share something interesting about himself or herself. • Always ask for audience input when posing a question or proposing an idea, which helps to stimulate group discussion. • Do anything you can think of to simulate face-to-face meetings and keep attendees attentive and engaged.

SOURCE: Thomas, F. (2010, December 20). 5 tips for conducting a virtual meeting. *Inc.* Retrieved and adapted from www.inc.com/guides/2010/12/5-tips-for-conducting-a-virtual-meeting.html

PRODUCTIVE CONFLICT

By now, you may be convinced that conflict is a necessary part of teams, but you still may not be excited about the idea of engaging in conflict, especially if you've experienced negative, counterproductive conflict in the past. Achieving professional excellence in teams involves the utilization of positive, productive conflict as a valuable resource.

STAGES OF TEAM DEVELOPMENT

Conflict is present in three of the five stages that make up team development (Posthuma, 2012; Tuckman & Jensen, 1977). The five stages of team development include forming, storming, norming, performing, and adjourning. During the *forming stage*, group members tend to be polite and impersonal as they test the waters. Conflict appears in the second stage, known as storming. During the *storming stage*, members engage in infighting and often clash with the leader. In the *norming stage*, the group develops procedures for organizing, giving feedback, and confronting issues. In the *performing stage*, the members carry out the duties of the group. In the final stage, *adjourning*, the group completes its work, resolves issues, and comes to a close. This is not a linear process. Group members don't march neatly from stage to stage. It's normal for groups to revisit stages and circle through the process repeatedly. The point here is that groups encounter conflict in the storming, norming, and performing stages of development. If a group is going to become a team, it will encounter conflict in the storming stage, develop productive ways to handle conflict in the norming stage, and utilize the kind of innovative thinking in the performing stage that can come only through productive discussion or conflict.

HANDLING CONFLICT

To achieve professional excellence, you must determine the best way to handle conflict so that it's both positive and productive. Every time you are faced with a conflict, you must select one of three modes of conflict resolution: flight, fight, or unite. Let's take a look at each.

Flight occurs when you choose not to engage or deal with a conflict. There are times when this is the appropriate strategy. Some issues are not worth the time or the energy. However, if there is a problem that must be solved or a behavior that must be changed, flight is not the appropriate response and avoidance only makes the problem worse.

Fight is another alternative for handling conflict. Using the fight approach will require you to engage in some type of confrontation. This approach is also known as a win-lose approach to problem solving. Both parties face off as opponents, and one party will come out the winner, while the other party will come out the loser. Clearly, this approach can have some negative consequences. In fact, the losing party often holds a grudge, which can damage relationships in the long run. However, there are times when an issue is important enough to warrant the fight approach. If handled properly, even conflicts that are solved using the fight approach can be positive.

THE UNITE APPROACH

The third mode for conflict resolution is the unite approach, which requires team members to move away from stating positions to exploring interests (Fisher, Ury, & Patton, 1991; Hackman, 2012). The unite approach defines team members as joint problem solvers rather than as adversaries. Instead of approaching the conflict as team member against team member, it becomes the team united against the problem. A position is a demand that includes each person's solution to the problem. Under the unite approach, team members look beneath the surface of each position to see all the interests. Interests are the needs and concerns underlying each position.

An example of two competing positions might be, "The wait staff should only wait tables and not do side jobs such as filling ketchup bottles or rolling silverware in napkins" and "The wait staff must wait on tables and do side jobs." There are only two positions, but under each position are many interests. For example, under the wait staff position are interests (needs and concerns) such as, *I want to be a good employee. I like working here. I want to do a good job. I want to be a team player. I do need to have the ketchup filled and silverware rolled. I do not have time to do side jobs and properly serve my customers. I want to earn the most tips possible. Not all the wait staff take turns with the side jobs. Hostesses and busboys do not do side jobs. I am paid only $2.00 an hour, while hostesses and busboys are paid $6.00 per hour.* Under the manager position are some similar needs and concerns: *My wait staff are excellent servers. I want to retain this wait staff. I want my wait staff to get the most tips possible. I want the customers to have an excellent dining experience. The side jobs must be done. Traditionally, wait staff do the side jobs. I want the entire staff to function as a team.*

When the team looks beyond the positions and focuses on the interests, they are able to identify interests they share and establish common ground for joint problem solving. Instead of arguing positions, the team can look for solutions that support the interests or common ground they share.

RAISE THE ISSUE

For this approach to work, it's critical for the opening communication to reflect the unite attitude. According to Fisher et al. (1991), you should begin by preparing to raise the issue. Preparation includes many of the elements we have already discussed, such as considering the meeting environment, meeting participants, and meeting topic. Because this process can take some time, be certain to schedule the meeting at a time when participants are not rushed (Chen, Zhao, Liu, & Wu, 2012).

Begin the meeting by stating the issue concisely and in a neutral tone. Focus on behaviors and facts, not opinions. For example, you would not want to begin by saying, "Clearly, the wait staff think they're too good to take care of the side jobs, and it's causing us to lose business. Do I have to fire someone in order to get this problem resolved, or do you have a better idea?" Rather, begin with something such as, "Recently, there has been a shortage of rolled silverware and filled condiments during peak serving times." The latter statement is concise with a neutral tone.

When stating the problem, be as brief as possible. As illustrated in the example above, you should keep it to a sentence or two. Leaders have a tendency to state the problem and the solution without allowing others to talk—this will shut down the entire communication process.

INVITE COOPERATION

Once the problem is stated, invite cooperation (Fisher et al., 1991; Kress & Schar, 2012). For example, you might say, "How can we solve this problem together?" By listening, you and the other team members will gain a better understanding of everyone's perceptions of the issue.

If your team is not familiar with this approach, you may need to guide team members through the process. Prior to addressing any issues, talk to the team about the benefits of using the unite approach. Have the team imagine themselves on one side of the table, united against whatever issue or problem arises. Emphasize that the unite approach requires effective listening and participation from all team members. To develop listening and participating as a norm, incorporate the round robin technique. After you've raised the issue and invited cooperation, go around the circle and allow everyone to share his or her perceptions of the issue. The round robin technique requires members to listen and not interrupt while other team members are speaking. Team members may ask one another clarification questions to improve understanding, but they can't argue for or against positions. As the team discusses their perceptions of the issue, the underlying interests will become clearer. Only then can the team begin generating options and select the best solution(s).

KEYS TO EXCELLENCE IN TEAM COMMUNICATION

Refer back to the discussion of Target's company-wide approach to teamwork, at the beginning of this chapter. When thinking about how you interact with others in a team setting, be aware of the KEYS process to improve your communication. During the first step, *know yourself*, do a self-inventory of how you have interacted with others in the past and how your team members reacted to your communication. Did they react positively or negatively to the way you communicated with them? Understanding different workplace cultures is critical to avoid offending the people you work with.

The second step, *evaluate the professional context*, requires you to identify what is considered professional communication and what is not. What types of jokes are tolerated in your working environment? Is cursing frowned upon or ignored? What behavior is considered acceptable when venting your frustrations to your coworkers? Try to make sure that your team communication fits the culture of your workplace.

The third step, *your communication interaction*, requires you to be critical of your communication while talking with your team members. Be sensitive to others' nonverbal cues, and try to notice when somebody feels threatened or offended by your communication. Take what you have learned from evaluating your professional context to craft a message that can be well received by your coworkers.

The final strategy, *step back and reflect*, involves taking a reflexive inventory of your communication with other team members. Both verbally and nonverbally, how did your coworkers react to what you said? Was your body language offensive or threatening, or did you choose a more amiable approach in your communication? Continually be aware of how others react to your communication, and make the proper changes to your approach when necessary.

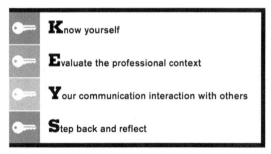

Know yourself

Evaluate the professional context

Your communication interaction with others

Step back and reflect

Think of a group or team to which you belong. How does that group or team make decisions and handle conflict? Are your decisions innovative? Are your conflicts productive? Based on what you have learned, could you improve the communication in your group or team?

EXECUTIVE SUMMARY

Now that you have finished reading this chapter, you should be able to:

Distinguish between a group and a team:

- A group is defined as three or more individuals who are working toward a common goal or share a common purpose (p. 138).
- A team is defined as a group in which members share leadership responsibility for creating a team identity, achieving mutually defined goals, and fostering innovative thinking (p. 138).

Explain the impact of the environment, the topic(s), and the participants on communication within meetings:

- Location is an important component in creating a positive meeting environment. In fact, you should consider the convenience, aesthetics, and comfort of the location (p. 140).
- An agenda is a useful channel for informing team members about meeting topics; if used properly, an agenda can serve as a communication tool for facilitating meetings (p. 143).
- Leaders with professional excellence avoid the trap of inviting a representative of each department just to be politically correct. Invite people who can contribute to the purpose of the meeting. Take time to assess the meeting's purpose, and then determine who can best serve that purpose (p. 144).

Analyze the roles and norms displayed by a group or team:

- Within every team, members can play a host of possible roles. Some of these roles are functional roles that help the team achieve goals or maintain positive relationships among members. These roles are known as task roles and relationship roles (p. 145).
- A norm is an unwritten rule of behavior. All groups have both positive and negative norms. The important thing is to step back and reflect on the norms and assess how various norms are affecting your group (p. 145).

Discuss the concepts involved in effective problem solving:

- Problem solving involves not only making a choice but also coming up with quality alternatives from which to select and then working to implement the choice your team selects (p. 147).

- Remember John Dewey's Reflective Thinking Process. According to Dewey (1910), five steps make up problem solving. These steps include describing and analyzing the problem, generating possible solutions, evaluating all solutions, deciding on the solution, and planning how to implement the solution (p. 147).

Describe ways to foster innovative thinking in a team context:

- One way to foster innovation in team problem solving is to incorporate Von Oech's (1986) explorer, artist, judge, and warrior into the process (p. 154).

Discuss the need for conflict and the strategies for productive conflict:

- Lack of conflict is a strong sign that your group has some serious problems, will not develop innovative ideas, and will never reach "team" status. The whole purpose for having meetings is to get different people together to share a variety of ideas and develop innovative solutions to problems. If this is to occur, then conflict must also occur (p. 156).
- To achieve professional excellence, you must determine the best way to handle conflict so that it's both positive and productive. Every time you are faced with a conflict, you must select one of three modes of conflict resolution: flight, fight, or unite (p. 160).
- To develop listening and participating as a norm, incorporate the round robin technique. After you've raised the issue and invited cooperation, go around the circle and allow everyone to share his or her perceptions of the issue (p. 161).

Apply the KEYS process to professional excellence as you develop your groups into teams:

- Know yourself. Be aware of the strengths and weaknesses you bring to the group or team (p. 162).
- Evaluate the professional context. Know your workplace culture and the personalities of other people in your group or team. This will enable you to foster a positive group interaction (p. 162).
- Your communication interaction. Develop an agenda and send it to the group a week before the meeting, giving everyone time to acquaint themselves with it (p. 162).
- Step back and reflect. Listen to the input from your peers to better understand what is important to the group and the company as a whole (p. 162).

EXPLORE

1. Find an example of a team-building exercise from your previous school or work experience. Did you find the exercise beneficial or effective? Write a brief response weighing positive and negative consequences from your experience.
2. Watch a video detailing some type of team-building function (e.g., military boot camp, exercise classes, athletics). Attempt to identify the purpose of the team-building exercise, as well as why it is important in the given context. Offer another

example of how the same exercise could be used in a different setting.
3. Form several small teams within your classroom with the goal of reaching a shared objective (e.g., solving a math problem, logic riddle, or anything else applicable). Have the teams try to complete the project while keeping track of who finished the fastest while also solving the problem. Have the team offer reasons as to why their team-building exercise was successful.

REVIEW

Check your answers to these questions at **http://edge.sagepub.com/quintanilla3e.**

1. Define a team.
2. A(n) _____ is a guide or an overview of the topics that will be covered during the meeting.
3. A(n) _____ is an unwritten rule of behavior.
4. Explain the difference between task roles and relationship roles.
5. _____ is the act of choosing among a set of alternatives under conditions that necessitate choice.
6. Identify the steps in John Dewey's Reflective Thinking Process.
7. _____ are the standards used to make a decision.
8. _____ is the tendency among members of highly cohesive groups to self-censor, suspend critical thinking, and make faulty decisions.

DISCUSSION QUESTIONS

1. Think about the last project you worked on with others. Would you define that as a group or a team experience? Why would you use that label?
2. Step back and reflect on some meetings in which you have participated. How did the environment, topics, and participants contribute to the communication in those meetings?
3. During meetings, do you share in the leadership? What roles do you play? When you have a designated leadership title, do you act as a coach? What norms do you use to help facilitate effective communication and shared leadership?
4. When it comes to innovative problem solving, in which role (explorer, artist, judge, or warrior) do you excel and which role must you work to develop?
5. How do you handle conflict? Have you ever tried a unite approach? Why or why not?

TERMS TO REMEMBER

Review key terms with eFlashcards. **http://edge.sagepub.com/quintanilla3e.**

agenda (p. 143)
artist (p. 154)
coach (p. 145)
compromise (p. 152)
conflict (p. 156)
consensus (p. 152)
criteria (p. 149)
decision by the leader (p. 151)
decision making (p. 147)
devil's advocate (p. 150)
explorer (p. 154)
false empowerment (p. 158)
fight (p. 160)

flight (p. 160)
group (p. 138)
groupthink (p. 157)
interests (p. 160)
judge (p. 155)
lead (p. 153)
meeting environment (p. 139)
meetingthink (p. 157)
norm (p. 145)
overload (p. 158)
overtalker (p. 144)
position (p. 160)
problem solving (p. 147)

Reflective Thinking Process (p. 147)
relationship roles (p. 145)
round robin technique (p. 161)
self-centered roles (p. 145)
stages of team development (p. 160)
task roles (p. 145)
team (p. 138)
undertalker (p. 144)
unite (p. 160)
voting (p. 151)
warrior (p. 155)

Organizational Systems Thinking and Problem Solving

Ziegenfuss, J.

> *Synergy means behavior of whole*
> *systems unpredicted by the behavior of their parts.*
> —Robert F. Fuller, *What I Have Learned*

Work teams collapse into conflict. New software products fail to meet delivery dates. Some executives quit, while whole departments are "downsized" out of existence. Morale and job satisfaction are at an all-time low. At various times, we could be talking about hospitals, Internet companies, steel producers, computer manufacturers, or schools. These situations represent only a few of the organization and management problems sometimes facing leaders at all levels of our public and private organizations. Problem-solving teams and consultants are at work in North America and Europe (Kipping, 1999) as well as in Asia (Vieira, 1997). In the public sector, subjects include Utah's personnel management department (Burrington, 1985), university admissions (Gose, 1999), and professional practices such as law (Dennis, 1999). Because *no* organization is perfect, we all become problem solvers—as "insider managers" or "outsider consultants."

Two questions are the focus of this book:

- How can academics, professional managers, and consultants use organization theory and systems thinking in teaching and practicing problem solving?
- Can a view of the nature of organization enhance our ability to teach and practice problem solving and consultation?

This book presents one organization and management problem-solving model used in a graduate management program and in a variety of field projects where the concepts were tested by public and private sector cases. The model and the cases have proved to be quite helpful to both managers and students, some of whom have had "McKinsey 101" experiences in learning consulting and problem solving in real projects (Hayes & Setton, 1998).

Introduction

This first chapter defines the philosophy, concepts, and analytical tools needed to attack organization and management problems from a systems point of view. The model is integrationist in approach, using the thinking and methods of many researchers and problem solvers. The model is a unique combination of diverse viewpoints that, as a whole, contribute to a new perspective on organization and management problem solving. In short, problems are viewed as systems design and redesign challenges.

In graduate schools of business and public administration, as well as in day-to-day management activities, we often forget that assumptions about the nature of organization form the basis of our thinking about organizational problem solving. Academics, executives, and practicing consultants continually search for methodologies and concepts that will help to develop their organizations. When managers engage consultants, they seldom talk directly about their own mental models of the organization, nor do they ask about the consultants' models. This often is the case when we teach students in M.B.A. programs as well. Managers, academics, and consultants need to respond to these shortfalls in two ways:

- Underlying assumptions that guide our organization and management problem solving must be surfaced.
- Practical models useful to managers, consultants, and students must be presented and field-tested.

Organizational problem solving and consultation often are presented in business school courses as a part of strategic management, management policy, organizational behavior, and organizational development. In schools of public administration, problem solving and policy analysis and development appear in courses in public management, program planning and evaluation, and public policy. In too few of these courses do we spend time considering our conceptual starting point. Senior managers only rarely engage in dialogue that clearly surfaces the assumptions of their organizational views of the world—a habit that, unfortunately, began in their primary education.

To understand this systems and consulting approach to organization and management problem solving (Figure 1.1), we must have answers to three questions:

1. *What* is the architecture of the organization we propose to fix?
2. *Who* are the problem-solving consultants?
3. *How* do the consultants work?

The first question leads us to a systems view of the organization. The second requires us to understand the consultant's role, skill, and preparation. The third is about the problem-solving process itself.

In this first chapter, I introduce the elements of a systems approach to organization and management problem solving. The approach can be used both to teach students and to assist practicing managers. The following topics comprise the approach to problems and their solutions:

- Needs
- Nature of problems
- Organizational and sociotechnical systems concepts
- Action research and organization development
- Stakeholders
- Organizational model and development process
- Consultation and problem-solving phases
- Problem-solving intervention concepts

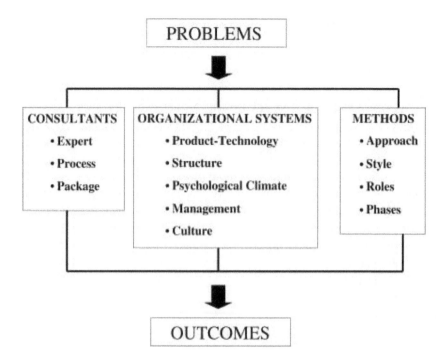

Figure 1.1. Problem Solving: The Systems and Consulting Approach

- Problem solvers: Consultant types and roles
- Problem-solving outcomes
- Engagement analysis: Case reports

To help us understand the many diverse parts of this approach, we use the case of the "problems" at the Internal Revenue Service (IRS) in Washington, D.C. We all have "experienced" taxes, and many of us complain about the inadequacies of the IRS. In a recent *Fortune* article, the author opened the discussion with this comment on technology currency:

> However badly you think the IRS is, it is worse. The agency that processes 209 million of the most complicated forms known to humankind uses computer systems mostly designed in the 1950s, built in the 1960s, and jury-rigged ever since. . . . Charles Rossotti, the new commissioner, told *Fortune* that upgrading his vacuum tube era technology "will be like rebuilding Manhattan while we're still living in it." (Birnbaum, 1998)

The article came on top of many public media reports of taxpayer abuse (e.g., auditors threatening and abusing taxpayers [Bovard, 1998]), poor service, and congressional hearings on the troubled state of this federal agency. We use these problems to illustrate our approach because of the multiple dimensions of organization involved—technical, attitudinal, structural, and managerial.

With all the public commentary, it seems that the IRS is a problem-laden organization. A composite of some of the outstanding issues includes the following:

- Inadequate taxpayer assistance
- Undone revisions of forms and publications to reflect new tax law
- Telephone response problems, such as hours of availability
- Audit demeanor of IRS staff
- Internal quotas for revenue collection
- Inadequate staffing for high-demand periods
- Unfinished electronic filing capability
- Lack of currency in computer technology
- Bar code misprints on address labels
- Incomplete Web site development
- Fragmented authority structure

With 100,000 employees, as well as many millions of forms and telephone transactions, this is a very large organizational problem.

There have long been calls for reinventing the IRS (Lear, 1993). We have the option of continuing to criticize, or we can attempt to continuously improve the agency (Lear, 1996). Efforts have been directed toward restructuring (Laffie, 1997; National Commission on Restructuring the IRS, 1997). In addition, there is renewed attention to customer service (Bigelow, 1994).

Many times, the first solutions proposed are one-dimensional. We could fire the IRS commissioner. Or, we could reorganize—a favorite of many public leaders. For example, structural changes such as eliminating districts have been proposed for the IRS (Phillips, 1999). Commissioner Rossotti would create separate divisions for individual taxpayers, big business, tax-exempt entities, and small business. Changing the structure is the "quick-fix" focus; this "redesign of the order" is only one of many changes needed to fully dissolve the IRS problems. A systemic approach would help create an enriched view of the diagnosis, planning, and actions needed for an IRS turnaround.

To successfully attack the organization and management problems at the IRS, we should (a) know more about their nature and root causes in a diagnostic sense, (b) approach the problems of organization development and learning with experience in mind, (c) identify and use stakeholder opinions, (d) employ a process with phases and steps, (e) be aware of our multiple roles in problem solving, and (f) seek outcomes that demonstrate positive impact. We will continue to work on the IRS case, but let us begin our presentation of this approach with a discussion of some of the reasons why executives and managers need both inside and outside help.

Needs for Problem Solving and Consulting

We sometimes hear company executives say "We never use outside consultants; we have no need for them." Implied in this statement are both positive and negative assumptions. On the positive side, executives are expressing confidence in their internal problem-solving teams, even as they sometimes work on the wrong systems (Ackoff, 1993). Certainly, large corporations have both the range and the depth of talent to tackle many problems.

On the negative side, the statement can imply the following: "The company is so strong that all the managerial ideas and skills are in-house now and forever. We rarely have the need for problem solving because we are so well managed." On closer examination, this reveals a misunderstanding of the dynamic complex organization. No organization runs perfectly—or even close to it. Recognizing the ongoing need for problem solving is a throwing off of denial and an acceptance of the never-ending search for better harmony and continuous improvement. Too often, the failure stems from an inability to act (Sull, 1999).

At Southwest Airlines, consultants are thought to be helpful in adding capability, managing workload and risk, adapting to change, and providing influence and power (Sartain, 1998). Some years ago, Blake and Mouton (1982) listed some reasons for using consulting help, such as morale, change, conflict, missing competencies, "taking the heat," and disposing of funds. A survey listed two top reasons as providing expertise and providing an external detached viewpoint (Oakley, 1994). On occasion, an engagement begins as follows: "We are not sure what the problem is." The client has not self-diagnosed but instead is asking for help in defining the problem (e.g., "Why is morale low?"; "Why have we lost market share?"; "Why do we have a shortage of new product ideas?"). But consultants often are asked to go beyond specific problems, contributing to permanent skills through coaching and teaching (Bergholz, 1999).

Internal teams of problem solvers and outside consulting groups are engaged for two reasons: in *reaction* to problems and/or in an effort to be *proactive*. For example, "How can we reduce and better manage our production and transaction costs?" (Canback, 1999) is a reaction to cost problems and can be a preventive strike. We solve existing problems, or we confront the never-ending question of how to continuously improve. Leaders must respond to problems, and they also should address the question of how to be more effective next year than they were this year (no matter how good they currently are). This sounds reasonable enough, but throughout the process they must manage resistance to change (Lipton, 1996)—only one of the barriers to smooth and quick resolutions.

The Nature of Problems

What exactly is a problem? A dictionary definition may offer us a starting point. A problem can be one of the following:

- A question proposed for solution or consideration
- A question, matter, situation, or person that is perplexing or difficult

We are addressing organization and management problem solving, so we are interested in tackling the difficult questions, situations, and persons in public and private organizations. Problems include the never-ending quest for quality products, the development and maintenance of teamwork, and the adjustment of the company's traditional mission to an ever-changing environment.

Because the organization is a complex set of interlocking social and technical systems, we face not just isolated problems but also connected ones. Ackoff (1981) defined these organization and management problems as follows:

> A set of two or more interdependent problems constitutes a *system*. The French call such a system a *problematique;* for lack of a corresponding word in English, I call it a *mess*. (It seems appropriate to think of planning as mess management.)
>
> A mess, like any system, has properties that none of its parts ha[s]. These properties are lost when the system is taken apart. In addition, each part of a system has properties that are lost when it is considered separately. The solution

to a mess depends on how the solutions to the parts *interact*. Therefore, a plan should be more than an aggregation of independently obtained solutions to the parts of a mess. It should deal with messes as wholes, systematically.

In brief, planning is here conceptualized as a participative way of dealing with a set of interrelated problems when it is believed that unless something is done, a desirable future is not likely to occur, and that if appropriate action is taken, the likelihood of such a future can be increased. (p. 52)

How do we typically address problems in organization and management? We try to make them go away—quickly. But there are several options available, even though we rarely consider them directly.

There are three ways of dealing with these or any other problems; they can be resolved, solved, or dissolved. To *resolve* a problem is to find a means that does well enough that satisfies. To *solve* a problem is to find a means that performs as well as possible that optimizes. To *dissolve* a problem is to redesign the relevant system or its environment so that the problem is removed. This idealizes. It is better to solve than resolve, and better to dissolve than solve, because few problems stay solved for long. Dissolution requires more creativity than solution, and solution more than resolution. Unfortunately, creativity is a very scarce commodity. (p. 248)

In this organizational systems approach, we take the position that creative dissolution of the causal condition is the most desired problem-solving mission. The IRS can be fixed, as is, with basic components in place. Computer capability is enhanced, auditors become customer sensitive, and new business units are created. This would be a solution—the IRS at optimal effectiveness. Or, we could try radical dissolution such as a flat tax or the use of a sales tax, thereby dissolving some or all of the troubling conditions of the IRS.

Exactly what are problems in organization? Are they difficulties in reporting structure, management behavior, or personality and leadership style? When executives, managers, and consultants approach organizational problems, several characteristics of their styles are apparent:

- Problems are approached from a narrow one-dimensional perspective.
- Solutions are thought of as compromises between two or more opposing points of view.

These two assumptions and patterns of behavior dramatically limit the effectiveness of our problem solving in the complex organization.

We need a model of organization to begin our discussion of diagnosis and response.

Organizational and Sociotechnical Systems Concepts

Enhancing organizational effectiveness requires a conceptual picture of the whole organization (Fuqua, 1993; Ridley, 1993). Two points are keys to this perspective of problem solving and consulting:

- A view of the nature of organization enhances our ability to teach and practice organizational problem solving and consultation.
- Academics and professional managers must increase their use of organization theory and systems thinking in consultation, teaching, and practice.

The roots of the model used here are the sociotechnical concepts of Trist and colleagues beginning during the 1950s (Trist & Bamforth, 1951; Trist, Higgins, Murray, & Pollack, 1963). They recognized that the organization was a social system and that, along with the task and technology demands, designers must address the social psychology of the company (Katz & Kahn, 1978). This thinking has continued to contribute to our understanding of autonomous work group functioning (Susman, 1979) and the design of the organization (Pasmore, 1988; Trist & Murray, 1993). Current texts build this thinking into the perspectives on organization design, change, and development (Cummings & Worley, 2001; Daft, 1998).

Several commentators have given us a view of the scope of organization and management problems in field efforts to promote change and development. In their presentation of reengineering concepts, Hammer and Champy (1993) used a diamond to outline four problem areas: business processes, values and beliefs, management and measurement systems, and jobs and structures (p. 80). Cowan (1993) presented points of potential organizational problems in the views of executives as including external environment, strategy, production, operations, management information systems (MIS)/data processing, accounting, marketing, communications, customer management, and personnel (p. 122). Harrison (1994) listed eight elements as potential sources of problems: inputs, outputs, technology, environment, goals and strategies, behavior and processes, culture, and structure (p. 29). Hammer and Stanton

(1999) emphasized attention to organization processes as the means to improvement. All these authors were giving us conceptual maps to help us with diagnoses. Importantly, all were asking us to target the rich and "deep structure" of the organization (Old, 1995).

Organizations: Definition and Systems

The following comments on the history of organization theory will bring us to the durable organizational point of view presented by Kast and Rosenzweig (1970). Their model, expanded over the past 10 years with the work of other theorists and practitioners, will be used to guide our systems analysis of organization and management problems of many types.

We can view the history of organization theory through the emergence of various schools of thought that proposed, at their time, to present the correct theories of the architecture and functioning of the organization (Shafritz & Ott, 1996). Each new theory became the accepted perspective on the nature of organization as each school of thought replaced another's popularity and position of authority. Theorists competed for dominance or for recognition that they had found the truth. Peaceful coexistence with previous theorists was not possible, at least until more recently.

Each school of theory—named in an early Scott (1961) review as *classical/structural, neoclassical/human relations,* and *modern/systems*—attempted to develop a picture of the "reality" of corporate evolution and operation. Each group of organization theorists presents a description of complex reality and teaches its followers (e.g., students, researchers, practicing executives) to "see" reality in that way. Unfortunately, this tutoring has hindered the ability of new theorists to see other dimensions as parts of a more complex whole. Thus, the main schools that have evolved over the history of organization theory, adding more recent views of stakeholder networks and culture as the essence of organization, actually are emergent dimensions of the same reality. Through many arguments, there are no winners because proponents of "opposing" theories are fighting over and through different dimensions of organizational reality. Problem-solving failures can be attributed, at least in part, to this inadequate understanding.

For example, we could define the IRS problems in relation to the period of organization theory development. During the classical period, the IRS would be troubled by structural and technological deficiencies—the emphasis of organization theorists at that time. The answer would be to fix the table of organization and restructure.

During the human relations period, IRS problems would be defined as psychological. The causes would be individual attitudes, motivation, and satisfaction. The answer would be team building, sensitivity groups, and motivational seminars.

In our ongoing period of systems thinking, IRS problems are viewed as a complex set of interlocking deficiencies. The causes lie in the pattern of interrelationships, for example, an incentive system that distorts citizen relationships and leads to employee dissatisfaction and turnover. The answer lies in multiple interventions to change technology, structure, management style, and culture. The newer focus is on interlocking structures and especially on the processes of organization management (Garvin, 1998).

Systems theory proposes general principles as the formative guidelines for all organizations. These general principles are either characteristics (e.g., environment, purpose, structure, hierarchy, boundary) or actions (e.g., adaptation, differentiation, integration). The principles are viewed by systems-thinking organization theorists as primary elements for understanding the nature of organization for all organizations—from the IRS, to Microsoft, to the Hospital of the University of Pennsylvania. During the late 20th century, theorists viewed the organization as a whole guided by values and principles, by interacting subsystems, and by structures and processes of integration. A complex web of interlocking systems (both social and technical in nature), these systems include the task and core technology, the skills and abilities needed to complete the work, and the individual and group behaviors that comprise a social system.

We must know what an organization is if we are to solve organizational problems. Some years ago, Kast and Rosenzweig (1970) offered a model that is described and elaborated throughout this book. According to Kast and Rosenzweig (1985),

> We view the organization as an open, sociotechnical system composed of a number of subsystems. Under this view, an organization is not simply a technical or a social system. Rather, it is the structuring and integrating of human activities around various technologies. The technologies affect the types of inputs into the organization, the nature of the transformation processes, and the outputs from the system. However, the social system determines the effectiveness and efficiency of the utilization of the technology. (p. 113)[1]

This model—a sense of the organization as an interlocking set of five sociotechnical subsystems—is derived from the history of organization theory.

Kast and Rosenzweig's 31-year-old conception of the organization is consistent with current sociotechnical thinking accepted in the field. They viewed the organization as open to the environment and as composed of several subsystems under the following five titles:[1]

1. The product and technical subsystem
2. The structural subsystem
3. The psychosocial subsystem
4. The managerial subsystem
5. The culture, goals, and values subsystem

The subsystems and their relation to the organizational environment are represented in Figure 1.2. In this approach to problem solving and consulting, this mental model is the underpinning—the architectural target for design, development, and change (Nadler, Gerstein, Shaw, & Associates, 1992). It is necessary to briefly describe the nature of each of these subsystems because they will become the targets of our diagnostic and problem-solving work. The following descriptions of the subsystems are based on Kast and Rosenzweig's original work and adapted with the research and thinking of other theorists.

1. *The product and technical subsystem.* This refers to the knowledge required to design, develop, distribute, and support goods and services. The product and technical subsystem includes the "core work" of the public agency or private company—retail sales, manufacturing, teaching, providing medical care, collecting taxes, and so on. The product and technical subsystem develops as a result of the task requirements of the organization and varies depending on the particular activities of the organization as a whole and of its subunits (e.g., departments). The technology for manufacturing automobiles differs significantly from that used in an oil refinery or a software company. Similarly, the products and technology of a hospital emergency room are different from those in a university department. The product and technical subsystem is shaped by the production and delivery process, by the specialization of knowledge and skills required, by the types of machinery and equipment involved, and by the layout of facilities.

We can examine manufacturing processes. For example, at Lockheed, managers were concerned about growing workers' compensation claims. A se-

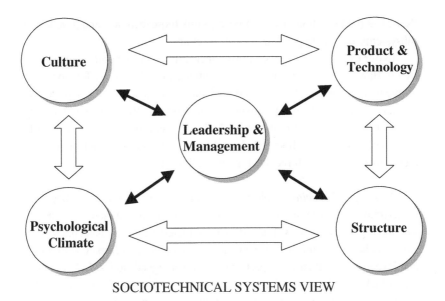

SOCIOTECHNICAL SYSTEMS VIEW

Figure 1.2. Organization and Management Problem Solving: The Diagnostic Targets

nior ergonomics engineering specialist led an internal team with representation from manufacturing, engineering, operations, production, materials processing, medical personnel, and safety engineering. The team was searching for a technical system flaw (Kelley, 1995).

In our case, the technologies used to assess, track, and collect taxes are the "technical system components" of the IRS. These include tax forms, tax tables, and audit processes. The product and technology help determine the organization's structure as well as its psychosocial climate, two more of the subsystems.

2. *The structural subsystem.* This involves the ways in which the tasks of the organization are divided (differentiation) and coordinated (integration). Organization charts, position and job descriptions, and rules and procedures define the structure in a "formal sense." Structure also is defined by patterns of authority, communication, and workflow. The organization's structure is the basis for establishing formal relationships between the production processes and worker psychology. Many examples of flawed performance are encouraged by wrong-headed reward systems that provide structural support for undesired behaviors

(Kerr, 1995). Interactions and relationships link those technical and psychosocial subsystems and can bypass the formal structure.

In our example, the IRS commissioner thinks that the unit structure at the IRS is flawed and is a prime cause of citizen dissatisfaction. Responding to problems of poor coordination and inefficiencies caused by the separation of specialists, he has proposed a business unit structure. IRS offices will be organized into four or more units: individual taxpayers, big business, nonprofits, and small business. With knowledge, skills, and resources better integrated in these units, citizens will receive higher quality service.

3. *The psychosocial subsystem.* Every organization has such a subsystem—the psychosocial dynamics of individuals and groups in interaction. Forces outside the organization, as well as internal characteristics such as technology and structure, help to establish the organization's psychological climate within which employees act out their roles performing their assigned duties. Subsystem elements include individual behavior and motivation, status and role relationships, and group dynamics as well as the values, attitudes, expectations, and aspirations of the people in the organization. As a result of this unique mix, psychological climates differ significantly from organization to organization. Certainly, the climate in which a computer analyst works is different from that of a nurse on a pediatric unit or a doctor in emergency surgery. Psychosocial aspects of the organization are both shaped and supported by management.

In our example of a federal agency, abusive, surly, and unfair treatment by IRS agents has come to the attention of congressional committees. Agents work in a climate where citizen abuse is tolerated, may be rewarded, and is thought to be helpful in management success. What will federal executives do to attack the problem that is here defined as psychosocial in nature—a combination of attitudes, motivation, and rewards? Behavioral strategies will be part of the solution (Berry, 1999).

4. *The managerial subsystem.* This is the integrator relating the organization to its environment; setting the goals; developing comprehensive, strategic, and operational plans; designing the structure; and establishing evaluation and control processes. Managerial activities traditionally have been described in terms of planning, organizing, developing, directing/leading, and controlling. More recently, the focus is on design, education, and stewardship as core duties (Senge, 1990). These duties are performed through a series of management roles—interpersonal, informational, and decisional (Mintzberg, 1975). Manage-

ment coordinates and integrates the production, structural, psychosocial, and cultural subsystems.

In our case of the IRS, the commissioner is responsible (*leadership*) for creating an organizationwide plan that will improve tax collection and audit processes (*product and technology*) with a new *structure* and a more "citizen-friendly" *psychological climate.* Deficiencies in IRS performance may be viewed as a *management* failure.

5. *Organizational culture.* This is the last of the five subsystems. To be successful and survive, the organization must meet social requirements—the goals and values of the external environment. Here we include the concept of corporate culture (Schein, 1990; Smircich, 1983) and the ability to understand culture as part of the problem-solving and consultation process (Lundberg, 1993). This subsystem links the goals and values of the members of the organization with those of the broader society. In our example, the IRS was created for social system purposes—the assessment and collection of monies for the support of our collective government. The IRS must fairly fulfill its purpose—collecting taxes—or else it will lose citizen support. Failure to complete the task due to technological breakdowns or inequitable application would erode societal support.

These five subsystems are considered "internal" to this perspective of the organization. There is an "external suprasystem." The environment is considered to be all forces outside the "boundaries" of the organization (defined by the five systems). These forces can include a diversity of issues such as national and international trends as well as climatic and competitive situations (Figure 1.3). A sample of the rich mix of aspects includes the following:

- Economics
- Politics
- Technology
- Social factors and demographics
- Law
- Education
- Culture
- Natural resources
- Globalization

Environment

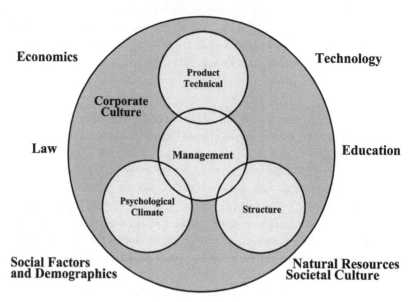

Figure 1.3.   System View of the Organization

We could add others that are related—communications, transportation, and so on. All can potentially affect problem solving from outside the organization.

With this perspective, every organization and management problem is potentially a five-system problem—plus the environment. This approach to problem solving both evolves from and reinforces our understanding of organizational thinking. Early views of organization failures and of problem-solving approaches emphasized the structural and technical subsystems. The human relationists and behavioral scientists advocated for the importance of the psychosocial subsystem, focusing their attention on motivation, group dynamics, and related people-oriented factors. The systems school (multiple subsystems) concentrated on methods of integration and linkage processes. Each approach to organization and management, or each school of theory, emphasized a particular subsystem with little recognition of the importance of the others. Figure 1.4 presents the full richness of subsystem variables in this view of the organization. Importantly, they all are potential points of trouble—targets for organization and management problem solvers.

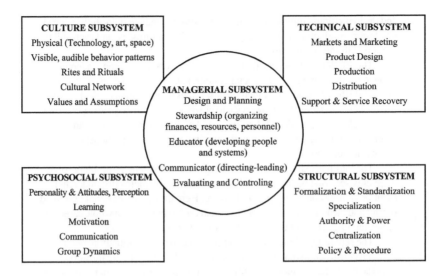

Figure 1.4. Organizational Analysis: Key Subsystem Variables

Quality of work life efforts, popular over the past two decades, increasingly took a whole organization perspective, changing climate, reward structure, and management style (Weisbord, 1987). For example, problem solvers at Continental Airlines address values, expectations, and teamwork as well as schedules and hub structures (Davidson, 1997).

This model of the organization is not without criticism. A summary of commentators' concerns, with some advice on the model's use, would include the following:

> There is incomplete knowledge of the five systems so that they are somewhat "black box like" (no one really knows what is in each). Subsequently there is little work on the validity of these contributors to the design and operation of companies. A problem solving team could use the model just as a discussion tool, keeping in mind that it is a somewhat artificial and not completely tested model of organization. If this is accepted, the group should proceed to use it but with the following additional limitations.
>
> *The model fosters system-by-system attention with limited focus on the interactive effects.* Because of the complexity in each of the topic areas—product, psychological climate . . .—consultants should remember that in reality all of the systems are working simultaneously and that their interactions are key. When the leaders commit to change beginning with statements of core values

and desired culture, they are also implying possible change in incentives, product design, production and delivery system, different attitudes, and even collaboration with the community.

The model is static in orientation, so the perspective can undercut our
knowledge that companies are social systems and as such are constantly changing. While the IRS leader is launching task forces to look into technical issues of
performance and a shortfall in service to citizens, staff may have already moved
to make changes in policy and procedure. And when those changes are made,
others are in the design stage, where ongoing efforts to continuously improve
quality do not stop.

The intuitive clarity of the five systems of the model helps problem solvers
to quickly see what must be done, but it simultaneously helps [to] undercut recognition of how complex organizations are. Here the culture material presented
is brief and clear. In practice, executives and researchers devote whole careers to
understanding what culture is and how to change it.

The separating of the systems is necessary for the presentation, but it is an
artificial construction that can cause us to forget the nature of organizations—as
integrated whole, product with structure with climate with leadership. At the
IRS, we are trying to consider whether a culture change is necessary. But it is
hard to separate out the potential effects of psychological climate, product quality, and leadership (determined commitment to serve the nation). Thus, as you
pay attention to culture or product, you must constantly keep the other systems'
effects in mind.

Each of the system's variables is not yet specific and quantifiable, i.e., the
metrics are as yet not fully developed and cannot take us easily beyond the qualitative judgment. When a senator suggested we change the IRS culture, he was
questioned by a second senator asking: "How citizen friendly is the IRS culture
now?" This is a very good question—one very hard to answer with the level of
science that the senators are accustomed to. We have made great strides in measurement, but each of the systems is a construction of reality that is open to
much interpretation. (Ziegenfuss & Bentley, 2000)

Sociotechnical Systems Thinking

Although we use the label, we have not fully discussed what we mean
by *sociotechnical systems* thinking and what the implications are for problem
solving. Several classic articles offer detailed descriptions of the elements of
sociotechnical theory (see, e.g., the earlier writings of Cherns, 1975; Cummings & Srivastva, 1977; Trist et al., 1963). The development of this theory and
practice was summarized by Fox (1995) and Trist and Murray (1993). Here we
review the main assumptions and concepts underlying the view that the organi-

zation is both *social* (culture, goals, values, psychology) and *technical* (production processes, structure, management, planning and control systems). We use the IRS case for illustration.

Sociotechnical systems theory is based on optimistic assumptions about human behavior in the workplace, as was noted some years ago:

- Many employees have the capacity and desire to make greater contributions through their jobs than ordinary organizational structures, processes, and workplace designs allow.

- To unleash employee motivation, organizations should allow employees to carry out activities relevant to their job tasks.

- Employees are not fixed as to their abilities but [rather] have the capacity to become either more or less than they currently are. (Chisholm & Ziegenfuss, 1986b, p. 318)

Experiences in the workplace also affect employees' needs and expectations. In short, one product of the organization is people. Because individual employees' skills and the motivation to employ these skills constitute key elements of, for example, the technology of health care delivery systems, the organization truly needs to view its employees as human resources.

Sociotechnical systems theory suggests that work roles and work units can be designed to respond flexibly to changing demands related to tasks performed and the environment. The capacity to perform in various ways and the ability to select appropriate responses are built into a sociotechnical systems work system. This approach contrasts sharply with traditional organization design principles of organizations that dictate the breaking of jobs into simple elements—so that the costs of training and replacing personnel may be eased—and otherwise follow closed-system principles derived from the concept of scientific management.

The term *sociotechnical systems* implies several types of internal and external congruence for work systems. The concept of congruence—or joint optimization—between technical and social systems is a design principle. The support systems of the organization, including those providing training, selection, payment, and so on, should be designed to foster and reinforce desired behaviors (Cherns, 1975). For example, wage incentives tied to individual performance actually inhibit efforts to develop work teams with group goals.

How does this perspective relate to our public agency's problems? In our IRS case, systems thinking implies several points about problem solving. First, we expect that IRS employees are responsible and interested in doing good work. They are not the villains painted in news reports. Rather, they are caught up in conflicting structures and system performance demands that compel them to "lean on" taxpayers. Because the IRS is divided into hierarchical structures, employees are unable to make discretionary judgments in a timely and flexible fashion. And because of incentive systems, they are put in a position of under-cutting the service function that we, as taxpayers, think we are paying for. The problems are both social-psychological and technical in nature, calling for consultation that recognizes this duality (Cummings, 1993). In short, the IRS systems are not consistent; they are incongruent.

The concept of congruence (Nadler & Tushman, 1980) implies the need for a fit among the culture, reward, and control systems of an organization and the design of specific work processes, employee roles, and departments. Efforts to make changes in one area affect other areas of the organization. System congruence requires interrelated attempts delivered in a coordinated fashion to improve organizational functioning and impact such as production, productivity, and quality of work life. This approach is based on several assumptions.

- *Whole* organizations, not just individual *parts,* contribute to high- or low-quality problem solving. The wide array of IRS problems will not be solved with a new computer system.
- *Whole* means that both *social and technical* aspects of the organization are considered as appropriate targets of improvement action. Congressional hearings cited the lack of modern computer technology *and* surly behaviors by agents.
- Quality organization designs require *attention to structure* (components and policies) and *process* (decision making and group dynamics). IRS leaders are now considering redesign of their structure, a revision of the quota system for judging job performance, and streamlined decision making.
- *Relations between the parts* of an organization are crucial to the improvement of quality of the whole—to problem solving. Treatment of citizens may improve when the IRS quota structure is revised. But management also must revise its control and performance assessment methods when beginning to institute culture change.
- Quality is viewed as *synergistic,* meaning that the whole is more than the sum of the parts and that multiple initiatives (rather than single actions) are called for to solve problems (multisystem actions). IRS leaders now plan to restructure, to upgrade computer technology, and to address agent behaviors that are making the IRS seem "customer unfriendly."

- Both producer and user *inputs* are crucial for problem definition and understanding, meaning that information from key stakeholders is necessary to develop problem solutions. Congressional hearings were held to collect feedback about the IRS from citizens and to provide political leaders with an opportunity to review current agency operations.

- *Transformation processes* are the focus of attention because they lead to and explain problematic outcomes and are the means to improvement. How the audits are chosen, whether IRS teams are focused on similar markets (e.g., small business, nonprofits), and methods of electronic processing all are receiving attention.

- Avoiding *entropy* (organizational decay) is an underlying assumption because, in a dynamic environment, quality will decrease if aggressive actions are not taken to periodically assess and continue improvement). Congressional hearings were both reactive and proactive in that the IRS received a top-to-bottom review that some citizens and staffers viewed as a reaction to public problems, whereas others viewed it as an overdue periodic assessment.

- The approach recognizes the importance of *open systems thinking,* meaning that the external environment influences problem solving and that external opinions and measures (benchmarks) are important. The IRS "problems" surfaced when political leaders began to receive many complaints. Politicians and citizens from the "outside environment" (beyond the walls of the IRS) are forcing the changes.

- *Contingency* and *equifinality* thinking means that organizing for problem solving is dependent on the situation and that each organization must create its own unique improvement plan. Although IRS leaders can learn about successful development and redesign of other public and private companies, they must devise their own unique plan for improvement. And there are many ways of solving problems.

- This philosophy and practice imply that *systems are purposeful and planned,* meaning that problem solutions in structures, processes, and outcomes also are purposeful and planned. The IRS problems will not be solved by accident. Their resolution will occur only by a planned attack that recognizes the complex interrelated aspects of product/technology, structure, psychological climate, management, and culture.

Organizational Systems and Development Processes

Systems thinking is critical to addressing organization and management problems because a model of the organization is *implicit* or *explicit* at four points in the problem-solving process: diagnosis, planning, action, and evaluation.

First, managers and consultants must *diagnose* the organizational "locale" of their problems. To put it in quality management language, in what systems are the root causes? Diagnosis requires an understanding of the nature of organization, as Harrison (1994) argued so effectively. From the brief organization theory history, we know that in the not-too-distant past, diagnosis would focus on technology and structure as the key sets of variables. When a performance problem such as the one at the IRS surfaces, one mental set leads us directly to structure. A change in the table of organization—a reorganization—is the quick recommendation. This is not necessarily the cause of the problem, but it is the implicit mental model followed by the problem solvers. Problem solvers would "see" a structural problem as a cause of the organization's poor performance. We even have recent examples of this non-systems thinking. The writings and work of the reengineering advocates are a prime example of this limitation. In the very popular book *Reengineering the Corporation,* Hammer and Champy (1993) focused their attention on the product manufacturing and delivery processes of private companies. Although great gains were made in process efficiency, they did not "transform" the organization. In a follow-up book, *Reengineering Management,* Champy (1995) admitted that there was a missing piece—the managerial system. A broad perspective of the organization promoted by the systems model expands the diagnostic targets right from the start.

So, we have found that narrowly defined technological and structural views of the organization no longer are appropriate. The systems view has brought in the external environment, the psychological system, management behaviors, and corporate culture and has exposed the complexity of this "mess" of connected problems. Each approach to organization and management problem solving, like that of the reengineers, emphasized a particular subsystem with little recognition of the importance of the others and with little understanding that problem solving and consulting is multisystem in nature.

More recent approaches view the organization as an open sociotechnical system with subsystems and interactions that, in total, are *co-producers* of organization and management behavior (and of problems). Organization behaviors are explained as a result of the *converging influences* of goals and values, technology, structure, and psychosocial and managerial characteristics and actions.

How is organizational systems thinking used to teach and practice problem solving and consultation (Ziegenfuss, 1992)? The sociotechnical systems view is both a general perspective and a specific model that defines all public and private organizations. The five subsystems are the internal elements examined when teaching and practicing problem solving through internal and external consulting. As a whole, these subsystems and their interrelationships *are* the organization to be analyzed, planned for, and acted on—the targets of interventions.

Teaching. To teach graduate management students about the consulting process, students are asked to analyze cases using the model to create a diagnosis, a plan for action, and impact measures of the changes (Ziegenfuss, 1996). The model drives group presentations of diagnosis, planning, action, and evaluation, and it helps students match problems with intervention tools and techniques.

Practice. In consulting practice, the model has been used regularly to guide board members' and senior managers' analyses of their organizations' strengths and weaknesses as a part of strategy formation. Between 800 and 1,000 senior managers and board members have used the model during the past 10 years as part of a strategic planning process. Along with internal "diagnosis" of the internal state of the organization, the model guides vision building (descriptions of the desired corporate future) by outlining a rich perspective of the organization future (Massie-Mara & Ziegenfuss, 2000; Ziegenfuss, 1989).

Research. The model also has been used in a series of research studies, for example, to attack medical malpractice (Ziegenfuss & Perlman, 1989), to identify barriers to quality improvement (Ziegenfuss, 1991), to create a conceptual plan for actions to improve quality (Ziegenfuss, 1992, 1993), as part of the scheme for a Delphi study of desired characteristics of departments of medicine (Jacques, Bauer, & Ziegenfuss, 1993), as a conceptual map for understanding the impact of organization change (Ziegenfuss, Munzenrider, & Lartin-Drake, 1998), and for organizing health care cost containment efforts (Ziegenfuss & Bentley, 2000).

The organizational systems model, as adapted here, has been used extensively as a part of a way of teaching consultation and engaging in consultative practice. It offers both elegance and simplicity, making it accessible to both students and managers. We can use the model to help us address the many problems of the IRS. And we can use it as a conceptual model for attacking problems of all types from diagnoses to action in many fields and industries.

Stakeholders

We now must consider who is involved in any given problem because we need their ideas, we need their advocacy, and we need to address their resistance to change (Golembiewski, 1993; Mitchell, Agle, & Wood, 1997). The IRS case is only one example. Each problem in any field involves a set of interested parties, labeled by some authors as *stakeholders*. To address the problem effectively, we must know who has a "stake" in a successful change (problem solving). For example, a team created to address the IRS problems would list the involved "parties to the problems." Who are they? Politicians, employees, tax attorneys, and citizens would be a good start.

Tschirhart (1996) defined stakeholders and the reasons why we attempt to manage them in problem-plagued organizations such as the IRS and in virtually all problem-solving and consulting engagements:

> Skilled management of the interactions of organizations with their stakeholders may help organizations achieve their missions by reducing the negative effects of dissatisfied stakeholders and encouraging support from key stakeholders. An organization's stakeholders include its employees, volunteers, board members, funders, suppliers, clients/consumers, regulators, contractors, competitors, collaborators, and any other actors who have a stake in the organization's performance and/or the power to affect organizational performance. A stakeholder's claims or interests in an organization may be economic, legal, or moral. (p. 1)

In the IRS case, business owners have an economic stake. Audited citizens have a legal one. And all citizens have a moral stake in the fairness of this key governmental agency. In each case, the stakeholders must be identified, and their positions must be understood.

In his book *Stakeholders of the Organizational Mind,* Mitroff (1983) identified seven categories of stakeholders that help us develop an "inclusionary net" of interested persons (Table 1.1). Starting engagements with a stakeholder analysis tells us who we will have to attend to during the problem-solving process. Stakeholders always are present. To attack organization and management problems, stakeholders must be identified, and their values and positions must be understood. Without systematic understanding of their views, problem solving proceeds as if their needs will be met by chance. The identification and involvement of stakeholders helps us expand the range and depth of problem solutions. And by including those with a stake in the problem, we can begin to address and minimize resistance to change.

Table 1.1 Stakeholders

1. The *imperative* approach identifies stakeholders who feel strongly enough about an organization's proposed policies or actions to act on their feelings.

2. The *positional* approach identifies those stakeholders who occupy formal positions in a policy-making structure, whether internal or external to the organization (e.g., government).

3. The *reputational* approach is a sociometric one. It entails asking various knowledgeable or important persons to nominate those who they believe have a stake in the system.

4. The *social participation* approach identifies individuals or organizations as stakeholders to the extent that they participate in activities related to a policy issue.

5. Because one of the reasons for identifying stakeholders is to assess their leverage and influence in a policy system, it sometimes is adequate to identify only those who tend to shape the opinions of other stakeholders. The *opinion-leadership* method does this.

6. The *demographic* approach identifies stakeholders by characteristics such as age, sex, race, occupation, religion, place of birth, and level of education.

7. The final method selects a *focal organization* in a policy system and seeks to identify the individuals and organizations that have important relationships with the focal organization. Typical relationships include those of (a) supplier, (b) employee, (c) customer or client, (d) ally, (e) competitor or adversary, (f) regulator or controller (e.g., government), and (g) regulatee or controlee (e.g., subdivisions of a parent organization, legally controlled entities).

SOURCE: Mitroff (1983).

How does this view of the organization as interrelated sociotechnical systems relate to problem-solving action by internal teams or outside consultants?

Action Research and Organizational Development

We now know what problems are, we have a definition of the organization, and we can identify and call on stakeholders for their help and involvement. What processes do we use to attack problems?

In this approach, organizational problem solving is considered to be both "action research" and "organizational development." A brief definition from a popular text introduced the philosophy and method:

Action research is a data-based problem-solving process of organizational change that closely follows the steps involved in the scientific method. It represents a powerful approach to organizational change and consists of three essential steps:

- Gathering information about problems, concerns, and needed changes from the members of an organization.

- Organizing this information in some meaningful way and sharing it with the employees involved in the change effort.
- Planning and carrying out specific actions to correct identified problems.

An organizational change program may go through repeated cycles of data gathering, information sharing, and action planning and implementation. The action research often concludes with a follow-up evaluation of the implemented actions. (Hellriegel, Slocum, & Woodman, 1998, p. 592)

Action research has received increasing attention from both researchers and practitioners during the past 10 years, and the strategy often is used to address problems (Greenwood & Levin, 1998; Reason & Bradbury, 2001; Stringer, 1999). Organization and management problem solving can be viewed as an *action research activity that is part of an overall strategy of organizational development.* This "system and whole organization" orientation to problem solving has meaning for how problems are engaged. When we confront situations such as the IRS case, we can too easily be led to the replacement of leaders and the notion that restructuring will "fix" the organization. But in cases where problems, as in Ackoff's language, are an interconnected "mess," we will need multiple actions in multiple systems along with follow-up data and reevaluation. The IRS problem really is one of long-term change and development that will require experimental action and a wide range of methods. It is not simply a problem of a flawed leader.

Organization development is an umbrella term for the philosophy and methods of continuous improvement of every aspect of the company (e.g., performance quality, productivity, efficiency, culture, leadership). Some leading organizational development activities and concepts currently in common use were presented by French and Bell (1990) some years ago and are listed in Table 1.2. In a problem-solving engagement, one, two, or several of these activities may be used and integrated into a "whole organization" strategy for improvement. Although some of these are not systems thinking in orientation, we can employ them as part of a rich strategy that is based in systems. We advocate the use of different methods in a pluralistic and complementary manner (Jackson, 1995).

Organization and management problem solving involves the use of one or several of these methods to dissolve the conditions that have given rise to problems, conditions that may be rooted in product/technology, structure, psychological climate, management, and culture systems.

Table 1.2 Organization Development Activities

---

      1. Diagnostic activities
      2. Team-building activities
      3. Intergroup activities
      4. Survey-feedback activities
      5. Education and training activities
      6. Structural activities
      7. Process-consultation activities
      8. Coaching and counseling activities
      9. Life and career planning activities
    10. Open-systems planning
    11. Action research

SOURCE: French and Bell (1990).

For example, at the IRS, the new commissioner might select a number of activities to foster organization development including the following:

- A diagnostic inquiry to determine the breadth and depth of the troubles at the IRS
- Survey feedback activities to collect and consider information from citizens and employees about both the problem diagnosis and some remedial actions
- Training in conflict resolution and conflict avoidance as well as in customer service sensitivity
- Coaching and counseling to improve supervisory skills
- Restructuring of the quota and incentive systems for monitoring performance

This "package" of organizational development activities will produce improvement because of the multisystem targets and the recognition of interactive effects. Now how does the problem-solving work flow?

Problem Solving and Consultation Phases, Interventions, and Engagement Questions

Exactly what happens when a problem-solving or consulting team addresses a problem? Managerial problem solving and consulting often, but not always, follows a series of phases or steps. Regardless of whether the problem solvers and consultants have a role within the organization, are located outside the organization, or are some combination of "insiders" and "outsiders," there are certain basic patterns of interaction between the client and the consultant. These are the "steps" of the process of problem solving and consulting. Here they are presented as phases, building on Lippitt and Lippitt's (1975) work. These authors described the consultant-client working relationship throughout a problem-solving experience with the description of the workflow applying to both inside and outside teams. When a team is formed to address the problems at the IRS or at any other public agency or private company, five phases comprise the flow of the "engagement" or task:

1. Contact, entry, and relationship building
2. Contract formulation and diagnosis/engagement parameters
3. Planning the goals, steps, and actions of problem solving (change effort)
4. Action taking and continuity of effort
5. Evaluation and termination

Each of the phases can involve joint and individual work activities between client and consultant (or problem solver). Each of these phases is now described in more detail.

Phase 1: Contact, entry, and relationship building. In the first phase, problem solvers and consultants must make contact with the organization and the relevant executives. The contact can be seen as the start of the consultation (Quick & Kets de Vries, 2000; Schein, 1987). As insiders, the staff might already know about the problem. Outside consultants must somehow learn that a problem exists. Most engagements begin with a referral, with the first contact being critical (Bowers & Degler, 1999). In our ongoing case, word of the internal problems of the IRS must be passed on to outsiders so as to stimulate outside pressure for change and to present a "call for help." Of course, this is a public agency with congressional hearings and front-page coverage. Still, "would-be consultants" must make contact with key insiders. Consultants, or an inside problem-solving team, must explore the need and readiness for change, the potential for collaborative work, and whether the willingness and courage to proceed are present. Both internal and external consultants must strive to "understand" the client (Long, 1999). In a high-profile problem such as that at the IRS, courage is especially needed.

Phase 2: Contract development and diagnosis/engagement parameters. In the second phase, we more fully define the nature of the problem and come to an agreement about the task (Norris, 1994). We may launch into a formal diagnostic process, sometimes with an engagement letter (Zabrosky, 1999) or, if an inside team, a "committee charge." At this point, we find out whether the client has fully developed a diagnosis of the problem. Organizational diagnosis, fully addressed as systems thinking by Harrison (1994), can be described as "the process of using conceptual models and methods from the behavioral sciences to assess an organization's current state and find ways to solve specific problems or increase its [the organization's] effectiveness" (p. 1). Harrison's view of diagnosis drifts into implementation activity. Diagnosis, in a more limited sense, is used here to guide the development of proposals for organizational change and improvement by consultants and their clients. At this point, stakeholders are identified and recruited.

When the diagnosis is complete and has shared agreement by inside and outside problem solvers, the team selected is often composed of *expert, process,* and *package of service* consultants. When diagnosis is unclear, process consultants are engaged early in the project to help the client understand the breadth and depth of the problem and to create and manage the problem-solving process.

This phase includes parceling out the roles and responsibilities including task assignments and time frames. Specific outcomes (in some contracts called "deliverables") also are defined and agreed on.

In the IRS case, experts in computer systems would be engaged to provide a second opinion on the degree of technological adequacy including how to bring hardware and software up-to-date. In recognition of the nature of tax work and citizen customers, training consultants might be engaged to offer workshops on dealing with difficult customers and team building. Both groups would have start dates, training delivery dates, and total costs clearly specified.

Phase 3: Planning. In this phase, the diagnostic activity is completed, with relevant data collected, analyzed, and fed back to the client and executives. In these early phases, the feedback of data in regard to the diagnosis is crucial. In the first several phases, the problem solvers collect data to develop or to confirm/disconfirm what the contact client has deemed to be the problem. The way in which feedback is handled as both art and science (Kuhnert, 1993) is vital to the development and maintenance of the relationship between consultants and the client. *High-quality* feedback emphasizes the "here and now," individual acts, and being nonjudgmental; it facilitates change, provides psychological safety, and helps to build the problem-solving community (Golembiewski, 1993, p. 331). Harrison (1994) added that feedback is effective when it is relevant, comparative, timely, believable, sensitive, limited, and practical (p. 76). The success of the plan for intervention depends on high-quality feedback.

Plans for intervention are defined with responsibilities and time frames. In this phase, the diagnosis is used to lead us to multiple actions targeting multiple systems of the organization.

What does the IRS problem-solving plan include? To this point, we have discussed several types of interventions:

- Exploring the nature of the problem/shared agreement on diagnosis
- Expert technical advice regarding hardware and software requirements
- Training packages to build customer service and teamwork competencies
- Restructuring of the IRS into business units
- Analysis and redesign of the quota and reward systems

A full plan includes clear task assignments with responsible persons and completion dates identified.

Phase 4: Action. In this phase, actions are taken by individuals, by groups in one or more departments, or by leaders throughout the organization. Restructuring, training, hiring, firing, new compensation systems, and/or new work policies are used to address the issues raised in the diagnostic and planning phases. This implementation work is recognized as both critical and challenging (Bates & Dillard, 1993).

Phase 5: Evaluation and termination. In this final phase, the success of the interventions is tested. We ask whether the problem has been solved, that is, whether the correct actions were taken to address the problems raised at first contact and verified in the diagnostic stage. This is, in some models, a pilot-testing effort with a cycling back to diagnosis and new action if negative results are found. If successful, the engagement is terminated. The termination process is actually a complex mix of technical completion of consultant duties and the psychodynamics of assessing the degree of success (Gilmore, 1993). The problem-solving partners agree that the task has been successfully completed.

At each of the stages, there is a need to communicate and, if necessary, to reframe (Kesner & Fowler, 1997). The flow of the phases seems a bit linear and rational, sometimes not well representing the fluid nature of real problem solving. But if we think of it as a broad "directional path," with movement back to earlier stages when appropriate, then it works as a descriptor of the process.

Problem-Solving Actions:
Philosophy and Style of Interventions

We solve a problem by *intervening* in it. "Interventions," or actions and activities designed to help, can be classified in many different ways, with Blake and Mouton (1982) listing five types or categories of interventions. These categories represent an amalgamation of philosophy style and methods, some of which are not compatible with our other philosophies of organizational development and action research. But they are common styles. Think of the problem solvers or consultants as puzzling out a broad approach that will guide their selection of tools and techniques as well as their demeanor during the engagement. Table 1.3 presents the original descriptions.

What interventions would we use in the IRS case? By following the Blake and Mouton model, we could consider a mix of actions reflecting different philosophies and styles, thereby adapting to client needs for different approaches to the helping process.

1. We could conduct seminars that explain the theories and principles of customer service to IRS employees, believing that the education would lead to changed behavior (*theories and principles*).
2. We could prescribe a set of management, technical, and structural solutions in a report to Commissioner Rossotti (as outside experts, we are asked for answers) (*prescription*).
3. We could confront IRS senior managers and employees with data from surveys of citizens about the state of customer service and their unfortunate experiences as taxpayers (*confrontation*).
4. We could help an internal team conduct a fact-finding and data analysis process that would be the stimulus action leading to change (*catalytic*).
5. We could meet regularly with the commissioner and senior managers to provide psychological support and security as they begin to move through a series of major actions leading to change (while in a fishbowl of political attention) (*acceptant*).

In other words, as problem solvers, we categorize our style and methods of responding to problems, a set of philosophy/style options that is used selectively. We can *prescribe* answers or *confront* the client with unsettling data or customer feedback. We can *teach* and *stimulate* or just provide *support*. The approach can be a mix that, in its diversity, promotes change. When catalytic efforts are successful, they (a) are unpredictable, (b) distribute power, (c) have power, (d) are intolerant of nonsupporters, and (e) are ongoing (Collins, 1999).

Table 1.3 Intervention Types

1. *Theories and principles.* By making theories and principles that are pertinent to the client's situation evident, the consultant helps the client to internalize systematic and empirically tested ways of understanding and acting. When learned so well as to be personally useful, these principles permit the client to view his or her situation in a more analytic, cause-and-effect fashion than has hitherto been possible. Thus, the client becomes able to diagnose and deal with present and future situations in more valid ways. From the outset, he or she can correct an immediate problem or can plan for long-range improvements on the basis of proven effective approaches. Interventions that bring theories and principles into use involve joining education and consultation in a single action. . . .

2. *Prescription.* The consultant tells the client what to do to rectify a given situation or else does it for him or her. The consultant assumes responsibility for formulating the solution as a recommendation to be followed. . . .

3. *Confrontation.* This action challenges a client to examine how the present foundations of his or her thinking—usually value-laden assumptions—may be coloring and distorting the way [in which] situations are viewed. Possible alternatives that might lead to more effective solutions may then come clearly into view. . . .

4. *Catalytic.* A catalytic intervention assists the client in collecting data and information to evaluate and possibly reinterpret his or her perceptions as to how things are, based on better or more extensive knowledge of the situation. In this way, the client may arrive at a better awareness of underlying causes of a problem and how to address or resolve it. . . .

5. *Acceptant.* The intention is to aid the client to develop a basic sense of personal security so that he or she will feel free to express personal thoughts without fear of being judged or rejected. The client may be helped to sort out his or her emotions and, in this way, get a more objective view of the situation.

SOURCE: Blake and Mouton (1982).

During each engagement, problem solvers and consultants must decide which engagement approaches should be used for what reasons.

How do these interventions fit into this model of problem solving and consulting? Problem-solving consultants and managers can ask themselves questions about their cases (as can students in a management class). These self-reflective questions are used to define the philosophical, stylistic, and methodological approaches to problem solving in any given engagement. Although the following list does not describe all options, four key questions help us define *the* approach to the problem (building on Blake & Mouton's, 1982, model):

Who is leading the engagement?

- The consultant and problem solvers (outsiders and insiders)

To whom is the work directed? Who is the client?

- Individual
- Group
- Intergroup
- Organization
- Large social system

Why is the team working on the problem? Is it to address an issue in one or more of the following systems?

- Product/technology
- Structural
- Psychosocial
- Managerial
- Culture, goals, and values

What is the general approach? Is it some kind of intervention philosophy and strategy, such as the following?

- Theory and principles
- Prescriptive
- Confrontational
- Catalytic
- Acceptant

The "why" in the model is very much driven by the diagnostic work based on this five-system conceptual view of the organization. The "what," in a broader sense, includes getting second opinions or technical assistance on topics such as computer technology and training systems (given the intervention approach). As we add more understanding to our knowledge of problem-solving and consulting practices, the options will expand.

The first question—"Who is leading the engagement?"—can be answered in several ways.

Problem Solvers: Consultant Types and Roles

What type of problem solvers do we need at the IRS? What roles will they play? In a basic way, we can think of problem solvers as experts, as skilled pairs of hands, or as facilitators (Long, 1999). Within the overall approach of a systems-oriented problem-solving model, different types of consultants and consulting products (packages) can be used effectively if they are delivered within the total system context. Several writers have described types of consultants. Schein (1993a) referred to content experts, doctors, and process consultants (p. 653). No definitions of consultant types have yet gained full consensus, but they are described here with the labels *packaged service* consultant, *expert advice* consultant, and *process* consultant. Keep in mind that managers and their problem-solving teams can act as consultants as they solve problems, so these options apply to internal agents as well.

The *packaged service* consultant is an individual who provides a specific "prefabricated" program, usually an "off-the-shelf" item. Training, new hardware installation, and turnkey operations of all sorts are examples. Here we can think about the positive and negative images of "pre-fab." Characteristics such as speed of construction, standardization, quality, and volume come to mind. As we consider projects developed to high-quality specifications, we can come to see consulting packages as effective because they are well tested, are delivered repeatedly in different environments, and conform to expectations of high quality.

For example, employees in every field have received fliers and brochures that invite participation in a professional education program of one kind or another. It may focus on team building, conflict management, time management, or any one of a number of management concerns. A current list might include searching the Web, managing stress, giving effective presentations, improving computing skills, and using quality analysis tools. Such programs frequently are available through executive development centers at colleges and universities and often are designed and conducted by selected staff of the institutions. They are developed as "standard models" (products) designed to be offered in similar fashion to many organizations. Other programs also are offered by private groups or practitioners. During the 1990s, total quality management training and reengineering programs were popular examples.

According to Schein (1987), four assumptions underlie the use of the packaged service consultant:

1. The client has correctly diagnosed the problem.
2. The client has correctly identified the consultant's capabilities to provide the expertise.
3. The client has correctly communicated the problem and the nature of the expertise or information that is to be purchased.
4. The client has thought through and accepted the potential consequences of obtaining the information or the service. (p. 23)[2]

Think about these important assumptions. One must get the diagnosis right—on one's own. The programs are helpful when the registrants are certain that the contents of the programs are directly related to their professional or organizational needs. Most of the time, the fliers include descriptions of the programs being offered, the names and backgrounds of the people who will conduct the programs, and other information regarding fees, locations, and registration. The major advantage to packaged service activities are relatively low cost, opportunities to meet people with similar needs from other organizations, and concentration of effort (most seminars are designed to be 2- or 3-day intensive learning programs). In our example, the IRS team might use packages of consultation for training, for new technology implementation, for individual staff development, and for a new performance incentive structure.

A major disadvantage to such programs is that they cannot, by virtue of their target audience, be company specific. They rarely are designed to deal with each participant's particular or unique problems; they can lead to "cookie-cutter" thinking (Pringle, 1998). Another disadvantage is that the learning is not easily transferable to employees' company environments. By definition, there is limited follow-up, there is no ongoing education, and only rarely is there any evaluation of results. Finally, predesigned programs succeed because of their standardization (bringing efficiency and low cost) and fail due to lack of flexibility. The contents and teaching methods for the programs usually are "locked in." Only rarely can participants redesign the programs if they do not meet their expectations.

This packaged service consultant mode, then, assumes that clients can use a set of "predeveloped products" that can be applied in generic fashion across industries. For example, whole product packages are delivered repeatedly in almost identical fashion to the IRS and to companies in transportation, health care, and banking. Although there are some consulting services that can be offered in this way, not all such services can be. Expert advice on a problem specific to only one organization might be needed on an individual basis.

The second type of problem solver is the *expert advice* consultant. Four assumptions underlie the use of the expert consultant, sometimes referred to as the doctor-patient model of consultation. According to Schein (1987), this model is effective when the following conditions apply:

1. The diagnostic process itself will be seen as helpful.
2. The client has correctly interpreted the organization's symptoms and has located the sick area.
3. The person or group defined as "sick" will reveal the pertinent information necessary to make a valid diagnosis; that is, [the person or group] will neither hide data nor exaggerate symptoms.

4. The client will understand and correctly interpret the diagnosis provided by the consultant and will implement whatever prescription is offered.
5. The client can remain healthy after the consultant leaves. (p. 25)[2]

These expert consultants are asked to visit the organization to diagnose its "state of health or illness" or to examine a particular technical activity. This usually is done through observations of staff meetings and employee activities and through interviews with specialists and managers. Sometimes, extensive data are collected about an aspect of technology or of the production and delivery process. After gathering the necessary data, a comprehensive report is prepared, typically containing a description of the corporation and situation, an analysis of the problems, listings of key findings and recommendations, and a cost of implementation analysis. Here the consultants offer procedures and strategies for accomplishing recommended changes.

Expert consultants are brought in because, in theory, they are objective and minimize internal biases. But the consultants selected often result from clients' biases about the nature of the problems and solutions. Problem solving using outsiders is "given over" to acknowledged experts in specialty fields of organization (e.g., marketing, production, finance, human resources) and specific technology (e.g., information systems, engineering). Deep training and much experience and ability are added. The studies can be very expensive and often include the analyses and recommendations that would have come from the companies' own employees. Follow-up and implementation can fail because of the "light" commitment to the outsiders' analysis and recommendations. The diagnosis–planning–action–evaluation cycle is not so much a partnership with the client as it is a partnership with organization development approaches.

These two types of consulting approaches—packaged and expert—are used frequently, but there are reservations about their use. We often reject packaged programs because organizations have *specific* and *unique* problems, not *general* ones. The transferability of standard solutions is questioned. Expert consultation uses outsiders to solve company problems. Unless the organization happens to learn the problem-solving process—typically not a part of the assignment—it will have to call in the experts each time the problem comes up.

The third consultant type, the *process* consultant, is a professional group or individual focusing attention on how work is accomplished. This model is advocated by organization development specialists. According to Schein (1987), six conditions underlie the process consultation model:

1. The client is hurting somehow but does not know the source of the pain or what to do about it.

2. The client does not know what kind of help may be available and which consultant can provide the kind of help that may be needed.

3. The nature of the problem is such that the client not only needs help in figuring out what is wrong but also would benefit from participation in the process of making a diagnosis.

4. The client has "constructive intent," is motivated by goals and values that the consultant can accept, and has some capacity to enter into a helping relationship.

5. The client is ultimately the only one who knows what form of intervention will work in the situation.

6. The client is capable of learning how to diagnose and solve his [sic] own organizational problems. (p. 32)[2]

The process consultant analyzes and redesigns the way in which organization problems are defined and addressed. This problem-solving capability is the target of the help, which is focused on the needs of the client, much like a clinical inquiry in personal therapy (Schein, 1995). In this model, a diagnosis is made, the results of the diagnosis are shared with employees and management, and the needs of the organization are identified and clarified as a part of the consulting process. In collaboration with company staff, problems are prioritized, including the need for education and training. Problem-solving process helpers can be internal, such as a process improvement director in a medical center (Shimkus, 2000), or can be brought in from the outside. Consultants and the client jointly develop a program designed to meet the organization's needs. It is not generic or prepackaged; instead, it is client specific (Jacobsen, 1990). Education efforts are planned, conducted, and evaluated in a continuing cycle until organizationwide competence exists. Process consultation requires a long-term relationship between consultants and the client, in the process developing a shared interest in the success of the outcome. Although not completely analogous, "corporate coach" is another label (Miller & Brown, 1995).

For example, a process consultant could be hired to lead a search for an IRS future (Cahoon, 1993). The process consultant would not prescribe what that future would be (as a package or an expert might). Instead, the process consultant would establish a means by which the participants could analyze their environment and stakeholder needs, self-reflectively assess the conditions of the IRS as it is, and jointly begin to craft a vision of the IRS's future. Participation, commitment, and creativity are fostered by the design of the process. No expert directives are issued, and no "standard package" of public agency futures is likely to exist. Instead, the client is taught and coached, building continuing capability to problem solve (Washburn, 1995).

Although this is not an exhaustive comparison of the models, the presentation has highlighted significant differences in the approaches to the problem-solving and consulting functions. Many organization development and systems practitioners do not believe that package and expert engagements are helpful unless they are conceived as part of "whole organization interventions." As a conclusion to this review (and as a statement of my bias), the Organizational Development Institute (1981) further commented on the differences and strengths of the process approach:

> In the *purchase-of-service model,* it is the participants who must determine the value of what was learned. If they are satisfied, they wait for some sort of "follow-up program" to provide the next level of learning; and such follow-ups are relatively rare.
>
> In the *expert advice model,* the client system must determine the value of the information and recommendations provided. They [client system] must also take responsibility for putting these recommendations to work. The problem here is that many client systems often lack the skills necessary to do that and, consequently, these "best-laid plans" never materialize.
>
> In the *process consultant model,* the implementation of action plans is typically a mutual effort between the consultant and the client system. The client system wants the plans to work because it developed them. The consultant wants the plan to work because consultant success is very closely tied to the success of the client system. The major disadvantages of the process consultant model are that client systems may have to share with the consultant in the investment of time and energy during all phases of the project. Organization development (OD) projects are long-term efforts, usually taking 2 years or more, and OD requires a learning commitment on the part of the organization as well as a financial investment.

Now we increasingly recognize the change management aspects of successful organization development.

How would these three types of consultants appear in our IRS case? First, we could engage a firm to provide a package of customer service training seminars to all our employees. We would have determined that surly behavior toward taxpaying citizens was caused, in part, by the lack of training—"not knowing" how to behave with clients.

Or, we could hire an information systems expert to help us determine how to move the IRS data system into the 21st century. This outside expert would prescribe a set of technical solutions regarding the acquisition of new hardware and software.

Or, we could hire a process consultant to work with an internal team of IRS employees to diagnose the problems in organization and technology and to develop a shared plan for corrective action. The process consultant would not prescribe answers; instead, the consultant would teach and support problem solving by the internal team.

In fact, we probably would need to employ all three types of consultants to address the wide range of IRS problems.

All the consultants must draw on power to make change. Each type of consultant—expert, package, and process—uses some or all of the following five sources of influence (French & Raven, 1968) plus an amalgamation that I think of as "personal" power, meaning charisma plus:

- Legitimate
- Coercive
- Reward
- Expert
- Referent
- Personal

Expert consultants draw on their legitimacy and expertise and on their referent linkage to senior managers (with their coercive and reward power). Process consultants often have strong interpersonal skills—a contributor to their personal power.

As we consider the three types of consultants and problem solvers, we should remember that they can be internal or external to the organization or a team with a combined locus. In large organizations, there are experts of all types, including very well-developed education and training groups and quality improvement and reengineering teams.

For internal consultants, the advantages to being based inside the organization include the following:

- Knowledge of the culture
- Knowledge of power sources and levers
- Track record of success and credibility

- On-site availability
- "Sunk" and somewhat hidden costs
- Pressure for follow-up
- Awareness of the whole problem environment

For external consultants, the advantages to being based outside the organization include the following:

- Free of bias and political linkages
- Power of the "external expert"
- Freedom to offer unpopular recommendations
- New skills and knowledge and "extra hands"
- Direct costs (often high)
- Natural termination points

In each engagement, there is a combination of advantages and disadvantages in the makeup of the team that will influence the decision to use insiders or outsiders. An inside-outside collaboration often is used, but there can be problems of clashing perspectives and methods (Lacey & Samuels, 2000).

When problem solving, managers or consultants can deliver predeveloped packages, offer advice, or use process skills to help clients and employees problem solve. The stated advantages/disadvantages inform us about each model's applicability. The preceding arguments seem to favor process work. But *all three types* are in constant use by consultants and managers in all kinds of profit and nonprofit organizations. This situation will continue. The task is to *match* the type of consultant with the appropriate problem situation and the organization's needs. The matching process is helped by considering the roles that the consultants are expected to play in solving the organization's problems.

Consultant Activities and Roles

We need to further describe the activities that consultants and internal problem-solving teams undertake for their clients. Some years ago, Turner (1982) listed eight activities central to the consulting and problem-solving process:

1. Providing information to a client
2. Solving a client's problems
3. Making a diagnosis, which may necessitate redefinition of the problem

4. Making recommendations based on the diagnosis
5. Assisting with implementation of recommended solutions
6. Building a consensus and commitment around corrective action
7. Facilitating client learning, that is, teaching clients how to resolve similar problems in the future
8. Permanently improving organizational effectiveness

Each of the three types of consultants—packaged service, expert, and process—contributes some but usually not all of these activities, which are engaged in through the performance of roles.

When consultants work in organizations, they do so with a variety of purposes and functions. Lippitt (1975) defined eight roles that consultants can act in as they problem solve. This role set has been used to describe the roles of the ombudsman and the quality management specialist (Ziegenfuss, 1987a, 1988b). Both specialists are internal consultants. Others have defined the problem solver's roles as initiator, expert, and facilitator (Geberlein, 1989). Think of how the IRS team of inside staff and outside consultants will need to act in each of the following roles. Note that the roles fit managers engaged in participative problem-solving teams as well as outside consultants.

The roles are separated into *process* and *content,* language that distinguishes the *way* we work from the *substance* of the problems. In process roles, consultants and problem-solving teams contribute their efforts to developing and improving the way in which problems are attacked and resolved. In content roles, consultants are relied on for expertise and skills relevant to the specific nature of the problems. Acting in a process role, consultants can facilitate a meeting between two "warring" department directors. Acting in a content/expert role, consultants may give an opinion about the safety of a bridge design or the options for new IRS software. Some consultants stay with one role, whereas others operate in a repertoire of ways (Lundberg, 1994).

The process roles of the consultant include the following four roles, with some examples of representative actions:

1. *Facilitator/Human dynamics specialist.* The consultant addresses the work process itself as a way of enhancing client competence. Here the consultant attempts to help the client to be more responsive to organization problems and more effective in solving them. In this role, the consultant helps to plan and facilitate meetings, engages in "shuttle diplomacy" to negotiate conflicts, and reports observations about meeting style and effectiveness to the client. At the IRS, managing the human dynamics of taxpayer and congressional relations

might require help to control emotions, constrain politics, and maintain a focus on solutions.

2. *Advocate role.* Some consultants are hired to be advocates for change and continuous improvement. As an advocate, the consultant works to influence the client to change in some way such as becoming informed about and use total quality management. For example, a consultant may be engaged to assist in strategic planning process design while simultaneously acting as an advocate for adaptation to a changing environment. Consultants could become advocates for new hardware and software or for improved customer service at the IRS.

3. *Collaborator in problem solving.* In this process role, the consultant partners with the client, announcing a desire to share the challenge of the task and the responsibility for success. The helping role complements the client work on the problem but does not displace it with a unilateral outside prescription. Consultants could work with the IRS commissioner to begin to change the culture and to develop a new structure of the agency.

4. *Reflector.* This role is defined by supportive active listening. As a reflector, the consultant assists in client decision making by asking questions that offer empathy and help to clarify, modify, or change a situation. The consultant is a "sounding board" to enable the client to verbalize and test possible diagnoses and solution alternatives—a "safe haven" for thinking out loud. Beset by angry citizens and congressional watchdogs, the IRS commissioner needs a secure and safe sounding board.

As a whole, these four roles are directed toward enhancing the client's understanding of the dynamics of problems and solutions. Content roles include the following: technical expert, fact finder, teacher, and alternative identifier.

5. *Technical expert.* One role of an internal or external consultant is providing specialist expertise in a field or function. The technical specialist, through his or her special knowledge, skill, and professional experience, is engaged to complement or supplement the skills and knowledge in the client organization. Consistent with the assumptions of the doctor-patient model, the client is responsible for problem diagnosis, for establishing the objectives of the consultation, and sometimes for implementation. Technical experts provide opinions and answers, for example, offering a recommended set of technical specifications for new computer hardware and software at the IRS.

6. *Fact finder.* All consulting involves some sort of investigative work. Fact-finding is an integral part of solving both technical and social-psychological problems. With an action research approach, the fact-finding can become applied research with methodological rigor. The depth, breadth, and length of the engagement define the thoroughness of the fact-finding process and related analysis (applied science). In this role, the consultant employs a wide range of qualitative and quantitative methods, from personal interviewing to statistical analysis. The IRS commissioner, confronted by public complaints and press reports, might ask consultants to survey citizens to determine the depth and breadth of their dissatisfaction with the agency.

7. *Teacher.* Consultants act as educators and trainers both directly and indirectly during engagements (Palmer, 1998). Some consultants provide training and education as a primary service, whereas others see the teaching as, for example, an "add-on" to survey work. Training programs (packaged consultation) offered to client organizations call for the teaching role almost exclusively. For example, in supporting strategic planning at the IRS, consultants hired to assist with the design of the planning process might be required to "teach" IRS staff and executives about strategy-making processes including methods for analyzing environmental changes.

8. *Identifier of options and recommendations.* Some consultants are employed specifically to offer options and recommendations. Other consultants help identify options in collaboration with the client. This role is particularly strong in the expert consultation model and is less apparent or absent in the process consultant approach. When the IRS commissioner began to see that the organization's structure was flawed, consultants hired by the agency could provide three alternative ways of organizing the agency with advantages, disadvantages (including especially costs), and feasibility.

In many engagements of significant size and duration, problem-solving managers and consultants act in a variety of the roles just noted, acting as both expert fact finders and process specialists at different points in the projects.

Consultant Skills and Competencies

Who will perform effectively as consultants or as members of insider-dominated problem-solving teams? McLean and Sullivan (1993) identified key competencies, and some years ago, Greiner and Metzger (1983) defined the essential personal characteristics required for success in this work. Now being developed is a uniform body of knowledge (International Council of Management Consulting Institutes, 1994), including codes of conduct, standards, and continuing education (Lightbown, 1993).

Many years ago, Sherlock Holmes demonstrated a number of key consulting skills in his famous cases—data gathering, determining vital facts, attending to detail, validating data, and analyzing alternatives (Webb, 1995). Some commentators with a bias toward the expert role have viewed the necessary skills as primarily technical and technological (Cooper, 1992). Others have indicated that the skill set is both social-psychological and technical, requiring the ability to develop trust and to sensitively provide feedback and support (Tagiuri, 1992). Moline (1990) identified categories of capability including orientation, consulting skills, project management skills, and industry or market skills. And once these skills have developed, practitioners and staff of both inside and outside teams must be retained. Otherwise, both expertise and client relationships are adversely affected (Morrell & Simonetto, 1999).

Skills and competencies can be tied to a single person, or they can reside in a team—the team collectively presenting the attributes required for a successful engagement. Large consulting firms and academic consulting teams (Kolenko, 1994) both bring this multifaceted perspective. When the IRS leadership looks for help, what are the selection criteria? Building on Greiner and Metzger (1983), the following competencies and skills are a good start.

Seven attributes comprise the leading professional skills and competencies required of members of inside problem-solving teams and outside consultants:

1. *Industry and/or functional expertise and experience.* This refers to background in an industry such as health care, retail, or manufacturing or in a specialty such as finance, marketing, or personnel. Background experience in public administration and tax law would fit the IRS engagement.

2. *Analytical and diagnostic.* This refers to the ability to integrate diverse streams of data to arrive at an understanding of the problem. Experience with collaborative diagnosis and problem solving is required if the approach is client centered. At the IRS, joint diagnosis would bring the client into the process, which would be very politicized from the outset.

3. *Methodological.* This refers to the ability to frame an approach to data collection, analysis, and feedback and to identify and employ change methods. In

a large engagement such as the IRS project, team members must have applied social science skills to enable them to define, collect, and analyze data.

4. *Teamwork.* This refers to the ability to appreciate and work with diverse internal and external team members (Drozodow, 1997). In the IRS project, members might represent management and information science, tax law, politics, and public policy, among other fields.

5. *Teaching.* This refers to the ability to interact with the client in an "educational mode," functioning as a teacher of technical and human relations skills (Senge, 1990). One view of surly IRS agents is that they were hired with that behavioral set. Another view is that they need to be taught new options and strategies for working with citizens.

6. *Writing and oral presentation.* This refers to the ability to develop and present project proposals (Minto, 1998) and final reports in high-quality writing and stimulating oral presentation. In some engagements, strategic storytelling works (Brown, 1998; McConkie & Boss, 1994). IRS consulting teams might need to present to both the agency management and congressional oversight committees. For the committees in particular, presentation and response skills will be key.

7. *Project management.* This refers to the ability to integrate multiple contributions, coordinate sometimes competing demands, and meet client deadlines. In high-profile projects such as the IRS case, delivery on time is critical.

All members of the consulting team must have base levels of the following personal attributes, including a strong bias and capability for self-inquiry (Badaracco, 1998). All members must know themselves and their contributions to the team.

1. *Tolerance for ambiguity.* This refers to the ability to work with uncertainty in diagnoses, work processes, and outcomes. The IRS case is a mix of organization design, politics, public policy, and law with no clear and easy answers.

2. *Openness to quantitative and qualitative data.* This refers to the ability to work with and integrate both objective numbers-oriented data and "softer" material from interviews and focus groups. IRS attention to quantitative measures of performance only is part of the problem.

3. *Relationship skills.* This refers to the ability to develop and maintain relationships with clients (Schaffer, 1997) and team members (Pick, 1992) including alliances (Sabath, 1992). IRS leaders will need both staff and congressional allies.

4. *Energy and stamina.* This refers to personal reserves that allow long days under pressure over long periods of time. For example, few congressional committees allow project teams to stop and rest.

5. *Ethics.* This refers to a desire to help within the boundaries of professional conduct (Prager, 1992). What can be done fairly in a sometimes hostile political environment? In a highly charged public engagement, consultants at the IRS will find that the truth has been "adapted" to fit positions and news headlines.

In building an internal change group or an outside consulting team, we search for candidates with these qualifications, recognizing that strengths and weaknesses can be balanced with other team members.

Problem-Solving Outcomes

How is the very real IRS case going? As reported in *USA Today,* the IRS commissioner gave an update on audits—one part of the progress:

> Rossotti says the reasons for the decline in audits include: a decade-long staff slide, antiquated computers, and IRS legislation—passed in 1998 amid a furor over alleged IRS abuses—that gave taxpayers new rights and IRS agents new customer service responsibilities that have taken them from enforcement. Even as its workload increased under the new law, the IRS's employment fell by 18,800 from the height of more than 116,000 in 1992. Many of those who remain have been reassigned from enforcement to training and customer service, the IRS says.[3]

Why do we often struggle to successfully implement solutions? Coates (1997) identified a number of reasons why organizational problem-solving efforts fail. Some of the leading reasons include inconsistencies between management's words and actions, unclear or overreaching expectations without a good measurement system to evaluate change, failure to realize that successful organizational change takes persistent effort that may last for years, absence of any long-term perspective dealing with systemic issues, capabilities of the consultant not being known or understood by management, and consultants tending to be proponents of one approach exclusively to help manage change. Sometimes, the failure is dramatic and costly. AT&T complained that it spent $500 million in a failed development and change effort (Puri, 1997). The failures are driven by a lack of understanding of the task and by poor execution. Let us think more about the task.

What do we expect to occur as a result of our consulting and problem-solving engagement? Shared understanding of the problem and commitment to resolution actions are two outcomes (Covin & Fisher, 1991). Do we want two department directors to end their conflict and work together as a team? Do we want our political critics to appreciate the turnaround at the IRS? We can consider a range of expected outcomes, from those that optimize the current conditions, to those that produce compromise from both sides, to a significant and dramatic redesign.

Ackoff (1987) helped us toward this perspective of problem dissolution:

> A problem is said to be solved when the decision maker selects those values of the controlled variables which maximize the value of the outcome, that is, when he [sic] has optimized. If he selects values of the controlled variables that do not maximize the value of the outcome but produce an outcome that is good enough, he has resolved the problem by satisficing. There is a third possibility: He may dissolve the problem. This is accomplished by changing his values so that the choices available are no longer meaningful. For example, the problem of selecting a new car may be dissolved by deciding that the use of public transportation is better than driving oneself. It may also be dissolved by moving to within walking distance from work so that driving is no longer required. We use "solving" loosely to cover all three alternatives. (p. 221)

How does this sense of outcome possibilities apply to the case of the IRS? There are three outcomes:

- *Satisficing* could be accomplished with incremental improvements in current IRS policies and procedures, some small changes in audit practices, and improved access to agents through expanded hours of operation and technologies such as 800 numbers and Web-based information.
- *Optimizing* could be accomplished by radically transforming the whole public agency. Computer hardware and software is acquired, the agency is restructured into business units, and agencywide training is employed to improve service, which is now measured by indicators and compared to other industry benchmarks. From the subject of jokes, the IRS is transformed into a model of a high-performance public agency.

- *Dissolving* of the problems could occur by creating a national flat tax or a sales tax, significantly reducing or eliminating many of the functions and structures of the IRS.

The approach to problem solving in this book, including the cases, requires us to consider both how we *solve problems* and how we *dissolve the conditions* that produce the problems in complex social organizations. Sometimes we are successful, and sometimes we are not.

What are some of the common and practical points of failure experienced by inside teams and outside consultants? Seven often encountered flaws in outsider engagements are when consultants offer fads; consultants rubber-stamp management decisions; teams answer questions when the answers already are known; senior consultants negotiate contracts but juniors are sent in to do the work; project length and scope are expanded; recommendations are not understood, thereby undercutting action; and consultants recommend what they do, thereby locking in the client (Shapiro, Eccles, & Soske, 1993). Not all consultants work in this manner, but the problems have a familiar feel.

When projects "work," what happens? In some cases, it is believed that the results come from incremental gains (Fishman & Moses, 1999). In other cases, problem solving represents a stretch or strategic leap forward (Hamel & Prahalad, 1993). One view of "high-impact" consulting specifies the key elements of problem solving success as a focus on results, willingness to change, speed, ongoing cycles (e.g., diagnosis, solutions, evaluations), and teamwork ("High Impact Consulting," 1997). Another suggests that successful outcomes result from top management support and a sponsor, consultant competence, and the consultant mode (Jang, 1998). Still other authors insist that it is results—not activity—that should drive problem solving (Schaffer & Thomson, 1992). In all cases, we are looking for specific tangible results expressed in the client's terms (Schaffer, 1995).

Analyzing Engagements: The Case Report

The preceding description of the consulting and problem-solving engagement can be combined to describe the full experience of moving through a problem, from *diagnosis* to *approach* to *impact*. The questions that drive the problem solving are represented on the checklist in Table 1.4 and are used to guide case discussion both in class and in professional assignments.

Table 1.4 Case Analysis Guidelines/Instructions

Step 1: Diagnosis

    a. *Problem identification.* What are the critical diagnostic issues/problems and the reasons for seeking help?

    b. *Sociotechnical systems analysis.* Develop the diagnosis and identify expected primary and secondary subsystem involvement—product-technology, structural, psychosocial, managerial subsystems, and culture.

    c. *Stakeholders.* Who are the critical stakeholders in the case? Describe them as types— imperative, positional, reputational, social participation, opinion leadership, demographic, and organizational.

Step 2: Approach and plan

    a. *Plan for action.* Identify the consulting approach, process, and methods to be used:
        • *Consultants:* expert–process–package
        • *Why:* information, facilitation, second opinion, objectivity, etc.
        • *Needed activities:* diagnostic, team building, survey, education and training, restructure, process, coaching, counseling, strategic planning, action research, etc.
        • *Methods:* theory, prescriptive, confrontational, catalytic, acceptant, etc.
        • *Roles:* content/fact finder, technology expert, educator, alternative identifier, process reflector, advocate, process specialist, etc.
        • *Power:* expert, reward, coercive, legitimate, referent, personal, etc.
        • *Who:* individual, group/team, intergroup, organization, larger social system, etc.

    b. *Personnel needs.* Define who is to be used in the consultation and why.

    c. *Time and responsibility.* Who does what and when?

    d. *Costs.*

Step 3: Evaluate problem and organization impact

    a. *Sociotechnical organization changes.* Define any long-term macro and micro system changes expected (system by system, if appropriate).

    b. *Problem.* resolved–solved–dissolved

    c. *Additional data needs.* What additional data would you like and why?

Summary

    This first chapter presented a description of a systems and consulting approach to organization and management problem solving. We can summarize the elements of the model by again using the IRS example. First, we consider the IRS problem to be sociotechnical in nature. It is more than creating an up-to-date information system; it also includes the culture and psychology of the agency. We can take this beginning diagnostic view further by analyzing whether the problems at the IRS are primarily technical, structural, psychosocial, managerial, or cultural in attempting to identify the leading problematic systems so as to initiate the first corrective action. As we begin our diagnosis, we consider that there are many stakeholders with a critical investment in the problems and the proposed solutions—employees, senior managers, citizens, politicians, tax lawyers, and others. Each stakeholder's position must be considered for the solution to be successful, and many stakeholders will have contributions to the problem's resolution.

Once the diagnosis is complete, we can select an internal or external consulting team. In many engagements, this selection is decided prior to diagnostic work. The IRS team's recommended actions will be prescriptive, catalytic, and educational, and they will rely on a range of methodologies dependent on the type of problems defined. For example, the IRS problem of computer inadequacy may require outside experts who will offer a prescriptive set of hardware and software suggestions. A process consultant may be brought in to help the agency plan for the future and to conduct some team-building sessions with the demoralized staff (under political attack in Washington, D.C.).

Consultants will be expected to offer second opinions as outside experts, or they will be counted on as a process team engaged in internal organization development. Frequently, the approach chosen is an action research one. Not all solutions to the IRS problems can be defined in a "master solution plan." Instead, they will emerge from some action/evaluation/redesign strategies, converting problem solving into organizational learning. Finally, the problems will be solved with a transformed IRS, or we will have successfully dissolved the conditions that produced it in the first place (e.g., with a flat tax).

The balance of the book offers further information on the locale of the problems—five organizational systems—and cases illustrating problem-solving interventions in those systems. The variety and depth of the cases are purposeful, reflecting what real teams and managers face. As you read the cases, consider how you and your own team would address the problems.

Notes

1. From F. E. Kast, *Organization and Management: A systematic contingency approach.* Copyright © 1985 by The McGraw-Hill Companies. Reprinted with permission.
2. From E. H. Schein, *Process consultation* (Vol. 2). Copyright © 1987 by Pearson Education, Inc., Upper Saddle River, NJ. Reprinted with permission.
3. From USA TODAY, Copyright 2001. Reprinted with permission.

PART 4

PROFESSIONAL CAREER
DEVELOPMENT

Resumes, Interviews and Negotiation

Quintanilla, K.M. and Wahl, S.T.

Many job seekers focus so much on answering interview questions that they forget they need to ask questions as well. Asking questions is important for two reasons: First, when done correctly, the questions you ask can confirm your qualifications as a candidate for the position. Second, remember that you are interviewing the employer as much as they are interviewing you; it is critical to learn if the organization is one you would like to work for (Konop, 2014). Writing in *Forbes* magazine, Joe Konop (2014) recommends preparing three to five questions for each interview, and planning on asking three of them. Here are three of his examples:

- **What skills and experiences would make an ideal candidate?** This is a good open-ended question that has the interviewer(s) state exactly what the employer is looking for.

- **What is the single largest concern facing your staff, and would I be in a position to help you solve this problem?** This question shows that you are immediately thinking about how you can help the team and encourages the interviewer to imagine you working in the position.

- **What is the next step in the process?** This is a critical last question and one you should definitely ask. It shows that you're interested in moving along in the process and invites the interviewer to disclose how many people are going for the same position.

As you read this chapter, remember that there is no one-size-fits-all type of résumé, cover letter, or interview strategy. It is important to do your homework on the company and tailor your job hunting strategy to the goals of the company. After reading this chapter, you should have the tools necessary to make your pre- and post-interview impression stand out with potential employers.

What do you want to be when you grow up? This is a question you have been asked from the time you were old enough to speak. Back then, you probably had no trouble responding. "I want to be an astronaut/a movie star/a princess." These are all common responses from children and, indeed, all interesting occupations. However, as you aged, most of you probably became less certain about what you wanted to be when you grew up.

This uncertainty makes selecting a major in college a daunting task for many students. Once you *have* selected, the uncertainty remains as you face the plethora of career choices available to every major. For example, communication is a highly sought-after skill but not a job title. So in a way, a degree in communication makes you qualified for nothing and everything all at once. The communication major must explore various areas of the discipline to find his or her individual focus. Within each of those areas are countless opportunities that can be both exciting and overwhelming.

Even seemingly defined majors such as nursing, accounting, and teaching require career exploration. You may want to be a nurse, but what kind of nurse? Do you want to work for a doctor's office, a clinic, or a hospital? With what kind of population do you wish to work? Would you prefer to work with children, women, the elderly, diabetics, burn victims, or cancer patients? The choices are many.

Fortunately, there is no need to fear. Considering that the average person holds numerous jobs in his or her lifetime, you'll have your entire career to grow, develop, and find your perfect fit. However, getting started on the right path can help maximize success and minimize frustration. By applying KEYS to the job-seeking process, you can start on the right path.

THE JOB-SEEKING PROCESS

What is the job-seeking process? What does it entail? Seeking a job is a multifaceted process that is part research, part performance, and part roller-coaster ride. The job-seeking process involves six stages: exploring, researching, applying, interviewing, following up, and negotiating.

We have integrated the KEYS process into our discussion of the stages of job seeking. By doing this, we hope that you will begin to see how the KEYS process can be applied to this communication situation, as well as to others that we cover in later chapters. Our discussion of the job-seeking process will be skills based. In other words, we are going to focus on communication skills (e.g., writing résumés, being interviewed) that will help you excel in the job-seeking process.

As a student of communication, it's important to realize that the discussion of communication skills is, in fact, the application of communication theory. As you read about the various skills, reflect on the theories and concepts we covered in Chapters 1, 2, and 3. For example, you learned that communication is a transactional process, not a pipeline. In this chapter, you will apply that concept by developing audience-centered messages. You also learned in the opening chapter that the communication context affects messages. Being offered a job changes the context and thereby changes the rules. So the question "What is the salary range and the benefits package?" sends two very different messages depending on when it is asked during the interviewing process. You learned in Chapter 2 that nonverbal communication is a vital component in any message. This chapter shows how the regulative rules for nonverbal communication (e.g., clothing, handshakes, eye contact) matter in the job-seeking process. In Chapter 3, you learned strategies to improve your listening. Excellent listening is a critical first step to successfully answering questions during interviews.

STAGE ONE: EXPLORING

The exploring stage begins with you, the job seeker. During this stage, you will need to explore both yourself and potential careers.

SELF-EXPLORATION

The first step in the KEYS approach is *know yourself*, so begin there with self-exploration. Take time to explore your goals and priorities. Here are just a few questions you should consider: What are you best at? What do you enjoy doing the most? What motivates you? What salary range do you need to live the lifestyle you desire? Is a family-friendly career a priority for you? Would you prefer to work in a large or small organization?

Taking time to think about your goals and priorities is an important part of the job-seeking process—it will help you determine what type of career you wish to pursue and what types of organizations you wish to work for.

CAREER EXPLORATION

Career exploration requires you to research opportunities in your major that correspond with your goals and priorities. Being a foreign correspondent may sound like a wonderful career, but if being a highly involved parent is your top priority, foreign correspondent would not be a wonderful career for you. Instead, you could use that same skill set to work for a local public relations firm, which would not require you to spend long periods of time away from your children.

As you narrow down career opportunities, it's important to develop a clear understanding of what each career entails. When you find a career that seems interesting, you need to do some investigating. Interview several people in that line of work and find out what the job involves. Ask questions that will help you determine if this career lines up with your goals and priorities. If it seems like a good fit, try shadowing someone in the field for a week or two. Then seek an internship that will allow you to develop a clearer understanding of this career choice. To many people, this may seem like an unnecessary step, but the interviewing phase of the job-seeking process isn't about finding the candidate with the most qualifications; it's about finding the person who is the best fit for the job and the company. The more you know about a given occupation, the more effectively you will be able to describe how your skills line up with the position.

STAGE TWO: RESEARCHING

The researching stage of the job-seeking process comprises two components: researching openings and researching potential employers.

RESEARCHING OPENINGS

Once you have an idea of what you are looking for in theory, you must begin to seek positions that exist in reality. For some students, this can be disappointing. Your dream job may require 5 years of experience that you do not have. The honest truth is that few students land their dream job right out of college. So become aware of the steps or experiences you'll need to get to your dream job, and begin working your way up the ladder.

Know Yourself:
RON EXPLORES HIS CAREER

As you read the passage below and answer the questions, think about how this knowledge can help you with your career search.

Ron was an outstanding student who was driven to succeed. As graduation approached, however, he was shocked to realize he had never clearly defined his goals for his future career or for his life. He had never thought about his priorities as they related to the type of position he wanted after graduation. "I guess I just thought I would graduate and someone would knock on my door and say, 'Come work for us. We have the perfect job for you!'" When he came to the realization that such a knock was never coming, he began with the first step in the KEYS approach to professional excellence, *know yourself*. He determined he wanted a position that gave him autonomy, allowed him to lead groups, would pay for graduate school, and would not make him wear a tie. He also discovered that his interviewing skills needed some polishing. Armed with this insight, Ron began searching for a position that would meet his criteria, simultaneously

practicing his interviewing skills. After a few months of searching and interviewing, Ron found a position that was the perfect fit. Five years later, he has completed his master of arts degree, received a promotion, and not worn a tie since his initial interview. If you find yourself in the same position as Ron, use the following questions to guide your career exploration.

QUESTIONS TO HELP
YOU EXPLORE YOUR CAREER

1. What are my greatest strengths?
2. What are my greatest weaknesses?
3. What kind of organization do I want to work for? What kind of organization do I not want to work for?
4. What do I know about this organization?
5. Where do I really want to work?
6. Why do I want to change jobs?
7. What do I expect as far as salary and benefits?
8. Where do I see myself going in the next few years?
9. What makes me stronger than other applicants?

When should you start your job search? This is a process that will take months, so plan accordingly. A good rule of thumb is for graduates to allow between 3 and 6 months to find that first job after graduation.

Where should you look for a job? The answer is simple: everywhere! Begin by using the resources available at your college or university. Most institutions of higher education have career planning centers. Your center may go by a slightly different name, such as career services, career placements, career development, or career consulting; regardless of the name, these centers are a vital resource in your job search.

Career services centers will often hold job fairs on campus or have information about job fairs in the surrounding community. Find out the dates for these job fairs and come ready to be interviewed. This means you should dress in business attire and have a résumé with you.

Once upon a time, the classified/help-wanted ads in the newspaper were the place to go when looking for a job. When job seeking, you should make it a habit to check the newspaper(s) in the city or cities that interest you. However, realize that in the 21st century, many organizations no longer post positions in the newspaper.

The Internet has become an excellent tool for locating employment opportunities. Multiple websites are dedicated to matching employees to jobs, including monster .com, snagajob.com, careerbuilder.com, Job.com, jobs.com, Jobs.net, jobsonline.net, USAJOBS.gov, and the like. In addition to employment-based websites, many organizations now post job openings on their company websites.

Another useful tool for finding openings is word of mouth. Tell everyone you know that you are job searching, making certain to be specific about the kind of job you are looking for. Saying "I am looking for a job in business" is very different from saying "I am looking for a job in hotel management." Who should you tell? Tell family, friends (your friends and your parents' friends), classmates, professors, former employers, people at church, contacts from your internships— tell anyone who will listen.

One family member you should be certain to contact is your Uncle Sam. Yes, Uncle Sam (aka the U.S. government) can help you find a job. If you are looking for jobs with the federal government, you must go through the U.S. Office of Personnel Management, which is easily accessed via www .opm.gov.

If you don't wish to work for the federal government, Uncle Sam can still be of help. According to the U.S. Bureau of Labor Statistics' (2010) *Occupational Outlook Handbook*,

> The State employment service, sometimes called the Job Service, operates in coordination with the U.S. Department of Labor's Employment and Training Administration. Local offices, found nationwide, help job seekers to find jobs and help employers to find qualified workers at no cost to either. To find the office nearest you, look in the State government telephone listings under "Job Service" or "Employment." (p. 21)

Today's job-seeking process may entail a lot of time spent using online employment systems.

In addition to state employment agencies, which are run by the government, private employment agencies, also known as head hunters, can assist you in your job search. Unlike state agencies, private agencies are for-profit organizations that charge a fee for their services. The amount of the fee and who pays it vary.

An often overlooked place to find openings is professional associations. Almost every industry has a professional association that sponsors meetings and conferences. Joining the local, regional, or even national chapter of a professional association will greatly enhance your ability to network with other professionals who may be looking to hire. When joining a professional association, be certain to inquire about outlets for job postings as well as student membership fees or dues.

RESEARCHING POTENTIAL EMPLOYERS

At this point, it should be clear that job searching is time-consuming. Therefore, you do not want to waste valuable time and energy on positions and organizations that do not fit your desires, goals, and priorities. Think about this stage of the job-seeking process as job researching, not job searching. You are not simply searching for vacant positions. You are researching positions and companies to find the right fit between your skills and desires and their needs and opportunities.

Before applying, take a few moments to research the position and the company. This research not only will help you determine if you truly wish to apply for this position with this organization but also will help you down the line when you customize your résumé and prepare for your interview. Remember, excelling as a communicator means you must be audience centered. You can't be audience centered if you do not know your audience.

Where do you find information on potential employers? You can begin by researching their websites, but remember that the purpose of company websites is to make the organization look appealing, so you do not want to end your research there. If you know anyone who works for the organization in question or has a similar type of position with a different organization, interview him or her for insights. Other sources of information that may be helpful include the Chamber of Commerce, Better Business

TOOLS FOR PROFESSIONAL EXCELLENCE 4.1
HOW TO USE LINKEDIN

To use LinkedIn for your job search and professional networking, follow these useful tips:

KEY POINTS	PRACTICAL TIPS
Make a findable and visually appealing profile.	• For your profile picture, use a headshot that is as professional looking as possible. • Write a headline that is sharp and to the point, yet says a lot about who you are. Use the 120 characters to express your creativity and give viewers a clear vision of the kind of person you are. • Use keywords that relate to your career or field of work, which will make your profile easier to find.
Use your profile to showcase everything that doesn't fit on your résumé.	• Fill out as many of the description areas as possible; this gives viewers even more insight into you as a professional and individual, and it says more about you than your headline gives you the room to do. • Link to outside sources (i.e., previous employers, examples of previous work) to further highlight your skills and accomplishments. • The more you develop your profile, the more likely you are to establish new connections.
Strategically connect with others.	• Connect with existing contacts (whether professional or personal) to establish a foundation for forging new relationships. • If you receive a connection request from someone you don't know, or you wish to connect with someone you don't know, research the person to find out whether it is worth connecting with him or her. • When connecting with someone new, craft a personal, detailed message that lets the person know who you are and why you want to connect with him or her. This will help you get your foot in the door, without scaring off the prospective new connection. • If connecting on LinkedIn fails, approach the person about connecting somewhere less formal, such as in person or on another social media site.
Snoop on your valuable network.	• If you're interested in a specific company, or you are hiring for your own company, don't be afraid to look through other users' profiles for any information that could give you a leg up, or help you find the perfect employee. • Keeping tabs on the connections you've made can help open doors you may not know existed, or give you the opportunity to help someone else.
Stay active on the site.	• You get the most out of LinkedIn by using it consistently, not just when you need it for a specific purpose. • Treat your profile as you would any other social media account by logging in on a consistent basis and keeping your account information current and updated. • Staying active on the site will also keep you in the loop of any site changes and help you adapt to these changes.

SOURCE: Shin, L. (2014, June 26). How to use LinkedIn: 5 smart steps to career success. *Forbes*. Retrieved and adapted from www.forbes.com/sites/laurash-in/2014/06/26/how-to-use-linkedin-5-smart-steps-to-career-success/

Bureau reports, the *College Placement Annual*, and CollegeGrad.com. According to Crosby (2000),

> Public libraries and career centers have valuable information about employers, including companies' annual reports to shareholders, reports kept by local chambers of commerce, trade journals, and business indexes, such as *Hoover's Business Index* and *Dun and Bradstreet*. (pp. 15–16)

STAGE THREE: APPLYING

Once you have researched a place you would like to consider for employment, it's time to turn your attention to résumés and cover letters.

DEVELOPING RÉSUMÉS

A résumé provides a picture of who you are as an employee by highlighting your skill set. An excellent résumé illustrates how you fit this position and this organization and highlights the skills you possess relevant to the skills required by the position for which you are applying.

There is no one standard form for a résumé—it's not one size fits all. When selecting the format for your résumé, select a format that will highlight your strengths and downplay your weaknesses. Regardless of which format you select, whenever possible, you should customize your résumé to each position and organization. Although formats vary, every résumé should be no more than one page and must be visually appealing.

Chances are you'll be applying for multiple positions while you are job seeking. Therefore, it's important to develop a generic résumé that you can use as a starting point for the customized résumé you develop for each position.

When developing your résumé, you will have to determine if you plan to use a chronological, functional, or combination résumé. These résumé types are defined in the sections that follow.

CHRONOLOGICAL

This is the most common form and probably the easiest to prepare. The chronological résumé emphasizes employment and/or experience history, listing elements in reverse chronological order (i.e., your most recent experience first). This format is especially useful to new graduates or those with limited work experience.

FUNCTIONAL (SKILL BASED)

This functional résumé emphasizes skills and attributes that can be applied to a variety of employment situations; your skills are broken down into categories that quickly communicate to employers what you can do for them. This format is useful for candidates without direct employment-related experience or for those who wish to work in fields unrelated to their academic major.

WRITE YOUR NOTES HERE

Your résumé is one of the most important factors in the job application process.

COMBINATION

For many candidates, a combination of elements from the chronological and functional résumé formats works best. Regardless of which résumé type you select, your résumé will include some or all of the following sections.

CONTACT INFORMATION

Begin your generic résumé by listing your contact information (see Figure 4.1). You should include your name, address, phone number, and e-mail address. Believe it or not, many prospective job seekers are taken out of the running due to problems with their contact information. You should make certain the address you provide will be valid throughout your job search. The same holds true for phone numbers and e-mail addresses.

When it comes to the telephone, remember that your ring tone and message are going to make an impression on prospective employers. If you want to communicate with professional excellence, use a standard ring tone (no songs) and record a professional message for your voice mail. This same level of professionalism should extend to your e-mail address. An e-mail address such as "partygirl2010" or "mrtequila" is going to land your résumé in the trash. Addresses such as "snugglebear" or "cutiepie" are unprofessional as well. Choose an e-mail address related to your name, and be certain to check your e-mail account regularly.

It's also important to make sure there is nothing in cyberspace that you would not want your future employer to see. What comes up when you "Google" your name? What information can be found on your Facebook and Instagram accounts? If you think prospective employers don't bother to check these sites, you're wrong. Not only do employers use Google and Yahoo to run background checks on potential employees; they also check Facebook, Twitter, and other forms of social media (Finder, 2006; Slovensky & Ross, 2012).

OBJECTIVE AND SUMMARY

An objective is a one- or two-sentence declarative statement about your career goals. An example of an objective would be: "To obtain a position as a reading specialist with the Altoona Area School District." The benefit of including an objective is debatable. Some people argue it can be beneficial and has been a résumé standard for years. Others argue that since the objective is clear (to obtain the position), there is no need to waste space stating the obvious. Many résumés have moved away from the objective to a summary of skills and traits.

EDUCATION

If you're a recent college graduate, your education is, in all likelihood, the most important thing you want future employers to consider, so your education section should be displayed prominently. Include the name of any college or university from which you have graduated or that you are currently attending. As a general rule, a college graduate should not list his or her high school education or high school accomplishments.

List the name of your degree and your major (e.g., bachelor of science in biology). You may also wish to state a minor if you have one. Include the date of graduation (e.g., "Degree conferred December 2011"). If you're in your final semester, you can use something such as "Degree anticipated May 2013."

You may also wish to list some relevant courses. For the purposes of the generic résumé, list all the courses you think may be relevant during your job-seeking process. You can narrow the list during the customizing step.

GENERIC RÉSUMÉ

FIGURE 4.1

Heather Gutiérrez

3606 Bon Soir Drive   Houston, Texas 78044   361.815.4949
heather.gutierrez@gmail.com

Your generic résumé should include any and all information you could utilize for constructing a résumé for a prospective job opening.

Summary of Qualifications

- Strong interpersonal skills
- Bilingual (Spanish, speak, read and write fluently)
- Conduct audits procedures, create reports and implement corrective/preventive measures
- Perform inventories, create reports and reconcile results
- Expert in Microsoft Office
- Prepared professional presentations
- Ability to manage multiple projects
- Effective problem solving techniques
- Purchases supplies and conduct inventory using on-line procedures
- Skilled in normal administrative processes
- Experience in training staff in software and administrative duties

Include an e-mail address that is professional and appropriate.

Include any skills and abilities you have gained.

Education

University of Houston
   Spring 2013 – Expected Graduation Date August 2016
   Bachelor of Arts in Communication
   3.5 GPA

If you decide to include your GPA, be certain it will reflect positively.

Coursework

Interpersonal Communication	Public Speaking
Business and Professional Communication	Intercultural Communication
Communication Theory	Small Group Communication
Persuasion	Media and Society
Graphic Design	Research Methods
Digital Journalism	Voice and Diction

Class Project

Coordinator, ABC: Read With Me   October – December 2014
   Duties – Leading team discussions, planning meetings, collaborate with team members, develop
   and promote campaign, develop relationship with donors, and create data report.

Work Experience
Office Assistant, Texas
University of Houston – Dean's Office   August 2014 – June 2016
   Duties – General Administrative including: answer phone, create correspondence, supply
   inventory, record retention, and maintain personnel files.

   Other assignments: planned special events, designed web content, developed brochures, flyers,
   press releases, and presentations, drafted letters, and oversaw two major projects to revamp the
   personnel files and records retention processes.

Include your assigned duties, as well as other duties and experiences you have had on the job. Always seek opportunities that will expand and utilize the skills you are learning while completing your degree.

Office Administrator, Zales, Inc.   August 2010 – Febuary 2014
   Duties – General Administrative including: answer phone, pay invoices, create correspondence,
   inventory responsibility, handle money, reconcile statements, conduct inventory, customer service,
   and inventory audit control.

Student Organizations

Lambda Pi Eta, National Communication Honor Society	Inducted May 2016
Leadership Award Recipient, Communication Club	2015
National Society of Leadership and Success	Inducted February 2015
Student Reading Council	2013 – 2014

References available upon request

ETHICAL CONNECTION
MAYA'S FACEBOOK PROBLEM

As you read this passage and answer the questions, consider how the way you communicate has an ethical dimension.

Maya had excellent experience, credible references, and an outstanding grade point average. Nonetheless, she was repeatedly passed over while less-qualified friends were interviewed and then hired. Maya could not understand what was going wrong, so she went to her university's career service center for some help. Her counselor commended her on her résumé and cover letter but told her she must do something about her Facebook account. Maya was shocked. She could not believe her private social-networking account was being viewed by employers.

QUESTIONS TO CONSIDER

1. Do you think it's ethical for employers to run background checks using search engines or to evaluate job candidate information posted on social-networking sites such as Facebook? Why? Why not?
2. If you were Maya, would you change your Facebook account?
3. What do you believe should be the appropriate, professional response in this situation?
4. Has the visibility and permanence of online disclosure changed the way you portray yourself on social-networking sites?

Students often ask if they should include their grade point average (GPA) on their résumé. The answer is simple—it depends on your GPA. If your GPA is a 3.0 or higher, include it. For some students, the overall GPA is under a 3.0 but the GPA for coursework in their major is much higher. If that's the case, then list your major GPA.

EXPERIENCE

A section on experience is a standard part of the résumé. As you advance in your career, you will most likely label this section as employment experience, which will take precedence over your education. Yet, for most college graduates, including relevant experience, not just employment experience, is more beneficial. Using the general title "Relevant Experience" allows you to incorporate a broader range of information. In this section, you can list your relevant employment history as well as internships, relevant class projects, relevant work with student organizations, or volunteering. For example, you may be applying for a job that requires leadership and grant-writing experience. During college, you worked as a waitress, but you were also the president of two student organizations, and as part of an English course, you wrote a grant for the local food bank, which was funded. All this information can be included in the "Relevant Experience" section because it's relevant to the position for which you are applying.

SKILLS

Skills may be incorporated under your experiences or may be a separate category. Some students opt for a résumé format that includes a separate skills section or lists skills rather than integrating them into the "Relevant Experience" section. Which format should you use? The answer is, whichever format does a better job of highlighting you.

EMPLOYMENT EXPERIENCE

If you've been lucky enough to work at a job that's relevant to the position you're seeking, prominently display that experience and your job duties. For most college graduates, however, this will not be the case.

Let's look at a few possible scenarios. In the first scenario, your work history is by and large unrelated to the career you are pursuing, but your work on campus through class projects, internships, and student or volunteer organizations is related. To best showcase your skills in this situation, list the class projects, your internship, and your work with the Sociology Club under "Relevant Experience," as previously discussed. Give some details about each experience. Then you can simply list your places of employment, job titles, and employment dates later in the résumé in a section titled "Employment Experience," "Employment History," or "Work History."

If your work history is not directly related to the position you are pursuing, list the place of employment, job title, employment dates, and some skills you acquired at this job. Even if the job is not directly related to your career, you likely gained or honed some skill(s) that will make you a more appealing applicant. For example, if you worked as a waiter, you have developed your customer service skills, worked both independently and as part of a team, handled difficult situations with professionalism, and demonstrated the ability to multitask.

AWARDS AND HOBBIES

Should you include awards and hobbies on your résumé? As always, the answer is, it depends. Include an awards and honors section only if you have multiple listings and they are relevant to the position. Academic awards and honors strengthen you as a candidate, but noting that you were homecoming queen does not. If you have only one award or honor but you think it is relevant, make sure to include it somewhere but do not set aside an entire section of the résumé to highlight it. It may be best to discuss it in your cover letter.

As for hobbies, do not put a hobbies and interests section in your résumé. If you do have a hobby or interest directly relevant to the position, work it into your résumé as a skill or experience. Otherwise, leave it out.

REFERENCES

References should not be listed on your résumé. You can make a note about references at the bottom of the page (e.g., "References available on request"), but the purpose of the résumé is to highlight you, so don't waste space listing references. This is not to imply that securing good references is not an important step in the job-seeking process; references are an extremely important part of the process.

Do not ask your references for generic letters of recommendation. You should submit letters of recommendation only to positions that request such letters. If letters of recommendation are required, then and only then should you solicit them from your references.

CUSTOMIZING RÉSUMÉS

The second step in the KEYS model is to *evaluate the professional context*, which includes your audience and the organization. All the research you have gathered during the previous stages of the job-seeking process will enable you to do just that. During the remaining stages of the process, you must take the information you have gathered and apply it to your communication interactions. These interactions include customizing your résumé and cover letter, as well as being interviewed (see Figure 4.3 on page 78).

REVIEW YOUR AUDIENCE

The research you have done on the organization will give you some insight into the organization's mission and values. In addition, the job posting will tell you exactly what they are looking for in terms of this position.

How do you customize your résumé? Begin with the generic résumé you have already developed. Systematically go through the generic résumé, identifying the information that is most relevant to this position. During the first round of cuts, delete all the information that is not relevant to the position. If the remaining information does not fit on one page, go back and eliminate the information that is least relevant to the position. When customizing your résumé, the goal is to include information about yourself that addresses every qualification noted in the job posting without exceeding the one-page limit.

Your first audience may be an employee in the Human Resources (HR) Department whose job is to determine if you meet the minimal qualifications for this position. In some cases, the HR Department may use a computer scanning program that counts the number of key words from the job posting found in each résumé. Because of these types of HR screening processes, you must make certain that the language on your résumé matches the language in the job posting exactly. Once you have determined which information will be included in this customized résumé, go back and customize the language. Let's say, for example, that you have applied for a position that requires "proven leadership experience." You believe your 2-year tenure as the president of the Kinesiology Club demonstrates your leadership experience. In your generic résumé, you've listed this experience and you've included "leadership" as one of your skills—this is not enough. The job posting specifically states "proven leadership experience," so you should not imply or dance around the wording used in the posting. To customize your résumé, change the wording in the skills section from "leadership" to "proven leadership experience."

CREATING VISUAL APPEAL

Although résumés can come in a variety of different forms, all résumés should be visually appealing and utilize a parallel structure. In terms of visual appeal, you need to include a balance between text and white space. Too much white space indicates a lack of qualifications. On the flip side, too much information jammed on a page does not make you look more qualified. Instead, it makes your résumé difficult to read, which makes you less appealing. Remember, a résumé is a snapshot. You can't include every detail of your life, so make sure to include the information that is most relevant to this position at this organization.

The font you select for the text of the résumé should be 12 point—no less than 11 point if you need more space—for easy reading. When selecting a font, you want to stick with standard fonts such as Arial, Helvetica, and Times New Roman to ensure easy electronic transfer.

As for parallel structure, decide on a heading system, and keep it consistent throughout the résumé. If your first major heading is bold, 14 point, and all capitals, then all major headings should be bold, 14 point, and all capitals.

The use of a parallel structure can also be applied to your word choices. For example, when listing your duties/work experience, use active verbs (see Figure 4.2). In addition, you may utilize a list of bulleted duties/skills. Whichever format you select, remember to use that format throughout that section of the résumé.

It's also critical to edit résumés, applications, and cover letters carefully. Make it a habit to check, double-check, and triple-check. Spelling errors seem to jump off the page at potential employers. If you want to be considered for an interview, your résumé can contain no spelling errors. Remember, spelling and grammar check catches only misspelled words, not incorrect words. Also, make certain your grammar is correct. For example, when discussing a former job or experience, use past tense; when discussing a current job or experience, use present tense.

Once your résumé and cover letter are complete, you should laser print them onto 8½-by 11-inch bond paper, also known as résumé paper. Pink paper with a spritz of perfume may have helped Elle Woods get into Harvard Law School in *Legally Blonde*, but that works only in the movies. Your best bet is to select white or off-white paper—unscented, of course.

Achieved	Evaluated	Managed	
Administered	Examined	Mediated	
Analyzed	Expanded	Motivated	
Budgeted	Expedited	Negotiated	Recommended
Built	Explained	Obtained	Recruited
Calculated	Facilitated	Operated	Reduced
Composed	Formulated	Organized	Reinforced
Conducted	Generated	Participated	Researched
Created	Handled	Performed	Reviewed
Delivered	Implemented	Planned	Scheduled
Demonstrated	Improved	Presented	Supervised
Developed	Increased	Processed	Translated
Directed	Initiated	Produced	Updated
Distributed	Launched	Programmed	Utilized
Established	Maintained	Proposed	

FIGURE 4.2
RÉSUMÉ ACTION WORDS

DEVELOPING ELECTRONIC AND SCANNABLE RÉSUMÉS AND ONLINE APPLICATIONS

Back in the day, résumés and cover letters were either mailed or hand-delivered to organizations. Today, organizations are requesting that résumés be submitted electronically or that the information traditionally found in a résumé be submitted via an online application.

When it comes to submitting electronic or scannable résumés, you must be sensitive to the style and formatting of the document. Electronic résumés should be prepared in common programs, such as Microsoft Word. Scannable résumés should be simplistic; so avoid any decorative fonts or graphics.

For electronic applications, you'll most likely be cutting information from your résumé and pasting it into the application. Although this may allow you to include more information than the standard one-page résumé, the information presented should still be concise and relevant.

DEVELOPING COVER LETTERS

Cover letters accompany your résumé and serve to introduce you as a potential employee, highlight your résumé, and demonstrate your writing skills. According to Buzzanell (1999),

> The goal of the cover letter is to get prospective employers to look at your résumé, the goal of a résumé is to get the prospective employer to ask you on an interview, and the goal of the interview is to get you the job. (p. 155)

Begin the cover letter by stating that you're interested in a specific position (state the exact position title). In the next paragraph or two, highlight why you are qualified for this position, making specific reference to the required skills and qualifications noted in the job posting. End the letter by expressing your desire to discuss your qualifications further during an interview. Like the résumé, your cover letter should be concise, no more than one page. Use the same paper and font for both your résumé and your cover letter.

Evaluate the Professional Context
CUSTOMIZING THE RÉSUMÉ

As you evaluate the passage below, how effectively Heather adapts her experience for this professional context.

Heather Gutierrez will soon be graduating from college. She has taken time to know herself and has developed clearly defined career goals. She is currently pursuing positions that will allow her to combine her love of communications and campaign development. She has found a position with HDS Live, Inc. (see the job posting below). After doing some research on HDS Live, she is certain she would be a good fit for both the position and the organization. In Figures 4.1 (page 73) and 4.3 (below), you will find (1) her generic résumé, (2) her cover letter, and (3) her customized résumé.

QUESTIONS TO CONSIDER

1. How does the customized résumé differ from the generic résumé?
2. Has Heather effectively adapted her experience to this professional context?
3. Has she done an effective job in customizing her résumé and cover letter?
4. Do they reflect the information found in the job posting?
5. Are they visually appealing?
6. What advice would you give Heather?

FIGURE 4.3

CUSTOMIZED COVER LETTER AND RÉSUMÉ

Advertisement for Position

HDS Life, Inc. seeks an Assistant Director of Communications

Position Description
The Assistant Director of Communications actively develops and promotes the HDS Life, Inc. narrative to key external and internal audiences and stakeholders. This role works across businesses to help build HDS Life's strategic communications message, and promotes efforts to achieve business goals and growth targets. The Assistant Director of Communications will provide administrative assistance for the Director of Communications, provide high-profile communication support to the HDS Project Management Office and to a variety of stakeholders.

Position Requirements
Proven administrative experience and expertise interacting with Leadership with strong execution and results orientation. Excellent organization and project management skills. Excellent communication (oral, written, and design). Effective problem-solver with expertise at anticipating and resolving issues; solution oriented, proactive and team-spirited. Strong collaborator. Advanced software skills in PowerPoint, Visio, Word, Excel and industry experience preferred. Bachelor's degree required; communication field preferred. Ability to stay up to date on presentation technology and capabilities.

CUSTOMIZED COVER LETTER

Heather Gutiérrez

3606 Bon Soir Drive • Houston, Texas 78044 • 361.815.4949
heather.gutierrez@gmail.com

Be certain to maintain the font and format for both the resume and the cover letter.

July 1, 2016

HDS Life, Inc.
2727 Allen Parkway
Houston, Texas 77019

Attention: Ms. Natalie Contreras

Re: Assistant Director of Communications

Dear Ms. Contreras:

I am writing in regard to the job description for the Assistant Director of Communications position. I believe my skills, education, and experience are an excellent match for the job duties and requirements listed. My resume is attached for your review. The document includes information regarding my Bachelor of Arts degree in Communication and work experience. Also enclosed is a list of references.

Include which position you are interested in.

Include education.

I have proven success and direct experience in all position requirements. During my time at the University of Houston, I created brochures and other marketing materials; wrote the web content that developed the narratives of the College of Liberal Arts and provided support to senior management and all other stakeholders. I am proficient in Microsoft Office, have experience with event planning, preparing and delivering professional presentations, preparing correspondence, conducting inventories, responding to audits, maintaining accounts payable and receivable, and handling all aspects of customer service.

Use specific language the job posting requires for the candidate.

Include any skills and abilities that qualify you for that particular position.

Strengths I would bring to the Assistant Director of Communications position include my ability to learn quickly, attention to detail, initiative, and strong communication skills. I pride myself on my professional and organizational skills, as well as my strong work ethic. I would appreciate the opportunity to interview for this position.

Express desire to further discuss your qualifications during an interview.

Thank you in advance for your consideration. I look forward to speaking with you.

Sincerely,

Cover letter should be limited to one page.

Heather Gutierrez

CUSTOMIZED RÉSUMÉ

Heather Gutiérrez

3606 Bon Soir Drive • Houston, Texas 78044 • 361.815.4949

heather.gutierrez@gmail.com

Summary of Qualifications

- Excellent oral and written skills
- Excellent organization and project management skills
- Proven interpersonal, customer service, and collaborative skills
- Proactive problem solving skills
- Bilingual (Spanish, speak, read and write fluently)
- Advanced software skills including, PowerPoint, Visio, Word, and Excel
- Ability to manage multiple projects
- Highly experienced at developing professional presentations and reports

Education

University of Houston

Bachelor of Arts in Communication, 3.5 GPA

Spring 2013 – Expected Graduation Date August 2016

Relevant Coursework

Interpersonal Communication	Public Speaking
Business and Professional Communication	Intercultural Communication

Relevant Experience

Office Assistant, University of Houston   August 2014 – June 2016

Office Administrator, Zales, Inc.   August 2010 – Febuary 2014

Relevant Duties – Provided outstanding customer service, created correspondence, paid invoices, planned event ranging from 10–200 attendees, served as project manager, developed a variety of communication and marketing materials, and designed web content.

Coordinator, ABC: Read With Me   October – December 2014

Duties – Facilitated team discussions, planned meetings, collaborated with team members, developed and promoted public relations campaign, develop relationship with donors, and create data report. Exceeded fundraising goals by 150%.

Student Organizations and Awards

Lambda Pi Eta, National Communication Honor Society	Inducted May 2016
Leadership Award Recipient, Communication Club	Received 2016
National Society of Leadership and Success	Inducted February 2016
Student Reading Council	2013 – 2014

References available upon request

Side annotations:

"The most important information that potential employers should remember about you should go in the F-zone" (Diaz, 2013). Be certain to use font that is easily legible.

Include an e-mail address that is professional and appropriate.

Use specific nouns and keywords to describe job duties and qualifications. If applicable, adjustments should be made to match those specified in the job posting.

If you decide to include your GPA, be certain it will reflect positively.

Creating distinctive headings and subheadings make a document easier to read. Instead of "Work Experience," it is often better to have "Relevant Experience" as you may include class projects, student organizations, and internships.

Provide information that helps describe the nature of your student organization. For example: honors societies, social organizations, and service organizations often are named with Greek letters.

Highlight anything that demonstrates your proven leadership skills.

Formatting should be consistent through the entirety of the résumé. Balancing white space and margins creates a document that is appealing.

STAGE FOUR: INTERVIEWING

When your average college graduate thinks of the job-seeking process, he or she thinks about the fourth stage, interviewing. But for students such as yourself who wish to achieve professional excellence, the work you have done in the previous stages will benefit you immensely during the interviewing stage. As you prepare for the interview, you already have a clear sense of who your audience is and what they are looking for in a candidate. Furthermore, your first communication interactions with the potential employers (your résumé and cover letter) not only highlighted you as a candidate but also began to demonstrate how you'll fit into their organization.

Although securing an interview is an exciting milestone in the job-seeking process, you're still several steps away from being hired. To land the position, you must do two important tasks: prepare and practice.

BEFORE THE INTERVIEW

To demonstrate professional excellence, you will need to prepare your message, anticipate the questions, script your answers, practice your answers, prepare your appearance, and reduce your nervousness.

PREPARING YOUR MESSAGE

A student once remarked, "Preparing for an interview would be simple if we knew the questions in advance." The bad news is that you do not have a crystal ball that will magically reveal your interview questions, but the good news is that you have something almost as telling. By reviewing your skills, the job posting, and your research, you can determine exactly what information to present during the interview.

Prior to walking into your interview, you should have a clear understanding of the information you plan to present. Begin by looking at the job posting. What qualifications are a must for this position? How do you meet each of these qualifications? For example, if the position states that the candidate must be highly organized, make a list of examples that demonstrate your organizational skills. Review the duties you'll be responsible for in this position. If you'll have to write, make a list of examples that show you are an effective writer. Then gather some samples of your writing to bring along to the interview.

Next, review your résumé and cover letter. Are there areas where you might need to elaborate? What information do you want to restate in the interview? What are some examples or experiences that illustrate the skills highlighted on your résumé? In the end, you should be ready to discuss specific examples, stories, and experiences that are relevant to the position.

Finally, make a list based on important points you learned while doing your research. This list should include things you learned about this company that made it appealing to you and questions you may have about the position or the organization.

ANTICIPATING QUESTIONS

Once you have completed your lists and reviewed your research, it's time to practice answering questions. You can never be 100% certain about what's going to be asked during the interview, but you can make some educated guesses.

Begin by imagining yourself as the interviewer. If you were going to hire someone for this position, what questions would you ask? How could you learn more about the interviewee's qualifications and skills? What would you be looking for in his or her answers? This exercise can help you anticipate possible questions, but it should also help you formulate stronger answers to those questions when the time comes for you to answer them.

Next, check out some resources that include sample interview questions as well as some helpful tips. Books such as *Best Answers to 201 Most Frequently Asked Interview Questions*, *301 Smart Answers to Tough Interview Questions*, and *The 250 Job Interview Questions You'll Most Likely Be Asked* provide a variety of possible questions.

Be certain to practice both behavioral questions and traditional questions. Behavioral questions explore how you have handled past situations and ask you to respond to hypothetical situations. For example: "Tell me about a time when you had to meet a very short deadline" or "Give me an example of a time you served as a leader." Traditional questions include some of the old standards listed below:

Tell me a little about yourself.

Why did you apply for this position?

What makes you qualified for this position? Why should we hire you?

What are your strengths? What are your weaknesses?

What would your former employer (professor, friend) say about you?

What are three words that describe you?

What are your short-term goals? What are your long-term goals?

Do you have any questions for us?

SCRIPTING ANSWERS

When it comes time for the interview, remember you are in control of your answers. The interviewer may ask slightly different questions from the ones you've practiced. Yet the information you present during the interview should be the same information you practiced prior to the interview. The purpose of practicing is not to guess the exact questions that will be asked—it's to learn to professionally present important information about your qualifications for the position and your fit in the organization.

If possible, you should prepare by scripting answers that follow a three-part formula. First, directly answer the question. Then, back up your answer with a specific example that supports your answer. Finally, connect the answer back to the company and/or the position.

Let's say you are applying for a position managing a retail team for Company A. The interviewer asks, "Have you had much experience working with groups?" Begin by answering the question: "Yes, I have had extensive experience working with groups, both as a group member and as a leader." That would be an average answer.

Some interviewers will inquire further about your experience; others may not. You do not want to miss this opportunity to highlight your experience, so extend your answer to include an example:

Yes, I have had extensive experience working in groups, both as a group member and as a leader. For example, last semester, I worked with a group of graduating seniors on a semester-long marketing project. It was a challenging experience, because the majority of the group had senioritis. At first, they didn't care much about the assignment, but I knew I could change that attitude, so I volunteered to be the leader. Once I was elected, I made certain everyone in the group participated when selecting the topic. This helped get everyone involved from the beginning. Then we divided the project into manageable pieces that allowed everyone to have a balanced workload and a sense of ownership. In the end, we received the highest grade in the class.

This is a good answer, but to turn it into an excellent answer, the job seeker needs to take one more step by relating the answer back to the position and the organization:

In fact, one of the things exciting to me about working for Company A is the opportunity to lead teams. I realize the challenges on the job will be different from what I faced in the classroom, but that is precisely the kind of challenge I am looking for in a position.

When it comes to answering questions, you want to be strategic. Answering strategically means discussing and emphasizing your skills and experiences that relate to this position. It means applying the KEYS of knowing yourself and evaluating your professional context. It does not mean you can lie, exaggerate, or fudge your answers. Lies, even little white lies, are unethical in any interview situation. If you have to lie to get the job, then this is not the right job for you.

How do you answer questions strategically? Let's say that during your research you learned that Company A has won awards for its customer service. During your interview, you might emphasize your desire to work for a company that has been recognized for excellence and/or highlight your excellent customer service skills—assuming, of course, that both these things are true.

In many interviews, the interviewer will allow some time at the end for you to ask a few questions. Therefore, you should prepare several questions for the employer. Although you would love to ask about salary, benefits, and vacation, this is not the time. That comes after they offer you the job. At this stage in the process, your questions are more about showing your research and interest in the position than about getting additional information. It is an opportunity for you to demonstrate that you have researched this company and will be a valuable asset. So you might ask something like, "When researching Company A, I noticed you have a 6-month training program. Can you tell me a little more about what that program entails?"

ACTION ITEMS
SKILLS FOR THE JOB INTERVIEW

SKILL	STRATEGY	APPLICATION
Review your résumé/cover letter	Check to see if your résumé/cover letter fits the job requirements and adjust if necessary.	Align your skills and experience to correlate with requirements listed in the job description.
Understand your personal selling points	Identify what key skills and experience you can offer to the employer.	Do a self-assessment that highlights your strongest qualities, and intertwine those with your listed professional skills.
Prepare answers to expected questions	Be prepared to answer what can be expected of you about the job, and identify the key message you want to get across.	Gain feedback from other professionals already in the industry, as well as their own personal job interview experiences.
Practice delivery	Make sure you can deliver your answers with the utmost confidence.	Practice several times in front of family, friends, or any other willing audiences.

WRITE YOUR NOTES
HERE

PRACTICING ANSWERS

Reading questions and thinking through the answers is an effective way to begin practicing, but to be fully prepared, you must take part in mock interviews. Enlist the help of family members and friends to run through questions with you. Have different people take different approaches to the interview. Have some mock interviewers smile and give you a lot of feedback. Have others be stern and cold and provide little feedback.

One of the best tools in improving your skills as an interviewee is the video recorder. On most college campuses, the career services center can help you in this process. Receiving professional feedback from the career services staff will be helpful, but watching yourself in action is the most powerful tool available for improvement. If your campus does not have a career center or if your career center does not tape mock interviews, find someone with a smartphone or tablet and record it yourself.

When practicing, keep in mind that there are a wide variety of interview formats. The good news is, although the settings vary, the basic rules for an effective interview remain the same across situations.

Telephone interviews are often used during the early screening phases of the interview process. When doing a phone interview, remember to block the call-waiting feature if you have it. Using a land line is preferred to using a cell phone; however, if you have access only to a cell phone, make sure the battery is charged. Never chew gum, smoke, eat, drink, or use the bathroom during a phone interview, because the noise will be picked up on the other end. When you have finished delivering your answer, wait for the next question. Even if it takes the interviewer(s) a moment or two to ask the next question, do not try to fill that silence. When being interviewed via videoconference, try to imagine the camera is a person and respond accordingly. This means making eye contact with the camera and smiling.

Face-to-face interviews also come in a variety of formats, which include the standard one-on-one interview, a series of one-on-one interviews, panel interviews, and interviews with multiple interviewees. The same rules that apply in the standard one-on-one interview apply in each of these settings, but keep a few things in mind for each context. If you have a series of one-on-one interviews, you may feel as though you are repeating yourself. But remember, each interviewer is hearing your information for the first time, so not only it is okay to repeat yourself, it is necessary. If you find yourself answering questions for a panel of interviewers, always acknowledge the person who asks the question but address your answer to (and make eye contact with) the entire group when responding. If you find yourself being interviewed with a group of other candidates, always treat your competition with respect and professionalism. The way you treat the other candidates is indeed part of how you will be assessed.

On occasion, your interview may be conducted during a meal. In this context, answering questions, not eating, is your priority. Keeping this in mind, order food that will be easy to eat. This is not the time to order barbequed ribs or crab legs, even if the interviewers order it for themselves. The same goes for alcohol. During the meal, follow all the basic rules of etiquette. If you are not certain of all the rules, review an etiquette book prior to the interview—at the very least, review the different types of silverware. And never talk with your mouth full.

PREPARING YOUR APPEARANCE

For many students, preparing for the interview begins and ends with purchasing a suit. Although presenting a professional image is an important part of your nonverbal communication in the interview, wearing an Armani suit will not land you the job. Your interviewing attire is in a sense a uniform that identifies you as a professional. Many books and articles have weighed in on the subject of appropriate interview attire (Dorio & Axelrod, 2000; Molloy, 1988, 1996; Ruetzler, Taylor, Reynolds, Baker, & Killen, 2012). In the end, these books can be summarized in a few basic rules that job seekers should follow when putting together their interviewing uniform.

The main piece in an interviewing uniform is the standard business suit. For men, that suit includes a jacket and pants. For women, it includes a jacket and skirt. Many female students question the necessity of wearing a skirt. For better or worse, even in the 21st century, the standard interviewing uniform for women is the suit with a skirt. Some interviewers may not think twice if you elect to wear pants, but some might. The jackets, pants, and skirts should be black, dark gray, or dark blue. The business suit should be coupled with a light-colored shirt or blouse, preferably white. Men should wear a silk tie with a conservative pattern.

Interviewers do not expect to see new college graduates in expensive, designer-label suits, nor do they expect to see them in ill-fitting suits. When purchasing your suit, the fit is extremely important. There is nothing professional about sleeves that cover your hands or a too-short skirt. Spend the extra $20 to have your suit professionally altered.

Female job seekers should wear a black or dark blue, closed-toe pump with a small heel, no higher than 2 inches. If you are not comfortable walking in heels, practice far in advance of your first interview. Your pantyhose should be flesh-colored. (Always keep an extra pair of hose on hand in case you get a run. Runs look very unprofessional.) You can wear jewelry during the interview, but you want to keep it simple. The rule of thumb for women is no more than five pieces of jewelry. Those five pieces consist of a watch, a

---

Your Communication Interaction
MEGAN'S SKYPE INTERVIEW

As you read the passage below, consider what would be a more effective communication strategy in this situation.

Megan is preparing for a Skype interview with a company to which she has applied. She wants to be comfortable for the interview, so she grabs her laptop, a cup of coffee, and settles into bed in her favorite plush bathrobe. A few minutes later, her laptop beeps and the chat screen pops up with the interviewer. Megan and the interviewer exchange introductions, and the interview begins. A minute later, Megan's dog begins barking loudly down the hall, which causes Megan to yell for it to be quiet. The interviewer then asks Megan a series of questions about why she wants to work for the company, what she enjoys most about the work she does, and so on. Megan suddenly cannot remember any of the answers she had come up with the night before, and when she nervously goes to take a sip of coffee, she spills it all over herself and curses

out loud. Toward the end of the interview, Megan's laptop begins beeping loudly, indicating that it is running out of battery power. The interviewer asks what the beeping noise is. Megan replies that she does not hear anything, all while frantically searching for her laptop charger. A few seconds later, the laptop runs out of power and the screen goes black. Megan stares at the blank screen before pulling the covers over her head and sinking deeper into bed.

QUESTIONS TO CONSIDER

1. What do you think was Megan's most critical mistake during the interview?
2. What are some things Megan could have done differently when preparing for the interview? What about during the interview?
3. What do you think Megan's next move should be?
4. How are video or Skype interviews similar to face-to-face interviews? How are they different?

Modern technology has opened the door for videoconferences hosted by interview committees, which saves company money on travel. How would you prepare for a phone or videoconference interview?

WRITE YOUR NOTES HERE

---

pair of earrings (counts as two pieces), a necklace, and a wedding/engagement ring. The earrings should be small posts, and the necklace should be very simple.

Men should wear basic black dress shoes. Both men and women need to polish their shoes prior to the interview. Men should wear dark, over-the-calf dress socks that correspond with the outfit. (When you sit down, your pant leg will rise and the interviewer will see if you have on your white running socks!) Men should keep a two-piece rule in mind for jewelry: one watch, as long as it appears professional with the suit, and one ring, such as a wedding band or college class ring.

Both men and women should carry a briefcase, portfolio, or some sort of professional bag. Under no circumstances is it acceptable to carry your backpack. For women, it is a wise idea to put your essentials in your briefcase and leave your purse at home. Carrying two bags can make you appear cluttered. Your bag must look professional and correspond with your outfit. Inside your bag, you should include extra copies of your résumé, contact information for your references, samples of your work, and mints or a breath freshener. What you should not have in your bag is your cell phone. Nothing will lose you a job faster than your phone going off during the interview. Don't take any chances; leave it in the car.

When it comes to makeup, men are advised not to wear any and women are advised to wear only light makeup. Dark lipsticks, dark eye shadows, and fake lashes should be avoided. Everyone's nails should be clean and filed. If women wear polish, it should be a light, neutral color. With the exception of one small pair of earrings for women, all other piercings should be removed. In addition, tattoos should be covered. Both men and women should also avoid perfumes and colognes when interviewing. Your interviewer may not like your fragrance or, worse yet, may be allergic to it. If you are a smoker, take extra measures to ensure that you do not smell like smoke. If possible, don't smoke in your suit, wash your hands after smoking, and freshen your breath.

As for your hair, it should be neat and clean. If you have long hair, pull it back. If you wear it short, make sure to schedule a trip to the hairstylist prior to your interview. You don't want to look like a shaggy dog. Men should avoid facial hair, which includes beards, mustaches, goatees, soul patches, and sideburns. Women should avoid big hair, mall hair, pageant hair—whatever you call it, it went out in the 1980s.

Where do the personal touches fit into the interviewing uniform? They don't fit in anywhere. Putting on the interviewing uniform may make you feel like a bit of a conformist, but in the end, it's your interviewing skills and qualifications that will set you apart as an individual, not your clothes or tattoos.

REDUCING NERVOUSNESS

For many job seekers, interviewing is an uncomfortable communication interaction for several reasons. First, it is a high-pressure situation in which all eyes are on you. Next, your desire to land the job increases whatever anxiety you might normally feel when communicating with strangers. Finally, many job seekers do not feel comfortable "tooting their own horns." Although you will not be able to eliminate these feelings completely, you can minimize them by practicing. Learning to feel comfortable talking about

TOOLS FOR PROFESSIONAL EXCELLENCE 4.2
HOW TO INTERVIEW ONLINE

Nowadays, job interviews using online video communication channels, such as Skype, are becoming more common. Take note of these practical tips to help you nail the online video interview:

INTERVIEW STAGE	PRACTICAL TIPS

Before your interview:	• Determine the best device to use for the interview (i.e., computer, tablet, cell phone).
	• Make sure the interview will be conducted in the proper location:
	  o Secluded enough so as to prevent any outside interference or distractions
	  o With a generic background, such as a plain white wall
	  o With diffused lighting to prevent shadows or glare
	  o Where you can be seen from the waist up, not just your head
	• Test all technological devices: Make sure all batteries are charged, Internet connections are working, and the volume is at an appropriate level.
	• Conduct a mock interview with a friend or family member so that you can practice your interview skills, as well as test the technology.
	• Have at least one backup plan in place in case of any technological glitches.
	• Prepare for the actual interview by researching the company, preparing any responses to potential questions, and making sure you look professional.

During your interview:	• Even though it is online, treat the interview as if it were face-to-face: Use your nonverbal skills (solid eye contact, smiling, hand gestures, good posture) to impress the interviewer. • Always make direct eye contact with the camera, not the screen. • Have a series of notes off to the side to aid you in the interview, but don't overuse them or you'll end up looking away from the camera too often. • Pause before answering any questions to compensate for any blips in the Internet signal.
After your interview:	• As with any type of interview, follow up by sending the interviewer a thank you letter. • Follow up occasionally with the interviewer to remind him or her of your interest in working for the company.

SOURCE: Hansen, R. (n.d.). Top tips for how to ace your online video job interview. *Quintessential Careers.* Retrieved from www.quintcareers.com/acing_online_video_interview.html

Step Back and Reflect:
TRYING TO FIT IN

As you read this passage and answer the questions, step back and reflect on what went wrong in this professional situation.

Malia was excited about the possibility of working as a computer programmer with Company Y. Company Y had a reputation for being an organization with high-quality professionals who enjoyed a laidback environment. It was not uncommon for these award-winning employees to come to work in shorts and flip-flops. Given their reputation, Malia took a more relaxed approach to her attire when interviewing with Company Y. She wanted to demonstrate that she could fit in

at the organization, so she came to the interview dressed in a business-casual outfit (khakis and a blouse). Although her interview went well, Malia was not offered the position.

STEP BACK AND REFLECT

1. What went wrong?
2. How should you dress for an interview?
3. Should organizational culture influence interview attire? Why or why not?
4. How could Malia use the KEYS approach to improve her communication?

---

your skills and accomplishments is a must for successful interviewing. After all, if you don't promote yourself, no one will.

Being at your best mentally and physically reduces nervousness. Preparing and practicing will help you be at your best mentally. But you also need to be at your best physically. This means getting a proper night's sleep before the interview. If you have failed to prepare in advance, staying up all night prior to your interview will only make you look and feel less than your best.

If you have to travel to the interview, it is wise to scout out the location a day or two in advance. Be certain you know the route to the building and the interview location inside the building. Always allow plenty of extra time for unexpected obstacles, such as traffic. If the interview is outside your local region, it's wise to drive or fly there the day before the interview and stay in a hotel or with friends. This will allow you to come to the interview fresh and well rested—as opposed to tired, wrinkled, and sleep deprived, all of which will increase your nervousness.

DURING THE INTERVIEW

Arrive for the interview at least 10 minutes early. When waiting for your interview to begin, show patience and professionalism. Remember that you are being interviewed during every interaction with the organization, whether you're interacting with the official interviewer or not. So treat everyone from the parking attendant to the receptionist to the CEO with the same level of professionalism and respect. When you meet the interviewer, look him or her in the eye and shake his or her hand. Your handshake should be firm. This means you do not want an overpowering, bone-crushing shake, nor do you want a wimpy, limp-wristed shake (Bass, 2010; Ivy & Wahl, 2014).

First impressions are extremely important when interviewing. Research has found that it takes as much as double the information in the opposite direction to change an interviewer's initial impression of an interviewee (Huffcutt, 2010; Judge, Higgins, & Cable, 2000). This means if you make a good first impression, you will have to work pretty hard to turn it into a negative impression.

During the interview, try to monitor your nonverbal communication. Sit up straight, maintain eye contact, and avoid speaking too quickly or using vocal fillers. If you are asked a question that you need a moment to think about, take that moment to think. Do not fill the silence with "umms" and "aahs." The bottom line is that nonverbal cues do bias interviewer ratings (Bass, 2010; Dipboye, 1992).

Central to being an excellent interviewee is being an excellent listener. Focus on each question asked. If you are unclear about what the interviewer wants, ask for clarification. If the interviewer asks a question with multiple parts, make a mental note of each part and then begin to answer.

If you have prepared and practiced, you will be ready to answer the questions. Include as much of the information you practiced as possible in your answers. Ask the follow-up questions you prepared. Know that your preparation and practice will help you stand out as a candidate.

Remember to remain positive about your qualifications, your experiences, your former employers, your major/field, the job, and the organization. It's important to remain positive even when discussing weaknesses or failures. This can be accomplished by discussing a weakness or failure that will not affect you in this position (Crosby, 2000; Gray, 2011).

ILLEGAL QUESTIONS

Ideally, you will never encounter an interviewer who asks illegal questions, but you should prepare in case it happens. What is an illegal question? According to the Civil Rights Act of 1964, Title VII, and subsequent legislation, employers may not consider race, color, religion, sex, national origin, disability, or age when hiring or promoting employees. Therefore, they legally can't ask questions related to these categories.

When an interviewer said to Yelena, "I see you worked for the Jewish Community Center. Are you Jewish?" she was not sure how to respond. There are several ways Yelena could approach this question. First, she could answer it directly and move on: "Yes, I am Jewish." She could directly answer the question with a follow-up: "Yes, I am Jewish. Why do you ask?" She could use humor to deflect the question: "Is this a test to see if I know which questions are illegal?" Or she could refuse to answer: "I do not see how that question is relevant to my qualifications." What is the correct way to handle this situation? Although many students would prefer to use one of the last three approaches, they often are afraid such an answer will hurt their chances of getting the job. Regardless of how you answer the question, make note of what occurs. If you believe your answer negatively affected your chances of being hired, then you have a discrimination case on your hands. If you are offered the job, you may decide not to take it because this question might be an indicator of a hostile work environment. At the very least, you should report this behavior to someone higher in the organization.

SALARY QUESTIONS

Although you should never bring up the issue of salary prior to being offered the position, you should be prepared in case the interviewer asks about your salary expectations. To prepare, research the appropriate pay for the position you are seeking. Be sure to examine pay-scale variations related to credentials, experience, and location. If asked, you can give a vague response such as, "I expect a salary that is competitive in this market." If the interviewer requests something more specific, give a range starting with the employer's probable salary and ending with a little above what you are willing to accept.

Know yourself

Evaluate the professional context

Your communication interaction with others

Step back and reflect

WRITE YOUR NOTES HERE

Thank you letters, especially handwritten ones, are an excellent way to follow up after an interview.

STAGE FIVE: FOLLOWING UP

When the interview ends, be certain to thank your interviewer verbally. Once you return home from the interview, formalize your thank you with a card. A handwritten thank you card for the interviewer not only demonstrates professional excellence but also guarantees that the interviewer will think of you favorably after the interview. If you were interviewed by more than one person, you can either send a thank you card to everyone who interviewed you or send just one card to your main contact and mention the other parties in the message (Crosby, 2000; Vanevenhoven, Delaney-Klinger, Winkel, & Wagner, 2011). If you have been communicating with the interviewer via e-mail, then you can send the thank you message through e-mail.

If any additional information was requested during the interview, get that information to your potential employer immediately. This will demonstrate your enthusiasm for the position and your attention to detail.

For many, what comes next is the most emotionally draining part of the job-seeking process—the waiting. It may be days, weeks, or even months until you hear back about the position. Remain patient. Under no circumstances do you want to appear like a stalker, calling twice a day to see if a decision has been made.

Use this time to engage in the last of the KEYS, *step back and reflect*. How would you rate your communication interactions? How did you perform during the interview? What did you do well? What can you improve for next time? What have you learned about the job-seeking process? What have you learned about interviewing? What have you learned about yourself?

STAGE SIX: NEGOTIATING

Although it may seem at times that the job-seeking process will never end, it will—and it will end with you accepting an offer. Yet the sixth stage of the job-seeking process involves more than just saying yes.

Once an offer is made, the ball is in your court. This is the time to ask clarifying questions about salary, benefits, work conditions, and the like. This is also the time to negotiate. A negotiation is a discussion between two or more parties to reach an agreement that concludes some matter. In this case, the matter being concluded is the terms of your employment. However, the skills and strategies used to engage in employment negotiations are the same skills and strategies needed to successfully negotiate personnel issues, contracts, legal matters, and other workplace issues.

The first rule to good negotiation is to act with professional excellence. In fact, negotiation experts often stress the need to maintain a polite, collegial, and collaborative tone. During negotiations, both parties should be looking for the best solution to meet the needs of both sides. Using the unite approach, described in detail in Chapter 7, is an excellence strategy for achieving this objective.

According to Hansen (n.d.), you should let the employer make the first offer, but you should not feel obligated to accept that offer if it is inadequate. How will you know if it is inadequate? You must do your homework and research salary norms, as well as benefits and other perks, for the industry, the region, and this organization. In fact, doing your homework and thoroughly researching the situation is critical for all types of negotiation. You can't negotiate a contract if you have no idea what is acceptable and expected in the industry.

According to Johnson (2012), you must also research your value. Your value is based on factors such as education, length of experience, certifications, and management responsibility. Throughout your career, your value will increase, as will your ability to negotiate better contracts for yourself. In other words, the need to negotiate effectively becomes increasingly important as your career progresses.

One common mistake made during negotiations is failing to negotiate for things other than salary. For example, performance expectations, benefits, moving expenses, equipment, and vacation time are all extremely valuable. It may be beneficial to accept a lower salary if the offer includes a company car and great health benefits. Again, keep in mind that your counteroffer must be reasonable and in line with the research you have done.

To make a counteroffer, you can state something such as, "I am very interested in working for your company. Although I would love to be a part of your team, I would like to discuss a few small issues. First, would it be possible to increase the salary offer by $5,000? This would put my starting salary in line with other entry-level salaries for folks with similar education and experience in your organization."

Once you have received the final offer, *step back and reflect*. Take into account all you have learned about the organization and the position during your research and the interviewing process. Compare this information with your goals and priorities. If you believe you are a good fit for the position and the organization and that the organization is a good fit for your goals and priorities, accept the offer. If it's not a good fit, then politely and professionally decline the offer. Declining may be difficult if you do not have another job lined up, but saying yes to the wrong job will be more difficult in the long run.

WRITE YOUR NOTES HERE

You may have to make a difficult decision in the process of negotiating your salary.

KEYS TO EXCELLENCE IN THE JOB-SEEKING PROCESS

At the beginning of this chapter, Joe Konop offered several excellent examples of interview questions to help land a job. When examining the first key, *know yourself*, it is important to know exactly how you want to describe yourself as a valuable asset to an employer. Before you ask any of Konop's sample questions, make sure to do a self-inventory to highlight your unique skills and motivations that set you apart from other applicants.

The next key, *evaluate the professional context*, would be an excellent time to ask Konop's first question: What skills and experiences would make an ideal candidate? It gives you an excellent idea of what the employer is specifically looking for while also giving you an in-depth look at the character and context of the organization.

The third key, *your communication interaction*, would be the time to use other intelligent and relevant questions to bolster your interview credentials. Besides Konop's examples, it is also a good idea to develop your own thoughtful questions that can pertain specifically to the company or organization to which you are applying.

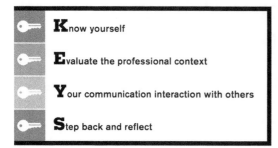

Know yourself

Evaluate the professional context

Your communication interaction with others

Step back and reflect

After the interview has concluded, it is time to *step back and reflect* over how your questions were received. Did the interviewer(s) respond positively to your inquiries? How useful were the answers you were given? Although no one wants go through numerous interviews, over time this practice can give you some reliable and helpful information as to what companies are looking for. Asking specific questions allows you to show great interest in an organization, indicates that you have already done some work studying the organization, and emphasizes your drive to work there.

Want a better grade?

Get the tools you need to sharpen your study skills.
Access practice quizzes, eFlashcards, video, and multimedia at
http://edge.sagepub.com/quintanilla3e.

$SAGE edge™

EXECUTIVE SUMMARY

Now that you have finished reading this chapter, you should be able to:

Identify the six stages of the job-seeking process:
- The exploring stage begins with you, the job seeker. During this stage, you will need to explore both yourself and potential careers (p. 67).
- The researching stage of the job-seeking process comprises two components: researching openings and researching potential employers (p. 67).
- Once you have researched a place you would like to consider for employment, it's time to turn your attention to résumés and cover letters in the applying stage (p. 71).
- The interviewing stage involves using your work from the previous stages to project a professional and competent image of yourself to a potential employer (p. 81).
- Following up after the interview is the next stage. A handwritten thank you card to the interviewer not only demonstrates professional excellence but also guarantees that the interviewer will think about you favorably after the interview (p. 90).

- Although it may seem at times that the job-seeking process will never end, it will—and it will end with you accepting an offer. Yet the sixth stage of the job-seeking process, negotiating, involves more than just saying yes (p. 90).

Explain the important role of exploring and researching in the job-seeking process:
- Self-exploration is important; taking time to think about your goals and priorities is an important part of the job-seeking process—it will help you determine what type of career you wish to pursue and what types of organizations you wish to work for (p. 67).
- As you narrow down career opportunities, it's important to develop a clear understanding of what each career entails. When you find a career that seems interesting, you need to do some career exploration (p. 67).
- You do not want to waste your valuable time and energy on positions and organizations that do not fit your desires, goals, and priorities. Think about this stage of the job-seeking process as job researching, not job searching. You are not simply searching for vacant positions; you are researching

positions and companies to find the right fit between your skills and desires and their needs and opportunities (p. 69).

Develop a customized résumé and cover letter:

- There is no one standard form for a résumé—it's not one size fits all. When selecting the format for your résumé, choose one that will highlight your strengths and downplay your weaknesses (p. 71).
- Cover letters accompany your résumé and serve to introduce you as a potential employee, highlight your résumé, and demonstrate your writing skills (p. 77).

Discuss examples of how to interview and negotiate successfully:

- To demonstrate professional excellence, you will need to prepare your message, anticipate the questions, script your answers, practice your answers, prepare your appearance, and reduce your nervousness before the interview (p. 81).
- During the interview, remember that you are being evaluated during every interaction with the organization, whether you're interacting with the official interviewer

or not. So treat everyone from the parking attendant to the receptionist to the CEO with the same level of professionalism and respect (p. 88).

Apply the KEYS approach to conduct yourself with professional excellence throughout the job-seeking process:

- Know yourself by capitalizing on your strengths and realizing your weaknesses (p. 91).
- Evaluate the professional context by searching for positions, researching each company, and then customizing your résumé and cover letter for each position (p. 91).
- Your communication interaction begins when your résumé and cover letter are reviewed, making it important to treat each step with care and diligence (p. 91).
- Step back and reflect. Your preparation and practice have served you well. If you do not land this position, you will continue to present the same level of professional excellence with other companies until you do land a job (p. 92).

EXPLORE

1. Visit a business news website (such as *Forbes* or a similar organization) and identify three types of employment advice they offer that you haven't learned in class. Do you find this advice to be beneficial or possibly effective? How important is it to gain feedback from the business community to supplement your academic knowledge?
2. Watch a YouTube video (or some other type of multimedia example) that shows a realistic mock interview. Put yourself

in the place of the interviewee and use the KEYS process to analyze his or her performance. What (if any) insight did this activity give you?
3. Visit your campus employment aid center. Many colleges and universities will offer to guide you in creating your résumé and cover letter, as well as do mock interviews. Take advantage of the advice they can give you, and also take the opportunity to create a professional connection if you can.

REVIEW

Check your answers to these questions at **http://edge.sagepub.com/quintanilla3e.**

1. Identify the six stages of the job interview process.
2. _____ requires you to research opportunities in your major that correspond with your goals and priorities.
3. A(n) _____ provides a picture of who you are as an employee by highlighting your skill set.
4. A(n) _____ is a one- or two-sentence declarative statement about your career goals.
5. A(n) _____ accompanies your résumé and serves to introduce you as a potential employee, highlight your résumé, and demonstrate your writing skills.

6. _____ explore how you have handled past situations, as well as asking you to respond to hypothetical situations.
7. A(n) _____ is a discussion between two or more parties to reach an agreement that concludes some matter.
8. It is _____ for an interviewer to ask an interviewee questions relating to race, color, religion, sex, national origin, disability, or age.

DISCUSSION QUESTIONS

1. Discuss the experiences you've had interviewing. How did the interviews go? Were you nervous? What will you strive to do differently in preparation for future interviews?
2. Take a moment to reflect on your dream job. Have you conducted an electronic search of the organization? What is it about the organization that makes you want to work there?
3. What are the qualities you're looking for in an employer? Related to some of the information in this chapter, how

could you retrieve information to see if those qualities exist?
4. Discuss the resources your campus has in place to support the job-seeking process. Do you plan to use these resources?
5. Take an inventory of your e-mail address and any virtual networks such as Facebook or Instagram where you have a membership or maintain a profile. Is there any information an employer could retrieve from the Internet that may be perceived as negative?

TERMS TO REMEMBER

Review key terms with eFlashcards. **http://edge.sagepub.com/quintanilla3e.**

awards and honors (p. 75)
behavioral questions (p. 82)
career exploration (p. 67)
career planning centers (p. 68)
classified/help-wanted ads (p. 68)
contact information (p. 72)
cover letters (p. 77)
customized résumé (p. 71)
education (p. 72)
electronic résumés (p. 77)
employment experience (p. 74)
exploring stage (p. 67)
face-to-face interviews (p. 84)
generic résumé (p. 71)
hobbies and interests (p. 75)

illegal questions (p. 89)
Internet (p. 68)
internship (p. 67)
job fairs (p. 68)
job seeker (p. 67)
job-seeking process (p. 66)
mock interviews (p. 84)
negotiation (p. 90)
objective (p. 72)
one-on-one interview (p. 84)
online application (p. 77)
panel interview (p. 84)
private employment agencies (p. 69)
professional associations (p. 69)
references (p. 75)

relevant experience (p. 74)
researching stage (p. 67)
résumé (p. 71)
scannable résumés (p. 77)
scripting answers (p. 82)
self-exploration (p. 67)
shadowing (p. 67)
skills (p. 74)
State employment service (p. 69)
summary (p. 72)
telephone interviews (p. 84)
traditional questions (p. 82)
videoconference (p. 84)
white space (p. 76)
word of mouth (p. 68)

Finding Work

13

Neugebauer, J. and
Evans-Brain, J.

What you will find in this chapter:

'I am a psychology graduate

What is the hardest thing about being a psychologist?

Finding a job'

(Debra Barraud, Humans of Amsterdam, Foto
Exhibition Openbare Bibliotheek Amsterdam, 2015.
Used with Permission.)

Introduction and Preparing for Applications

Preparing work application is a massively time-consuming process. There are very few shortcuts in the process. In this chapter we recommend how to prepare yourself for this process. With the number of graduates applying for roles, applications will receive only a very short period of consideration: those which have obvious gaps in background, competences, appropriate qualification or which contain gaffs and errors (see below) will be quickly discarded. If you cannot submit a well-prepared application, it is usually best not to waste your time. Here we present some tips for creating good applications.

Be Organised, and Get Organised Early

Being well organised throughout the process is important: it will help you to make the most of individual applications, and help when there are time pressures on application dates.

Make sure that you check the application deadlines of the employers you are most interested in. Your target employer(s) may have deadlines in the first term of your final year, so check, plan and prepare in the summer before your final year.

To be organised, you need:

- A generic CV with all your personal work history details on it. The generic CV is your 'library copy'. You would not send it to an employer but instead edit it down to the two sides which are most appropriate for that application. We cover CV preparation in more detail in the following section, 'Smart CVs'.
- A list of competence examples. See Table 3.2 for details about how to summarise examples of your competences. Again, this is a library copy for your personal use: you will take examples from this list to illustrate your suitability for the role for which you are applying. Your own list of competences, kept up to date throughout your career, will also enable you to attend job interviews and discuss positive examples of how you meet the job requirements.
- Sufficient time to understand what is required in the application; answer all the questions; and ensure that spelling and grammar are correct.

Here are some examples of the most common gaffs in job applications. Despite having spent time in the application, these gaffs ensure that your application is immediately discarded:

- spelling errors
- applying for unsuitable jobs
- poor grammar
- failing to read the job requirements and linking your background to the job requirements
- failing to answer all the employers' questions
- rushing to use a previous generic application – and showing your commitment to a competitor organisation!

Most importantly: When you have finished your application, ask a friend or family member to check it for you.

Demonstrate Your Passion for the Role for which You Are Applying

In preparing this book, every employer we spoke to and every placement agency emphasised the need to show your passion for the role being advertised. How does the role fit with what you have done already? How does the role fit with your longer-term plans? What immediate contribution can you make to the organisation? Check the employers' websites to see how you can align your skills with their needs.

Write a Convincing Covering Letter

It is useful to have a high-quality covering letter ready and amendable for each application. The covering letter may be:

- used as the covering letter for which it was intended
- to copy into application forms where you are invited to 'tell us in your own words' why you are suitable for the job
- useful to edit as a top four lines for a personal summary in your CV.

Not all employers require a covering letter, and the evidence is mixed as to whether this makes a big difference or no difference at all (with some employers preferring to rely on the application form or the CV).

Typically, your covering letter will be:

- one side maximum, therefore clear and concise
- businesslike but not too formal, nor over-familiar
- a summary with evidence and short examples of how you meet the job requirements
- a demonstration of your passion for the organisation's objectives (without being creepily sycophantic!)
- typed, perfectly set out and free of grammar and spelling errors.

A sample covering letter is shown at Appendix C.

Be Ready for the Next Steps

Keep a copy of your application and the job description to hand so that you are ready when a reply comes in. Some organisations will reply quickly, others will feel like black holes. Be especially ready for unexpected phone calls, which may be to do a quick check on your application details, pre-screen you or invite you for interview. In particular, if you answer the phone from a number you don't recognise, make sure you answer it in a businesslike manner: it may just be that call you have been waiting for.

Smart CVs

Your CV is your core document for applications. Even if you apply online, your CV will be the document that informs most of the content of your online application.

There are many sources of advice and help for getting your CV right. In this section we suggest the best way to organise yourself to have a smart CV – one that you can tailor quickly and effectively to specific roles.

Much of the advice on CV preparation suggests, correctly, that a CV of more than two sides will not be read as carefully as a shorter CV. So the CV you submit needs to be two sides. However, different roles will require different emphases on your suitability and experience, and two sides are unlikely to be sufficient to cover this. Therefore we suggest you organise your CV as follows:

- First, to have a generic CV, which covers all your experience to date, wherever you are in your career. This generic version can be several pages long.
- Second, you use the generic CV to edit your pitch in a smart CV – one that is tailored and specific for the post for which you are applying .

Your smart CV is the CV tailored by you from the generic CV to show how you are the most suitable person for this specific role. Link what you say to the role requirements. The smart CV should contain:

Short personal profile of 4–5 lines: This links your key skills and passion to work in that role for that employer. You may have one or two generic models, but this statement needs to be tailored to each role you apply for.

Summary of education: As with career history, show first your most recent qualifications (or studies towards an imminent qualification). Don't bend the truth – this is the first thing you will be found out on. Emphasise qualifications and distinctions, and play down grades if you were not so good at some stages of your education. GCSE grades don't need to be shown, but make sure that successes in Maths and English are shown.

Career history: In reverse chronological order, with the most recent roles first. For each role show: the employer; dates in role; job title; key aspects of the role; key achievements in the role (use 'I' not 'we' to show your contribution to the achievements. Practise 'I' not 'we' for job interviews, as employers want to understand *your* contribution, not what the team did). This section needs to be accurate, pithy and relevant to the job.

Competences and skills summary: In the section on 'Competencies' in Chapter 3, we explain competences and skills. Employers still place a big emphasis on transferable skills. See what competences are required for the role you are applying for (which should be on the job or role specification or description) and tailor your answers accordingly. You may not have enough space for competences in your CV: if not, summarise them in the covering letter you write or, if you are applying online, use them to amplify your application in the box for 'additional information' or 'tell us more about why you consider yourself suitable for this role'.

Additional training and skills: Show that you have a breadth of interests and experience, from lifeguarding to cashing up the shop/bar at the end of the day, to a Duke of Edinburgh's award and so on . For almost any job for which you apply, don't forget to show your IT skills. For more specialist roles, say which software you have used. Show also your language skills, with an honest assessment of your capability (basic, good, conversational, fluent and bilingual).

Additional Posts of Responsibility

Pastimes: include three or four, but do not include 'socialising' as a hobby or pastime. Some advisers doubt the value of including pastimes. We disagree. Showing, briefly, that you have a range of interests shows a well-rounded candidate. A further advantage for applicants is that interviewers may pick up on their shared interest in your hobbies and sports – it helps to develop relationships during selection stages.

Don't bother with: referees' names and addresses (they'll get them if they are interested, but ensure that you have three referees lined up – you will usually need two); photographs (in the UK); fancy layout and design using software packages (use Word, set it out well, use narrow margins but don't overcrowd the page).

The order of your smart CV will probably be as shown in the above checklist, but there are variations. For example, if you have a high level of work experience, your personal statement may say 'Graduate with substantial experience in …', with your work experience shown first and qualification further down the list.

We strongly recommend that you have a careers adviser, friend or family member check your smart CV for comprehensiveness and to check spellings and grammar (the most common reasons to reject CVs outright). Don't forget to have a two-sided CV with your LinkedIn page (see Exhibit 3.3).

CVs are an art, not a science. There are good practices, but the best CVs are the ones which most appeal to the person who receives them. The most challenging part of the CV is getting started. In Appendix B we show a typical CV, with annotated comments to get you started. Linked with your CV, Appendix C shows a sample covering letter.

What You Can Expect in Selection and Assessment

Employers want to process applications as quickly and cost effectively as possible. In the early stages of selection you may find that you have little direct contact with the organisation. Here we discuss the types of selection procedures you may encounter. We look at how to succeed, but we also look at how to fail by considering some of the most common mistakes which are made at each stage.

Telephone Interviews

Some organisations will use initial telephone screening to check whether you are worth bringing to further interview. You may be given advance notice of a telephone interview. Sometimes there will be little notice of a telephone interview, especially where organisations are running assessment centres and realise there are not a sufficient number of candidates attending. Provided that you have done the necessary preparation, it should not be difficult to pass an initial telephone interview, but you need to be ready at short notice. See Table 4.1 for a summary.

Your minimum aim: To pass

TABLE 4.1   Succeeding and failing in telephone (and video) interviews

How to fail	How to pass	How to excel	Preparation and practice
Get caught on the hop and unprepared. Organisations may call you at short notice to ask you questions about your application	Be prepared so that you have your personal information and application ready and accessible at short notice, and can deal with 'unexpected' phone calls	If you are given advance notice, treat the interview as a business meeting – have a quiet place for the call, get ready about 15–30 minutes beforehand; some candidates also feel more confident if they are standing up during the discussion	Make sure you have information about the organisation and have your application to hand

Numeracy, Oral and Spatial Reasoning Tests

Many organisations use online tests in numeracy, verbal skills or spatial reasoning for initial candidate screening. Most graduates should have the ability to do these tests, but the main reasons for failing are often being rusty, understanding the 'rules' of the tests too slowly, and failing to finish enough questions on time.

If you have not undertaken these tests recently it will help you to practise. It is especially important to get into the right tempo for doing these tests, which are usually timed. You may be able to answer a few of the questions by glancing at the tests without time pressures, but it is much more challenging to do a battery of tests under live conditions. So do practise!

Websites such as http://cebglobal.com/shldirect/index.php/en/ practice-tests offer useful practice sessions. Practise on these sites before you start the selection processes, and practise again when you have been told that you will be undertaking these types of tests.

Your aim is to show that you have these basic skills, so passing is usually enough. See Table 4.2 for a summary.

Your minimum aim: To pass

TABLE 4.2   Succeeding and failing in numeracy, or verbal, spatial reasoning communication

How to fail	How to pass	How to excel	Preparation and practice
Assume that you will be OK on the day – don't practise	Spend a few hours on practice sessions, and repeat this shortly before you do the online tests or attend an assessment centre	Not usually necessary though some roles may require high levels of personal fitness, hand–eye coordination or excellent results in mental agility tests	Spend time with online test and practice sessions Don't be put off by these tests – treat them as enjoyable challenges
	Stay focused during the tests. Keep an eye on time. Move on to the next question if you are stuck and the tests allows you to move on	Consider whether you are going into a specialist field where these types of tests will be more critical to your success in the selection process. Find out what is required in advance and practise	

Interviews

Whilst you may be able to afford to be good (rather than excellent) in many of the selection methods used so far, you need to excel during face-to-face interviews. In part these are about checking your ability, experience and commitment. But they are also about making an assessment: Is this the type of person we want working here? Is this someone I would wish to work with? Do this candidate's values fit with the values of the organisation?

You can expect two types of interview, structured and unstructured. You need to be ready for both.

In **structured interviews**, all candidates will be asked the same or very similar questions. Typically these will be based on job competences, and you will be asked to show how your competences meet – or exceed – the competences of the role for which you are applying. Structured interviews often begin with a simple question such as 'Tell me a bit about yourself.'

Structured interviews need quite a bit of preparation if you are going to show yourself at your best. Prepare yourself for the most typical questions you may be asked (see Exhibit 4.3), and practise giving these answers with a friend or mentor. You can prepare by completing the competence inventory, which is shown in Table 3.2.

For **unstructured interviews** it is less easy to prepare and less easy for you to manage during the interview. The interviewers themselves may be highly skilled at unstructured interviews. On some occasions, and more difficult for you to manage as a candidate, the interviewers may not be fully prepared to see you, may lack training in selection interviewing, or feel that they have some special insight (often erroneously) in how to pick a successful future employee.

Unstructured interviews are more difficult to prepare for, but there are still some things which you can do. First, share interview experiences with your friends and see what kind of questions they have had to deal with. For example, if you were asked 'If you were an animal, what kind of animal would you be?', think about what kind of answer you would give and the reasons for your choice. Unstructured interviews may also push your patience to the limits (in some cases that is intentional): stay calm.

Whether you find yourself in a structured or unstructured interview, be true to yourself and to your values. It should go without saying that you need to keep your cool as well; especially in unstructured interviews, bear in mind that interviewers may be looking to see how you react when pushed to the limits. State your points clearly, but don't rise to the bait of a contrived argument and debate which becomes emotional. See Table 4.3 for a summary.

Your minimum aim: To excel

Group Exercises, Role Plays and Presentations

Group exercises and role plays may be used to see how you may operate in real-life situations. Group exercises can be difficult (and quite subjective) for recruiters to assess. So a good tip is to make your mark against the criteria which will enable you to 'pass' (see below), rather than stand out as a candidate for good or not-so-good reasons. See Table 4.4 for a summary.

TABLE 4.3   Interviews

How to fail	How to pass and excel
Don't read the job details	Make a strong start.
	Be ready with a 60-second summary about yourself.
Don't align your experience and skills with the job requirements	Be ready with your CV and competence examples (see Exhibit 4.3, Typical questions asked during structured interviews).
Treat it as another interview	Check the job details and organisation details carefully.
	Show passion – and if you can show genuine passion, even better!
	Practise direct eye contact with a range of interviewers.
	Be ready with great questions.
Lying. Mark Twain is reported to have written that 'if you tell the truth, you don't have to remember anything'. Anywhere in the selection process, lying is a sure way to fail. It may take a while for your deceit to be uncovered, but in the end, the system is likely to catch up with you: you may even lose your job as a result of it	Position your experience assertively and confidently. Don't lie about your actual or expected degree class, nor your previous experience. If you have unspent criminal convictions (or spent convictions but are applying for roles where you cannot claim exemption from disclosure), make sure that you declare them and that you can articulate what you have learned from the experience.

Your minimum aim: To pass (although in some selection processes such as for leadership roles you will need to excel)

TABLE 4.4   Succeeding and failing in role plays

How to fail	How to pass	How to excel	Preparation and practice
Feel a bit lost on the day – not sure what the topic is, be disorientated by the exercise	Know that you will need to make 3–4 really good interventions in the session – make sure that you do	For specialist roles where leadership is a key requirement, you may need to excel rather than pass. Check this in advance	You need to practise these skills in advance. How do you do in society or tutorial meetings?
			Discuss with friends going through similar selections, and give feedback to each other

(Continued)

TABLE 4.4   (Continued)

How to fail	How to pass	How to excel	Preparation and practice
Say nothing Say 'I agree with that' (without adding to the conversation) Say too much: dominate the conversation and block out other team members	As well as making your contributions, be a good team player – keep an eye on timing for the group; if members are quiet, say 'I'd like to hear X's view on this point'; when the discussion has progressed, use phrases to summarise the group position, e.g. 'so to summarise, are we saying …'		Demystify the process by finding out more about group dynamics. Read: Tuckman, 1965 (Group working dynamics) Belbin, 1981 (Working Style in Groups) Janis, 1971 (Group Thinking) See Chapter 6 for further details
Think that the assessors want to watch a run-through of *The Apprentice* – instead, they are looking for people who can listen to others, keep an eye on group progress and timing, come up with good ideas and act as good team members	Have these objectives clearly in mind and make sure that you make your mark		

Presentations

A pre-prepared presentation, or an unprepared presentation, is a regular feature of assessments centres. Assessors will tend to have a stronger positive impression of a candidate whom they have seen present well. See Table 4.5 for a summary.

Your minimum aim: At least good, and preferably to excel

What Can Go Wrong – with Your Assessors

Having looked at assessment processes, we now look at what can go wrong with your assessors, and with you, during the process. Selection processes are notoriously difficult for predicting future role suitability.

TABLE 4.5   Succeeding and failing in presentations

How to fail	How to pass	How to excel	Preparation and Practice
Don't prepare. As authors, we have know times when even though candidates are given advance notice of the need to present, and the topic, they may come unprepared on the basis of being 'too busy'. They usually fail, as this also suggests poor work prioritisation	If you have been given the presentation title in advance, practise, especially with content, timing and dealing with questions	Engage your audience: • Maintain scanning eye contact with the audience • Inject some originality in content or style – but avoid being quirky	Make and take opportunities to present: e.g. in seminars (even if – perhaps especially if – these are the least comfortable environments for you, they enable you to develop your techniques), club and society meetings etc.
Tell yourself that you are not good in presentations. Instead, take time in your studies to get as much experience and good technique as possible	Use good presentation skills during this assessment. They do not come without practice and technique, so prepare this in advance	Be a bit different – but don't be a clown	Use a formula for every presentation: 1. Title 2. Aims 3. Content 4. [Recommendations where appropriate] 5. Conclusion Envisage yourself doing a great presentation – and then deliver it!
Learn to 'rise above' your nerves and tension – we are all tense in presentations – the issue is controlling nerves	Take control of your presentation environment. Arrive in good time and set the room – or at least the presentation position – to how you want it and how you feel comfortable		

Even in more structured selection interviews, assessors make mistakes and errors of judgment. These have been called 'unconscious bias' – either making an over-flattering assessment of a candidate or finding an early fault in a candidate which then impairs further objective assessment of the candidate.

Many of the recruitment and assessment techniques used by organisations have been challenged for their effectiveness in picking the best candidate. So if you have not succeeded in an assessment centre or other type of selection test it might be you – but then again, you can take comfort that the assessors may have made an error of judgment too. Mistakes electors make during interviews are shown in Exhibit 4.1. The challenge for you, however, is to ensure that the same mistakes are not repeated!

Exhibit 4.1

Mistakes Selectors May Make in Interviews

Selective attention: Interviewer only considers selected information and data, rather than looking at all information available on a candidature. As a result selectors may decide that a candidate is 'suitable' or 'unsuitable' in the first few minutes of the interview, and spend the rest of the meeting finding information to confirm the original decision.

Halo effects: Interviewer draws conclusions on the basis of only one criterion (e.g. intelligence or appearance) and interprets all other interview data in the same positive way irrespective of how positive or negative that data is.

Contrast effects: Interviewers may look at a fairly strong performer in the interviewee and consider that candidate to be much stronger than in reality because the interviewer has just seen a much weaker candidate.

Projection: Interviewer assumes other people 'are like us', (e.g. conscientious) and makes an error of judgment as a result.

Stereotype: Interviewer does not look at the individual attributes of a particular candidate but judges the candidate based on the perception of the characteristics of the group in which they are classified or stereotyped (e.g. too old, too young, immigrant, well brought-up, elite university, lesser ranked university etc.).

Heuristics: Interviewer tries to simplify complex decisions by taking shortcut judgments.

Source: based on Newell and Shackleton, 2001

Exhibit 4.2

Uncovered lies in the selection process

Even people who should know better still get found out. Here is a sample from professional people who got caught – and what happened to them.

NHS HR manager who lied on her CV and was given a six-month suspended prison sentence and ordered to pay £9,600 in compensation. The employee falsely claimed that she held a degree in Human Resource Management and said she was part way through a Chartered Institute of Personnel and Development course. She had been working as an HR manager for six years.

Barrister dismissed for falsely claiming degrees from Harvard and Oxford.

New Zealand Defence Force's chief scientist failed to declare a job he had been fired from the previous year for incompetence. Failing to spot this and errors in the CV were described as 'seriously embarrassing' (Sands, 2010). The chief scientist was dismissed.

Nurse manager sacked and given a suspended prison sentence after falsely claiming a degree (she had dropped out of university) and forging documents.

According to an article in *The Guardian* (Rowley, 2014), the Higher Education Degree Datacheck reports that about one-third of graduates misrepresent their degree class or results, even though this is so easy to check. The national press also report that graduates misrepresent the subjects they have studied in order to submit job applications.

Exhibit 4.3

Typical questions asked during structured interviews

These questions, and the answers, may seem predictable. Candidates often fail on the easiest questions, so make sure you are genuinely ready.

'I've read your CV, but tell me a bit about yourself, in your own words.' (Limit your answer to one minute, maximum.)

'Why have you applied to us?' (Research the organisation and show how you can make a difference to them. Be enthusiastic! Avoid over-long answers on what you think you can get from working for that organisation.)

'Which other organisations have you applied to?' (Only mention a couple, and only where the role is very similar to the one you have applied for; make clear your preference for this organisation.)

'Give me an example of when you demonstrated the competence of ...' (To answer this type of question – and you will probably have many questions framed in this way – you must have pre-prepared examples of competences based on your earlier experiences. See Chapter 3 on competences.)

'Give me an example of when you have failed to demonstrate the competence of ...' or 'What has been your greatest disappointment?' (Again, use

(Continued)

(Continued)

your pre-prepared competences to answer this question. Use examples where you have turned round a difficult situation and succeeded, or learned a deeper lesson for the future. Do not use the worst-case example you have – the assessors are looking for resilience and learning.)

'What would you like to ask us?' (Use this opportunity to get further information, but also impress the assessors. See the next section on 'Killer questions to ask'.)

Killer Questions to Ask in Interviews

Often you will be asked for any questions you have about the organisation or the proposed role. This is an opportunity to find out more information about the organisation. But if you handle it appropriately, it may be an additional opportunity to impress the assessors.

As with answers to your interview questions, the questions you ask of the interviewers should be prepared in advance. The questions you ask can also be a chance for you to show again your passion and interest in the organisation.

'I've read [make sure you have!] and heard a lot about the organisation's main goals and objectives looking forward, but I would be interested to hear your own views on what you think is important.'

Asking this question may give you additional insight into the organisation. Seeing how the interviewers handle the question may also give you some idea of the culture within the organisation. Also some interviewers will be impressed with your question.

'What happened to the previous person [or graduate intake cohort] and how and why did they move on?'

You will usually get a stock answer, but it shows you are interested.

'I really want to focus on my learning and development over the next couple of years. Can you tell me how this will be supported?'

Again, this shows that you want to progress, but without directly asking when you can expect your first promotion. The answer given, as well as being of value in helping you decide whether to join them, will also give you an idea of the culture of the organisation, particularly whether they want to develop you and how they would do this.

'Looking forward three to five years, where would you reasonably expect someone for this year's intake to be?'

This shows you focus on the longer term, but may also show that you have not read the recruitment literature properly, so make sure you do read it before you use this question.

'What attracted you to join the organisation and how has this developed in practice?'

Answers will help you judge the organisation and may help you connect further with the interviewer.

Questions to avoid include detail on the contract of employment, which you can sort out and negotiate once you have been offered a role, when you will be in a much stronger position to negotiate. Similarly, do not ask when you will hear more about your application (they usually tell you this in the interview wrap up), so don't waste a question on it unless they fail to tell you at the end.

Assessment Centres

Assessment centres are expensive and time-consuming for employers to run, but well-structured assessment centres are regarded as having the best predictor of future job success. Even so, their predictive values of finding the best person for the job varies between 0.41 and 0.66 (see e.g. Pilbeam and Corbridge, 2006: 173).

Assessment centres will usually incorporate: structured (and possibly unstructured) interviews; presentations; psychometric exercises; role play and group exercises; and some form of work simulation.

In practice, if your assessment centre simulates the workplace or work events, both you and the employer will have a good idea about future success. If you feel you are not ready for the assessment centre, then you may need to prepare yourself better or practise further.

As an example of what you may expect from less conventional assessment centres, Virgin Money won the CIPD 2015 Award for Best Recruitment and Talent Management Initiative with assessments that included a half-time talk to an England football team, talk to an unresponsive bouncer, and getting through a smoke-filled room. Virgin Media focused on activities which were not competence based (in their terms), but difficult to prepare for. No doubt Virgin Money had their reasons for this unorthodox approach, and claim that it is very successful in picking the right people. In the meantime, it also demonstrates the range of differences which you may need to be ready for in an assessment centre.

Possible Final Round Interview with Senior Management

After all this, some organisations still ask you to see a senior manager before a job offer is made. Don't think that you are home and dry until this important step is completed. Remember also that this is a two-way process – can you see yourself working with that type of senior manager in future?

Exhibit 4.4

Top tips for a successful application

We asked some employers for their top tips for a successful employer. Here are some of their answers.

1. Always read each question and answer it. If you don't answer questions, your application is unlikely to progress.
2. Balance the technical details in your application with how you show that your values align with the employer's values.
3. Once you have completed your application, get someone to check it carefully on your behalf.
4. If there is an opportunity to have an informal discussion with the recruiter in advance, take it.
5. Make a connecting phone call.
6. Get interview practice before you attend the employment interview.
7. Show your enthusiasm: make the employer feel that they are your number one choice.
8. If you are called to interview, make sure you arrive in good time and plan the journey. Even better, visit the area and the site in advance to get an impression of what it may be like working there.
9. From the moment you arrive on site until the moment you leave, people will be making judgments about you.

Jane Hadfield, Head of Learning & Development, Learning & Development, Human Resource & Development Directorate, North Bristol NHS Trust

Be bespoke for the role for which you are applying. Really focus your application on that role, rather than a generalised application. This usually means you need to tailor your CV for particular job roles. Really make your CV stand out – adapt it to what that employer is looking for.

Apply the 'so what?' factor. With a CV or application, you probably have about 20 seconds of the reader's attention, so make your application relevant to the job and relevant to your strengths – otherwise don't waste your time!

Avoid over-long and complicated covering letters.

Be realistic about what you really want. Avoid being general and vague. Stick to your passions and learn to use your time wisely.

Get experience. If, at the moment, you genuinely don't have what they are looking for, put yourself out into the market to get work experience – either in voluntary work or internships – to get the experience to use in interviews.

Ask really good – brilliant – questions at interview.

Befriend relevant agencies and consultants to build a good relationship with them and to make sure they know you and are fighting your corner.

Prepare yourself thoroughly for the interview – know the organisation

Allie Whelan, Director, LeapUK

Understand the values of the organisation and really make sure that you are aligned with them. If not, it will quickly become apparent during the interview, or worse still, when you have started work.

Develop great relationship skills, not just about emotional intelligence but also ensuring that you know yourself and can relate well to others.

Develop a continuous learning attitude and learn from relational interaction by keeping an insight journal.

Learn to be critically reflexive; this is not about being critical of others, but understanding how much we as individuals create or complicate situations.

Be self-aware, which is not about being humble or self-effacing, but about being appropriately self-aware and self-regulating: in this way, you contribute more effectively within the team.

Patrick Goh, Head of Global HR People & Organisation Development, Tearfund

Learning from Failure

If you have got past the written application stage of the selection process, but then after an failed interview, find out why. It is not enough to hear that there were 'many other candidates whose skills and abilities more closely matched the role requirements'. Neither is it enough to know, as we have seen earlier in this chapter, that assessment methods may not always chose the best candidate.

You need to find out where the specific gaps were in your application and make sure those gaps are closed the next time you apply. So phone the people who interviewed you, say you want feedback and agree with the assessors a time when you can call back for more detailed feedback. Not all potential employers will help you in this way, but the better ones will. This is too important to leave. You have invested time and emotional commitment in your application – make the most of it by identifying where you may need to do things differently next time round.

If You Get Stuck

Getting stuck – scores, or more applications, without getting anywhere – is a very dispiriting experience, and draws heavily on reserves of resilience and self-efficacy and self-belief (see Chapter 7).

Try to avoid longer periods without work. Apart from not wishing to be unemployed, there is some evidence that the longer we are unemployed, the more difficult it becomes to find new employment. Unemployment can become a self-fulfilling prophecy if we allow ourselves to lose heart in the search.

But it is not simply our own motivations which can lengthen periods without work. Kroft et al. (2012) submitted 12,000 fictitious CVs for 3,000 jobs in America, each with similar backgrounds but different lengths of unemployment of up to 36 months. The longer a person had been without work, the lower the chances of being called for interview, despite the similarities of experience and qualifications with other candidates. There may be several reasons for this. Employers may feel that job skills of longer-term unemployed candidates were getting rusty, although the likelihood of being called for interview was actually higher where unemployment was higher in a particular region or city. But one other explanation was that human decisions on shortlisting (as conscious or unconscious bias) and even software to sift through applications may discriminate against candidates with increasing periods of unemployment. Kroft et al. therefore suggest, as we do, that taking work to get on your CV is better than waiting for the perfect job to come along. You are more likely to get work when you are in work.

> You have to keep trying and stay positive. It took me 9 months of interviewing for different roles and getting several rejections before finding my current job. **Employability Panel law graduate, now a full-time qualified Solicitor**

PRACTICAL APPLICATION

For the wide range of graduate opportunities and disciplines that are available, there cannot be a 'one size fits all' approach to getting unstuck. However, the overall principles should apply and encourage you to look at new ways to find a way forward.

The first thing is to realise that you are not the only one, even though it feels that way.

Do not try to deal with this alone. This is particularly a time to:

- work with your careers adviser or with a mentor, someone outside your family and friends who can give you support, objective advice and think about different ways to approach your job search. In addition, having a third party to work with helps to give a renewed sense of purpose.
- network. This is an important time to make renewed use of your networks, and to make new networks as well. This may be face to face or via social media (see Chapter 3).
- make full use of your university careers service. As we have already seen in Chapter 2, our Employability Panel did not always have positive experiences of careers services, and careers services themselves felt that graduates did not make effective use of their service. Do remember that their services will often be available for a period after you leave university, and their help can include workshops and so goes beyond just having a look at CVs.
- think about getting work through employment agencies. This will often only be temporary and may not be that well paid, but it can help develop the skills and competences you need for a permanent role. Agencies need you to be working to earn their own fees, so the better agencies will give you direct and relevant feedback on your application.
- volunteer. Doing something – anything – is almost always better than doing nothing, provided that you keep sufficient time available for the commitment needed to submit high-quality applications. One graduate we spoke to found a trainee role at Harvey Nichols based on experience of several weeks work in a charity shop, learning to display merchandise to maximum effect. Another found a job as an automotive engineer after an unpaid internship with Jaguar Land Rover. Volunteering and internships also give you additional material to include in your competence examples and demonstrate to potential employers that you are actively working.
- look critically at your applications. At what stage do they break down (initial application, shortlisting, interview or assessment centre)? Use this chapter to ensure that your applications are positioned as strongly as possible.
- consider whether you are being flexible enough. Are you too demanding on the type of job, location, salary and so on? Getting started is more important than getting the perfect role at the first attempt.
- look after yourself, physically (taking exercise as well) and in your personal appearance.
- remember that you don't need multiple job applications to be successful. You just need one. Sometimes that in itself will seem challenging, but out there, there is someone who could just do with somebody like you.
- remember that it won't last forever (though it may feel like that at times). In the end, based on all our experience and the Employability Panel experience, you *will* find that role and get your career started.

Onboarding and Induction

This section has been contributed by Dr Jenny Chen.

'A good start is half way to success.'

Chinese Proverb

This proverb is particularly true for those of you who have just joined a new organisation and wish to achieve long-term success and satisfaction in your career. In this section we look at the research and practical advice to help you make a great start.

What Is Onboarding?

'Onboarding' is a set of processes through which newcomers learn knowledge, information, skills, behaviours, organisational norms and values required to function effectively as a member of an organisation. It is also used to describe the onging process of orienting, socialising and engaging newcomers to ensure that they are able to make a positive start with the organisation. Onboarding programmes may include a series of both formal and informal activities, aiming to speed up the process of adjustment and increase newcomers' productivity.

Based on attempts of earlier socialisation theorists, Feldman (1976) developed a stage model to demonstrate what newcomers are likely to experience after entering an organisation. Building on Feldman's stage model, Louis (1980) suggested that newcomer adjustment was not only a process of 'adding new roles to their portfolio of life roles', but also involved a process of leaving a former role. Differing from Feldman's overwhelming emphasis on activities newcomers may engage in after entering an organisation, Louis focused on the newcomers' experience in coping with surprises and making sense of the new settings. Specifically, Louis identified 'change', 'contrast' and 'surprise' as key features of the newcomers' experience after organisational entry. He pointed out that individuals could not erase all the memories of former roles before settling into the new role. Therefore newcomers were inclined to subconsciously undertake role change by interrelating with new settings and using previous experiences to manage surprise.

Feldman (1981) also suggested that role clarity, task mastery and social integration are three typical adjustment outcomes that reflect to what extent you are successfully settling in the new workplace.

Table 4.6 illustrates best practices to help you settle in. Feldman's (1981) Three adjustment outcomes are often regarded as 'proximal'

TABLE 4.6   Best practices to help you settle in

Aims and objectives	Organisational approach
Reducing uncertainty	• Share realistic job previews • Provide a written, in-depth and up-to-date file/guideline on job responsibilities and duties • Set specific goals and clarify expectations • Connect orientation programmes to job roles
Increasing productivity	• Provide on-the-job training and/or work shadowing opportunities • Provide job-specific training • Give continuous and developmental feedback • Provide tools, facilities and resources • Train line managers on how to support new employees • Assign mentors and/or buddies • Organise social events (e.g. welcome party, group lunch) to enable new employees to meet others • Help newcomers to nurture their networks and socialise with others • Implement formal orientation programmes

Source: Adapted from Bauer, 2011

socialisation outcomes in organisational socialisation studies, and proximal in the sense of occurring in the shorter term. Closely related to these are attitudinal variables (job satisfaction and organisational commitment) and behavioural variables (performance and turnover) as indicators of longer-term adjustment outcomes (see Table 4.7).

TABLE 4.7   Successful vs unsuccessful adjustment

Successful adjustment	Unsuccessful adjustment
• Greater knowledge about the organisation and the team	• Role ambiguity, unstable progress
• Increased self-confidence	• Lack of confidence
• Increase productivity	• Anxious and stressful
• Trusting work relationship	• Lack of trust, unmet expectations
• Accepted by the team members	• Feeling lonely and isolated
• Increased job satisfaction and commitment	• Unhappy, lack of commitment, and intent to leave the organisation

Source: Adapted from Ashforth et al., 2007

PRACTICAL APPLICATION

Whilst most newcomers experience some type of onboarding programmes, the formality, expectation and breadth of the programmes can vary considerably across occupations and industries. For example, doctors and nurses are usually required to attend long periods of formal onboarding programmes before they are allowed to work on their own due to the complexity involved in the work and the serious consequences of getting it wrong. Another example of the formal approach is when technical workers are required to attend formal training programmes to learn how to use specialised equipment before they are allowed to perform by their own. Those formal programmes are expected to 'minimize risk by providing each new recruit with standard training that emphasizes the proper and accepted ways to accomplish things in the organization' (Salisbury, 2006: 22). In contrast, some organisations prefer a less structured and less systematic method where newcomers are left to the work team and learning usually takes place 'on the job'. Under this approach, newcomers are provided with a greater control of their learning process. They learn the norms and principles usually from the interactions with other colleagues and master the skills from assigned tasks.

Some organisations tend to accept newcomers as they are and newcomers are valued for what they bring to the organisation, whilst others deny these personal attributes and ensure that newcomers accept prescribed standards of membership. For example, in police onboarding training, new cadets are informed that they are no longer ordinary citizens and their behaviour needs to be strictly regulated. Table 4.6 highlights some of best organisational approaches used to help newcomers settle down.

What Can You Do to Settle in Successfully?

To reduce uncertainty and stress associated with the onboarding process, you should learn about your organisations, job roles and social relations (see Table 4.8).

In addition to learning, research has found positive relationships between newcomers' information-seeking behaviours and a number of socialisation outcomes, such as job satisfaction, organisational commitment, job performance and negative relationships with work anxiety and intention to turnover (Chen, 2010; Bauer et al., 2007). The implication is that it is vitally important for you to engage in various proactive behaviours during and after the onboarding process. You should actively take part in those behaviours without being asked.

More recently Cooper-Thomas and Burke (2012) revealed a list of proactive behaviours that newcomers may take part in to make sense of the workplace and reduce the levels of uncertainty, which they

TABLE 4.8   Content of learning during onboarding

Learning areas	Examples on what to learn
Understanding of the company	• Organisational strategies, mission statement, values, culture, history, code of ethics, core business and services • Rules and policies: compensation and benefits packages (e.g. forms and procedures), health and safety guidelines • Housekeeping: eating facilities, equipment, parking guidelines • Communication information: key executives, key contact, reporting system, union representatives, help line
Knowledge of the job role	• Performance review: how, when and by whom your performance will be evaluated • Work hours, job location, requirements, key tasks and duties, expectations, priorities, responsibilities and authorities • Promotion opportunities, career paths, professional training, role models, career sources and available support
Information within the team	• Both formal and informal power structure within the team • Unwritten rules of conduct and behaviours developed by the team members • People to contact for learning about job skills • Information on self-position and self-image

Source: Adapted from Jablin, 2001 and Morrison, 1993

classified into three categories: mutual development (e.g. networking, boss relationship building); change self (e.g. performance feedback seeking, monitoring); and change role or environment (e.g. redefine job, change work procedures). Details are presented in Table 4.9.

TABLE 4.9   Your can-do list: examples of proactive behaviour

Dimension	Examples of proactive behaviour
Mutual development	• Developing workplace networks with your colleagues • Exchanging resources with your colleagues • Negotiating job duties and the methods of performing tasks • Building a good work relationship with your boss • Taking part in social activities organised by the group and the organisation
Change self	• Seeking performance-related information from your colleagues and supervisors • Trying to respond to situations in a positive way • Trying to emulate the ways your colleagues behave in order to achieve better outcomes

(Continued)

TABLE 4.9   (Continued)

Dimension	Examples of proactive behaviour
Change role or environment	• Minimising new role requirements to achieve a better fit to your current skills and abilities • Redefining the job duties and work methods • Testing limits by carrying out work in your preferred way and seeking if it works • Gaining credibility in order to have more influence • Delegate responsibilities

Source: Adapted from Cooper-Thomas and Burke, 2012

In conclusion, onboarding is a continuous process and you are expected to become a functional organisational member by the end of it. Most organisations are able to provide various practices to help you to settle in. Even so, you should also take the initiative to learn and to integrate into the team and culture as quickly as you can with an eye to your own personal development.

Conclusion

For some, finding their niche in the employment market – employability – is a sprint. But for others it will take longer, and may turn into a marathon. The more preparation you put into it, from school, early years at university and in the application process itself, the more successful you are likely to be. In this chapter we have looked at how to make the most of the opportunities we discussed in Chapter 3.

So far we have undertaken the challenging task of preparing for your career and successfully finding work. Settling into the new organisation is, of course, the start of the next stage. For the remainder of the book, we will look more carefully at the world of work and how you can really develop your hard-won career and make the most of it. We start with what has consumed most of your life so far – learning – but with a new emphasis on learning at work.

ACTION

• Having read this chapter, we suggest that you think about the following action points: If you think you want to run your own business, there are many sites offering advice, and organisations offering more tangible support too. See The Start Up Donut at www.startupdonut.co.uk/startup/

start-up-business-ideas/running-a-business/eight-reasons-to-start-your-own-business-when-you-graduate and the UK Government website www.gov.uk/starting-up-a-business/start-with-an-idea.

- Look again at the key stages in the process of finding work, and our sections on competences, smarter CVs and preparing for assessment. Have you done as much as you can? Have you prioritised time to do this?

Further Reading

Browse your careers service for ideas.

One good source of information – and thinking about your next steps – is *Postgrad* magazine, published by Prospects (see www.prospects.ac.uk). Updated regularly, this contains articles and advertisements for opportunities after your degree, and includes ideas on postgraduate study. Disciplines covered include arts and humanities, science technology and engineering, business, consulting and management, social sciences, and teaching and education.

Workplace Learning and Development

Neugebauer, J. and Evans-Brain, J.

What you will find in this chapter:

In this chapter we consider the main tools for your personal learning and longer-term development. There are three key reasons for the emphasis on workplace learning:

- First, and most obviously, to align your values with those of your work organisation and to enable you to perform effectively in that first role.
- Second, to enable you to develop professionally, inside or outside the organisation, in the short to medium term.
- Third, for your longer-term career development and your employability – maximising your longer-term potential to align with your dreams and ambitions.

The first of these reasons is the most obvious to manage, and is most likely to be supported by your work organisation. In contrast, the third is the most nebulous – not least because it is very possible that you are preparing yourself for a longer-term role which may not even exist yet. All three need careful attention. The difference between these aims and your earlier learning is that, this time, you have the personal responsibility for what you do.

Exhibit 5.1

Learning and Long-term Employability

For longer-term employability I look for how well people express their ideas and thinking: to see how far they have an appetite for further knowledge – a hunger, and a reason, for further growth; and to understand their future career dreams. Some of this can be judged from what candidates have done earlier in their education, such as travel, Duke of Edinburgh scheme, societies and positions of responsibility. They show how someone is keen to develop.

Allie Whelan, Director, LeapUK

Understanding How We Learn

Before we look at the resources available to help us learn, it is worthwhile to review how we learn – and think about our personal learning styles.

Most commonly used is Honey and Mumford's (1986) learning styles approach. They suggested that we learn in four ways:

Activists: who learn by having an active involvement in concrete tasks and relatively short-term tasks.

Reflectors: who review and reflect, stand back, listen, and think. Reflectors need to take care not to be seen as 'quiet' or day-dreaming.

Theorists: who learn by taking on new situations, but need to relate these to theory. Reflectors need to be aware that absorbing new ideas might distance them from day-to-day situations.

Pragmatists: who learn by linking between new information and real-life problems. Pragmatists like techniques which can be applied immediately.

Individuals can evaluate their current learning styles by undertaking one of the many Honey and Mumford learning styles inventories, which are widely available. Whilst there is no 'right' or 'wrong' learning style mix, it is better to have a good balance of each style. For example, if your learning style is mainly reflector, you may achieve deep insight into what is happening around you, but you may be seen in the workplace as not living in the here and now. In contrast, activists, who certainly do live in the here and now, may find that in their desire to get things done they fail to notice things and repeat previous mistakes.

PRACTICAL APPLICATION

This short review of learning styles reminds us that to be fully effective learners we need a range of styles. In this way we are more likely to take full opportunity of learning and development from our work environments.

Furthermore, it is worthwhile to bear in mind that our preferred styles may also reflect on how we come across in the workplace. In this way, learning styles are not only important for understanding how we develop, but they also give good clues to how we may be perceived in the workplace. For example, reflectors may feel uncomfortable speaking up in team meetings or in giving presentations. It is therefore worthwhile to consider your learning styles: if you have areas of weakness, look for opportunities in the workplace to find new balance with these. Table 5.1 gives some practical ideas on how you could manage this.

Training, Learning and Development

You may hear the terms 'training', 'learning' and 'development' being used interchangeably. In fact they have different points of emphasis, and it is important to recognise those differences:

- **Training** is the process to enhance work performance and improve current or special personal knowledge, skills and attitudes so that a job is performed accurately, effectively and ensures continuing improvement of work quality (Romanowska, 1993). On the other hand, Bramley (2003: 4) defines training as the process 'which is planned to facilitate learning so that people can become more effective in carrying out aspects of their work.'
- **Learning** aims to deliver qualitative and relatively permanent change in how an individual sees, experiences or understands something in the real world (Marton and Ramsden, 1988).
- **Development** is a more wide-ranging, longer-term concept. Nadler and Wiggs (1986) see development as preparation of employees for an uncertain future. It may include linking the organisation's strategy and retention strategy for employees, and linking career with learning plans. In terms of employability, development may also include learning and experience outside the immediate organisational boundaries.

TABLE 5.1   Balancing learning styles

Learning style	Strengths	Possible weakness: why this matters	Practical steps to address
Activist	Seen as getting on with it. Less likely to be resistant to change	The work usually gets done, but at what cost? May do too much yourself (or try to give that impression). May take risks in determination to deliver	You get the work done, but how effective are you? Balance your style with stepping back and thinking about things – use a learning journal or read a few articles or books – lift your head above the parapet!
Theorist	Understands the wider, deeper issues. May be leading edge as new ideas are explored	Too interested in theory and not living in the real world. May be seen as indecisive, or slow to complete work	Look at activist and pragmatist styles. How, particularly, can you make decisions or explain actions in more practical terms?
Reflector	Thoughtful and careful. Sees the deeper meaning. Good at problem solving. Good at data review and listening	Too much a day-dreamer, questions the 'what, why and how' without getting on with work. May be seen as indecisive or slow to complete work	How comfortable are you in group situations? Make and take opportunities to speak up in team meetings or give presentations. If it helps, get a colleague to give feedback in how you did. Build your confidence
Pragmatist	Down to earth, and happy to put new ideas into practice	A focus on technique and practical application may mean that people or policy may be overlooked	Spend more time listening to others, especially on implementation practicalities. Be careful of those shortcuts: they could yet get you into serious trouble

As you look at your learning plan, remember that you will have each of these elements, and access a range of different facilities to develop your learning.

Reflective and Action Learning

Action learning (and its closely linked concept of reflective learning) is an approach to practical learning originally developed by Professor Reg Revans. Revans believed that real learning only took place when it was supported by real-world experiences – not in formal courses and lecture theatres. Despite being a business school professor himself, Revans was damming of the position of those business school professors who had little or no experience of the real world – so much so that, in the end, he resigned from his position at Manchester Business School.

Although recognising that the detail of action learning may vary, Marquardt and Banks (2010) note that the underlying common principles of the approach are:

- **Real work experience:** learning is acquired in the midst of action and dedicated to the task at hand.
- **Based on actual organisational experience and personal development:** participants work on problems aimed at organisational as well as personal development and the intersection between them.
- **Peer learning:** learners work in peer learning teams to support and challenge each other.
- **Learning to learn:** users demonstrate learning-to-learn aptitude entailing a search for fresh questions over expert knowledge (based Marquaradt and Banks, on 2010: 159–160).

There is limited empirical evidence as to why action learning should be as successful but it is claimed that action learning repays the cost of the learning by five to twenty-five times. Even so, as a form of learning, its practicality and closer link with real-life workplace issues means that it remains a popular and widely used concept.

PRACTICAL APPLICATION

Reflective and action learning need your personal investment in time and thinking about workplace successes and failures. In Appendix E we show a model action learning log.

Best Value Learning and Development?

Despite the investments made in designing and delivering learning and development solutions, it does not follow that those which are the most expensive (e.g. attendance on an external course or conference) are the most effective.

CIPD surveys consistently suggest that learning closest to the workplace is the most effective. In-house development programmes (52 per cent), coaching by line managers (46 per cent), on-the-job training (29 per cent), job rotation, job shadowing and secondments (23 per cent) are consistently rated as the most effective (CIPD, 2012). Other forms of training, such as audio and video tapes (2 per cent), e-learning (11 per cent), external conferences and workshops (14 per cent), and formal education and courses (12 per cent) are rated amongst the least effective. Learning methods such as non-managerial coaching, mentoring, action learning sets and internal knowledge-sharing events fall within the mid-range of perceived effectiveness (CIPD, 2012).

PRACTICAL APPLICATION

For long-term employability, including development within your role, developing your workplace learning is important throughout your career. Therefore whether you are in an organisation that organises training for you or in one where little attention is given to your learning, you need to keep an up-to-date learning plan covering what you need to do in the next 12–18 months.

Your learning comes from a number of sources:

- Ensuring that you have the ability to deliver all elements of your role description and performance objectives.
- If, as we recommend, you keep a reflective learning log (see Appendix E for an example), look at gap areas in your performance and work out how to close them.
- Keep examples of your competences up to date (see Table 3.2). Look at areas of competence strength – how can you develop these for the future? Look at areas of weakness in your competences – how will you cover these?
- Express your learning plan in SMART terms (Specific, Measurable [what success looks like], Achievable, Realistict and Timed).
- Look at your longer-term objectives and what you need to develop to be credible in those areas.
- Check your plans with your line manager.
- Discuss your plans with your mentor.

Some organisations (including an aerospace company we spoke to) in the UK use a 70:20:10 ratio to guide a balance of learning, with 70 per cent related to the job and role, 20 per cent from social learning such as mentoring and networking, and 10 per cent related to course attendance. Other organisations, such as the RHP Group, have a nominal monetary budget to support individual learning, which is used in addition to direct work-related training. Mentoring and how professional bodies require undertaking continuing professional development with your professional bodies are also important in developing your learning, and we discuss these now.

Mentoring

We share seeing the understanding of the role of mentor, as defined on the Alta Mentoring Scheme:

> A mentor has relevant knowledge and experience, and works on a short or long term basis with a mentee to give advice, guidance and support to assist the mentee's career, learning and development.[1]

Mentoring offers the following benefits:

- A separate, objective sounding board.
- A source of experienced advice and guidance on a range of work-related issues.
- An adult-to-adult relationship, which may include constructive criticism.
- An independent role model.
- Someone you can turn to when you feel 'stuck'.

Despite the advantages of having a mentor, they are not a panacea. In particular, they will not tell you what to do (you will need to sort that out yourself), neither will they substitute for the role of the line manager. Mentoring can be used in conjunction with other types of learning, including coaching.

Exhibit 5.2

The Value of Mentors – Employers' Views

Mentors can be hugely valuable in a number of ways: giving feedback and advice, expanding your network and acting as a sponsor for you at a more senior level. The right mentor pairing is important in order that you have effective communication between you and a high level of trust and respect. When you are starting out in your career the best approach is to take all the help you are offered and use these relationships to further your network and enhance your experience. **Sarah Harper, Goldman Sachs**

Graduate 'work readiness' and employability is now very much improved. Even so, we use coaches and mentors during their early development. **Jane Hadfield, Head of Learning & Development, Human Resource & Development Directorate, North Bristol NHS Trust**

---

[1]See http://alta-mentoring.com/ – used with permission.

So what are the benefits of having a mentor? They may be summarised as:

- time for personal learning/reflection
- broader organisation awareness
- broader network via the mentor
- builds competence and confidence
- helps to deal with difficult circumstances
- learns from the experiences of others
- maintains a focus on both current work issues and longer-term career progression and personal development
- gaining independent, third-party advice.

We also know that there are benefits for being a mentor as well. Even if you are an undergraduate, or a recent graduate progressing through professional training, you may have a lot to offer people a few years behind you:

- time for personal learning/reflection (as mentors support the development of others, many report that they develop a different perspective of the organisation, or that it helps them to stay in touch with issues outside their immediate organisational levels)
- leadership: sets an example that can be 'passed down the line'
- learning from the perspective of others
- passing on knowledge and experience
- helping others to 'grow'
- contributes to organisational performance
- gives something back
- supports organisational learning.

Mentoring others is usually enjoyable, and demonstrates to potential employers that you have transferable skills.

Although mentoring benefits are usually expressed as being for the mentees, organisations benefit as well. They offer improved access to, and retention of, scarce talent and present new opportunities for employees. It is a cost-effective way to develop people and, pursued appropriately, should lead to an increase in employee loyalty and commitment. The direct benefits of a good mentoring relationship as you develop your employability portfolio are that it will give you:

- honest, candid, and objective feedback
- support and a different perspective.

Once you are in employment your manager may, at times, also give you advice as a mentor. But it is best for you to find a mentor outside your usual line. Your employing organisation may have a formal mentoring scheme. Alternatively, look to see if your professional body has a mentoring scheme, or ask your HR department for recommendations. If you are not employed, look for a mentor, who may be a family member or friend. There are professional-specific mentoring schemes and, increasingly, special schemes for women (see details at the end of this chapter).

Women specialist mentoring schemes recognise the particular needs of women, especially for those who are working in male-dominated organisations where female role models and confidantes may be harder to find and women colleagues form only a low proportion of the overall workforce. Examples include:

The Mentoring Foundation, www.mentoringfoundation.co.uk/, a UK scheme to help more women reach the very top of large organisations.

Alta, http://alta-mentoring.com/, for women in aviation and aerospace.

Women in Film and Television UK, www.wftv.org.uk/mentoring-scheme, for those with at least 5 years' experience.

Women-only schemes are designed to supplement male/female mentoring; mentoring does, of course, remain open and valuable for men as well. Women-only schemes are usually structured and formalised. The schemes are lawful in the UK as part of 'positive action' or 'positive support' diversity programmes. The value of the schemes can be judged by some of the comments that mentees have given on the value of their schemes, For example:

'The mentoring scheme fosters an incredibly supportive and safe environment to openly identify obstacles (both professional and personal), push boundaries, learn new skills, ask questions and take risks.' **Fleur Jago, Producer (Mentee 2014) WFTV Mentoring Scheme, used with permission**

Continuing Professional Development (CPD)

Whether CPD is a voluntary or mandatory part of your professional development, it should keep you up to date with the technical aspects of your work and help you to ensure that your personal skills remain appropriate and relevant. Friedman (2012) surveyed 102 professional bodies and found that 55 had their own definitions of CPD. Our own definition of CPD is:

A methodical approach to maintain and improve professional and personal skills, to enable personal work effectiveness throughout an individual's career.

Looking at the overall effectiveness of CPD, Friedman (2012) found that use of CPD was widespread (indeed, Gold and Smith, 2010, estimated that about 20 per cent of UK employees had their own CPD plans). However, there were some concerns about the use of CPD. For example, some regulatory bodies may see CPD as a form of public protection; however, it may equally be thought of as weak unless it is underpinned by legislation. On the other hand, where organisations wish to reinforce their own distinctive brand or culture, they may prefer to reinforce their own learning styles rather than rely on generic CPD approaches from national professional bodies.

PRACTICAL APPLICATION

We see CPD as an essential part of employability, though we recognise that employers may or may not see it as important in your development. If you are in an organisation which encourages your learning, CPD provides an invaluable framework for your development. If you are in an organisation which pays little attention to your development, your CPD programme will help you to maintain the skills that will enhance your employability where you are, and support you if you leave that employer.

Many professional bodies have their own CPD frameworks. As an example, abstracts from the CPD framework for dentistry are shown in Exhibit 5.3. Review your CPD twice a year and make sure that it is realistic and continues to develop your skills and competences.

Your CPD may include an action plan for:

- Your developing competences – how you work with others, not just your technical skills (Table 3.2).
- Developing technical knowledge and skills.
- Coaching and mentoring (see Table 5.2 at the end of the chapter).
- Ensuring that you use all types of learning styles in your development (see Table 5.1).
- Reflective practice and action learning (see Table 5.1 and the example in Appendix E).
- Conventional learning through formal courses.
- General reading and activities which are 'outside the box' and enable you to take a broader perspective.

Exhibit 5.3

CPD and Professionalism – an Example for Dental Professionals

Some professional bodies have strict CPD requirements, which may also be established in law. In the example below we have shown an abstract from the General Dental Council's (GDC) requirements for CPD. Dental professional are advised to refer to the original source for the full requirements.

Notice the breadth of CPD examples which are given, as well as the importance attached to formal recording of CPD activities and minimum time commitments. Notice also that CPD is a legal requirement.

Keeping skills and knowledge up to date throughout your career is at the heart of what it means to be a dental professional.

We require you to do CPD because the GDC's purpose is to protect patients and the public. CPD helps to maintain public confidence in the dental register by showing that dental professionals are staying up to date. This is so you can give your patients the best possible treatment and make an effective contribution to dentistry in the UK.

The CPD scheme

CPD makes an important contribution to patient safety and is a requirement for continued registration with the GDC.

The GDC's current requirements have been in place since 2008 and they are set out in law. These can be found at the GDC's website at www.gdc-uk.org/governancemanual. You must meet our requirements to maintain your registration or restore to the register. Our requirements are based on a minimum number of hours of CPD that you must do during the five-year CPD cycle that applies to you. We will require you to tell us about all the CPD you have done at the end of your five-year CPD cycle. We will also invite you to provide us with certain information each year about the CPD you have done during your CPD cycle.

Definition of CPD

CPD for dental professionals is defined in law as lectures, seminars, courses, individual study and other activities that can be included in your CPD record if it can be reasonably expected to advance your professional development as a dentist or dental care professional and is relevant to your practice or intended practice.

Examples of types of CPD may include:

- courses and lectures
- training days
- peer review

- clinical audit
- reading journals
- attending conferences
- e-learning activity.

Visit www.gdc-uk.org for some suggestions on how to carry out your CPD.

Source: Abstract taken from 'Continuing Professional Development for Dental Professionals', General Dental Council (2013) and used with permission

Performance Reviews

Assessment doesn't stop at university, and most employers adopt some form of employee performance review (also known as 'performance appraisals'). The aims of the performance review process are objectives, feedback and evaluation (Storey and Sisson, 1993). In turn, this typically involves:

- linking your work objectives to those of the team and the organisation
- monitoring progress against SMART (**S**pecific, **M**easurable, **A**chievable, **R**ealistic and **T**imed) work objectives
- looking at your current and future learning and development needs
- understanding how the work environment may have helped, or obstructed, your performance
- updating your SMART work objectives for the coming review period
- accepting the results of 360-degree feedback (in some organisations) (see following section)
- understanding whether there is any additional support you may need to do your job effectively
- giving feedback to your manager.

In some organisations, especially in the commercial sector, performance reviews are often linked to pay or bonus reviews; a minimum threshold of good performance will be required for you to receive a pay review. Some performance review schemes may end with an 'overall rating' – that you were 'good', 'very good', 'not good enough' and so on. Furthermore, and especially during graduate development periods, your performance reviews and an updated assessment of your competences (see Chapter 3) will often be used as part of your development assessment, and possibly of your standing on talent management programmes (see 'Talent Programmes' below). Where there are internal job selection processes, they may be used as part as selection assessment. In those occasions where organisations either restructure or need to implement redundancy programmes, performance reviews may also be used as an important de-selection criterion, so it is important to get them as right as possible.

So what might go wrong with performance reviews? Important as they are, performance reviews can go wrong. Poor reviews may be:

- infrequent (e.g. only annually)
- a monologue from the manager
- a review only of failures and omissions (or an excessively glossy review which fails to look at setbacks)
- based on impressions, not measurement of work against objectives
- a disagreement between the employee and the manager
- that both parties are left feeling disgruntled and the employee demotivated.

Qualitative performance objectives may be difficult to assess objectively, whereas quantitative goals (budget management, hitting date objectives, sales, project time lines etc.) concentrate too much on the numbers and not enough about the circumstances (good or bad) in which you worked.

The research on performance management systems underlines many of the problems associated with this technique of management. For example, it is not always easy for managers to make objective distinctions in performance (Heneman, 1992; Wiese and Buckley, 1998). In turn, this makes overall ratings more difficult to get right. Managers themselves may feel ill prepared or insufficiently trained to undertake appraisals. Crush (2013) noted that appraisals can go wrong when neither party comes away from the review meeting 'any the wiser', an excessive focus on what needs to be done rather than how it is done, a failure to have clear work objectives, a tendency for employees to feel disengaged and a failure to give praise. Overall, it is little wonder that so much has been expected of performance review as a process, and yet that potential has not yet been fully delivered.

Against the difficulties associated with performance reviews, organisations are often looking both to improve appraiser training and develop clear policy. One area of emerging interest is 'abolishing' the formal annual performance appraisal. In its place, organisations such as Accenture (management consultants), Microsoft, Gap, and Expedia are said to be introducing more frequent, less formalised schemes (Kirton, 2015:10). For many, this would in any case reflect the type of good practice which could already be integrated into current schemes. It will be interesting to see how these schemes develop, and whether they genuinely achieve the aims of a good review suggested by Stone and Heen (2014): appreciation, evaluation, coaching.

360-Degree Feedback

As part of your performance reviews (sometimes used for graduate development, though typically used from junior management roles and above), you may take part in 360-degree feedback.

This feedback on your work performance should remain relevant to the role, but benefit from a broad range of stakeholders. You will be invited to gather feedback from a range of contributors (subordinates, peers, managers and customers) (Chen and Naquin, 2006).

As to how effective and useful 360-degree feedback is, CIPD (2012) found that 22 per cent of organisations rated 360-degree feedback as effective for talent management (against only 3 per cent for assessment centres).

But 360-degree feedback also has its critics. These include lack of clarity on purpose, use only to deal with under-performers (in some cases), potential breach of confidentiality, lack of measurement effectiveness, treating it as an end in itself, not part of a wider process, and poor communication with those involved (Wimer and Nowack, 1998). At a more practical (and potentially cynical) level, the value of the feedback may also depend on who chooses the 360 responders, and whether the review is for genuine, confidential development or is constructed as part of a flattering performance review.

PRACTICAL APPLICATION

Some colleagues may be relaxed at the prospect of their reviews, whilst other may be cynical, tense or non-committed. This is a pity. Well executed, performance reviews are a very important part of working life and can give you realistic and supportive feedback on how you are doing. You must prepare for a performance review and not leave it to your manager to give a monologue report on your process. Indeed, a well-trained manager should let you do most of the talking during the review. You can prepare by:

- keeping your performance review papers safely (though increasingly, reviews are kept online)
- checking your performance against your SMART objectives under regular review – certainly not leaving it until the next review before you look at them again
- knowing how well (not so well) you have done since the last review meeting (give actual data and examples)

(Continued)

(Continued)

- not assuming that, just because performance reviews have not been mentioned, they will not happen (some line managers still find formal performance reviews a chore and do not prepare adequately for them; make sure that *you are* prepared and have considered your learning needs as part of that review)
- keeping notes on what has gone well and not so well, and why (give actual data and examples)
- thinking about your own learning and development needs (remember, you should have your own learning plan)
- agreeing to new objectives for the coming review period without underestimating the potential for other factors to interfere with your ability to deliver – this is not a mandate for playing games in performance reviews, however, a good adage is to be cautious in promising what you think you can do and then seek to exceed expectations in quality and timing of delivery
- arranging your review date with your manager in good time – don't let your manager, or yourself, be rushed into getting results together at short notice.

In conclusion, the performance review is a widely used system, in all sectors and globally. Despite this, it can still be seen as a complication, even a barrier, to what should be constructive and valuable feedback between the employee and the manager. We have included a candid review here so that you may have an objective perspective of the process. It is important for you to have an informed and 'can do' attitude towards your own review, and use this section to minimise some of the pitfalls in the system.

If your organisation has a talent management programme, your potential participation in the programme will be based on how you perform in your role and how your future potential is judged. We will now look at talent programmes in more detail.

Talent Programmes

Organisations use talent development programmes to develop key employees for future managerial or specialist roles. Graduates may initially be put on talent programmes to focus learning and development investment in what is often an expensive resource to recruit, and one which organisations hope will provide at least some of their longer-term specialist and managerial resources. Other organisational talent programmes may be focused on specialist functions, graduates or to develop more senior – and the most senior – executives of the organisation.

CIPD (2015a) found that about 60 per cent of commercial organisations and 40 per cent of public sector organisations used talent development programmes. Of these, 54 per cent include all staff in their talent development programmes, whilst about 35 per cent focus on higher potential employees only; about 17 per cent of graduates were allocated to some form of talent development programme (CIPD 2015a).

Talent management programmes should link organisation strategy with employee performance and potential in order to provide the organisation with its longer-term functional and management needs. This does not happen as frequently or as systematically as you might expect. Charan noted the paradox that organisations focused time and resources to managing finances, but commented on a 'scant approach' (2010: 2) to identifying and developing their leaders.

Blass (2007) emphasised the interdependencies between talent management and performance management and also noted that performance management (linked with a systematic review of future potential) should be a good basis for talent management systems. For Charan et al. (2011) talent can be identified by ranking current performance and future potential; individuals with high performance and high potential will be ready for early promotion, following a path of development aimed at developing self and progressively leading larger teams and groups within the organisation. Those with lesser talent potential may make slower progress, and not to such senior levels, whilst those with low performance and low potential would come under further review, either for development or for leaving the organisation.

Given the profile and money spent on them, do talent programmes work? At the individual level, Blass (2007) found that only 31 per cent of managers had any real confidence that their organisation could identify high-potential talent. At organisational level, Gutridge et al. (2006) found strategic failures to link talent management and business strategies. Blass noted that although the necessary alignment with business strategy was considered critical, 'in practice they are too often developed in isolation' (2007: 3). Research by CIPD (2012) found that only 6 per cent of organisations regarded their talent management activities as 'very effective', 50 per cent 'fairly effective', but 15 per cent as 'fairly ineffective or very ineffective'. As a result, they observed a slight fall in organisations using these programmes: to 54 per cent in 2012 from 61 per cent the previous year. By 2015, the organisation behaviour specialist Adrian Furnham expressed the view that 'telling someone they are talented is disastrous' (2015: 44): in part, this reflects the difficulty in identifying 'talent' in the first place, but also recognises the raised expectations (which may not be achieved) of those identified as talent.

┌─────────────── **PRACTICAL APPLICATION** ───────────────┐

If you find yourself in a talent programme, what can you expect from it? We don't want the experience to be 'disastrous', but for you to make the most of the opportunity without losing your head and sense of proportion. Typically, this may include work rotation, promotions, project work, management training schemes, qualifications, mentoring, secondments, transfers and job shadowing (Blass, 2007). Throughout this time you can expect that your performance will be monitored through regular performance management reviews and future potential assessed though competence assessment. The talent pool is usually kept under regular review, with new opportunities for newly identified talent and dropping for those who are not making the required level of progress. Talent development programmes are not a panacea for long-term tenure in an organisation. Indeed some organisations (including accounting and financial services) will terminate employment of graduates who fail to make the required standards during or on completion of the talent programme.

And what should you do if you find that your organisation does not have a talent development programme? Or that it does, and that you are not part of it? Of course, this does not mean that your development is of no value to the organisation (in reality, whilst talent programmes help to focus development spend on those who are most likely to benefit from it, they are also regarded as potentially elitist). Instead, you should develop your own talent programme. This is not as difficult as it may seem, though it will mean that you need to invest time to do so – indeed, it is central to the purpose of this book on employability. Use the chapters in this book to develop your personalised talent development programme. Once you have done this, use it as the basis for working with your mentor (see 'Mentoring' in this chapter) on your personal development.

└───┘

In conclusion, talent programmes are still widely used, and graduates may often find themselves on an organisation-based programme. Despite the hype which surrounds them, they have weaknesses in design and implementation. Even so, they are an important opportunity to take and make the most use of – so much so that if you are not on one, we do suggest that you prepare your own programme (see Table 5.2 for an example).

Conclusion

Effective learning and development – throughout your career – is key to long-term employability.

The techniques for learning at work may still include development of theoretical knowledge through reading and professional studies, but will now rely more on learning from your work performance, including reflective learning.

Mentoring and CPD have important roles in your continued learning and development, so do get organised to make the most of these resources.

TABLE 5.2 Sample individual learning plan

	What	By when	Support needed
My personal goals	Achieve 'chartered' status in professional exams	3 years from now:	Can my employer provide financial or time resources to support?
	Enhance all work-related competences in preparation for career advancement		
	Gain further experience in [subject] to prepare for new job applications	Review competence examples every 3–4 months. Look out for new roles from 12 month's time	Line manager
	Keep a broad view of wider developments in my area of work through reading and external conference attendance	Next 18 months: Request short-term attachment to [name of] department	
		Read professional journal. Attend 3 professional body events each year.	
		See if local university has relevant public seminars	
Learning to achieve this	Complete professional exams, review chartered criteria	Ensure I complete at least three exam modules each year	Use competences examples to see what gaps I need to close
	List out my competences examples (Table 3.2), and review strengths and areas of development	Every 3–4 months	Discuss with line manager; keep an eye open for secondments
	Get better at [competency] and discuss with line manager how I can improve in this/these areas	By year end	
		In next 18 months	
	Gain experience outside current role with a secondment/ placement	Within 2 months	
	Find a mentor and discuss development plans with mentor. See mentor every 6 weeks	Ask [trusted colleague] to give me feedback on team effectiveness over next month	Check if mentoring scheme available, or via my professional body
	Is there 360-degree feedback available as part of organisation learning schemes? If not, do I have a trusted colleague who could give me feedback on how I come across, especially in team meetings and presentations	See HR information for possible 360-degree feedback	

Performance reviews are also an integral part of your learning and tracking the impacts of your development. It is very important that you prepare yourself thoroughly for your performance reviews – don't simply leave it to your manager.

Some organisations will still give good support for your learning, others less so. You may also find yourself part of an organisation talent programme, or find yourself excluded from it. Whichever of these apply, remember that managing your learning is in the end your own responsibility. Do take time to manage it effectively.

ACTION

Having read this chapter, we suggest that you think about the following action points:

- Commit yourself to your long-term personal development with a personal learning plan.
- As you start work it is worthwhile keeping a journal, especially in the first year. This will help you to move up the learning curve more quickly. Keep notes on what you did, things you achieved, problems you encountered. Topics to include are:
  - who does what
  - your first impressions (and see how they develop over time)
  - a sketch map of who works where (useful as you get bombarded with new names)
  - learning plans which you need to achieve
  - things going well (how will you replicate this in other areas of work?)
  - things going not so well (and how you will fix these).
- Set aside regular time for that personal development.
- Find a mentor – or two.
- If you are on a professional development track, look at professional qualifications and requirements for CPD.
- Think about how *you* could develop your mentoring skills.
- Take the opportunity to look outside the box for learning opportunities, for example: mix your learning styles; visit a library and browse through the books; think about how the full range of arts, science, technology, social changes and culture could impact your work; go to a talk which does not seem relevant to your field – what can you learn from it?
- Read your professional journals; think about writing an article.

Further Reading

Find a copy of Honey and Mumford's learning style questionnaire (Honey, 1986); look at your learning styles and think about what you can do to make fullest use of each of the four learning styles.

Graduate Skills

Dowson, P.

15

A NOTE FROM THE AUTHOR

Many of you will be well aware of intelligent and talented graduates who have not secured what we might term befitting employment. These are young adults who have got their university degrees but these have not led them as of yet into graduate work. Some may be doing work that could have been secured without a university degree. Others may even be unemployed and living again with their parents in their early twenties. This all goes to show that there is more to securing a desirable graduate job than going to university and getting a degree. What are the reasons for this?

There are a number of things at play here. Firstly, there are more qualified people chasing fewer jobs. In the economic downturn the supply of graduates is outstripping demand. In this extremely competitive environment employers can and will seek ever *more* from prospective employees. For example, they might start by only considering those who have secured a top classification from a top university.

Secondly, it has always been the case that employers attach much significance to what are known as employability skills. This causes them to value work experiences and other responsibility experiences which permit graduates to slot into employment openings more easily. Added to this certain university courses more overtly than others offer the skills development that employers seek.

Thirdly, much responsibility still rests with the graduate themselves to make the very most of the opportunity at university. This applies not only to looking on a university education as a chance to develop significant skills but also being more deliberate about documenting and evidencing such skills development in job applications.

Fourthly, it may be the case that in certain sectors and with certain jobs some degrees would be more highly regarded than others. For a whole manner of reasons sometimes graduates are not able to offer employers the most appropriate specialized degree with a skills development most attuned to the specific employment opportunity. All other things remaining equal, the employer will probably select the candidate with the most relevant degree subject.

Learning outcomes

When you have completed this chapter you will be able to:

- evaluate the job opportunities available to graduates
- profile the skills offering graduates are expected to offer employees
- define the options that give graduates employability edge
- appreciate the significance of planning in making progress
- understand and define differentiating factors for the contemporary age.

GRADUATE JOBS

For the majority of occupational areas there is a starting job suited or exclusively designed for graduates as the examples in Table 4.1 show.

Table 4.1   Graduate jobs and their job titles on entry

Accountancy	trainee accountant
Advertising	trainee account executive or trainee account handler
Architecture	architectural assistant
Armed Forces	officer cadet
Banking	graduate trainee
Charity	project assistant, fundraising assistant or admin assistant
Chemical and pharmaceutical	graduate scientist
Civil Service	fast streamer
Construction	construction trainee
Energy and oil	trainee analyst
Engineering and industry	graduate engineer
Film and TV	production assistant or programme assistant
Hospitality	trainee manager
Human resources (HR)	HR trainee
Insurance	graduate trainee
Investment banking	trainee analyst
IT and telecoms	IT trainee
Law	trainee solicitor
Management consultancy	analyst
Marketing and social media	marketing assistant
Medicine	foundation doctor
Pilots and air traffic control	first officer or student air traffic controller
Police and Fire Service	probationer constable or trainee firefighter

Recruitment	trainee recruitment consultant
Research and development	postdoctoral or research associate
Retail	trainee manager
Sales	trainee sales executive
Surveying and property	trainee surveyor
Teaching	newly qualified teacher

Susanne Christian in her book *Top Jobs: Discover the Best Graduate Jobs and How to Get One* profiles 29 graduate job areas. As you can see from Table 4.1, which lists these jobs along with the respective graduate job title on entry, there is no shortage of options. Speaking to business students, if you consider that virtually all these job areas consist of organizations that are run as businesses there are even more possibilities. The challenge here is possibly knowing where to start, or just getting started. For a whole manner of reasons it is easy while at university to put off career enquiries and research and not doing justice to the opportunity one has to be working towards a satisfying job opening, no matter how competitive the current situation is.

All the job areas above offer graduate schemes often referred to as graduate development programmes. Information about such schemes is available at your university careers service. Obviously there is competition and a limited number of places, but if you are successful this is an ideal introduction to a specific job area and will consist usually, over two years, of gaining vital experience of the employing organization and being rotated in a number of roles or departments, where your performance will be assessed. This enables the trainee to gain an understanding of what they're most suited to. Very helpfully it also involves on-the-job training supported by more formal classroom training, in some cases studying for more qualifications.

Christian is right to point out that you need to be determined to secure one of these graduate places reflected in the following process:

- Enquiring about such openings towards the end of your first year at university. Some schemes have application processes in your final year but others may be during the second year and it is important not to miss out through lack of planning.
- Graduate scheme employers look for candidates offering not only graduate knowledge and aptitude but also demonstrating varied interests and early responsibilities in sporting and other leisure activities. Former and existing part-time work experience is also valued as is demonstration of employability skills.
- The selection process almost always includes what is known as an assessment centre where candidates are required to do a number of things including: give a presentation; do group and individual exercises; sit psychometric tests; be interviewed; and consider case studies.
- Like applying to any organization it is essential to research it. This is an expectation on the part of the employer.

KEY CONCEPT – THE GRADUATE JOBS FORMULA

Paul Redmond (2010) developed the graduate jobs formula which is:

$$E = Q + WE + S \times C$$

Where:

E = employability
Q = qualifications
WE = work experience
S = strategies
C = contacts

It is a very concise way of bringing together all the elements needed for a graduate to access a desirable career in what Redmond refers to as the job market 'AD' (after the downturn). How Redmond understands these essential elements is summarized below:

Employability – Redmond's 'employability redux' (Redmond, 2010) as he calls it is the recognition that employability is essentially about self-sufficiency. Added to this he fleshes out (see embodiment box) the important distinction between being in employment (which is good) and being 'employable' (which is even better).

Qualifications – Business degrees have the great potential to deliver commercial awareness which Redmond says, is an 'essential skill sought by thousands of recruiters' (Redmond, 2010). If you're not doing a business degree you may want to plan how you can alternatively gain this significant employability skill.

The biggest recruiters of business students are in order:

- The retail sector, with some retailers offering two-year graduate management training programmes
- The professional services sector including management and human resources
- Financial services including accountancy, baking, insurance and investment banking

Work experience – 'It is now widely recognised,' Redmond argues, 'that work experience is the *key* to employability' (Redmond, 2010). Work placements are particularly useful making students who have gone on them more marketable and where of a good quality deliver:

- personal development
- new learning and skills development

- assessment and feedback
- clear aims and objectives
- on-going support and contact.

Strategies – In Redmond's strategies section he deals with applications and CVs, interviews and assessment centres. Here he emphasizes how the growth of the internet and the drive to reduce recruitment costs on the part of the employer are changing the rules of engagement as far as recruitment is concerned. But as ever, successful candidates will be those who are well prepared and have approached the recruitment process strategically.

Contacts – Redmond argues, 'It's not what you know, it's not who you know. It's who knows you' (Redmond, 2010). The key to networking for Redmond is knowing exactly what you're wanting to achieve through it and the resulting interaction – what you might call adopting a very deliberate approach. Students he says should have business cards not only because they are more likely to be retained than say CVs and emails, but also because they are a symbol of being professional and prepared.

GRADUATE SKILLS

In this section we shall present the findings of three pieces of research about what constitute what we might term as graduate skills. The reader will note that there is some contrast in the results. Rather than suggesting that one piece of research has more validity than another, in this case, we should probably pool the findings and reflect on their implications.

INSTITUTE FOR EMPLOYMENT STUDIES (2000) RESEARCH

A piece of Institute for Employment Studies research summarized in a report entitled *The art of getting started: graduate skills in a fragmented labour market* (La Valle et al., 2000) highlights a number of relevant things in this area of graduate skills.

Firstly, the notion of what employers refer to as a 'skills gap' – this is the gap between what an employer looks for in hiring an employee by way of their skills offering and what skills the successful candidate actually brings. It is also the case that graduates themselves, securing employment, can be become conscious of this skills gap and would like to be in the position of offering more.

Secondly, the research lists the skill areas as follows:

- self-confidence and self-esteem
- decision making
- time management

- self-promotion
- problem-solving skills
- motivation/commitment to learning
- developing creative ideas
- pro-active/entrepreneurial skills
- visual/verbal/written communication
- cope with uncertainty
- specific craft/technical skills
- networking
- teamwork
- negotiating.

While one can immediately see that these skills are by no means *exclusive* to graduates, at the same time it is undoubtedly the case that university provides an opportunity to develop these skills not just in relation to the course of studies, but also in the life the student leads around their study in leisure, part-time employment and volunteering.

Thirdly, the research suggested that all these skills were important in the graduates' employment activity but their relative importance is reflected in the order of the above listing. This is not the same as the 'skills gap' which was much more significant in certain areas than others. The largest gaps related to negotiating and networking. Smaller, but still significant gaps related to self-confidence, self-promotion, entrepreneurial skills, time management and the ability to cope with uncertainty.

FUTURETRACK (2012) RESEARCH

The Futuretrack research (2012) headed by Professors Peter Elias and Kate Purcell (2013) casts important light on what skills are particularly associated with graduate jobs and defines three groups of graduate jobs requiring high level skills.

- The *expert* group of jobs focus on specialist knowledge gained from a degree course. Examples include chemical scientists, civil engineers, pharmacists, solicitors, physiotherapists, chartered surveyors and airline pilots.
- The *orchestrators* group of jobs draw on a host of strategic skills including managerial skills, problem-solving skills, planning skills and decision-making skills. Managers and Directors often occupy this group as do senior officers from the armed forces and other public sector organizations. Since it requires extensive experience of the particular field in question to operate as an orchestrator Elias and Purcell suggest that it is not an area occupied by many recent graduates (Elias and Purcell, 2013).
- The *communicators* group require high level communication skills, whether oral or written. Examples include web design and development,

marketing associate professionals, journalists, actors, conference and exhibition organizers. Communicators use interactive skills whether interpersonal, creative, technological or about manipulating and directing information.

PRINCE'S (2013) NEW SKILLS FOR THE WORLD WE NOW LIVE IN

Emma-Sue Prince's book *The Advantage: The 7 Soft Skills You Need to Stay One Step Ahead* endorses the development of the skills highlighted already. In addition to these, and because of a number of trends and changes, she advocates seven more, to strengthen ability to focus, communicate and collaborate as follows:

1 adaptability
2 critical thinking
3 empathy
4 integrity
5 optimism
6 proactivity
7 resilience.

Prince's understanding of these skills is outlined below:

Adaptability – this is not just about being flexible and able to change to fit altered circumstances but also about being open to new ways of operating and venturing outside our comfort zone. She outlines ten ways to become more adaptable.

1 Challenge limiting beliefs and 'mental scripts' and be prepared to open yourself up to new ways of thinking and responding.
2 Develop resilience and complete tasks through focus and self-discipline.
3 Travel more and so gain confidence in handling varied situations.
4 Seek to learn something new, be prepared to try new things and draw conclusions from new situations.
5 Look for ways to expand your comfort zone and through time reinvent yourself.
6 Practise being spontaneous and improvising. Take an opportunity now rather than putting it off.
7 Try exercising three types of flexibility: cognitive flexibility, or new ways of thinking; emotional flexibility, adjusting how you deal with your emotions and those of others; and dispositional flexibility, balancing realism and optimism.
8 Train yourself to respond more positively to changes and even setbacks.

9 Be more creative and experiment with different ways of problem solving.

10 Develop a survivor rather than a victim mentality.

Critical thinking – we introduced critical thinking in Chapter 3. As you will recall critical thinking is all about how we evaluate a situation or come to a judgement incorporating rationality, creativity and reflection. Prince describes six ways in which critical thinking is changing.

1 Making sense of information is increasingly significant in view of our being constantly bombarded with so much of it. This necessitates high level thinking skills.

2 Most high-skill jobs now demand what is known as 'situational adaptability' – the ability to respond quickly to the unexpected.

3 So called 'computational thinking' is required to correctly interpret large amounts of data.

4 New media literacy is a must, reflected in, for example, user-generated media like blogs and podcasts.

5 Optimum cognitive functioning will be required through discriminating and filtering information.

6 Being 'T-shaped' as a worker means having depth of expertise in at least one area but having the capacity to apply critical thinking and reasoning across a breadth of fields.

Empathy – Prince suggests this is 'the ability to enter the internal world of the other person' and understand their situation, feelings and motives (Prince, 2013).

Empathy is now a much sought after quality reflected in how people want to connect with others, even relative strangers, via social network sites. It has become something which one would wish to find in friendships and even collegiate relationships in the workplace. Finally, managers and leaders who can extend empathy are also appreciated and more likely to be followed.

Integrity – we shall be dedicating a chapter to integrity (Chapter 8) but this also makes Prince's list of essential soft skills. As Prince highlights, integrity is derived from the Latin word *integer*, meaning whole or intact. Her profile of integrity (as follows) is also useful in building up a picture of what integrity looks like:

- demonstrating authenticity – a life aligning with a person's values
- displaying consistency
- taking responsibility
- following through – doing what they said they would do
- being accountable
- communicating truth respectfully
- actively listening and seeking to understand 'other'
- being emotionally receptive and articulate
- acting without hidden agendas.

In the workplace, this might look like this:

- not just saying what others want to hear
- displaying depth of character
- 'walking the talk'
- being reliable
- keeping promises
- being up front in a respectful way.

Optimism – the hallmarks of optimism for Prince are threefold:

1 realistically and accurately assessing a situation
2 an 'overcoming' attitude to problems
3 a sense of empowerment to tackle something.

Prince's distinction between optimism and the cult of positive thinking is a helpful one. She warns of an 'irrational optimism where mind-set is all that matters' (Prince, 2013) and adds that 'we cannot change outcomes by thoughts and affirmations alone'. Optimism isn't blind positive thinking but looks for the big picture – all the facts and possibilities in a given situation.

Being proactive – for Prince being proactive has four elements as follows:

1 Self-awareness – this is about becoming aware of your reactions, seeing yourself if you like – so you can choose to act differently.
2 Willpower – this has to be built up over time and practised.
3 Responsibility – this is the ability to respond with conscious choices.
4 Self-mastery – this is having complete control not only of your actions but the thoughts, emotions and beliefs that underpin actions.

Resilience – how resilient someone is, Prince argues, comes down to two things and their interaction:

1 Resilience is a factor in someone's personality and, as Prince remarks, some people are just 'far better able to handle set-backs than others'.
2 Resilience also depends on your environment – not only what happens (your experiences), but also the strength of support in the form of family, friends and the social environment.

Resilience, Prince argues, is essentially about taking control given inevitable adversity or problems. It is a quality that is associated with contemporary senior leaders forever facing business and operational uncertainties and competitiveness. It is supported by having strong social networks expressed in sites such as LinkedIn.

Pulling together these three pieces of research, what observations can we make about so called 'graduate skills'? Firstly, the research may suggest that the term graduate skills means different things to different people and critically to different employers. It could indicate at least three things:

1 An expected standard – skills an employer would expect to come with employing a graduate. It is, for example, reasonable that employers should expect graduates to spell well and show a good standard in their written communications.
2 High order skills – as well as possessing all the skills that an employer would expect to find in a graduate, there is often an added expectation of graduates possessing high order skills, for example critical thinking skills.
3 Cutting edge skills – because universities are often at the forefront of new thinking reflected in the latest research, it would be reasonable for employers to expect to find the latest and most progressive thinking in university graduates, particularly in the sort of areas highlighted by Prince above.

Secondly, looking at this research another way, perhaps to be highly skilled is a multifaceted and expanding notion – the idea that a lot of things come with a highly skilled individual who is often the product of a good and prolonged education and/or upbringing.

Thirdly, the research raises the issue of how skills are acquired and developed. Some skills development is progressed through practice even without being particularly conscious of this, for example, what is gained by practising working in small groups. At the same time, training input and strategy takes skills development forward in a deliberate fashion.

EMBODIMENT BOX – THE EMPLOYABILITY EDGE

Paul Redmond's (2010) distinction between what it means to be employable and how this trumps in many respects being purely in employment is a useful tool for reflection, as shown in Table 4.2:

Table 4.2 A comparison of being employable and being in employment

Being Employable	Being in Employment
career	job
contacts	contract
who knows you	what you know
ongoing training	previous qualifications
works with …	works for …
global worldview	'local' worldview

EMPLOYABILITY FOCUS – VOLUNTEERING

Employers look upon graduates who have volunteering experiences very favourably. Not only does this communicate other interests on the part of the student, it also can help students develop the employability skills so sought after by employers. A key here is for students to demonstrate the added value of their time given to volunteering. This distils down into how the student is going to ably communicate and summarize what their volunteering experience consisted of and what skills and other learning they acquired through the volunteering placement.

There are innumerable opportunities to volunteer both in one's country of study and internationally. Perhaps the best way to make the most of any volunteering experience is to select an organization working for a cause that is a genuine area of interest to the student. We cannot identify with all needs and all causes, but there are some that would be more inspirational than others depending on the individual.

There are options regarding the length of the placement. This could occupy a year out or university summer vacation or it is something students can do part-time to coincide with their studies. Charities are now very much businesses in their own right and some of them are extremely large and influential. There may be future employment opportunities in such charities and volunteering is sometimes a way into employment.

Consider some of the advantages of volunteering summarized below:

- network contacts and potential referees
- skills development opportunities
- trial responsibilities to define performance areas
- CV and application enhancement
- demonstration of commitment and motivation
- application of subject area learning in the workplace
- widening of experience
- potential intercultural learning.

GRADUATE NETWORKING

University represents a near perfect training ground for professional networking and therefore it is included in this chapter on graduate skills. Divan defines networking as 'developing and maintaining contact with people who work in the same field as you or in a related field' (Divan, 2009).

From the very beginning of university it is both professional and sensible to adopt a networking mentality for the following reasons:

1 It is a means by which you can share, develop, refine and revise your ideas. Conversations and meetings yield useful feedback and information that you may not otherwise acquire.
2 Networking constitutes a resource base for a whole manner of things including references, recruitment opportunities and the latest news and developments in your field.
3 It can also be a source of support and even fun, meeting with like-minded people.

There are a number of ways of networking and students should consider their prospects for adding new spheres to their network activity. Below are a number that are outlined by Divan:

Departmental networking – this is obviously a natural place to start, in your own department or business school. Don't limit yourself to talking with friends, but find out what other students are doing and are interested in. Don't be afraid to approach researchers and other staff attached to your school or department.

Attending added seminars and events – in addition to the academic timetable with its lectures and seminars there will be a host of added events and seminars not only in your department, but in the university and at neighbouring universities. As far as priorities allow these all have potential for developing your network.

Attending conferences – sometimes there are opportunities to attend conferences. Like the above opportunity these are also useful for your studies as well as for networking. Be sure to note down contact details and exchange cards if possible.

Other networking opportunities – these might include joining a professional society relevant to your subject area and getting involved in any relevant local groups pertinent to your academic specialism and interests.

In addition to face-to-face networking there are of course opportunities to network through web-based media.

DEVELOPMENT POINTER – USING LINKEDIN

Launched in 2003, LinkedIn is regarded by many as the number one business social networking site (Peregrin, 2012). A social media specialist, Kristina Jaramillo argues that LinkedIn has great significance as a job networking site (Peregrin, 2012), but it also doubles as a tool to stay connected to professional contacts. Marisa Moore adds in Tony Peregrin's (2012) article, 'LinkedIn profile makeover: optimizing your professional online profile,' that the site is a 'great way to get your name out there and to increase your exposure and visibility'.

The article proposes eight ways to optimize your LinkedIn profile as follows:

1 Highlight only the most relevant information – avoiding the temptation to include everything about yourself.
2 Build a complete profile – where LinkedIn records it is 100 per cent complete and not missing sections.
3 Always include a picture – one, Marisa Moore adds, that 'puts your best face forward'.
4 Develop guidelines for adding individuals to your network – approach this strategically avoiding a catch all 'numbers game'.
5 Limit recommendations to people you trust – approach only people best able to endorse your skills.
6 Join groups – this increases your visibility in relevant and strategic areas.
7 Provide credible, accurate information when contributing to discussions and answering questions.
8 Maintain e-professionalism.

The advice from Peregrin's article sits well alongside Susan Joyce's (2013) piece, 'Be visible on LinkedIn', which outlines how to get 'good' LinkedIn visibility. Joyce speaks of playing nice on LinkedIn (Joyce, 2013), resisting any temptation to slip into negativity, crankiness and profanity. This is linked to Joyce's advice to practise smart self-promotion on LinkedIn, involving taking responsibility to be your own publicist. The art of doing this well is how to profile yourself and highlight your accomplishments without resorting to something which comes across as 'bragging' (Joyce, 2013).

Joyce, an online job search specialist, suggests LinkedIn is not optional for job seekers and sets out three targets for using LinkedIn to this end:

1 Establish a LinkedIn profile and connect with 100 people you know, building your network from there.
2 Join 20 LinkedIn groups relevant to your job search.
3 Connect with recruiters.

Blogs where information is posted on a regular basis are one means of professionally connecting and gaining information. Since content is not peer reviewed you need to be both critical and discerning. Authoring a blog is another option, but like all dealing with information, time spent is key.

Contributing to discussion forums, wikis and mailing lists constitutes other electronic opportunities for networking. Mailing lists have the disadvantage that they can deliver too much information.

EMBODIMENT BOX – A YEAR ABROAD

On many degrees there is an opportunity to have a spell where you study abroad, sometimes for a whole academic year. In Europe we have what is known as the Erasmus scheme which permits a period of time in another European university. There are a number of reasons why students often don't pursue this opportunity as follows:

- they don't get around to organizing it
- relationships and friendships (at university) make it appear too radical
- fear of it being an isolating experience
- they are unaware of what is available
- they don't appreciate its contemporary value and significance.

Enlarging on the latter point, time spent studying abroad will differentiate you from the next student and its potential for enhancing a CV and job applications is significant. From the perspective of your personal development it also has great promise. It demonstrates that if you are able to adapt to living and studying in a foreign country, then you will feel more confident about the next challenge in life. But the point to really emphasize is the relevance of such a venture in a globalizing world – a chance to encounter 'other', another country, another experience, other ways of looking at the world (worldviews), other ways of living. This is not an easy option and it can bring on all sorts of challenges. However, if you talk to students who have done this you can see that it has often enlarged them as people – given them more confidence, a greater ability to cope and adapt, sometimes it has been great fun and a wonderful opportunity to experience as a young adult. An experience of another culture often changes your outlook, if only the way you now look at yourself.

Make enquiries early with your course as to the provision of exchange opportunities. You may consider doing this with another student, who you may or may not know really well before you in some sense share this experience.

ETHICS BOX – A NEW ORDER OF DISCOURSE

Sarah Mann writes in *Study, Power and the University* (2008):

> in choosing to study a 'new' subject, an individual enters a new order of discourse, that of higher education and academic practice and that of their chosen discipline. The encounter will challenge their existing representation of the world, their social relations and their sense of identity. While this challenge may potentially undermine the ground the

student stands on, if their engagement with it is constructive, it will produce a richer ground, a more differentiated understanding, new ways of acting, and new ways of being. But the negotiation of this new discourse is complex.

This is a lengthy quotation but Mann here takes us to the very heart of what it means to be a graduate. We enter a new world when we become students of higher education – and universities have their own particular ways of thinking, vocabularies (ways of talking), and cultures (ways of being). As Goldberg (2007) points out, it is not possible to stand outside such systems and as the quotation from Mann suggests this changes the student in some way.

Goldberg takes us a step further by highlighting that the discursive framework found in such places as universities is 'defined by the contradictory discourses it contains', that is, all manner of ways of thinking and of talking and of being. He continues, 'discourses are multivalent and intertwined, and … at any given time an individual may be positioned differently depending on which discourses she is at any given time enmeshed in' (Goldberg, 2007). This is characteristic of a university and what it means to be a graduate – to be exposed to difference and to graduate with a broader understanding and comprehension of such differences.

THE GLOBAL GRADUATE

An important aspect of becoming a graduate is having been a part of a genuine global community. The force of Clement Katulushi's (2005) chapter in the book *Values in Higher Education* is expanding on the significance of this important dimension of what it means to be a university student.

Katulushi cites Roger King (2003) who says, 'historically universities are more global than national in their academic and intellectual orientations'. The presence of international students is one dimension of this adding to the range and diversity of a university's clientele.

Added to this Katulushi argues that 'most universities see themselves as part of a global community' – a community where the appreciation of diversity is central to the substance of being a university. This is powerfully summarized by Katulushi where he writes, 'a genuine experience of higher education is that which enables interaction between and among the diversities of learning communities, respecting their idiosyncrasies while at the same time holding true to the tradition of university education, helping individuals and societies to transcend themselves'.

The ideal here from an educational perspective is tolerance and dialogue between students and staff from different cultures – 'enabling different types of literacies' as Katulushi puts it and resulting in genuine collaboration.

In the second half of Katulushi's chapter majoring on this idea of the university as a global community, he builds on the thinking of Whitehead (2002) who considers the intrinsic values which characterize higher education (as listed below) as essentially the values of *humanity*:

- critical and original thinking
- enquiry
- learning
- freedom
- loving relationships
- the education of social formations.

This takes Katulushi to his argument that the twin functions of a university, teaching and research, 'are both activities of humanity transcending cultures and boundaries'. In other words, university is the place where we can overcome difference and learn together. He closes his chapter with the following challenge, 'to genuinely embrace the global dimension demands effective partnership at the level of learning, and management, in terms of global collaboration and global responsibility'.

The implications of Katulushi's thinking in relation to the global graduate, as we have termed it, are as follows:

1 To have a university education is to participate in a global community.
2 To have a university education is an opportunity to inculcate tolerance and learn dialogical skills.
3 To have a university education is not just about crossing and negotiating boundaries but seeking the transcendent thinking and answers that can arise from cross-cultural collaboration.
4 To have a university education is to be exposed to the values of what it means to be (more) human.
5 The end of all this, to have a university education means that we can pursue global collaboration and global responsibility.

CASE STUDY: JAMIE SMART'S DEEP DRIVERS

Jamie Smart in his book *Clarity* (2013) identifies eight what he calls deep drivers – these are qualities and traits people already possess and can remain purely innate resources if not drawn upon. The eight drivers are:

1 clarity
2 direction
3 resilience
4 creativity
5 connection

6 authenticity
7 intuition
8 presence.

There are two aspects to this thinking by Smart. The first is to more fully comprehend what exactly is meant by these terms. This permits one to identify this innate resource within oneself. The second is to more fully appreciate the profound application of each of these resources to drive all manner of professional and personal activity.

The essence of Smart's thinking is outlined below:

Clarity – achieving a clear mind and being fully present in the moment, discerning the way forward without getting distracted by the 'noise' and complexity in the system. Clarity drives many things including effective leadership, insight, detecting opportunities and decision making.

Direction – a clear sense of direction and a motivation to pursue something without a sense of undue pressure. Direction drives strategic planning, authentic leadership, resolving uncertainty and achieving shared vision and purpose.

Resilience – an ability to bounce back after (inevitable) setbacks and implicitly involving security and trust in oneself and the world. Resilience drives dealing with change, thriving through uncertainty, responsiveness and confidence.

Creativity – not the exclusive domain of 'creatives' but the driver behind innovation and problem solving. Creativity drives strategic thinking, product and service design, brand narrative and customer delight.

Connection – strong connections and relationships that are genuine and warm extending to colleagues, suppliers and customers. Connection drives collaboration, employee engagement, persuasion and influence and effective teams.

Authenticity – being who you are, speaking and doing what is genuine, differentiating those that 'walk the walk' from those who only 'talk the talk'. Authenticity drives trust and credibility, transparency, authentic leadership and integrity.

Intuition – often associated with 'gut feel', an internal guide it is risky to ignore. Intuition drives effective decision making, opportunity identification, strategic thinking and innovation.

Presence – associated with enhanced awareness and characterized by connectedness to one's mind, body and the world around. Presence drives charismatic leadership, influencing others, clear view of reality and trend detection.

THE GRADUATE IDENTITY APPROACH

A piece of research funded by the UK Higher Education Academy entitled 'Employer concepts of graduate employability' (Higher Education Academy, 2009) sought to define what skills, competencies, attributes and personal qualities were most valued by employers from a full range of organizations in Norfolk, England.

Overall what emerged from the research was a search for graduates with four identity elements as follows:

1 values
2 intellect
3 performance
4 engagement.

What exactly these labels encompass is outlined below but some of the other details from the research are also both illuminating and significant.

Turning first to the top ten employer expectations on appointment of a graduate, these were the things that employers expected all graduates to display from day one:

1 Demonstrates honesty and integrity.
2 Is someone I can trust.
3 Is able to listen to others.
4 Is able to integrate quickly into a team or department.
5 Is able to present ideas clearly, both verbally and in writing.
6 Can assimilate information quickly.
7 Works safely.
8 Demonstrates good time management.
9 Can plan and manage their time.
10 Can demonstrate attention to detail and thoroughness.

A point to emphasize here is that these ten expectations came ahead of 37 others.

The expectation is for graduates to be 'able to fit quickly into a team' and to be good communicators, both verbally and in writing.

Another part of the research asked employers to rank groupings of employability skills relative to one another. This 'forced' ranking produced the following results in rank order of importance:

1 interpersonal skills
2 written communication skills
3 IT skills
4 experience of work environment
5 commercial/business awareness
6 numeracy skills
7 presentation skills.

This, of course, does not suggest that presentation skills are not important. Rather, that the most important skill area for these employers was interpersonal skills. Note also how written communication skills came out ahead of IT skills.

Turning now to the four elements of 'graduate identity':

Values – the research found that values which universities are concerned to foster were also valued by the employers. This included:

- diversity awareness
- citizenship
- environmental awareness
- an interest in culture.

An important point here is that such values also have significance from an employer's business perspective, encompassing customers and clients and relating to business opportunities in the areas of environmental and global awareness.

Intellect – employers look to the subject discipline to deliver cognitive abilities and to furnish graduates with a body of knowledge that both the graduate and the employer can draw upon. It is important for the graduate to be able to articulate the intellectual value of their degree.

Performance – although graduate performance in employment is essential, when they select graduates employers only assess potential and here the research discovered that employers conceive this potential through the idea of graduate identity.

Engagement – according to the research, employers expect graduates to have the ability to interact with others in a whole variety of situations. Employers were suspicious of graduates who had chosen a narrow student experience and valued those graduates who made the most of opportunities available to them, who had gained a broad-based experience through volunteering, university societies and events.

APPLIED PERSONAL DEVELOPMENT

What skills do you have or are you going to develop that mark you out as a graduate – and not just a graduate, but a graduate of distinction? What can you do to differentiate yourself from the next intelligent and talented student chasing the same opportunity? What is going to be distinctive about you?

Looking at the expectations of employers, is there anything here that makes you feel a little 'exposed' – a skill area where you are not up to standard. There is likely to be at least one or two things to work on. The time to work on these things is not later or towards graduation, but now. It is something you could mention to your personal tutor and it is something you could incorporate into your personal development plan. Beware of any suggestion or temptation to think of oneself as the 'complete item'. Everybody has what you might call a profile.

This is not just about plugging gaps but developing into excellences where your greatest potential lies. You may be exceptionally analytical. You might have the potential to be an outstanding communicator (like many of the people we see in the media). Otherwise, you might have the makings of being an inspirational leader. From the list of graduate skills you can see there are many areas where you might excel.

It is good to be working out from your first year onward which industry sectors or business cultures you find yourself most drawn to. Get hold of some highlighter pens (a green one, a yellow one and a pink one) and run down the list of job areas at the beginning of the chapter. 'Traffic light' your interest areas as follows. If you are naturally drawn to an area highlight it green. If you are naturally disinterested by another area colour it pink. If you are unsure either way highlight it yellow. Analyse the pattern this produces. Do any of those areas you have highlighted the same colour have anything in common and what does this suggest about you? Or ask yourself why you are particularly attracted to a certain area?

What can you do to start to explore your areas of interest? Could you secure a work placement in that area? Or perhaps you could do some volunteering? If you want to explore a particular responsibility, for example a leadership or communication role, consider exercising this in the context of a university club or society. Set yourself the objective of doing one thing in addition to your studies and your social life and think of this one thing as your opportunity to enhance your CV, explore an area of interest and experiment with developing skills and confidence.

Some of the skills covered in this chapter would be a big ask for any adult. Some of them which are metaphorically in line with the current of where the contemporary river is flowing – 'skills' such as collaboration, dialogue, empathy and integrity – have enormous potential. If at first you don't fully comprehend the significance of something or don't completely understand it, don't just dismiss it. Try your hand at becoming an early adopter of a certain skill or technology. Give it a go. You may surprise yourself.

For example, why not be the first person from your year group or school to study abroad at a specific university? By all means follow certain trends, but why not lead or innovate in other things. Sometimes risk takers are more highly rewarded than the risk averse. Don't let fear rob you of great opportunities.

Finally, work out what you want. Don't be tempted just to please others with your career selections and the interests you pursue. For some of you this will come naturally. For others, you may have to work really hard to figure this out or work this through. Seek support and guidance from the career service and your personal tutor. Explore in conversation with friends and fellow students the possibilities.

REFERENCES

Christian, S. (2012) *Top Jobs: Discover the Best Graduate Jobs and How to Get One*. Richmond: Trotman Publishing.

Divan, A. (2009) *Communication Skills for the Biosciences: A Graduate Guide*. Oxford: Oxford University Press.

Elias, P. and Purcell, K. (2013) 'Futuretrack working paper 5: classifying graduate occupations for the knowledge society'. Warwick: Institute for Employment Research, University of Warwick. Available at: www2.warwick.ac.uk/fac/soc/ier/futuretrack/findings/elias_purcell_soche_final.pdf (accessed 15 July 2013).

Futuretrack (2012) 'The changing relationship between higher education and the graduate labour market: evidence from Futuretrack', conference paper, Manchester, 7 November.

Goldberg, M. L. (2007) 'Discourse'. Available at: https://faculty.washington.edu/mlg/courses/definitions/discourse.html (accessed 16 July 2013).

Higher Education Academy (2009) 'Employer concepts of graduate employability'. York: HEA.

Joyce, S. P. (2013) 'Be visible on LinkedIn', *Career Planning and Adult Development Journal*, Fall: 88–90.

Katulushi, C. (2005) 'Diversity, values and international students in higher education', in S. Robinson and C. Katulushi (eds), *Values in Higher Education*. St Bride's Major: Aureus Publishing.

King, R. (2003) 'Globalization and the national context: finding a balance', *The Bulletin*, May.

La Valle, I., O'Regan, S. and Jackson, C. (2000) *The Art of Getting Started: Graduate Skills in a Fragmented Labour Market*. Brighton: The Institute for Employment Studies.

Mann, S. J. (2008) *Study, Power and the University*. Maidenhead: McGraw-Hill Education.

Peregrin, T. (2012) 'LinkedIn profile makeover: optimising your professional online profile', *Journal of the Academy of Nutrition and Dietetics*, 112 (1): 23–25.

Prince, E. (2013) *The Advantage: The 7 Soft Skills You Need to Stay One Step Ahead*. Harlow: Pearson Education.

Redmond, P. (2010) *The Graduate Jobs Formula: How to Land Your Dream Career*. Richmond: Trotman Publishing.

Smart, J. (2013) *Clarity: Clear Mind, Better Performance, Bigger Results*. Chichester: Capstone Publishing.

Whitehead, J. (2002) 'Transforming embodied values of humanity into educational standards of judgement for use in creating the new disciplines approach to educational theory', draft paper, 11 June, University of Bath Department of Education.

Getting a Handle on Costs and Financial Aspects

Valentin, E.

Dollars do better if they are accompanied by sense.

—Earl Riney

Implementing a market strategy and a business model costs money. Equipment and facilities must be bought or leased. Employees and utilities must be paid. Various raw materials, components, or goods for resale, also, may have to be purchased. All such expenditures will have to be identified and estimated sooner or later. The best time to start is now.

Getting an early start on estimating expenditures is advisable for two reasons. First, collecting cost data and refining cost estimates may take some time. Fortunately, other planning tasks can be completed in parallel. Second, expenditure estimates are needed to conduct preliminary financial viability checks. If results are disappointing, cost estimates and key assumptions should be reexamined along with the intended market strategy and business model. Of course, adjustments must never be driven by wishful thinking.

This chapter offers suggestions for itemizing and estimating capital, leasing, and operating expenditures attendant to launching a new venture or expanding an existing business. Additionally, it explains how estimated expenditures can be used to conduct preliminary assessments of a venture's financial prospects.

GETTING STARTED

Expenditure estimates are never perfectly accurate, but they must be reasonably close to serve their purpose. Begin with rough approximations, if necessary; then, refine your estimates as the planning process moves forward. Get started by identifying anticipated expenditures on capital items and operations.

Estimating Expenditures on Capital Items

Make a list of land, facility, and equipment needs. If your business is an existing enterprise, only needs that arise from planned changes should be listed. For example, if you plan to expand a business in a way that requires more warehouse space, then list only the additional space needed, not warehouse space in total.

Next, sort out which items probably will be purchased and which leased or rented. For instance, leasing office space usually is a better option for startups than buying land and building an office. Leasing is less risky and usually has a less severe impact on precious debt capacity. Leasing versus buying decisions are complex in large part due to tax and accounting regulations. Fortunately, you need not make definite commitments to leasing or buying at this early stage. Further, the financial viability checks introduced later in this chapter turn out about the same, regardless of whether capital items are bought or leased.

Figure 4-1 shows what an initial *capital budget*, or summary of initial capital expenditures, might look like for a new nine-station hairstyling salon. Note that the last line item implies the facilities will be leased. Accordingly, the monthly or annual cost of the lease should be noted in a table of operating expenditures.

In Figure 4-1, all sources of cost information are cited, which lends credibility to the summary and the plan. When citing information obtained via e-mail, telephone, or personal interviews, include the provider's name, organizational affiliation, position, and other credentials that bear on credibility. If listed items require clarification, provide explanatory footnotes or footnotes that direct readers to explanatory appendices. All footnotes that apply to listings within an exhibit should be part of that exhibit, as Figure 4-1 illustrates.

Building from scratch could be considered. If it were, land and construction costs would be added as separate line items to Figure 4-1, and the lease improvements line would be removed. Long lists of capital items should be organized meaningfully under such headings as "Land & Facilities," "Production Equipment," and "Office Furnishings & Equipment."

Where you may find credible cost information depends on the item in question. If you need PCs, you can find relevant cost information easily on several websites, including Dell's. Finding cost information on branded equipment should not be too difficult. But if you cannot find cost information on the web, ask a vendor for a quote. If you need a building, try scouring the real estate pages of your newspaper, or search online for suitable facilities.

Estimating Operating Expenditures

Operating expenditures commonly include payroll; expenditures on materials, components, or goods for resale; and other items, such as utilities and office sundries. Summarize these expenditures in a table that lists expense categories and amounts. Aim to make your summary table so clear that readers can grasp it at a glance. Use explanatory footnotes to clarify anything that requires clarification, and cite sources of cost information. A complete listing of operating expenditures is an *operating budget*.

Figure 4-1	Sample Capital Budget

Item	Quantity	Cost/Unit	Total
Wilmington Genesis stations[a]	9	Mix of Items	$15,000
Televisions and mounting hardware[b]	6	$700	$4,200
Reception station[c]	1	$2,500	$2,500
Reception sofas[c]	2	$1,050	$2,100
Employee lockers & coat rack[d]	1	$500	$500
Computer Equipment[e]	1	$800	$800
Outdoor sign[f]	1	$1,800	$1,800
Software (MS Office & Quickbooks)[b]	1	$650	$700
Plumbing, electrical, and other lease improvements[g]			$15,000
Total			$42,600

Notes:

[a] Nine stions: Includes styling stations, chairs, backwash systems, dryer chairs, and hooded dryers. Source: http://www.minervabeauty.com/salon-packages/

[b] http://www.costco.com

[c] http://www.bestpriceseating.com/gurewaro.html?gclid=CIyC_v-t7bICFWThQgodZBAAgg

[d] Includes 16 lockers. Source: http://www.globalindustrial.com

[e] http://www.dell.com

[f] http://www.signtronix.com/product-crystalite.asp

[g] Western Plumbing & Electrical Improvement; G. Smith, Estimator (800-555-5555)

Human Resources

What kinds of employees will you need? How many of each type will you need? What will your payroll cost be?

Begin to answer these questions by constructing a simple spreadsheet like the one in Figure 4-2. List positions, and note the number of people needed per position. Be sure to list all workers, even those who do not draw salaries or wages. Next:

- Estimate hours and wages for each hourly position on a weekly or a monthly basis.

- Estimate compensation for each salaried position on a weekly or a monthly basis.

- Factor in compensation for workers who do not draw salaries but, nevertheless, benefit or expect to benefit financially.

Figure 4-2	Payroll Spreadsheet

Employees	Number	Weekly[a]					Annual	
		Avg. Hrs./ Employee	Total Hours[a]	Avg. Loaded Hourly Rate[b]	Loaded Payroll	Total Hours[c]		Loaded Payroll
Hourly Employees								
Stylists (8 booths)	14	24	336	$26	$8,736	17200		$447,200
Nail Technicians (1 station)	2	22	44	$26	$1,144	2250		$58,500
Receptionists	2	30	60	$15	$900	3050		$45,750
Total Hourly	18		440		$10,780	22500		$551,450
Salaried Employees								
Manager	1	40	40		$1,000			$52,000
Accountant	1	10	10		$400			$20,800
Total Salaried	2				$1,400			$72,800
Total Loaded Payroll					$12,180			$624,250

Notes:

[a]Mondays through Saturdays; open 60 hours per week. Full capacity per booth is 60 hours per week; actual usage is estimated at 70%.

[b]Includes Employer's FICA @ 7.65%.

[c]The salon will be open 307 days per year.

Owners are the most likely people to say they will work for "free." In fact, however, they expect to be paid in some way. For present purposes, add reasonable amounts of compensation for such people to the payroll. Reasonable compensation is equivalent to the salaries or wages competent replacements would require. If you cannot find pertinent information about salaries and wages in newspapers, try searching the Internet. CareerBuilder.com and state government websites may be helpful.

Your complete payroll spreadsheet should list each position, note the number of people per position, and show loaded wages and salaries. Loaded payroll includes all employee-related expenses, such as direct compensation, and company contributions to

FICA and healthcare premiums. Again, cite information sources, and aim to make your spreadsheet so clear that readers have no difficulty following calculations or finding total loaded payroll.

Materials and Goods for Resale

If your business is a manufacturing company, it surely will have to buy materials from outside suppliers. If it entails buying and reselling, it will have to buy the goods it resells. Prices are fairly stable for some materials and goods for resale, but for others, such as petrochemicals, they may fluctuate wildly. Flying J, for example, refined oil and sold gasoline at its 220 travel centers throughout the USA and Canada. The value of the oil it bought in July of 2008 for close to $150 per barrel declined to less than $45 per barrel six months later. Flying J had too much high-cost oil in its system, could not absorb the loss, and ended up bankrupt.

If the prices of the materials you need are volatile, then estimate high, low, and expected values for at least three years. Sensitivity analysis, explained later in this chapter, can be revealing and useful when prices are highly unstable.

If you understand hedging and intend to use it to lock in prices, then explain your hedging scheme very concisely and note its cost. But do not write a treatise on hedging. Also, make sure you are merely locking in prices, not speculating in commodities.

Box 4-1

The Tragic Tale of Flying J

In early 2008, Flying J looked like a thriving company, at least from all outward appearances. When it filed for bankruptcy in December of that year, it operated about 220 travel centers in the USA and Canada, and was the largest retailer of diesel fuel in North America.

The company blamed its demise largely on a collapse in oil prices, which dropped sharply from $147 a barrel in July, 2008, to $42 in less than six months. Flying J had too much high-priced oil in its system—oil that was losing value day by day. Investments in an oil refinery and a pipeline made a few months earlier had already put the company in a difficult cash-flow position. The decline in oil prices was the proverbial straw that broke the camel's back.

Hedging might have saved Flying J. It entails placing two offsetting bets on a particular commodity, such as oil: One bet generates a profit if prices go up during a specified period, such as 90 days, and a loss if prices go down. The opposite is true of the second bet. In effect, then, placing such bets locks in current prices for a specified time because gains and losses cancel out, except for the cost of placing the bets.

Source: P. Beebe, *The Salt Lake Tribune*, August 7, 2009.

Other Operating Expenditures

Itemize other major operating costs, such as utilities. Lump miscellaneous items, such as pencils and paperclips, together under "Sundries."

Outsourcing and Cost

If you outsource production and your company is small, your source's bargaining position is apt to be much stronger than yours. Therefore, expect one or more of the following when outsourcing and fixed production costs are high:

- Expect to pay very high prices for small orders.

- Expect having to order much larger quantities than you would like.

- Expect to pay all or some fixed costs up front.

Finding reliable cost information may be difficult. Suppose, for example, that you have envisioned a small, cheap, portable alarm designed to help locate people who are lost outdoors. Prospective customers would include hikers, skiers, hunters, and the Boy Scouts. Suppose further that you have some idea of how the product would work, but do not have a schematic diagram of its circuitry. Before you could outsource production, you would need a working model. You might build it yourself, hire someone to build it for you, or take on a partner who has the required technical skills.

Apple Computer's initial need for capital was to defray the cost of outsourcing production of the circuit board that founding partner Steve Wozniak had designed for the Apple I. More recently, Eric Migicovsky had an idea for a "smart" watch that became the Pebble E-Paper Watch. With the help of Y Combinator, a business incubator, he was able to construct a working model. After that, he needed capital for outsourcing production of the watch. Migicovskye hoped to raise around $100,000 online using crowdfunding. He ended up raising more than $10 million.[1]

CONDUCTING FINANCIAL REALITY CHECKS

A business' viability depends on cash inflows from sales and cash outflows attendant to starting and operating the business. Cash outflow results from everything that costs money.

For new ventures, outflows usually can be estimated much more accurately than sales and revenue. Payback analysis and breakeven analysis, discussed next, can provide early indications of viability and potential profitability without relying on accurate sales forecasts.

Payback Analysis

The focal question in payback analysis is, How long will it take for cumulative cash inflows to equal cumulative cash outflows? Remember that new businesses usually incur startup cost before they open. For instance, they may have to pay rent, buy equipment, and pay employees before making the first sale. For present purposes, assume sales are in cash and all expenditures are in cash.

Payback analysis entails estimating cash outflows, including capital expenditures and operating costs, and cash inflows, mainly operating revenue. The number of months or years that it takes for cumulative inflows to equal cumulative outflows is the payback period.

The following example illustrates how payback analysis may be used to get an indication of a venture's viability when sales forecasts are too unreliable. Assume that money spent on facilities, equipment, and employee wages before the business opens is $100,000. Also assume that variable cost is 75 percent of revenue, and annual fixed costs come to $80,000. How much revenue would the business have to generate to keep the payback period below five years?

In the given example, five-year cash outflow due to startup expenditures and annual fixed costs would be

$$\$100,000 + 5(\$80,000) = \$500,000.$$

Therefore, over its first five years, the business would have to generate at least

$$\$500,000 / (1 - 0.75) = \$2,000,0000$$

Anything less than that would result in a longer payback period.

Now, the question is this: Is the five-year payback objective realistic? Attaining it would require generating revenues of $2,000,000 in five years. Equivalently, it would require average annual revenues of $400,000; average monthly revenues of $33,333; and, assuming a six-day work week, average daily revenues of $1,282. Such breakdowns often shed light on whether expectations are realistic. Sometimes, what seems plausible on an annual basis appears decidedly implausible when reduced to daily or hourly averages.

If $2,000,000 over five years is not realistic, then payback will take longer. But even a 10-year payback would require average annual revenues of $360,000. The longer the payback, the less attractive the investment. A 10-year payback is unlikely to offer investors ample returns.

What would happen to the payback period if fixed costs were reduced to $75,000 per year? And what if prices were raised or variable costs were reduced so that variable costs would be only 70 percent of revenue? Answering such questions is the essence of sensitivity analysis, which can illuminate just how sensitive the business' profitability is to particular assumptions and variables.

If fixed costs were reduced to $75,000 per year and variable costs were only 70 percent of revenue, then only $317,000 in average annual revenue would be required to attain the five-year payback goal. A big risk with such analyses is that they promote wishful thinking, which makes remote optimistic possibilities appear realistic.

Keep in mind that the point of this exercise is not to reach definitive conclusions. It is merely to get a feel for a venture's chances.

Breakeven Analysis

Breakeven (BE) analysis also facilitates assessing a venture's prospects. Look three or four years ahead; then, estimate annual operating costs for the third or fourth year of operation, add a charge for the use of capital items, and calculate the amount of revenue that would have to be generated to cover operating costs plus the charge for capital. To be more exact, do the following:

1. *Define the unit of analysis*. If your venture is a new business, then the pertinent unit of analysis is the entire new business. If your venture is some sort of expansion from an existing base, then the pertinent unit of analysis is the increment you envision, not the entire business.

   You may approach incremental assessment by focusing directly on the increment or by comparing your business as it is with how it would be if your plan were followed. For instance, expansion plans that require adding employees should address payroll as it would be if the plan were implemented and payroll as it would be if the plan were not implemented. Expansion plans that call for replacing facilities or equipment currently in use should focus on net cost: the total price of assets to be acquired less estimated proceeds, if any, from the sale of assets they will replace.

2. *Choose a point in time*. The first year of operation seldom is typical or indicative of a venture's prospects, especially if the venture is a new business. Therefore, for present purposes, consider your venture three or four years after launching it.

3. *Estimate gross margin*. Estimate gross margin by pondering how many dollars in sales every dollar spent on cost of sales or variable cost will generate. *Cost of sales* applies to retailers and wholesalers. It is the price they pay their suppliers for the merchandise they resell. *Variable* cost stems from expenditures on materials used in production and from such variable items as direct labor.

4. *Estimate out-of-pocket operating costs.* They are likely to include rent, leases, utilities, and administrative overhead. They exclude capital expenditures, depreciation, and amortization. For present purposes, they also exclude interest charges and taxes. Assume for now that you have enough equity capital to implement your plan and, therefore, will not need loans or incur interest charges. If the business is not feasible without paying interest and taxes, then it will not be feasible when interest and taxes are included.

5. *Estimate a fair annual charge for facilities and equipment*. If you lease or rent your facilities and equipment, then a fair annual charge is the annual cost of leasing or renting. But, if you buy land and build on it, buy existing facilities, or buy equipment, you will have to estimate a fair annual charge for such items to assess whether your venture has real economic value. When you actually pay for such items is irrelevant for present purposes.

   The simplest way to estimate a fair annual charge entails finding out how much leasing or renting the assets in question would cost. The annual cost of leasing office space, for example, usually can be estimated with sufficient accuracy by looking at ads for office space in newspapers or online.

Alternately, you could use annual straight-line depreciation as a rough estimate of the fair annual charge. Refer to IRS Publication 946, Table B-1, to find the expected life of each depreciable asset.[2] Find each asset's straight-line depreciation and fair annual charge by dividing its cost by its life expectancy. For instance, if a piece of equipment that cost $50,000 were expected to last 10 years, then a fair annual charge for that asset would be $5,000. Land is not depreciable. But for present purposes, treat land as if it had a 25-year life expectancy.

A third approach to estimating a fair annual charge entails assuming that the assets of interest are financed by a bank loan and calculating corresponding annual payments. It is a little more difficult than using straight-line depreciation, but tends to be more accurate and more conservative. For assets other than land and buildings, begin by estimating each depreciable asset's life expectancy; consult IRS Publication 946, Table B-1, if necessary. Next, per asset, calculate the annual payment that would have to be made if the asset were financed over its expected life. For instance, if a piece of equipment is expected to last 10 years, assume it will be financed using a 10-year loan. Search for *business loan rates* on the web for an estimate of the applicable interest rate, which tends to be 3 to 6 percent higher than the prime rate.[3] So, if a piece of equipment cost $50,000 and were expected to last 10 years, and the interest rate were 10 percent, then a fair annual charge would be approximately $7,900. This amount is equivalent to the annual payment on a 10-year mortgage of $50,000 at an interest rate of 10 percent. Accordingly, the payoff calculator at Bankrate.com is quite handy for calculating fair annual charges.[4] To use it, set both the "number of years remaining" and "mortgage length" to the life of the asset, enter the asset's cost, set "additional monthly payment" to $0, enter the interest rate, and click "Calculate." The mortgage calculator will give you the monthly amount, which you should multiply by 12 to get the annual fair charge. Assume that land and buildings will be financed by 30-year loans.

6. **Estimate the sales volume needed to break even**. Apply one of the following formulas:

$$BE_Q = C_F/(P-C_V)$$

or

$$BE_S = C_F/(M_G)$$

where BE_Q=break-even quantity, BE_S=break-even revenue, C_F=fixed cost, P=price, C_V=variable cost, and M_G=gross margin. Again, exclude capital expenditures and depreciation from cost calculations, but do include the charges for facilities and equipment that you estimated in Step 5. You may change your analysis to a *profit target analysis* by replacing C_F with $C_F+\pi$, where π is your profit target.

7. **Ponder whether your venture is likely to surpass the BE point or profit target**. Ask yourself, How likely is the venture to generate enough revenue to cover costs? Answer this question not only within the context of an annual time frame, but also

within the context of a daily or an hourly span. In other words, calculate how much revenue, on average, the business must generate per day or per hour to break even; then, ponder whether corresponding average daily or hourly volumes are attainable.

Such an analysis was conducted for a small specialty bookstore. At first glance, annual volume required to break even appeared well within reach. But further analysis showed that, on average, the store would have to sell five books per hour while open for business. Five books per hour seemed very unlikely in view of the store's location and narrow appeal. The store was opened, nevertheless, and lost money every day of its brief existence.

8. *Conduct sensitivity analyses*. Vary key assumptions, and note how changes in assumptions affect the BE point. For example, assess the impact of somewhat higher and lower margins and of using three times the prime rate when estimating fair annual charges for fixed assets. Sensitivity analyses facilitate assessing risk.

REMEMBER THIS

Implementing a market strategy and a business model requires equipment, facilities, employees, utilities, and more. Various raw materials, components, or goods for resale, also, may have to be purchased. The best time to identify such items and find out how much they cost is early on in the planning process. *Capital budgets* itemize anticipated expenditures on capital items, such as facilities and equipment, while *operating budgets* itemize anticipated operating expenditures on the likes of human resources, rent, and utilities.

Conclusions drawn from payback analyses should be considered along with those drawn from BE analysis. At this juncture, such analyses provide only rough preliminary assessments. However, if both are discouraging, the chances that the final result will look much better are slim, unless substantial mistakes were made in estimating costs or in making further calculations. If results are disappointing, cost estimates and key assumptions should be reexamined along with the intended market strategy and business model. Of course, adjustments must never be colored by wishful thinking.

If no realistic adjustments render the venture profitable, then it probably should be scrapped. However, a final decision need not be made until more sophisticated and detailed financial projections have been derived. These projections are addressed in Chapter 11.

Questions for Review and Discussion

1. Why is getting an early start on estimating costs advisable?

2. What is the difference between capital expenditures and operating expenditures?

3. Outline the process of estimating payroll costs.

4. What is meant by "loaded payroll"?

5. What is the purpose of financial reality checks?

6. How is the payback period defined?

7. How is the payback period calculated?

8. What is the point of estimating fair annual charges for purchased facilities and equipment?

Notes

1. Learn more about the Pebble E-Paper Watch and crowdfunding, respectively, at getpebble.com and kickstarter.com.
2. http://www.irs.gov/publications/p946/13081f31.html
3. http://www.bankrate.com/rates/interest-rates/wall-street-prime-rate.aspx
4. http://www.bankrate.com/calculators/mortgages/mortgage-loan-payoff-calculator.aspx

PART 5

BUSINESS PLANNING AND
MARKET STRATEGY

Writing and Pitching a Business Plan

Valentin, E.

I keep six honest serving-men

[They taught me all I knew];

Their names are What and Why and When

And How and Where and Who.

—Rudyard Kipling

Hard writing makes easy reading.

Easy writing makes hard reading.

—William Zinsser

Writing and pitching a business plan amount to telling and selling, but without overselling. By the time you are ready to write your business plan and a corresponding script for pitching it, you should have performed the tasks outlined in earlier chapters and accumulated plenty of notes and numbers along the way. In particular, you should already have

- a vivid description of the business, including the business model (Chapter 3);

- a thorough situation analysis, including competitor profiles and assessments of the competitive environment and the market outlook (Chapters 8 and 9);

- a market strategy and sketches of corresponding action plans for implementing it (Chapters 2 and 5);

- well-documented estimates of capital expenditures and operating costs (Chapter 4); and

- financial projections that are consistent with all other items in this list (Chapter 11).

Writing a business plan proceeds with assembling the various notes and numerical exhibits amassed so far in a logical order and filling in gaps. The resulting document's narrative must be consistent with all financial estimates. Further, it must advance a cogent argument for implementing the plan. Polishing wording and flow is the final step in writing a business plan.

Both content and packaging are critical. No matter how enthusiastic, upbeat, or optimistic they may be, plans that lack substance are mere speculation. Poorly packaged plans are hard to follow and, thus, are apt to be misunderstood.

This chapter addresses packaging—in essence, organizing content and writing effectively. The chapter outlines a general structure for writing business plans, which should be tailored to resonate with specific audiences and to tell readers what they need to know when they need to know it. Suggestions for writing the plan, reviewing it, and pitching it to prospective investors and lenders follow. The appendix after the last chapter illustrates what a proper business plan looks like.

WRITING A BUSINESS PLAN

Every proper business report begins with an executive summary that encapsulates the report's main points. In complex reports, such as business plans, appendices often follow the body. Further, proper business reports include a table of contents when lengthy and a letter of transmittal when sent to a client.

Writing Executive Summaries

To be effective, a business plan's executive summary must capture the gist of the entire plan. But if it exceeds 10 percent of the body, it probably is too long. Draft the executive summary before writing the rest of the document. Doing so will help you stay on track when writing the body of the plan.

Immediately provide a vivid snapshot of the business—one that enables your audience to clearly envision the enterprise, the means by which it creates value for customers and shareholders, the goods and services it offers, and the benefits customers derive from offerings. Ensure it conveys how the business works and that it is not just a sales pitch. However, do include a value proposition. Recall that value propositions are not hype; they are concise objective answers from a customer perspective to the question, Why buy from us?

Next, you may summarize findings from your situation analysis, including market and competitor analyses; list objectives; outline actions to be taken; state capital requirements; and note expected financial results. Be as specific as possible without getting into inessential details.

Effective executive summaries include a few key numbers in concise informal tables like the one in Figure 12-1, which shows sales and operating income projections for the next five years. It could be introduced using a sentence much like the one directly above the table in Figure 12-1. Details not needed to make key points should be omitted from informal exhibits. Accordingly, costs are not shown in Figure 12-1.

Figure 12-1   Excerpts from an Executive Summary

... The company expects to realize the following sales and operating income during the first five years of operation:

	Year 1	Year 2	Year 3	Year 4	Year 5	Year 6
Sales	$300,000	$400,000	$550,000	$700,000	$900,000	$900,000
Operating Income	−$10,000	$5,000	$20,000	$35,000	$60,000	$60,000

As shown, sales and profits are expected to increase each year. However, ...

Reporting key numbers in one or two simple, informal tables is much more effective than weaving them into the narrative of the executive summary. When interspersed with verbiage, numbers tend to get lost along with their meaning. When reported in simple well-organized tables, numbers stand out and their significance is more apparent.

Although pie charts and histograms have visual appeal, they usually are either too simple or too complex for inclusion in an executive summary. For instance, three-dimensional pie charts that show only two or three slices seldom convey information that readers would not derive from reading the underlying numbers alone. Charts that show many more slices are too complex for an executive summary.

Do not confuse the executive summary with an introduction. A proper introduction orients readers by noting the purpose of the document and the topic sequence. A proper executive summary, in contrast, encapsulates key points from the entire plan.

Crafting the Body

The body of a proper business report elaborates greatly on matters highlighted in the executive summary. When writing it, keep the following in mind:

- Readers should not have to read the executive summary to understand anything in the body, nor should they have to read the body to understand the executive summary.

- The sequence in which topics are addressed should be about the same in the body as in the executive summary. The order must be logical and easy to follow.

- The body of a business plan should be sufficiently detailed to paint a vivid picture of the venture and its prospects and to render critical assertions credible. But it should not be so detailed that readers are overwhelmed or distracted from the main points of the story that the document is intended to tell. Details that would distract readers or would interest only the most inquisitive readers are best deferred to appendices.

Begin the body with a section labeled "Introduction" that conveys the purpose of the document and the basic nature of the venture under consideration. Inclusion of a concisely worded value proposition tends to help readers grasp the nature of the business.

End the introduction by telling readers what lies ahead. For example, you might say, "The pages that follow address the business model, the market outlook, competitive and economic conditions, market strategy, financial needs, financial performance, and implementation."

Although your topic sequence should resemble this one, you may choose somewhat different topic headings and should move topics around a bit if doing so improves readability. For instance, you may elect to address the market outlook, the competitive environment, competitor profiles, and environmental forces beyond the competitive environment under separate rubrics. Or, you could discuss all such topics under "Situation Analysis."

Always strive to make your writing as readable as possible and sufficiently informative to fully answer readers' most urgent questions. As much as possible, anticipate readers' questions and address them before they arise. Unanswered questions lodged in readers' minds are distractions that impede understanding.

Nature of the Venture

As in the executive summary, depict the business venture very near the beginning. Until readers can envision the venture, they will be unable to follow the rationale of the plan. If the business is simple or the intended audience knows it well, then the business may have been described adequately in the introduction. But if it is complex and readers are unlikely to be familiar with it, then readers must be given enough detail to enable them to picture the venture clearly in their minds.

Depict the business venture from both the supply side and the demand side. When describing the supply side, address the mechanics of the business. For instance, if the business is a value chain, note what goes in, what comes out, and what happens in between. A flow diagram, such as the one shown for R. C. Willey in Chapter 3, may help explain how the business works. It also may highlight competitive advantages and disadvantages. For instance, the R. C. Willey diagram highlights cost advantages rooted in superior scale economies that, in home furnishings retailing, accrue to the local or regional market-share leader.

Be clear about the scope of your business, particularly about its participation in creating value for end users. For instance, if the business sells a product, make clear whether it designs, manufactures, wholesales, or retails the product.

When describing the venture from the demand side, profile targeted customers, and delineate the needs your offering fulfills, the problems it helps customers solve, or the benefits it conveys. In a value proposition, encapsulate why targeted customers should choose your offering rather than alternatives.

Box 12-1

What About Mission And Vision Statements?

Mission statements are commonly included in business plans. Their purpose is to express why the business exists, but their value in painting a vivid picture of the business is doubtful. Look at the following mission statements, and try to figure out whose they are:

- To make people happy

- To push the leading edge of aviation, taking huge challenges doing what others cannot do

- To solve unsolved problems innovatively

Respectively, these once were Disney's, Boeing's, and 3M's mission statements.* While they make sense and have a certain inspirational flair, they are too abstract to convey the nature of any business.

Vision statements, which are intended to express what an organization aspires to be, are not very helpful either in painting a vivid picture of a business. Take Disney's "Be the leader in the delivery of entertainment experiences," for instance.

Much more helpful than mission or vision statements in conveying what a business is about and how it works are the means introduced in Chapter 3, "Devising a Business Model." Particularly useful are value propositions in conjunction with business definitions that identify targeted customers, the benefits that attract them, and the mechanisms, or technologies, by which the business delivers benefits to targeted customers.

If you feel compelled to include mission and vision statements, go right ahead. They're harmless and do afford some insights into organizations. Just don't expect readers to get a clear idea of how the business works from such statements alone.

*http://www.fastcompany.com/ 1821021/defining-your-companys-vision.

Situation Analysis

Recall that situation analysis requires thorough internal and external appraisal. Moreover, external appraisal entails analyzing the market and the competitive environment. Assessments of the market and the competitive outlook often are reported in separate sections that precede the "Situation Analysis" section. Separate sections are perfectly alright and may help readers and writers stay on track. Review Chapters 8 and 9 for good advice about performing situation analyses and reporting results.

Market Strategy

Articulate your market strategy by telling readers where and how you intend to compete and why your strategy will work. To convince readers of your venture's prospects, reiterate your value proposition and address competitive position by identifying critical current advantages and disadvantages. If you expect your venture's competitive position in cost or differentiation to change over the next several years, note the changes and explain their causes.

Marketing

Be sure to address all relevant aspects of marketing noted in Chapter 5 under "More about Marketing Plans." Per targeted segment, note key marketing activities and explain how they will serve to acquire and retain customers. If applicable, also address how they will increase wallet share and profit margins.

Functional Matters not Addressed Elsewhere

Potentially, other pertinent functional matters include operations and human resources. With regard to human resources, address staffing needs and costs. If details are voluminous and likely to interest only the most curious readers, defer them to appendices, but always provide summaries in the body.

Major Capital Expenditures and Leases

If you have not done so already, construct an itemized list of capital expenditures by category (e.g., land, facilities, office equipment, and improvements), note quantities required, cost per unit, and total cost. Recall that capital items appear on the balance sheet. With the exception of fully depreciated assets, a charge for the depreciation of facilities and equipment appears in the income statement. If capital expenditures will be incurred over several years, then note when they will be incurred. Additionally, note all major leases and their annual cost.

Implementation

Address what is to be done and when. Gantt charts often are useful devices for depicting implementation schedules graphically.[1]

Expected Financial Results

Closely follow the template for five-year pro forma statements shown in Figure 11-2. As noted in Chapter 11, fine details that underlie some line items, such as fixed assets and parts inventories, should be shown in appendices. For instance, one of the several supporting schedules in an appendix may show sales and gross profit broken down by product line, type of customer, or sales territory. Restaurants may show sales and gross profit broken down by breakfast, lunch, and dinner traffic. Begin with annual pro formas; then derive monthly pro formas for the ensuing 12 or 24 months.

Risk

Summarize how changes in critical assumptions are apt to affect financial results. Apply the sensitivity analysis techniques outlined in Chapters 4 and 11. Also estimate how much investors would stand to lose if the venture failed within a few years. Very likely, nothing spent on lease improvements would be recoverable, and equipment would have to be sold for much less than the purchase price.

Appendices

Appendices should provide supporting details, such as customer survey results, itemized equipment lists and prices, and staffing charts complete with estimated salaries and wages. However, readers should have no trouble making sense of your plan without referring to any appendix. Therefore, only details that would not interest most readers or would detract from central issues and arguments should be relegated to appendices. For instance, product functions and benefits should be described in the body of a plan, but technical specifications and schematic diagrams usually should be deferred to an appendix.

A FEW WRITING TIPS

Use informative headings liberally to keep readers and yourself on track. Everything discussed under a particular heading must correspond to the topic heading. For example, if "Competitor Profiles" is the heading, then the corresponding section should describe competitors, not outline a strategy for besting competitors.

Heed the "branching rule," which requires at least two headings at the same level. In effect, the title of your document is the tree trunk, while headings and subheadings are the branches. Likewise, bulleted lists must contain at least two items.

All same-level headings and subheadings must have the same look throughout your document. Lower-level headings should be less prominent than higher-level headings. Refer to any textbook or scholarly article for examples.

Construct a table of contents from headings and subheadings. Rearrange topics in your report that seem out of place. As much as possible, avoid addressing topics in fragments. Instead, try to cover each topic completely right after introducing it.

By and large, avoid repetition; however, a few ideas are worth repeating. Among them is your value proposition. Include it in your description of the business and in the marketing portion of your plan.

All exhibits, including tables, figures, and charts, must be relevant. For instance, the Top Shape business plan, mentioned in Chapter 10, includes a population breakdown by race. However, the race statistics are irrelevant because they are not used for anything—not for segmenting the market, tailoring advertisements, or anything else. They clarify nothing and support no claims or arguments.

All exhibits must be numbered and must have descriptive titles. "Exhibit 1," for example, is a label, but not a title. "Five-Year Financial Projections" is a title. Rows and columns of tables, like the titles of exhibits, must have informative labels. Aim to make exhibits self-explanatory, which entails making them so clear that they can be understood easily without reading any surrounding narrative. You may have to include a few concise footnotes at the bottom of some exhibits to achieve this goal. If longer explanations are necessary, then provide them in the narrative surrounding the exhibit or refer readers to appendices.

Figures and tables are types of exhibits and often are labeled as such. However, using the label "Exhibit" to refer to both types has advantages. First, it precludes having to distinguish between figures and tables. Second, figures and tables need not be tracked separately. For instance, Figure 2, Table 9, and Figure 3 could be the sequence in which these items are introduced in a report. If all figures and tables were labeled "Exhibit," Figure 2 would be Exhibit 10, Table 9 would be Exhibit 11, and Figure 3 would be Exhibit 12.

Introduce exhibits, whether they be figures or tables, in the body of your report. Do not simply insert them without referring to them first. The same goes for appendices. For example, "Exhibit 1 shows the US trend for . . . ; see Appendix A for trends by state."

Comply with numbering conventions. For instance, if all types of exhibits are labeled "Exhibit," then the first one mentioned in the narrative should be labeled "Exhibit 1." The second appendix mentioned should be labeled "Appendix B." In appendices, number exhibits by including the letter of the appendix. For example, "Exhibit A-1" denotes the first exhibit in Appendix A. Remember, each exhibit requires a title in addition to a label.

When possible, avoid displaying part of an exhibit on one page and the rest on another. You may have to use a small font to make an exhibit fit on a single page, but do not use fonts smaller than 9 points. If you must split an exhibit, split it in the least disruptive way. For example, if your balance sheet is so detailed that is does not fit on one page, put the "Assets" portion on one page and the "Liabilities and Equity" portion on another. If the balance sheet is Exhibit 3, then label the portion that appears on a new page "Exhibit 3: Balance Sheet, Continued."

Business plans and reports should never be mysteries imbued with twisted plots that culminate in surprise endings. They should inform rather than entertain.

CONDUCT A FINAL REVIEW

Read the finished document carefully. As you read, ask yourself whether the plan provides the background information readers need to understand it. Does it clearly explain the business venture, what the business offers targeted customers, who its targeted customers are, and why these customers are targeted? Does it portray the competitive environment and the broader surrounding environment thoroughly?

Most importantly, ask whether the plan makes a cogent argument for implementing it. Do pro forma financial statements support implementation? Are the pro formas consistent with the market strategy, the situation analysis, and cost estimates? Are critical assumptions reasonable? Is credible supporting evidence cited? Is the plan internally consistent?

Polish the plan until the answers to all such questions is "yes." Use a spelling checker, but realize it will not catch every spelling mistake. Also, use a grammar checker to identify possible grammatical problems, including poor punctuation. Most flags raised by your grammar checker may have no merit, but some will be valid and helpful. Proofread carefully. Remove mysterious verbiage, spelling errors, and grammatical flaws. Leave no loose ends, and be sure exhibits are relevant, intelligible, properly labeled, and properly introduced.

PITCHING A BUSINESS PLAN

If you need money to move forward, you will have to pitch your plan to prospective investors, such as angels or venture capitalists, a lending institution, or, if the business is one of several in a corporate portfolio, higher management. Of these audiences, angels and venture capitalists are the toughest. They are willing to incur big risks for a chance at big rewards. Often, they are bombarded with investment opportunities, but have little time to sort them out. Accordingly, they tend to decide quickly whether an opportunity is worth a second look. Opportunities that survive the first cut are scrutinized meticulously.

Bankers want assurances that loans will be repaid, while corporate executives want to allocate available funds to maximize shareholder value. The ensuing paragraphs address pitching your plan to the toughest audience, investors. But, in large part, they also apply to persuading more patient audiences.

Realize from the outset that persuading investors to part with their money requires convincing them that prospective returns are attractive in light of risks. Your business plan and corresponding presentation, therefore, must convince prospective investors of the following: (a) that an ample market exists for what your business has to offer, (b) that the market is not fiercely contested by formidable competitors, (c) that you know how to go to market, (d) that a genuine opportunity exists from an investor perspective, and (e) that your management team has what it takes to make the venture successful. Offer the following in support:

- *A compelling value proposition*—preferably, one that articulates superior benefits or a superior solution to a significant problem experienced by targeted customers

- *A sound business model*—one that expresses concisely, yet vividly, what the business does to generate revenues and how it incurs costs in the process of generating revenues

- *A sound market strategy*—one that explains the venture's prospects within targeted markets in terms of competitive advantages and disadvantages

- *Evidence of a competent management team*—a team that has convincing credentials, including a proven track record

- *Concise complementary pro formas* that are consistent with all preceding items in this list. Include financial summaries in your slide presentation, but keep them brief. If you have not given a copy of your business plan to your audience, then offer detailed financials as handouts.

REMEMBER THIS

Plenty of sample business plans and topic outlines are available online. Search for them, and glance at a few to get ideas for organizing your plan. As you glance at each plan, critique it by asking yourself whether the plan is truly informative, credible, and easy to follow. If you model your plan after one of the samples, modify whatever needs to be modified to make your plan as informative, credible, and readable as possible. Keep the following in mind as you proceed:

- Although all proper business reports have the same general structure, no single template is best for all occasions.

- Writers must determine the order in which data, findings, and the like are presented most effectively. However, the purpose of the document and the nature of the business venture it covers should be among the first topics addressed.

- To be persuasive, recommendations must be supported by valid arguments and credible evidence.

- To be effective, plans must be rich in effectively packaged content. Content is lost when packaging is inadequate—for instance, when organization is poor, wording is awkward, critical assertions are unsupported, and irrelevancies distract readers.

- Language appropriate to textbooks seldom is appropriate to business communications. Textbooks and business communications generally have different purposes and different audiences. Therefore, "talk" to your audience, and never sound like a textbook or as if you were lecturing.

Questions for Review and Discussion

1. What are the three main parts of proper business reports, including business plans?

2. How does an introduction differ from an executive summary?

3. Why does it make sense, in most instances, to state the claim before the grounds and the warrant? (Refer to Chapter 6 if you cannot recall the answer.)

4. What do you think of the paragraph in the following box as an opening for a business plan? Does it grab you? Is it effective? What do you like or dislike about it? Is it risky if the plan is intended to obtain a bank loan or attract investors?

Box 12-2

How Do You Like This Opening?

Imagine two bright young men joining forces to start a company that, within three years, of its founding dominates its industry. Are they Microsoft's Bill Gates and Paul Allen? Are they Steve Jobs and Steve Wozniak of Apple? Perhaps they are Google cofounders Larry Page and Sergey Brin? Although they could be any one of these dynamic duos, they are, in fact, Clark Kent and Peter Parker. Moreover, they are not in high tech, but in high-end prêt-à-porter fashions. Today, their success can only be imagined. But three years from now, it will be the talk of the high-fashion world and financial analysts alike.

Note

1. Learn more about Gantt charts at http://www.netmba.com/operations/project/gantt.

Raising Capital and Choosing a Business' Legal Structure

Valentin, E.

Borrow money if you have to from your parents; start a business.

—Mitt Romney

When asking for something, make it easy to give it to you.

—E. K. Valentin

Alan Hall, like many a consummate entrepreneur, struck out a few times before striking it rich. First, it was diamond-tipped dental drills; next came Netline printer-sharing software.[1]

What these ventures have in common is this: Mr. Hall believed in them, and both were undone by distribution woes. In a last-gasp attempt to save Netline, he hired and trained 25 computer-savvy college students to demonstrate Netline's printer-sharing software in computer stores, which abounded at the time. In-store software demonstrations aimed at customers were common, but Hall set his sights on sales personnel. Netline's biggest problem, he sensed, was not the product itself, but lack of attention at the retail level. To retailers, Netline's software was just a few boxes among several hundred displayed in every store. Consequently, it did not get the push it needed to generate profitable volume.

Hall's Netline squad visited more than 3,000 stores throughout the continental USA during a three-month period. It showed sales staff how the product worked and how to sell it. Although these efforts boosted Netline's sales, the company soon failed.

All was not lost, however. Far from it. As Netline went under, Mr. Hall fathomed and then pursued his next business opportunity. Other companies, he figured, could use his help to overcome obstacles akin to those that Netline had experienced. On that hunch, he founded TempReps (TR) in 1987.

Early TR clients included both startups and notables, such as Microsoft and HP. The company operated by organizing four national campaigns per year and offering four product slots per campaign. Thus, TR could represent as many as four or as few as one client per campaign, depending on whether clients bought multiple slots. Each campaign began with tutorials near TR's headquarters in Ogden, Utah. Clients were the teachers; TR reps were the students. After mastering clients' products, TR reps visited resellers for the next two months.

TR quickly evolved into MarketStar, which operates on a much larger scale than TR ever did. Further, its clients are more diverse, and its services are broader in scope. In 1999, MarketStar joined Omnicom, a global leader in advertising and marketing communications. Omnicom had the financial resources MarketStar needed to keep pace with the ever-increasing demands of its best clients.

Mr. Hall remained MarketStar's CEO for a few years after the merger, but later left to pursue other interests. His current passion is helping entrepreneurs achieve the kind of success he experienced. He is the managing director of Mercato Partners, a venture capital fund that invests in high-growth technology companies. He also is the founder and chairman of Grow Utah, a not-for-profit organization dedicated to stimulating economic development through entrepreneurship.[2] In addition, he is the founder of Grow America, which he described as "Grow Utah on steroids."[3]

Hall's recent efforts have involved providing entrepreneurs with access to both good advice and capital. Various contests serve to give thousands of dollars away to entrepreneurs with promising ideas. Winners get free money with no strings attached. Additional help with funding includes putting entrepreneurs in touch with lenders, venture capitalists, and angel investors.

This brief chapter passes along some good advice from Alan Hall and many other experienced consultants, entrepreneurs, angel investors, and venture capitalists about seeking funding. In addition, it outlines matters worth considering when choosing a business' legal structure.

The chapter is not intended to make you an expert on financing or on business structure. Instead, its intent is to make you aware of various financing and legal structuring options, impress on you the importance of making wise financing and structuring decisions, and encourage you to seek help from competent professionals before entering into financing agreements or deciding on a legal structure.[4] The chapter applies predominantly to independent startups and fledgling ventures. In multi-business corporations, external financing arrangements and corporate structuring decisions are made at the top and do not involve business-level executives.

RAISING CAPITAL

Sources of capital may be personal or non-personal. Further, funds may come with or without strings attached.

Personal Resources

Personal sources of funds include your own money, salable assets, and unused credit card capacity. However, founding a business with personal credit card debt rarely is wise, since interest rates are high.

Starting a company seldom is possible without investing some personal funds in the business. Even Steve Jobs and Steve Wozniak had to scrape up over $1,000 to start Apple. Their first product, the Apple I, was a kit with a printed circuit board that Wozniak designed. The two partners needed money to buy parts and get the boards printed. So, Wozniak sold his HP calculator for $370, and Jobs cashed in his VW bus for nearly $1,000.[5]

Respectively, Jobs and Wozniak were 21 and 25 years old when Apple was founded in 1976. They had no idea where their venture would lead, but agreed that being able to say they once had their own company was well worth risking their investment.[6] Few entrepreneurs would be satisfied with so little.

Family members and close friends also are potential personal sources. Alan Hall suggested inviting family and friends to contribute without promising them anything, not even repayment. Wait to reward contributors, he advised, until you can afford it.[7]

Unfortunately, not everyone with a bright business idea is surrounded by exceedingly generous people who can afford to give much money away. Typical contributors, regardless of whether they do or do not know you, will expect something in return, especially if the business is ever profitable. Be careful about what you promise and get a professional to draw up agreements.[8]

Funds without Strings Attached: Free Money

Contrary to what myriad web sites and some infomercials suggest, free money is hard to get. Ventures that qualify for scientific or economic development grants under federal or state rules have the best chance. The Small Business Administration (SBA) has a "Loans and Grants Search Tool" that may help you find legitimate sources of free funds, given your particular requirements and qualifications.[9] Also check out the US Economic Development Administration (EDA).[10] If you surf the web for potential giveaways, be careful: Scammers are always on the lookout for people who search for deals and freebies.

Competitions sponsored by legitimate entrepreneurial organizations, such as Grow America and Grow Utah, also are potential sources of seed money. Examples include Grow America's Innovative Product Competition.[11] Keep in mind that, while many enter such contests, few win significant prizes.

Crowdfunding, which took root with the passing of President Obama's JOBS Act in 2012, encompasses several ways of raising startup or growth capital. In one form, it simply entails using social media to solicit donations from family, friends, and strangers while promising nothing in return. But even people who know you and think highly of you are unlikely to chip in without knowing something about your venture. Free money is most likely to roll in if you give potential donors an ample intangible reason to contribute. That reason might be a cleaner planet, for example, if the business involves recycling or making biodegradable packaging.[12]

Funds with Some Strings Attached

When crowdfunding entails offering something in return for contributions of a specified amount, that something might be cheap, yet effective. For instance, in the case of a recycling venture, it may be nothing more than a "Save Our Planet" bumper sticker.

Pebble Technology offered something more substantial, namely, a Pebble Jet Black smart watch in return for a donation of $115. The Pebble crowdfunding campaign boils down to soliciting pre-paid orders well in advance of making and shipping the product. Call it what you will, the campaign generated 100 times more revenue than expected, partly because the Pebble Watch would be an intriguing gadget even at $200 or $300 per copy and partly because the company's video was professional, engaging, and compelling.[13]

Even though crowdfunding is fairly new, numerous safe crowdfunding web sites have emerged.[14] Look for many more to come.

Non-Personal Sources with Lots of Strings Attached

Non-personal sources that usually come with lots of strings attached include angel investor funding, venture capital funding, and bank loans.

Angels and Venture Capital

Soon after founding Apple Computer, Steve Jobs and Steve Wozniak realized their little company had immense potential. Unexpectedly high sales of Apple I kits inspired their vision of the Apple II. In Wozniak, they had all the technical expertise they would need to design the Apple II. What they did not have and needed urgently was cash. They found an angel investor in Mike Markkula, who later led them to the man who coined the term *venture capital*, the legendary Arthur Rock.

Angels provide capital during the early stages of a business' existence, usually in exchange for convertible debt or ownership equity. Often, they contribute more than capital. Mike Markkula, for example, contributed both money and expertise to Apple. He became Employee No. 3. His financial contribution—$80,000 in the form of an equity investment and $170,000 in the form of a loan—made him a one-third owner of Apple. With Markkula's help, Apple was incorporated on January 3, 1977, just nine months after its founding as a partnership.

Markkula was Apple's CEO from 1981 to 1983 and served as its chairman from 1985 to 1997. His contributions were varied and lasting. He helped Apple obtain credit and capital and guided the company over many a rough spot. In 1978, he facilitated the sale of 640,000 shares of Apple to Arthur Rock, who then became an influential director of the company. Rock's investment of roughly $57,000 was worth $14 million three years later when Apple's stock became available to the public.

The dividing line between angel investors and venture capitalist is imprecise. Generally, both angels and venture capitalists are willing to invest substantial sums, both expect high returns, both want some say in managing the businesses in which they invest, and both are very selective. Of the two, venture capitalists usually are prepared to contribute more financial resources, generally insist on becoming major shareholders or partners, and expect higher returns on their investments. Angels typically expect compounded annual returns of at least 20 percent; venture capitalists expect more.[15]

Angels and venture capitalists take high risks in hope of reaping high rewards. They understand their investments are far from safe, but are ready to put large sums at risk for a chance to win big. What makes them different from casino gamblers is that they have good reason to believe they can skew the odds of coming out ahead in their favor. Thorough inquiry informed by experience and expertise, they believe, can help them discover the most promising opportunities. Apple's Mike Markkula, for example, was an electrical engineer who had worked for Fairchild Semiconductor and Intel before retiring in 1972 at age 32. Unlike some other prospective investors whom Jobs had tried to persuade, Markkula had the background to appreciate Wozniak's wizardry and to share Jobs' vision.

Nowadays, angels can be located easily online or with the help of financial planners, investment advisors, and consultants.[16] Most angels manage their own money rather than investment pools funded by multiple partners. But the number of angel groups, or angel networks, is growing.[17] Typical investment pools are structured as limited partnerships, with one of the partners being the managing, or controlling, partner.

On July 10, 2013, the Securities and Exchange Commission (SEC) ruled that "sophisticated" investors, such as angels and venture capitalists, may be solicited directly over the Internet. Nevertheless, online equity crowdfunding remains highly restricted.[18]

Conventional Business Loans

Lending institutions—mostly banks, but also credit unions—operate under a set of principles and rules that differ greatly from those that apply to angels and venture capital funds. Instead of seeking equity positions, they make loans that are to be repaid with interest. Loan officers are expected to exercise due diligence before approving business loans and lines of credit. Generally, they are expected to verify that income from applicants' business operations is sufficient to service debt, which means pay interest and repay the principal in accordance with the loan agreement. They also are expected to examine and render judgment on the quality of collateral and the creditworthiness of the borrower. Additional matters of consideration may include the business' debt/equity ratio and life insurance on key people. Both affect loan risk.[19]

Having assets that can be pledged helps secure business loans, but apparent capacity to service debt generally is the lender's predominant concern. Accordingly, businesses that have no appreciable operating history are unlikely to secure conventional business loans.

Government Guaranteed Business Loans

Government guaranteed business loans are obtained through banks and other conventional lending channels. US government institutions do not make business loans directly, but the SBA may offer lenders guarantees that take most of the risk out of making loans to qualified applicants. The SBA may even help entrepreneurs obtain startup loans.

Whether the SBA can guarantee a business loan, how SBA guaranteed loans can be used, and who qualifies depends on factors too numerous to explain here. Refer instead to the "Loans & Grants" tab on the SBA's home page (http://www.sba.gov) and the documents linked to it. If you are a veteran, also check the "Business" tab on the Veteran Administration's home page (http://www.va.gov). Many universities have Small Business Development Centers (SBDCs) that can help entrepreneurs navigate the financing maze.

CHOOSING A BUSINESS' LEGAL STRUCTURE

A business' legal structure affects personal liability, control, taxation, and ease of adding investors.[20] Fundamentally, businesses may be structured as sole proprietorships, partnerships, or corporations. A current favorite, the Limited Liability Company (LLC), is a hybrid structure that affords the liability protections of a corporation and the tax benefits and operational flexibility of a partnership.[21]

To appreciate the gravity of a business' legal structure, consider the founding of Apple, which has become one of the world's most valuable corporations. Along with Steve Jobs and Steve Wosniak, Ronald G. Wayne became a founding partner in Apple Computer on April 1, 1976. However, Wayne was the lone partner with any tangible personal assets—assets that the partnership exposed to Apple's creditors. Liability exposure made Wayne so nervous that he sold his 10 percent interest to the two remaining partners for $800 on April 13, 1976, less than two weeks after becoming a partner. Less than a year later, Apple incorporated, thus, shielding owners' personal assets from the business' creditors. Wayne's share would have been worth around $35 billion in 2013.

While reorganizing Apple as a corporation had its advantages, it also had unpleasant consequences. In particular, Steve Jobs had lost so much control over Apple by 1985 that he was relieved of managerial responsibilities by then CEO John Sculley, a man Jobs had recruited. Jobs left Apple before the end of 1985, but was asked to return a decade later.

Deciding which particular legal structure is best is a matter of weighing tradeoffs. The advantages of a *sole proprietorship* are that it is easy and inexpensive to form one, full control remains in the hands of the proprietor, and tax forms can be prepared with relative ease because business income is taxed as personal income. Its disadvantages are that the proprietor is exposed to unlimited personal liability for the debts and obligations of the business. Further, sole proprietorships often find raising capital difficult.[22]

In *general partnerships*, profits, liability, and managerial duties are divided equally among the partners, unless the partnership agreement specifies otherwise. However, partners whose participation in managing and profit sharing may be relatively small may have the greatest personal liability exposure. Such was the case with Apple's Ronald G. Wayne.

Most major corporations are *C Corporations*. Owners of C Corporations are shielded from the company's debts and obligations; however, they are subject to double taxation, since C Corporations must pay corporate income taxes and their owners must pay personal income taxes on dividends.[23]

Currently, the favorite structure among small businesses is the LLC. Owners, who may be called "members," enjoy the liability protections of a C Corporation and the tax advantages of a partnership. LLCs themselves pay no income taxes; instead, all profits and losses accrue to the LLC's owners, who report their portions on their personal tax returns the same way that owners of partnerships report profits and losses.

To learn more about business structure, click the "Starting & Managing" tab on the SBA's home page (http://www.sba.gov); then click "Choose Your Business Structure," and go from there. Familiarize yourself as much as possible with the advantages and disadvantages of the various business structures, but see a qualified professional before you file any papers.

REMEMBER THIS

Financing and formal business structuring decisions are consequential. This brief chapter provides but a glimpse of the many financing possibilities, the several structuring options, and their advantages and disadvantages. The *Ernst & Young Business Plan Guide* provides a more thorough introduction to both topics and echoes the advice given here: Seek professional advice before entering into financial agreements and before deciding on a legal structure.[24] The SBA's introduction to financing and legal structure is very similar to the one in the *Ernst & Young Business Plan Guide*. A major difference is that the SBA's advice is free. Much valuable additional information about starting a business, also, is accessible at http://www.sba.gov.

In sum, inform yourself about financing possibilities and various legal structures, but see a qualified professional before you sign any papers. Better safe than sorry!

Questions for Review and Discussion

1. Does the SBA make loans? How does it facilitate getting a business loan?

2. What is crowdfunding, and how did Pebble Watch use it?

3. How do the goals of angels and venture capitalists differ from those of bankers?

4. Generally, what is a banker's greatest concern when making a business loan? Is it collateral?

5. What are the advantages and disadvantages of a sole proprietorship?

6. What are the advantages and disadvantages of a general partnership?

7. Why are LLCs so popular among entrepreneurs?

Notes

1. E. K. Valentin and H. Hess-Lindquist, "MarketStar: A Channel Services Pioneer," *Business Case Journal*, 14, Issue 2, Winter 2006–2007.
2. http://www.growutahventures.com.
3. J. Bruder, "Grow America's Unusual Approach to Spurring New Ventures and Creating Jobs," *New York Times*, February 19, 2013, http://boss.blogs.nytimes.com/2012/11/13/grow-americas-unusual-approach-to-spurring-new-ventures-and-creating-jobs.
4. B. R. Ford, J. M Boorstein, and P. T. Pruitt, *The Ernst & Young Business Plan Guide*, Hoboken, NJ: John Wiley, 2007.
5. In July 2013, an Apple I sold for $387,750. See http://www.tuaw.com/2013/07/09/rare-apple-i-sold-for-387-750-in-online-christies-auction/.

6. S. Wozniak with G. Smith, *iWoz*, New York: Norton, 2006.
7. http://www.forbes.com/sites/alanhall/2012/10/20/5-means-of-funding-a-small-business-how-to-get-your-piece-of-the-pie.
8. B. R. Ford et al., *op. cit.*
9. See http://www.sba.gov/ loans-and-grants.
10. See http://www.eda.gov.
11. For details, see http://www.growam.com/competition.
12. T. Prive, "What Is Crowdfunding and How Does It Benefit the Economy," *Forbes*, November 27, 2012, http://www.forbes.com/sites/tanyaprive/2012/11/27/what-is-crowdfunding-and-how-does-it-benefit-the-economy.
13. http://www.kickstarter.com/projects/597507018/pebble-e-paper-watch-for-iphone-and-android.
14. D. Thorpe, "Eight Crowdfunding Sites for Social Entrepreneurs," *Forbes*, September 10, 2012, http://www.forbes.com/sites/devinthorpe/2012/09/10/eight-crowdfunding-sites-for-social-entrepreneurs.
15. B. R. Ford et al., *op. cit.*
16. See, for example, https://www.equitynet.com/angel-investors.aspx?gclid= CPiQyLGFy7UCFQxx QgodywIAUg.
17. B. R. Ford et al., *op. cit.*
18. T. Berry, "Today's SEC Ruling on Crowdfunding Is a Mixed Bag," *The Huffington Post*, July 10, 2013, http://www.huffingtonpost.com/ tim-berry/todays-sec-ruling-on-crow_b_3575958.html.
19. The FDIC's "Underwriting Standards for Small Business Loans Originated under the Small Business Lending Fund Program" exemplifies the standards that business loan officers generally should apply. See http://www.fdic.gov/news/news/financial/2010/fil10090.pdf.
20. B. R. Ford et al., *op. cit.*
21. http://www.sba.gov/content/limited-liability-company-llc.
22. http://www.sba.gov/content/sole-proprietorship-0.
23. For advantages and disadvantages of the corporate structure, see http://www.sba.gov/content/corporation.
24. B. R. Ford et.al., *op. cit.*

Developing Communication Management Skills: Integrated Assessment and Reflection in an Experiential Learning Context

Cyphert, D., Dodge, E.N. and Duclos, L.K.

Abstract

The value of experiential learning is widely acknowledged, especially for the development of communication skills, but students are not always aware of their own learning. While we can observe students practicing targeted skills during the experiential activity, the experience can also color their explicit understanding of those skills. Transfer of applied knowledge to managerial contexts requires an explicit grasp of the skills as appropriate solutions to the problems they encounter within the experiential team. This article reports the adaptation of assessment processes to encourage the reflection steps necessary for developing the desired managerial perspective on team communication.

Keywords

assessment, experiential learning, team communication

Competent communication within group settings is essential in the contemporary workplace (Worley & Dyrud, 2001), widely recognized as essential to quality practices (M. W. Allen & Brady, 1997; Terziovski, 2002) and participative management more generally (Drehmer, Belohlav, & Coye, 2000). Although employees who have

[1]University of Northern Iowa, USA

received training have been shown to exhibit better conflict resolution and team skills (Hartenian, 2003), team communication instruction remains one of the more challenging aspects of a university business curriculum. The communication used by effective teams is complex and sophisticated (Yeatts & Hyten, 1998), including knowledge, skills, and abilities that involve a sensitivity to a specific organizational environment (M. J. Stevens & Campion, 1994).

Previous investigations have demonstrated the utility of contextualized communication instruction (Hoover, Giambatista, Sorenson, & Bommer, 2010). Business courses can teach group process skills along with discipline knowledge (Young & Henquit, 2000), and MBA programs, especially, have long recognized the value of integrating conceptual knowledge and practical advice with experiential learning through workshops, case studies, or field experiences (Bogert & Butt, 1996; Navarro, 2008; Saunders, 1997), internships (Dillon, McCaskey, & Blazer, 2011), or external consulting projects (Glazer, 2010). Experiential learning has been shown to have positive effects on student self-awareness and collaboration skills (Brzovic & Matz, 2009), creativity and flexibility (Bush-Bacelis, 1998), commitment and motivation (Cyphert, 2006; Judge, 2006; Littlefield, 2006), and emotional intelligence (Sigmar, Hynes, & Hill, 2012). All of these effects demonstrably enhance students' team communication expertise, but assessing the experience's direct effect on learning goals is a more difficult proposition.

One recommended solution is to embed assessment within the experiential learning process (O'Toole, 2007), designing prompts for student reflection that guide learning toward desired outcomes even as they provide evidence that learning has occurred. Implementation within a complex, time-sensitive, and emotionally intense consulting project is not simple. Nevertheless, the experience of the University of Northern Iowa's MBA program suggests that the integration of instruction, assessment, and practice within an experiential learning project can enhance student development in the elusive, but important domain of team communication. This article presents a model for integrating learning goals, learning assessments, and reflection prompts to enhance the development of a managerial perspective of team communication.

Managerial Communication Goals

The MBA program at the University of Northern Iowa aims to meet the needs of mid-level management or prospective management employees of small- to midsized companies in the U.S. upper Midwest. One learning objective involves " . . . the ability to effectively participate as a team member, facilitate group processes, and manage team projects," with a focus on managerial skill. As with any aspect of communication, managerial applications require an ability to encourage and develop others, along with strategic application of one's own skills. To effectively assign, train, or coach teams within an organization, a manager must be cognizant of the impact of relationships, skills levels, and specific behaviors. It is not enough to *be* an adequate team player; a manager must *be mindful* of the impact of various behaviors on team outcomes in order to effectively create and manage teams within a business environment and proactively develop effective team skills of her own employees. A qualitatively different realm of action is involved when the learning objective is *managerial* expertise rather than simply team participation.

Peer assessments were collected within a learning assurance program that includes data from peer evaluations for each student, EBI Alumni Surveys, within-course evaluations of team performance, program evaluation surveys, and course evaluation surveys. Assessments collected annually over 5 years indicate generally proficient communication within self-managed teams (see Table 1). On a scale of 0 (*does not meet*) to 7 (*proficient*), peer assessments cluster between 3.74 and 5.53, indicating that students exhibit personal team skills at an adequate level for each of the College's team communication learning goals.

In any one year, teams might experience unusually difficult circumstances, and each year a few students fall below the norm (typically international students without work experience who face vocabulary or culture issues). Conversely, a few students exhibit proficiency in one or more areas because of career experience or specialized training. Overall, however, students in the program are demonstrably able to work within self-managed teams to plan and execute successful projects.

Graduating students and recent alumni of the MBA program affirmed that team experiences were a valuable part of the program, but questions remained about the nature of that value. Students' ability to practice targeted team skills during the program do not predictably translate into a mindful managerial capacity to develop, supervise, or coach effective teams after graduation. Exit surveys suggested students were highly engaged and reported learning from the ambiguities, conflicts, and problems inherent in the experiential learning process but simultaneously failed to report (and seemingly even resisted any responsibility for) management steps designed to resolve those ambiguities, conflicts, and problems.

Instructional Resources

The general philosophy of the MBA program reflects a "learned-behavior approach" (Hunt & Sorenson, 2001), which emphasizes the development of various skills in an inductive learning process that leads to conceptual understanding. Because students are judged to be generally proficient in the target skills, there is no explicit attention to team communication instruction (i.e., demonstrations, role-play exercises, case discussions, etc.), and the curriculum instead prioritizes conceptual knowledge and mindful management of team processes. Opportunities for self- and peer assessment allow students to identify their own developmental needs, with the assumption that students in the MBA program "are capable of using printed material, demonstrations, and discussion to identify areas in which they need to improve" and are willing to take responsibility for enhancing their skills (Cyphert, 2002, p. 85).

Given the emphasis on management of team communication, the most important element of the instructional process is a culminating consulting project known as the Capstone Experience. This final application of the MBA curriculum content requires teams of three to five students to work with a regional business, government,

Table 1. Peer Assessment Averages in Capstone Experience.

	2010	2011	2012	2013	2014	2015
Individual behavior (peer assessment)						
Communication skills and task-related behaviors that support team participation						
Oral communication skills	5.14	4.36	5.38	4.50	4.00	3.84
Task competence	5.13	4.33	5.74	3.75	4.39	3.95
Engagement	5.42	4.51	5.88	3.83	4.19	4.03
Team orientation	5.27	4.54	5.58	4.08	3.92	4.08
Conformity to group norms	5.53	4.49	6.21	4.00	3.92	4.27
Facilitation of group processes						
Communication management	5.03	4.43	5.65	4.33	4.50	4.03
Conflict resolution	4.93	4.44	5.50	4.50	3.75	4.35
External communication	4.87	4.53	5.58	4.50	4.11	3.86
Leadership	4.73	4.48	5.38	4.17	4.14	3.74
Team behavior (self-assessment)						
Efficiency in team project management						
Goal identification	5.13	4.87	5.85	4.29	4.28	4.07
Task identification	4.93	4.62	5.67	4.17	4.35	3.97
Goal achievement	5.30	4.51	5.65	4.31	4.33	4.18
Use of norms and resources	5.04	4.56	5.67	4.23	4.25	3.92
Communication processes	5.03	4.80	6.04	4.10	4.25	4.28
Teams	5	3	4	4	3	5
Assessments completed	21	13	14	16	13	18

Note. Scale: 0-1 = *does not meet*, 2-3 = *developing*, 4-5 = *adequate*, 6-7 = *proficient*.

or nonprofit organization, taking approximately 6 months to identify, analyze, and propose solutions for a business problem or opportunity.[1] Its educational intent is twofold:

1. Develop problem-solving and decision-making techniques in a dynamic business environment, giving students a real understanding of the complexities of applying theoretical knowledge in an environment characterized by incomplete information, unclear goals, competing stakeholders, and dynamic political and economic conditions.
2. Develop the managerial skills of MBA graduates in the areas of team dynamics, business writing, professional presentations, organizational dynamics, and cross-cultural communication.

The Capstone Experience features active coaching of team processes, intended as a remedy for the typical business school assignment, which asks for team products without providing training in effective team processes (Hansen, 2006; Vik, 2001). Instead, mentoring and coaching occur at appropriate stages within the Capstone Experience project. Following the model introduced by Hackman and Wageman (2005), team formation guidance is provided as teams are first meeting, while process and strategy advice is delayed until status report discussions after the first half of the project. Teams disband at the end of the project, making moot the collective after-action review process recommended by Hackman and Wageman (2005) as appropriate to workplace teams. Instead, individuals and teams are encouraged to meet with their assigned faculty mentors, the capstone coordinator, and the MBA program director to discuss team problems, options, and outcomes.

Within this mentoring and coaching structure, teams must nevertheless function autonomously as consultants to regional businesses and nonprofit organizations. The program's core student, a midcareer business professional, might come into the program as a proficient team member, but within the context of a high-stakes consulting team, students must take a more proactively robust managerial role. Rather than simply giving students yet another team experience, the instructional goals of the MBA program require that the Capstone Experience allow students an opportunity to develop mindful team management skills.

In practical terms, instruction relies heavily on students' self-directed learning. Because each team of students faces a different client situation, there is no way to anticipate exactly the instructional needs with respect to team facilitation or management skills over the course of a specific project. Furthermore, because students' cultural backgrounds, communication competence, and work histories vary widely, there is no consistent baseline knowledge on which to build a meaningful curriculum. While the faculty can be sure that the Capstone Experience will teach students a great deal about team processes, there is no good way to predict exactly what the lessons should be for any one student.

Experiential Learning and Learning Outcomes

Research consistently shows experiential learning yields positive effects (Brzovic & Matz, 2009; Bush-Bacelis, 1998; Cyphert, 2006; Judge, 2006; Littlefield, 2006; Sigmar et al., 2012), but assessing a direct effect toward learning goals is not simple. The learning situations reflect variability in student background, preparation, and motivation, compounded in the experiential context by differences among the students' projects, clients, locations, or team composition. There is no question that students learn though experiential projects, but there is little evidence that they are all learning the same thing. As a result, most experiential learning programs do not attempt to assess individual learning. Instead, program assessment is "the easiest and the most common type of assessment" to do (Qualters, 2010, p. 57); success is measured with quantitative data such as the number of participants, student characteristics, or clients served.

With more than a hundred business and nonprofit organizations served since 1999, Capstone Experience success measures include client testimonials and estimates of value of consulting for the regional economy. The faculty and alumni consider the consulting experience a "distinct advantage" of the program, providing students with an opportunity to integrate knowledge and skills under the pressure of working for a vested client (Wilson, 2011). Such measures can be gratifying, and the College regularly points to the impact of Capstone Experience teams within the regional business community. However, such accolades cannot indicate whether the Experience has enhanced managerial team communication skills.

A program exit survey frequently garnered comments about team processes, as did a final reflection paper required of all capstone participants. While these provide only self-reports, the students' comments were reviewed for insights. Over 10 years, 118 students (72.4% of all graduates) completed exit surveys. The authors categorized comments related to "strengths" and "weaknesses" of teamwork in the MBA program.

General Strengths and Specific Weaknesses

The most obvious insight was that students both valued and complained about group work, or perhaps, some students appreciated it, while others did not. In either case, the nature of comments varied with respect to specificity. Students reported the value of the team experience with broad descriptors such as "project management skills" or "group work," but never in terms of specific skills developed or used. Conversely, they described team-related weaknesses in terms of specific problems or events within the project. There were a few holistic complaints about "too much" group work, but most students named specific situations related to workload distribution, slackers, unequal skill levels, or communication with international students.

This result suggests that students did not recognize their development in terms of specific, strategically useful managerial skills, even though they might have developed more holistic skills such as self-confidence, empathy, or emotional intelligence. This is not to say they had not gained management skills, but until students have developed a strategic awareness of those skills, we could not claim to have met our managerial communication learning goals.

Recognizing Management Issues

A second observation was that the very things that students list as disadvantages of teamwork are the common problems that effective managers must solve:

- appropriate size of teams
- differences in resources allocated or work expectations across teams
- interpersonal relationships within teams
- cultural and language differences
- within-group differences in work ethic, competitiveness, or performance standards
- background differences in educational preparation or work experience
- conflicting work schedules
- organizational policies/work rules

For instance, students consistently listed unbalanced workloads as a "weakness" of teams, sometimes tied to incompatible or "challenging" work schedules and sometimes to variations in technical preparation. Yet there was never a suggestion that the program should offer better instruction for developing and managing collaborative work methods. Similarly, difficulties with a "lack of accountability" were noted with the implied—and in a couple of cases, explicit—understanding of performance management as the "firing" of nonperforming team members. The sentiment echoes many professionals' secret wish to have management fire all their nonperforming colleagues so they do not cause any pain. However, managerial success requires taking steps to improve others' performance, skills, or motivation. The comments suggested that students respond to immediate team challenges, perhaps even solving the problems in productive ways, but without developing an ability to objectively analyze and troubleshoot team issues from a managerial perspective. We again judged the goals not to have been met.

Team Performance as an Ethics Problem

Perhaps most telling were the responses to a question on the final capstone reflection paper about ethical issues in the consulting process. When asked to describe any ethical challenges experienced during the Capstone Experience, students reported, almost without exception, team management situations. The faculty considered such incidents to be tests of managerial skill, but students perceived them as ethics violations on the part of their classmates. Research with workplace teams supports the connection; shared perceptions of fairness are a predictor of team performance (Roberson & Williamson, 2012). Even so, while an employee's good attitude, work ethic, or team orientation might be deemed desirable by coworkers, such traits as "initiative, trust, openness, helpfulness, flexibility, and supportiveness" are not generally amenable to managerial control (M. J. Stevens & Campion, 1994, p. 504).

The learning goal rubric for team communication had deliberately minimized attention to personality traits in favor of objective communication behaviors, but that instructional framework had obviously not eliminated students' willingness to explain dysfunctional behavior in terms of ethical choices. We might dismiss this finding as inevitable: the result of a fundamental attribution error. That would be an error, however, that an effective manager should strive not to make. Still, in practical terms, a manager does need to foster teams' *perception* of a shared justice climate, which has been shown to depend on team homogeneity, interpersonal expressiveness, and interdependent work relationships (Roberson & Williamson, 2012).

Enhancing Managerial Development With Experiential Learning

The tenuous relationship between experiential learning and an assessment of students' development as managers for a team environment did not deter the faculty from its commitment to the authentic consulting context, which offers a unique value for students. Classroom exercises and role-play might offer more opportunities for structured instruction and explicit conceptual understanding, but two key factors suggest the Capstone Experience remains the best option for developing team management skills: inherent emotional engagement with a project and the self-managed team environment.

The experiential learning model is successful *because* it triggers emotional cues to motivate and guide learning, especially implicit learning (Kolb, 1984), but this same feature can create stress, which makes explicit cognitive learning more difficult. Within the capstone project, we have seen this dynamic played out repeatedly. The factors that demand engagement are simultaneously sources of stress.

Every capstone team faces significant challenges, starting with the normal project issues of content and process. Furthermore, conceptual challenges are why MBA students are asked to apply their knowledge in the context of an existing business. Case studies present static, even sanitized, business questions, but practicing consultants must be prepared to face deceptive or imprudent clients, ambiguous instructions and requests, and situational changes.

Intellectual challenges might be the faculty priority, but the biggest challenge from the students' perspective is the sheer stress of meeting the expectations of the Capstone Experience. The time and peer pressure inherent in a culminating project, the ambiguities of an authentic consulting project, and the complex sense making required in a diverse project context are usually unexpected and sometimes overwhelming. However, these stressors drive a level of student engagement impossible within the structured parameters of classroom instruction.

The special situation of *self*-managed teams in the Capstone Experience similarly poses both unique challenges and unique learning opportunities. Team assignment depends primarily on students' expressed interest in working with a particular client or industry, with some attention to previous professional experience and students' requests to be placed on the same (or different) teams. No team leader is designated and, while each team is assigned a faculty mentor, the role is strictly advisory.

The absence of any supervisory alternative forces teams to perform managerial functions, but without an imposed supervisory structure, there is no explicit structure to guide students' development in this area. In these realms, the inherent variability of experiential learning compromises the value of fixed instructional materials. Learning goals include task knowledge as well as conflict resolution and leadership skills, but without any specific application to a self-managed context. Once projects are underway, students will sometimes request managerial advice from their mentor, capstone coordinator, or other faculty members, but typically present themselves as facing "personal" problems with situations or individuals.

Mentors sometimes suggest solutions when teams deem themselves unable to resolve issues, but, even with coaching, students might not understand themselves as part of a team that is experiencing problem-solving, decision-making, or leadership issues. Their focus is on solving an immediate problem, rather than learning how to solve problems in general. The self-managed team environment does seem to call on managerial skills, but it offers little structure to guide students toward a strategic perspective.

With any project, resource, goal, and process, conflicts are sure to arise, and self-managed collaboration necessarily involves conflict resolution skills. The program goals name conflict resolution as a targeted skill set, but without any presumption of a specific method, perspective, or context. Once again, the self-managed environment invites the application of important skills, but it offers no systematic supervision, coaching, or instruction to encourage the development of strategic managerial expertise.

Reflection in Experiential Learning

The experiential learning environment offers both emotional and concrete incentives to develop skillful team behavior, but both the emotional engagement and autonomy can also preclude the development of explicit awareness of the managerial skills or appropriate strategies for applying them. The faculty determined that the experiential learning activity needed instructional enhancements in order to achieve its potential to develop critical insights surrounding team management skills. A revision of the assessment process to incorporate student reflection prompts seemed to offer promise.

Concrete experience is just one part of the experiential learning process, which necessarily includes reflection, theorizing, and subsequent application (Kolb, 1984). Reflection is often incorporated into experiential assignments as an important part of the learning process (Mahin & Kruggel, 2006), and self-assessment prompts can be used to guide students' reflection toward the essential steps of metacognitive theorizing and setting application goals (O'Toole, 2007). Reflection is generically understood as a moment of detached, dispassionate self-observation—a quiet moment away from the emotional complications of concrete experience.

The experiential learning works because of the inherent tensions. Emotions must be "available for use" in order for the learner to formulate and achieve goals (Moon, 2004, p. 46). Emotions guide students' attention toward those aspects of the experience that warrant learning. Structured reflection on the emotion-inducing elements of the capstone project might thus allow students to more accurately identify managerial situations and assess their own capacity for skillful response. Furthermore, the reflection process can direct the student's attention toward strategic choices made—or not made—at the point of emotional engagement. As with team formation steps and managerial resources, even consulting contexts that do not consistently require tools or foster good choices during the project can nevertheless provide learning opportunities for the students involved.

As one element of the College's ongoing learning assessment process, the students in the Capstone Experience had been required to produce a final reflection paper, originally designed to assess student writing and technical knowledge relevant to the project scope. In view of the need for better development of managerial team skills, we revised this assignment and added additional reflection prompts designed to better capitalize on the educational potential of the Capstone Experience. Furthermore, both coaching and oral prompts to reflect on the management situation had been administered on an ad hoc basis, so systematic prompts were developed to optimize their instructional effectiveness.

Hackman and Wageman (2005) have shown that asking students to reflect on behaviors that are appropriate to the stage of the team's work is most effective. The assessment process was thus redesigned to prompt reflection at key points across the students' Capstone Experience.

Table 2. Initial Rubric Self-Assessments.

	All students	Native speakers	ESL speakers
Familiarity with individual communication skills	3.67	4.43	2.60
Familiarity with individual facilitation skills	4.25	4.86	3.40
Familiarity with collective team functions	4.25	4.57	3.80
MBA teams have been well managed	4.11	4.00	4.20

Note. ESL = English as a second language.

Initial Individual Reflections. During an early course in the MBA program, students had been oriented to the team communication learning goals and skill vocabulary, and they were prompted to reflect on their own team management skills with a self-assessment instrument (see Appendix A). These documents have not been consistently collected, however, making an independent assessment of that step problematic. A second prompt was introduced at the first meeting of the Capstone Experience. The team skills rubric is collapsed into three categories of communication, facilitation, and group skills within which students are asked to self-assess their own skills as well as their team management and coaching expertise on a 1- to 5-point Likert-type scale. Three open-ended questions encourage higher level reflection in the key areas of problem-solving, decision-making, and collaborative work (see Appendix B).

With just 1 year of results, we draw no conclusions other than to note that the results support our own observations of teams over the years (see Table 2).

All students rated themselves lowest in the area of individual skills (i.e., conversational skills, technical task competence, engagement, etc.), with the average falling midway between "I can do these things myself" (3) and "I know the goal but not how to coach a team" (4). The difference was much greater for English as a second language students, many of whom are uncomfortable with the fast-paced and sometimes heated conversations that characterize U.S. work teams, but all students felt unqualified to coach or train their future reports in these areas. Most U.S. employers label individual communication competence as a baseline entry-level skill (National Association of Colleges and Employers, 2012), which employees ought to have mastered during their educational preparation, and remedial skills training is not typically considered a managerial function.

Students, particularly native speakers, reported that they understood the team facilitation and process goals, but even native speakers approached managerial confidence only in the area of team facilitation skills, skill sets that are often discussed in management textbooks and practitioner publications. All students were generally unsure about coaching toward effective collaborative work processes, and their open-ended reflections suggest the cause might be a lack of strategic mindfulness—the very outcome we aim to achieve with additional reflection on their experiential learning.

Asked to reflect on effective and ineffective problem-solving methods they had used in previous MBA teams, students universally discussed foundational communication skills, particularly face-to-face conversation. Not one student named a specific problem-solving method, even though the MBA curriculum is filled with such tools. Similarly, they named no specific decision-making methods. Students focused instead on the relative merits of consensus, consultative, voting, or command methods, although without using that vocabulary. Nearly all students described elements of collaboration as effective methods, but mentioned no generalized organizational methods to foster collaboration.

Initial Team Reflection. Shortly after Capstone Experience teams form, students are asked to discuss and report orally on their own task readiness and team processes. This activity is now given additional emphasis as an assessment instrument (see Appendix C) that includes a reflection prompt asking the team to offer itself objective management advice for enhancing its own performance. With just one round of results, we claim no new insights on teams' development with respect to managerial team skills. We anecdotally note that teams highly engaged in the in-class discussion were also on track with team tasks and rated themselves at what appeared to be accurate levels, although the request for managerial advice was met with either superficial advice (e.g., "Don't be afraid of creative solutions") or a status justification (e.g., "Scope still under construction"). A third team, which was dealing with a nonperforming member and clearly avoiding discussion, rated themselves higher than their actual output warranted and gave themselves no advice at all.

These behaviors might turn out to be typical over many teams, but even within the highly variable contexts of experiential learning, we find both the assessment results and reflection process to be useful. Rather than depend on summative numeric data, we find ourselves discussing the dynamics of real teams in real situations. The reflection exercise gives the faculty a chance to reflect as well. Given this relatively unusual situation of a team with significant dysfunction, the formative assessment process gives us a tool for initiating an intervention. We expected the first few years to yield too little information for any further analysis; but, we have found ourselves with extremely useful qualitative assessment data.

Midproject Reflection. We have added a formal midproject reflection on the team's process and managerial strategies (see Appendix D), shown by Hackman and Wageman (2005) to be a point when teams intuitively reassess team processes and often make major changes in their internal processes. Students have often commented at this point on their implementation of team formation steps, client relationships, and problem-solving frustrations. The formal reflection prompt encourages them to think systematically about the managerial skills of leadership, decision-making, and conflict resolution and their systematic application.

We can never anticipate the specific issues that a team will face, but research with teams (Yeatts & Hyten, 1998) has identified critical functions: internal processes to reach decisions and solve problems; the logistics of team meetings, including scheduling, technical support, and developing a clear agenda; and good working relationships with external stakeholders. The midproject prompt again asks students to review their success with a managerial troubleshooting mind-set.

Postexperience Reflection. A final prompt appropriately occurs at the end of the project, after the anxieties are largely over and individuals are better able to reflect dispassionately about their experience. This activity remains in place with some revisions to elicit more insightful responses and thus more learning.

First, the current open-ended questions typically yield description or descriptive reflection, Hatton and Smith's (1995) two lowest levels of reflection. The prompt now solicits reflection about diverse team perspectives on the team's processes and interaction, potentially encouraging the higher levels of dialogic and critical reflection. Secondly, a 360° peer review/self-evaluation tool is used to foster more accurate self-assessments of leadership capability (Mayo, Kakarika, Pastor, & Brutus, 2012). Those data are incorporated with qualitative reflections to assess context-specific influences on managerial lapses, such as attribution error, which is potentially causing students to confuse ethical and managerial issues, or cross-cultural challenges, which might require specialized management tools.

Finally, the artifact provides individual data on writing and content knowledge skills, providing a mechanism to identify underperforming students within the team environment. Students also identify gaps between project requirements and curriculum coverage, allowing faculty to assess the degree to which the MBA program prepares students for typical problems found among regional businesses. These subjective, open-ended responses have not been included in the College's assessment of team skill outcomes, but a qualitative analysis of their content suggests these reflections offer powerful insights into the effectiveness of experiential learning.

Nine papers from members of three client teams written in 2006, the earliest available set of reflections, were compared with 18 papers from five teams in the most recent cohort available, 2015. All comments relevant to team dynamics and project planning were highlighted, generating 184 items (an average of 20.4 per student) in 2006 and 227 (an average of 12.6 per student) in 2015. Two of the authors had worked closely with teams in both years, while the third had participated in a capstone project as an MBA student in the program. All comments could thus be interpreted in the context of a specific known client and project.

As noted earlier, the extreme variability across experiential projects and contexts makes generalizations of any kind difficult, but a comparative analysis of their content yields several insights. Comments were first matched for causal or explanatory connections. When a description of events or behavior appeared within a sentence or two of the student's assessment of how or why it occurred, the two comments were coded as a single reflection. Multiple explanatory factors were treated as a single reflective comment. The results of this first sort (see Table 3) suggest that overall mindfulness has increased over the years, with most students now reporting on team processes with attention to causal factors. This does not, in and of itself, indicate accuracy or appropriateness of those factors; items were paired regardless of the causal validity or

Table 3. Percentage of Observations With Explanatory Reflection.

Capstone year	Total behaviors observed	Observations without corresponding reflection	Observations with reflection	Percentage of comments with reflection
2006	99	27	72	72.7
2015	117	13	104	91.5

managerial perspective invoked. However, it would appear that students have become more aware that team-related situations, events, and behaviors can be traced to explanatory factors of some kind.

Comments were then categorized in terms of learning goals. Our primary question was whether students observed team-related issues that were not captured within our assessment rubric. Although the students' vocabulary differed at some points, we found a straightforward correspondence with the top-level learning goals (see Table 4).

The Capstone Experience focuses on the management of team-level functions, but comments were often made about team members' foundational communication skills or group facilitation skills. These were included as aggregate totals, referring almost exclusively to individual or collective task competence (90% of total across both years) or external communication (77% of total across both years), generally involving the client.

We observe variation across skill areas and across years but attribute these to the normal variations across experiential learning contexts. For example, two teams in 2015 found themselves dealing with a member who lacked relevant technical skills, driving a high percentage of comments in that category. Further analysis of the comments will allow faculty to assess instruction and coaching methods relevant to specific rubric elements.

Conclusions and Implications for Pedagogy

Assessment of communication skills in any context is challenging, but the complexity and variability of an experiential learning context adds complications. The systematic use of the learning goals rubric as a guide for reflection should make experiential learning more effective, but objective measures of effectiveness remain elusive. In practice, much reflection occurs during mentoring or coaching conversations, with only a small proportion expressed in written documents that are available for later analysis. Furthermore, learning continues to occur after graduation—sometimes long after graduation—and we expect some lag time between program changes and evidence from alumni or employer reports.

Still, we are confident that systematically incorporating reflection prompts into the assessment process yields both better assessment data and better student learning. We also recognize points where further improvements can be made in both instruction and

Table 4. Reflections on Team Management Skills.

Team-level skills	Percentage of 2006 comments	Percentage of 2015 comments
Goal setting and project scope	14.3	12.2
Project planning and scheduling	14.3	1.6
Resource identification and use	14.3	14.6
Collaborative work methods	9.8	16.3
Internal communication processes	18.8	18.7
Individual foundational skills	8.0	16.3
Individual group facilitation skills	20.5	20.3

assessment of our students' team management skills. In fact, the degree to which we recognize the need for a continuous improvement mind-set draws from our first conclusion.

Conclusions

Closing the loop is an iterative process. On paper, an assessment program typically appears as a single feedback loop. Students score poorly on a goal, and changes are made to instruction, leading to some measurable change. In reality, even the simplest learning scenario involves double-loop learning (Argyris & Schön, 1996), and within the complex contexts of experiential learning, we can expect to find emergent knowledge structures. Self-referential, recursive feedback loops (Hofstadter, 1979, 2007) create small but meaningful cognitive shifts in understanding with each task or assignment repetition.

In practical terms, this means new faculty insights also emerge with each round of assessment, and we must be patient with our search for a seemingly illusory end of the rainbow. In our case, for instance, after a first round of assessment several years ago, faculty focused on skills associated with self-managed teams and sought to align goals and instruction more closely to those specific skills. With the next iteration, students reflected on self-management issues in terms of ethics, which we first assumed to stem from fundamental attribution error. As these topics were more closely parsed during subsequent course instruction and team coaching, however, we suspected individual variations in task competence as the root cause of most team management issues. Principles of internal team dynamics or conflict resolution skills tend to assume a level playing field among equally competent peers. These are not merely self-managed teams; they are also student teams. In a workplace, weak team members might be reassigned or terminated; academic institutions issue lower grades. On our fifth iteration since the review of the team skills learning goal, we find ourselves returning to instructional resources—not for self-managed team techniques, however, but for ways to scaffold academically weak students through the experiential project.

Student reflections offer important insights for the definition and assessment of learning goals. Those who argue for the instructional value of assessment or scoring rubrics

(D. Allen & Tanner, 2006; Panandero & Jonsson, 2013; Reddy & Andrade, 2010; D. D. Stevens & Levi, 2013) suggest designers utilize vocabulary and concepts that reflect student usage and understanding. Rather obviously, student reflections can offer insights into their use of terminology and concepts, but we found them equally useful for understanding student priorities, concerns, and challenges during the experiential learning process. We were correct in our initial assumption that students would each learn something different from the experiential project, but we had not realized there would also be similarity across the diverse contexts.

For us, the key step was mapping student descriptions of their team processes back to the assessment rubric. Outcome assessment had previously been done by reading the final reflection paper as a writing artifact, noting only whether team processes were understood and vocabulary was used appropriately. With a focus on the reflection itself as the assessment artifact, we found ourselves categorizing *all* student ideas. We were gratified to find they did fit within the goals rubric, but we were also able to discern patterns. For instance, all student comments regarding collaborative work processes dealt with just two of the four subgoals, *initial planning* and *decision-making processes*, and we will now parse these topics more fully during instruction and coaching. We expect additional insights to emerge, causing yet another zig in our path toward that pot o' gold, but we look forward to making thoughtful and important adjustments to our team communication learning goal at the next 5-year review.

Reflection prompts offer a tool for the integration of outcomes assessment and student learning. The value of assessment rubrics as instructional tools has been previously noted (Panandero & Jonsson, 2013; Reddy & Andrade, 2010), as has the instructional value of well-timed reflection prompts within experiential learning contexts (Brockbank & McGill, 2007; Kolb, 1984; Mahin & Kruggel, 2006; O'Toole, 2007). Our faith in the value of coordinating the assessment rubric with a reflection prompt appears to have been rewarded, and we remain confident that student learning has been enhanced with the addition of rubric-based reflection prompts.

At a more subtle level, we have also found faculty conversation around both learning goals and student performance has grown richer and more useful. As we interpret student reflections, we find ourselves doing so in terms of specific team members, client situations, and business contexts. Instead of looking at numbers that tell us the proportion of students who seem to understand team management skills, we can see the range of options a specific team had as it dealt with a client's internal politics or a team member's lack of technical skill. Systematic interim reflections have moved the faculty beyond anecdotal conversations about current projects toward our own reflective assessment of the timing and content of our coaching and instruction. Perhaps most intriguingly, assessment that occurs within the single capstone course has become interesting enough to spark conversation among all faculty in the program, leading to both better coaching within that culminating experience and better instructional preparation in the prerequisite courses.

Qualitative, formative data offer rich insights. Like many faculty, we have favored quantitative data in our assessment methods, both for its convenience in data collection and reporting, and for its promise of generalizable results. We began, as this article does, with the recognition that variable contexts make outcomes assessment difficult within experiential learning events, but we understood summative, quantitative assessment data as an unmet ideal. We were willing to assume that learning was taking place, even though we could not hope to measure it directly.

Implications for Pedagogy

As so many qualitative scholars will attest, convenience and generalizability offer no inherent advantage over systematic immersion in the data and richly detailed understanding of the idiosyncratic workings of specific projects and project teams. The key seems to lie in the quality of the underlying data. Having moved from ad hoc, oral, anecdotal conversation to systematic, carefully timed, and thoughtfully aimed reflection prompts, we are building a grounded theory of our own instructional processes and student outcomes.

The actual steps of integrating reflections with assessment are deceptively simple: create simple prompts that utilize learning outcomes goals and vocabulary, administer them at points in the experiential learning process in which the use of the targeted skills might be expected, and systematically analyze the results in terms of the assessment rubric. The results have been powerful, leading to instructional changes that give more than lip service about closing the loop.

Furthermore, the elements involved in assessing the outcomes within an experiential learning context seem to offer promise for other applications. Service learning, increasingly popular as a mechanism for engaging students in their educational process, is similarly context specific and often experiential in design. Learning goals that include subjective and idiosyncratic applications, such as critical thinking, creativity, and interpersonal communication, are similarly difficult to standardize for quantitative assessment. Learning in general, when understood as a cycle of activity, reflection, integration, and application, might be usefully assessed with attention to students' subjective reflections on their own process.

Finally, as management faculty, we have recognized some of our own assessment biases as a broader bias toward objectivist managerial practice. Our learning goals assume the successful graduate of an MBA program will possess the capacity to diagnose and fix problems faced by his or her team-based reports. Drawing from a tool kit of communication principles, team practices, and established intervention points, the skilled manager would assess the situation and administer successful coaching and instruction. We now approach our own interventions as formative assessment, recognizing the team's reflection process as an essential element of its own identity as a team; stepping in to fix a team destroys the team. Objectivist management traditions face the same challenge within any complex learning organization (Clippinger, 1999; Gharajedaghi, 1999; Stacey, Griffin, & Shaw, 2000). An iterated, multiple-loop assessment process never closes; the reflection raises new questions and leads to new knowledge with which to revise the learning goals themselves.

Appendix A

Team Skills Self-Assessment and Planning Tool

Now that you have completed a team project, review the rubric of targeted team skills. Remember, the goal is for you to be a mindful and objective manager of team processes. You do not gain anything by inflating your own scores; you do gain a great deal by dispassionately assessing all aspects of a team's performance, including your own participation.

This sheet will be returned to you as you begin the MBA Capstone Experience. At that point, it will function as a planning tool for your learning within that team environment.

Name:

Individual Communication Skills	Had no clue	Highly proficient
Able to converse clearly and effectively in a group.	0......1.......2....3.......4.......5.......6........7	
Able to complete tasks with high quality, timeliness, and anticipation of others' needs and abilities.	0......1.......2....3.......4.......5.......6........7	
Knowledgeable about all aspects of the project.	0......1.......2....3.......4.......5.......6........7	
Effective leadership and conflict resolution skills.	0......1.......2....3.......4.......5.......6........7	
Aware of and responsive to group norms.	0......1.......2....3.......4.......5.......6........7	
Individual Facilitation Skills	Had no clue	Highly proficient
Skillful use of various communication technologies to facilitate group productivity.	0......1.......2....3.......4.......5.......6........7	
Understands and uses proactive conflict prevention strategies.	0......1.......2....3.......4.......5.......6........7	
Proactive networking activities to facilitate external communication and resources.	0......1.......2....3.......4.......5.......6........7	
Uses leadership skills to facilitate group's ability to meet goals.	0......1.......2....3.......4.......5.......6........7	
Group-Level Project Management Skills		
These are, by definition, collaborative tasks. The question is how well the team actually did, not how well you think you could have done as an individual.	Had no clue	Highly proficient
Goal development processes to accommodate all stakeholders and serve multiple purposes.	0......1.......2....3.......4.......5.......6........7	

(continued)

Appendix A (continued)

Task identification accurately represents and facilitates multiple and multistep group goals.	0......1.......2....3.......4.......5.......6........7
Effective and efficient use of resources to meet team goals.	0......1.......2....3.......4.......5.......6........7
Effective use of team development techniques to maximize team efficiency in meeting goals.	0......1.......2....3.......4.......5.......6........7
Effective and efficient use of appropriate communication processes.	0......1.......2....3.......4.......5.......6........7

Appendix B

Team Management Self-Assessment

1. Rate your familiarity with the individual communication skills that affect an employee's success within a collaborative work team (i.e., conversational skills, technical task competence, engagement, etc.).

☐	☐	☐	☐	☐
no clue what is involved	know the words but not the skills	I can do these things myself	know goal but not how to coach a team	confident in how to coach reports

2. Rate your familiarity with the individual communication skills involved in effectively facilitating team tasks and processes: (i.e., meeting facilitation, external communication, communication technology, etc.).

☐	☐	☐	☐	☐
no clue what is involved	know the words but not the skills	I can do these things myself	know goal but not how to coach a team	confident in how to coach reports

3. Rate your familiarity with the team functions that must be collaboratively accomplished within a productive work team: (i.e., goal identification, task planning, resource allocation, decision-making, etc.).

☐	☐	☐	☐	☐
no clue what is involved	know the words but not the skills	I can do these things myself	know goal but not how to coach a team	confident in how to coach reports

4. To what extent have the self-managed teams in your MBA courses been *well-managed*? (Do not consider dyads or work supervised directly by the instructor, assigned or external leader.)

☐	☐	☐	☐	☐
not at all	few, unsuccessful attempts	we tried, with limited success	generally effective with some lapses	excellent results

5. What problem-solving methods (if any) have you found to be particularly effective or ineffective within MBA teams?
6. What decision-making methods (if any) have you found to be particularly effective or ineffective within MBA teams?
7. What collaborative work methods (if any) have you found to be particularly effective or ineffective within MBA teams?

Appendix C

If you were your team's manager . . .

Having worked together for more than two months, you should "take stock" of your own performance as a team. This is the time to make any needed changes in your internal processes and procedures to ensure timely completion of your Capstone project.

Rate your own team's effectiveness in five categories of project management.

Team proposed a project to meet Capstone Experience goals.			
☐ Acted without concern for organizational and stakeholder goals.	☐ Set general goals but failed to clarify some elements with organizational or external stakeholders.	☐ Appropriate and complete goals were set with attention to all external and organizational goals.	☐ Team negotiated goals to accommodate diverse or conflicting stakeholder interests.
☐ Acted without identifying overall team objectives.	☐ Set overall team objectives without clarifying all steps to reach those goals.	☐ Project plan included complete and relevant subgoals for the project to support project goals.	☐ Project plan involved creative development of subgoals to serve multiple purposes.
☐ Acted without clarifying project scope and constraints.	☐ Project scope is not completely supportive of overall team goals.	☐ Project scope is clearly supportive of team goals.	☐ Project scope included multiple stages or contingency plans to accommodate conflicting or complex goals.

If you were this team's manager, what advice would you give the team to improve its collective goal setting and project-scoping processes?

(continued)

Appendix C (continued)

Team created a work plan to accomplish the proposed project.

☐ Team did not prepare a task-level work plan.	☐ Task-level work plan is incomplete or inconsistent with team goals.	☐ Team's task-level work plan supports project goals.	☐ Team created a sophisticated or complex work plan to support multiple goals or interests.
☐ Team did not define clear objective deliverables.	☐ Deliverables are vaguely defined, incomplete, or inconsistent with team goals.	☐ Team identified appropriate deliverables.	☐ Team project required multistage or complex deliverables.
☐ Team did not develop clear benchmarks for tracking progress.	☐ Project benchmarks are incomplete or inappropriate.	☐ Team identified and used appropriate benchmarks.	☐ Team developed unique or creative benchmarks to effectively manage a complex project.
☐ Team did not develop clear metrics of success.	☐ Completion and success metrics are incomplete or inconsistent with team goals.	☐ Team identified and used appropriate metrics of completion and success.	☐ Team developed unique or creative metrics to determine completion or success in a complex project.

If you were this team's manager, what advice would you give the team to improve its collective project-planning processes?

Team is utilizing its internal and external resources efficiently.

☐ Team failed to meet project milestones, produce deliverables as agreed, or produce an outcome that met specifications.	☐ Team met project milestones but used excessive resources, failed to maximize team abilities, or failed to meet specifications in quality, quantity, timeliness, or cost.	☐ Team completed project milestones effectively, meeting all specifications in quality, quantity, timeliness, and cost.	☐ Team efficiently met milestones while exceeding expectations with respect to quality, quantity, timeliness, and cost.
☐ Team was unable to identify sufficient resources to meet its goals.	☐ Team did not adequately define and utilize necessary resources.	☐ Team identified and utilized resources to accomplish goals efficiently.	☐ Team utilized fewer resources than expected or leveraged them for outstanding results.
☐ Team did not schedule all tasks necessary for meeting its goals.	☐ Project scheduling was generally inadequate, with tasks inequitably distributed over the project period.	☐ Project schedules were accurately planned and executed as planned.	☐ Project schedules included sufficient slack to meet contingencies or exceed expectations.

If you were this team's manager, what advice would you give the team to improve its collective resource planning processes?

(continued)

Appendix C (continued)

Team is working collaboratively.

☐ Team engaged in internal or external conflict over procedures or work organization.	☐ Team procedures were not clearly predetermined; team engaged in ad hoc work assignments.	☐ Effective work procedures were determined prior to the start of the project.	☐ Effective work procedures had a significant positive impact on project outcome.
☐ Team member roles/tasks as defined or allocated were inappropriate for skill sets or work styles of individuals.	☐ Team member roles/tasks were not clearly defined or allocated.	☐ Team member roles/tasks were reasonably defined and allocated.	☐ Team roles and tasks were effectively reassigned to meet changing project requirements.
☐ Work plan was clearly unfair or inappropriate to team resources.	☐ Work distribution was unreasonable or unfairly distributed among team members.	☐ Project scheduling was appropriate, with tasks fairly distributed over the project period.	☐ Project schedule was effectively revised to meet changing project requirements.
☐ Decision-making processes were not determined prior to project start.	☐ Decision-making processes were inadequate for project requirements.	☐ Decision-making processes were effective and appropriate to project needs.	☐ Team engaged in creative or sophisticated decision-making to accommodate team diversity or project. requirements.

If you were this team's manager, what advice would you give the team to improve its collaborative work processes?

Internal communication processes.

☐ Team failed to plan communication events to support team goals.	☐ Team failed to consistently plan or use appropriate project management communication.	☐ Team planned communication that was appropriate and effective in meeting project goals.	☐ Team effectively accommodated unplanned communication requirements over the course of the project.
☐ Team meetings were unplanned, undocumented, or not effectively facilitated.	☐ Meeting facilitation was inadequate to ensure planned communication met goals.	☐ Team efficiently facilitated meetings, information systems, and other communication practices to effectively meet team goals.	☐ Team devised efficient methods to facilitate unfamiliar or unplanned communication needs.

(continued)

Appendix C (continued)

Internal communication processes.

☐ Project documentation was inadequate.	☐ Project or meeting documentation was sufficiently incomplete, late, or inappropriate to negatively impact project success.	☐ Team created meeting and project documentation that supported team requirements.	☐ Team created sophisticated or highly effective documents to support difficult, changing, or complex project requirements.

If you were this team's manager, what advice would you give the team to improve its internal communication processes?

Is there any other advice you'd like to give yourselves that is **not** covered in one of the categories above?

Appendix D

Midpoint Turnaround Reflection

*Complete and return a TEAM response before or at your ETS exam on **May 5**.*

1. Research shows that project teams will usually undergo a "major" upheaval at the midpoint of a project. This might be triggered by external factors (poor outcomes, missed deadlines, major holidays, etc.) or by internal factors (processes are not working, individuals are unwilling to continue dealing with problems, a person quits the company, etc.). Not all events are negative, although negative events will be the more obvious triggers. As a result, the team makes major changes in goals and/or processes to "solve" the problem and presumably achieve better outcomes (e.g., change meeting processes, hire a resource, etc.).

For Capstone teams, the trigger point is often the end of Mod. 3 classes. This is perceived as a transition point, which can be motivating ("Hey, let's finally get organized!") or simply a "natural" point to take stock, either as individuals or as a team. Your own team might have been triggered a little earlier for other reasons.

Summarize any "major" upheaval your team has experienced, including the timing, the trigger, and the changes you have made as a team.

2. Based on final reflections provided by 10+ years of Capstone teams, these areas cause the most problems for teams:
    *   One or more team members lacked technical skills to accomplish an assigned task, which was either discovered too late or ignored.

- One or more team members took time at the end of Mod. 3 for travel, family visits, or catching up on work, and the team had either failed to create a detailed work plan in the first place or failed to realize how much time would be needed to do the project.
- Teams failed to deal with internal problems (including but not limited to skills or the May hole) or conceptual problems (generally involving a failure by one or more members to grasp the overall project strategy) until too late. The "too late" moment seems to be the MOU. If your MOU is done, and you haven't yet had a team upheaval, you might want to take stock anyway.

Summarize your team's status with respect to (a) technical skills available to do the planned analysis, (b) planned or unplanned "time off" the project for any reason, and (c) anything else you see lurking on the horizon that warrants "taking stock."

[Use more space as needed, but this is not meant to be a lengthy document.]

Authors' Note

Preliminary results of the research reported here were presented at the annual convention of the National Communication Association, Assessment Division, Chicago, IL, USA, 2014.

Declaration of Conflicting Interests

The author(s) declared no potential conflicts of interest with respect to the research, authorship, and/or publication of this article.

Funding

The author(s) received no financial support for the research, authorship, and/or publication of this article.

Note

1. Scheduled as the final course in the MBA program, the Capstone Experience involves self-managed consulting. Specific client needs vary, but teams are required to determine the strategic issues involved, conduct both secondary and primary research, analyze the results, and make a recommendation to the client. Each team works with a graduate faculty mentor with expertise in the client's industry or the functional area of focus, but the teams have access to the expertise and resources of the entire college faculty, including the business and community outreach division's resources for entrepreneurship, intellectual property, market research, and economic development professionals. The teams meet together several times with the capstone coordinator, a faculty member in business communication. The students share experiences; report on key milestone documents (project proposal, memo of understanding with the client, industry analysis, and methodology plan); discuss the managerial applications

of written, presentational, interpersonal, and team communication; and rehearse the formal presentations (project proposal and final recommendation) to the MBA faculty. Managerial writing, persuasion, team facilitation, communication operations, and crisis communication, previously offered as separate courses in the MBA curriculum, are developed and coached within the authentic managerial context of the Capstone Experience consulting project.

References

Allen, D., & Tanner, K. (2006). Rubrics: Tools for making learning goals and evaluation criteria explicit for both teachers and learners. *CBE–Life Sciences Education, 5*, 197-203.

Allen, M. W., & Brady, R. M. (1997). Total quality management, organizational commitment, perceived organizational support, and intraorganizational communication. *Management Communication Quarterly, 10*, 316-341.

Argyris, C., & Schön, D. A. (1996). *Organizational learning II: Theory, method, and practice.* Reading, MA: Addison-Wesley.

Bogert, J., & Butt, D. (1996). Communication instruction in MBA programs: A survey of syllabi. *Business Communication Quarterly, 59*(2), 20-44.

Brockbank, A., & McGill, I. (2007). *Facilitating reflective learning in higher education* (2nd ed.). Maidenhead, England: Open University Press.

Brzovic, K., & Matz, S. I. (2009). Students advise Fortune 500 company: Designing a problem-based learning community. *Business Communication Quarterly, 72*, 21-34.

Bush-Bacelis, J. L. (1998). Innovative pedagogy: Academic service-learning for business communication. *Business Communication Quarterly, 61*(3), 20-34.

Clippinger, J. H., III. (1999). Order from the bottom up: Complex adaptive systems and their management. In J. H. Clippinger III (Ed.), *The biology of business: Decoding the natural laws of enterprise* (pp. 1-30). San Francisco, CA: Jossey-Bass.

Cyphert, D. (2002). Integrating communication across the MBA curriculum. *Business Communication Quarterly, 10*(3), 81-86.

Cyphert, D. (2006). Real clients, real management, real failure: The risks and rewards of service learning. *Business Communication Quarterly, 69*, 185-189. doi:10.1177/1080569906069002 07

Dillon, M., McCaskey, P., & Blazer, E. (2011). MBA internships: More important than ever. *Journal of Education for Business, 86*, 44-49. doi:10.1080/08832321003774764

Drehmer, D. E., Belohlav, J. A., & Coye, R. W. (2000). An exploration of employee participation using a scaling approach. *Group & Organization Management, 25*, 397-418.

Gharajedaghi, J. (1999). *Systems thinking: Managing chaos and complexity: A platform for designing business architecture.* Boston, MA: Butterworth-Heinemann.

Glazer, E. (2010, September 2). At some companies, students are teaching. *The Wall Street Journal.* Retrieved from http://online.wsj.com/article/SB10001424052748703467004575463931414473468.html

Hackman, J. R., & Wageman, R. (2005). A theory of team coaching. *Academy of Management Review, 30*, 269-287.

Hansen, R. S. (2006). Benefits and problems with student teams: Suggestions for improving team projects. *Journal of Education for Business, 82*, 11-19.

Hartenian, L. S. (2003). Team member acquisition of team knowledge, skills, and abilities. *Team Performance Management, 9*, 23-30.

Hatton, N., & Smith, D. (1995). Reflection in teacher education: Towards definition and implementation. *Teaching and Teacher Education, 11*, 33-49.

Hofstadter, D. R. (1979). *Gödel, Escher, Bach: An eternal golden braid*. New York, NY: Basic Books.

Hofstadter, D. R. (2007). *I am a strange loop*. New York, NY: Basic Books.

Hoover, J. D., Giambatista, R. C., Sorenson, R. L., & Bommer, W. H. (2010). Assessing the effectiveness of whole person learning pedagogy in skill acquisition. *Academy of Management Learning & Education, 9*, 192-203.

Hunt, J. G., & Sorenson, R. L. (2001). A learned-behavior approach to management skill development. *Journal of Management Education, 25*, 167-190.

Judge, T. M. (2006). Service learning on campus. *Business Communication Quarterly, 69*, 189-192. doi:10.1177/108056990606900208

Kolb, D. A. (1984). *Experiential learning: Experience as the source of learning and development*. Englewood Cliffs, NJ: Prentice Hall.

Littlefield, H. (2006). Service learning in business communication: Real-world challenges develop real-world skills. *Business Communication Quarterly, 69*, 319-322.

Mahin, L., & Kruggel, T. G. (2006). Facilitation and assessment of student learning in business communication. *Business Communication Quarterly, 69*, 323-327.

Mayo, M., Kakarika, M., Pastor, J. C., & Brutus, S. (2012). Aligning or inflating your leadership self-image? A longitudinal study of responses to peer feedback in MBA teams. *Academy of Management Learning & Education, 11*, 631-652.

Moon, J. A. (2004). *A handbook of reflective and experiential learning: Theory and practice*. New York, NY: RoutledgeFalmer.

National Association of Colleges and Employers. (2012, October 24). *The skills and qualities employers want in their Class of 2013 recruits*. Retrieved from https://www. roanestate.edu/webfolders/HARRISKB/placement/articles/students/The_Skills_and_ Qualities_Employers_Want_in_Their_Class_of_2013_Recruits.pdf

Navarro, P. (2008). The MBA core curricula of top-ranked U.S. business schools: A study in failure? *Academy of Management Learning & Education, 7*, 108-123.

O'Toole, K. (2007). Assessment in experiential learning. *Education Research and Perspectives, 34*(2), 51-62.

Panandero, E., & Jonsson, A. (2013). The use of scoring rubrics for formative assessment purposes revisited: A review. *Educational Research Review, 9*, 129-144. doi:10.1016/j. edurev.2013.01.002

Qualters, D. M. (2010). Bringing the outside in: Assessing experiential education. *New Directions for Teaching and Learning, 2010*(124), 55-62.

Reddy, Y. M., & Andrade, H. (2010). A review of rubric use in higher education. *Assessment & Evaluation in Higher Education, 35*, 435-448. doi:10.1080/02602930902862859

Roberson, Q. M., & Williamson, I. O. (2012). Justice in self-managing teams: The role of social networks in the emergence of procedural justice climates. *Academy of Management Journal, 55*, 685-701.

Saunders, P. M. (1997). Experiential learning, cases, and simulations in business communication. *Business Communication Quarterly, 60*(1), 97-114.

Sigmar, L. S., Hynes, G. E., & Hill, K. L. (2012). Strategies for teaching social and emotional intelligence in business communication. *Business Communication Quarterly, 75*, 301-317. doi:10.1177/1080569912450312

Stacey, R. D., Griffin, D., & Shaw, P. (2000). *Complexity and management: Fad or radical challenge to systems thinking?* New York, NY: Routledge.

Stevens, D. D., & Levi, A. J. (2013). *Introduction to rubrics: An assessment tool to save grading time, convey effective feedback, and promote student learning* (2nd ed.). Sterling, VA: Stylus.

Stevens, M. J., & Campion, M. A. (1994). The knowledge, skill, and ability requirements for teamwork: Implications for human resource management. *Journal of Management, 20*, 503-530.

Terziovski, M. (2002). Differentiators between high and low performing manufacturing firms: An empirical study. *International Journal of Manufacturing Technology and Management, 4*, 356-371.

Vik, G. N. (2001). Doing more to teach teamwork than telling students to sink or swim. *Business Communication Quarterly, 64*(4), 112-119.

Wilson, L. K. (2011). *MBA program self-study*. Cedar Falls, IA: College of Business Administration, University of Northern Iowa.

Worley, R. B., & Dyrud, M. A. (2001). Managing student groups. *Business Communication Quarterly, 64*(4), 105-106.

Yeatts, D. E., & Hyten, C. (1998). *High-performing self-managed work teams: A comparison of theory to practice*. Thousand Oaks, CA: Sage.

Young, C. B., & Henquit, J. A. (2000). Viewpoint: A conceptual framework for designing group projects. *Journal of Education for Business, 76*, 56-60.

Author Biographies

Dale Cyphert is an associate professor of management at the University of Northern Iowa. She coordinates the Capstone Experience in the MBA program, works with the College of Business Administration's Professional Readiness Program, and teaches undergraduate courses in business communication.

Elena Nefedova Dodge is an assessment specialist for the College of Business Administration, University of Northern Iowa, administering assessment of student learning for curriculum management at graduate and undergraduate levels. She researches academic engagement and learning of students of diverse cultural backgrounds.

Leslie K. Duclos (Wilson) is a professor of management and the Dean of the College of Business Administration at the University of Northern Iowa. Formerly, she served as the MBA program director and provided leadership in learning assurance in the MBA program.

Working better together? Empowerment, Panopticon and Conflict Approaches to Teamwork

Crowley, M., Payne, J.C. and Kennedy, E.

Abstract

Scholars often offer competing accounts of the consequences of workplace teams. Researchers in the *empowerment* tradition describe autonomy in teams as generating satisfaction and pro-social behaviors. The *panopticon* approach emphasizes the disciplinary aspect of teamwork – arguing that peer monitoring elicits intense effort and discourages resistance through visibility and normative control. The *conflict* school highlights variation in experiences of and responses to teamwork, calling particular attention to worker resistance. This study uses mixed methods to investigate these perspectives simultaneously, analyzing content-coded data on 204 work groups. Though evidence supports both empowerment and panopticon theories, especially when used in combination, the conflict perspective emerges as pivotal to understanding not only worker resistance but also consent to empowerment and even panoptic control.

Keywords

Autonomy, citizenship, collective action conflict, empowerment, job satisfaction, panopticon, sabotage, team management, teams, teamwork

Introduction

For a quarter century, scholars have investigated how participation in workplace teams influences worker experiences and behavior – offering different and sometimes competing accounts based on disciplinary emphasis and points of view. Rooted primarily in the human relations approach, the *empowerment* perspective explores use of teams to solve managerial challenges related to inflexibility, turnover and collective action – making the case that opportunity to exercise discretion in teams enhances satisfaction, promotes

Corresponding author:
Martha Crowley, Department of Sociology and Anthropology, North Carolina State University, Campus Box 8107, Raleigh, NC 27695-8107, USA.
Email: martha_crowley@ncsu.edu

effort and weakens the impulse to resist (Appelbaum et al., 2000; Hodson, 2001). The panopticon approach draws on postmodern Foucauldian (1977) notions of power and control, arguing that task-group self-monitoring promotes peer discipline and internalization of production norms, thereby limiting solidarity necessary for collective action and opportunities to engage in sabotage (Barker, 1993; Sewell, 1998).[1] Like the panopticon tradition, the *conflict* perspective has foundations in critical sociology, but assumes that managers lack the totalizing power assumed in many panoptic accounts. Rooted in Marxist-oriented understandings of the labor process, this approach emphasizes varied implementation of teams and workers' resistance to arrangements that fail to meet their needs and/or expectations (Ezzamel et al., 2001; Vallas, 2003a; Vidal, 2007a).

With the exception of a few studies, primarily in the empowerment tradition, much research on teamwork is based on qualitative case studies that provide rich accounts of work sites and illustrations of particular theoretical paradigms, but are not conducive to evaluating the range of theoretical perspectives side-by-side (but see Niemelä and Kalliola, 2007). This study uses content-coded data on 204 work groups to investigate how teamwork influences worker citizenship, sabotage and collective action through mediators specified in the three paradigms: job satisfaction, co-worker estrangement and conflict with management. Quantitative analyses based on ordinal and ordinary least squares (OLS) regression confirm expectations associated with the empowerment perspective, which also emerges as important for explaining reductions in sabotage usually highlighted by the panopticon approach. Conflict theory not only receives support in the quantitative models, but likewise proves immensely important in the second phase of our analysis, wherein we return to the qualitative case studies to explore processes not easily discernible from the quantitative data. This 'reimmersion' in the text (see Roscigno et al., 2009) reveals a pervasive pattern whereby workers evaluate and respond to teamwork on the basis of explicit comparisons to experiences and perceptions of work in other times/places. Consistent with the conflict perspective, these contrasts suggest that workers perceive most employment options as alienating and oppressive, and respond favorably to teamwork largely because it appears comparatively humane. We conclude that an expanded emphasis on worker agency and its diverse influences, including perceptions of opportunities available to working people in general, is necessary to understand not only resistance to teamwork as emphasized in the conflict approach, but also consent to empowerment and/or panoptic control.

Theoretical perspectives on teamwork

Across the occupational spectrum, teamwork has become an increasingly important aspect of work organization. Long a part of work in craft manual environments, teamwork expanded rapidly into other manual sectors as firms replicated practices associated with Japanese firms' mounting success in an expanding global market (Piore and Sabel, 1984; Womack et al., 1990). In manual production, small groups of workers with bounded decision-making authority and flattened hierarchies help firms adapt to rapidly shifting markets and consumer tastes (Cappelli et al., 1997). Teamwork has also emerged as increasingly important in white-collar work, where it promotes creativity, effort and normative control (Crowley et al., 2010; Kunda, 2006; Sennett, 1998). Scholars have devoted a great deal of attention to what these shifts mean for workers and firms. Although their explanations overlap to some degree, those in the empowerment, panopticon and conflict traditions highlight different forms, functions and impacts of teamwork, depending on disciplinary origins and points of view.

Empowerment in teams

Most commonly associated with the human relations approach to management, the empowerment perspective regards teamwork as a managerial strategy aimed at solving problems of inflexibility and resistance associated with reliance on more coercive control (Pruijt, 2003; Womack et al., 1990). Opportunities for bounded autonomy communicate to workers that the firm values employees and their contributions (Friedman, 1977). Research in this tradition highlights how discretion in teams enhances workers' daily satisfactions, fostering a sense of trust, fairness and reciprocity that enhances commitment to employers (Appelbaum et al., 2000; Batt, 2004; Batt and Appelbaum, 1995). These in turn promote pro-social behaviors at work including cooperation and effort (Cappelli and Rogovsky, 1998; Huselid, 1995).

According to Paul Adler (1995: 218), worker empowerment requires managers to relinquish some of their own authority to gain control overall: 'the loss of management's *power over* workers seems to be more than compensated by the competitive benefits of the associated increases in the organization's *power to* accomplish its goals' (emphasis in original). Indeed, the positive impacts of team participation are in part realized through reduced reliance on hierarchical controls known to impinge upon worker dignity (Hodson, 2001; Pruijt, 2003; Shaiken et al., 1997). Firms that go much further – expanding the scope of efficacious action beyond the bounds of the immediate work group – may secure even greater consent by shifting loyalties from the work group to the organization as a whole (Gecas and Schwalbe, 1983).

Teamwork as panopticon

Rooted in postmodern Foucauldian (1977) notions of discipline, the panopticon approach regards teamwork as a managerial strategy intended to increase effort and deter sabotage through heightened visibility and normative control. The panopticon, a penitentiary plan designed by Jeremy Bentham in the late 1700s, serves as a metaphor for how this is accomplished. In it, a circular cell structure allows unseen guards to view the activities of prisoners from a central observation tower through one-way backlit windows. Visibility presents a continuous threat of discipline for malfeasance, thus encouraging prisoners to internalize regulations and police their own behavior.

The panopticon perspective applies Foucault's metaphor to workplaces, arguing that firms install teams in ways that promote peer surveillance – thus heightening visibility, peer discipline and internalization of work rules while eroding solidarity necessary for collective action (Sewell, 1998). Many firms link pay and bonuses to group output, encouraging workers to monitor and discipline one another on the basis of productivity, and/or augment normative control with organizational cultures emphasizing peer accountability (Casey, 1999; Fernie and Metcalf, 1998; Townsend, 2007; Van den Broek et al., 2004). Workers deemed as failing to keep pace are targeted for formal or informal group discipline, motivating them to meet or exceed team expectations (Barker, 1993; Collins, 2001).

Similar to the empowerment perspective, research in the panopticon tradition posits that teams increase work effort, but primarily through visibility and normative control (Barker, 1993; Kunda, 2006). Whereas empowerment scholars regard worker autonomy as essential to the successful operation of teams, researchers in the panopticon tradition contend that managers rarely relinquish it (see Townsend, 2007; Van den Broek et al., 2004); indeed, teamwork may result in even greater restrictions on workers. The panopticon approach also differs from the empowerment perspective in that it places much greater emphasis on use of teams to deter sabotage and collective action (see especially Sewell and Wilkinson, 1992).

Although firms structure the overall functions of teams to profit from an increasingly intense work pace, managerial control nevertheless recedes into the background – obscured by new work roles and a discourse that denies responsibility for organizational arrangements (Kraft, 1999). According to some, workers themselves become the 'bearers' of control – the face of oppression and constraint (Kunda, 2006; Sewell and Wilkinson, 1992). If so, the workplace panopticon exceeds Bentham's prison in terms of effectiveness and sophistication; whereas Foucault imagined prisoners internalizing control in response to the ever-present possibility of surveillance by unseen guards, the workplace panopticon exposes workers to a more diffuse threat seemingly removed from authority within the organization.

The conflict approach

In contrast to the empowerment and panopticon perspectives, which emphasize managerial perspectives and strategy, respectively, the conflict approach calls attention to how worker agency shapes teamwork on the shop floor. Rooted in labor process research and thus Marxist perspectives on work, this approach situates teamwork in the context of ongoing class conflict – placing workers, their varied responses to teams, and especially resistance to participative regimes at the center of analysis (Edwards, 1979; Knights and McCabe, 1998; Thompson and Ackroyd, 1995; Vallas, 2003a; Vidal, 2007a). Rather than assuming workers will uniformly respond to teamwork as management intends, conflict scholars contend that worker sentiments and behaviors depend on team implementation and social context.

Research in the conflict tradition emphasizes processes underlying changing work organization and employees' responses – underscoring the influence of both local and macro political, economic, historical and industrial contexts (Thomas, 1994; Vidal, 2007b, 2010; Weeks, 2004). Such contexts form a milieu that can support or undermine the realization of teamwork as envisioned by scholars in the empowerment and panopticon perspectives. For instance, a legacy of Taylorist and Fordist management practices runs counter to entrusting workers with decision-making, which is crucial to effective teamworking (Niemelä and Kalliola, 2007). Even good-faith efforts to install participative teams may fail due to inertia and a legacy of top-down control, since flexible practices are superimposed onto arrangements organized around rationalized procedures and hierarchy (Vallas, 1999). Context helps explain why many ethnographic accounts reveal 'teams without teamwork' – superficial or rhetorical team initiatives, lacking any indication of actual workplace transformation (Townsend, 2007; Van den Broek et al., 2004).

Employee responses in turn vary with implementation and individual preferences. Many workers – especially those who have long desired greater 'say' in production – embrace opportunities to express ideas and make decisions on-the-job; those preferring predictability and routine, however, can become frustrated with the added responsibility, stress and disorder that sometimes accompany participative arrangements (Bélanger et al., 2003; Townsend, 2007; Vidal, 2007a). In some cases, employees embrace the idea of empowerment or self-management, but become frustrated with the realities of teamwork as implemented in their workplaces (Stewart et al., 2009; Vallas, 2003b). Likewise, some work groups enthusiastically embrace peer monitoring roles, even using them to 'tighten the iron cage' of bureaucratic control (see Barker, 1993), while others, especially those who are skeptical of managerial ends, reject such changes (Stewart et al., 2009). Unwanted efforts to introduce these controls have been met with sustained sabotage, as workers refused to participate in the introduction of teams, rejected management's appeal to their interest in autonomy and engaged in overt subversion of managerial authority (Ezzamel and Willmott, 1998; Ezzamel et al., 2001).

Furthermore, implementation and workers' responses may change over time. For example, Mexican garment workers in newly organized teams willingly consented to intensification because they believed their interests were bound with those of management. However, when layoffs called into question the normative foundations of this 'community of fate', it collapsed into widespread resistance including slowdowns, walkouts and sabotage (Plankey Videla, 2006). Similarly, Graham (1995) describes how workers initially enthusiastic about workplace transformations ultimately used teams and empowerment rhetoric as a vehicle for undermining managerial control and resisting work intensification. Such evolving worker responses to teamwork likely reflect the tendency of anti-Taylorist team initiatives to devolve into neo-Taylorist practices (Pruijt, 2003; see also Crowley et al., 2010).

Summary and hypotheses

In sum, the perspectives outlined above offer overlapping, but distinct and sometimes competing explanations regarding the impact of teams on job satisfaction, workplace relationships and worker behavior. The empowerment perspective emphasizes teamwork's capacity to enhance effort through opportunities for autonomy and intrinsic rewards. According to this approach, autonomy in teams should increase satisfaction with positive implications for worker citizenship. Autonomy may also hedge against collective action and sabotage since it fosters psychological rewards and facilitates understanding of constraints faced by management (Smith, 1996, 1997, 2001; Snape and Redman, 2010). Some scholars in this tradition have also suggested that self-monitoring teams enhance workplace dignity by reducing reliance on more demeaning controls (Hodson, 2001). If this is the case, teamwork may increase satisfaction and/or reduce conflict with management.

The panopticon approach characterizes teamwork as a means of increasing effort and limiting sabotage and collective action, but through processes associated with peer monitoring and co-worker estrangement rather than autonomy and intrinsic rewards. According to this perspective, teamwork entails peer monitoring that lateralizes conflict – estranging workers from their peers while limiting conflict with management. These relationships should in turn increase citizenship and limit sabotage and collective action.

Like the empowerment and panopticon approaches, the conflict perspective has often highlighted how levels of autonomy, fulfillment and solidarity relate to both consent and resistance. However, the conflict perspective diverges from these traditions in that it considers political, economic, historical and industrial contexts as constraining both employers' ability to effectively implement idealized forms of teamwork and also worker responses to it. When successful, teams may indeed yield the benefits specified by the empowerment perspective. Notably, the conflict approach also suggests that incomplete workplace transformations engender mistrust of and conflict with management, eroding consent and encouraging resistance.

Data and measures

We evaluate our hypotheses using content-coded data on 204 work groups derived from the population of English-language workplace ethnographies. These data, collection of which was orchestrated by Randy Hodson, offer detailed information on a range of work-related attributes (organizational characteristics, work arrangements, worker sentiments, behaviors and relationships) for hundreds of work groups (individuals doing the same job in a single work organization) across a broad array of industries and occupations (Hodson et al., 2011; see Gamson, 1975 and www.yale.edu/hraf/index.html for similar approaches to aggregating qualitative data on social movement histories and cultures, respectively). Although the data do not reflect a random sample of work groups, they offer variation needed to analyze relationships among workplace characteristics, including complex/ nuanced phenomena difficult to capture and thus not typically reported surveys or other quantitative data sources. Coding of ethnographies inevitably results in loss of information, especially connections to localized meanings. However, aggregation widens the scope of analysis allowing for detection of patterns across cases – helping to offset these losses. Furthermore, 'reimmersion' in the ethnographic sources allows researchers using these data to zoom in on particular settings for inductive reasoning valuable for illuminating processes, anomalies and patterns not readily evident in the quantitative data (see Roscigno et al., 2009). The coding project (described in detail at www.sociology. ohiostate.edu/rdh/ Workplace-Ethnography-Project.html), proceeded in three stages: (1) selection of workplace ethnographies to be coded, (2) preparation of the instrument and (3) coding of cases.

Selection of cases

Roughly 800 books were identified for potential inclusion in the coding project via electronic and physical search of libraries, archival research and examination of bibliographies in books already selected for review. Texts lacking sufficient length or detail to code variables pertaining to the organization and experience of work for at least one

Table 1. Industrial and occupational locus of organizational ethnographies (*N* = 204).

	%
Industry	
Extractive and construction	5.9
Nondurable manufacturing	19.7
Durable and electronic manufacturing	12.8
Transportation equipment	8.4
Transportation, communication and utilities	8.9
Wholesale and retail trade	10.8
Finance, insurance, real estate and business services	8.4
Personal services	6.4
Professional and related services	14.8
Public administration	3.9
Occupation	
Professional	21.1
Managerial	7.8
Clerical	5.9
Sales	3.4
Skilled trade	9.8
Assembly	27.5
Unskilled labor	6.9
Service	15.2
Farm	2.5
Employment size	
Fewer than 100 employees	29.4
100–499 employees	18.6
500+ employees	52.0

clearly identifiable work group were eliminated (e.g. organizational histories, strike histories, occupational studies not limited to a specific work organization). Additionally, dissertations, which have not undergone editorial review, were excluded as a quality control. Most books that were selected for coding pertained to a single work group, although some of the lengthier titles contained sufficient information to code data on multiple cases. For example, Rosabeth Moss Kanter's (1977) *Men and Women of the Corporation* generated two cases: managers and clerical workers.

A broad range of industrial, occupational and organizational settings are represented in these data (see Table 1). Although the data are non-random, meaning that descriptive information and statistical significance levels should be approached with caution, they offer ample variation necessary for detecting relationships among variables. These, too, should be approached with the understanding that many of the ethnographies pertaining to teamwork were published in the 1980s and 1990s, a time when teamwork spread rapidly and became the subject of scholarly attention and debate. It is thus possible that the cases include more intense (very positive and/or very negative) responses to teamwork than might have been found in a random sample.[2]

Instrument preparation and coding

After developing a draft of the coding instrument reflecting core concepts in the sociology of work, Hodson collaborated with two graduate assistants to complete a trial coding of eight selected ethnographies. This process generated lengthy discussions regarding concepts, response categories and complex themes, some of which were not prominent in the existing work literature (e.g. chaos, abuse, co-worker infighting). The instrument was revised and select cases were re-coded when measures and values defined early on were later deemed insufficient or flawed (see Hodson et al., 2011).

Once the instrument was finalized, the full set of selected ethnographies was coded by a larger team of researchers, including participants in a year-long graduate practicum and graduate assistants supported by a grant from the National Science Foundation. Coders worked individually, using a common coding protocol and recorded the pages where information relevant to their coding decisions could be found (when too little information was available to code a variable, it was coded as missing). As each case was completed, team members met as a group to review coding decisions and resolve questions. Where there was disagreement about how to code an item, the entire team reviewed relevant passages and came to a consensus regarding the best answer.

Measures

We assess the effect of teamwork and attendant processes using variations present in the entire sample of 204 work groups. Table 2 presents means, standard deviations and codes for dependent and independent variables used in our models. The focal independent variable, *teamwork*, observed in 23% of work groups, is measured with a binary indicator of formal team organization of work. Teamwork is hypothesized to influence *job satisfaction, co-worker estrangement* and *conflict with management* (all measured ordinally) by way of variations in *autonomy* (measured ordinally) and *peer monitoring* (measured dichotomously). These variables, like all others in the data, were coded using information presented in the case studies. Very low satisfaction, for example, is illustrated in a case study of a factory producing parts for high-tech products:

> After about two weeks of work at Biomed, Sam showed me the jobs that he had been working on that day. One job involved placing metal clips on small plastic parts. The other job was punching out the circular tin elements for the disc anterior pads. Performing such jobs prompted Sam to say, 'I don't think there is one happy employee at Biomed. All the jobs in this place are miserable. There are no good jobs.' (Devinatz, 1999: 58)

We measure behavioral outcomes with scale measures of *citizenship, sabotage* and *collective action* (see Table A1 in the Appendix for scale components, codes, loadings and alphas). Sabotage, for example, is on display in Graham's (1995: 125) account of work on an automobile assembly line:

> Whenever one of their team members fell behind and the 'coast was clear' … they stopped the line and the entire car side went down. This not only allowed people on their team to catch up,

Table 2. Means and standard deviations of dependent, independent and control variables.

	Definition	Mean	SD
Teamwork	0-no 1-yes	.23	.42
Autonomy	1-none 2-little 3-average 4-high 5-very high	2.95	1.24
Peer monitoring	0-no 1-yes	.36	.48
Job satisfaction	1-very low 2-moderately low 3-average 4-high 5-very high	2.96	1.07
Co-worker estrangement	1-strong solidarity 2-average solidarity 3-little or no solidarity	1.86	.82
Conflict with management	1-never 2-infrequent 3-average 4-frequent 5-constant	2.92	1.05
Citizenship	Mean of standardized measures of extra time, extra effort, good soldiering and cooperation (see Table A1)	−.01	.80
Sabotage	Mean of standardized measures of procedural sabotage, social sabotage, subverting a manager and playing dumb (see Table A1)	.04	.74
Collective action	Mean of standardized measures of union participation, strikes during research, history of strikes and organized group action (see Table A1)	−.03	.75
Unemployment	1-low 2-medium 3-high	2.24	.89
Organization size			
Fewer than 100 employees	0-no 1-yes	.29	.46
100–499 employees	0-no 1-yes	.19	.39
500+ employees	0-no 1-yes	.52	.50
Post Taft–Hartley Act	0-no 1-yes	.97	.17

it gave everyone time away from the line. In addition, it provided entertainment as workers watched management scramble around trying to find the source of the line stoppage. ... [T]he workers who were aware of the sabotage never told management. Whether the reason for complicity was selfish, because of the appreciated breaks, or was based on loyalty to other workers, their silence was a direct act of resistance and evidence of lack of commitment to the company.

Because disposition to opportunities and protections afforded by teamwork may vary as a function of the availability of work more generally, we include statistical controls for level of *unemployment* in the community. We also control for *organization size*, which influences availability of resources associated with satisfaction, consent and resistance (Godard, 2001). Finally, because our behavioral outcomes include collective action, we add to our final models a binary indicator of whether the case study was initiated after passage of the Taft–Hartley Act – legislation that crippled union activity in the US (Fantasia and Voss, 2004).[3]

Analytic strategy

Quantitative analysis

Reflective of hypotheses drawn from the empowerment, panopticon and conflict perspectives, our analyses model teamwork as impacting worker behavior through job satisfaction, co-worker estrangement and conflict with management, which are themselves
shaped by levels of autonomy and peer monitoring. In our first set of analyses, we
investigate the first part of this causal chain. We use ordinal regression to investigate
whether teamwork impacts job satisfaction, co-worker estrangement and conflict with
management (all measured ordinally) and to determine whether these impacts are attributable to autonomy and peer monitoring as hypothesized. Independent variables entered
in Model 1 include teamwork and control variables; Model 2 adds autonomy and peer
monitoring.

 In our second set of analyses, we use ordinary least squares (OLS) regression to investigate the full process – that is, how teamwork influences behavioral outcomes including
citizenship, sabotage and collective action (these are continuous measures requiring OLS
rather than ordinal regression), and whether impacts are attributable to the processes
addressed in our first set of analyses. Model 1 includes teamwork and controls, Model 2
adds autonomy and peer monitoring and Model 3 adds job satisfaction, co-worker
estrangement and conflict with management.

Qualitative analysis

The final stage of our analysis, reimmersion in qualitative case studies, involves returning to the qualitative case studies to investigate processes exemplifying or anomalous to
quantitative patterns. While quantitative models provide evidence of patterns spanning
organizations, the original qualitative texts embody workers' experiences and speak
directly to theory. Where quantitative analyses reveal an unexpected relationship between
variables, for example, we can use the data to locate cases with the relevant attributes,
and adjust our focus to zoom in on those cases in order to better understand – and inform
– the relevant theories. This back-and-forth movement between qualitative and quantitative methods allows the inductive, subjective and contextualizing tendencies of the former to inform the deductive, objective and generalizing tendencies of the latter, and vice
versa (Morgan, 2007: 71).

Results

Quantitative models

Results of regression models predicting job satisfaction, coworker estrangement and
conflict with management are presented in Table 3. As the empowerment perspective
suggests, teamwork has a positive impact on *job satisfaction* and this relationship is
mediated through autonomy. We were somewhat surprised to find that peer monitoring
has a sizable positive impact on job satisfaction, given emphasis on concertive control
and fear in the panopticon approach. Findings for models predicting *co-worker*

Table 3. Unstandardized ordinal regression coefficients for models predicting job satisfaction, co-worker estrangement and conflict with management.

	Job satisfaction		Co-worker estrangement		Conflict with management	
Teamwork	.80*	.24	−.11	.08	−.26	−.06
Autonomy		.95***		−.04		−.18
Peer monitoring		.58†		−.81*		−.65*
Unemployment	−.04	.00	−.21	−.22	.54**	.53*
Organization size						
Under 100 (ref.)						
100–499 employees	−.54	−.27	.25	.26	−.12	−.14
500+ employees	−.01	−.08	−.09	−.04	.12	.21
Intercept 1	−2.81***	−6.48***	−.51	−.17	−4.07***	−3.42***
Intercept 2	−.59	−3.82***	.86	1.25†	−1.89***	−1.18†
Intercept 3	.61	−2.20***	−	−	−.75	.01
Intercept 4	2.47***	.09	−	−	1.52**	2.34***
Model fit[a]	8.09†	81.54***	1.93	9.30	8.80†	18.42**
df	4	6	4	6	4	6
N	190	190	160	160	177	177

[a]Likelihood ratio test.
***$p < .001$, **$p < .01$, *$p < .05$, †$p < .1$, two-tailed tests.

estrangement and *conflict with management* are consistent with the conflict perspective in that teams affect neither of these outcomes – suggesting contextual contingencies. Peer monitoring, however, has a significant negative impact on both. This finding contradicts hypotheses derived from the panopticon perspective regarding lateralization of conflict in the context of teams. But the negative impact of peer monitoring on conflict with management, along with the positive impact of peer monitoring on job satisfaction, supports views of some empowerment scholars regarding potential benefits of replacing hierarchical controls with more participative arrangements – an issue we explore further in our qualitative reimmersion.

Results of regressions predicting worker citizenship, sabotage and collective action are presented in Table 4. Analyses predicting *citizenship* also lend support to the empowerment perspective. Teamwork positively impacts citizenship, and this relationship is mediated by a positive impact of autonomy, which itself is mediated by job satisfaction. It appears that teams can enhance quality of work life and foster consent, provided they truly enhance opportunities to use discretion and exercise skill.

In keeping with the key focus of panopticon research, teamwork reduces rates of *sabotage*, and this relationship is mediated by peer monitoring. Taken alone, this finding could suggest that teamwork encourages peers to police one other and enforce normative control. Interestingly, however, the effect shrinks to non-significance when job satisfaction and conflict with management (both of which are significant) are added in Model 3. These findings, combined with results of analyses presented in Table 3, suggest that heightened job satisfaction (which reduces sabotage) and reductions in conflict with

Table 4. Unstandardized OLS regression coefficients for models predicting citizenship, sabotage and collective action.

	Citizenship			Sabotage			Collective action		
Teamwork	.37**	.23†	.20	−.30*	−.23	−.22	−.25*	−.20	−.18†
Autonomy		.21***	.11*		.01	.09		−.09*	−.08†
Peer monitoring		.11	.05		−.27*	−.20		−.01	−.08
Job satisfaction			.22***			−.16*			−.03
Co-worker estrangement			.07			−.04			−.46***
Conflict with management			−.04			.11†			.16***
Unemployment	−.11	−.09	−.08	.15†	.15†	.11	.07	.06	−.02
Organization size									
Under 100 (ref.)									
100–499 employees	−.49**	−.37*	−.37*	.06	.10	.11	.43**	.37*	.43***
500+ employees	−.29*	−.29*	−.29*	.07	.09	.08	.58***	.58***	.56***
Post Taft–Hartley Act	.73*	.60†	.74*	−.06	−.03	.18	.63†	−.58†	−.54†
Intercept	−.32	−.87*	−1.37**	−.22	−.20	.00	.10	.35	.92*
Adjusted R^2	.068	.175	.221	.017	.034	.078	.120	.134	.384
N	202	202	202	175	175	175	199	199	199

***$p < .001$, **$p < .01$, *$p < .05$, †$p < .1$, two-tailed tests.

management (which increases it) mediate the negative impact of peer monitoring on sabotage. The empowerment tradition thus plays a role in explaining a key hypothesis drawn from panopticon research: reductions in sabotage associated with peer monitoring are attributable to positive implications of teamwork for satisfaction and reductions in conflict with management.

Consistent with hypotheses derived from the empowerment tradition, we find that teamwork reduces *collective action*, seemingly owing to a small negative effect of autonomy, which diminishes somewhat with the addition of co-worker estrangement and conflict with management to the model (co-worker estrangement and conflict with management have negative and positive effects on collective action, respectively). Yet, the absence of any significant impact of autonomy on either of these variables (see Table 3) suggests that reductions in collective action are more reflective of selective hiring practices and/or selective incorporation of teams than the empowerment of workers or the impact of teams per se (see Crowley et al., 2010; Graham, 1995). Furthermore, the coefficient for job satisfaction is small and non-significant – suggesting that the negative impact of autonomy on collective action is not mediated by quality of work life.

In sum, our quantitative findings lend support to both the empowerment perspective (especially with regard to job satisfaction and citizenship) and the conflict approach (in that teamwork has no straightforward connection to co-worker estrangement, conflict with management or collective action). Findings do not support hypotheses derived from the panopticon perspective regarding citizenship or lateralization of conflict; peer surveillance does not necessarily elicit extra effort, nor does it estrange workers from one another. Results do suggest that peer monitoring curtails sabotage, but the full models indicate that the relationship is attributable to job satisfaction and reduced conflict with management – something more consistent with benefits accruing from reduced hierarchical control than with fear of sanctioning by peers.

Qualitative reimmersion

To obtain a more nuanced understanding of these processes, we returned to the original ethnographies, focusing on the 47 cases where teamwork was present, with particular emphasis on cases in which: (1) teams lived up to the empowerment ideal – enhancing both satisfaction and citizenship; (2) teams came closest to panopticon predictions associated with peer monitoring and sabotage, but also enhanced satisfaction and reduced conflict with management; and (3) teams failed to generate citizenship, reduce sabotage or curb collective action, consistent with the conflict approach. Given the limits of our data, we refrain from commenting on how frequently these patterns would be encountered in the 'real world', instead using ethnographic data to refine theoretical perspectives and understand relationships between them. In the text that follows – organized by theme – quoted passages help to explain how and why teamwork influences citizenship, sabotage and collective action; how the panopticon perspective may be developed in light of our findings; and why even well-intentioned attempts to incorporate teamwork can fail. Notably, this phase of our analysis also highlights how workers' comparative evaluations of teamwork play a subtle but important role in shaping their responses – a phenomenon that has tended to go unnoticed in individual accounts of teamwork, but emerges as a prominent theme when multiple cases are examined simultaneously.

Realizing the empowerment ideal. Burawoy's classic study *Manufacturing Consent* (1979) demonstrates that even narrow and informal windows of opportunity to exercise discretion can effectively secure consent, in part by allowing workers to derive psychological rewards such as pride from routine jobs. Terry Besser's (1996) case study of teamwork in a Toyota manufacturing facility likewise shows how *formal* provisions for autonomy generate satisfaction and willingness to go the extra mile – exerting effort on behalf of the firm, willingly and not unwittingly:

> That's what I do while I'm working, I think of new ways to improve the area that I'm in. I just recently redid the whole job since I've been there. It took a lot of time and effort on my part, but I wanted to show them I could do it. It saved all kinds of time as far as labor is concerned. Now my next project will be a safety task that I'm working on. (Besser, 1996: 69–70)

Besser's research goes somewhat further, however, in demonstrating that positive reactions to the firm and its implementation of teamwork reflect *comparisons between their current situation and employment opportunities perceived elsewhere*. The worker quoted above illustrates this point:

> I know how cold it can be sometimes. I'm not saying that Toyota could not be cold if it has to be. But I'm saying that I think they have more of a concern for their employees than other organizations. If an employee has a problem of something, they'll bend over backwards to do something about it. (Besser, 1996: 108)

Another echoes her sentiments:

> Toyota is fantastic … I mean if there's a group consensus by the team members that something is perceived as not being as it should be, then Toyota tries to revise that, and you don't get that other places. (Besser, 1996: 109)

Toyota's responsiveness to employee input leads workers to feel valued and invested in the company. Knowing that management takes their insights seriously, workers voluntarily go above and beyond formal job expectations to improve production. Having some say, even within relatively narrow bounds, promotes satisfaction. Because employers rarely offer employees such opportunities, workers evaluate their jobs in an especially positive light. In other words, what other companies fail to do emerges as a significant part of how 'empowerment' in teams is received. A worker explains how working for Toyota has made him feel: 'They trust their employees. I feel real confident that they do trust me. Basically I feel real good about my job. I feel like I'm important to them' (Besser, 1996: 109).

Revising the panopticon approach. As noted in the quantitative results section, causal processes emphasized in the empowerment perspective emerge as key to explaining a hypothesis derived from the panopticon approach. That is, reductions in sabotage associated with peer monitoring are rooted not in fear, but are mediated by increased satisfaction and reductions in conflict with management. Barker's (1999) ethnographic case study of a telecommunications equipment manufacturing firm exemplifies this pattern. Consistent with panopticon accounts of teamwork, the transfer of supervisory roles to employees heightens visibility and promotes peer discipline and internalization of production norms. But in keeping with our quantitative findings, the case study suggests that peer monitoring also allows for a more favorable work experience in comparison to traditional hierarchical controls.

In the passage below, a new employee struggles with a difficult task and intense performance pressure associated with peer surveillance. Yet, he is startled by the respect he is afforded in the process – something that strengthens his resolve to overcome the challenges and do what is asked:

> When Greg got a board from Karen, he first had to check her work (a team rule) and then very carefully install three tiny diodes. … He then checked his work and slid the board to Diego, who repeated the checking process. Greg was having trouble getting the diodes in right, … He was only 1½ hours into the day, and already Diego had to correct several errors that Greg had let slip. Diego was not really angry with him yet. He just pointed out the error and told Greg, 'Just keep watching what you are doing and check your work. You'll get it. It takes a while to learn how we do things out here.'
>
> Greg's last mistake, which Diego had caught, had been about a half hour ago. But now Greg saw Martha and Grace Anne coming toward him, which could mean only one thing … Greg sank low in his chair …
>
> 'Hey Greg,' Martha said, 'Let's talk for a minute.' Her voice was not angry, which surprised Greg. He let out his breath … 'Take a look at this board and tell me what's wrong … Look,' she said, in a coaching voice, 'we know that you are just starting out and that you're going to make

some mistakes. But you have to do two things.' ... 'First, you have to put the diodes in right ... But more importantly, you have to check your work. That's what we do on our team ... We're all big believers in that because it keeps us all straight ... Got it?' ...

'Yes, I know. It's just hard right now.'

'Don't worry. You're learning how we work on this team. We always check our own work. We always check each other's work. That's the thing to remember.'

[Greg:] 'I'll get it right.' (Barker, 1999: 94–95) [4]

This passage provides a powerful illustration of peer control, but a closer look also reveals how *experiences with hierarchical control outside the firm* can set the stage for a favorable response to teamwork. Note the distress Greg exhibits at the team leader's approach; his surprise at her lack of anger; and how his body relaxes in response to her calm demeanor. Prior negative experiences with traditional supervision have primed him for a generally positive comparative evaluation of, and response to, peer control.

Elsewhere, the same case underscores how workers' perceptions are influenced by explicit comparisons to experiences with more traditional forms of work organization. An employee's account of teamwork highlights both the normative and disciplinary aspects of peer surveillance and favorable comparisons relative to the 'old system', especially the unpleasantness of reporting to a boss:

[W]e are like a family in a twisted sort of way. It happens like that with the people that you are working with here. You get to where you know what they're gonna do, and they know what you're gonna do. You don't let them do something like miss a part because they can't. They don't let you do that because they know you can't. That part is really nice. There may be a few bad apples, but, on the whole, we're pretty close to each other ... [W]ith the old job, you had some days when you didn't want to come to work 'cause you didn't want to face your boss. Well, [sometimes] ... you don't want to come to work because you don't want to face your team. But I still come in, I still face them. No matter what, I still don't want to go back to the old system. Would you? (Barker, 1999: 164)

Barker (1999: 132) summarizes: 'team members ... seemed to find their control by identification to be less objectionable than the hierarchical control [used previously]. Whereas before they might have rankled at being told what to do, now they "told themselves," and that felt better to them.' In other words, as co-workers assume supervisory functions formerly carried out by a boss, workers feel empowered *relative to prior arrangements*. They are unlikely to engage in sabotage not simply because peer monitoring leads to subjective experiences of fear and anxiety, but because peer discipline is preferable to the direct and abusive controls workers regard as normative.

Unfulfilled promises and resistance. Comparisons vis-a-vis previous experiences are especially notable in the conflict tradition, which documents how *absence of anticipated change relative to prior forms of work organization* takes center stage in workers' rejection of teamwork. For example, Andrew Scott's (1994) case study of frozen food production demonstrates how installation of peer monitoring failed to diminish rates of sabotage. The 'new' working practices differed little from the old ones, and repeated supervisory interference reminded workers who was really in control. Workers thus perceived teamwork not as an improvement relative to prior controls, but as part of longstanding efforts to erode solidarity and increase pace. Rather than submit to new arrangements, they adhered to a tradition of sabotage and collective action. Indeed, some managers felt that worker resistance actually increased in the wake of workplace change:

> The new working practices are just a sham – things are going back to the old way of working. Supervisors keep interfering. They want to put certain people in certain jobs, they're here to spy on us … it's just the same old story. If a machine's supposed to run at fifty an hour, this company will try to make it run at seventy five. It's always been the same for as long as I can remember. (Scott, 1994: 55)

Failed promises of 'having a say' seem to have even stronger negative impacts on worker orientations toward management – and workers frequently make reference to prior arrangements in explaining their dissatisfaction. Ruth Milkman's (1997) study documenting reaction to a failed empowerment program at General Motors illustrates how workers evaluate 'new' methods in light of earlier experiences. Despite (and perhaps because of) a long history of adversarial relationships with management, workers welcomed the possibility of change. They emerged from an 80-hour training program, developed by Louis Tice, deeply committed to its principles, but when managers facing organizational pressures reverted to top-down orientations and abusive practices, workers angrily noted the absence of change relative to their prior experiences with hierarchical control:

> Louis Lambert exclaimed … 'That's all bullshit. They're not doing it the way they said they were going to do it.' … As Ellen Thomas explained: 'You still have the management that has the mentality of top down … they don't listen to … the workers … So that's why … people say it's a farce. Because you do not feel mutual respect … This is a manufacturing plant; they do have to produce. But you can't just … give me this big hype, and then … have the same old attitude.' (Milkman, 1997: 174)

Cynicism in this context reached new heights – seemingly fueled by the frustration of wasted time. Workers repeatedly referenced the 80 hours they spent in training, and the time wasted in weekly (paid) meetings wherein they submitted ideas that were repeatedly ignored (Milkman, 1997: 173). Indeed, the waste of effort seems to add an additional layer of insult, despite the pay – a notion resonating with experimental research conducted in the field of behavioral economics (see Ariely et al., 2008) and with anecdotal accounts of the distinct, 'almost unbearable' kind of 'moral torture' experience by workers assigned senseless tasks (such as digging foundations for facilities that would never be built) in forced labor camps (Coser, 1990: 168).

The case study also strongly suggests that hope itself becomes an instrument of injury and the training received serves as a point of comparison (see also Vallas, 2003a). Even among workers long-critical of management, the rhetoric of empowerment conveyed in the 80-hour course engendered hope – and an expectation – that the firm would shift away from top-down controls and embrace a more democratic ideal based on respect. When those expectations failed to materialize, workers drew on *comparisons highlighted in the training* to express their dissatisfaction. A worker states:

> If management was to get a grade score [based] on that Louis Tice course, if I were to grade them, I'd give 99 percent of them an F … [I]f you have a problem … they all try to keep it … under the rug, and [they say,] 'Don't bother me about it – just fix it and let it slide.' And that is not the teachings we went through in that 80-hour course! (Milkman, 1997: 175)

> [According to another,] You are sent to a two-week, eighty-hour course, and *paid* [to attend] … Then … go back to work. And … they *still* don't listen to people! This bullshit about working together! I mean, there is more anger in that plant now, you know … [I]t's supposed to change, and that's what's offending people. (Milkman, 1997: 169, emphasis in original)

Following the training, workers seem less willing to accept conditions to which they were once accustomed – and wielded the rhetoric of empowerment as a weapon in subversion of management:

> [T]his was the idea that … [Louis Tice] was trying to get over to the people … See, we are not children; we are men. I used to work upstairs, and I had a problem, no water around. I called the foreman, and he told me, 'When you have a break, you can get water … But I didn't do that. When I got ready for water, I just made it my business, went out, and got the water … I mean, we are not slaves! … [I]f you know you need it, then it's up to you. That's what … [Tice] told me! (Milkman, 1997: 175)

Discussion and conclusion

In this article, we use content-coded data on 204 work groups to investigate hypotheses derived from empowerment, panopticon and conflict perspectives on teamwork. Our quantitative analyses confirm the empowerment perspective regarding potential for autonomy in teams to increase satisfaction and in turn citizenship, and support the conflict approach in that teamwork has no straightforward connection to co-worker estrangement, conflict with management or collective action. They highlight a need for a revision of the panopticon perspective on teamwork, however, especially with respect to co-worker relationships and mechanisms underlying how peer monitoring reduces sabotage. Panopticon theorists traditionally posit that peer monitoring in teams operates in a manner akin to Bentham's hypothetical prison – with co-worker enforcement of normative standards resulting in a diffuse, sophisticated and subjectively oppressive disciplinary mechanism of self-control. Yet, our quantitative models suggest that reductions in sabotage associated with peer monitoring are due primarily to heightened satisfaction and declines in conflict with management, *not* surveillance and fear. Qualitative reimmersion further reveals that workers prefer peer surveillance to traditional hierarchical control, and they enjoy the feeling of being part of, rather than simply subject to, the authority structure of an organization.

Even more interesting is how close examination of cases across all three theoretical traditions illustrates how contrasts evident *from the point of view of workers* come to the fore in explaining not only workers' rejection of teamwork, but also *positive* reactions to team-based production. Workers who accept teamwork do so not because they are manipulated or subject to managerial co-optation, but because they have evaluated their circumstances favorably in comparison to previous experiences inside and outside the organization, as well as their perception of arrangements available to workers in general, and have determined that returns to teamwork are sufficient to justify their embrace (e.g. less demeaning supervision, more opportunity for efficacious action, or a greater sense that the employer values workers and their ideas). This finding underscores the importance of worker agency in the full range of responses to teamwork and expands the conflict approach – which has tended to emphasize both agency and workers' comparative estimation of work arrangements – by highlighting comparisons to conditions encountered across places, over time and by other workers.

Although teams in our non-random sample may differ from the broader population in ways that potentially bias our results, our findings resonate with other accounts stressing the power of contextual factors to influence individuals' perceptions of and responses to their circumstances. In the field of economics, psychology-based critiques of decision-making models premised on rational choice and expected utility maximization have made the case that individuals do not pursue a single, static utility; rather, their goals are flexible and reflect evaluations of what others have and as well as their own potential for gains and losses (Frank, 1997; Hastie and Dawes, 2001).

Likewise, workers evaluate work arrangements in light of their individual appraisal of alternatives, which are informed by their own circumstances, conditions encountered by others and what they have come to expect (Handel, 2005; Ouellet, 1994: 198; Vidal, 2007a). In a symposium on Michael Burawoy's (1979) *Manufacturing Consent*, Robert Freeland (2001) notes that it is necessary to consider not only self-interested rationalities generated in production relations endogenous to the organization, but also normative, non-rational commitments generated externally. Matt Vidal (2007b), building on Robert Thomas's (1994) characterization of worker dispositions as reflecting collective worldviews and institutionalization of organizational forms, suggests that worker receptiveness to teamwork reflects local context, including plant-specific history and the nature of implementation. The results of this study point to even more far-reaching influences on individual workers' expectations, which may be met, exceeded, or go unfulfilled in a given employment setting.

In many ways, a major conclusion of this research is that many workers tend to regard employment options as undesirable and/or oppressive, and the important role this plays in their responses to teamwork. Poor conditions in workplaces at-large form a relatively low standard against which to evaluate teams, and thus contribute to willing acceptance of even narrow opportunities for empowerment and pressure-cooker peer monitoring regimes. Empowerment feels like empowerment because so many workers are deprived with respect to autonomy. Peer monitoring engenders satisfaction, improves relationships among co-workers and minimizes conflict with management because it represents a departure from infantilizing and/or abusive hierarchical controls that humiliate workers and in some cases promote co-worker conflict (Crowley, 2012; Crowley, in press). What is more, many employers formally espousing the transformative effects of teamwork informally acknowledge and play off workers' limited labor market opportunities. As Steven McKay (2004) demonstrates, commitment may occasionally surface as loyalty to and goodwill toward an employer, but more often, it appears as tepid satisficing culminating from conditions of worker powerlessness, desperation and insecurity. Workers may indeed pledge to stay with their organization and work hard, but their actions are best understood as reflecting 'alienative commitment', not empowerment.

Future studies can improve our understanding of teamwork by exploring factors that contribute to feelings of true empowerment in successful teams, factors underlying workers' evaluation of employment alternatives with special attention to workers' personal histories, and emergent processes associated with combinations of team attributes – not only those addressed here, but also others, such as gender/race composition – for team functioning and success. Finally, future investigators may consider further exploring the patterns we identify in our quantitative models using larger samples with representative data if they become available. Such studies would be particularly useful for understanding how commonly employers adopt different approaches to teamwork and how frequently they produce the patterns identified here. Although our study suggests use of teamwork to elicit citizenship and quell resistance requires a shift away from obtrusive hierarchical controls, this need not mean that employees would lack oversight. On the contrary, our qualitative reimmersion shows that workers willingly assume the task of monitoring each other, and do so effectively, without the negative consequences of hierarchical control, when they are given genuine authority to do so. Our reimmersion also provides important precautionary advice: disingenuous or superficial implementations of teamwork cause more damage than doing nothing at all. Workers invariably become hostile when management fails to live up to the obligations that they themselves have established. Stated bluntly, it is better to give workers no hope for a better tomorrow than to promise it and fall short.

Even when implemented in ways that improve the work experience, reduce sabotage and elicit citizenship, teamwork often has limited impact on power relations within a firm. Small but meaningful changes, however, may pave the way for more substantial ones, and they proliferate as a result of institutional pressures encouraging adoption of flexible practices (Minssen, 2005; Zbaracki, 1998). Scholars have suggested that teamwork arose in part to meet rising expectations and capacities of an increasingly educated workforce (Hodson, 2001). Our findings suggest that, once exposed to the principles of teamwork, and especially practices associated with empowerment, workers integrate those principles into the evaluative framework by which they judge current and future employers. As such, they may promote further supply-side pressure for change that would offer more freedom and responsibility to those who want it.

Acknowledgements

The authors would like to thank the editors and two anonymous reviewers for helpful comments on an earlier version of this manuscript. We are also indebted to Randy Hodson, who orchestrated collection of data used in this research.

Funding

This research received no specific grant from any funding agency in the public, commercial, or not-for-profit sectors, but draws from data collected with support from the National Science Foundation under Grant 0112434. Any opinions findings and conclusions or recommendations expressed in this material are those of the author and do not necessarily reflect the views of the National Science Foundation.

Notes

1. The panopticon refers to a circular prison in which small cells separated by windowless walls surround an observation tower, offering limitless opportunities for unseen guards to observe misconduct through one-way glass. According to Foucault (1977), continuous exposure to risk of discipline causes prisoners to internalize regulations and ultimately control themselves.

2. Because there is no sampling frame from which to draw a random sample of work groups, we cannot evaluate the degree to which these data represent work groups more generally.

3. Early models included controls for industry, occupation, region, job insecurity, percent female in the organization and percent minority in the organization. None of these rose to significance in our models and they were subsequently removed from analyses.

4. Peer control is not always carried out with such good humor. Yet, a careful reading of Barker's (1999: 117) case study demonstrates that even the strongest rebuke, which hints at the 'ultimate penalty ... banishment from the team community', was carried out without assaults on employee dignity that generally accompany direct supervision. A worker describes her approach to correcting a worker giving less than 100%:

   John [a relatively new team member] was really ticking us off. ... He ... kept missing the training classes. ... So ... I went up to him and said, 'Why are you doing this? Do you think that everybody on the team can act this way? ... I want you to wake up and smell the coffee. ... You had better get to that training.' And he did. Sometimes you have to say that to people, whether they've been around here a long time or what. 'Wake up, smell the coffee. You are living in a dream world, come back down.' (Barker, 1999: 131)

References

Adler P (1995) 'Democratic Taylorism': The Toyota production system at NUMMI. In: Babson S (ed.) *Lean Work: Empowerment and Exploitation in the Global Auto Industry*. Detroit, IL: Wayne State University Press, pp. 207–219.

Appelbaum E, Bailey T, Berg P and Kalleberg AL (2000) *Manufacturing Advantage: Why High-performance Work Systems Pay Off*. Ithaca, NY: Cornell University Press.

Ariely D, Kamenica E and Prelec D (2008) Man's search for meaning: The case of Legos. *Journal of Economic Behavior and Organization* 67(3–4): 408–437.

Barker JR (1993) Tightening the iron cage: Concertive control in self-managing teams. *Administrative Science Quarterly* 38(3): 408–437.

Barker JR (1999) *The Discipline of Teamwork: Participation and Concertive Control*. Thousand Oaks, CA: Sage.

Batt R (2004) Who benefits from teams? Comparing workers, supervisors, and managers. *Industrial Relations* 43(1): 183–212.

Batt R and Appelbaum E (1995) Worker participation in diverse settings: Does the form affect the outcome, and if so, who benefits? *British Journal of Industrial Relations* 33(3): 355–378.

Bélanger J, Edwards PK and Wright M (2003) Commitment at work and independence from management: A study of advanced teamwork. *Work and Occupations* 30(2): 234–252.

Besser TL (1996) *Team Toyota: Transplanting the Toyota Culture to the Camry Plant in Kentucky*. Albany: State University of New York Press.

Burawoy M (1979) *Manufacturing Consent: Changes in the Labor Process under Monopoly Capitalism*. Chicago: University of Chicago Press.

Cappelli P and Rogovsky N (1998) Employee involvement and organizational citizenship: Implications for labor law reform and 'lean production'. *Industrial and Labor Relations Review* 51(4): 633–653.

Cappelli P, Bassi L, Katz H et al. (1997) *Change at Work.* New York: Oxford University Press.

Casey C (1999) 'Come, join our family': Discipline and integration in corporate organizational culture. *Human Relations* 52(1): 155–178.

Collins J (2001) *Good to Great: Why Some Companies Make The Leap ... and Others Don't.* New York: Harper Business.

Coser LA (1990) Forced labor in concentration camps. In: Erikson K and Vallas SP (eds) *The Nature of Work: Sociological Perspectives.* New Haven, CT: American Sociological Association Presidential Series and Yale University Press, pp. 162–169.

Crowley M (2012) Control and dignity in professional, manual and service-sector employment. *Organization Studies* 33(10): 1383–1406.

Crowley M (in press) Class, control and relational indignity: Labor process foundations for workplace humiliation, conflict and shame. *American Behavioral Scientist.*

Crowley M, Tope D, Chamberlain LJ and Hodson R (2010) Neo-Taylorism at work: Occupational change in the post-Fordist era. *Social Problems* 57(3): 421–447.

Devinatz VG (1999) *High-tech Betrayal: Working and Organizing on the Shop Floor.* East Lansing: Michigan University Press.

Edwards RC (1979) *Contested Terrain: The Transformation of the American Workplace in the Twentieth Century.* New York: Basic Books.

Ezzamel M and Willmott H (1998) Accounting for teamwork: A critical study of group-based systems of organizational control. *Administrative Science Quarterly* 43(2): 358–396.

Ezzamel M, Willmott H and Worthington F (2001) Power, control and resistance in 'the factory that time forgot'. *Journal of Management Studies* 38(8): 1053–1079.

Fantasia R and Voss K (2004) *Hard Work: Remaking the American Labor Movement.* Berkeley: University of California Press.

Fernie S and Metcalf D (1998) (Not) hanging on the telephone: Payment systems in the new sweatshops. *CEP Discussion Paper 390.* London: Centre for Economic Performance.

Frank RH (1997) The frame of reference as a public good. *Economic Journal* 107(445): 1832–1847.

Freeland RF (2001) Consent and rational choice. *Contemporary Sociology* 30: 446–448.

Friedman AL (1977) *Industry and Labor: Class Struggle at Work and Monopoly Capitalism.* London: Macmillan.

Foucault M (1977) *Discipline and Punish: The Birth of the Prison.* New York: Vintage Books.

Gamson WA (1975) *The Strategy of Social Protest.* Belmont, CA: Wadsworth.

Gecas V and Schwalbe ML (1983) Beyond the looking-glass self: Social structure and efficacy-based self-esteem. *Social Psychology Quarterly* 46(2): 77–88.

Godard P (2001) High-performance *and* the transformation of work? The implications of alternative work practices for the nature and experience of work. *Industrial and Labor Relations Review* 54(4): 776–805.

Graham L (1995) *On the Line at Subaru-Isuzu.* Ithaca, NY: Industrial and Labor Relations Press.

Handel MJ (2005) Trends in perceived job quality, 1989 to 1998. *Work and Occupations* 32(1): 66–94.

Hastie R and Dawes RM (2001) *Rational Choice in an Uncertain World: The Psychology of Judgment and Decision Making.* Thousand Oaks, CA: Sage.

Hodson R (2001) *Dignity at Work.* Cambridge: Cambridge University Press.

Hodson R, Chamberlain LJ, Crowley M and Tope D (2011) Coding ethnographies for research and training: Merging qualitative and quantitative sociologies. *Sociological Perspectives* 54(1): 125–131.

Huselid MA (1995) The impact of human resource management practices on turnover, productivity and corporate financial performance. *Academy of Management Journal* 38(3): 635–672.

Kanter RM (1977) *Men and Women of the Corporation*. New York: Basic Books.

Knights D and McCabe D (1998) Dreams and designs on strategy: A critical analysis of TQM and management control. *Work, Employment and Society* 12(3): 433–456.

Kraft P (1999) To control and inspire: U.S. management in the age of computer information systems and global production. In: Wardell M, Steiger TL and Meiksins P (eds) *Rethinking the Labor Process*. Albany: State University of New York Press, pp. 17–36.

Kunda G (2006) *Engineering Culture: Control and Commitment in a High-tech Corporation*, rev edn. Philadelphia: Temple University Press.

McKay SC (2004) Securing commitment in an insecure world: Workers in international high-tech subsidiaries. *Economic and Industrial Democracy* 25(3): 375–410.

Milkman R (1997) *Farewell to the Factory: Auto Workers in the Late Twentieth Century*. Berkeley: University of California Press.

Minssen H (2005) Challenges of teamwork in production: Demands of communication. *Organization Studies* 27(1): 103–124.

Morgan DL (2007) Paradigms lost and pragmatism regained: Methodological implications of combining qualitative and quantitative methods. *Journal of Mixed Methods Research* 1(1): 48–76.

Niemelä J and Kalliola S (2007) Team membership and experiences of work in the Finnish context. *Economic and Industrial Democracy* 28(4): 552–588.

Ouellet LJ (1994) *Pedal to the Metal: The Work Lives of Truckers*. Philadelphia: Temple University Press.

Piore M and Sabel CF (1984) *The Second Industrial Divide: Possibilities for Prosperity*. New York: Basic Books.

Plankey Videla N (2006) It cuts both ways: Management and the construction of a 'community of fate' on the shop floor in a Mexican garment factory. *Social Forces* 84(4): 2099–2120.

Pruijt H (2003) Teams between neo-Taylorism and anti-Taylorism. *Economic and Industrial Democracy* 24(1): 77–101.

Roscigno VJ, Lopez SH and Hodson R (2009) Supervisory bullying, status inequalities and organizational context. *Social Forces* 87(3): 1561–1589.

Scott A (1994) *Willing Slaves?* Cambridge: Cambridge University Press.

Sennett R (1998) *The Corrosion of Character: The Personal Consequences of Work in the New Capitalism*. New York: WW Norton.

Sewell G (1998) The discipline of teams: The control of team-based industrial work through electronic and peer surveillance. *Administrative Science Quarterly* 43(2): 397–428.

Sewell G and Wilkinson B (1992) 'Someone to watch over me': Surveillance, discipline and the just-in-time labor process. *Sociology* 26(2): 271–289.

Shaiken H, Lopez S and Mankita I (1997) Two routes to team production: Saturn and Chrysler compared. *Industrial Relations* 36(1): 17–45.

Smith V (1996) Employee involvement, involved employees: Participative work arrangements in a white-collar service occupation. *Social Problems* 43(2): 166–179.

Smith V (1997) New forms of work organization. *Annual Review of Sociology* 23: 315–339.

Smith V (2001) Teamwork versus tempwork: Managers and the dualisms of workplace restructuring. In: Campbell K, Cornfield D and McCammon H (eds) *Working in Restructured Workplaces: New Directions for the Sociology of Work*. Thousand Oaks, CA: Sage, pp. 7–28.

Snape E and Redman T (2010) HRM practices, organizational citizenship behavior, and performance: A multi-level analysis. *Journal of Management Studies* 47(7): 1219–1247.

Stewart P, Richardson M, Danford A et al. (2009) *We Sell Our Time and No More: Workers' Struggles against Lean Production in the British Car Industry*. New York: Pluto.

Thomas RJ (1994) *What Machines Can't Do: Politics and Technology in the Industrial Enterprise*. Berkeley: University of California Press.

Thompson P and Ackroyd S (1995) All quiet on the workplace front? A critique of recent trends in British industrial sociology. *Sociology* 29(4): 615–633.

Townsend K (2007) Who has control in teams without teamworking? *Economic and Industrial Democracy* 28(4): 622–649.

Vallas SP (1999) Rethinking post-Fordism: The meaning of workplace flexibility. *Sociological Theory* 17(1): 68–101.

Vallas SP (2003a) The adventures of managerial hegemony: Teamwork, ideology, and worker resistance. *Social Problems* 50(2): 204–255.

Vallas SP (2003b) Why teamwork fails: Obstacles to workplace change in four manufacturing plants. *American Sociological Review* 68(2): 223–250.

Van den Broek D, Callaghan G and Thompson P (2004) Teams without teamwork? Explaining the call center paradox. *Economic and Industrial Democracy* 25(2): 197–218.

Vidal M (2007a) Lean production, worker empowerment, and job satisfaction: A qualitative analysis and critique. *Critical Sociology* 33(1–2): 247–278.

Vidal M (2007b) Manufacturing empowerment? 'Employee involvement' in the labor process after Fordism. *Socio-Economic Review* 5(2): 197–232.

Vidal M (2010) Review of We sell our time and no more: Workers' struggles against lean production in the British car industry. *British Journal of Industrial Relations* 48(3): 646–648.

Weeks J (2004) *Unpopular Culture: The Ritual of Complaint in a British Bank*. Chicago: University of Chicago Press.

Womack JP, Jones DT and Roos D (1990) *The Machine that Changed the World*. New York: Rawson Associates.

Zbaracki MJ (1998) The rhetoric and reality of total quality management. *Administrative Science Quarterly* 43(3): 602–636.

Author biographies

Martha Crowley is an Associate Professor in the Department of Sociology and Anthropology at North Carolina State University, USA. Her work-related research emphasizes the labor process and workplace dignity. Recent projects include investigations of workplace stress and abuse, gender inequality in workplace control and dignity, and changes in manual and professional work.

Julianne Payne is a doctoral candidate in the Department of Sociology and Anthropology at North Carolina State University, USA. Her dissertation is an ethnographic study of variations in how workers experience and respond to workplace monitoring. Her other research interests include workplace insecurity, production teams, economic sociology and public health.

Earl Kennedy received his master's degree from the Department of Sociology and Anthropology at North Carolina State University, USA. His research interests include social stratification, education and employment.

Table A1. Dependent variable scale components, loadings and alphas.

		Loadings (alpha)[a]
Citizenship		
Extra time	0-no 1-yes	.73
Extra effort	0-no 1-yes	.79
Good soldier	1-none 2-some 3-half 4-most 5-all	.77
Cooperation	1-absent 2-mixed 3-widespread	.85
Alpha		(.79)
Sabotage		
Procedural sabotage	0-no 1-yes	.72
Social sabotage	0-no 1-yes	.82
Subverting management	0-no 1-yes	.81
Playing dumb	0-no 1-yes	.70
Alpha		(.76)
Collective action		
Union participation	0-no 1-yes	.77
Strikes during research period	0-no 1-yes	.71
History of strikes	1-no 2-infrequent 3-frequent	.84
Organized group action	1-absent 2-infrequent 3-average 4-widespread 5-pervasive	.80
Alpha		(.79)

[a] Extraction method: Principal component analysis. All first eigenvalues are greater than 1, and all second eigenvalues are below 1. Every component matrix reported only one factor.

Interpersonal Communication in the Workplace: A Largely Unexplored Region

Dekay, S.H.

Recent research has identified interpersonal communication skills as critical attributes for new employees and more experienced workers seeking promotion. However, despite the significance of interpersonal communication in the workplace, our knowledge of these skills and how they may be taught is limited. The two articles comprising this theme section are intended to extend our understanding of these skills.

Nineteenth-century maps of the African continent—at least those printed in the United States and Europe—contain a rather strange entry in the central section of that land mass. If you consult one of these old maps, you will notice, south of the "Mountains of the Moon" and north of the land of Moologa, a large territory labeled the UNEXPLORED REGION. Apparently, there yet remained a portion of the continent unoccupied by the soldiers and merchants of colonial powers.

The topic of this themed section, Interpersonal Communication in the Workplace, also resembles a largely "unexplored region." The reasons for our scanty knowledge are complex. Certainly, it is not due to a lack of research: The two articles comprising this section offer useful bibliographies concerning numerous studies examining the people skills, the "soft" skills, and the personal skills often associated with interpersonal communication. Yet the studies fail to provide us with clear definitions of these skills, their interrelationships, and their relevance to communication. In fact, much of the cited research informs us that managers and human relations professionals maintain that "interpersonal skills" and communication represent two distinct sets of behavior. It has proven difficult to explore the terrain of interpersonal communication when we can't agree on a common nomenclature with which to ask questions, frame hypotheses, conduct studies, and report findings.

[1]St. John's University, USA
[2]BNY Mellon Corporation, USA

Nor is our knowledge of interpersonal communication in the workplace an unexplored region because the topic is deemed trivial. In their presentation at the Association for Business Communication's Annual Convention in Montreal, Reinsch and Gardner (2011) reported the results of a national survey revealing that senior business executives maintain that employees with strong interpersonal skills are most likely to be considered for promotions. The study also indicated that writing ability—the development of which occupies considerable attention in most business communication courses—was not viewed as a primary concern when considering executives for promotion. The articles in this theme section extend the findings of Reinsch and Gardner by indicating that employers would rather hire employees with well-developed interpersonal skills than those with demonstrated writing ability.

I recently conducted an informal experiment to gain some sense of the significance of interpersonal communication skills in work-related environments. For a 5-month period—from February through June 2012—I collected every e-mail message received from vendors of business communication training. (I work in a technical communication function.) During that period, I received 38 offers from service providers. Here are the results, arranged by type of training offered, number of offers, and the percentage of total offers represented by each specific type:

Having Difficult Conversations	*17 (44.7%)*
Speaking as a Leader	*7 (18.4%)*
Giving Presentations	*5 (13.3%)*
Coaching/Motivational Speaking	*4 (10.6%)*
Communicating With Customers	*3 (7.8%)*
Facilitating Meetings	*2 (5.2%)*

I found the results interesting because they reveal the sorts of communication training that, to the thinking of profit-minded companies that specialize in providing instruction to large corporations, will be most wanted.

All of the training offerings focus on speaking skills—none were concerned with writing. The most popular topic, "Having Difficult Conversations," comprised a mélange of courses, each focusing on very specific problems: reducing "drama" in the workplace, giving and receiving criticism, dealing with insubordination, handling employees with "bad hygiene," resolving conflicts, making the transition from "buddy to boss," dealing with rude employees, disciplining workers, conducting performance reviews, counseling employees, handling terminations, avoiding "bad boss" behaviors, working with disabled employees, and repairing relations with other departments. Most of the vendors promised that these issues could be resolved by the use of videos, audio programs, written scripts, flash cards, or a combination of these methods. In most instances, course content focused on various "rules" that would permit managers to modify the undesirable behaviors of employees. (Some courses, though, devoted attention to rules intended to modify the behaviors of managers.)

The listing of possible "difficult conversations" presents a brief catalog of certain interpersonal communication in the workplace—especially those dealing with situations that hold the potential of embarrassing managers, employees, or both. But the other types of training offerings, including "Speaking as a Leader" and "Coaching/Motivational Speaking," are also forms of interpersonal communication. Clearly, from the standpoint of vendors whose business consists of providing corporations with the kinds of training deemed most saleable, interpersonal communication in the workplace is considered a moneymaker. These trainers for hire agree with Reinsch and Gardner (2011), as well as the articles in this section: Interpersonal skills are critical attributes, necessary for successful employees.

But even this plethora of behavior modification training does not add greatly to our knowledge of interpersonal communication. We are merely told that certain "rules" or scripts, if followed correctly, will cause certain problems to disappear. In short, the vast terrain of interpersonal skills in the workplace remains an "unexplored region."

The two articles presented in this section represent genuine attempts to explore the terrain and invite future researchers to join this ongoing effort.

Robles contributes to our knowledge by developing a clear nomenclature with which to discuss "interpersonal skills" and its relation to communication. According to Robles's formulation, the term *soft skills* is a composite of *interpersonal (people) skills* and *personal (career) attributes*. Personal attributes consist of behavioral traits unique to an individual, such as effective time management. Interpersonal skills, however, involve traits exemplified when the individual engages in social interaction. The ability to communicate effectively—to handle difficult conversations in such a manner that problems are resolved—is an interpersonal skill. "Soft skills" refers to all attributes or traits associated with personal skills as well as those dubbed "interpersonal."

Hynes describes a consulting engagement in which she developed a curriculum intended to provide training in interpersonal communication competencies to employees of a major corporation. Her discussion emphasizes that assessment is a complicated matter when interpersonal skills are the focus of instruction. (The nettlesome topic of assessment was never broached by the 38 vendors who forwarded to me their training proposals.) Hynes reveals to us that thorough assessment involves not only the reactions of employees who have been trained but also the observations of managers who are requested to assess employees many weeks after training has concluded. Conducting surveys and interviews and then collating and interpreting their results are time-consuming tasks.

Both Robles and Hynes, working independently, reach similar conclusions. One of these findings, which may also partially explain why the topic of interpersonal skills is largely an "unexplored region," is that organizations have not developed methods for measuring the long-term value of training. Many of the participants find employment with other companies; others transfer to different departments within the organization. Thus, the actual return on investment of interpersonal skills training is elusive.

The second finding, with which both authors concur, is that business communication curricula at the college and graduate school level are well served by including an interpersonal skills component. As Hynes indicates, most curricula currently include instruction in business writing and verbal presentations. However, given the significance attributed to interpersonal communication in business environments, the topic should not be ignored or given short shrift. Perhaps, if this recommendation were seriously considered and implemented by instructors of business communication, the topic of interpersonal communication in the workplace would not remain largely unexplored.

Reference

Reinsch, N. L., Jr., & Gardner, J. A. (2011, October). Do good communicators get promoted? Maybe not! In L. G. Snyder (Ed.), *Proceedings of the 76th annual convention of the Association for Business Communication.* Retrieved from http://businesscommunication.org/wp-content/uploads/2011/10/2011-ABC-01-REINSCH.pdf

Bio

Sam H. DeKay, Section Editor, is a vice president for corporate communications at BNY Mellon Corporation in New York City. He is also an adjunct associate professor at the Graduate School of Education, St. John's University, Jamaica, Queens, New York.

Soft skills and employability: Evidence from UK retail

Nickson, D., Warhurst, C., Commander, J., Hurrell, S.A., Cullen, A.

Abstract

This article contributes to ongoing debates about soft skills in front-line interactive service work in considering employability in the UK retail sector. It recognizes how UK government policy has emphasized the importance of qualifications in enhancing employability. However, it suggests that for front-line work in retail it is soft skills that are required to access entry-level jobs. The article notes how these soft skills have traditionally been dominated by debates about emotional labour. Drawing on a survey of 173 clothing, footwear and leather goods retailers, the article argues for a need to recognize the broadening of soft skills to also include aesthetic labour. The article concludes by discussing the implications of the broadening of soft skills with regard to policy initiatives to encourage the long-term unemployed into the retail sector.

Keywords

Aesthetic labour, emotional labour, employability, entry-level jobs, interactive service work, long-term unemployed

Introduction

In the UK, as across the EU as a whole, employability is a concern of government. This concern arises through a desire by government to prepare workers to be able to participate in what is perceived as a dynamic and transforming labour market (Cullen, 2008). In levering employability, the UK government has largely concentrated on supply-side interventions in the labour market; in practice having more workers with better qualifications. As the then Prime Minister of the UK, Tony Blair, explained when Labour came to power in the UK, 'education is the best economic policy we have' (cited in DfEE, 1998). At the expanding top end of the labour market for managers, professionals and associate professionals (see Dickerson et al., 2006) the most obvious manifestation of this policy is the expansion of higher education and the number of degree or Level 4 and above qualified workers.[1] Likewise at the expanding bottom end the labour market, for sales and customer service occupations for example, the UK government similarly wishes to encourage a qualifications uptake, most obviously and recently flagged through the Leitch Review of Skills, which wants more unskilled and low skilled workers qualified to Level 2 and, more recently, Level 3 (UKCES, 2009).

However, there is some indication that qualifications are only part of the answer, and that soft skills are also an important feature of employability for jobs at both the top and bottom end of the labour market (Brown and Hesketh, 2004; Lafer, 2004). At the bottom end of the labour market much of the literature on front-line interactive service work has pointed to the importance of so-called soft skills. Soft skills are defined by Moss and Tilly (1996: 253) as 'skills, abilities and traits that pertain to personality, attitude and behaviour rather than to formal or technical knowledge'. Other authors have, however, revealed that soft skills are more than simply individual traits and dispositions. Hurrell (2009: 397), for example, defines soft skills as 'involving interpersonal and intrapersonal abilities to facilitate mastered performance in particular contexts'. To date analysis of these soft skills in interactive service work has been dominated by debates about emotional labour and workers having to manage their own and customers' emotions (following, most obviously, Hochschild, 1983; but see also Bolton, 2004). Within this analysis workers having the right personality and attitude have become *proxies* for these soft skills (see, for example, Callaghan and Thompson, 2002). This current focus on the management of emotions as the required soft skill needs to be complemented by an awareness that employers are also concerned with the management of employee appearance, or what is termed 'aesthetic labour' (Nickson et al., 2001; Warhurst et al., 2000). This labour refers to the hiring of people with corporeal capacities and attributes that favourably appeal to customer senses and which are then organizationally mobilized, developed and commodified through training, management and regulation to produce an embodied style of service. In short, employers seek employees who 'look good' and 'sound right' and can best either embody the brand or appeal to the senses of customers.

Thus there is a relative lack of demand for qualifications among employers in interactive service work and especially the industry that is the focus of this article, retail (Lewis et al., 2008). Indeed, there is a strong recognition that front-line service workers in industries such as retail primarily require soft skills both to get and do jobs. In seeking to assess this issue the article takes up the challenge of writers such as Korczynski (2005a) and Gatta et al. (2009) who argue for the need to develop a fuller understanding of what skills are important in interactive service work. The latter argue, for example, that:

Sociologists need to develop a research agenda that recognises skills in service work, both at the level of worksites and within national skills certification systems; that understands how service work can be organised so skills are rewarded and quality of jobs is improved; and that develops training and education protocols to ensure that current and future workforces possess the necessary skills. (Gatta et al., 2009: 985)

This debate about employability and soft skills demand is not an academic one. Bunt et al. (2005) note that the UK government targets retail as an industry that might usefully provide jobs for the unemployed. Similarly, retail-led regeneration is suggested as reconnecting communities to economic opportunity, providing employment, business support and investment (DTZ Consulting, 2009). Within the industry, sales and customer service and elementary occupations, such as sales and retail assistants, retail cashiers and checkout operators are identified as possible entry-level jobs into the labour market. However, research on the long-term unemployed by Cullen (2008) reveals that training organizations, guided by UK government funding, are not providing appropriate training for the unemployed who are seeking front-line service work. It is important therefore to understand how employability is understood by different employers (see, for example, Lanning et al., 2008) and specifically what retail employers are seeking in prospective employees. This article examines this issue. It focuses on entry-level jobs in the retail sub-sectors of clothing, footwear and leather goods – sub-sectors described by Skillsmart (2007: 48) as 'significant categories in UK retailing'.

The research suggests that qualifications feature low in employers' perceptions of employability and that soft skills matter more. The findings in this article are pertinent, it is argued, not only because Korczynski (2005a) and Gatta et al. (2009) argue for new research agendas but also because they challenge current policy orientations with regard to employability, particularly for the unemployed. We argue in the concluding remarks that the focus on qualifications ignores some key issues in skill formation within the labour market that creates the potential for the social exclusion of the unemployed.

Understanding employability in retail

Despite its equation with qualifications by government, employability is not a straightforward or one-dimensional concept. Indeed, it is a matter of some debate. Employability cannot be solely equated with skill as measured by qualifications. Brown and Hesketh (2004) make the point that it is 'personal capital', or the sum of various personal qualities that employers value. Employers, they suggest, place importance on hard currencies, such as qualifications and work experience *and* soft currencies such as personal skills and appearance and accent. Brown and Hesketh (2004: 35) highlight that ' "who you are" matters as much as "what you know" '. Certainly soft skills, such as friendliness and team working ability, and traits such as emotional intelligence have been highlighted as the skills that are of greatest importance in the current labour market (Lafer, 2004).

While recognizing the importance of workers' knowledge, skills and attitudes as employability assets, Hillage and Pollard (1998) also point out that employability is affected by context, such as individual personal circumstances and external socioeconomic factors. Likewise, Brown et al. (2003) argue that for the most part it is the labour market rather than personal factors that determines employability. McQuaid and Lindsay (2005) also argue a narrow supply-side conceptualization of employability does not take adequate account of employer demand issues. Their broader conceptualization of employability allows, as McQuaid et al. (2005: 194) point out, 'the additional consideration of vital demand, personal circumstances and other factors that influence employability'. A duality of employability therefore exists that encompasses supply and demand, as well as qualifications and soft skills.

A key issue however is what constitutes the soft skills being supplied or demanded. In this regard analysis of skill issues is particularly pertinent in UK retail. Retail is now a significant part of the UK economy, accounting for £256 billion in sales and one-third of all consumer spending (Skillsmart, 2007). Indeed, it might be said that the UK is no longer a nation of shopkeepers but instead shopworkers. It is the largest private sector employer in the UK, employing 3 million workers or one in 10 of the working population. It is a relatively gendered industry with 60% of the workforce being women, many of whom work part-time. Retail also tends to be a young industry with a third of all workers under 25, a figure far higher than the economy as whole (Skillsmart, 2007). A large proportion of these young workers are students, such that they are now considered to be a structural part of the retail labour market (Huddleston and Hirst, 2004). There is a strong indication that employers have skill deficits particularly in sales occupations, which is the largest occupational group in retail (Skillsmart, 2007). In this respect there are both skills gaps in existing employees and skills shortages when employers are recruiting. For example, Hart et al. (2007) note that skills gaps in retail are higher than across the economy as a whole (26% vs 22%). Skills gaps are particularly acute for sales and elementary occupations, with customer handling skills especially lacking (Skillsmart, 2007). Retail employers face skill shortages which create difficulties in recruiting appropriate employees. These skills deficits create particular problems for retailers that can include 'difficulties in meeting customer needs, providing quality service and also increased organisational costs' (Hart et al., 2007: 272). With the job growth provided by the industry and employers facing such labour problems it is unsurprising that government is targeting retail as an opportunity to regenerate local economies and lever the unemployed back into the labour market, particularly as most jobs in retail are entry-level jobs (BMG, 2006; Bunt et al., 2005; DTZ Consulting, 2009; Skillsmart, 2004a).

While all retail work requires some knowledge, for example of hardware such as computerized tills and payment processing systems, the need for product knowledge varies across retail sub-sectors. Unlike in supermarkets, where goods sell themselves, fashion retail requires employees to sell the jumpers, dresses and shoes for example. In other words fashion goods have to be sold rather than sell themselves (Buchanan et al., 2003). Korczynski (2005b), perhaps over-egging the distinction, claims that such employees have to 'enchant' the customer. However there is little demand from retail employers for workers with qualifications – even job-relevant qualifications. Recent analysis of Labour Force Survey data undertaken by Skillsmart (2006) suggests that for sales and customer service occupations in retail, 17% of employees had no qualifications at all (compared to 10% across the economy as a whole), with 20% having a qualification below National Vocational Qualification (NVQ) Level 2 and 26% being qualified at NVQ Level 2.[2] Similarly, the take-up of apprenticeships is well below average in the retail sector (LSC, 2008). Moreover even when apprenticeships are undertaken, completion rates are lower than for other industries (Lewis et al., 2008). Qualifications therefore may only be one, arguably marginal, component of providing for employability for the unemployed in obtaining front-line, entry-level jobs in the industry.

Instead employers are more concerned with soft skills. In their review of retail and related occupations as entry-level jobs for the unemployed, Bunt et al.'s (2005) employer survey found that the skills demanded by retail employers in new recruits for sales and retail assistants, retail cashiers and checkout operator jobs centred on self-presentation, verbal communications and interpersonal and team work skills.[3] There is further evidence that it is these skills and their shortages that most concern employers. For example, Huddleston and Hirst (2004: 8) recognize that:

> While few organisations have difficulty recruiting sales assistants, attracting the right candidate is often difficult. A lack of people with the right 'attitude' has been seen as a major barrier to success . . . some retailers may be looking specifically for young people who 'look a certain way', this is especially important in some designer fashion retail outlets.

The 'personality market' described by Mills (1956) centred on employee attitude and appearance. Attitude was proxied by Mills in terms of employees being 'friendly, helpful, tactful and courteous' to customers (1956: 183) but appearance quickly disappeared from his analysis, perhaps because empirically Mills could find no evidence of organizational intervention to shape it. This analytical myopia has been compounded in debate about emotional labour, which, following Hochschild (1983), has become the dominant research paradigm in service work. As such, attitude has become a proxy for the soft skills required of emotional labour (see, for example, Callaghan and Thompson, 2002). Having the right attitude is regarded as a prerequisite of employees appropriately managing their own as well as customers' feelings in order to affect the desired service encounter. To this end, feeling rules prescribe employees being responsive, courteous and understanding with customers for example (for an overview of the emotional labour literature, see Korczynski, 2002). For this reason, attitude has come to be conceived as constituent of the soft skills necessary within interactive service work.

However, this conceptualization of soft skills is partial. While the importance of employee attitudes has been extensively researched as a feature of emotional labour, the issue of appearance or employees 'looking a certain way' to use Huddleston and Hirst's phrase, has tended to be overlooked or at best marginalized. Its importance has been acknowledged but not analysed not only by Mills but also Hochschild and by subsequent research within the emotional labour paradigm (for a fuller discussion of the theoretical boundaries between emotional, aesthetic and sexualized labour, see Warhurst and Nickson, 2009).

Recent research of interactive services has sought to rectify this omission and draw attention to not only the organizational management of employee feelings but also employees' corporeality, and has led to the development of aesthetic labour. This concept points to the increasing importance of the demand for employees to embody the product in industries such as retail and hospitality (see, for example, Warhurst and Nickson, 2007; Warhurst et al., 2000). As part of this process of embodiment, employees are now expected to demonstrate not only soft skills with regard to their attitude but also their appearance to customers. The short-hand for this soft skill as demanded by employers is employees having to 'look good' or 'sound right'. As such employers are concerned with managing and monitoring employees' body language, dress and speech for example. Employees are hired because of the way they look and talk; once employed, they are instructed how to stand while working, what to wear and how to wear it and what to say to customers (Nickson et al., 2001). Indeed, Leslie (2002) suggests that fashion retail is distinct from other forms of retail employment in its strict enforcement of image and presentation rules suggesting that 'like models, retail workers have to conform to specific bodily criteria' (2002: 69). As she further notes, what stores are seeking may also differ depending on the style they wish to portray. Consequently there is a matching process between stores and the recruitment of retail workers to ensure that employees are the 'right type' for the brand (and see also Pettinger, 2004, 2005). Although most of the focus has been on the manner in which fashion retail is concerned with creating feminized performativity (Leslie, 2002; McRobbie, 1997; Pettinger, 2004, 2005), recent research by Walls (2008) reveals that this process of styling is equally true for men working in the industry. As he notes, the men in his study of fashion retailers would use their aesthetic capital in seeking employment and 'workers had to offer more than just masculinity, they had to also offer "cool", style and "trendiness" ' (2008: 110).

Thus any account of what potentially comprises employability in fashion retail has to include not just qualifications and technical skills but also the soft skills deemed constituent of both emotional and aesthetic labour. It is this range of requirements that are explored in this article. As the next section outlines, the location for the research was Manchester – a former industrial city which has recently reinvented itself as a retail hub for the North West of England.

An outline of the research project

The article draws on a postal survey focused on standard industrial classification (SIC) codes 52.42 and 52.43, clothing, footwear and leather goods retailers in the Greater Manchester area and undertaken as part of a broader comparative project with teams from Australia and Sweden. This geographical focus reflects the fact that the Greater Manchester area is a major shopping destination in the North West of England and that retail is a key driver of the area's recent economic development (Skillsmart, 2004b). Prior to the economic downturn the North West had the largest amount of construction activity of new shops and stores in the UK (Skillsmart, 2007), with obvious implications for employment opportunities for the unemployed. Moreover in some of the shopping districts in Greater Manchester, clothing and footwear comprises nearly half of all retail business (BMG, 2005, 2006). Significantly, retailers in Greater Manchester have stated that a key reason for the existence of hard-to-fill vacancies for sales and customer service staff is a low number of applicants with the required soft skills (Skillsmart, 2004b).

The survey was administered to a sample of 500 SIC 52.42 and 52.43 retailers in Manchester. The sample drew upon a database collated by the Manchester Chambers of Commerce but was updated and extended by the researchers targeting public and business directory listings of the main shopping centres and districts. The shopping centre databases were provided by the centre managements. The shopping districts' sample was confirmed as being representative of the identified sub-sectors by telephoning each retailer in advance of including them in the final sample. From the sample of 500 retailers a final response rate of 35% (*n* = 173) was achieved. This response rate is close to the average rate of 35.7%

for surveys of organizations relying on managerial respondents as reported in Baruch and Holtom (2008).

The questionnaire included sections on recruitment and selection, skills demand and whether skills shortages in potential recruits or skills gaps in the current workforce existed. Questions in these sections explored employer demand for aspects of emotional and aesthetic labour as well as qualifications and other job-related needs. Data analysis was conducted using SPSS. The data were coded and cleaned with results first drawn using descriptive statistics and frequencies. Differences between types of establishment were also ascertained on key variables. Multiple regression analyses were conducted to ascertain whether the characteristics sought during recruitment and selection (qualifications, experience and the 'right' personality and appearance) and the overall importance of the appearance of front-line staff differed by a number of establishment and workforce variables, while controlling for other variables in the models. Establishment variables included the ownership structure of the establishment (chain or independent) and customer preference for style, cost and quality. Workforce variables that may have potentially affected the characteristics sought during recruitment included the proportion of male and female staff, the proportion of students in the workforce, the age profile of staff and the ideal level of education for recruits. The size of the establishment, measured by the number of staff employed, was also included as a further control variable.

Research findings

Establishment and workforce characteristics

Tables 1 and 2 provide an overview of the characteristics of the sample establishments and their workforces. There were some problems with missing data, with a minority of variables having greater than the benchmark of 5% missing cases (Little and Rubin, 1987) (the number of staff and the proportion of the staff that were female, students, full-time and had a retail qualification). Indeed for the proportion of students, over 30% of respondents did not provide an answer, although for most variables the number of missing cases was considerably lower. Analysis of the missing data revealed that respondents may have simply left the categories blank when they had no staff fitting the criteria or where the proportion of staff in a group may have been difficult to recall or data were unavailable to them.[4] Although the student data must be interpreted with some caution, the data on the whole remain robust.

The vast majority (73%) of the 173 establishments were branches of multi-site chain establishments. Such organizations may be expected to have centralized practices in place regarding skills policies (Kersley et al., 2006) and also more formalized branding strategies (Lury, 2004). Establishments were also small with an average of 22 employees. All establishments in the sample catered for customers of a variety of ages and typically for both males and females. Quality and style were seen as more important to customers than cost by the respondents. Only 39% of establishments rated cost as 'very important' or 'essential' to customers, compared to 80% for quality and 82% for style.

Respondents were asked about the demographics of their front-line workers. On average, 74% of staff in each establishment were female, supporting the view that fashion retailing is more gendered than the sector as a whole (Leslie, 2002; McRobbie, 2002;

Table 1. Sample characteristics: frequencies.[a]

Question	Categories	% establishments
Type of establishment (N = 172)	Independent single-site shop	22
	Independent franchised shop	5
	Branch in a chain	73
Ideal required level of education for front-line staff (N = 168)	None	38
	GCSE/NVQ Level 1/2 or equivalent	49
	A levels/NVQ advances/Level 3 or equivalent	9
	Further/higher education short of a degree	2
	Bachelor's degree	2
	Higher degree	0

[a]Frequencies reported are valid exclusive of missing data.

Table 2. Sample characteristics: descriptives.

	N	Range	Mean	SD
Number of staff employed in establishment	164	1–600	21.70	60.11
Approx % of female staff	158	10–100	74.03	26.43
Approx % of full-time staff	156[a]	7–100	46.96	26.19
Approx % of staff who were students	118	0–80	41.18	21.57
Approx % of staff aged 16–20	165	0–100	28.83	25.81
Approx % of staff aged 21–25	165	0–100	29.68	24.52
Approx % of staff aged 26–30	165	0–100	13.28	19.32
Approx % of staff aged 31–40	165	0–100	11.75	17.65
Approx % of staff aged 41–50	165	0–80	7.51	15.83
Approx % of staff aged > 50	165	0–100	7.50	19.91
Approx % of staff with specialist retail qualification	152	0–100	15.16	23.13

[a]Included two extreme low values that were removed after analysis.

Pettinger, 2005). Front-line staff were also, typically, young with, on average, almost 60% of establishments' workforces aged between 16 and 25. Approximately 41% of staff in each establishment were students and only 47% of staff worked full-time, reflecting varied labour demand and that many staff were in education. Despite hiring many students, respondents typically reported that to get the job staff needed either no education or only basic school leaving standard education. These findings reaffirm that front-line retail staff need little formal education. Additionally, very few staff had a specialist retail qualification. As with the size of establishments there was a large degree of variation for each characteristic, highlighting the diversity of retail establishments.

Employer demand for employees getting and doing the job

Table 3 examines the criteria stated by employers to be important for employees in *getting* the job. Employers were asked to rate whether the characteristic was 'not at all important', 'not very important', 'fairly important', 'very important' or 'essential'. The table also presents

Table 3. Factors important in staff selection.[a]

	N	% reporting 'very important' or 'essential'	Range	Mean	SD
Right personality	170	79.7	3–5	4.15	0.71
Right appearance	170	68.2	1–5	3.84	0.80
Previous experience	170	41.1	1–5	3.36	0.85
Qualifications	169	4.6	1–5	2.14	0.86

[a]All factors measured on a five-point scale ranging from 'not at all important' to 'essential'.

Table 4. Significant regression coefficients: importance of factors in selecting front-line staff.

Model	R^2	Variable	Coefficient
1 – Qualifications	0.31	Approx % of staff aged 21–25	0.37**
		Approx % of staff aged 26–30	0.31**
		Approx % of staff aged 31–40	0.23*
		Approx % of staff aged > 50	0.27*
		Ideal required education level of staff[a]	0.41***
		Importance of quality to customers[b]	0.19*
2 – Experience	0.12	Ideal required education level of staff	0.17*
		Importance of style to customers[b]	0.17*
3 – 'Right' personality	0.17	Approx % of staff aged 16–20	−0.30*
		Approx % of staff aged 31–40	−0.30**
		Approx % of staff aged > 50	−0.40**
4 – Appearance	0.13	Importance of style to customers	0.18*

*$p \leq .05$, **$p < .01$, ***$p = .000$.
[a]Measured on an ascending six-point scale with categories: none; GCSE/NVQ Level 1 or 2 or equivalent; A levels/NVQ advanced/Level 3 or equivalent; Further/higher education short of a degree (e.g. HND, HNC); First (bachelor's) degree; Postgraduate degree.
[b]Measured on a five-point scale ranging from 'not at all important' to 'very important'.

the mean perceived importance of these criteria to employers. The maximum possible mean score was 5 indicating that an aspect is 'essential' in the work of front-line staff.

As shown in Table 3, just over 41% viewed previous experience as either essential or very important while only 5% rated qualifications in this manner. Of more importance are the proxies for emotional and aesthetic labour. Reflecting the findings of Bunt et al. (2005), employers rated personality and appearance as the most important aspects when selecting front-line staff with 80% suggesting that personality was either 'essential' or 'very important'. Sixty-eight percent of employers also stated the importance of having the 'right' appearance as either 'essential' or 'very important' when selecting staff.

Any differences between establishments in the importance of particular factors in selecting staff were determined using the multiple regression analyses described in the methods section.[5] Table 4 shows those establishment characteristics that significantly affected selection criteria. Where organizations reported a higher ideal education level for front-line staff, qualifications and, to a lesser extent, experience were deemed as more important during selection. Where establishments reported that customers were more

Table 5. Characteristics important in performing front-line work.[a]

	N	% reporting 'very important' or 'essential'	Range	Mean	SD
Ability to work with others	170	85.0	2–5	4.25	0.69
Ability to deal with customers	171	84.0	2–5	4.30	0.74
Availability and rostering	166	65.9	1–5	3.84	0.79
Product knowledge	170	65.5	1–5	3.86	0.88
Work ethic	166	63.0	1–5	3.68	1.03
Outgoing personality	169	60.2	1–5	3.72	0.83
Dress sense and style	168	57.2	1–5	3.68	0.88
Knowledge of store operations/procedures	170	54.3	1–5	3.66	0.93
Ability to use equipment	169	48.0	1–5	3.47	1.00
Voice and accent	170	27.2	1–5	2.89	1.06
Previous job experience	166	28.3	1–5	3.07	0.84
Overall physical appearance	156	21.4	1–5	2.72	1.05
Formal education/qualifications	170	8.6	1–5	2.35	0.87
Age	164	7.4	1–5	2.07	0.92
Height	162	4.6	1–5	1.72	0.84
Weight	162	4.1	1–5	1.83	0.85

[a]All characteristics measured on a five-point scale ranging from 'not at all important' to 'essential'.

concerned with quality, the importance of qualifications in selecting staff also increased. The importance of style to customers was also associated with a greater emphasis on both appearance and experience when selecting front-line staff. These findings suggest that appearance was more important in conveying a certain style within establishments and that where employers were looking for experience this experience related to style markets. Selection requirements were thus not ubiquitous.

There was no set pattern regarding the effects of the age profile of staff and no significant effects in terms of the importance of selection characteristics depending on the size of the establishment, the proportion of male/female staff or students, the ownership structure of the establishment or the importance of cost to customers. Customer requirements for style and to a lesser extent quality were, therefore, the establishment characteristics that most affected what was deemed important during selection.

Table 5 shows the mean importance of staff characteristics in actually *doing* the job. As Table 5 shows factors that might be regarded as features of emotional labour were regarded as most important to employers. These aspects were followed by workers' availability and rostering, product knowledge, work ethic, outgoing personality, some elements of aesthetic labour (dress sense and style), knowledge of store operations and procedures and use of equipment. All of these factors were rated on average as 'very important'. Still above average in terms of mean importance (> 2.5) were other aspects of aesthetic labour, such as overall physical appearance and voice and accent, plus job experience. This latter finding suggests that the aesthetic requirements of customer-facing work were related more to clothing and style than physical appearance per se, consistent with the importance

Table 6. Significant regression coefficients: overall importance of the appearance of front-line staff.

R^2	Variable	Coefficient
0.23	Branch in a chain of shops[a]	0.30***
	Ideal required education level of staff[b]	−0.16*
	Importance of style to customers[b]	0.24**

*$p \le .05$, **$p < .01$, *** $p = .000$.
[a]Variable uses standard dummy coding and is reported relative to reference category; belonging to an independent establishment. For this analysis being an independent single-site store and being an independent franchised store were collapsed due to the relative small numbers of establishments in these categories.
[b]See notes to Table 4.

that establishments believed customers placed on 'style' and the workers that can best embody that style (Pettinger, 2004, 2005).

Formal education and qualifications clearly lack importance to employers both as a percentage and a below average mean score. The relative lack of importance attributed to formal qualifications is consistent with employers' low educational requirements. Age, weight and height were also, apparently, not a great concern for employers. It may be the case that employers were aware of the delicacy of these potentially sensitive physical characteristics and were underplaying their importance.

Establishments were also asked to rate the importance of the overall appearance of front-line staff (see Table 6). Multiple regression determined whether the importance of appearance differed between establishments. The importance of style to customers was positively related to the overall importance of appearance, while the ideal level of education for staff was negatively related to the same. Chain stores were also significantly more likely to attribute the appearance of front-line staff as important, perhaps reflecting standardized style and branding requirements across the organization (see Lury, 2004). These results are again consistent with the earlier reported analyses that the appearance of staff is especially important in style markets and is demanded at the expense of qualifications.

Recruitment and selection methods

Recruitment and selection methods are an important element in determining how organizations ensure that they are staffed with the appropriate skills. As with other research focusing on service industries (see, for example, Kersley et al., 2006; Lockyer and Scholarios, 2004), there was a reliance on informal recruitment methods, the most popular being referrals from current staff (64%) and window adverts (60%). Two formal methods were the next most frequently reported categories; 48% used recruitment agencies and job centres while 42% used company websites. Other formal and informal methods such as advertising in the local press, rehiring old staff and accepting casual callers were reported by 23–32% of establishments. The use of informal methods such as referrals suggests that employees may be recruited who 'fit' with employees already in the establishment and possibly, therefore, the establishment's brand (Hurrell and Scholarios, 2011; Warhurst and Nickson, 2009). It is also the case that casual callers and those responding to window adverts typically present themselves in person, which may be advantageous in allowing employers to screen for soft skills, especially those associated with appearance (Nickson et al., 2005).

Table 7. Characteristics difficult to recruit.[a]

	N	% reporting 'very difficult' or 'impossible'	Range	Mean	SD
Product knowledge	169	26.0	1–5	3.01	0.82
Knowledge of store operations/procedures	168	21.4	1–4	2.76	0.86
Work ethic	165	14.5	1–4	2.55	0.90
Ability to deal with customers	167	13.9	1–5	2.61	0.85
Availability and rostering	164	11.0	1–5	2.59	0.81
Previous job experience	166	10.4	1–5	2.50	0.84
Voice and accent	165	8.7	1–4	2.21	0.89
Formal education/qualifications	164	8.7	1–5	2.22	0.87
Outgoing personality	166	7.5	1–5	2.27	0.83
Ability to use equipment	166	4.6	1–4	2.19	0.69
Dress sense and style	166	4.1	1–5	2.23	0.75
Ability to work with others	167	2.9	1–5	2.21	0.67
Age	157	2.3	1–5	1.83	0.75
Weight	152	1.2	1–4	1.61	0.65
Physical appearance	156	1.2	1–4	1.74	0.61
Height	152	–	1–3	1.58	0.60

[a]All characteristics measured on a five-point scale ranging from 'not at all difficult' to 'impossible'.

Employers tended to use the 'classic trio' of application forms/CVs (60/78%), interviews (71%) and references (60%) when selecting front-line staff. In addition to this classic trio, 24% of the Manchester employers reported using role plays to select front-line staff, 17% product knowledge tests, 11% requested photographs of applicants and 10% used job simulations.

Employers were then asked to rate which methods were the most useful for selecting front-line staff. Resonating with the point about employers wanting to filter in or filter out appropriate staff, almost two-thirds of respondents stated that interviews were the most useful method. This finding gives a 'usefulness' ratio of 0.87 when dividing the proportion of employers finding interviews 'most useful' by the proportion using this selection method. The usefulness/use ratios for CVs, application forms and references were 0.40, 0.48 and 0.22 respectively. For role plays the usefulness ratio was 0.58. These findings indicate that employers prefer the opportunity to directly interact with potential employees, finding interviews and role plays most useful in selecting new employees, although role plays were relatively under-used. These techniques allow employers to make an immediate assessment of potential employees' emotional and aesthetic labour potential. That employers in interactive services wish to assess the interactive potential of applicants is not surprising and indeed seems to be a standard feature of the purpose of the use of interviews more widely in other forms of service work (Nickson, 2007).

Skills shortages

Managers were asked to rate the difficulty of recruiting applicants from a range of characteristics related to the job, ranging from skills through to product knowledge and qualifications (see Table 7).

Contrary to Huddleston and Hirst's (2004) claim about skills shortages related to applicants' attitudes and appearance, only a minority of employers had any significant difficulty recruiting the desired soft skills among potential employees. Where most difficulty did exist was in recruiting employees with the appropriate knowledge of products or store operations and procedures. It should be noted, however, that both types of knowledge can be very basic, as employees reported to Warhurst and Nickson (2007). As one fashion retail worker from the study explained, 'I'd never worked in retail before in my life and they threw me in at the deep end and I just got on with it, but when we got a new manager . . . she gave out sheets about brands and all that and we had one till-training session' (Warhurst and Nickson, 2007: 114).

Aside from these most 'difficult' aspects only four characteristics were reported as 'very difficult' or 'impossible' to recruit by over 10% of establishments (previous job experience, availability and rostering, the ability to deal with customers and work ethic). All had mean scores of 2.5 or greater suggesting a tendency for these characteristics to be rated as 'fairly difficult' rather than 'not very difficult'. It was, therefore, harder and more technical skills, abilities and knowledge that were generally perceived as causing skills shortages rather than factors such as personality, dress sense and style.

One explanation for this finding is that fashion retail has greater cachet than other types of retail. The Retail E-Commerce Task Force found that 'trendy', aspirational sub-sectors, such as fashion, music/video, sport and software/games appealed most as employment opportunities to young people. Similarly Walls (2008) in his ethnography of fashion retail found his co-workers would often contrast the 'coolness' of jobs in fashion retail to retail jobs in supermarkets, for example. As a consequence those applicants who possess the appropriate attitudes and appearance are more likely to be attracted to fashion retail. This finding would support the work of Leslie (2002) and Pettinger (2004, 2005), who recognize that many workers in fashion retail see a blurring between their identities as workers and consumers. Often they already have a strong identification with the brand as consumers before they become workers; a process that is further reinforced when they go to work in the store. A number of respondents in Warhurst and Nickson (2007) noted how they were recruited to work in establishments for which they were previously consumers. Consequently employers have least difficulty in recruiting the right emotional and aesthetic labour.

Discussion and conclusion

Retail has been targeted by the UK government as an industry that can provide jobs for the unemployed (Bunt et al., 2005) and is particularly appropriate for employability initiatives to assist the long-term unemployed (Lindsay and Sturgeon, 2003). In order for such initiatives to work, however, there is clearly a need to develop an appropriate understanding of what employers are seeking in front-line retail workers, and in terms of those workers not only getting but also doing the job.

The survey findings reported in this article clearly indicate that Manchester fashion retail employers are more concerned with the soft skills of applicants, particularly having the 'right' attitude and appearance, than qualifications and technical skills. The requirement specifically for appearance is more associated with displaying a certain sense of 'style'.

Where recruitment problems existed it was for operational and product knowledge rather than for soft skills. It was, therefore, clearly easier to find applicants with the 'right' personality, attitude and appearance than such knowledge. There is a need to consider this finding within the particular context of the clothing, footwear and leather goods fashion retail sub-sector. Although not the main focus of this article, it is important to note that the retail sector is not homogeneous in terms of product markets, labour markets and skill utilization. There is some emergent evidence that different types of retailers may draw on different labour markets, and within fashion retail employers are able to source employees with the required soft skills with greater ease than supermarkets for example (see Buchanan et al., 2003). Thus, there may be greater cachet attributed to fashion retail compared to other sub-sectors in retail (Walls, 2008) and there is evidence to suggest that young people are more attracted to fashion than other retail sub-sectors (Retail E-Commerce Task Force, 2002). This point is useful in indicating the need to recognize heterogeneity in retail and although these results are likely to be generalizable to fashion retail in other parts of the UK, they may not be generalizable to other parts of the retail sector. This need to develop a more nuanced understanding of the 'retail sector' is one worthy of further research as the implications of this finding suggest that context is indeed important in shaping employability, as Brown et al. (2003), Hillage and Pollard (1998) and Lanning et al. (2008) assert, and this has significant implication for initiatives aimed at levering the unemployed into jobs in the retail sector.

Understanding the soft skills demands of employers is important and needs to inform policy discussion of employability in the UK and elsewhere. This need for a more nuanced understanding is particularly pronounced because, as Crouch (2004) points out, skill formation systems may not operate effectively during periods of change such as the current growth of the service economy generally or now specifically during the economic downturn (for a discussion of the latter, see Innovation, Universities, Science and Skills Committee, 2009). Thus existing methods of equipping individuals with skills may not be effective when there is little understanding of skill demands. Moreover, as Witz et al. (2003: 41) note, the 'embodied dispositions', or what can be perceived as aesthetic capacities and attributes, that are recast as part of the soft skills demanded by employers in much interactive service work 'are not equally distributed socially' and as such many individuals may lack the required soft skills to access employment in the interactive service sector. Indeed, Lindsay (2005) and Lindsay and McQuaid (2004) recognize that a significant proportion of the long-term unemployed in Glasgow and Edinburgh would never consider entry-level jobs in retail. One of the key reasons was that these unemployed respondents felt that they lacked the appropriate soft skills. As Lindsay and McQuaid state: 'those who had not previously worked in services and perceived themselves as lacking the "soft" skills required for such jobs were also particularly hostile to working in services' (2004: 309). This issue may be particularly pronounced in fashion retail, as argued earlier, which attracts more students who are more likely already to possess the desired soft skills if these skills are really associated with middle-classness as Hochschild (1983) and Warhurst and Nickson (2007) state respectively of emotional and aesthetic labour. In recruiting this emotional and style-driven aesthetic labour employers seem geared to excluding the unemployed.

If effective training and educational protocols are to be developed, Gatta et al. (2009) assert that a new research agenda is required that recognizes skills in service work. However, how these skills are formed also needs to be part of that agenda we would add. If what is deemed a skill is socially constructed (Grugulis et al., 2004), then the findings in this article indicate that those skills demanded by employers relate to being middle-class. Certainly the relatively high level of student labour reported in the findings would be consistent with such an argument. Warhurst and Nickson (2007) suggest that there is a displacement effect in much service work, with students, who in the UK generally have middle-class backgrounds, filling positions in the service sector that other types of workers – those from working-class backgrounds and the long-term unemployed – may have been expected to fill. Likewise Leslie (2002) and Walls (2008) suggest that both the feminine and masculine performativity required in fashion retail is overwhelmingly middle-class. The implication here is that middle-classness is being recast as a skill. The consequence is that the demand for soft skills may thus benefit the middle classes to the disadvantage of unemployed job seekers.

Although there was no evidence in our study of any gender differences in employer skills demand,[6] as part of its social construction, Leslie and Walls also point out the gendered performativity required in fashion retail. Scott (1994) too highlights the inherent 'feminine' skills that are perceived as being synonymous with the soft skills required by retail employers, Indeed, MacDonald and Merrill (2009) note that interactive service workers' 'performance' has to align with certain customer and management expectations and in that sense, 'the service performance may be more or less aligned with the gender and ethnic identity of the worker' (2009: 116). This latter point is also picked up by Leslie (2002) in her claim that the skills required in retail align with being white (see also Moss and Tilly, 1996). While in the past research on the social construction of skill has tended to focus on the effect of gender (Grugulis et al., 2004), it is clear from these data that more research is required into the intersection of gender, ethnicity, age and class on the social construction of skills in retail. Clearly the construction of these skills also has the scope for significant discrimination based on these aspects.[7] Further research also needs to consider attendant implications with regard to concerns about job quality and the relative value ascribed to 'feminine' soft skills and particularly why such skills continue to be undervalued (Gatta et al., 2009; Korczynski, 2005a).

With the increasing recognition of the primacy of soft skills for front-line service work there is some evidence of piecemeal attempts across the UK to offer soft skills training for the unemployed. For example, Learndirect[8] offer various courses that encompass the soft skills associated with customer care, which is suggested as being particularly useful for the unemployed looking to return to work. The creation of a Retail Academy in Glasgow is also intended to facilitate work placements for those seeking a career in retail by offering short-term, pre-employment training programmes that include soft skills to attract the young unemployed into retail (Glasgow Chamber of Commerce, 2007). Similarly in Milton Keynes in England there are programmes designed specifically to encourage the long-term unemployed into retail, with most of the training geared to enhancing the self-confidence of the unemployed and also ensuring they understand the importance of attitude and appearance (Ridge, 2006). When there has been an appreciation of the broad range of soft skills required by retail employers there has been some success in developing appropriate training. For example, Nickson et al. (2003), reporting on a short-lived training programme for the long-term unemployed who were seeking work in the retail and hospitality industries, found that that upon completion of the training participants had developed an appreciation for and understanding of the soft skill demands of employers. Participants also reported an increase in confidence, a better understanding of the performance-related nature of front-line service work and a clear appreciation of the importance of both looking good and sounding right in front-line service work. Such attempts to incorporate soft skills into the enhancement of the employability of the unemployed however remain piecemeal and incremental.

It is vital that UK government employability initiatives are geared to meeting the demands of employers in targeted industries such as retail. Recent research by Cullen (2008) highlights the weaknesses of existing job training for the unemployed. Part of the problem lies in the narrow view held by some policy-makers of the skills demanded in front-line service work and, consequently, the lack of appropriate training being provided related to these skills. What employers actually demand, as revealed by this article, resonate with arguments about the need for a wider conceptualization of employability, and so the type of training needed to be encouraged by government if it wishes to address the issue of social exclusion by enhancing employability, particularly for the unemployed. Overcoming social exclusion and levering the unemployed into the labour market by equipping them with employability takes into account both labour supply and demand and achieving an appropriate balance between qualifications and soft skills. Currently, UK government policy aims to address employability by focusing on enhancing workers' qualifications without looking at the broader factors that also impact upon employability. It is clear from the research reported here that a combination of approaches is required so employment opportunities in the retail industry can be accessed by the unemployed.

Funding

We would like to acknowledge and thank the Nuffield Foundation for funding the research on which this article is based.

Notes

1. The Qualifications and Credit Framework covers England, Wales and Northern Ireland and has eight levels. Level 2 denotes basic school leaver skills and Level 4 and above, degree-level study and equivalent. Although differing slightly in the number of levels, a similar qualifications and credit framework exists in Scotland.
2. NVQs are work-related, competence-based qualifications. They reflect the skills and knowledge needed to do a job effectively, and show that a candidate is competent in the area of work the NVQ represents. NVQs are based on national occupational standards.
3. Indeed, the National Occupational Standards for Retail, devised after extensive consultation with employers, outline core competences at NVQ Level 2 for providing customer service suggesting that employees should 'give the customers a positive impression of yourself and your organisation' by being aware of the organization's appearance and behaviour standards (Skillsmart, 2008).
4. The establishments not providing answers on the proportion of students were more likely to report that no education was required for staff and that they had higher numbers of full-time staff (with students typically working part-time). The same was true for missing data on female employees, which was also more likely to occur where establishments had greater numbers of full-time staff (women also more likely to work part-time). The establishments missing data on whether a specialist retail qualification was required were also more likely to report that no education was required for staff, with very few employees holding such qualifications. Independent

single-site stores were also more likely to have missing data on the number of staff and the proportion of full-time, female and student staff than other types of establishment. This response may reflect less standardized record keeping or the more informal staffing policies of smaller independent retailers.

5. The missing data on some independent variables would affect the statistical power of the model given the large number of independent variables. As the patterns of missing data were related to other variables of interest (see note 4) the missing values were replaced using the commonly used regression method (Little and Rubin, 1987). The other independent variables in the model were used to predict the missing values, while also adding a randomly selected residual to each value given the error associated with regression models and to avoid over homogeneity in the replaced values (Little and Rubin, 1987).

6. Such aligning of soft skills with women tends to be ahistorical, based on the current growth of service work and the feminization of these services (see also Hochschild, 1983). In an earlier age, when bank clerks were only male, these workers too were emotional labourers, required to deploy the soft skills now claimed to be feminine, as McKinlay's (2009) exposition of Mr Notman's employment history powerfully highlights.

7. See, for example, Fleener (2005) for a discussion of the recent Abercrombie and Fitch case in which the company in late 2004 agreed an approximately US$50 million settlement with a number of plaintiffs from minority ethnic groupings, including African Americans, Latinos and Asian Americans. These plaintiffs either failed to get jobs or were excluded from sales floor positions as their natural physical features did not represent the company's conception of 'natural classic American style'. It was argued by the plaintiffs that the 'A&F look' was 'virtually all white' and as Corbett (2007: 155) notes 'these plaintiffs succeeded when the attractive look the employer was seeking was not just pretty, but pretty and *white*' (emphasis in original).

8. Learndirect is a not-for-profit organization created by the UK government in 1998 to transform the skills and employability of the working population in order to improve the UK's productivity.

References

Baruch Y and Holtom B (2008) Survey response rate levels and trends in organizational research. *Human Relations* 61(8): 1139–1160.

BMG (2005) Retail workforce development survey: The Arndale Centre. BMG Research Report.

BMG (2006) Retail workforce development survey: The Trafford Centre. BMG Research Report.

Bolton S (2004) Conceptual confusions: Emotion work as skilled work. In: Warhurst C, Grugulis I and Keep E (eds) *The Skills that Matter*. London: Palgrave.

Brown P and Hesketh A (2004) *The Mismanagement of Talent*. Oxford: Oxford University Press.

Brown P, Hesketh A and Williams S (2003) Employability in a knowledge-driven economy. *Journal of Education and Work* 16(2): 107–126.

Buchanan J, Evesson J and Dawson M (2003) Retail trade. In: Buchanan J and Hall D (eds) *Beyond VET: The Changing Skill Needs of the Victorian Services Industries*. Sydney: ACIRRT, University of Sydney.

Bunt K, McAndrew F and Kuechel A (2005) *Jobcentre Plus Employer (Market View) Survey 2004*. Norwich: HMSO.

Callaghan G and Thompson P (2002) 'We recruit attitude': The selection and shaping of call centre labour. *Journal of Management Studies* 39(2): 233–254.

Corbett W (2007) The ugly truth about appearance discrimination and the beauty of our employment discrimination law. *Duke Journal of Gender Law and Policy* 14(1): 153–178.

Crouch C (2004) Skill formation systems. In: Batt R, Ackroyd S, Thompson P et al. (eds) *The Oxford Handbook of Work and Organization*. Oxford: Oxford University Press.

Cullen A (2008) *The demand for aesthetic skills in interactive service work: The implications of this demand upon unemployed job seekers' access to this work.* Unpublished Doctoral Thesis, University of Strathclyde.

DfEE (Department for Education and Employment) (1998) *The Learning Age.* Nottingham: DfEE.

Dickerson A, Homenidou K and Wilson R (2006) Working futures 2004–2014. Institute for Employment Research, University of Warwick.

DTZ Consulting (2009) Retail-led regeneration: Why it matters to our communities. Available at: www.bcsc.org.uk/media/downloads/Retail-ledRegeneration.pdf.

Fleener H (2005) Looks sell, but are they worth the cost? How tolerating looks-based discrimination leads to intolerable discrimination. *Washington University Law Quarterly* 83(4): 1295–1330.

Gatta M, Boushey H and Appelbaum E (2009) High-touch and here-to-stay: Future skills demands in us low wage service occupations. *Sociology* 43(5): 968–989.

Glasgow Chamber of Commerce (2007) Glasgow's academy of retail. *Glasgow Business: The Journal of Glasgow Chamber of Commerce*, March/April, 29.

Grugulis I, Warhurst C and Keep E (2004) What's happening to 'skill'? In: Warhurst C, Grugulis I and Keep E (eds) *The Skills that Matter.* Basingstoke: Palgrave Macmillan.

Hart C, Stachow G, Farrell A and Reed G (2007) Employer perceptions of skills gaps in retail: Issues and implications for UK retailers. *International Journal of Retail and Distribution Management* 35(4): 271–288.

Hillage J and Pollard E (1998) *Employability: Developing a framework for policy analysis.* Research Report No. 85. London: Department for Education and Employment.

Hochschild A (1983) *The Managed Heart.* Berkeley: University of California Press.

Huddleston P and Hirst C (2004) Are you being served? Skills gaps and training needs in the retail sector. SKOPE Research Paper No. 53, Universities of Oxford and Cardiff.

Hurrell SA (2009) *Soft skills deficits in Scotland: Their patterns, determinants and employer responses.* Unpublished Doctoral Thesis, University of Strathclyde.

Hurrell SA and Scholarios D (2011) Recruitment and selection practices, person-brand fit and soft skills gaps in service organizations: The benefits of institutionalized informality. In: Brannan M, Parsons E and Priola V (eds) *Branded Lives: The Production and Consumption of Identity at Work.* Cheltenham: Edward Elgar.

Innovation, Universities, Science and Skills Committee (2009) *Re-skilling for Recovery: After Leitch, Implementing Skills and Training Policy.* London: The Stationery Office.

Kersley B, Alpin C, Forth J et al. (2006) *Inside the Workplace.* London: Routledge.

Korczynski M (2002) *Human Resource Management in the Service Sector.* Basingstoke: Palgrave.

Korczynski M (2005a) Skills in service work: An overview. *Human Resource Management Journal* 15(2): 3–14.

Korczynski M (2005b) The point of selling: Capitalism, consumption and contradictions. *Organization* 12(1): 69–88.

Lafer G (2004) What is 'skill'? Training for discipline in the low-wage labour market. In: Warhurst C, Grugulis I and Keep E (eds) *The Skills that Matter.* Basingstoke: Palgrave Macmillan.

Lanning J, Martin R and Villeneuve-Smith F (2008) *Employability Skills Examined: Ten Key Messages from LSN's Quest to Understand Employability Skills.* London: Learning and Skills Network.

Leslie D (2002) Gender, retail employment and the clothing commodity chain. *Gender, Place and Culture* 9(1): 61–76.

Lewis P, Ryan P and Gospel H (2008) A hard sell? The prospects for apprenticeship in British retailing. *Human Resource Management Journal* 18(1): 3–19.

Lindsay C (2005) 'McJobs', 'good jobs' and skills: Job-seekers' attitudes to low-skilled service work. *Human Resource Management Journal* 15(2): 50–65.

Lindsay C and McQuaid R (2004) Avoiding the 'McJobs': Unemployed job seekers and attitudes to service work. *Work, Employment and Society* 18(2): 297–319.

Lindsay C and Sturgeon G (2003) Local responses to long term unemployment: Delivering access to employment in Edinburgh. *Local Economy* 18(2): 159–173.

Little R and Rubin D (1987) *Statistical Analysis with Missing Data.* New York: John Wiley and Sons.

Lockyer C and Scholarios D (2004) Selecting hotel staff: Why best practice does not always work. *International Journal of Contemporary Hospitality Management* 16(2): 121–135.

LSC (Learning and Skills Council) (2008) *Research into expanding apprenticeships: Final report.* Coventry: LSC.

Lury C (2004) *Brands: The Logos of the Global Economy.* London: Routledge.

MacDonald CL and Merrill D (2009) Intersectionality in the emotional proletariat: A new lens on employment discrimination in service work. In: Korczynski M and MacDonald CL (eds) *Service Work: Critical Perspectives.* Abingdon: Taylor and Francis.

McKinlay A (2009) Banking, employment and masculinity, 1900–39: The peculiar case of Mr Notman. In: *Management History Research Group Conference,* University of York.

McQuaid R and Lindsay C (2005) The concept of employability. *Urban Studies* 42(2): 197–219.

McQuaid R, Green A and Danson M (2005) Introducing employability. *Urban Studies* 42(2): 191–195.

McRobbie A (1997) Bridging the gap: Feminism, fashion and consumption. *Feminist Review* 55: 73–89.

McRobbie A (2002) Fashion culture: Creative work, female individualisation. *Feminist Review* 71: 52–62.

Mills CW (1956) *White Collar.* New York: Oxford University Press.

Moss P and Tilly C (1996) 'Soft' skills and race: An investigation of black men's employment problems. *Work and Occupations* 23(3): 252–276.

Nickson D (2007) *Human Resource Management for the Hospitality and Tourism Industries.* Oxford: Butterworth Heinemann.

Nickson D, Warhurst C, Cullen AM et al. (2003) Bringing in the excluded? Aesthetic labour, skills and training in the new economy. *Journal of Education and Work* 16(2): 185–203.

Nickson D, Warhurst C and Dutton E (2005) The importance of attitude and appearance in the service encounter in retail and hospitality. *Managing Service Quality* 15(2): 195–208.

Nickson D, Warhurst C, Witz A et al. (2001) The importance of being aesthetic: Work, employment and service organization. In: Sturdy A, Grugulis I and Wilmott H (eds) *Customer Service.* Basingstoke: Palgrave.

Pettinger L (2004) Brand culture and branded workers: Service work and aesthetic labour in fashion retail. *Consumption, Market and Culture* 7(2): 165–184.

Pettinger L (2005) Gendered work meets gendered goods: Selling and service in clothing retail. *Gender, Work and Organization* 12(5): 460–478.

Retail E-Commerce Task Force (2002) *Destination Retail: A Survey of Young People's Attitudes Towards a Career in Retailing.* London: Foresight.

Ridge M (2006) A perfect fit. *Guardian Education,* 3 October. Available at: education.guardian. co.uk/print/0,329590633-108283,00.html.

Scott A (1994) Gender segregation in the retail industry. In: Scott A (ed.) *Gender Segregation and Social Change.* Oxford: Oxford University Press.

Skillsmart (2004a) *Retail Sector Skills and Productivity Alliance Action Plan.* London: Skillsmart.

Skillsmart (2004b) *Manchester Enterprises ASP Sectoral Research: Retail Sector.* London: Skillsmart.

Skillsmart (2006) *A Qualified and Trained Workforce?* London: Skillsmart.

Skillsmart (2007) *Sector Skills Agreement Stage One: Assessment of Current and Future Skills Needs.* London: Skillsmart.

Skillsmart (2008) Units for the retail N/SVQs at Levels 1, 2 and 3. Available at: www.skillsmartretail. com/pdfs/retail_nsvq_units_sep_08.pdf.

UKCES (United Kingdom Commission for Employment and Skills) (2009) *Ambition 2020: World Class Skills and Jobs for the UK*. London: UKCES.

Walls S. (2008) *Are you being served: Gendered aesthetics among retail workers*. Unpublished Doctoral Thesis, University of Durham.

Warhurst C and Nickson D (2007) Employee experience of aesthetic labour in retail and hospitality. *Work, Employment and Society* 21(1): 103–120.

Warhurst C and Nickson D (2009) 'Who's got the look?' Emotional, aesthetic and sexualized labour in interactive services. *Gender, Work and Organization* 16(3): 385–404.

Warhurst C, Nickson D, Witz A et al. 2000) Aesthetic labour in interactive service work: Some case study evidence from the 'new' Glasgow. *Service Industries Journal* 20(3): 1–18.

Witz A, Warhurst C and Nickson D (2003) The labour of aesthetics and the aesthetics of organization. *Organization* 10(1): 33–54.

Dennis Nickson is professor and head of the Department of Human Resource Management, University of Strathclyde. His research interests include labour markets and skills and HRM issues in interactive service work. He has published widely in these and other areas and sole and co-authored books include *Human Resource Management for the Hospitality and Tourism Industries* (Butterworth Heinemann, 2007).

Chris Warhurst is Professor of Work and Organizational Studies at the University of Sydney. His interest centres on employment policy, with current research examining skill utilization, job quality, creative labour and aesthetic labour. He undertakes advisory work for a number of governments' skills bodies. With colleagues, his latest book is *Are Bad Jobs Inevitable?* (Palgrave, 2012).

Johanna Commander is a research fellow with the Scottish Centre for Employment Research at the University of Strathclyde. She is currently working on projects that examine skills utilization, management in new economy industries, job quality and pay inequality.

Scott A Hurrell is lecturer in work and employment studies in the University of Stirling's Institute for Socio-Management. His research interests include skills, work organization, recruitment and selection and labour market issues particularly in interactive service work and the non-profit sector. Scott has published in international journals and edited collections and has worked with Scottish public policy bodies.

Anne Marie Cullen gained her PhD from the University of Strathclyde. Her research interests concern aesthetic labour and access to work. Specifically her research and publications focus on unemployed job seekers access to interactive service work.

Writing a Successful Business Plan

Haag, A.B.

ABSTRACT

In creating and building a business, the entrepreneur assumes all the responsibilities for development and management, as well as the risks and rewards. Many businesses do not survive because business owners fail to develop an effective plan. The business plan focuses on major areas of concern and their contribution to the success of a new business. The finished plan communicates the product or service to others and provides the basis for the financial proposal.

American corporations are downsizing, outsourcing, and flattening their hierarchies. As a result, advancement opportunities are shrinking. Conversely, workers are looking for security, new opportunities, and rewards from their work. In search of a more rewarding lifestyle, increasing numbers of individuals are determined to become their own bosses or to work more independently by starting their own businesses and becoming entrepreneurs.

Entrepreneurs are considered the catalysts for change in today's business world (Bangs, 1995). Most businesses in the United States are small, with 20 or fewer employees. Yet, in total, small businesses account for most of the new jobs created each decade. New business owners are becoming the life blood of the Ameri-

can economy. They are developing new ideas, products, and services that are on the "cutting edge" of the economy. Their success brings profits and a competitive environment spawning more ideas and innovation. This entrepreneurial spirit is evident in occupational health and safety including safety personnel, industrial hygienists, physicians, and occupational health nurses forming their own businesses.

About 600,000 new businesses are started each year in the United States, not including all the small home online businesses. Of these, approximately 200,000, or 1 in 5, will survive to see their fifth anniversary. Considerable time, energy, and resources go into staffing a business, so why do so few survive the first 5 years? Most of these business owners did not have a business plan. Although business and industry have found no simple equation for success, one basic rule holds true: "A business owner who fails to plan, plans to fail" (Covello & Hazelgren, 1995, p. 2).

The author recently attended a meeting at her local Chamber of Commerce during which the importance of developing a business plan was discussed. When entrepreneurs were asked why they did not develop a business

ABOUT THE AUTHOR
Ms. Haag is occupational health nurse, Drug Delivery Systems Division, 3M, Northridge, CA.
The author has disclosed no potential conflicts of interest, financial or otherwise.
Address correspondence to Annette B. Haag, MA, RN, COHN-S/CM, FAAOHN, Drug Delivery Systems Division, 3M, 19901 Nordhoff Street, Northridge, CA 91324. E-mail: ahaag@mmm.com.

plan, typical responses included, "It requires a lot of hard work and time," "I am able to self-fund my business and developing a plan is not critical at this time," and "I have my plan in my head." Many felt that the rapidly changing economic environment invalidated their plans. The discussion concluded that although no plan will ever be 100% accurate or current, an effective business plan enables an entrepreneur to quickly make necessary changes to meet competitive environmental changes.

Success requires hard work and careful planning. A business plan is the owner's road map for a successful enterprise—a blueprint, a statement of goals and hopes, a compass, and a guideline to planned action. It is the current and futuristic image of the business.

A business plan is key to securing financing, maintaining focus, communicating, and preparing for the unexpected. "Your business plan is the heart and soul of your operation and the most important set of documents provided by you to any lending institution or potential investor" (Covello & Hazelgren, 1995, p. 2). The business plan is evidence of the business owner's initiative and allows the owner to communicate a step-by-step agenda for reaching goals. It enables the owner to take an objective, critical, unemotional look at the business in its entirety. Developing a business plan forces the owner to assess the competition and establish competitive alternatives and advantages.

The plan incorporates the possibility of uncertain outcomes and provides for contingency strategies. Bankers and investors expect to see negatives as well as positives in the business plan. They are further impressed when the entrepreneur has included a plan to handle the unexpected.

THE BUSINESS PLAN PROCESS

Many individuals believe that a business plan is only needed to raise funds and document business parameters for investors. However, business plans are actually the road maps that enable individuals to execute excellence. Many entrepreneurs establish their businesses without business plans; however, this may take more time and result in higher costs. Without a business plan, the owner has no concrete foundation or direction to keep the business focused. The owner might not even know when the business is headed in the wrong direction. The business plan should clearly and concisely define the mission, values, strategy, measurable objectives, and key results the owner expects.

It is important to set aside enough time to formulate the plan. Experts recommend starting the planning process at least 6 months before initiating a new business. The owner should not wait until resigning from a current workplace. Many individuals start researching their ideas and writing their business plan during evenings and weekends while they are employed in another position. The employment situation today is not as secure as it once was. Since the 2008 stock market crash, many individuals have unexpectedly lost their jobs. For many it has taken years to find a new position, and often the new position is not the job they want. They just need a job to pay the bills. On the positive side, for many individuals losing a job is the impetus to start the business they had wanted to start for many years.

An effective plan may take from 50 to 100 hours to research, document, analyze, and review. Some consultants may accomplish the task in a shorter period. However, a poorly conceived plan can set the company back several months or years, or can result in business failure. Building a business plan is a dynamic process; execution is the primary task. Once it is formulated, the plan is fine-tuned and updated on a continuous basis. The business planning process entails a variety of steps.

Define the Business Concept

During this stage, business owners must determine the types of services and products they will provide, who will buy the services and products, and how these products and services will be different from those provided by competitors. Even Thomas Edison recognized this fact when he said, "Anything that won't sell, I don't want to invent" (Abrams, 2010, p. 4). Questions for the business owner to ask include:

- Is this something new?
- Is it something better?
- Does it have a niche in an underserved or new market?
- Would I buy it or use it?

Gather Data on the Feasibility and Specifics of the Concept

Before an owner can develop the body of a business plan, information and reliable data about all aspects of the business must be compiled. For example, if the concept is to develop a self-study guide to assist individuals in preparing for an examination, the needed data might include:

- How many other self-study guides currently exist in the specialty targeted?
- How profitable is the company's marketing of the self-study guide?
- In what format will the self-study guide be distributed (printed manuals, online, CD-ROMs)?
- What type of information is presented in the self-study guide?

If the concept is to conduct educational seminars, the data needed might include:

- What type of educational seminars currently exist in the specialty area targeted?
- Are the seminars an overview on the subject area, or do they offer an in-depth program on the topics covered?
- Do the seminars offer continuing education credit?
- What are the length and price of the seminars?
- Where are the seminars conducted?

After formulating a list of questions, the next step is to look for the answers. Most information can be found through the Internet, local libraries, government resources, business publications, professional organizations, and trade associations. Paid research services are also available. Because funding is always a consideration, the owner can find some of the information and have a research firm handle more complicated tasks. Research firms can be recommended by various professional and trade organizations that support the owner's market niche.

It is advisable not to over-research and collect more data than needed. During this phase, it is necessary to answer some basic questions about the business. If the entrepreneur is creating a product or service that does not exist, data may not be available. To make the plan more compelling and persuasive to investors, the owner should use the most current data and the most reliable sources. Whenever possible, it is best to use conservative figures and translate data into financial units.

Focus and Refine the Concept

At this point, the owner analyzes the information gathered and decides whether the original idea is still viable or should be revised. Does a market still exist for the products and services? Will the time, energy, and money invested in starting and operating the business generate sufficient return on investment to create a venture worth pursuing? Will the product or service survive in both good and bad economic times? For example, it is difficult for a construction industry to make money when the number of new homes being built is low; another revenue source is the remodeling market. It is often tempting to offer too much. Focus is critical. The first phase of a business should be narrowly defined.

Outline the Specifics of the Business

At this point in the process, the owner crafts a concise statement of the purpose of the business. A helpful exercise is to write a mission statement outlining what will be provided, to whom the product or service will be provided, and what will differentiate the business. "A rule of thumb: If you can't describe your idea clearly and simply, you haven't thought it through" (Bangs, 1995, p. 9). This information should be included in the executive summary. If financing is needed, which has been more difficult to secure in the recovering economy, the owner must capture the interest of investors within the first few sentences of the executive summary. The owner must instill a positive impression the first 5 minutes. Investors rarely read the entire business plan. The most important aspects of the plan must ignite the interest of the reader to avoid being rejected and encourage the reader to finish the plan.

Using a Compelling Form for the Plan

The format of the plan may vary according to the intended use and readership. However, the author must remember that readers' time is extremely valuable. Bankers, venture capitalists, and other investors rarely have time to give each proposal and business plan the attention deserved. Each owner will be competing with other entrepreneurs for needed support. Highlighting key areas and summarizing as needed will allow investors to easily review the data contained in the plan.

Most experts suggest the business plan be no longer than 15 to 35 pages, not including the financials and appendices; 20 pages are sufficient for nearly every business. Anything fewer than 10 pages may be viewed as

---

Sidebar 1
Business Plan Components

Cover letter

Executive summary

Table of contents

Business description and history

Business structure

Product or service description

Market analysis and trends

Operations

Technology plan

Management and organization

Social responsibility and sustainability

Development, milestones, and exit plan

Financial data

Appendix

---

insubstantial. The appendices are limited to no more than the length of the plan. If investors are interested, they will ask for more information. Most plans should project 3 to 5 years into the future or until the owner has reached the proposed exit strategy (Abrams, 2010).

BUSINESS PLAN COMPONENTS

At a minimum, a business plan must contain the components listed in Sidebar 1.

Cover Letter

A cover letter should entice the reader to give careful consideration to the business opportunity and to read further. The cover letter should include:
• Why the owner has chosen this funder to receive the plan.
• The nature of the business.
• The development stage of the business.
• The amount of funds sought.
• The type of funding sought (e.g., investment or loan).
• The principals of the company and contact information.

The cover letter must be simple, attractive, concise, and tailored to each investor.

Potential investors should be contacted again about a week after the plan is submitted; it is acceptable to ask when the funding source might contact the owner for further conversation. Inquiries should be brief. Most contacts will be through e-mails and voicemail messages. The owner should have a message that quickly explains the nature of the business.

Sources of funding and department financing include:
• Banks and lending institutions.

- Loans or investment from family and friends.
- Cash advances and personal or company credit cards.
- Venture capitalists.
- Private investors.

Owners must have a well-conceived financial plan to secure the money needed to start and sustain the business.

Executive Summary

The executive summary captures the essence of the business plan. This section is an abstract of the company's present status and future direction but is prepared after the plan is completed. The executive summary is the most important section of the business plan. The executive summary:

- Summarizes the basic concepts and highlights key points.
- Identifies the company's main concept, objectives, and purpose.
- Identifies the target or niche market and competitive advantage and position.
- Outlines the marketing and sales strategy.
- Identifies growth opportunities.
- Highlights benchmarks (e.g., financial and non-financial targets).
- Quantifies resources.
- Describes work and management experience and past successes of the management team.

Investors will look for entrepreneurs who can articulate their vision, passion, and dreams.

If an owner is submitting a financing proposal, the executive summary is more complex and contains additional information about the structure of the corporation. In addition, it includes the amount of money needed and the purpose. Finally, the owner will articulate how the funds will benefit the business and be repaid.

The executive summary is targeted to the audience. Current technology enables the entrepreneur to change, update, and tailor the business plan as needed. The importance of the executive summary cannot be overstated. Some investors may prefer reviewing the executive summary and financials before reviewing the plan. The executive summary is usually no longer than 2 to 3 pages, although a 1-page executive summary is acceptable. Bullet points are effective and make the executive summary more appealing to the reader. A busy funder should be able to read the executive summary in 5 minutes (Abrams, 2010).

Table of Contents

The table of contents serves as a guide to writing and organizing the business plan. It also assists readers to understand and easily access the information presented.

Business Description and History

The objective of this section is to describe the business, how the entrepreneur will manage it, and why the business will succeed. If the business is new, the following questions should be answered (Bangs, 1995):

- What is the legal/corporate name of the business?
- What is the legal form of the business?

- What is the mission of the company?
- Where is the business located and what geographical areas will it serve?
- What hours of the day and days of the week will the business operate?
- Will the business be seasonal?
- What is the nature of the business (i.e., its products and services)?
- How will the business succeed and what is its growth potential?
- What is each individual's experience in the business and what positions will individuals hold?
- What type of staff will be needed?
- What makes this business special or different?
- What is the financial status of the company (i.e., income and expenses)?
- What is the structure of the business?
- Why will the business be profitable or continue to grow?
- What types of patents, trademarks, copyrights, and licenses are needed?

For an existing business, the owner should state whether the business is expanding or if the plan is to subsume an existing business. Focus is the aim. When entrepreneurs are clear, concise, and knowledgeable about the business, they are able to concentrate their efforts and use resources effectively.

The business will need a name; naming a business requires a legal name search. The name of the business should be memorable and easy to spell and include information about what the business does. Information on the purpose of the business should be provided so that potential customers and clients can find the business online or in telephone books and directories. What the name implies should be considered. The name of the company is usually the first introduction investors and prospects have to the company.

Business Structure

In this section of the plan, owners include historical facts supporting any request for financing or acquisition objectives. The legal form of the business is listed (i.e., sole proprietorship, partnership, corporation, Subchapter-S corporation, C-corporation, limited liability company). Most new businesses start as sole proprietorships or partnerships. Structural, management, or ownership changes are documented. Present or past successes are recorded.

Product or Service Description

The purpose of this section of the plan is to provide a description of the product or services offered. Unique features that provide a competitive advantage are highlighted. Products and services provided by competitors are analyzed. Entrepreneurs should list the advantages of the product or services provided, along with improvements over existing products and services. The entrepreneur must explain the strategy for meeting or dominating the competition.

A plan to introduce new products and services should be included. When completing this segment of the plan, a sales breakdown by product, region, and industry type is essential. New products might include selling informational material presented at a seminar, such as manuals and audio recordings, or webinars to clients who are unable to attend the program. The product life cycle and seasonality of the product or services are noted. Professional textbooks and references have a shelf life of approximately 3 to 5 years; they should be updated periodically to remain current with trends, technology, research, regulations, and legislation. Discussing the duration and impact of the product or services on competitive advantage and whether the product has a limited shelf life is essential. The owner provides documentation when a patent, copyright, or exclusive agency is involved.

The owner includes responses from clients and inquiries from prospective clients that illustrate the demand for the product or service. Relationships with leading companies and major accounts and accomplishments are documented, substantiating the company's fitness for growth. If the owner is concerned about proprietary information, a non-disclosure agreement is created.

Market Analysis and Trends

This segment describes the existing marketplace in which the entrepreneur will introduce the company, its products, and services. It can be viewed as a plan within a plan. At its most basic level, the marketing strategy (plan) sets forth the product's or service's marketing mix and includes product, price, promotion, and place (distribution) for the coming year with projections for at least 5 years. Marketing (including sales) is the revenue-generating part of the company.

The product is the tangible aspect of the product or service itself, such as a professional textbook or health and safety seminar. Price and value work together. Clients consider durability, reliability, service, and quality in addition to cost. The approach to pricing strategies should be logical and justified and should produce ample return on investment while leaving room for a margin of error. Promotion, the amount and nature of the marketing activities, might include advertising online, in professional publications (e.g., *Workplace Health & Safety,* American Association of Occupational Health Nurses, Inc. [AAOHN] News, American Board for Occupational Health Nurses, Inc. Continuing Education Resource Guide), in local constituent newsletters, or via direct mail by purchasing mailing labels from targeted groups (e.g., AAOHN, Association of Occupational Health Professionals in Healthcare, American Society of Safety Engineers). Distribution includes the convenience and decor of the location in which the product or service is presented. For example, are the meeting facilities comfortable, reasonably priced, and near convenient air and ground transportation?

Market Research. Marketing involves research to learn what people want to purchase. Business owners should put themselves in the client's place to determine client needs. What is the client base demographically: age, income, gender, family, location, and occupation? What motivates a client to purchase a product or service: lifestyle, motives, needs, or interests? The client is the sole focus (Bangs, 1995). Marketing plans and strategies are not valuable unless supported by accurate data. Current technology facilitates the process of collecting needed data. Even with historical and current data, predicting the future is a challenge. The owner must be realistic and alert for market changes.

Marketing Strategy. Marketing strategy also includes analysis of the alternative opportunities and risks to the company with informed consideration of the competition, social environment, and company's internal production capability (Arkebauer, 1994).

Entrepreneurs survey the existing market to determine size, diversity, and location. They define the competitors and their pricing policies, promotional strategies, and relative share of the market. Is the market growing or shrinking? The owner should outline trends, implied opportunities, and expectations of industry forecasters for the next 2 years, including projections.

Strengths and Weaknesses. Strengths and weaknesses should be listed. When discussing strengths, entrepreneurs should place at least as much emphasis, if not more, on marketing as on the product. Strengths include how the product or service is favorably differentiated from the competition in actual performance, quality, and reliability, breadth of line and options, distribution, pricing, and awareness and image.

When documenting weaknesses and barriers, the entrepreneur must explain how the problems or threats will be overcome. The discussion also includes opportunities to justify the potential with logical rationale. For unexploited opportunities, it is crucial to include the estimated cost of entry, time required, and risk.

Target Marketing. The business must establish target market segment and a strategic fit, a match, between the company's abilities and resources vis-à-vis the basic criteria needed to compete in a market, also known as a market "niche" or "target marketing." Strategies may include feasibility testing and competitive analysis. A business owner may consider engaging a qualified and experienced market research firm to analyze the market, using techniques such as focus groups. Typically, a group of 5 to 10 individuals (from the target industry) are gathered together with a moderator. The moderator works with prepared questions. The findings are used to determine the viability of the product and service and enable the business owner to focus on short- and long-range marketing, advertising, and promotion plans.

Market Potential—Positioning. An additional issue to address is the size of the market niche. Is it large enough to sustain business profitably? Do enough clients and effective and economically justifiable ways exist to reach the target market? The business owner must be sure that the niche is large enough for growth. Positioning also includes location, pricing, benefits, and testimonials. Positioning may be as simple as locating the business in high consumer traffic areas and away from other similar competitors, or concentrating on selected market segments. Will the price of the product or service be targeted to the high, middle, or low end of the market? This may depend on the target niche.

It is important for the business owner to differentiate the business from other competing businesses by promoting the benefits of the product or service. A common question asked is, "What's in it for me?" It is important for owners to place themselves in the client's shoes. Positioning strategies include testimonial letters and references. The owner should never hesitate to ask clients for referrals and permission to place quotes and comments in advertising literature.

Pricing Strategy. Lack of courage in pricing may be the single most significant marketing error small business owners make (Bangs, 1995). A common mistake is thinking that offering the lowest price is the key to success. Some clients may be price sensitive, whereas others may be prestige sensitive. Knowing what clients want is crucial to this phase of the marketing plan. The nature of the market will affect the pricing strategy. Three types of market, monopoly, oligopoly, and competitive, are defined by the competition operating within that market.

Monopolistic Market. This market is one in which one business controls the vast majority of supply. It has a unique or protected product (e.g., a patented invention), or a temporary edge on the competition due to an existing business structure. The optimum price is that amount which will allow marginal revenues to equal marginal costs.

Oligopolistic Market. This market is characterized by few participants with little meaningful product differentiation. In this case, pricing is a function of competitor pricing. If the business owner reduces the price of the product, competitors reduce their price. However, if the owner increases the price, competitors may not.

Competitive Market. This type of market is characterized by numerous participants with almost no product differentiation and little or no economic barriers to market entrance. In this market, customers, as a whole, determine the prices. All of these markets have critical implications for businesses. However, to stay viable, the business must generate a profit (Brenner, Ewan, & Custer, 1990).

Distribution, Advertising, and Promotion. Business owners must demonstrate that the price and profitability of the product or service justifies the costs of sales (e.g., presentations, advertising, website, commissions, telephone, travel) and the distribution channels selected. The marketing strategy must establish the optimum channels of distribution, including executive selling, direct sales force, manufacturers' representatives, distributors, retailers, national and regional chains, independents, mail order and direct response, catalogs, telemarketing, original equipment manufacturers, international distribution, the media (i.e., radio, television, print, social), and the Internet. Occupational health and safety professionals have found successful distribution and advertising channels exhibiting at national, state, and local conferences, placing advertisements in professional publications, and using direct mail (i.e., flyers, brochures).

Social media offers an enormous range of marketing opportunities. The public is now connected to the online universe virtually all the time via smartphones and mobile devices. The result is a huge number of individuals constantly attached to the web, their phones, and each other. The consultant must determine if the strategy is to reach consumers or businesses. Does a mass-market site (e.g., Facebook, Twitter, Friendster), a special interest site (e.g., Chowhound for food and Linked Musicians for music lovers), or a professional networking site (e.g., LinkedIn or Nurse Linkup) better suit the business? Once the right site (or sites) is chosen, the owner must provide relevant and interesting content to raise the company's visibility nationally and internationally (Abrams, 2010).

The Internet is a global network of computers that communicate using a common language. It is simply a "network of networks." Although important, the ability to buy and sell online is not the only part of the Internet commerce equation. Entrepreneurs and established companies are finding more outlets for marketing "the Net." Examples include traditional product sales, selling advertisements on popular websites, collecting demographics, and selling access to target markets.

The most obvious way to market on the Net may be to establish a website that showcases the company's products and services and accepts orders. One of the best features of the Internet is its ability to level the playing field. Every company can look as significant as the next company. Entrepreneurs do not need a storefront operation to present a professional image and can target customers within or beyond their geographical area. Some major types of online website advertising opportunities are (Abrams, 2010):

- Portal sites and directories—online hubs usually grouped together around a common theme, product, topic, or location.
- Website ads (banner and interstitial ads)—a banner ad is similar to a newspaper ad, including graphics, photographs, and text; and an interstitial advertisement is similar to an advertisement used in a TV commercial. When an individual types in a website address, the website changes to another advertisement instead of the intended website.
- Sponsorships—website sponsors will give an advertiser visibility and recognition on their websites.
- Online classified—text with pictures like a classified ad.
- Affiliate auction sites—eBay has created numerous marketing opportunities. On these sites, the owner can create stores and list products as "Buy It Now."
- Affiliate programs—advertise on other websites and arrange pay-per-sale ads for which the website is paid if the ad results in a sale.

A realistic budget should be allocated for an advertising and promotional campaign. The owner may need someone to advertise, as advertising can be time consuming. Business owners should devote the majority of their time to running and growing the business. As the business grows, additional sales and marketing personnel may be needed. Business owners must also decide if they intend to market their product and service internationally.

Which products and services are well suited for international sales, and which countries are the best prospects? Advertising and promotion strategies also include logos, stationery, business cards, and packaging design. As mentioned earlier, the marketing section of the business plan is a plan within a plan. The entrepreneur can significantly impact investors and customers if a simple rule is followed: keep the message concise and clear. The owner must remember that the marketing plan and sales strategy are the heart of the company's business.

Operations

The operations section of a business plan explains the day-to-day functions of the company. This section varies, depending on the type of business. The differing requirements are best illustrated by considering retailing and manufacturing. The operation of a retail establishment is conceptually straightforward; businesses manufacturing technical products are more complex, but the mechanics are easier to understand. Operations for a retail business simply involve buying the product, transporting it, storing it, selling it, and delivering it. For the manufacturing business, the product's quality and reliability depend on how it is assembled. Readers may lack the technical knowledge to understand the process. Being too technical in the plan may present a problem (Lasher, 1994). Illustrations can be extremely helpful. Areas included in the operations section are:
- Facilities (square footage, acquisition, future needs).
- Location (accessibility to clients, suppliers, labor force).
- Operating costs (heat, light, phone, Internet, water, general upkeep).
- Manufacturing capability (equipment, materials, personnel, space).
- Processes (productivity, fabrication, assembly, test inspection, inventory control).
- Suppliers, distribution channels (includes outsourcing).
- Labor (unskilled, skilled, special requirements or talents).
- Research and development (creating new products and services or improving on an existing product).
- Quality control (Total Quality Management, Continuous Process Improvement philosophy).
- Contingency planning (problems addressed and overcome).
- Customer satisfaction feedback.

This section does not need to be thoroughly detailed; rather, the plan should be brief and to the point. Bulleted points are helpful. The business owner must be cognizant of safety and health issues, labor regulations, protecting the environment, legal considerations, government regulations, adequate insurance protection, and imported or exported goods.

Technology Plan

Every business needs technology; the owner will need to determine what functions require or could benefit from technology. With the numerous technology systems available today, the owner may benefit greatly by using the services of a technology consultant to assist in choosing the best products and systems to meet business needs. Key issues when choosing technology include (Abrams, 2010):
- Function.
- Ease of use.
- Cost.
- Security.
- Ability to be upgraded and expanded.
- Integration with existing data and technology systems.

Management and Organization

Various studies analyzing key factors in small business failures have determined that 98% of failures stem from managerial weaknesses. Only 2% of the failures are due to factors beyond the control of those involved. Dun and Bradstreet grouped the failures into categories (Lasher, 1994):
- Poor choice of business type.
- Owner not suited to small business.
- Emotional selection of location.
- Lack of knowledge of advertising or attracting clients.
- Failure to obtain proper professional advice.
- Insufficient planning and investigation.
- Poor choice of legal form.
- Insufficient capital.
- Too many non-critical assets.
- Poor pricing practices.
- Owner living beyond income from business.
- No knowledge of finances and record-keeping.
- Poor credit-granting practices.
- Poor inventory management.
- Inadequate borrowing practices.

The majority of these factors do not involve a lack of knowledge of the product or service of the business; rather, they are related to operating the business (Lasher, 1994). When preparing the management section, five areas should be addressed (Bangs, 1995):
1. Personal history of the principals.
2. Related work experience.
3. Duties and responsibilities.
4. Salaries.
5. Resources available to the business.

The personal history of the principals documents their business background, education, special abilities, interests, and personal financial status. Investors usually have two concerns. First, they do not want to see lavish spending on living expenses. Second, they do not want to see frugal spending on living expenses. Both could lead to business failure.

Work experience should explain whether the experience is directly related to the business venture. Unrelated business experience can indicate a weakness in the management structure. Investors are also looking for transferable skills. Investors want to lend to individuals, not companies. The owner must convince decision makers that management personnel are serious and levelheaded and have every intention of focusing on the business venture and repaying the loan.

Sidebar 2

Start-up Costs

List the specific details of the initial cash requirements. These are expenses incurred before business launch. Post-launch expenditures should be entered in the income statement.

	Cost
Facilities	
Land purchase	
Building purchase	
Initial rent	
Deposits (security, utilities, etc.)	
Improvements/remodeling	
Other	
Other	
Equipment	
Furniture	
Production machines/equipment	
Computers/software	
Cash registers	
Telephone/telecommunications	
Vehicles	
Other	
Other	
Materials/supplies	
Office supplies	
Stationery—business cards	
Brochures/pamphlets, other descriptive material	
Other	
Other	
Fees and other costs	
Licenses/permits	
Trade or professional memberships	
Attorneys	
Accountants	
Insurance	
Marketing/management consultants	
Design/technical consultants	
Advertising/promotional activities	
Other	
Total	

Note. *Adapted with permission from Abrams (2010, p. 293).*

Investors want to see balance and the ability to provide the four essential elements of management: planning, organization, control, and leadership. It is necessary to designate who will be in charge of particular responsibilities and tasks and have a plan outlining the formal structure of the organization. When developing a management team, the owner must determine the types of managers and employees needed (e.g., top decision makers—president, chief executive officer, chief operating officer, chief financial officer, division presidents), key production personnel, plant managers, key technology personnel, management information systems director, systems administrator, principal marketing and sales staff, human resource staff, training directors, and head of research and development. In smaller businesses, responsibilities are shared by many individuals. Each business is unique in the type of personnel needed and will depend on the products and services being provided.

Support professionals and resources outside the company such as researchers, technical advisers, accountants, and attorneys are also included on the management team (Covello & Hazelgren, 1995). An organizational chart is one way to describe the management structure, along with job descriptions detailing job duties and responsibilities.

Proposed salaries, including bonuses, profit sharing plans, and other compensation arrangements for each member of the management team, should be listed. In general, salaries should be based on industry averages. However, deferred compensation (e.g., stock options) is desirable, as it demonstrates long-term commitment. When issuing stock, it is advisable to make it available to key executives over a period of several years. This strategy encourages executives to think strategically and enhances the likelihood of the employees remaining with the company for an extended period (Schilit, 1990). A simple statement of management compensation is sufficient. Being realistic and factual is crucial. Because of its importance to the success of the company, investors may review management expertise and structure before reviewing any other section of the plan.

Social Responsibility and Sustainability

Abrams (2010) stated, "Increasingly, companies judge their performance not merely on profit, but on the concept of the 'triple bottom line'—or people, planet, profile" (p. 240).

- *People.* How do you affect other people (employees, community, specific groups like the disadvantaged, or society as a whole)?
- *Planet.* How do individuals' actions affect the environment, not just now but in the future?
- *Profit.* How do owners achieve financial sustainability, as the company must be profitable to remain in business? Without focusing on profits, no company can long meet any of its other goals.

As the business and business plan are constructed, the owner must consider the triple bottom line and not just the financial bottom line. Being socially responsible brings many benefits to a company. It will attract employees and gain visibility for the company.

Sidebar 3					
Income Statement: Annual by Quarter					
For Year: _____	*1st Quarter*	*2nd Quarter*	*3rd Quarter*	*4th Quarter*	*Total*
Income					
Gross sales					
(Commissions)					
(Returns and allowances)					
Net sales					
(Cost of goods)					
Gross profit					
Expenses—general and administrative					
Salaries and wages					
Employee benefits					
Payroll taxes					
Professional services					
Marketing and advertising					
Rent					
Equipment rental					
Maintenance					
Depreciation					
Insurance					
Telecommunications					
Utilities					
Office supplies					
Postage and shipping					
Travel					
Entertainment					
Interest on loans					
Other					
Other					
Total expenses					
Net income before taxes					
Provision for taxes on income					
Net profit					

Note. *Adapted with permission from Abrams (2010, p. 296).*

Financial Data and Projections

This section contains a set of financials, including income and expense statements (i.e., profit and loss), balance sheet, and cash flow statement. These reports are standard for most companies. The business owner must understand how each of these documents is developed. The new business owner can learn about financial statements through workbooks, courses, and consultants. Computerized spreadsheets permit changes in financials.

To the financial backer, the heart of the plan lies in its financial projections. The rest of the plan is material that makes the financial backer believe that the financial projections will come true (Lasher, 1994). Financial forecasts in the business plan should be conservative, realistic, and supported with actual orders, client demographic information, and accurate production costs. A fundamental truth of financial planning is that dollar projections should follow projections of physical activity (Lasher, 1994).

IN SUMMARY

Writing a Successful Business Plan

An Overview

Haag, A. B.

Workplace Health & Safety 2013; 61(1), 19-29.

1 In creating and building a business, the entrepreneur assumes all the responsibilities for development and management, as well as the risks and rewards. Many businesses do not survive because business owners fail to develop an effective plan.

2 The business plan focuses on major areas of concern and their contribution to the success of a new business. The finished plan communicates the product or service to others and provides the basis for the financial proposal.

3 The plan identifies customers, target markets, pricing strategy, and competitive conditions. It aids in decision making and is an essential guide for operating a business successfully and measuring progress.

4 The business plan not only serves as a mechanism for obtaining any needed financial resources, but also indicates the future direction of the company.

It is important to produce a complete fiscal plan of what is expected to happen in the future (i.e., products to be sold, personnel, materials, equipment, and services needed by the company). Financial considerations include origination costs (Sidebar 2) and the use of funding proceeds (i.e., marketing and advertising, salaries, facilities, capital equipment, research and development, operating expenses, and capital).

The income and expense forecast statement (e.g., profit and loss) is described as the operating statement expected for the business at the end of the period for which the forecast is prepared (Sidebar 3). The balance sheet is a position statement, not a historical record. It shows what is owned and owed on a given date. The cash flow statement measures the flow of money, both expenses and revenue, for the business (Gray, 1995). Projected financials are an estimation of future financial earnings and expenses. Projections are usually divided into monthly projections for the first 2 years, and annually thereafter, up to and including year 5.

Financial ratio analysis is also used to provide a formalized system of relating elements of the balance sheet to the income statement. The mathematical effort of creating a ratio lessens the importance of individual numbers and allows the owner to evaluate trends, industry standards, and acquisitions. The ratio analysis allows the owner to project asset needs based on historical ratios. Seeking assistance from a certified public accountant simplifies the task. Investors will review financial projections carefully to determine if they are realistic and attainable. Other financial measures used to evaluate success include market share, sales, inventory management, and profit margin.

Another aspect of the business for which an accountant is valuable is deciding whether to create financial records on an accrual or cash basis. Most small companies are advised to conduct business on a cash basis, meaning that income and expenses are entered in the books at the time money actually changes hands. In accrual-based accounting, income and expenses are counted at the time of the transaction. The latter is often used by larger businesses. Even if business owners are not responsible for preparing the financials, it is critical that they have an understanding of financial statements so they have better control of their companies. Financial statements provide the information needed to make informed decisions and assess the condition of the business.

Appendix

The appendix is used to reinforce the content of the business plan. The appendix includes the conclusions outlined in the plan. Information that can be provided in this section includes:

- Letters of intent.
- Key contacts.
- Endorsements and testimonials.
- Definitions of technical words.
- Client listings.
- Photographs.
- News articles.
- Résumés of key management personnel and consultants.
- Contracts.
- Trademarks or copyrights.
- Marketing materials (e.g., brochures).

A FINAL THOUGHT ON PLANNING

To avoid problems, delays, or rejection from investors, it is best to present the business plan to impartial outsiders for review. An accountant should review the financial statements and assess business and personal tax considerations. An attorney can evaluate those areas that may have legal implications. The business plan is typed neatly and placed in a folder or spiral binder for presentation or e-mailed to the investor as needed.

The business plan components listed above are the main core elements commonly included in most plans. However, no single way of preparing a business plan is required. Alternative formats can be found in various references and in computer programs specifically designed to take the business owner step by step through the process.

The importance of planning cannot be overemphasized. Well prepared and executed, the business plan is the entrepreneur's most crucial business document. Investors expect a higher level of expertise and preparation from entrepreneurs they choose to fund. The successful business plan is convincing because it not only discusses the business idea but also demonstrates the author's business competence through a thorough, detailed discussion of what must be done to implement the idea.

The business plan is not merely a report prepared and then forgotten. It is used by the entrepreneur to make daily decisions. It enables the entrepreneur to focus on the tasks at hand. The business plan is reviewed monthly, quarterly, or, at a minimum, semi-annually. Entrepreneurs without a business plan often react intuitively to business conditions without properly thinking through all appropriate alternatives. Consequently, they may find it difficult to make appropriate choices that are strategically important to the business. A sound business plan gives the entrepreneur the ability to maneuver more efficiently and change course when needed. A well-composed business plan offers a true strategic advantage.

A business plan does not have to be perfect. The owner is not able to anticipate every situation. Endless revisions waste time. No business plan is ever finished—it is a work in progress. As mentioned earlier, the owner will need to update the plan on an ongoing basis.

As the number of new businesses increases each year, competition for funding is greater than ever. Owners who provide business plans with a clear definition of the business, evidence of strong management, thoughtful marketing capabilities, and an attractive financial structure have the competitive advantage and are more successful in obtaining necessary funding. However, the greatest beneficiary of this project is not the investor, but rather the business owner. A well-conceived business plan is still the most effective tool for reaching long-term goals and achieving success.

REFERENCES

Abrams, R. M. (2010). *The successful business plan: Secrets & strategies* (5th ed.). Palo Alto, CA: The Planning Shop.

Arkebauer, J. B. (1994). *The McGraw-Hill guide to writing a high-impact business plan: A proven blueprint for entrepreneurs.* New York, NY: McGraw-Hill.

Bangs, D. H., Jr. (1995). *The business planning guide: Creating a plan for success in your own business.* Chicago, IL: Upstart Publishing.

Brenner, G., Ewan, J., & Custer, H. (1990). *The complete handbook for the entrepreneur.* Englewood Cliffs, NJ: Prentice-Hall.

Covello, J., & Hazelgren, B. (1995). *Your first business plan.* Naperville, IL: Sourcebooks.

Gray, D. A. (1995). *Start and run a profitable consulting business: A step-by-step plan.* Bellingham, WA: Self Counsel Press.

Lasher, W. (1994). *The perfect business plan made simple.* New York, NY: Doubleday Dell.

Schilit, W. K. (1990). *The entrepreneur's guide to preparing a winning business plan and raising venture capital.* Englewood Cliffs, NJ: Prentice-Hall.

PART 6

JOURNAL ARTICLES

Left to Their Own Devices: College Students' "Guilty Pleasure" Media Use and Time Management

Panek, E.

Abstract

New media provide college students with an unprecedented number of ways to spend their unstructured time. Research on decision making suggests that choosers low in self-control presented with proximate options will eschew tasks that provide delayed benefit in favor of immediate gratification and will experience guilt when they are aware of the tradeoff between immediate gratification and long-term benefits. A survey of college students (N = 458) suggests that users are aware of overuse of leisure media because of deficits in self-control, in particular two proximate media experience (social networking sites [SNS] and online video). Of these, only online video viewing is associated with less time spent on schoolwork. Though this study is correlational and thus does not definitively establish causality, the evidence suggests that the interaction between the high-choice media environment and users' self-control may account for a decline in learning among college students.

Keywords

Facebook, social media, college students, Internet, self-control

The transition from high school to college represents a profound change in the lives of young people, from the highly structured, highly supervised home environment to the relatively unsupervised, unstructured campus environment. Though many college students have as many curricular and extracurricular demands on their time as they did

[1]Drexel University, Philadelphia, USA

before coming to college, they are not required to physically be in a single building for 8 hours each day nor are their leisure activities monitored by parents. Without these external constraints, college students are free to spend their time as they wish: socializing, completing schoolwork, or engaging in entertainment experiences at various times throughout each day.

The generation making its way through college at the start of the second decade of the 21st century has an unprecedented number of options as to what to do with their leisure time. Their adolescence coincided with the popularization of new media that served to multiply the quantity of experiences and the places and times in which these experiences could be accessed: mobile communication devices (e.g., cell phones), time-shifting television viewing technologies (e.g., digital video recorder or "DVR"), and the Internet. There is concern over the possibility that time spent using some or all of these leisure media may be substituting for time spent on school-related activities. Evidence suggests that the amount of media use a student engages in can affect the student's scholastic performance. Children aged 8 to 18 who spend less time using media do better in school than those who use more media (Kaiser Family Foundation, 2010). Though these survey findings are correlational and thus cannot account for all third variables, they do suggest that time spent using media for leisure purposes may be time that students are not studying, leading to lower grades.

Of the students who are unable to maintain a balance between schoolwork and leisure pursuits, it is likely that some make deliberate decisions to neglect their schoolwork, which offers a delayed gratification in the form of better grades and a better job, in favor of other pursuits. The preference for activities offering smaller, short-term gain over those offering larger, long-term gain is not necessarily an irrational or uncommon behavior. Such a preference may be indicative of a difference in values. These students' failures to devote more time to schoolwork are the results of rational, deliberative choices based on their valuation of expected outcomes of activities. At the same time, other students may not deliberately choose to spend less time on schoolwork but may end up doing so anyway. Such behavior comes about when students low in self-control make choices in an environment that offers sufficiently tempting alternatives. Knowing the difference between extracurricular activities that are selected based on a rational consideration of options and experiences that are selected when self-control has failed is essential to understanding college students' time budgeting.

Individuals' susceptibility to temptation may vary as well as the extent to which choice environments test the resolve of individuals. Some leisure activities may be seen by students as temptations—such as alcohol consumption or video game playing—while others are more often chosen by those who decide that they are more important than schoolwork—such as athletics or club activities. Media researchers have noted the frequency with which the term "guilty pleasure" is used to refer to certain types of media use, including reality-based television viewing (Baruh, 2010; Pozner, 2010), reading romance novels (Radway, 1984), or personal Internet use at work (i.e., "cyberloafing") (Stratton, 2010). Gauntlett and Hill (1999) found that many television viewers refer to TV viewing as a guilty pleasure regardless of the content being viewed. New media technologies—mobile devices and the Internet—are not obviously or exclusively used for activities regarded as "guilty pleasures" or for activities that one consciously values as much or more than schoolwork such as professional advancement. Researchers must differentiate among specific uses of the Internet and mobile devices to determine the extent to which various uses of new media are indicative of lapses in self-control and to determine what characteristics of some of these media experiences make them particularly tempting.

This study establishes evidence indicating the extent to which popular leisure media experiences function as distracting temptations for college undergraduates. Determining whether media use correlates with trait levels of self-control, feelings of guilt, and the amount of time students dedicate to schoolwork is an important step in understanding media selection behavior in a choice environment in which more options are temporally and physically proximate to choosers than ever before. This article presents a review of the literature on temptation and self-control, followed by a review of literature on self-control and media choice, leading to the hypotheses.

Media Temptations and Self Control

Goods and experiences from which individuals choose can be more or less tempting. Options that are experienced as initially tempting during the preconsumption phase are often pleasurable during the consumption phase and are associated with feelings of guilt during the postconsumption phase. These "guilty pleasures" appeal to one's desire for immediate pleasure rather than one's belief that they *should* partake of a product or experience so as to obtain long-term benefits such as cultural enrichment, enhanced ability to perform the duties of a responsible, informed citizen, or increased earning potential (Shiv & Fedorikhin, 1999). Guilty pleasures can be thought of as offering smaller, earlier rewards in contrast to options that offer delayed gratification value. In media terms, one might consider a lowbrow comedy to be a guilty pleasure, while an intellectually challenging foreign film would not be a guilty pleasure (Read, Loewenstein, & Kalyanaraman, 1999).

To forgo guilty pleasures, choosers may call on self-control or willpower: the conscious act of restraining one's self from engaging in an activity (Baumeister, 2008; LaRose, 2009). Hoch and Loewenstein (1991) make the distinction between two means of preventing one's self from making such selections: reducing desire by avoiding or distracting one's self from the tempting options or overcoming desire by exercising willpower. If those who are low in self-control are put in environments that have tempting options, the tendency to select such options increases (Babin & Darden, 1995; Baumeister, Sparks, Stillman, & Vohs, 2008; Gul & Pesendorfer, 2004).

The close physical proximity of various leisure media experiences via mobile communication technology amounts to having a temptation nearby in all places at all times. In addition, various "time-shifting" on-demand entertainment technologies such as DVR and online video (e.g., Hulu) bring desired entertainment experiences out of the scheduled availability choice environment in which desired options are often temporally remote from a media user into a choice environment in which all options are unscheduled and are thus always in close temporal proximity to the user. This constant presence of tempting media options makes it difficult for choosers who are low in self-control to resist these options.

Users' exposure to various leisure media experiences is contingent on the availability of the users (Webster, 1985). For example, prime-time (8 p.m.-10 p.m.) television ratings have, historically, been the highest partly due to the fact that most individuals are not at work and are not asleep at that time (Webster, 1985). However, the constraints of work hours are not the same for all populations. The lack of regular structure in college students' lives, relative to that of high school students or those working full-time jobs, and their relative autonomy present them with opportunities to select leisure media experiences immediately before use (Chak & Leung, 2004; Young, 2001). Given these conditions, college students are more apt to use more tempting, proximate media than their counterparts who either have restrictive schedules or do not possess technologies that give them access to tempting options in various places. This proximate temptation effect has been shown to be moderated by self-control (Babin & Darden, 1995): those with higher levels of self-control are capable of refraining from temptations despite their constant presence.

Media Selection

To the extent that the research on media selection conceives of media use as influenced by users' levels of self-control, much of it concerns so-called abuse of a medium or addiction. There has been much debate over what it means to be addicted to a medium. Byun et al.'s (2009) meta-analysis of 39 quantitative studies of Internet addiction from 1996-2006 concludes that there is little consensus on how to define addiction in this context. Nevertheless, Internet addiction studies continue to proliferate. In many of these studies, Internet addiction is regarded as a behavioral impulse control disorder in which individuals who exhibit loneliness, depression, or low self-esteem use the Internet to temporarily alleviate feelings of emotional tension (e.g., Dell'Osso, Altamura, Allen, Marazziti, & Hollander, 2006; Young, 1998, 2007).

By focusing on the relatively small portion of the population that suffer from what might be called addiction, researchers may be missing an opportunity to understand the basic dynamics of motivations and rewards that underlie all new media use. There are circumstances, which have been referred to as "benignly problematic" use (Hall & Parsons, 2001) or "unregulated media behavior" (LaRose, Lin, & Eastin, 2003), in which use does not interfere significantly with one's life and, therefore, does not meet the clinical criteria for addiction. Still, this behavior is not entirely under one's conscious control and can, over time, interfere with users' abilities to achieve long-term goals. The ability to forgo immediate gratification in favor of distant goals (i.e., future-oriented self-control) is associated with superior scholastic performance, superior coping skills, and better relationships (Shoda, Mischel, & Peake, 1990; Tangney, Baumeister, & Boone, 2004). This suggests that there is merit in not limiting studies of the negative consequences of Internet use to include only those who exhibit signs of addiction.

Among a general sample of undergraduate Internet users, the amount of Internet usage was found to be positively correlated with deficiencies in self-regulation (LaRose et al., 2003). Research on television viewing has shown that the amount of time adults spend on television viewing is negatively associated with self-control (Kubey & Csikszentmihalyi, 1990). Though these studies demonstrate negative correlations between various media use and self-control, their approach provides a limited insight as to what characteristics of the media, the content, and the audience explain these correlations. LaRose et al.'s (2003) study does not indicate what applications or websites on the Internet are used more by those who have deficient self-regulation. Given the wide variety of social and entertainment leisure activities one can engage in via new media technology, it is essential to establish correlations between certain popular online activities and self-control rather than treating all Internet use as the same. Similarly, in their analysis of self-control and television use, Kubey and Csikszentmihalyi assume a certain degree of homogeneity to the leisure media choice environment and to the television viewing experience in particular. Benesch, Frey, and Stutzer (2010) find that the likelihood that individuals with low self-control watch more television than they had intended to was positively related to the number of available television channels. This suggests that the relationship between the amount of leisure media use and self-control depends on the number of leisure options from which one chooses. Since the finding linking television use to deficits in self-control, the number of alternative leisure activities has grown significantly. Assuming that the user has access and flexibility in his or her schedule, portable networked devices (e.g., laptops) are often physically and temporally proximate to the user and, thus, are just as (if not more) likely to test the willpower of users as television.

The aforementioned research on the effects of proximity on the tendency of low self-control choosers to select immediately gratifying options and the research on self-control and media selection lead to the hypotheses that the level of students' self-control will be negatively associated with the amount of leisure media use.

Hypothesis 1 (H1): College students' self-control is negatively associated with amounts of leisure media use.

Experiences of failed self-control in the face of temptation are likely to be coupled with the self-reactive attitude of guilt (Bandura, 1991; LaRose et al., 2003). Guilt has been hypothesized to be a symptom of deficient self-control (Ainslie, 1996), but it may also be an indication that the individual is *aware* that they have lost control, indicative of some degree of successful self-monitoring (LaRose & Eastin, 2002) and allowing for subsequent improvement in self-control (Baumeister & Heatherton, 1996). The constant presence of tempting, proximate media options is hypothesized to result in more lapses in restraint and thus lead to greater feelings of guilt.

Hypothesis 2 (H2): College students' guilt about media use is positively associated with amounts of leisure media use.

After leaving for college, young people spend significant amounts of time using these media for various leisure activities, ranging from text messaging to social networking websites to online video viewing, in addition to the dominant form of leisure media use: television viewing (Junco & Cole-Avent, 2008). One survey found that college students spent 51% of their time on socializing and recreation while spending only 7% of their time studying (Arum & Roksa, 2011). The amount of time college students dedicate to studying has steadily declined over the past five decades (Babcock & Marks, 2010), which suggests that the recent advances in technology are not entirely to blame for the decline. Nevertheless, the combination of an unscheduled time environment and an unprecedented multiplicity of appealing diversions make the leisure time choices of these individuals somewhat unique and, based on extant knowledge of self-control and decision making in high-choice environments, are likely to exacerbate the existing trend. It is thus hypothesized that time spent using leisure media will substitute for time spent on schoolwork.

> *Hypothesis 3 (H3)*: The amount of time college students spend on schoolwork is negatively associated with amounts of leisure media use.

College students' leisure media use may be explained or predicted in other ways. Media users' stated that "gratifications sought" have proved an effective means of predicting amounts of use of traditional and new forms of media (e.g., Papacharissi & Rubin, 2000). It is possible that the amount of time students spend using leisure media can be better explained by their stated motives rather than their levels of self-control. To address the argument that greater amounts of use of these leisure media are attributable to certain motives rather than the user's level of self-control, an analysis was performed that compared the power of factors derived from Flanagin and Metzger's (2001) measure of motivations for Internet use with that of self-control to predict the amount of use of two popular online applications used by students—SNS and online video. It is hypothesized that self-control will predict amount of media use to a greater degree than stated motivations for using media.

> *Hypothesis 4a (H4a)*: Self-control will predict amounts of SNS use by college students to a greater extent than students' stated reasons for Internet use.
> **Hypothesis 4b (H4b):** Self-control will predict amounts of online video use by college students to a greater extent than students' stated reasons for Internet use.

Much of the research on self-control and media use examines different media (e.g., cell phones, television) in isolation. To provide an insight into which media or online applications are the most tempting or distracting to students and which media or applications interfere with students' abilities to complete schoolwork, an analysis was conducted that compares the significance and the strength of the relations between amounts of use, self-control, guilt, and the amount of time on schoolwork across various popular leisure media and online applications.

Research Question 1: What media or online applications have the strongest associations with self-control, feelings of guilt, and time spent on schoolwork among students?

Method

Participants

A survey was administered online during the fall 2010 semester and winter 2011 semester to students enrolled in a communications class at a large Midwestern university. Participants received credit in exchange for participation. Four hundred fifty eight students took the survey; 74% (336) of these participants were female and the median age was 19 ($M = 18.8$, $SD = .80$). The entire sample's ethnic make-up was not determined; however, a subsample of 173 students drawn from the sample consisted primarily of Caucasians (70%) and Asians or Asian Americans (15%).

Measures

The survey to assess media use was developed after consulting the most recent studies tracking the media habits of adolescents (Kaiser Family Foundation, 2010; Lenhart, Purcell, Smith, & Zickuhr, 2010). To verify that this information accurately and exhaustively reflected the ways in which college students were using media, a round of individual interviews were conducted with 30 undergraduate students in 2010. From this, several leisure media or applications emerged as popular among the population of interest: SNS use, watching television as it is broadcast, watching online video, watching previously recorded programs on a DVR, and watching DVDs.

To assess various kinds of video use, participants were asked, *"On average, how much time do you spend engaging in these activities with your TV or laptop each day?"* and told to provide the answer in minutes. There were four video use measures: *"watching online video," "watching recorded programs when you want (On-demand, DVR, or TiVo)," "watching DVDs," "watching TV programs at the times they are broadcast (not recorded programs).* Amount of SNS use was assessed by asking students how many times each day they visited an SNS site such as Facebook and, on average, how much time they spent on the site each time they visited.[1] These variables were added together to create a single daily leisure media use variable (known hereafter as "leisure media use").

To assess individual differences in self-control, Tangney et al.'s (2004) 13-item measure of self-control was used. Participants rated 13 statements based on the degree to which they felt each statement described them (1 = *"not at all like me"* to 5 = *"just like me"*; example of an item: *"Rate the degree to which you feel these statements describe you: 'I am good at resisting temptation'"*). This measure was considered appropriate for this study given the fact that it was conceived by its creators as a way to assess, in particular, individuals' abilities to "interrupt undesired behavioral tendencies (such as impulses) and refrain from acting on them" (p. 274). The internal reliability of the measure was .85 in this sample, which is comparable to validations in previous samples (alpha = .89; Tangney et al., 2004).

To assess guilt, participants were asked to rate the degree to which they felt the following four statements described themselves (1 = *"not at all like me"* to 5 = *"just like me"*): *"I often feel guilty about the amount of television I watch"; "I often feel guilty about having watched certain TV programs"; "I often feel guilty about the amount of time I spend online"; "I often feel guilty about having engaged in certain activities online."* These questions measured guilt associated with the amount and type of television and Internet consumption. Together, they had an alpha = .73 and were combined in a single measure of media guilt by adding them together and dividing them by four.

Given the amount and frequency of new media use among young people and given the increasingly "user-friendly" nature of the various online applications, it is likely that many young users have achieved a level of mastery of the use of such technologies and that self-efficacy plays a diminishing role in predicting amounts of use. To ensure that self-efficacy is not significantly predictive of media use within this population, a proxy for self-efficacy (e.g., age of media technology adoption) is included as another independent variable in the regression models. So as to control for differences in use between males and females, gender was also assessed (Female =1; Male = 2).

To assess the amount of time participants spent on schoolwork each day, they were also asked to report the number of hours they spent doing schoolwork on an average day.

To assess motivations for using SNS and online video, participants were asked to report the extent to which they used the Internet for 20 different reasons (examples of items: *"To get information," "To be entertained"*; 1 = *"Never"* to 5 = *Very Often"*).

Analysis

To test the first hypothesis, the composite leisure media use variable was used as a dependent variable in a two-step regression. Gender and the composite measure of age of media technology adoption were used as simultaneous independent variables in the first step, and self-control as the independent variable in the second step. To test the second hypothesis, a two-step regression was run with gender and the composite measure of age of media technology adoption as simultaneous independent variables in the first step, and the composite measure of media use as the dependent variable. In the second step, the composite measure of guilt over amount and type of media use was the independent variable. To test the third hypothesis, a regression was run with students' self-reports of the composite measure of media use as the dependent variable, gender and age of adoption of media technologies as simultaneous independent variables in the first step, and the amount of schoolwork per day as the independent variable in the second step.

To test the fourth hypothesis, principle component analysis was performed on the 20 item Internet users index. This yielded four factors with eigenvalues greater than 1 (see Table A1 of appendix). The following nine items loaded highest on the first factor: *"to generate ideas," "to learn more about myself and others," "to get to know others," "to impress people," "to have something to do with others," "to gain insight into myself," "to feel less lonely," "to feel important,"* and *"to stay in touch."* These items related primarily to social uses and are thus labeled "social" (alpha = .89). These seven items loaded heaviest on the second factor: *"to get information," "to be entertained," "to learn how to do things," "to do schoolwork," "to provide others with information," "to play,"* and *"to contribute to a pool of information."* These items relate primarily to information gathering and entertainment and are thus labeled "information/entertainment" (alpha = .89). The third factor consists of two items: *"to solve problems"* and *"to make decisions,"* both of which could be considered utilitarian use of the Internet and are thus labeled "utilitarian" (alpha = .70). Finally, the fourth factor consisted of two items: *"to pass time when bored"* and *"to relax,"* both of which connote using the Internet as a way to pass time and are thus labeled "to pass time" (alpha = .77). These four uses were used along with self-control as independent variables in two regressions, the first of which used SNS use as a dependent variable and the second of which had online video use as a dependent variable. As with the aforementioned regressions, gender and age of adoption were controlled for using stepwise regression.

Results

In this population, participants averaged just over 4 hours each day on schoolwork (4.20; $SD = 1.84$), roughly 95 minutes using SNS (95.51; $SD = 78.27$), about 25 minutes watching television as it is broadcast (24.87; $SD = 36.20$), roughly 23 minutes watching online video (23.19; $SD = 33.58$), 14 minutes watching prerecorded video (14.00; $SD = 28.58$), and 7 minutes watching DVDs (7.36; $SD = 22.00$). The total average amount of time spent using the five popular leisure media or applications was roughly 2 hours 45 minutes (164.43; $SD = 111.01$). The large variance in this sample reflected positively skewed kurtotic distributions in which many of the participants did not use media in some of these ways and several other participants used them frequently and/or for long durations. The mean score of the 5-point scale self-control variable was 3.1 with a standard deviation of .62, while the mean score of the 5-point scale composite guilt variable was 2.41 with a standard deviation of .80. In addition, the average age of media technology adoption was 12.26 with a standard deviation of 1.30, confirming that this sample is relatively homogenous in terms of its levels of experience with these technologies.

Hypothesis 1 was supported. Step 1 of the stepwise regression explained 2.3% of the variance in leisure media use ($R^2 = .023$, $p = .01$). Males used roughly 28 fewer minutes of use than females (unstandardized $B = -28.42$, $p = .02$). The age at which students adopted media did not significantly affect the amount of media they used (unstandardized $B = -7.86$, $p = .06$). The independent variable in step two of this regression explained 6.3% of the variance in leisure media use ($R^2 = .063$, $p = .001$). Self-control was negatively associated with leisure media use. For every point on the 5-point self-control scale, students used roughly 36 fewer minutes of leisure media (unstandardized $B = -35.61$, $p = .001$).

Hypothesis 2 was also supported. The variables in step two of the regression explained 8.1% of the variance in leisure media use ($R^2 = .081$, $p = .001$). Media use guilt was significantly positively associated with amount of leisure media use. For every point on the 5-point guilt scale, students consumed roughly 34 minutes of leisure media (unstandardized $B = 33.69, p = .000$).

Hypothesis 3 was not supported. Step two of the regression explained 3.1% of the variance in leisure media use ($R^2 = .031$, $p = .006$). The amount of time spent on schoolwork was not significantly associated with leisure media use (unstandardized $B = -5.46, p = .07$).

Accounting for Motivation

To assess the power of self-control to predict amounts of SNS use and online video use relative to that of students' reported uses, two regressions were conducted. Hypothesis 4a was supported. Step two of the first stepwise regression accounted for 14.4% of the total variance in the amount of SNS use ($R^2 = .144, p = .001$). Self-control significantly predicted the amount of SNS use (unstandardized $B = -31.10, p = .001$), while "social," "information/entertainment," "utilitarian," and "to pass time" were not significantly associated with the amount of SNS use. This indicates that for every point on the 5-point self-control scale, students spend roughly 31 fewer minutes using SNS. Hypothesis 4b was supported as well. Self-control significantly predicted the amount of online video use (unstandardized $B = -11.12$, $p = .001$), while the four uses were not significantly associated with the amount of online video use. This indicates that for every point on the self-control scale, students spend roughly 11 fewer minutes watching online video.

Self-Control, Guilt, Schoolwork, and Individual Media

To address the research question, a bivariate correlation was conducted with the following variables: SNS, online video, DVD, DVR, broadcast TV, self-control, guilt, and school-work (see Table 1). This disaggregation of media uses shows self-control to be negatively associated with SNS use and online video use. Self-control is not associated with DVD, DVR, or broadcast TV use. Feelings of guilt are positively associated with SNS use and, to lesser extents, with online video use and broadcast television use. Finally, online video use is negatively associated with the amount of time students' spend on schoolwork, while no other media use is significantly correlated with amount of schoolwork.

Discussion

This study provides support for the claim that students who are low in self-control are apt to spend more time using leisure media and are apt to feel guilty about doing so. Findings suggest that levels of self-control are a more accurate predictor of the amount of SNS use and online video use than the users' stated reasons for using the Internet. In addition, the analysis differentiates among many media activities engaged in by college undergraduates and establishes associations among self-control, guilt, and some uses, while demonstrating that no such associations exist for other uses. In doing so, it increases understanding of the characteristics of tempting media experiences beyond the basic medium-specific understanding of self-regulation and media use.

Table 1. Media Use, Self-Control, Guilt, and Schoolwork Correlation Matrix.

	SNS	Online video	DVR	DVD	TV	Self-control	Guilt	School-work
SNS								
DVR	.03	−.04						
DVD	−.05	−.04	.34**					
TV	.09	−.06	.17**	.11*				
Self-control	−.25**	−.21**	−.01	−.03	.06			
Guilt	.21**		.08	.06	.03*	−.32**		
Schoolwork	−.06	−.13**	.05	−.03	.02	.23**	−.05	

Note. Pearson correlation statistics presented.
*$p < .05$. **$p < .01$.

Specifically, this analysis suggests that online video use and SNS use are associated with deficits in self-control and feelings of guilt, while television viewing, DVR use, and DVD use are not. Despite the fact that SNS use functions as a temptation for college students, it does not take away from the amount of time students spend on schoolwork. Of the popular leisure media surveyed, only online video viewing is negatively associated with the reported amount of time spent on schoolwork. Together, these findings suggest that the constant presence of online video and SNS tests the self-control of students to a greater degree than other media in their choice environment, that students are aware of this, and that online video viewing displaces time spent on schoolwork. Though there is concern about the degree to which SNS and mobile phones distract students (e.g., Hanson, Drumheller, Mallard, McKee, & Schlegel, 2010), there is relatively little research concerning the extent to which streaming video applications do so. This study suggests that more research on the role of these applications is essential to understanding students' time budgeting.

The absence of a negative correlation between SNS use and the amount of time spent on schoolwork is consistent with some prior findings on this phenomenon (Junco, 2012) and inconsistent with others (Kirschner & Karpinski, 2010). Kirschner & Karpinski's (2010) finding that Facebook users spent less time studying was based on a sample that was nearly one-third nonusers and assessed SNS use with a yes/no question. Ninety-nine percent of the samples in this study used SNS that is roughly consistent with the proportion of Facebook users in Junco's (2012) sample. Similar to the results of the current study, Junco found no evidence of a strong negative correlation between the amount of time students spent using SNS and the amount of time they spent on schoolwork. This suggests that the negative correlation between SNS use and schoolwork is only observable when users are compared with nonusers. Given the extremely high rates of SNS adoption in the college student population, it will be more useful going forward to use the amount or type of SNS use in analyses of schoolwork and leisure media use.

One possible explanation for the absence of negative correlation between SNS use and time spent on schoolwork is that students are engaging in serial or sequential use of

SNS and schoolwork, rapidly toggling back and forth between the two activities (Koolstra, Ritterfeld, & Vorderer, 2009). It is easier for users to toggle between SNS and schoolwork than to toggle between watching a video and schoolwork by virtue of the fact that SNS requires attention for mere seconds, while online video typically requires attention for several minutes or more. It is also possible that SNS use may be substituting for other social activities such as spending time with dorm-mates or talking on the phone. Further research on time displacement should consider these possibilities.

Anytime/Anywhere Media and Self-Control

Physical and temporal proximity of the options are known to affect the extent to which products or experiences test the self-control of choosers: the closer one is to a tempting option, in time or in space, the more likely one is to choose that option over less tempting alternatives (Ainslie, 1975; Hoch & Loewenstein, 1991; Mischel, 1974). The past two decades have seen a steady shift toward increasingly physically and temporally proximate leisure media options; however, television viewing remains constrained by place and time—viewers typically watch only in their homes and content is only available at scheduled times. The presence of associations among self-control, guilt, and anytime/anywhere media such as online video and SNS, combined with the absence of such associations for television use, suggests that constantly present media may test the self-control of individuals with flexible schedules to a greater extent than media experiences constrained by time and place.

The study did not find any associations among self-control, guilt, and DVD or DVR use. Of the media use options presented in the survey, DVD and DVR had the lowest mean amount of use, suggesting that, at least for this population, they are not as attractive an option as the other temporally proximate leisure media options. Many students do not have access to DVR, while almost all students have access to the Internet and, hence, to SNS and online video. Regardless of how one accesses DVDs (e.g., via library loan or postal service), one must choose from fewer titles than when selecting an online video. There is also the possible influence of duration: DVDs and DVRs offer experiences of relatively long duration, typically between 30 minutes and 2 hours, while online video and SNS do not require users to commit such large chunks of time. A student asking herself whether she wants to watch a 2-hour movie may be making a deliberative decision that is not as prone to be affected by deficits in self-control as less deliberative decisions (Shiv & Fedorikhin, 1999). Finally, DVR users typically choose from a menu of predetermined options. This array of options is assembled at a time that is temporally remote from the moment of viewing and thus may be chosen in a deliberative, reflective way. The act of DVR viewing, then, may be an unscheduled act (one may sit down and view DVR programs whenever one likes) but the DVR viewers' options are circumscribed by available options assembled by a deliberating, reflective self.

Limitations

This cross-sectional survey relies on self-report data, which may misrepresent the actual amount of media use engaged in by the participants given individuals' tendencies to misestimate the amount of media they use (Collopy, 1996). Specifically, media users have tended to overestimate the amount of time they spend online and underestimate the amount of time they spend watching television (Bloxham, Holmes, Moult, & Spaeth, 2009), though one wonders whether this may change the more people associate time spent online with leisure.

Though this study uses self-report survey data to determine media users' durations and types of media use, it does not simply take the users at their word as to *why* they chose what they chose. By demonstrating that students' levels of self-control are better predictors of amount of various kinds of media use than stated reasons for use, this study establishes preliminary evidence that these experiences are, to some degree, not selected mindfully. Such evidence should prompt researchers interested in explaining why users select certain media experiences to supplement assessments of self-reported media use motivations with a measure of self-control, in particular when studying SNS use and online video viewing.

There was no measure of overall Internet use, nor any measure of cell-phone use or videogame playing, activities known to be engaged in more by those with lower levels of self-control (Billieux et al., 2011; Billieux, Van der Linden, d'Acremont, Ceschi, & Zermatten, 2007; Seay & Kraut, 2007), both of which are more prevalent than viewing online video (Nielsen, 2009). All these measures should be included in future studies.

Among the variables not assessed in this study that may affect media use, guilt, and self-control is the perception of social norms (LaRose, Mastro, & Eastin, 2001). Though guilt can be understood as evidence of knowledge of such norms and acknowledgment that one has violated them (Baumeister, Stillwell, & Heatherton, 1994), there are other feasible ways of isolating the effects of the perception of one's leisure media selection relative to social norms. In future studies, media users could be asked to estimate the average amount of daily use of various kinds of media and applications.

In this study of individuals with unstructured time, there is no comparison group comprising those who have more structured time. To address this, the findings in this study should be compared with survey results from a group of individuals of the same age (18-20 years old) who are currently employed at fulltime jobs. It may not be the lack of structure of the college environment that leads those with low self-control to use more SNS, but rather the fact that SNS happens to be an especially important mode of social surveillance, used to track minute changes in the status of peers among this population at this time. If there were a population that had more regular, regimented schedules that had similarly high needs for social surveillance and communication with peers, one might expect to see the same correlation between self-control and SNS use.

Conclusion

Medium-specific theories about overuse efface the difference between various types of Internet use, different media choice environments, and different media users. In some cases, the amounts of time users spend using various applications or functions of a medium are highly correlated with variables of interest such as self-control, guilt, and the amount of time students spend on schoolwork, justifying a medium-specific conceptualization of media use. In others, such as the case of online video, a particular application has different antecedents and consequences than other applications on the very same medium. It is therefore essential to develop theories of media use that conceptualize media uses in terms of attributes such as the degree to which their uses are constrained by time and place.

The continuing project of understanding college students' time budgeting as well as the project of defining, diagnosing, and treating problematic Internet use require a thorough understanding of the ways in which all users relate to media options in general, the unique attributes of new media experiences, and the circumstances in which users select such media from a variety of leisure-time options. Differentiating among uses and establishing the psychological mechanisms and choice environments that are associated with the repeated selection of leisure media options not only provide a basis for effective interventions aimed at improving college-student achievement but may help all individuals intending to curb the "guilty pleasure" use of media.

Appendix

Table A1. Principle Component Matrix of 20 Internet Uses (Flanagin & Metzger, 2001).

Uses	Social	Information/ entertainment	Utilitarian	To pass time
To get information	−.07	**.67**	.35	−.18
To generate ideas	**.61**	.21	.45	−.17
To learn more about myself and others	**.69**	.20	.09	.17
To be entertained	−.03	**.83**	.10	−.05
To get to know others	**.79**	.11	.18	−.01
To learn how to do things	.02	**.82**	.10	−.09
To impress people	**.83**	.01	.03	.16
To do school work	−.08	**.63**	.36	−.37
To have something to do with others	**.67**	.12	.37	.06
To provide others with information	.25	**.77**	.07	.06
To solve problems	.20	.13	**.76**	.05
To play	.23	**.76**	.01	−.07
To stay in touch	**.47**	.23	.47	−.13
To relax	.24	−.17	−.09	**.84**
To make decisions	.37	.07	**.67**	.04
To contribute to a pool of information	.33	**.72**	−.07	−.08
To gain insight into myself	**.75**	−.09	.16	.23
To pass the time away when bored	.09	−.20	.10	**.87**
To feel less lonely	**.72**	.08	.19	.07
To feel important	**.60**	.47	−.33	.00

Note. Bold values signify that they are part of the factor listed at the top of each column.

Acknowledgments

The author wishes to thank Sara H. Konrath at the University of Michigan Institute for Social Research for her insightful feedback on various drafts of this article.

Declaration of Conflicting Interests

The author declared no potential conflicts of interest with respect to the research, authorship, and/or publication of this article.

Funding

The author received no financial support for the research, authorship, and/or publication of this article.

References

Ainslie, G. (1975). Specious reward: A behavioral theory of impulsiveness and impulse control. *Psychological Bulletin, 82*, 463-496. doi:10.1037/h0076860

Ainslie, G. (1996). Studying self-regulation the hard way. *Psychological Inquiry, 7*, 16-20. doi:10.1207/s15327965pli0701_2

Arum, R., & Roksa, J. (2011). *Academically adrift: Limited learning on college campuses.* Chicago, IL: University of Chicago Press.

Babcock, P., & Marks, M. (2010). Leisure college, USA: The decline in student study time. *Education Outlook, 7.* American Enterprise Institute for Public Policy Research. Retrieved from http://www.aei.org/docLib/07-EduO-Aug-2010g.pdf

Babin, B. J., & Darden, W. R. (1995). Consumer self-regulation in the retail environment. *Journal of Retailing, 71*, 47-70. doi:10.1016/0022-4359(95)90012-8

Bandura, A. (1991). Social cognitive theory of self-regulation. *Organizational Behavior and Human Decision Processes, 50*, 248-287. doi:10.1016/0749-5978(91)90022-L

Baruh, L. (2010). Mediated voyeurism and the guilty pleasure of consuming reality television. *Media Psychology, 13*, 201-221. doi:10.1080/15213269.2010.502871

Baumeister, R. F. (2008). Free will in scientific psychology. *Perspectives on Psychological Science, 3*, 14-19. doi:10.1111/j.1745-6916.2008.00057.x

Baumeister, R. F., & Heatherton, T. F. (1996). Self-regulation failure: An overview. *Psychological Inquiry, 7*, 1-15. doi:10.1207/s15327965pli0701_1

Baumeister, R. F., Sparks, E. A., Stillman, T. F., & Vohs, K. D. (2008). Free will in consumer behavior: Self-control, ego depletion, and choice. *Journal of Consumer Psychology, 18*, 4-13. doi:10.1016/j.jcps.2007.10.002

Baumeister, R. F., Stillwell, A. M., & Heatherton, T. F. (1994). Guilt: An interpersonal approach. *Psychological Bulletin, 115*, 243-267. doi:10.1037/0033-2909.115.2.243

Benesch, C., Frey, B. S., & Stutzer, A. (2010). TV channels, self control and happiness. *The B.E. Journal of Economic Analysis & Policy, 10*(1), Article 86. doi:10.2202/1935-1682.2119

Billieux, J., Van der Linden, M., d'Acremont, M., Ceschi, G., & Zermatten, A. (2007). Does impulsivity relate to perceived dependence on and actual use of the mobile phone? *Applied Cognitive Psychology, 21*, 527-537. doi:10.1002/acp.1289

Billieux, J., Chanal, J., Khazaal, Y., Rochat, L., Gay, P., Zullino, P., & Van der Linden, M. (2011). Psychological predictors of problematic involvement in massively multiplayer online role-playing games: Illustration in a sample of male cybercafé players. *Psychopathology, 44*, 165-171. doi:10.1159/000322525

Bloxham, M., Holmes, M., Moult, B., & Spaeth, J. (2009). *Video mapping consumer study.* Retrieved from http://researchexcellence.com/committees/vcm_finalreport.pdf

Byun, S., Ruffini, C., Mills, J. E., Douglas, A. C., Niang, M., Stepchenkova, S., & . . .Blaton, M. (2009). Internet addiction: Metasynthesis of 1996-2006 quantitative research. *CyberPsychology & Behavior, 12,* 203-207. doi:10.1089/cpb.2008.0102

Chak, K., & Leung, L. (2004). Shyness and locus of control as predictors of Internet addiction and Internet use. *CyberPsychology & Behavior, 7,* 559-570. doi:10.1089/cpb.2004.7.559

Collopy, F. (1996). Biases in retrospective self-reports of time use: An empirical study of computer users. *Management Science, 42,* 758-767. doi:10.1287/mnsc.42.5.758

Dell'Osso, B., Altamura, A. C., Allen, A., Marazziti, D., & Hollander, E. (2006). Epidemiologic and clinical updates on impulse control disorders: A critical review. *European Archives of Psychiatry & Clinical Neuroscience, 256,* 464-475. doi:10.1007/s00406-006-0668-0

Flanagin, A., & Metzger, M. (2001). Internet use in the contemporary media environment. *Human Communication Research, 27*(1), 153-181. doi: 10.1111/j.1468-2958.2001.tb00779.x

Gauntlett, D., & Hill, A. (1999). *TV living: Television, culture, and everyday life.* London, England: Routledge.

Gul, F., & Pesendorfer, W. (2004). Self-control, revealed preference and consumption choice. *Review of Economic Dynamics, 7,* 243-264. doi:10.1016/j.red.2003.11.002

Hall, A. S., & Parsons, J. (2001). Internet addiction: College student case study using best practices in cognitive behavior therapy. *Journal of Mental Health Counseling, 23,* 312-327.

Hanson, T. L., Drumheller, K., Mallard, J., McKee, C., & Schlegel, P. (2010). Cell phones, text messaging, and Facebook: Competing time demands of today's college students. *College Teaching, 59,* 23-30. doi:10.1080/87567555.2010.489078

Hoch, S. J., & Loewenstein, G. F. (1991). Time-inconsistent preferences and consumer self-control. *The Journal of Consumer Research, 17,* 492-507. doi:10.1086/208573

Junco, R., & Cole-Avent, G. A. (2008). An introduction to technologies commonly used by college students. *New Directions for Student Services, 124,* 3-18. doi:10.1002/ss.292

Junco, R. (2012). Too much face and not enough books: The relationship between multiple indices of Facebook use and academic performance. *Computers in Human Behavior, 28,* 187-198. doi:10.1016/j.chb.2011.08.026

Kaiser Family Foundation. (2010). *Report: Generation M2: Media in the lives of 8- to 18-Year-Olds—Kaiser Family Foundation.* Retrieved from http://www.kff.org/entmedia/8010.cfm

Kirschner, P. A., & Karpinski, A. C. (2010). Facebook® and academic performance. *Computers in Human Behavior, 26,* 1237-1245. doi:10.1016/j.chb.2010.03.024

Koolstra, C. M., Ritterfeld, U., & Vorderer, P. (2009). Media choice despite multitasking? In T. Hartmann (Ed.), *Media choice: A theoretical and empirical overview* (pp. 234-246). New York, NY: Routledge.

Kubey, R. W., & Csikszentmihalyi, M. (1990). *Television and the quality of life: How viewing shapes everyday experience.* Hillsdale, NJ: Lawrence Erlbaum.

LaRose, R. (2009). Social cognitive theories of media selection. In T. Hartmann (Ed.), *Media choice: A theoretical and empirical overview* (pp. 10-31). New York, NY: Routledge.

LaRose, R., & Eastin, M. S. (2002). Is online buying out of control? Electronic commerce and consumer self-regulation. *Journal of Broadcasting & Electronic Media, 46,* 549-564. doi:10.1207/s15506878jobem4604_4

LaRose, R., Mastro, D., & Eastin, M. S. (2001). Understanding Internet usage. *Social Science Computer Review, 19,* 395-413. doi:10.1177/089443930101900401

LaRose, R., Lin, C. A., & Eastin, M. S. (2003). Unregulated Internet usage: Addiction, habit, or deficient self-regulation? *Media Psychology, 5,* 225-253. doi:10.1207/S1532785XMEP0503_01

Lenhart, A., Purcell, K., Smith, A., & Zickuhr, K. (2010). *Social media and mobile Internet use among teens and young adults*. Retrieved from http://pewInternet.org/Reports/2010/Social-Media-and-Young-Adults/Summary-of-Findings.aspx?r=1

Mischel, W. (1974). Processes in delay of gratification. In L. Berkowitz (Ed.), *Advances in experimental social psychology* (pp. 249-292). New York, NY: Academic Press.

Nielsen (2009). *How teens use media: A Nielsen report on the myths and realities of teen media trends*. Retrieved from http://www.nielsen.com/us/en/reports/2009/How-Teens-Use-Media.html

Papacharissi, Z., & Rubin, A. M. (2000). Predictors of Internet use. *Journal of Broadcasting & Electronic Media, 44*, 175-196. doi:10.1207/s15506878jobem4402_2

Pozner, J. L. (2010). *Reality bites back: The troubling truth about guilty pleasure TV*. Berkeley, CA: Seal Press.

Radway, J. (1984). *Reading the romance: Women, patriarchy, and popular culture*. Chapel Hill: University of North Carolina Press.

Read, D., Loewenstein, G., & Kalyanaraman, S. (1999). Mixing virtue and vice: Combining the immediacy effect and the diversification heuristic. *Journal of Behavioral Decision Making, 12*, 257-273. doi:10.1002/(SICI)1099-0771(199912)12:4<257::AID-BDM327>3.0.CO;2-6

Seay, A. F., & Kraut, R. E. (2007). Project massive: Self-regulation and problematic use of online gaming. *Proceedings of the SIGCHI Conference on Human Factors in Computing Systems* (pp. 829-838). New York, NY: Association for Computer Machinery.

Shiv, B., & Fedorikhin, A. (1999). Heart and mind in conflict: The interplay of affect and cognition in consumer decision making. *The Journal of Consumer Research, 26*, 278-292. doi:10.1086/209563

Shoda, Y., Mischel, W., & Peake, P. K. (1990). Predicting adolescent cognitive and self-regulatory competencies from preschool delay of gratification: Identifying diagnostic conditions. *Developmental Psychology, 26*, 978-986. doi:10.1037/0012-1649.26.6.978

Stratton, M. T. (2010). Uncovering a new guilty pleasure: A qualitative study of the emotions of personal web usage at work. *Journal of Leadership & Organizational Studies, 17*, 392-410. doi:10.1177/1548051809350893

Tangney, J. P., Baumeister, R. F., & Boone, A. Z. (2004). High self-control predicts good adjustment, less pathology, better grades, and interpersonal success. *Journal of Personality, 72*, 271-324. doi:10.1111/j.0022-3506.2004.00263.x

Webster, J. G. (1985). Program audience duplication: A study of television inheritance effects. *Journal of Broadcasting & Electronic Media, 29*, 121-133. doi:10.1080/08838158509386571

Young, K. S. (1998). Internet addiction: The emergence of a new clinical disorder. *CyberPsychology & Behavior, 1*, 237-244. doi:10.1089/cpb.1998.1.237

Young, K. S. (2001). *Surfing not studying: Dealing with Internet addition on campus*. Retrieved from http://www.studentaffairs.com/ejournal/winter_2001/addiction.html

Young, K. S. (2007). Cognitive behavior therapy with Internet addicts: Treatment outcomes and implications. *CyberPsychology & Behavior, 10*, 671-679. doi:10.1089/cpb.2007.9971

Author Biography

Elliot Panek is a Visiting Fellow at Drexel University. He examines new media uses and effects, persuasion, and narrative form from sociological and psychological perspectives using interviews, surveys, and experiments to understand the antecedents and consequences of media selection in high-choice media environments. He has published research on social networking site use and narcissism, media use and self-control, and the effects of parental restrictions on their children's media use.

Executive Perceptions of the Top 10 Soft Skills Needed in Today's Workplace

Robles, M.M.

Abstract

Hard skills are the technical expertise and knowledge needed for a job. Soft skills are interpersonal qualities, also known as people skills, and personal attributes that one possesses. Business executives consider soft skills a very important attribute in job applicants. Employers want new employees to have strong soft skills, as well as hard skills. This study identified the top 10 soft skills as perceived the most important by business executives: integrity, communication, courtesy, responsibility, social skills, positive attitude, professionalism, flexibility, teamwork, and work ethic.

Keywords

soft skills, interpersonal skills, people skills

Technology has had a profound impact on skills that employers want from business graduates today (Mitchell, Skinner, & White, 2010). The shift from an industrial economy to an information society and an office economy means that many jobs now place an emphasis on integrity, communication, and flexibility (Zehr, 1998). Historically, technical skills, also known as hard skills, were the only skills necessary for career employment; but today's workplace is showing that technical skills are not enough to keep individuals employed when organizations are right-sizing and cutting positions (James & James, 2004). Because soft skills are critical for productive performance in today's workplace, current and future business leaders are emphasizing the development of soft skills (Nealy, 2005). While technical skills are a part of many excellent educational curricula, soft skills need further emphasis in the university curricula so

---

[1]Eastern Kentucky University, USA

that students learn the importance of soft skills early in their academic programs before they embark on a business career (Wellington, 2005).

Much research has been done on the importance of soft skills in the workplace (Klaus, 2010; Maes, Weldy, & Icenogel, 1997; Mitchell et al., 2010; Nealy, 2005; Smith, 2007). One study found that 75% of long-term job success depends on people skills, while only 25% is dependent on technical knowledge (Klaus, 2010). Another study indicated that hard skills contribute only 15% to one's success, whereas 85% of success is due to soft skills (Watts & Watts, 2008, as cited in John, 2009). As employers are progressively looking for employees who are mature and socially well adjusted, they rate soft skills as number one in importance for entry-level success on the job (Wilhelm, 2004).

Purpose and Problem Statement

The purpose of this study was to determine the critical soft skills that employers want from their employees so that business educators can promote these skills in their curriculum to improve the employability of graduating business seniors.

Method and Procedures

Students in a junior-level business communication class were each required to interview two executives each semester for their final project. After the interview, the student gave the executive a "thank you" letter and an evaluation survey from the course professor, along with a self-addressed, stamped envelope. The evaluation survey asked the business executive to comment on the performance of the student during the interviewing process. Additionally, the survey asked about topics that the business executives deemed important for business graduates to study. During the spring semester 2011, the executives were also asked to list the 10 most important soft skills they wanted new employees to possess when hired for a position within their organization.

Forty-five students were enrolled in the two business communication courses during spring semester 2011, so 90 executives received the survey. Of those 90 business executives, 49 (54%) responded by returning the questionnaire in the self-addressed, stamped envelope. A list of 517 soft skills (with repetition) was created. Some executives listed more than 10 soft skills; therefore, more than 490 items were gathered. After the skills were coded with like terms and themes, 26 soft skills emerged. The 10 soft skills that were listed most often by the executives were then included in a questionnaire to be rated by importance. Some examples of the "like" terms that were categorized as one of the 10 most mentioned *soft skill attributes* are listed in Figure 1.

After the top 10 soft skills attributes were determined, a 5-point Likert-type scale was created that would measure the strength of importance of each attribute. During the fall semester 2011 and spring semester 2012, the questionnaire was distributed to the business executives (along with the "thank you" and evaluation survey) by the

- Communication – oral, speaking capability, written, presenting, listening
- Courtesy – manners, etiquette, business etiquette, gracious, says please and thank you, respectful
- Flexibility – adaptability, willing to change, lifelong learner, accepts new things, adjusts, teachable
- Integrity – honest, ethical, high morals, has personal values, does what's right
- Interpersonal Skills – nice, personable, sense of humor, friendly, nurturing, empathetic, has self-control, patient, sociability, warmth, social skills
- Positive Attitude – optimistic, enthusiastic, encouraging, happy, confident
- Professionalism – businesslike, well-dressed, appearance, poised
- Responsibility – accountable, reliable, gets the job done, resourceful, self-disciplined, wants to do well, conscientious, common sense
- Teamwork – cooperative, gets along with others, agreeable, supportive, helpful, collaborative
- Work Ethic – hard working, willing to work, loyal, initiative, self-motivated, on time, good attendance

Figure 1. Ten soft skill attributes categorized from executive listings

students after they conducted the interviews for their field report. There were 91 students in three classes over those two semesters, so the survey was sent to 182 executives. A response was received from 57 (62.6%) executives.

The questionnaire asked the executive to rate the level of importance of each of the 10 soft skills attributes. The range of *extremely important* (5), *very important* (4), *somewhat important* (3), *not very important* (2), and *not important* (1) was used.

Data Findings and Analysis

Executives overwhelmingly indicated that integrity and communication were the top two soft skills needed by employees in today's workplace. All 57 (100%) of the executives indicated that integrity and communication were very important or extremely important. Over three fourths of the respondents (84.2%) indicated that courtesy was an extremely important skill, and over half (71.9% and 61.4%, respectively) reported that responsibility and interpersonal skills were extremely important. The frequency of each response and the percentages that indicated the level of importance of each soft skill attribute as perceived by business executives can be seen in Table 1.

The mean score and standard deviation of each of the soft skill attributes related to its perceived level of importance is shown in Table 2. Each of the soft skill attributes had a mean score of ≥4.12 based on a 5.0 scale, where 5 = *extremely important*, 4 = *very important*, 3 = *somewhat important*, 2 = *not very important*, and 1 = *not important*. None of the soft skills attributes received a *not important* ranking. Teamwork skills and Flexibility each received one response for *not very important* (by different executives).

Table 1. Perceived Level of Importance of Each Soft Skill Attribute in Today's Workplace (N = 57)

Soft Skill Attribute	Not Important 1		Not Very Important 2		Somewhat Important 3		Very Important 4		Extremely Important 5	
	n	%	n	%	n	%	n	%	n	%
Integrity							4	7.0	53	93.0
Communication							5	8.8	52	91.2
Courtesy					2	3.5	7	12.3	48	84.2
Responsibility					5	8.8	11	19.3	41	71.9
Interpersonal skills					9	15.8	13	22.8	35	61.4
Professionalism					7	12.3	23	40.4	27	47.4
Positive attitude					6	10.5	25	43.9	26	45.6
Teamwork skills			1	1.8	16	28.1	15	26.3	25	43.9
Flexibility			1	1.8	12	21.1	20	35.1	24	42.1
Work ethic					14	24.6	22	38.6	21	36.8

Table 2. Mean and Standard Deviation of Each Soft Skill Attribute Relative to Perceived Level of Importance (N = 57)

Soft Skill Attribute	M	SD
Integrity	4.93	0.26
Communication	4.91	0.28
Courtesy	4.81	0.48
Responsibility	4.63	0.64
Interpersonal skills	4.46	0.75
Positive attitude	4.35	0.66
Professionalism	4.35	0.69
Flexibility	4.18	0.82
Teamwork skills	4.12	0.88
Work ethic	4.12	0.77

Defining Hard and Soft Skills

The term *soft skills* has been around a long time in both business and educational settings, in corporate meetings, and in curriculum development (Evenson, 1999). When people think about their skills, they usually reflect on practices that they have perfected, such as keyboarding with speed and accuracy or wiring the electronics in an automotive system. Basically, when individuals use the term *hard skills*, they typically are referring to the definition of skill as defined by Random House Dictionary: the ability, coming from one's knowledge, practice, aptitude, to do something well; competent excellence in performance; and a craft, trade, or job requiring manual dexterity or special training in which a person has competence and experience

Soft Skills = Interpersonal (People) Skills + Personal (Career) Attributes

Figure 2. Soft skills are more than interpersonal skills

(http://dictionary.reference.com/browse/skills). Hard skills are those achievements that are included on a résumé, such as education, work experience, knowledge, and level of expertise. Examples of hard skills include job skills like typing, writing, math, reading, and the ability to use software programs (Investopedia, 2012).

The real soft skills definition is not about skills in the traditional sense. The Collins English Dictionary defines the term *soft skills* as "desirable qualities for certain forms of employment that do not depend on acquired knowledge: they include common sense, the ability to deal with people, and a positive flexible attitude" (http://dictionary .reference.com/browse/softskills). Soft skills are character traits, attitudes, and behaviors—rather than technical aptitude or knowledge. Soft skills are the intangible, nontechnical, personality-specific skills that determine one's strengths as a leader, facilitator, mediator, and negotiator.

Soft skills are character traits that enhance a person's interactions, job performance, and career prospects (Parsons, 2008). The greatest feature of soft skills is that the application of these skills is not limited to one's profession. Soft skills are continually developed through practical application during one's approach toward everyday life and the workplace (Arkansas Department of Education, 2007; Magazine, 2003). Unlike hard skills, which are about a person's skill set and ability to perform a certain type of task or activity, soft skills are interpersonal and broadly applicable (Parsons, 2008).

Soft Skills Include More Than People Skills

People skills are a core component of soft skills (Cafasso, 1996; Klaus, 2010). People skills are the interpersonal attributes that characterize a person's relationships with others. Some researchers note that interpersonal skills are the most important skills at all levels of the job (Sheikh, 2009; Smith, 2007). While many authors equate interpersonal skills with soft skills (James & James, 2004; Perreault, 2004), interpersonal skills are only one facet of soft skills. In addition to interpersonal skills, soft skills include personal qualities and career attributes (James & James, 2004; Nieragden, 2000; Perreault, 2004). Personal attributes might include one's personality, likeability, time management prowess, and organizational skills (Parsons, 2008). Career attributes can include communication, teamwork, leadership, and customer service (James & James, 2004). People skills are the foundation of good customer service, and customer service skills are critical to professional success in almost any job (Evenson, 1999; Zehr, 1998). People skills promote a positive attitude, effective communication, respectful interaction, and the ability to remain composed in difficult situations (Evenson, 1999). Therefore, soft skills are made up of the combination of interpersonal (people) skills and personal (career) attributes, as shown in the equation in Figure 2.

Communication is an important interpersonal skill in today's global business environment (John, 2009; Timm, 2005). It is often assumed that communication is a fundamental skill that everyone knows and does well. Unfortunately, that assumption is usually not a reality. Communication, or the lack thereof, has been the reason for many tragedies and disasters that have taken place within the financial industry, health care, and the wider environment in recent years (Jelphs, 2006).

Businesses want resourceful employees with soft skills at all levels ("Employers Value Communication," 2004; John, 2009) with interpersonal qualities (Rodas, 2007) who can collaborate, motivate, and empathize with their colleagues (Klaus, 2010). Business leaders complain that graduates do not have soft skills such as work ethic, verbal and nonverbal communication, attendance, interview abilities, and positive attitude. As one employer said, "We want somebody who shows up on time, somebody who works hard and someone who's trainable" (Arkansas Department of Education, 2007, p. 13). When asking business educators' perceptions of the importance of specific soft skills for success in today's workplace, Mitchell et al. (2010) found ethics and general communication skills as extremely important, with 57% stressing written communication and 56% indicating time management and organization skills as extremely important.

Soft skills are employability skills that are transferrable in many jobs. Cleary, Flynn, and Thomasson (2006) define general employability skills as follows:

- Basic/fundamental skills: technical, knowledge of task, hands-on ability
- Conceptual/thinking skills: planning, collecting and organizing information, problem-solving
- Business skills: innovation and enterprise
- Community skills: civic and citizenship knowledge
- People-related skills: interpersonal qualities, such as communication and teamwork
- Personal skills: attributes such as being responsible, resourceful, and self-confident

Note that the "people-related skills" and the "personal skills" (attributes) above fit the definition of soft skills. "Soft" skills can also be called "applied" skills or "21st-century skills" (Gewertz, 2007). Soft skills have more to do with who we are than what we know. As such, soft skills encompass the character traits that decide how well one interacts with others, and are usually a definite part of one's personality. Whereas hard skills can be learned and perfected over time, soft skills are more difficult to acquire and change. Klaus (2010) compares the "bedside manner" needed by medical students to communication skills training needs for business curriculum. The soft skills required for a doctor, for example, would be empathy, understanding, active listening, and a good bedside manner. Alternatively, the hard skills necessary for a doctor would include a vast comprehension of illnesses, the ability to interpret test results and symptoms, and a thorough understanding of anatomy and physiology. The hard and soft skills must complement one another (Nieragden, 2000).

Importance in Today's Workplace

Soft skills are as important as cognitive skills (John, 2009; Zehr, 1998). Giving students soft skills could make the difference in their being hired for a job in their field (Evenson, 1999), and the lack of soft skills can sink the promising career of someone who has technical ability and professional expertise but no interpersonal qualities (Klaus, 2010). Wellington (2005) describes the soft skills of success based on his experiences in different management positions, primarily within human resources. Successful managers who were promoted had both excellent technical and soft skills, especially the willingness and ability to work positively with others. Cobanoglu, Dede, and Poorani (2006) concluded that soft skills were among the most important skills in the job requirements for a hotel information technology manager: Communication was the most important, followed by critical thinking, and then the knowledge of information technology.

The research for the 21st century shows that potential employers want to hire applicants with strong interpersonal skills ("Employers Value Communication," 2004; Glenn, 2008; Mitchell et al., 2010; Perreault, 2004; Sutton, 2002; Wilhelm, 2004), but new graduates are falling short of employers' expectations (National Union of Students, 2011). Employers stress that educators should be teaching their students how to cooperate with others in the workplace and successfully acquire customer service skills (Evenson, 1999). In fact, soft skills are so important that they are ranked as number one and extremely important for potential job hires in many occupations and industries (Sutton, 2002). Hiring applicants who have interpersonal skills is instrumental for successful organizations to maintain a competitive advantage (Glenn, 2008). Soft skills are critical in the technical workplace (James & James, 2004), and business professionals need these skills because employers value them (John, 2009).

Even though some money is devoted to training managers to comply with workplace rules and teaching them the financial basics, oftentimes little attention is given to soft skills (White, 2005). Many senior executives view the concept of training soft skills as simply a motivational seminar that inspires employees but offers little use for job application or value to the company that pays for the training (Onisk, 2011); and some will say that hard skills, such as those in construction, computer programming, or accounting, take precedence over knowing how to be diplomatic with an upset customer or show finesse as an effective team member (Evenson, 1999). In contrast, Klaus (2010) notes that she frequently finds senior managers complaining that their newest employees lack the interpersonal skills needed for success in the business world. Personality measures are equally important predictors of work success as cognitive ability and work accuracy.

Moad (1995) justifies the increases in training budgets driven by changes to client/server technologies and the need for soft skills in business. Soft skills must be quantifiable and measured in returns, with the benefit translated into the bottom line (Onisk, 2011). Hard skills are specific, teachable abilities that can be defined and measured. By contrast, soft skills are less tangible and harder to quantify (Bronson, 2007). Measuring the impact of soft skills training on the return on investment (ROI) versus the impact of hard skills training is a challenge (Georges, 1996; Redford, 2007). Calculating the ROI and measuring the effectiveness of communications training, ethics, teamwork skills, and other softer skills is extremely difficult; therefore, many corporate training departments are reluctant to provide soft skills training. However, Moad (1995) notes that the impact of softer skills on ROI much more than justifies the money spent on training. Hard skills alone may be meaningless without soft skills. For example, software testers need two types of skills: one skill set to perform technical duties at work and one skill set to approach work with a positive attitude (soft skills; Magazine, 2003).

As a result of economic restructuring, European and Welsh business executives are trying to raise the skill levels of the workforce in order to boost productivity and economic growth and reduce unemployment. To engage workers with negative experiences of formal learning (e.g., school), there has been an increase in more informal learning, much of which is focused on soft skills, such as self-confidence and communication skills (Holtom & Bowen, 2007). Corporate trainers are implementing in-house training that teaches how to read people, draw out clients, and build relationships: skill-oriented executive education that fills in the holes of their employees' formal educations "all while bringing their humanity and personality into the mix" (Klaus, 2010, p. 9). Another method of promoting soft skills in organizations is to team up a newly hired employee with an expert mentor, who has been in the industry for 20 to 35 years. One Texas company begins the mentoring process informally, then involves an official mentorship relationship, and then returns to informality. The mentee learns both technical and soft skills from the mentor, such as the ability to cooperate with managers, peers, and customers (Riley, 2006).

Implications for Business Educators

Today, the national concern among business executives and professors is that high school graduates do not have the set of soft skills they need to be successful in college or in the workplace (Gewertz, 2007; National Union of Students, 2011). A survey of 400 leading American corporate managers in 2007 indicated that 70% of high school graduates lack professionalism and work ethic skills (Bronson, 2007). Another report, analyzing data from the U.S. Department of Labor, indicated that even though managers value interpersonal skills most in new employees, business graduates were not being taught the people skills they needed (Mangan, 2007). As educators open the lines of communication with employers, soft skills continue to be a topic of discussion (Kilday, 1996).

Companies are continuing to rate their employees' interpersonal skills as more important than their analytical abilities (Klaus, 2010). It is often said that hard skills will get you an interview but you need soft skills to get (and keep) the job. Success is based not only on what you know but also on how you can communicate it (Klaus, 2010). Technical skills are taught so that graduates can meet the job expectations and know-how (Magazine, 2003). Hard skills are easily justified and quantified, but preparing students with soft skills could make the difference in whether they find, and keep, the job for which they earned a degree (Evenson, 1999). Even in the quantitative areas, educators must instill the importance and development of soft skills in addition to the specific discipline foundation. Surprisingly, most of one's education is time spent on learning technical skills (Magazine, 2003), but integration of soft skills with technical skills is critical (McGee, 2007). Information technology professionals, for example, can enhance their job security (i.e., safe from outsourcing) by integrating the required soft skills necessary for their job with their technical skills (Cafasso, 1996; McGee, 2007). The results can be easily quantified in information technology as returns are often immediate and the alternative costs would not be acceptable because the inherent value of these soft skills programs is intuitive at every level of the organization (Onisk, 2011).

Over a decade ago, the National Business Education Association's Policies Commission for Business and Economic Education (2000) noted the upcoming shortage of skills in today's workplace that stresses the need for interpersonal skills, above and beyond academics, technical skills, and hands-on training. Schools must do a better job of teaching "soft skills" if students are to succeed in the evolving American economy (Zehr, 1998). Nontechnical interpersonal skills are needed in addition to having technical competence. Integration of soft skills into the business curriculum promotes hiring of students in today's workforce (Glenn, 2008; James & James, 2004; Mitchell et al., 2010; Perreault, 2004; Wilhelm, 2004). Oftentimes, educators are already trying to cover more content than reasonably possible in the classroom, so asking for a unit on soft skills can be burdensome to those teachers who are already dealing with a tight curriculum schedule (Evenson, 1999). Schools must balance the preparation of students for both high-tech jobs and office jobs (Zehr, 1998).

Soft skills can be included into the curriculum easily by spreading the content throughout the semester (Evenson, 1999):

1. Introduce students to basic people skills so they understand how to get along with people.
2. Segue to teaching essential customer service skills.
3. Foster student understanding by facilitating a problem-solving discussion based on real-life situations.
4. Have students demonstrate the people skills they have learned using role-play exercises in a mock business setting.

One school in Great Britain requires secondary students to compile specialized electronic portfolios to measure their soft skills, such as teamwork, in completing various assignments, research projects, and presentations. This portfolio requirement and soft skills assessment is intended to improve the availability of vocational options for high school students (Mansell, 2006). Sacramento New Technology High School also assesses soft skills of the students. In addition to course content knowledge, math students are evaluated on team collaboration and oral communication. These two interpersonal skills are among 10 student learning outcomes that students must master as they advance through all of their academic courses. The embedded assessments in coursework were designed to build soft skills as well as subject matter content (Gewertz, 2007).

One of the main challenges of soft skills training faced by educators is that we still have not figured out how to teach soft skills, nor have we figured out how to assess them and capture the impact of such programs on learners (Holtom & Bowen, 2007; Zehr, 1998). The outcomes of soft skills training are often intangible and provide gradual or deferred returns (Onisk, 2011). If teachers have the proper resources, they can do a better job preparing the employees that businesses are seeking in today's environment (Kilday, 1996).

Faculty development for business professors should be designed to assist with integration of interpersonal skills into the business curriculum (Mitchell et al., 2010). Research indicates that the typical learning styles of all students are not necessarily suited to the acquisition of generic skills. Boyce, Williams, Kelly, and Yee (2001) use a learning theory framework to support the use of case studies as an instructional method to capture various learning styles and, therefore, develop soft skills. When designing business curricula, soft skills that ranked low should still be emphasized because there could be a lack of value placed on the skill, or a lack of understanding of how to integrate the soft skill into the business curriculum (Mitchell et al., 2010).

Summary

Research suggests that soft skills are just as good an indicator of job performance as traditional job qualifications (hard skills). Hard skills are the technical abilities and knowledge that one possesses, whereas soft skills are those personal attributes and interpersonal qualities that are intangible. Although soft skills are important to recognize and improve, hard skills are critical on the job as well. While employers exceedingly want new employees to possess strong soft skills, the hard and soft skills must complement one another.

This study identified the top 10 soft skills as perceived the most important by business executives: integrity, communication, courtesy, responsibility, social skills, positive attitude, professionalism, flexibility, teamwork, and work ethic.

Business executives consider interpersonal skills a very important attribute in job applicants. They want employees who are honest, can communicate well, get along with others, and work hard.

Conclusions and Recommendations

Corporate recruiters want candidates with soft skills who add value with their soft skills, and also have the ability to make a difference in the workplace. Business employees need to communicate effectively, get along well with their coworkers, embrace teamwork, take initiative, have high work ethic, and portray professionalism.

This study identified the top 10 soft skills attributes deemed critical by business executives. Even though all of the soft skills appear very important, not all are perceived by business executives to be equally important. This study found that communication, integrity, and courtesy are the most important interpersonal skills for success.

Soft skills are critical in today's workplace and should be viewed as an investment. Even though interpersonal skills are critical for employers, many job applicants and current employees in business do not have adequate interpersonal skills. Organizations need to train current employees to enhance their soft skills.

Although we see many challenges, we also have many opportunities to prepare business students for today's workforce. Business educators need to understand the importance of interpersonal skills for their students and include soft skills in their curriculum. Instructional strategies and methods can be applied in the classroom to enhance interpersonal skills. Soft skills and hard skills should be integrated to create a well-rounded business graduate.

Further research is needed to study interpersonal skills and determine if other soft skills are deemed as important as the attributes found in this study.

Declaration of Conflicting Interests

The author(s) declared no potential conflicts of interest with respect to the research, authorship, and/or publication of this article.

Funding

The author(s) received no financial support for the research, authorship, and/or publication of this article.

References

Arkansas Department of Education. (2007). *Combined research report of business leaders and college professors on preparedness of high school graduates.* Little Rock: Author.

Boyce, G., Williams, S., Kelly, A., & Yee, H. (2001). Fostering deep and elaborative learning and generic (soft) skill development: The strategic use of case studies in accounting education. *Accounting Education, 10*, 37-60.

Bronson, E. (2007). Career and technical education is ideally suited to teaching students the soft skills needed to succeed in the 21st century workplace. *Techniques: Connecting Education & Careers, 82*(7), 30-31.

Cafasso, R. (1996, April 1). Selling your soft side (people skills win you the job). *Computerworld, 30*, 97.

Cleary, M., Flynn, R., & Thomasson, S. (2006). *Employability skills from framework to practice: An introductory guide for trainers and assessors.* Canberra, Australia: Department of Education, Science and Training.

Cobanoglu, C., Dede, P., & Poorani, A. (2006). An analysis of skills and competencies of full service hotel technology managers. *Journal of Teaching in Travel & Tourism, 6*(4), 19-35.

Employers value communication and interpersonal abilities. (2004). *Keying In, 14*(3), 1-6.

Evenson, R. (1999). Soft skills, hard sell [Electronic version]. *Techniques: Making Education & Career Connections, 74*(3), 29-31.

Georges, J. C. (1996). The myth of soft-skills training. *Training, 33*, 48-50. Retrieved from http://www.jtemgt.com/PDF/TrainingMyths.pdf

Gewertz, C. (2007, June 12). Soft skills in big demand: Interest in teaching students habits of mind for success in life is on the rise. *Education Week, 26*(40), 25-27.

Glenn, J. L. (2008). The "new" customer service model: Customer advocate, company ambassador. *Business Education Forum, 62*(4), 7-13.

Holtom, D., & Bowen, R. (2007, March). *People and work unit: Evaluation of the equal development partnership 'valuing learning—strengthening communities' project*. Retrieved from http://www.equal-works.com/resources/contentfiles/2447.pdf

Investopedia. (2012). *Hard skills*. Retrieved from http://www.investopedia.com/terms/h/hard-skills.asp#axzz1lMzgjWjK

James, R. F., & James, M. L. (2004). Teaching career and technical skills in a "mini" business world. *Business Education Forum, 59*(2), 39-41.

Jelphs, K. (2006). Communication: Soft skill, hard impact? *Clinician in Management, 14*, 33-37.

John, J. (2009). Study on the nature of impact of soft skills training programme on the soft skills development of management students. *Pacific Business Review, October/December*, 19-27.

Kilday, J. (1996). Getting all the skills employers want. *Techniques: Making Education & Career Connections, 71*(11), 21-25.

Klaus, P. (2010). Communication breakdown. *California Job Journal, 28*, 1-9.

Maes, J., Weldy, T., & Icenogel, M. (1997). A managerial perspective: Oral communication is most important for business students in the workplace. *Journal of Business Communication, 34*, 67-80.

Magazine, A. (2003). *Soft skills that make a tester*. Retrieved from http://www.stickyminds.com/sitewide.asp?ObjectId=6752&Function=DETAILBROWSE&ObjectType=ART

Mangan, K. (2007, August 17). M.B.A.'s may need more "soft skills." *Chronicle of Higher Education, 53*(50), 1A0.

Mansell, W. (2006, February 17). Diploma to plug the "soft skills" gap. *Times Educational Supplement, 4673*, 4.

McGee, M. K. (2007, July 23). Stay ahead with soft skills. *InformationWeek, 36*.

Mitchell, G. W., Skinner, L. B., & White, B. J. (2010). Essential soft skills for success in the twenty-first century workforce as perceived by business educators. *Delta Pi Epsilon Journal, 52*, 43-53.

Moad, J. (1995, April 15). Calculating the real benefit of training. *Datamation, 41*(7), 45-47.

National Union of Students. (2011). *Working towards your future: Making the most of your time in higher education*. Retrieved from http://www.nus.org.uk/en/news/news/your-guide-to-better-employability-skills/

Nealy, C. (2005). Integrating soft skills through active learning in the management classroom. *Journal of College Teaching & Learning, 2*(4), 1-6.

Nieragden, G. (2000, September). The soft skills of business English (The Weekly Column: Article 28). *ELT Newsletter*. Retrieved from http://www.eltnewsletter.com/back/September2000/art282000.htm

Onisk, M. (2011, October). *Is measuring soft-skills training really possible?* (White Paper). Retrieved from http://www.appcon.com.au/Portals/0/Research_Case_Studies/Is_Measuring _Soft_Skills_Training_Really_Possible.pdf

Parsons, T. L. (2008). *Definition: Soft skills.* Retrieved from http://searchcio.techtarget.com/ definition/soft-skills

Perreault, H. (2004). Business educators can take a leadership role in character education. *Business Education Forum, 59,* 23-24.

Policies Commission for Business and Economic Education, National Business Education Association. (2000, October). *This we believe about teaching soft skills: Human relations, self-management, and workplace enhancement* (Policy Statement No. 67). Retrieved from http://www.nbea.org/newsite/curriculum/policy/no_67.pdf

Redford, K. (2007, July 17). *How to measure the impact of soft skills training.* Retrieved from http://www.personneltoday.com/articles/2007/07/17/41446/how-to-measure-the-impact-of-soft-skills-training.html

Riley, S. (2006, February 13). Mentors teach skills, hard and soft. *Electronic Engineering Times, 1410,* 1-14.

Rodas, D. J. (2007, September 21). What business students should know. *Chronicle of Higher Education, 54*(4), A39.

Sheikh, S. (2009, April). *Alumni perspectives survey: Comprehensive data report.* Reston, VA: Graduate Management Admission Council. Retrieved from http://www.gmac.com/~/media/ Files/gmac/Research/Measuring%20Program%20ROI/APR09Alumni_CDR_Web.pdf

Smith, L. (2007). Teaching the intangibles. *T+D, 61*(10), 23-25.

Sutton, N. (2002, August 9). Why can't we all just get along? *Computing Canada, 28*(16), 20.

Timm, J. A. (2005). Preparing students for the next employment revolution. *Business Education Forum, 60,* 55-59.

Wellington, J. K. (2005, August 1). The "soft skills" of success: Be it high tech, low tech, or no tech. *Vital Speeches of the Day, 71,* 628.

White, E. (2005, November 21). Learning to be the boss. *Wall Street Journal (Eastern Edition),* B1-B5.

Wilhelm, W. J. (2004). Determinants of moral reasoning: Academic factors, gender, richness of life experiences, and religious preferences. *Delta Pi Epsilon Journal, 46,* 105-121.

Zehr, M. A. (1998, February 18). New office economy putting greater demands on schools. *Education Week, 17*(23), 7.

Bio

Marcel M. Robles is a professor of corporate communication in the College of Business and Technology at Eastern Kentucky University. She teaches managerial report writing, entrepreneurship, web design, and MBA strategic business communication. Her research interests include assessment, education technologies, and teaching and learning strategies.

Teaching Teamwork and Problem Solving Concurrently

26

Goltz, S. M., Hietapelto, A. B., Reinsch, R.W., Tyrell, S.K.

Teamwork and problem-solving skills have frequently been identified by business leaders as being key competencies; thus, teaching methods such as problem-based learning and team-based learning have been developed. However, the focus of these methods has been on teaching one skill or the other. A key argument for teaching the skills concurrently is that the ability to solve an unstructured real-world problem within teams is what is needed outside the classroom and that this requires the use of both sets of skills simultaneously. Thus, the authors describe the design and implementation of a group problem-solving skills course for undergraduates, in which they engage in real creative problem-solving work together over a semester while learning and developing skills appropriate to their current stages in the team development and problem-solving processes. This method offers the potential to address criticisms by business leaders that new graduates often are technically proficient yet ill prepared to solve everyday organizational problems.

Keywords: *decision making; experiential learning; group process; interpersonal skills; problem solving; teams; team development*

In the information age, there is constant change, and an employee must be able to engage in problem-solving activities (Zorn, 2002). In addition, work teams dominate industry largely because business decision making is more effective when teamwork is used (Guzzo & Shea, 1992). This is especially the case when team players have good interpersonal and problem-solving skills (Bamber, Watson, & Hill, 1996; LaFasto & Larson, 2001). Thus, many businesses, professional associations, and other groups consider interpersonal and problem-solving skills to be core competencies and often assess these as part of the interview or accreditation process (e.g., American Institute of Certified Public Accountants, 1999; Association of American Colleges and Universities, 2002). Similarly, the Greater Expectations National Panel Report (Association of American Colleges and Universities, 2002) calls for the development of intentional learners in university education who have mastered critical skills such as communication, creative problem solving, and working in diverse teams, and who can integrate and adapt these skills from one setting to another. In addition, the National Survey of Student Engagement (NSSE, 2006) identifies five key indicators of effective educational practices, one of which is "active and collaborative learning."

However, even as problem solving and teamwork have become widespread in management education, the teaching of these skills in business schools has not been sufficient according to business leaders, who have complained that new recruits are technically proficient but socially ill equipped and unable to solve everyday organizational problems (Bailey, Saparito, Kressel, Christensen, & Hooijberg, 1997; Holt & Willard-Holt, 2000). There are numerous explanations for these problems, such as college instructors emphasizing individual over group achievement (Schmuck & Schmuck, 1997), assigning students to team projects without teaching interpersonal skills (Cox & Bobrowski, 2000), and using very structured problems rather than messy problems that are more characteristic of organizations (Bigelow, 2004). For instance, a survey at one university revealed that 72% of faculty in the College of Business assigned students to project teams in at least one class, but 81% of these provided modest, limited, or no teamwork guidance (Bolton, 1999).

Team-Based and Problem-Based Learning Methods

Two techniques that have been developed to address some of these issues are team-based and problem-based learning methods. Problem-based learning originated in medical schools, but has also been applied to

Authors' Note: The authors are grateful to Janet Gillespie, Courtney Hunt, and Jane Schmidt-Wilk, and to two anonymous reviewers, for their insightful comments and encouragement on this article. A workshop version of this article was presented at OBTC 2005 in Scranton, Pennsylvania; feedback from session participants is also acknowledged. Correspondence should be directed to Sonia M. Goltz, Michigan Technological University, School of Business and Economics, 1400 Townsend Drive, Houghton, MI 49931; e-mail: smgoltz@mtu.edu.

marketing and management curricula, such as at the University of Maastricht (http://www.fdewb.unimaas.nl/feba%5Fhome/mission/), which converted its entire marketing and management curriculum to a problem-based approach to provide students a learning community with skills "to evaluate business problems in their broader societal context." Problem-based learning refers to a range of methods from a very well-documented and rigid approach to any approaches that give problems, such as engineering, business, or social problems, a central place in learning (Bereiter & Scardamalia, 2000; Davis & Harden, 1999). Although problem-based learning approaches vary significantly, two key aspects are found in all approaches: (a) the problem is the center of attention and (b) the attempt to solve the problem is used as a basis for learning about a particular content area, such as medicine, law, or marketing (Sherwood, 2004). Problems are usually ill structured and multifaceted (Bigelow, 2004), offering the opportunity for real-life experience and creating a meaningful learning context (Sherwood, 2004). Based on a constructivist approach to teaching, problem-based learning generally requires students to be responsible for determining what they need to know about the problem in order to be able to define and solve it, which often includes defining learning issues and finding the appropriate learning material. Faculty are present primarily to facilitate this process (Major, 1988). Bolton (1999) has termed this coaching a "just-in-time" approach to learning. Thus, problem-based learning methods are used to teach substantive knowledge and to teach skills needed to apply that knowledge. For instance, substantive knowledge about how to play racquetball by reading or hearing a lecture may be of little use unless combined with an opportunity to practice and receive feedback by being coached in a real game, with its many unexpected twists and turns that have to be dealt with as they arise. Similarly, knowledge about medical diagnosis is not as useful as when an actual case with symptoms is presented for analysis, and knowledge about managing diversity is not as useful as when the learner has the opportunity to lead different personalities.

In problem-based learning, students may work individually or in groups; however, teams are often recommended to bring together various skills and foster collaboration (Duch, Groh, & Allen, 2001). Because collaboration requires that team members be able to both appreciate individual differences and communicate with each other (Duch et al., 2001), team dynamics should also be a part of the learning process of students in problem-based learning. However, even though the problem-based learning literature often assumes that there will be a use of teams, the team process—what the faculty member

must teach to have effective teams and what is learned through that process—
is usually not directly addressed.

The team-based learning approach, in contrast, is a specific instructional
strategy designed to support the development of high-performing teams and
provide opportunities for them to engage in learning tasks (Fink, 2002).
Team-based learning is similar to problem-based learning in that it has the
two learning goals of imparting a significant body of knowledge while at
the same time providing students with a structure that facilitates learning
how to apply the content (Fink, 2002). In addition, both instructional methods rely on timely feedback and coaching from the instructor as issues
emerge. The primary difference between the two methods is that one provides
the structure for learning to apply knowledge by emphasizing and developing
problem-solving skills and the other provides this structure by emphasizing
developing team interaction. In team-based learning, group-focused activities
largely determine the structure of the course. Students are members of an
ongoing team and become actively engaged, committing higher levels of
effort to the group, enabling the team to solve challenging and complex problems (Knight, 2002). In addition, team-based learning relies on students to
monitor and improve their interactions and performance over an extended
period of time, which helps increase their interpersonal skills (Fink, 2002).
Whereas the term "problem-based learning" is used to refer to a diverse range
of methods, the literature on team-based learning is narrower in scope and
thus is often associated with a very specific set of sequential steps used by
Michaelsen and his associates (e.g., Michaelsen, 2002). The principles of
design outlined by Michaelsen (2002) as being essential to team-based learning are the following: (a) careful attention is given to how permanent groups
were formed and managed, (b) students are made accountable for individual
contributions and high-quality team performance, (c) team assignments are
designed to both promote learning and team development, and (d) students
receive frequent and immediate feedback.

The Resultant Integrated Approach

Several years ago, our business school went through a curriculum revision process that had among other goals the better preparation of students
to solve business problems and work in groups both in their various business courses and in their careers. Not surprisingly, our curriculum structure
that resulted from this revision process was reflective of the state of the literature on teaching problem-solving and teamwork skills. These skills were

taught separately. One course borrowed from problem-based learning methods, in which defining and solving ill-structured problems are the focus of attention. Our students were taught about the content area of individual creative problem solving in a class in which they also developed these problem-solving skills using problem-based learning techniques. No assignments in the class concerned interpersonal processes. For interpersonal skill development, our students took a team skills course, in which the content area of focus was interpersonal skills in groups and which drew on team-based learning methods so students could develop skills as they learned about them. Our team skills course was individually developed to suit our curricular needs at the time and therefore was not designed to follow the specific sequence used by Michaelsen (2002). For instance, we did not use individual readiness assurance tests followed by team readiness assurance tests. However, the course was more similar to a team-based learning approach than to other approaches to team skills in a number of ways. Specifically, the course included all four design elements outlined by Michaelsen as being important for team-based learning: Permanent groups were carefully formed and managed, students were held accountable for individual and group performance, team assignments were designed for learning and team development, and frequent and immediate feedback was provided.

When our quarter system was changed to a semester system a few years later, the two separate courses had to be integrated into one course, forcing us to rethink the traditional problem-based and team-based methods. One argument for teaching the skills concurrently was that, although generally, the focus has been on teaching one skill or the other, the design of both problem-based and team-based learning courses often requires both skills. We discovered some of these overlaps between the two approaches when we taught the two separate courses under the quarter system. For example, as discussed, in problem-based learning, students usually are asked to solve problems in groups. Thus, although team skills are not the focus, team formation has been identified as a factor critical to the success of problem-based learning (Peterson, 2004), and problem-based learning benefits from the development of team skills (Sasse, Davis, & McConnell, 2000). Similarly, group-based learning methods offer various problem-solving opportunities. For instance, one advantage of group-based learning is that teams are more able to solve challenging and complex problems (Knight, 2002). Furthermore, it has been noted that many interpersonal skills such as conflict resolution, collaborative problem solving, and communication also require problem-solving skills (Stevens & Campion, 1994). Thus, it appeared to us that the concurrent teaching of the two skills together might strengthen each learning approach and reinforce the

Table 1
Integrative Individual and Group Problem-Solving Process Model

Week	Problem-Solving Stages	Group Process Stages and Interpersonal Skill Development
1	Intro to decision model	
2		Forming stage
3	Recognizing, conceptualizing the problem	
4	Identifying conceptual blocks	
5		Communicating supportively
6		Norming stage
7	Generating alternatives	
8		Individual differences, feedback
9	Evaluating alternatives	
10		Conflict and storming
11	Implementation planning	
12	Advocating the chosen alternative	
13		Performing stage
14		Performing stage

original strengths of each approach. In both approaches, learning does not take place isolated and insulated from real-world and social contexts; in addition, comprehension, critical thinking, and retention of learning is increased (Kearny, 2000; Knight, 2002). Furthermore, the concurrent teaching of the two would utilize various active and collaborative learning components NSSE (2006) advocates to enhance student engagement.

Therefore, we chose to integrate not only our course content but also our teaching methods by presenting the two skill sets concurrently. This new integrative course, which continues to be offered, has student groups engage in real creative problem-solving work together over a semester, while they are introduced to both problem-solving and team skills. Two key principles form the basis for the structure for this course. First, as indicated by Table 1, problem-solving and group development concepts are introduced at the point when students are at that specific stage of development. Second, concepts are introduced and then reinforced with increasingly complex exercises and assignments. Tables 2 and 3 illustrate the application of this second principle. Table 2 indicates the standard problem-solving steps students progress through in this integrative team-based and problem-based course design. As Table 2 indicates, concepts, tools, exercises, games, cases, movies, and assignments were used for each of these key decision steps in the problem-solving process. Similarly, Table 3 indicates the standard stages

Table 2
Problem-Solving Topics Level of Application

Decision Steps	Concepts or Tools	Exercises or Games	Cases or Movies	Problem Project
Recognizing, conceptualizing problem	Information collection and sorting, gap analysis, cause–effect diagram	Boyberik[a] Research scavenger hunt[b]	Challenger disaster[c]	Problem project assignment
Identifying conceptual blocks	Various assumptions, conceptual blocks (e.g., idea killing)	Scattergories Ring in toilet bowl[d] Ball in pipe	*Pearl Harbor*[e] Sony Walkman[e] *October Sky Apollo 13 Tucker*	Problem project assignment
Generating alternatives	Various creativity techniques (e.g., brainstorming, diametrics)	Scattergories Ring in toilet bowl[d] Ball in pipe The Deep Dive[f]	Sony Walkman[e] *October Sky Apollo 13 Tucker*	Problem project assignment
Evaluating alternatives	Decision biases, decision criteria and tools, political constraints	Flying to Rio[g]	*12 Angry Men Tucker The Mustang*[h]	Problem project assignment
Advocating the chosen alternative	Influence, persuasion, presentation methods	45-s punch[g] Listening exercise[g]	Whitewater simulation[i]	Problem project presentation
Implementing and evaluating the solution	Resistance to change, project planning, evaluation methods	Create Gantt chart for Quality Circles case	Resistance to change and Quality Circles incidents[j]	Problem project assignment

a. From Marcic (1995).
b. From Engleberg and Wynn (2000).
c. From Maier (1996).
d. Based on Scholz, Tinsmon, Rodney, and Polansky (1995).
e. From Whetton and Cameron (2005).
f. From Smith (1999).
g. From Iacocca & Novak (1984).
h. From Wohlberg and Weighart (1992).
i. From Fisher, Krieger, and Fisher (1994).
j. From Champion and James (1989).

Table 3
Group Topics Level of Application

Decision Steps	Concepts or Tools	Exercises or Games	Cases or Movies	Group Process Papers
Forming stage	Team creation, forming stage	Composing a team[a] Circle of Hands[e] Challenge course 1[b]	Ozark River Bank[c] *Little Giants*	Team document and grading contracts,[d] Group development and individual learning assignment
Communicating supportively	Supportive communication, high performing team talk	Blind and seek[e] Role plays[i]	*The Apprentice* clips	Communication assignment
Norming stage	Norming stage, functional, dysfunctional norms, and roles	Team self-analyses on roles and norms	*White Squall*	Group development and individual learning assignment
Individual differences	Managing diversity, MBTI dimensions	Build Your Dream House[f]	*White Squall* *12 Angry Men*	MBTI assignment, group development, and individual learning assignment Communication assignment
Feedback	Giving feedback, receiving feedback	Fishbowl feedback[d] Stop-Start-Continue[d] Team Development Scales[d]		Midterm, end of semester peer evaluations Final meeting with instructor
Conflict and storming	Functional, dysfunctional conflict, conflict response types	Role Plays[i] Whitewater simulation[j]	*12 Angry Men* *The Apprentice* clips	Group development and individual learning assignment

(continued)

Table 3 (continued)

Decision Steps	Concepts or Tools	Exercises or Games	Cases or Movies	Group Process Papers
Performing stage	Performing stage, supporting teams, evaluating teams	Challenge course 2[b] Hilarity greeting card[g]	Beer Sales and Delivery case[h]	Group development and individual learning assignment Group performance assessments Videotape analysis

NOTE: MBTI = Meyer-Briggs Type Indicator.
a. From Goltz (1998).
b. From Hietapelto, Tyrell, Tyrell, and Walck (2000).
c. From Wohlberg and Weighart (1992).
d. From Dyer (1995).
e. From Webster (1994).
f. From Moody and McLaughlin (2002).
g. From Mainiero and Tromley (1994).
h. From Saavedra (1990).
i. From Whetton and Cameron (2005).
j. From Fisher, Krieger, and Fisher (1994).

of group development and interpersonal skill development students progressed through in this course design and the concepts, tools, exercises, games, cases, movies, and assignments used for the group development process. (Nonoriginal material is referenced following Tables 2 and 3 in the notes, where possible, or in the article references. Syllabi, class notes, and assignment descriptions can be obtained from Sonia Goltz. See the authors' note for contact information.)

Thus, in the early portion of the course, teams are in the forming stage. First, they engage in an exercise using a hypothetical group that is designed to allow them to practice composing a diverse group in terms of backgrounds and skill sets. After this exercise, they select their own group members for their project groups. They then embark on a series of activities to jumpstart the forming stage, learning more about themselves and their team members. One of these activities is a challenge course session, in which team members engage in a series of physical and mental tasks together. While in the forming stage, teams are also at the beginning stages of problem solving; so during this time, they learn about information gathering and problem definition through a series of activities and assignments and select a significant, real problem, usually found at a local business, to solve for the semester. To aid this process, the instructor has a brainstorming session during class concerning local organizations students might want to work with. These organizations are then grouped by type of business: for example, governmental institutions, schools, service organizations, restaurants, retail clothing stores, and so forth. Each group of students then adopts one set of these possible organizations from which to identify the organization and problem they will be working on. Examples of organizations and problems that have been studied include getting more students to vote in the student government elections, attracting more customers to a downtown clothing store, and reducing the inventory problems at a discount store.

During the norming stage, teams learn conceptually about stages of team development, communication, and group process, while engaging in role plays and experiential activities to develop and hone skills in these areas. They also practice analyzing group process through in-class movie analysis. This is followed by reflection of their own group process, which occurs through videotaping their team meetings and completing team process written assignments. While in the norming stage, teams also learn about alternative generation and creativity topics and techniques, with class activities and assignments designed to provide skill practice.

We cover norming before storming because we have found that storming in teams tends to occur later during the semester. As the teams increasingly face class assignment and performance pressures, conflict typically emerges, with frustration with team members becoming evident. In addition, in the problem-solving phases typically occurring simultaneously with the storming stage, groups are focusing on generating criteria for evaluating alternative solutions, examining biases and constraints, and trying to come to a solution consensus, all of which are potential areas for conflict. Assignments are designed to teach teams to learn how to manage conflict by developing skills in the areas of communication, individual differences, and conflict management, consistent with recommendations from team-based learning research. Teams continue to engage in role plays, exercises, and experiential course activities, focusing on skill development in these additional areas. They continue to both analyze teams external to themselves, and to turn the lens on themselves analytically, completing team assignments on conflict management and Meyer-Briggs Type Indicator (MBTI) styles, and engaging in team feedback sessions with the instructor. Individual differences, such as MBTI styles, are introduced this point in the semester because we have found that students will then have more of an appreciation for individual differences given the conflicts they just experienced, which are often fueled by differing perceptions and expectations. In terms of feedback sessions, groups may meet privately with the instructor or the class can split up into teams in a large classroom to give and receive feedback, with the instructor floating from team to team. Students prepare feedback prior to the session for *every* member of their team, excluding themselves. It is important for the instructor not to dominate the session, but to encourage the group to raise issues critical to the group's performance and accept responsibility for changing those.

By the time the student teams have entered the performing stages, teams are planning implementation of the selected alternative for the problem their group chose to address. They are also writing their final written report and preparing their team presentations on their problem projects. Teams also write a team process paper analyzing their own movement through the stages of team development, including an assessment of whether they reached the performing stage. So that teams can analyze changes in dynamics and performance not only on their course assignments but also on other types of tasks, a second challenge course session, with new physical and mental challenges, takes place during this time. Then, in a final meeting with the instructor, students analyze their team development over time and their current strengths and weaknesses as a group.

Assessment

Throughout this article, we describe our observations of the benefits of the course based to a large extent on our knowledge of student assignments, videotapes of group meetings, and interactions with students that occurred throughout the years we have taught the course. However, more formal assessment results also indicate the effectiveness of this method. These assessment methods have varied over the years, reflecting changes in the Association to Advance Collegiate Schools of Business (AACSB) assessment expectations. In earlier years, Educational Benchmarking Incorporation surveys of graduating students and alumni were conducted. Graduating seniors and alumni who experienced the integrated course reported enhanced interpersonal and team skill development, and enhanced problem-solving and analytical skills. As a result, AACSB specifically cited the focus on team skill development as a program strength (Michigan Technological University, School of Business and Economics, 2000). Later, more course-embedded methods focusing on specific objectives were introduced. Recent 2006-2007 student peer assessment data from the integrative course substantiate earlier, more program-oriented findings. Each of these assessment results and some additional findings will be discussed further.

The integrative course we have described had been assessed intermittently and predominantly through self-report data until recently. For instance, following about 10 years of the implementation of this course, alumni cohorts were asked to answer, on a 5-point scale: "Relative to your peers from other schools, how well did your education here prepare you for your present job?" This rating varied by cohort, improving from 3.4 (1987 to 1990 cohort, where the course was absent in the curriculum) to 3.9 (1992 to 1995 cohort, where the course was present, but still two separate courses) to 4.5 (years 1997 to 2000 cohort, where the integrated course was created and implemented). The 4.5 for the 1997 to 2000 integrated course cohort group was the highest rating given of 12 questions asked. The second highest rating, for the "development of analytical/problem-solving skills," was 4.4. Both numbers were well above the rating for the "development of concepts in your major," which was 3.9.

The 1997 to 2000 alumni (integrated course cohort group) rated the importance of "team skills" in their jobs at 4.4, just behind the highest rating, which was 4.6 for "self-confidence", and equal to the rating of importance for "basic computer skills", rated 4.4. The importance of "analytical problem-solving skills" was next at 4.2. All other ratings were below these, including "the application of concepts in your major" at 4.1 (12 questions were asked here, also). In the 2000 senior exit survey, the ratings for the satisfaction of the quality of teaching of team skills (5.8 on a 7-point scale) was the second highest rating out of 70 questions about satisfaction with their education at the university.

In 2003, the Workplace Skills Survey was given to the strategy capstone class to assess how seniors compared on workplace skills to individuals in the external workforce. Thus, unlike the other assessment results, these data indicate how students who have taken the course compare to an external set of respondents on a standardized, validated scale that is used for personnel selection purposes. For the entire scale, students were at approximately the 80th percentile, with subscale scores in the 70th percentile for problem solving, 75th percentile for teamwork skills and adaptation to change, and the 90th percentile for communication.

More recently (fall 2006, spring 2007) four specific student learning objectives concerning effective teamwork skills were created for the undergraduate program and assessed in the integrated course. Although it is our observation that the benefits of the integrated course extend well beyond these four teamwork objectives created for the undergraduate program as a whole, assessment results for these objectives are still quite informative. In all sections of the course taught each semester, students anonymously assessed their team member peers on the following four dimensions: (a) commitment and dependability, (b) supportive communication, (c) contribution of ideas, and (d) focusing on the assigned task or tasks. Tables 4 to 7 display the results of this assessment. Results vary somewhat by semester; therefore, the following conclusions err on the side of caution. As demonstrated in Table 4, more than 84% of students in all courses evaluated their peers as displaying acceptable to good or excellent levels of commitment and dependability. As demonstrated in Table 5, more than 80% of students in all courses evaluated their peers as displaying acceptable to good or excellent levels of supportive communication. As demonstrated in Table 6, more than 84% of students in all courses evaluated their peers as displaying acceptable to good or excellent levels of contribution of ideas. As demonstrated in Table 7, more than 80% of students in all courses evaluated their peers as displaying acceptable to good or excellent levels of staying on track (e.g., task focus). Results of at least 80% acceptability on all dimensions support earlier assessment findings of effective team skill development. Efforts to broaden and sustain assessment are ongoing, such as assessing these dimensions in subsequent coursework.

Discussion

We have described a teaching strategy that structures the class to simultaneously focus on group development and on problem solving to teach both the content knowledge and the skill sets for understanding and applying creative problem solving and successful group dynamics. This is unlike the traditional use of problem-based and team-based learning methods for three major reasons. First, these past methods have tended to use *either* team-based *or* problem-based learning as the primary structure for the course. Second, both team-based and problem-based learning have traditionally focused on other content knowledge areas, rarely teaching the substantive knowledge in the areas of creative problem solving and group dynamics. Third, the simultaneous attention to both group and problem-solving skills we described serves to integrate the learning of two different knowledge areas, which has rarely been done in either problem-based or team-based learning. One exception that did focus on the teaching of multiple disciplinary concepts using team-based learning was the use of the "Integrated

Business Core" at the University of Oklahoma (Lucas, 2002; Michaelsen, 1999). Much like the results of that program, our course design of simultaneous application of problem-based and team-based learning methods to teach creative problem solving and group dynamics allows students to better see how course concepts, previously presented as discrete units, actually significantly overlap. This mirrors most business environments, in which various conceptual knowledge and skill sets need to be successfully integrated to achieve an objective. The benefits of the integrated approach are that students learn and practice both problem-solving and teamwork skills concurrently as they move through the stages of each process while working in teams on real problems. In addition, this learning happens in a rather messy way as issues emerge with both the problem and with interpersonal dynamics. This emergence of issues and learning more accurately reflects the nature of work settings that students are being prepared for and should therefore increase the relevance and retention of learning even beyond that which is found with either problem-based or team-based learning approaches.

The success of the course rests on the simultaneous focus on a real problem project and on actual group development while students are also learning the content knowledge of creative problem-solving steps and group dynamics. These are of great benefit to students particularly when instructors have ensured appropriately engaging and challenging problem projects and have fostered and enhanced team self-analysis and development. Each of these aspects will be discussed, along with other constraints and opportunities that may arise in teaching the course.

For the project in this course, students analyze actual problems that are currently being faced by business, educational, or nonprofit service organizations in the local area. We find that using a local actual problem that is identified by the students, rather than the instructor, is valuable for several reasons. First, students with little work experience are forced to interact with managers and workers in actual organizations, and students with work experience are exposed to problems in organizations different from the ones they have worked in. Over time we have observed that students, through their research and presentations, develop self-confidence in their ability to interact professionally with local businesses. We have also observed students form an appreciation for the experiences and efforts of local businesses that they previously may have had little awareness of, creating a meaningful learning context, consistent with research findings in problem-based learning (Sherwood, 2004). On the other hand, businesses are provided the opportunity to mentor students in their local university and obtain fresh insights regarding their

Table 4
Peer Evaluation Results: Commitment and Dependability

	Unacceptable (%)	Acceptable (%)	Good to Excellent (%)
Category description	Seems reluctant to engage fully in task assignments or provide quality work	Accepts assignments willingly and completes them on time	Volunteers for assignments and turns in high quality work on time
Fall 2006 ($n = 85$)	8.5	26.2	65.2
Spring 2007 ($n = 83$)	16.0	25.7	58.3

Table 5
Peer Evaluation Results: Supportive Communication

	Unacceptable (%)	Acceptable (%)	Good to Excellent (%)
Category description	Uncommunicative or communicates unclearly or in a way that puts down other group members	Communicates clearly without offending others	Addresses difficult group issues in a clear, supportive way that fosters group development and progress
Fall 2006 ($n = 85$)	5.8	34.3	60.0
Spring 2007 ($n = 83$)	19.4	29.4	51.1

Table 6
Peer Evaluation Results: Contribution of Ideas

	Unacceptable (%)	Acceptable (%)	Good to Excellent (%)
Category description	Rarely offers ideas or suggestions that contribute to problem solving	Frequently offers helpful ideas or suggestions	Contributes own ideas and also listens actively and builds on others' ideas
Fall 2006 ($n = 85$)	7.7	26.2	66.0
Spring 2007 ($n = 83$)	15.7	29.4	54.9

business problems for no cost. Further evidence of the value of this real-life application and interaction occurs when some of the businesses ask students to continue to work on the problem after the semester has ended. In these cases, students can be encouraged to engage in volunteer work for

Table 7
Peer Evaluation Results: Stays on Track

	Unacceptable (%)	Acceptable (%)	Good to Excellent (%)
Category description	Takes the group off track by initiating conversations or discussions unrelated to the task	Introduces suggestions and ideas that are relevant to the task at the appropriate time	Uses tact and diplomacy to alert group that focus has strayed from the task at hand
Fall 2006 ($n = 85$)	9.4	30.4	60.1
Spring 2007 ($n = 83$)	20.0	36.6	43.4

the organization, which can yield valuable business experience that can be listed in resumes or discussed in interviews. All of the above are consistent with the active, collaborative learning practices called for by NSSE (2006) to foster student engagement and enhance student learning.

Second, students are even more likely to be engaged in a problem they have chosen than one that was assigned to them. Also, instructors emphasize that students should choose an organization and problem they are really interested in because they will be working on the problem over the course of the whole semester. Students are also told that they must choose an organization that is willing to send one member to the group's class presentation on the proposed solution to the problem. This member and members from the other groups' organizations ask questions during the student presentations and also rate the presentations. This process holds the students more accountable for their problem solving than they would have been if they were only graded by the instructor, who knows less about the problem situation.

Finally, the analysis of actual local problems teaches students about the wide variety of the problems organizations face and how "messy" they usually are. One of the purposes of problem-based learning is to help students learn how to find the additional resources they need to solve the problem. In doing this for an actual business problem project, students often learn the difficulty in obtaining sufficient and accurate information, and this challenge can be used as a focus of class discussion. Students also learn about other obstacles to problem solving faced in organizations, such as constraints on the solutions that can be implemented, and so forth. Also, students are exposed during the semester to each of the other groups' organizations and problems, which generally range widely in terms of content and complexity.

Another key to a successful course is that teams make the initial transition from objective analysis of *other teams* to self-analysis of *one's own team*. This is a sensitive area, and students may at first resist, offering very cursory analysis of their team, such as by saying, "everything's fine." Thus, students will need coaching to overcome their fear of open communication and constructive conflict with their peers and with the instructor. Also, activities that make it difficult to avoid this transition are staged at critical moments. For example, feedback processes are designed to aid in the management of conflict. They are scheduled to coincide with periods of typically heightened conflict, such as one session around the middle part of the semester and another later in the semester. However, the course also accommodates conflict that does not occur linearly, but erupts early, or reoccurs repeatedly in a group, such as by scheduling additional feedback sessions as necessary.

Although fostering critical self-analysis by the groups can be initially challenging for instructors, we have found that roughly half to two thirds of the way through the semester, a huge mental and behavioral shift occurs in the classroom dynamics, and the class is typically transformed, reaching high levels of morale and team synergy. Late-semester feedback and end-of-semester teaching evaluations consistently reflect high positive affect. By the time groups have met several weeks on their problem projects, performed various class activities together, completed at least one feedback session, and have received feedback on team assignments, most members are relatively comfortable giving and receiving feedback. The group has typically navigated their conflicts and is demonstrating some competency in team self-management, so the need for instructor intervention for the majority of teams decreases fairly significantly. At this point, the students feel a sense of both cohesiveness and confidence from having been able to successfully deal with the various difficulties that have emerged in their groups, have an increased set of both interpersonal and problem-solving skills, and are often motivated to perform at a high level on remaining assignments. We have based these observations on assignments (Table 3; conflict, storming and performing stages) which have required detailed individual and group reflection about team development, and videotaped group meetings and our feedback sessions with student groups discussing team development. Furthermore, these observations are consistent with findings in both problem-based and team-based learning (e.g., Duch et al., 2001; Fink, 2002; Knight, 2002).

A number of other considerations should be taken into account when planning the course, including class size, instructor styles, and the timing of the course. For instance, because of the high level of student-student, student-team, faculty-student, and faculty-team interactions, as discussed above, it is advisable that class sizes not exceed 30 students, with approximately 4 to 5 teams per class. The recommended size for both groups and classes is below the sizes often suggested when the problem and team-based learning approaches are each used alone primarily because in the integrative approach, two skills sets are being simultaneously developed, requiring additional monitoring of processes and provision of feedback by the instructor. Also, in the integrative approach, students' workload is increased because they are being asked to analyze individual and team behavior and the problem being solved. Thus, reducing group size is essential for keeping student work manageable. (For instance, a group process paper requiring that the four MBTI profiles of each of seven group members be analyzed in addition to the overall group MBTI profile could get rather complex.) Another reason we have kept group membership to 4 to 5 students is because we have observed from experience that free ridership problems are typical in groups with 6 to 7 members.

The small class and group sizes are particularly needed if the class is being taught primarily at the freshman or sophomore level or to students with little teamwork experience because these types of students will need more guidance on both problem-solving and teamwork skills. Older or more experienced students may require less guidance, which may allow the instructor to teach a larger class or remove aspects of the course that encourage student accountability, such as having representatives from the organization being studied attend the presentations. On the other hand, older or experienced students sometimes have developed bad team habits that are harder to break. If so, these may pose a challenge for the instructor and additional activities focusing on these specific problems may be required.

In addition, instructors should model the interpersonal and team skills that students are being asked to develop and leadership styles that are compatible with the course design. Beyond this, instructors will need to be comfortable facilitating group interactions—the change in role from one who supplies information to one who guides and coaches may be difficult for some (e.g., Knowlton, 2003). This role requires, among other things, that the faculty member circulates through the class for in-class activities and is available to students for out-of-class projects (Lerner, 2004). Training in facilitation and debriefing group activities such as challenge course initiatives can increase instructor effectiveness at this coaching role in this course. Another characteristic of successful instructors of this course is a comfort with allowing learning to emerge, a very critical component of this course. The instructor structures the course and creates conditions to facilitate learning, but learning cannot be forced. Issues and insights need to come from the individuals and teams based on their learning experiences. The instructor should keep in mind that one of the goals of problem-based learning is to allow students to learn to become learners. The majority of the time, self-awareness does develop and emergent learning does occur, at both the individual and team levels.

The benefits of improved team management and problem-solving skills developed in this class have been apparent in later classes. Several of the authors have taught courses downstream from this course, including organizational behavior and the strategy capstone course, and have noted improved team management skills in students who have had the integrated course compared with students who have not taken it. Most of the students who have been through the course are able to coalesce their teams and be productive much earlier, needing much less help from instructors in managing team processes. Therefore, we suggest that students should take this course early in their undergraduate or graduate curriculum so they will benefit from these skills, and continue to practice them, in the rest of their courses. Introducing the course early also allows for extensions of the format or reinforcement of the material in later classes. For instance, we have found that instructors for other classes have asked for our materials from this course on creating a team document or conducting peer evaluations, so that they can ask students in upper level courses to continue to use some of the team skills they were taught earlier in the curriculum.

Conclusion

In an increasingly complex world, problem-solving and teamwork skills are more and more necessary. To meet this challenge, new integrative curricular models and educational practices are needed (e.g., Axley & McMahon, 2006). The integrated course described here uses various techniques, assignments, and experiences, presented in a timely manner, to facilitate conceptual learning and skill development in both problem solving and teamwork. The skills are presented and developed at the time during the group or problem-solving stages when the students most need those skills. Furthermore, they are reinforced within the course using increasingly complex exercises and assignments, and they are also reinforced in later courses. The success of the course rests not only on the sequencing of topics, but also on the focus on both a real problem project and actual group development. These aspects present a messy, emerging learning process, stimulating a more holistic treatment of teamwork and problem solving that is also more reflective of actual work situations.

Various types of assessment that have been conducted suggest that learning outcomes are both short and long-term. The immediate success of this holistic treatment is directly evident in student evaluations of their peers' teamwork skills at the end of the course. The persistence of this learning is evident from workplace skills assessment in subsequent coursework and from ratings and comments found in senior exit and alumni surveys. In conclusion, we believe the relevance of course concepts to the students' current experiences creates increased engagement in learning and retention of course concepts, and is an example of the kind of active, collaborative course design called for by the NSSE (2006).

References

American Institute of Certified Public Accountants. (1999). *Vision project*. Retrieved October 1, 2006, from http://www.aicpa.org/vision/index.htm

Association of American Colleges and Universities. (2002). *Greater expectations*. Retrieved October 1, 2006, from http://www.greaterexpectations.org

Axley, S. R., & McMahon, T. (2006). Complexity: A frontier for management education. *Journal of Management Education, 30*(2), 295-315.

Bailey, J. R., Saparito, P., Kressel, K., Christensen, E. W., & Hooijberg, R. (1997). A model for reflective pedagogy. *Journal of Management Education, 21*, 155-167.

Bamber, E. M., Watson, R. T., & Hill, C. (1996). The effects of group decision support systems technology on audit group decision making. *Auditing, a Journal of Theory and Practice, 15*(1), 122-134.

Bereiter, C., & Scardamalia, M. (2000). Commentary on part 1: Process and product in problem-based learning (PBL) research. In D. D. Evensen & C. E. Hmelo (Eds.), *Problem based learning: A research perspective on learning interactions* (pp. 185-195). Mahwah, NJ: Lawrence Erlbaum.

Bigelow, J. (2004). Using problem-based learning to develop skills in solving unstructured problems. *Journal of Management Education, 28*(5), 591-609.

Bolton, M. K. (1999). The role of coaching in student teams: A "just-in-time" approach to learning. *Journal of Management Education, 23*(3), 233-250.

Champion, J. M., & James, J. H. (1989) *Critical incidents in management* (6th ed.). Homewood, IL: Irwin.

Cox, P. L., & Bobrowski, P. E. (2000). The team charter assignment: Improving the effectiveness of classroom teams. *Journal of Behavioral and Applied Management, 1*(1), 92-103.

Davis, M. H., & Harden, R. M. (1999). AMEE Medical Education Guide No. 15: Problem-based learning: A practical guide. *Medical Teacher, 21*(2), 130-140.

Duch, B. J., Groh, S. E., & Allen, D. E. (2001) (Eds.). *The power of problem-based learning*. Sterling, VA: Stylus.

Dyer, W. G. (1995). *Team building* (3rd ed., OD Series). Reading, MA: Addison Wesley.

Engleberg, I. A., & Wynn, D. R. (2000). *Working in groups* (2nd ed.). Boston: Houghton Mifflin.

Fink, L. D. (2002). Beyond small groups: Harnessing the extraordinary power of learning teams. In L. K. Michaelsen, A. B. Knight, & L. D. Fink (Eds.), *Team-based learning: A transformative use of small groups* (pp. 3-25). Westport, CT: Praeger.

Fisher, J., Krieger, S., & Fisher, K. A. (1994). *Whitewater: A team building simulation*. Ann Arbor, MI: ORION International.

Goltz, S. M. (1998). Composing a team. *Developments in Business Simulation and Experiential Learning, 25,* 194-200.

Guzzo, R. A., & Shea, G. P. (1992). Group performance and inter-group relations in organizations. In M. D. Dunnette & L. M. Hough (Eds.), *Handbook of industrial and organizational psychology* (Vol. 3, 2nd ed., pp. 269-313). Palo Alto, CA: Consulting Psychologists Press.

Hietapelto, A., Tyrell, S. K., Tyrell, S. J., & Walck, C. (2000, June). *Challenge ropes course: Trust and team building inside and outside the 21st century classroom.* Preconference workshop presented at the Organizational Behavior Teaching Conference, Carrollton, GA.

Holt, D. G., & Willard-Holt, C. (2000). Let's get real: Students solving authentic corporate problems. *Phi Kappa Deltan, 82,* 243-246.

Iacocca, L., & Novak, W. (1984). *Iacocca: An autobiography*. New York: Bantam.

Kearny, T. (2000, December). *Problem based learning and education Queensland: The learning organization*. Paper presented at the Second Asia-Pacific Conference on PBL, Singapore.

Knight, A. B. (2002). Team-based learning: A strategy for transforming the quality of teaching and learning. In L. K. Michaelsen, A. B. Knight, & L. D. Fink (Eds.), *Team-based learning: A transformative use of small groups* (pp. 200-211). Westport, CT: Praeger.

Knowlton, D. S. (2003, Fall). Preparing students for educated living: Virtues of problem-based learning across the higher education curriculum. *New Directions for Teaching & Learning, 95,* 5-12.

LaFasto, F., & Larson, C. (2001). *When teams work best*. Thousand Oaks, CA: Sage.

Lerner, A. M. (2004). Using our brains: What cognitive science and social psychology teach us about teaching law students to make ethical, professionally responsible choices. *Quinnipiac Law Review, 23,* 643-706.

Lucas, L. A. (2002). Creating group assignments that teach multiple concepts in an interdisciplinary course context. In L. K. Michaelsen, A. B. Knight, & L. D. Fink (Eds.), *Team-based learning: A transformative use of small groups* (pp. 27-51). Westport, CT: Praeger.

Maier, M. (1996). A major malfunction: The story behind the space shuttle challenger disaster [Video]. In J. Schermerhorn, J. Hunt, & R. Osborn (Eds.), *Managing organizational behavior* (5th ed.). Hoboken, NJ: John Wiley.

Mainiero, L. A., & Tromley, C. L. (1994). *Developing managerial skills in organizational behavior* (2nd ed.). Englewood Cliffs, NJ: Prentice Hall.

Major, C. H. (1988). Connecting what we know to what we do through problem-based learning. *AAHE Bulletin, 51*(7), 7-9.

Marcic, D. (1995). *Organizational behavior: Experiences and cases* (4th ed.). St. Paul, MN: West.

Michaelsen, L. K. (1999). Integrating the core business curriculum: An experience-based solution. *Selections, 15*(2), 9-17.

Michaelsen, L. K. (2002). Getting started with team-based learning. In L. K. Michaelsen, A. B. Knight, & L. D. Fink (Eds.), *Team-based learning: A transformative use of small groups* (pp. 27-51). Westport, CT: Praeger.

Michigan Technological University, School of Business and Economics. (2000, June 1). *Application for initial undergraduate business accreditation self-evaluation report* (Vol. 1). Houghton: Author.

Moody, D., & McLaughlin, G. (2002, June). *Build your dream house: Explaining personality using the MBTI*. Paper presented at the Organizational Behavior Teaching Conference, Orange, CA.

National Survey of Student Engagement. (2006). *NSSE 2006 annual report: Engaged student learning: Fostering success for all students*. Retrieved June 24, 2007, from http://nsse .iub.edu

Peterson, T. O. (2004). So you're thinking of trying problem based learning? Three critical success factors for implementation. *Journal of Management Education, 28*(5), 630-647.

Saavedra, R. (1990). Beer sales and delivery teams. In J. R. Hackman (Ed.), *Groups that work and those that don't* (pp. 361-381). San Francisco: Jossey-Bass.

Sasse, C., Davis, J., & McConnell, C. (2000, September). *Using problem-based learning: A multidisciplinary investigation* (Rockhurst University Carnegie seminar project). Retrieved October 2, 2002, from http://cte.rockhurst.edu/carnegie/PBL.htm

Schmuck, R., & Schmuck, P. (1997). *Group processes in the classroom* (7th ed.). Chicago: Brown & Benchmark.

Scholz, E., Tinsmon, K., Rodney, C., & Polansky, A. (1995, Spring). *Diamonds in the rough* [Unpublished class exercise]. Binghamton: State University of New York–Binghamton.

Sherwood, A. L. (2004). Problem-based learning in management education: A framework for designing context. *Journal of Management Education, 28*(5), 536-557.

Smith, J. (1999, July 13). The deep dive [Television series episode]. In *Nightline*. New York: American Broadcasting Company.

Stevens, M. A., & Campion, M. J. (1994). The knowledge, skills and ability requirement for teamwork: Implications for human resource management. *Journal of Management, 20,* 207-228.

Webster, S. E. (1994). *Project adventure ropes course safety manual: An instructor's guide to initiatives and high and low elements*. Dubuque, IA: Kendall/Hunt.

Whetton, D. A., & Cameron, K. S. (2005). *Developing management skills* (6th ed.). Upper Saddle River, NJ: Pearson Prentice Hall.

Wohlberg, J. W., & Weighart, S. (1992). *OB in action: Cases and exercises* (3rd ed.). Boston: Houghton Mifflin.

Zorn, T. (2002). Converging with divergence: Overcoming the disciplinary fragmentation in business communication, organizational communication, and public relations. *Business Communications Quarterly, 65*(2), 44-55.